HAD I KNOWN

D0964949

The Worst Years of Our Lives:
Irreverent Notes from a Decade of Greed

The Hearts of Men:
American Dreams and the Flight from Commitment

Re-Making Love:
The Feminization of Sex

Women in the Global Factory

Complaints and Disorders:
The Sexual Politics of Sickness

Witches, Midwives, and Nurses:
A History of Women Healers

The American Health Empire:
Power, Profits, and Politics

Long March, Short Spring:
The Student Uprising at Home and Abroad

Had I Known

COLLECTED ESSAYS

BARBARA EHRENREICH

TWELVE
New York

Compilation copyright © 2020, 2021 by Barbara Ehrenreich
Cover copyright © 2021 by Hachette Book Group, Inc.

Hachette Book Group supports the right to free expression and the value of copyright. The purpose of copyright is to encourage writers and artists to produce the creative works that enrich our culture.

The scanning, uploading, and distribution of this book without permission is a theft of the author's intellectual property. If you would like permission to use material from the book (other than for review purposes), please contact permissions@hbgusa.com. Thank you for your support of the author's rights.

Twelve
Hachette Book Group
1290 Avenue of the Americas, New York, NY 10104
twelvebooks.com
twitter.com/twelvebooks

The essays in this collection were previously published and may have been slightly revised for this edition.

First trade paperback edition: March 2021

Twelve is an imprint of Grand Central Publishing. The Twelve name and logo are trademarks of Hachette Book Group, Inc.

The publisher is not responsible for websites (or their content) that are not owned by the publisher.

The Hachette Speakers Bureau provides a wide range of authors for speaking events. To find out more, go to www.hachettespeakersbureau.com or call (866) 376-6591.

Additional copyright/credits information is on page 000.

LCCN: 2019950073
ISBNs: 978-1-4555-4369-4 (paperback), 978-1-4555-4368-7 (ebook)

Printed in the United States of America

LSC

Printing 1, 2021

CONTENTS

INTRODUCTION

Back in the fat years—two or three decades ago, when the "mainstream" media were booming—I was able to earn a living as a freelance writer. My income was meager, and I had to hustle to get it, turning out about four articles—essays, reported pieces, reviews—a month at $1 or $2 a word. One of the things I wanted to write about, in part for obvious personal reasons, was poverty and inequality, but I'd do just about anything—like, I cringe to say, "The Heartbreak Diet" for a major fashion magazine—to pay the bills.

It wasn't easy to interest glossy magazines in poverty in the 1980s and '90s. I once spent two hours over an expensive lunch—paid for, of course, by a major publication—trying to pitch to a clearly indifferent editor who finally conceded, over decaf espresso and crème brûlée, "OK, do your thing on poverty. But can you make it upscale?" (Yes, I found a way to do this.) Then there was the editor of a quite liberal magazine who responded to my pitch for a story involving blue-collar men by asking, "Hmm, but can they talk?" (Actually, my husband was one of them.)

I finally got lucky at *Harper's*, where fabled editor Lewis Lapham gave me an assignment that turned into a book, which in turn became a best seller, *Nickel and Dimed: On (Not) Getting By in America*. Thanks to the royalties and subsequent speaking fees, at last I could begin to undertake projects without concern for the pay, just because they seemed important to me. This was the writing life I had always dreamed of—adventurous, obsessively fascinating, and sufficiently remunerative that I could help support less affluent members of my family.

In the years that followed, I wrote about America's shifting class contours, the criminalization of poverty, sexual harassment, the racial wealth gap, as well as any other subject that attracted me—from the automation of war to Americans' apparent belief that they can live forever if only they eat the right combination of veggies and nuts. I paid my bills and, better yet, I was having fun.

Meanwhile, though I didn't see it at first, the world of journalism as I had known it was beginning to crumble around me. Squeezed to generate more profits for billionaire newspaper owners and new media conglomerates, newsrooms laid off reporters, who often went on to swell the crowds of hungry freelancers. Once-generous magazines shrank or slashed their freelance budgets; there were no more free lunches.

True, the internet was filled with a multiplicity of new outlets to write for, but paying writers or other "content providers" turned out not to be part of their business plan. I saw my own fees at one major news outlet drop to one-third of their value between 2004 and 2009. I heard from younger journalists who were scrambling for adjunct jobs or doing piecework in "corporate communications." But

I determined to carry on writing about the subjects that gripped me, especially poverty and inequality, even if I had to finance my efforts entirely on my own. And I felt noble for doing so.

Then, as the kids say today, I "checked my privilege." I realized that there was something wrong with an arrangement whereby a relatively affluent person, such as I had become, could afford to write about minimum-wage jobs, squirrels as an urban food source, or the penalties for sleeping in parks, while the people who were actually experiencing these sorts of things, or were in danger of experiencing them, could not.

In the last few years, I've gotten to know a number of people who are at least as qualified writers as I am, especially when it comes to the subject of poverty, but who've been held back by their own poverty. There's Darryl Wellington, for example, a local columnist (and poet) in Santa Fe who has, at times, had to supplement his tiny income by selling his plasma—a fallback that can have serious health consequences. Or Joe Williams, who, after losing an editorial job, was reduced to writing for $50 a piece for online political sites while mowing lawns and working in a sporting goods store for $10 an hour to pay for a room in a friend's house. Linda Tirado was blogging about her job as a cook at IHOP when she managed to snag a contract for a powerful book titled *Hand to Mouth* (for which I wrote the preface). Now she is working on a "multimedia mentoring project" to help other working-class journalists get published.

There are many thousands of people like these—gifted

journalists who want to address serious social issues but cannot afford to do so in a media environment that thrives by refusing to pay, or pay anywhere near adequately, its "content providers." Some were born into poverty and have stories to tell about coping with low-wage jobs, evictions, or life as a foster child. Others inhabit the once-proud urban "creative class," which now finds itself priced out of its traditional neighborhoods, like Park Slope or LA's Echo Park, scrambling for health insurance and child care, sleeping on other people's couches. They want to write—or do photography or make documentaries. They have a lot to say, but it's beginning to make more sense to apply for work as a cashier or a fry cook.

This is the real face of journalism today: not million-dollar-a-year anchorpersons, but low-wage workers and downwardly spiraling professionals who can't muster up expenses to even start on the articles, photo essays, and videos they want to do, much less find an outlet to cover the costs of doing them. You can't, as I learned from Darryl Wellington, hop on a plane to cover a police shooting in your hometown if you don't have a credit card.

This impoverishment of journalists impoverishes journalism. We come to find less and less in the media about the people who work from paycheck to paycheck, as if 80 percent of the population had quietly emigrated while the other 20 percent wasn't looking. Media outlets traditionally neglected stories about the downtrodden because they don't sit well on the same page with advertisements for diamonds and luxury homes. And now there are fewer journalists on hand at major publications to arouse the conscience of editors and other gatekeepers. Coverage of poverty accounts for less than 1 percent of American news, or, as former *Times* columnist Bob Herbert has put it: "We don't have coverage of poverty in this country. If there is a story about poor people in the *New York Times* or in the *Washington Post*, that's the exception that proves the rule. We do not cover poverty. We do not cover the poor."

As for commentary about poverty—a disproportionate share of which issues from very well-paid, established columnists like David Brooks of the *New York Times* and George Will of the *Washington Post*—all too often, it tends to reflect the historical biases of economic elites, that the poor are different than "we" are, less educated, intelligent, self-disciplined, and more inclined to make "bad lifestyle choices." If the pundits sometimes sound like Republican presidential candidates, this is not because there is a political conspiracy afoot. It's just what happens when the people who get to opine about inequality are drawn almost entirely from the top of the income distribution.

It hurts the poor and the economically precarious when they can't see themselves reflected in the collective mirror that is the media. They begin to feel that they are indeed different and somehow unworthy, compared to the "mainstream." But it also potentially hurts the rich.

In a highly polarized society like our own, the wealthy have a special stake in keeping honest journalism about class and inequality alive. Burying an aching social problem does not solve it. The rich and their philanthropies need to step up and support struggling journalists and the slender projects that try to keep them going. As Nick Hanauer, a self-proclaimed member of the 0.01 percent, warned other members of his class in 2018: "If we don't do something to fix the glaring inequities in this economy, the pitchforks are going to come for us."

At an age when most people retire—or are pushed out of the workforce into low-paid work as home health aides, valet parkers, or babysitters—I am fortunate enough to be able to keep on writing about the things that inflame my curiosity or fill me with moral outrage. But mostly I try, through a nonprofit I helped create, the Economic Hardship Reporting Project, to launch struggling journalists who otherwise might never be heard from on account of their poverty or skin color, gender or sexual orientation, youth or age. It's a great joy to me to work with people like Darryl, Joe, Linda, and so many others, and to see them begin to thrive. In the spirit of torch-passing, I dedicate this book to them.

Barbara Ehrenreich
May 2019

HAVES AND
HAVE-NOTS

NICKEL-AND-DIMED: ON (NOT) GETTING BY IN AMERICA

Harper's Magazine, 1999

At the beginning of June 1998 I leave behind everything that normally soothes the ego and sustains the body—home, career, companion, reputation, ATM card—for a plunge into the low-wage workforce. There, I become another, occupationally much diminished "Barbara Ehrenreich"—depicted on job-application forms as a divorced homemaker whose sole work experience consists of housekeeping in a few private homes. I am terrified, at the beginning, of being unmasked for what I am: a middle-class journalist setting out to explore the world that welfare mothers are entering, at the rate of approximately 50,000 a month, as welfare reform kicks in. Happily, though, my fears turn out to be entirely unwarranted: during a month of poverty and toil, my name goes unnoticed and for the most part unuttered. In this parallel universe where my father never got out of the mines and I never got through college, I am "baby," "honey," "blondie," and, most commonly, "girl."

My first task is to find a place to live. I figure that if I can earn $7 an hour—which, from the want ads, seems doable—I can afford to spend $500 on rent, or maybe, with severe economies, $600. In the Key West area, where I live, this pretty much confines me to flophouses and trailer homes—like the one, a pleasing fifteen-minute drive from town, that has no air-conditioning, no screens, no fans, no television, and, by way of diversion, only the challenge of evading the landlord's Doberman pinscher. The big problem with this place, though, is the rent, which at $675 a month is well beyond my reach. All right, Key West is expensive. But so is New York City, or the Bay Area, or Jackson Hole, or Telluride, or Boston, or any other place where tourists and the wealthy compete for living space with the people who clean their toilets and fry their hash browns.[1] Still, it is a shock to realize that "trailer trash" has become, for me, a demographic category to aspire to.

So I decide to make the common trade-off between affordability and convenience, and go for a $500-a-month efficiency thirty miles up a two-lane highway from the employment opportunities of Key West, meaning forty-five minutes if there's no road construction and I don't get caught behind some sun-dazed Canadian tourists. I hate the drive, along a roadside studded with white crosses commemorating the more effective head-on collisions, but it's a sweet little place—a cabin, more or less, set in the swampy

---

1   According to the Department of Housing and Urban Development, the "fair-market rent" for an efficiency is $551 here in Monroe County, Florida. A comparable rent in the five boroughs of New York City is $704; in San Francisco, $713; and in the heart of Silicon Valley, $808. The fair-market rent for an area is defined as the amount that would be needed to pay rent plus utilities for "privately owned, decent, safe, and sanitary rental housing of a modest (non-luxury) nature with suitable amenities."

back yard of the converted mobile home where my land-lord, an affable TV repairman, lives with his bartender girl-friend. Anthropologically speaking, a bustling trailer park would be preferable, but here I have a gleaming white floor and a firm mattress, and the few resident bugs are easily vanquished.

Besides, I am not doing this for the anthropology. My aim is nothing so mistily subjective as to "experience poverty" or find out how it "really feels" to be a long-term low-wage worker. I've had enough unchosen encounters with poverty and the world of low-wage work to know it's not a place you want to visit for touristic purposes; it just smells too much like fear. And with all my real-life assets— bank account, IRA, health insurance, multiroom home— waiting indulgently in the background, I am, of course, thoroughly insulated from the terrors that afflict the gen-uinely poor.

No, this is a purely objective, scientific sort of mission. The humanitarian rationale for welfare reform—as op-posed to the more punitive and stringy impulses that may actually have motivated it—is that work will lift poor women out of poverty while simultaneously inflating their self-esteem and hence their future value in the labor mar-ket. Thus, whatever the hassles involved in finding child care, transportation, etc., the transition from welfare to work will end happily, in greater prosperity for all. Now there are many problems with this comforting prediction, such as the fact that the economy will inevitably undergo a downturn, eliminating many jobs. Even without a down-turn, the influx of a million former welfare recipients into the low-wage labor market could depress wages by as much as 11.9 percent, according to the Economic Policy Institute (EPI) in Washington, DC.

But is it really possible to make a living on the kinds of jobs currently available to unskilled people? Mathematically, the answer is no, as can be shown by taking $6 to $7 an hour, perhaps subtracting a dollar or two an hour for child care, multiplying by 160 hours a month, and comparing the result to the prevailing rents. According to the National Coalition for the Homeless, for example, in 1998 it took, on average nationwide, an hourly wage of $8.89 to afford a one-bedroom apartment, and the Preamble Center for Public Policy estimates that the odds against a typical welfare recipient's landing a job at such a "living wage" are about 97 to 1. If these numbers are right, low-wage work is not a solution to poverty and possibly not even to homelessness.

It may seem excessive to put this proposition to an experimental test. As certain family members keep unhelpfully reminding me, the viability of low-wage work could be tested, after a fashion, without ever leaving my study. I could just pay myself $7 an hour for eight hours a day, charge myself for room and board, and total up the numbers after a month. Why leave the people and work that I love? But I am an experimental scientist by training. In that business, you don't just sit at a desk and theorize; you plunge into the everyday chaos of nature, where surprises lurk in the most mundane measurements. Maybe, when I got into it, I would discover some hidden economies in the world of the low-wage worker. After all, if 30 percent of the workforce toils for less than $8 an hour, according to the EPI, they may have found some tricks as yet unknown to me. Maybe—who knows?—I would even be able to detect in myself the bracing psychological effects of getting out of the house, as promised by the welfare wonks at places like the Heritage Foundation. Or, on the other hand, maybe there would be unexpected costs—physical, mental, or financial—to throw off all my calculations. Ideally, I should do this with two small children in tow, that being the welfare average, but mine are grown and no one is willing to lend me theirs for a month-long vacation in penury. So this is not the perfect experiment, just a test of the best possible case: an unencumbered woman, smart and even strong, attempting to live more or less off the land.

On the morning of my first full day of job searching, I take a red pen to the want ads, which are auspiciously numerous. Everyone in Key West's booming "hospitality industry" seems to be looking for someone like me—trainable, flexible, and with suitably humble expectations as to pay. I know I possess certain traits that might be advantageous— I'm white and, I like to think, well-spoken and poised—but I decide on two rules: One, I cannot use any skills derived from my education or usual work—not that there are a lot of want ads for satirical essayists anyway. Two, I have to take the best-paid job that is offered me and of course do my best to hold it; no Marxist rants or sneaking off to read novels in the ladies' room. In addition, I rule out various occupations for one reason or another: Hotel front-desk clerk, for example, which to my surprise is regarded as unskilled and pays around $7 an hour, gets eliminated because it involves standing in one spot for eight hours a day. Waitressing is similarly something I'd like to avoid, because I remember it leaving me bone tired when I was eighteen, and I'm decades of varicosities and back pain beyond that now. Telemarketing, one of the first refuges of the suddenly indigent, can be dismissed on grounds of personality. This leaves certain supermarket jobs, such as deli clerk, or housekeeping in Key West's thousands of hotel and guest rooms. Housekeeping is especially appealing, for reasons both atavistic and practical: it's what my mother did before I came along, and it can't be too different from what I've been doing part-time, in my own home, all my life.

So I put on what I take to be a respectable-looking outfit of ironed Bermuda shorts and scooped-neck T-shirt and set out for a tour of the local hotels and supermarkets. Best Western, Econo Lodge, and HoJo's all let me fill out application forms, and these are, to my relief, interested in little more than whether I am a legal resident of the United States and have committed any felonies. My next stop is Winn-Dixie, the supermarket, which turns out to have a particularly onerous application process, featuring a fifteen-minute "interview" by computer since, apparently, no human on the premises is deemed capable of representing the corporate point of view. I am conducted to a large room decorated with posters illustrating how to look "professional" (it helps to be white and, if female, permed) and warning of the slick promises that union organizers might try to tempt me with. The interview is multiple choice: Do I have anything, such as child-care problems, that might make it hard for me to get to work on time? Do I think safety on the job is the responsibility of management? Then, popping up cunningly out of the blue: How many dollars' worth of stolen goods have I purchased in the last year? Would I turn in a fellow employee if I caught him stealing? Finally, "Are you an honest person?"

Apparently, I ace the interview, because I am told that all I have to do is show up in some doctor's office tomorrow for a urine test. This seems to be a fairly general rule: if you want to stack Cheerio boxes or vacuum hotel rooms in chemically fascist America, you have to be willing to squat down and pee in front of some health worker (who has no doubt had to do the same thing herself.) The wages Winn-Dixie is offering—$6 and a couple of dimes to start with—are not enough, I decide, to compensate for this indignity.[2]

I lunch at Wendy's, where $4.99 gets you unlimited refills at the Mexican part of the Super-bar, a comforting surfeit of refried beans and "cheese sauce." A teenage employee, seeing me studying the want ads, kindly offers me an application form, which I fill out, though here, too, the pay is just $6 and change an hour. Then it's off for a round of the locally owned inns and guesthouses. At "The Palms,"

---

2 According to the *Monthly Labor Review* (November 1996), 28 percent of work sites surveyed in the service industry conduct drug tests (corporate workplaces have much higher rates), and the incidence of testing has risen markedly since the eighties. The rate of testing is highest in the South (56 percent of work sites polled), with the Midwest in second place (50 percent). The drug most likely to be detected—marijuana, which can be detected in urine for weeks—is also the most innocuous, while heroin and cocaine are generally undetectable three days after use. Prospective employees sometimes try to cheat the tests by consuming excessive amounts of liquids and taking diuretics and even masking substances available through the internet.

let's call it, a bouncy manager actually takes me around to see the rooms and meet the existing housekeepers, who, I note with satisfaction, look pretty much like me—faded ex-hippie types in shorts with long hair pulled back in braids. Mostly, though, no one speaks to me or even looks at me except to proffer an application form. At my last stop, a palatial B & B, I wait twenty minutes to meet "Max," only to be told that there are no jobs now but there should be one soon, since "nobody lasts more than a couple weeks." (Because none of the people I talked to knew I was a reporter, I have changed their names to protect their privacy and, in some cases perhaps, their jobs.)

Three days go by like this and, to my chagrin, no one out of the approximately twenty places I've applied calls me for an interview. I had been vain enough to worry about coming across as too educated for the jobs I sought, but no one even seems interested in finding out how overqualified I am. Only later will I realize that the want ads are not a reliable measure of the actual jobs available at any particular time. They are, as I should have guessed from Max's comment, the employers' insurance policy against the relentless turnover of the low-wage workforce. Most of the big hotels run ads almost continually, just to build a supply of applicants to replace the current workers as they drift away or are fired, so finding a job is just a matter of being at the right place at the right time and flexible enough to take whatever is being offered that day. This finally happens to me at one of the big discount hotel chains, where I go, as usual, for housekeeping and am sent, instead, to try out as a waitress at the attached "family restaurant," a dismal spot with a counter and about thirty tables that looks out on a parking garage and features such tempting fare as "Pollish [sic] sausage and BBQ sauce" on 95-degree days. Phillip, the dapper young West Indian who introduces himself as the manager, interviews me with about as much enthusiasm as if he were a clerk processing me for Medicare, the principal questions being what shifts can I work and when can I start. I mutter something about being woefully out of practice as a waitress, but he's already on to the uniform: I'm to show up tomorrow wearing black slacks and black shoes; he'll provide the rust-colored polo shirt with HEARTHSIDE embroidered on it, though I might want to wear my own shirt to get to work, ha ha. At the word "tomorrow," something between fear and indignation rises in my chest. I want to say, "Thank you for your time, sir, but this is just an experiment, you know, not my actual life."

So begins my career at the Hearthside, I shall call it, one small profit center within a global discount hotel chain, where for two weeks I work from 2:00 till 10:00 P.M. for $2.43 an hour plus tips.[3] In some futile bid for gentility, the management has barred employees from using the front door, so my first day I enter through the kitchen, where a red-faced man with shoulder-length blond hair is throwing

---

3   According to the Fair Labor Standards Act, employers are not required to pay "tipped employees," such as restaurant servers, more than $2.13 an hour in direct wages. However, if the sum of tips plus $2.13 an hour falls below the minimum wage, or $5.15 an hour, the employer is required to make up the difference. This fact was not mentioned by managers or otherwise publicized at either of the restaurants where I worked.

frozen steaks against the wall and yelling, "Fuck this shit!" "That's just Jack," explains Gail, the wiry middle-aged waitress who is assigned to train me. "He's on the rag again"—a condition occasioned, in this instance, by the fact that the cook on the morning shift had forgotten to thaw out the steaks. For the next eight hours, I run after the agile Gail, absorbing bits of instruction along with fragments of personal tragedy. All food must be trayed, and the reason she's so tired today is that she woke up in a cold sweat thinking of her boyfriend, who killed himself recently in an upstate prison. No refills on lemonade. And the reason he was in prison is that a few DUIs caught up with him, that's all, could have happened to anyone. Carry the creamers to the table in a monkey bowl, never in your hand. And after he was gone she spent several months living in her truck, peeing in a plastic pee bottle and reading by candlelight at night, but you can't live in a truck in the summer, since you need to have the windows down, which means anything can get in, from mosquitoes on up.

At least Gail puts to rest any fears I had of appearing overqualified. From the first day on, I find that of all the things I have left behind, such as home and identity, what I miss the most is competence. Not that I have ever felt utterly competent in the writing business, in which one day's success augurs nothing at all for the next. But in my writing life, I at least have some notion of procedure: do the research, make the outline, rough out a draft, etc. As a server, though, I am beset by requests like bees: more iced tea here, ketchup over there, a to-go box for table fourteen, and where are the high chairs, anyway? Of the twenty-seven tables, up to six are usually mine at any time, though on slow afternoons or if Gail is off, I sometimes have the whole place to myself. There is the touch-screen computer-ordering system to master, which is, I suppose, meant to minimize server-cook contact, but in practice requires constant verbal fine-tuning: "That's gravy on the mashed, OK? None on the meatloaf," and so forth—while the cook scowls as if I were inventing these refinements just to torment him. Plus, something I had forgotten in the years since I was eighteen: about a third of a server's job is "side work" that's invisible to customers—sweeping, scrubbing, slicing, refilling, and re-stocking. If it isn't all done, every little bit of it, you're going to face the 6:00 P.M. dinner rush defenseless and probably go down in flames. I screw up dozens of times at the beginning, sustained in my shame entirely by Gail's support—"It's OK, baby, everyone does that sometime"—because, to my total surprise and despite the scientific detachment I am doing my best to maintain, I care.

The whole thing would be a lot easier if I could just skate through it as Lily Tomlin in one of her waitress skits, but I was raised by the absurd Booker T. Washingtonian precept that says: If you're going to do something, do it well. In fact, "well" isn't good enough by half. Do it better than anyone has ever done it before. Or so said my father, who must have known what he was talking about because he managed to pull himself, and us with him, up from the mile-deep copper mines of Butte to the leafy suburbs of the Northeast, ascending from boilermakers to martinis before booze beat out ambition. As in most endeavors I have encountered in my life, doing it "better than anyone" is not a reasonable goal.

Still, when I wake up at 4:00 A.M. in my own cold sweat, I am not thinking about the writing deadlines I'm neglecting; I'm thinking about the table whose order I screwed up so that one of the boys didn't get his kiddie meal until the rest of the family had moved on to their Key Lime pies. That's the other powerful motivation I hadn't expected—the customers, or "patients," as I can't help thinking of them on account of the mysterious vulnerability that seems to have left them temporarily unable to feed themselves. After a few days at Hearthside, I feel the service ethic kick in like a shot of oxytocin, the nurturance hormone. The plurality of my customers are hardworking locals—truck drivers, construction workers, even housekeepers from the attached hotel—and I want them to have the closest to a "fine dining" experience that the grubby circumstances will allow. No "you guys" for me; everyone over twelve is "sir" or "ma'am." I ply them with iced tea and coffee refills; I return, mid-meal, to inquire how everything is; I doll up their salads with chopped raw mushrooms, summer squash slices, or whatever bits of produce I can find that have survived their sojourn in the cold-storage room mold-free.

There is Benny, for example, a short, tight-muscled sewer repairman, who cannot even think of eating until he has absorbed a half hour of air-conditioning and ice water. We chat about hyperthermia and electrolytes until he is ready to order some finicky combination like soup of the day, garden salad, and a side of grits. There are the German tourists who are so touched by my pidgin *"Wilkommen"* and *"Ist alles gut?"* that they actually tip. (Europeans, spoiled by their trade-union-ridden, high-wage welfare states, generally do not know that they are supposed to tip. Some restaurants, the Hearthside included, allow servers to "grat" their foreign customers, or add a tip to the bill. Since this amount is added before the customers have a chance to tip or not tip, the practice amounts to an automatic penalty for imperfect English.) There are the two dirt-smudged lesbians, just off their construction shift, who are impressed enough by my suave handling of the fly in the piña colada that they take the time to praise me to Stu, the assistant manager. There's Sam, the kindly retired cop, who has to plug up his tracheotomy hole with one finger in order to force the cigarette smoke into his lungs.

Sometimes I play with the fantasy that I am a princess who, in penance for some tiny transgression, has undertaken to feed each of her subjects by hand. But the non-princesses working with me are just as indulgent, even when this means flouting management rules—concerning, for example, the number of croutons that can go on a salad (six). "Put on all you want," Gail whispers, "as long as Stu isn't looking." She dips into her own tip money to buy biscuits and gravy for an out-of-work mechanic who's used up all his money on dental surgery, inspiring me to pick up the tab for his milk and pie. Maybe the same high levels of agape can be found through-out the "hospitality industry." I remember the poster deco-rating one of the apartments I looked at, which said "If you seek happiness for yourself you will never find it. Only when you seek happiness for others will it come to you," or words to that effect—an odd sentiment, it seemed to me at the time, to find in the dank one-room basement apartment of a bellhop at the Best Western. At the Hearthside, we utilize whatever bits of autonomy we have to ply our customers with the illicit calories that signal our love. It is our job as servers to assemble the salads and desserts, pouring the dressing and squirting the whipped cream. We also control the number of butter patties our customers get and the amount of sour cream on their baked potatoes. So if you wonder why Americans are so obese, consider the fact that waitresses both express their humanity and earn their tips through the covert distribution of fats.

Ten days into it, this is beginning to look like a livable lifestyle. I like Gail, who is "looking at fifty" but moves so fast she can alight in one place and then another without apparently being anywhere between them. I clown around with Lionel, the teenage Haitian busboy, and catch a few fragments of conversation with Joan, the svelte fortyish hostess and militant feminist who is the only one of us who dares to tell Jack to shut the fuck up. I even warm up to Jack when, on a slow night and to make up for a particularly unwarranted attack on my abilities, or so I imagine, he tells me about his glory days as a young man at "coronary school"—or do you say "culinary"?—in Brooklyn, where he dated a knock-out Puerto Rican chick and learned everything there is to know about food. I finish up at 10:00 or 10:30, depending on how much side work I've been able to get done during the shift, and cruise home to the tapes I snatched at random when I left my real home—Marianne Faithfull, Tracy Chapman, Enigma, King Sunny Adé, the Violent Femmes—just drained enough for the music to set my cranium resonating, but hardly dead. Midnight snack is Wheat Thins and Monterey Jack, accompanied by cheap white wine on ice and whatever AMC has to offer. To bed by 1:30 or 2:00, up at 9:00 or 10:00, read for an hour while my uniform whirls around in the landlord's washing machine, and then it's another eight hours spent following Mao's central instruction, as laid out in the Little Red Book, which was: Serve the people.

I could drift along like this, in some dreamy proletarian idyll, except for two things. One is management. If I have kept this subject on the margins thus far it is because I still flinch to think that I spent all those weeks under the surveillance of men (and later women) whose job it was to monitor my behavior for signs of sloth, theft, drug abuse, or worse. Not that managers and especially "assistant managers" in low-wage settings like this are exactly the class enemy. In the restaurant business, they are mostly former cooks or servers, still capable of pinch-hitting in the kitchen or on the floor, just as in hotels they are likely to be former clerks, and paid a salary of only about $400 a week. But everyone knows they have crossed over to the other side, which is, crudely put, corporate as opposed to human. Cooks want to prepare tasty meals, servers want to serve them graciously, but managers are there for only one reason—to make sure that money is made for some theoretical entity that exists far away in Chicago or New York, if a corporation can be said to have a physical existence at all. Reflecting on her career, Gail tells me ruefully that she had sworn, years ago, never to work for a corporation again. "They don't cut you no slack. You give and you give, and they take."

Managers can sit—for hours at a time if they want—but it's their job to see that no one else ever does, even when there's nothing to do, and this is why, for servers, slow times can be as exhausting as rushes. You start dragging out each little chore, because if the manager on duty catches you in an idle moment, he will give you something far nastier to do. So I wipe, I clean, I consolidate ketchup bottles and recheck the cheesecake supply, even tour the tables to make sure the customer evaluation forms are all standing perkily in their places—wondering all the time how many calories I burn in these strictly theatrical exercises. When, on a particularly dead afternoon, Stu finds me glancing at a *USA Today* a customer has left behind, he assigns me to vacuum the entire floor with the broken vacuum cleaner that has a handle only two feet long, and the only way to do that without incurring orthopedic damage is to proceed from spot to spot on your knees.

On my first Friday at the Hearthside there is a "mandatory meeting for all restaurant employees," which I attend, eager for insight into our overall marketing strategy and the niche (your basic Ohio cuisine with a tropical twist?) we aim to inhabit. But there is no "we" at this meeting. Phillip, our top manager except for an occasional "consultant" sent out by corporate headquarters, opens it with a sneer: "The break room—it's disgusting. Butts in the ashtrays, newspapers lying around, crumbs." This windowless little room, which also houses the time clock for the entire hotel, is where we stash our bags and civilian clothes and take our half-hour meal breaks. But a break room is not a right, he tells us. It can be taken away. We should also know that the lockers in the break room and whatever is in them can be searched at any time. Then comes gossip; there has been gossip; gossip (which seems to mean employees talking among themselves) must stop. Off-duty employees are henceforth barred from eating at the restaurant, because "other servers gather around them and gossip." When Phillip has exhausted his agenda of rebukes, Joan complains about the condition of the ladies' room and I throw in my two bits about the vacuum cleaner. But I don't see any backup coming from my fellow servers, each of whom has subsided into her own personal funk; Gail, my role model, stares sorrowfully at a point six inches from her nose. The meeting ends when Andy, one of the cooks, gets up, muttering about breaking up his day off for this almighty bullshit.

Just four days later we are suddenly summoned into the kitchen at 3:30 P.M., even though there are live tables on the floor. We all—about ten of us—stand around Phillip, who announces grimly that there has been a report of some "drug activity" on the night shift and that, as a result, we are now to be a "drug-free" workplace, meaning that all new hires will be tested, as will possibly current employees on a random basis. I am glad that this part of the kitchen is so dark, because I find myself blushing as hard as if I had been caught toking up in the ladies' room myself: I haven't been treated this way—lined up in the corridor, threatened with locker searches, peppered with carelessly aimed accusations—since junior high school. Back on the floor, Joan cracks, "Next they'll be telling us we can't have sex on the job." When I ask Stu what happened to inspire the crackdown, he just mutters about "management decisions" and takes the opportunity to upbraid Gail and me for being too generous with the rolls. From now on there's to be only one per customer, and it goes out with the dinner, not with the salad. He's also been riding the cooks, prompting Andy to come out of the kitchen and observe—with the serenity of a man whose customary implement is a butcher knife— that "Stu has a death wish today."

Later in the evening, the gossip crystallizes around the theory that Stu is himself the drug culprit, that he uses the restaurant phone to order up marijuana and sends one of the late servers out to fetch it for him. The server was caught, and she may have ratted Stu out or at least said enough to cast some suspicion on him, thus accounting for his pissy behavior. Who knows? Lionel, the busboy, entertains us for the rest of the shift by standing just behind Stu's back and sucking deliriously on an imaginary joint.

The other problem, in addition to the less-than-nurturing management style, is that this job shows no sign of being financially viable. You might imagine, from a comfortable distance, that people who live, year in and year out, on $6 to $10 an hour have discovered some survival stratagems unknown to the middle class. But no. It's not hard to get my coworkers to talk about their living situations, because housing, in almost every case, is the principal source of disruption in their lives, the first thing they fill you in on when they arrive for their shifts. After a week, I have compiled the following survey:

- Gail is sharing a room in a well-known downtown flophouse for which she and a roommate pay about $250 a week. Her roommate, a male friend, has begun hitting on her, driving her nuts, but the rent would be impossible alone.

- Claude, the Haitian cook, is desperate to get out of the two-room apartment he shares with his girlfriend and two other, unrelated, people. As far as I can determine, the other Haitian men (most of whom only speak Creole) live in similarly crowded situations.

- Annette, a twenty-year-old server who is six months pregnant and has been abandoned by her boyfriend, lives with her mother, a postal clerk.

- Marianne and her boyfriend are paying $170 a week for a one-person trailer.

- Jack, who is, at $10 an hour, the wealthiest of us, lives in the trailer he owns, paying only the $400-a-month lot fee.

- The other white cook, Andy, lives on his dry-docked boat, which, as far as I can tell from his loving descriptions, can't be more than twenty feet long. He offers to take me out on it, once it's repaired, but the offer comes with inquiries as to my marital status, so I do not follow up on it.

- Tina and her husband are paying $60 a night for a double room in a Days Inn. This is because they have no car and the Days Inn is within walking distance of the Hearthside. When Marianne, one of the breakfast servers, is tossed out of her trailer for subletting (which is against the trailer-park rules), she leaves her boyfriend and moves in with Tina and her husband.

- Joan, who had fooled me with her numerous and tasteful outfits (hostesses wear their own clothes), lives in a van she parks behind a shopping center at night and showers in Tina's motel room. The clothes are from thrift shops.[4]

It strikes me, in my middle-class solipsism, that there is gross improvidence in some of these arrangements. When Gail and I are wrapping silverware in napkins—the only task for which we are permitted to sit—she tells me she is thinking of escaping from her roommate by moving into the Days Inn herself. I am astounded: How can she even think of paying $40 to $60 a day? But if I was afraid of sounding like a social worker, I come out just sounding like a fool. She squints at me in disbelief, "And where am I supposed to get a month's rent and a month's deposit for an apartment?" I'd been feeling pretty smug about my $500 efficiency, but of course it was made possible only by the $1,300 I had allotted myself for start-up costs when I began my low-wage life: $1,000 for the first month's rent and deposit, $100 for initial groceries and cash in my pocket, $200 stuffed away for emergencies. In poverty, as in certain propositions in physics, starting conditions are everything.

There are no secret economies that nourish the poor; on

---

4   I could find no statistics on the number of employed people living in cars or vans, but according to the National Coalition for the Homeless's 1997 report "Myths and Facts About Homelessness," nearly one in five homeless people (in twenty-nine cities across the nation) is employed in a full- or part-time job.

the contrary, there are a host of special costs. If you can't put up the two months' rent you need to secure an apartment, you end up paying through the nose for a room by the week. If you have only a room, with a hot plate at best, you can't save by cooking up huge lentil stews that can be frozen for the week ahead. You eat fast food, or the hot dogs and Styrofoam cups of soup that can be microwaved in a convenience store. If you have no money for health insurance—and the Hearthside's skimpy plan kicks in only after three months—you go without routine care or prescription drugs and end up paying the price. Gail, for example, was fine until she ran out of money for estrogen pills. She is supposed to be on the company plan by now, but they claim to have lost her application form and need to begin the paperwork all over again. So she spends $9 per migraine pill to control the headaches she wouldn't have, she insists, if her estrogen supplements were covered. Similarly, Marianne's boyfriend lost his job as a roofer because he missed so much time after getting a cut on his foot for which he couldn't afford the prescribed antibiotic.

My own situation, when I sit down to assess it after two weeks of work, would not be much better if this were my actual life. The seductive thing about waitressing is that you don't have to wait for payday to feel a few bills in your pocket, and my tips usually cover meals and gas, plus something left over to stuff into the kitchen drawer I use as a bank. But as the tourist business slows in the summer heat, I sometimes leave work with only $20 in tips (the gross is higher, but servers share about 15 percent of their tips with the busboys and bartenders). With wages included, this amounts to about the minimum wage of $5.15 an hour. Although the sum in the drawer is piling up, at the present rate of accumulation it will be more than a hundred dollars short of my rent when the end of the month comes around. Nor can I see any expenses to cut. True, I haven't gone the lentil-stew route yet, but that's because I don't have a large cooking pot, pot holders, or a ladle to stir with (which would cost about $30 at Kmart, less at thrift stores), not to mention onions, carrots, and the indispensable bay leaf. I do make my lunch almost every day—usually some slow-burning, high-protein combo like frozen chicken patties with melted cheese on top and canned pinto beans on the side. Dinner is at the Hearthside, which offers its employees a choice of BLT, fish sandwich, or hamburger for only $2. The burger lasts longest, especially if it's heaped with gut-puckering jalapeños, but by midnight my stomach is growling again.

So unless I want to start using my car as a residence, I have to find a second, or alternative, job. I call all the hotels where I filled out housekeeping applications weeks ago— the Hyatt, Holiday Inn, Econo Lodge, HoJo's, Best Western, plus a half dozen or so locally run guesthouses. Nothing. Then I start making the rounds again, wasting whole mornings waiting for some assistant manager to show up, even dipping into places so creepy that the front-desk clerk greets you from behind bulletproof glass and sells pints of liquor over the counter. But either someone has exposed my real-life housekeeping habits—which are, shall we say, mellow—or I am at the wrong end of some infallible ethnic equation: most, but by no means all, of the working housekeepers I see on my job searches are African Americans,

Spanish-speaking, or immigrants from the Central European post-Communist world, whereas servers are almost invariably white and monolingually English-speaking. When I finally get a positive response, I have been identified once again as server material. Jerry's, which is part of a well-known national family restaurant chain and physically attached here to another budget hotel chain, is ready to use me at once. The prospect is both exciting and terrifying, because, with about the same number of tables and counter seats, Jerry's attracts three or four times the volume of customers as the gloomy old Hearthside.

Picture a fat person's hell, and I don't mean a place with no food. Instead there is everything you might eat if eating had no bodily consequences—cheese fries, chicken-fried steaks, fudge-laden desserts—only here every bite must be paid for, one way or another, in human discomfort. The kitchen is a cavern, a stomach leading to the lower intestine that is the garbage and dishwashing area, from which issue bizarre smells combining the edible and the offal: creamy carrion, pizza barf, and that unique and enigmatic Jerry's scent—citrus fart. The floor is slick with spills, forcing us to walk through the kitchen with tiny steps, like Susan McDougal in leg irons. Sinks everywhere are clogged with scraps of lettuce, decomposing lemon wedges, waterlogged toast crusts. Put your hand down on any counter and you risk being stuck to it by the film of ancient syrup spills, and this is unfortunate, because hands are utensils here, used for scooping up lettuce onto salad plates, lifting out pie slices, and even moving hash browns from one plate to another. The regulation poster in the single unisex restroom admonishes us to wash our hands thoroughly and even offers instructions for doing so, but there is always some vital substance missing—soap, paper towels, toilet paper—and I never find all three at once. You learn to stuff your pockets with napkins before going in there, and too bad about the customers, who must eat, though they don't realize this, almost literally out of our hands.

The break room typifies the whole situation: there is none, because there are no breaks at Jerry's. For six to eight hours in a row, you never sit except to pee. Actually, there are three folding chairs at a table immediately adjacent to the bathroom, but hardly anyone ever sits here, in the very rectum of the gastro-architectural system. Rather, the function of the peritoilet area is to house the ashtrays in which servers and dishwashers leave their cigarettes burning at all times, like votive candles, so that they don't have to waste time lighting up again when they dash back for a puff. Almost everyone smokes as if his or her pulmonary well-being depended on it—the multinational mélange of cooks, the Czech dishwashers, the servers, who are all native-born American—creating an atmosphere in which oxygen is only an occasional pollutant. My first morning at Jerry's, when the hypoglycemic shakes set in, I complain to one of my fellow servers that I don't understand how she can go so long without food. "Well, I don't understand how you can go so long without a cigarette," she responds in a tone of reproach—because work is what you do for others; smoking is what you do for yourself. I don't know why the anti-smoking crusaders have never grasped the element of defiant self-nurturance that makes the habit so endearing to its victims—as if, in the American workplace, the only thing people have to call their own is the tumors they are nourishing and the spare moments they devote to feeding them.

Now, the Industrial Revolution is not an easy transition, especially when you have to zip through it in just a couple of days. I have gone from craft work straight into the factory, from the air-conditioned morgue of the Hearthside directly into the flames. Customers arrive in human waves, sometimes disgorged fifty at a time from their tour buses, peckish and whiny. Instead of two "girls" on the floor at once, there can be as many as six of us running around in our brilliant pink-and-orange Hawaiian shirts. Conversations, either with customers or fellow employees, seldom last more than twenty seconds at a time. On my first day, in fact, I am hurt by my sister servers' coldness. My mentor for the day is an emotionally uninflected twenty-three-year-old, and the others, who gossip a little among themselves about the real reason someone is out sick today and the size of the bail bond someone else has had to pay, ignore me completely. On my second day, I find out why. "Well, it's good to see you again," one of them says in greeting. "Hardly anyone comes back after the first day." I feel powerfully vindicated—a survivor—but it would take a long time, probably months, before I could hope to be accepted into this sorority.

I start out with the beautiful, heroic idea of handling the two jobs at once, and for two days I almost do it: the breakfast/lunch shift at Jerry's, which goes till 2:00, arriving at the Hearthside at 2:10, and attempting to hold out until 10:00. In the ten minutes between jobs, I pick up a spicy chicken sandwich at the Wendy's drive-through window, gobble it down in the car, and change from khaki slacks to black, from Hawaiian to rust polo. There is a problem, though. When during the 3:00 to 4:00 P.M. dead time I finally sit down to wrap silver, my flesh seems to bond to the seat. I try to refuel with a purloined cup of soup, as I've seen Gail and Joan do dozens of times, but a manager catches me and hisses "No eating!" though there's not a customer around to be offended by the sight of food making contact with a server's lips. So I tell Gail I'm going to quit, and she hugs me and says she might just follow me to Jerry's herself.

But the chances of this are minuscule. She has left the flophouse and her annoying roommate and is back to living in her beat-up old truck. But, guess what? she reports to me excitedly later that evening: Phillip has given her permission to park overnight in the hotel parking lot, as long as she keeps out of sight, and the parking lot should be totally safe, since it's patrolled by a hotel security guard! With the Hearthside offering benefits like that, how could anyone think of leaving?

Gail would have triumphed at Jerry's, I'm sure, but for me it's a crash course in exhaustion management. Years ago, the kindly fry cook who trained me to waitress at a Los Angeles truck stop used to say: Never make an unnecessary trip; if you don't have to walk fast, walk slow; if you don't have to walk, stand. But at Jerry's the effort of distinguishing necessary from unnecessary and urgent from whenever would itself be too much of an energy drain. The only thing to do is to treat each shift as a one-time-only emergency: you've got fifty starving people out there, lying scattered on the battlefield, so get out there and feed them! Forget that you will have to do this again tomorrow, forget that you will have to be alert enough to dodge the drunks on the drive home tonight—just burn, burn, burn! Ideally, at some point you enter what servers call "a rhythm" and psychologists term a "flow state," in which signals pass from the sense organs directly to the muscles, bypassing the cerebral cortex, and a Zen-like emptiness sets in. A male server from the Hearthside's morning shift tells me about the time he "pulled a triple"—three shifts in a row, all the way around the clock—and then got off and had a drink and met this girl, and maybe he shouldn't tell me this, but they had sex right then and there, and it was like, beautiful.

But there's another capacity of the neuromuscular system, which is pain. I start tossing back drugstore-brand ibuprofen pills as if they were vitamin C, four before each shift, because an old mouse-related repetitive-stress injury in my upper back has come back to full-spasm strength, thanks to the tray carrying. In my ordinary life, this level of disability might justify a day of ice packs and stretching. Here I comfort myself with the Aleve commercial in which the cute blue-collar guy asks: If you quit after working four hours, what would your boss say? And the not-so-cute blue-collar guy, who's lugging a metal beam on his back, answers: He'd fire me, that's what. But fortunately, the commercial tells us, we workers can exert the same kind of authority over our painkillers that our bosses exert over us. If Tylenol doesn't want to work for more than four hours, you just fire its ass and switch to Aleve.

True, I take occasional breaks from this life, going home now and then to catch up on e-mail and for conjugal visits (though I am careful to "pay" for anything I eat there), seeing *The Truman Show* with friends and letting them buy my ticket. And I still have those what-am-I-doing-here moments at work, when I get so homesick for the printed word that I obsessively reread the six-page menu. But as the days go by, my old life is beginning to look exceedingly strange. The e-mails and phone messages addressed to my former self come from a distant race of people with exotic concerns and far too much time on their hands. The neighborly market I used to cruise for produce now looks forbiddingly like a Manhattan yuppie emporium. And when I sit down one morning in my real home to pay bills from my past life, I am dazzled by the two- and three-figure sums owed to outfits like Club Body Tech and Amazon.com.

Management at Jerry's is generally calmer and more "professional" than at the Hearthside, with two exceptions. One is Joy, a plump, blowsy woman in her early thirties, who once kindly devoted several minutes to instructing me in the correct one-handed method of carrying trays but whose moods change disconcertingly from shift to shift and even within one. Then there's B.J., aka B.J.-the-bitch, whose contribution is to stand by the kitchen counter and yell, "Nita, your order's up, move it!" or "Barbara, didn't you see you've got another table out there? Come on, girl!" Among other things, she is hated for having replaced the whipped-cream squirt cans with big plastic whipped-cream-filled baggies that have to be squeezed with both hands—because, reportedly, she saw or thought she saw employees trying to inhale the propellant gas from the squirt cans, in the hope that it might be nitrous oxide. On my third night, she pulls me aside abruptly and brings her face so close that it looks as if she's planning to butt me with her forehead. But instead of saying, "You're fired," she says, "You're doing fine." The only trouble is I'm spending time chatting with customers: "That's how they're getting you." Furthermore I am letting them "run me," which means harassment by sequential demands: you bring the ketchup and they decide they want extra Thousand Island; you bring that and they announce they now need a side of fries; and so on into distraction. Finally she tells me not to take her wrong. She tries to say things in a nice way, but you get into a mode, you know, because everything has to move so fast.[5]

I mumble thanks for the advice, feeling like I've just been stripped naked by the crazed enforcer of some ancient sumptuary law: No chatting for you, girl. No fancy service ethic allowed for the serfs. Chatting with customers is for the beautiful young college-educated servers in the downtown carpaccio joints, the kids who can make $70 to $100 a night. What had I been thinking? My job is to move

---

5   In *Workers in a Lean World: Unions in the International Economy* (Verso, 1997), Kim Moody cites studies finding an increase in stress-related workplace injuries and illness between the mid-1980s and the early 1990s. He argues that rising stress levels reflect a new system of "management by stress," in which workers in a variety of industries are being squeezed to extract maximum productivity, to the detriment of their health.

orders from tables to kitchen and then trays from kitchen to tables. Customers are, in fact, the major obstacle to the smooth transformation of information into food and food into money—they are, in short, the enemy. And the painful thing is that I'm beginning to see it this way myself. There are the traditional asshole types—frat boys who down multiple Buds and then make a fuss because the steaks are so emaciated and the fries so sparse—as well as the variously impaired—due to age, diabetes, or literacy issues—who require patient nutritional counseling. The worst, for some reason, are the Visible Christians—like the ten-person table, all jolly and sanctified after Sunday-night service, who run me mercilessly and then leave me $1 on a $92 bill. Or the guy with the crucifixion T-shirt (SOMEONE TO LOOK UP TO) who complains that his baked potato is too hard and his iced tea too icy (I cheerfully fix both) and leaves no tip. As a general rule, people wearing crosses or WWJD? (What Would Jesus Do?) buttons look at us disapprovingly no matter what we do, as if they were confusing waitressing with Mary Magdalene's original profession.

I make friends, over time, with the other "girls" who work my shift: Nita, the tattooed twenty-something who taunts us by going around saying brightly, "Have we started making money yet?" Ellen, whose teenage son cooks on the graveyard shift and who once managed a restaurant in Massachusetts but won't try out for management here because she prefers being a "common worker" and not "ordering people around." Easy-going fiftyish Lucy, with the raucous laugh, who limps toward the end of the shift because of something that has gone wrong with her leg, the exact nature of which cannot be determined without health insurance. We talk about the usual girl things—men, children, and the sinister allure of Jerry's chocolate peanut-butter cream pie—though no one, I notice, ever brings up anything potentially expensive, like shopping or movies. As at the Hearthside, the only recreation ever referred to is partying, which requires little more than some beer, a joint, and a few close friends. Still, no one here is homeless, or cops to it anyway, thanks usually to a working husband or boyfriend. All in all, we form a reliable mutual-support group: If one of us is feeling sick or overwhelmed, another one will "bev" a table or even carry trays for her. If one of us is off sneaking a cigarette or a pee,[6] the others will do their best to conceal her absence from the enforcers of corporate rationality.

But my saving human connection—my oxytocin receptor, as it were—is George, the nineteen-year-old, fresh-off-the-boat Czech dishwasher. We get to talking when he asks me, tortuously, how much cigarettes cost at Jerry's. I do my best to explain that they cost over a dollar more here than

---

6 Until April 1998, there was no federally mandated right to bathroom breaks. According to Marc Linder and Ingrid Nygaard, authors of *Void Where Prohibited: Rest Breaks and the Right to Urinate on Company Time* (Cornell University Press, 1997), "The right to rest and void at work is not high on the list of social or political causes supported by professional or executive employees, who enjoy personal workplace liberties that millions of factory workers can only daydream about....While we were dismayed to discover that workers lacked an acknowledged legal right to void at work, [the workers] were amazed by outsiders' naïve belief that their employers would permit them to perform this basic bodily function when necessary....A factory worker, not allowed a break for six-hour stretches, voided into pads worn inside her uniform; and a kindergarten teacher in a school without aides had to take all twenty children with her to the bathroom and line them up outside the stall door when she voided."

at a regular store and suggest that he just take one from the half-filled packs that are always lying around on the break table. But that would be unthinkable. Except for the one tiny earring signaling his allegiance to some vaguely alternative point of view, George is a perfect straight arrow—crew-cut, hardworking, and hungry for eye contact. "Czech Republic," I ask, "or Slovakia?" and he seems delighted that I know the difference. "Václav Havel," I try, "Velvet Revolution, Frank Zappa?" "Yes, yes, 1989," he says, and I realize we are talking about history.

My project is to teach George English. "How are you today, George?" I say at the start of each shift. "I am good, and how are you today, Barbara?" I learn that he is not paid by Jerry's but by the "agent" who shipped him over—$5 an hour, with the agent getting the dollar or so difference between that and what Jerry's pays dishwashers. I learn also that he shares an apartment with a crowd of other Czech "dishers," as he calls them, and that he cannot sleep until one of them goes off for his shift, leaving a vacant bed. We are having one of our ESL sessions late one afternoon when B.J. catches us at it and orders "Joseph" to take up the rubber mats on the floor near the dishwashing sinks and mop underneath. "I thought your name was George," I say loud enough for B.J. to hear as she strides off back to the counter. Is she embarrassed? Maybe a little, because she greets me back at the counter with "George, Joseph—there are so many of them!" I say nothing, neither nodding nor smiling, and for this I am punished later when I think I am ready to go and she announces that I need to roll fifty more sets of silverware and isn't it time

I mixed up a fresh four-gallon batch of blue-cheese dressing? May you grow old in this place, B.J., is the curse I beam out at her when I am finally permitted to leave. May the syrup spills glue your feet to the floor.

I make the decision to move closer to Key West. First, because of the drive. Second and third, also because of the drive: gas is eating up $4 to $5 a day, and although Jerry's is as high-volume as you can get, the tips average only 10 percent, and not just for a newbie like me. Between the base pay of $2.15 an hour and the obligation to share tips with the busboys and dishwashers, we're averaging only about $7.50 an hour. Then there is the $30 I had to spend on the regulation tan slacks worn by Jerry's servers—a setback it could take weeks to absorb. (I had combed the town's two downscale department stores hoping for something cheaper but decided in the end that these marked-down Dockers, originally $49, were more likely to survive a daily washing.) Of my fellow servers, everyone who lacks a working husband or boyfriend seems to have a second job: Nita does something at a computer eight hours a day; another welds. Without the forty-five-minute commute, I can picture myself working two jobs and having the time to shower between them.

So I take the $500 deposit I have coming from my landlord, the $400 I have earned toward the next month's rent, plus the $200 reserved for emergencies, and use the $1,100 to pay the rent and deposit on trailer number 46 in the Overseas Trailer Park, a mile from the cluster of budget hotels that constitute Key West's version of an industrial park. Number 46 is about eight feet in width and shaped like a barbell inside, with a narrow region—because of the sink and the stove—separating the bedroom from what might optimistically be called the "living" area, with its two-person table and half-sized couch. The bathroom is so small my knees rub against the shower stall when I sit on the toilet, and you can't just leap out of the bed, you have to climb down to the foot of it in order to find a patch of floor space to stand on. Outside, I am within a few yards of a liquor store, a bar that advertises "free beer tomorrow," a convenience store, and a Burger King—but no supermarket or, alas, laundromat. By reputation, the Overseas park is a nest of crime and crack, and I am hoping at least for some vibrant multicultural street life. But desolation rules night and day, except for a thin stream of pedestrian traffic heading for their jobs at the Sheraton or 7-Eleven. There are not exactly people here but what amounts to canned labor, being preserved from the heat between shifts.

In line with my reduced living conditions, a new form of ugliness arises at Jerry's. First we are confronted—via an announcement on the computers through which we input orders—with the new rule that the hotel bar is henceforth off-limits to restaurant employees. The culprit, I learn through the grapevine, is the ultra-efficient gal who trained me—another trailer-home dweller and a mother of three. Something had set her off one morning, so she slipped out for a nip and returned to the floor impaired. This mostly hurts Ellen, whose habit it is to free her hair from its rubber band and drop by the bar for a couple of Zins before heading home at the end of the shift, but all of us feel the chill.

Then the next day, when I go for straws, for the first time I find the dry-storage room locked. Ted, the portly assistant manager who opens it for me, explains that he caught one of the dishwashers attempting to steal something, and, unfortunately, the miscreant will be with us until a replacement can be found—hence the locked door. I neglect to ask what he had been trying to steal, but Ted tells me who he is—the kid with the buzz cut and the earring. You know, he's back there right now.

I wish I could say I rushed back and confronted George to get his side of the story. I wish I could say I stood up to Ted and insisted that George be given a translator and allowed to defend himself, or announced that I'd find a lawyer who'd handle the case pro bono. The mystery to me is that there's not much worth stealing in the dry-storage room, at least not in any fenceable quantity: "Is Gyorgi here, and am having 200—maybe—250 ketchup packets. What do you say?" My guess is that he had taken—if he had taken anything at all—some Saltines or a can of cherry-pie mix, and that the motive for taking it was hunger.

So why didn't I intervene? Certainly not because I was held back by the kind of moral paralysis that can pass as journalistic objectivity. On the contrary, something new—something loathsome and servile—had infected me, along with the kitchen odors that I could still sniff on my bra when I finally undressed at night. In real life I am moderately brave, but plenty of brave people shed their courage in concentration camps, and maybe something similar goes on in the infinitely more congenial milieu of the low-wage American workplace. Maybe, in a month or two more at

Jerry's, I might have regained my crusading spirit. Then again, in a month or two I might have turned into a different person altogether—say, the kind of person who would have turned George in.

But this is not something I am slated to find out. When my month-long plunge into poverty is almost over, I finally land my dream job—housekeeping. I do this by walking into the personnel office of the only place I figure I might have some credibility, the hotel attached to Jerry's, and confiding urgently that I have to have a second job if I am to pay my rent and, no, it couldn't be front-desk clerk. "All right," the personnel lady fairly spits, "So it's housekeeping," and she marches me back to meet Maria, the housekeeping manager, a tiny, frenetic Hispanic woman who greets me as "babe" and hands me a pamphlet emphasizing the need for a positive attitude. The hours are nine in the morning till whenever, the pay is $6.10 an hour, and there's one week of vacation a year. I don't have to ask about health insurance once I meet Carlotta, the middle-aged African-American woman who will be training me. Carla, as she tells me to call her, is missing all of her top front teeth.

On that first day of housekeeping and last day of my entire project—although I don't yet know it's the last—Carla is in a foul mood. We have been given nineteen rooms to clean, most of them "checkouts," as opposed to "stay-overs," that require the whole enchilada of bed-stripping, vacuuming, and bathroom-scrubbing. When one of the rooms that had been listed as a stay-over turns out to be a checkout, Carla calls Maria to complain, but of course to no avail. "So make up the motherfucker," Carla orders me, and I do the beds while she sloshes around the bathroom. For four hours without a break I strip and remake beds, taking about four and a half minutes per queen-sized bed, which I could get down to three if there were any reason to. We try to avoid vacuuming by picking up the larger specks by hand, but often there is nothing to do but drag the monstrous vacuum cleaner—it weighs about thirty pounds—off our cart and try to wrestle it around the floor. Sometimes Carla hands me the squirt bottle of "BAM" (an acronym for something that begins, ominously, with "butyric"; the rest has been worn off the label) and lets me do the bathrooms. No service ethic challenges me here to new heights of performance. I just concentrate on removing the pubic hairs from the bathtubs, or at least the dark ones that I can see.

I had looked forward to the breaking-and-entering aspect of cleaning the stay-overs, the chance to examine the secret, physical existence of strangers. But the contents of the rooms are always banal and surprisingly neat—zipped up shaving kits, shoes lined up against the wall (there are no closets), flyers for snorkeling trips, maybe an empty wine bottle or two. It is the TV that keeps us going, from *Jerry* to *Sally* to *Hawaii Five-O* and then on to the soaps. If there's something especially arresting, like "Won't Take No for an Answer" on *Jerry*, we sit down on the edge of a bed and giggle for a moment as if this were a pajama party instead of a terminally dead-end job. The soaps are the best, and Carla turns the volume up full blast so that she won't miss anything from the bathroom or while the vacuum is on. In room 503, Marcia confronts Jeff about

Lauren. In 505, Lauren taunts poor cuckolded Marcia. In 511, Helen offers Amanda $10,000 to stop seeing Eric, prompting Carla to emerge from the bathroom to study Amanda's troubled face. "You take it, girl," she advises. "I would for sure."

The tourists' rooms that we clean and, beyond them, the far more expensively appointed interiors in the soaps, begin after a while to merge. We have entered a better world—a world of comfort where every day is a day off, waiting to be filled up with sexual intrigue. We, however, are only gate-crashers in this fantasy, forced to pay for our presence with backaches and perpetual thirst. The mirrors, and there are far too many of them in hotel rooms, contain the kind of person you would normally find pushing a shopping cart down a city street—bedraggled, dressed in a damp hotel polo shirt two sizes too large, and with sweat dribbling down her chin like drool. I am enormously relieved when Carla announces a half-hour meal break, but my appetite fades when I see that the bag of hot-dog rolls she has been carrying around on our cart is not trash salvaged from a checkout but what she has brought for her lunch.

When I request permission to leave at about 3:30, another housekeeper warns me that no one has so far succeeded in combining housekeeping at the hotel with serving at Jerry's: "Some kid did it once for five days, and you're no kid." With that helpful information in mind, I rush back to number 46, down four Advils (the name brand this time), shower, stooping to fit into the stall, and attempt to compose myself for the oncoming shift. So much for what Marx termed the "reproduction of labor power," meaning the things a worker has to do just so she'll be ready to work again. The only unforeseen obstacle to the smooth transition from job to job is that my tan Jerry's slacks, which had looked reasonably clean by 40-watt bulb last night when I handwashed my Hawaiian shirt, prove by daylight to be mottled with ketchup and ranch-dressing stains. I spend most of my hour-long break between jobs attempting to remove the edible portions with a sponge and then drying the slacks over the hood of my car in the sun.

I can do this two-job thing, is my theory, if I can drink enough caffeine and avoid getting distracted by George's ever more obvious suffering.[7] The first few days after being caught, he seemed not to understand the trouble he was in, and our chirpy little conversations had continued. But the last couple of shifts he's been listless and unshaven, and tonight he looks like the ghost we all know him to be, with dark half-moons hanging from his eyes. At one point, when I am briefly immobilized by the task of filling little paper cups with sour cream for baked potatoes, he comes over and looks as if he'd like to explore the limits of our shared vocabulary, but I am called to the floor for a table. I resolve to give him all my tips that night, and to hell with

---

7 In 1996 the number of persons holding two or more jobs averaged 7.8 million, or 6.2 percent of the workforce. It was about the same rate for men and for women (6.1 versus 6.2), though the kinds of jobs differ by gender. About two-thirds of multiple jobholders work one job full-time and the other part-time. Only a heroic minority—4 percent of men and 2 percent of women—work two full-time jobs simultaneously (From John F. Stinson Jr., "New Data on Multiple Jobholding Available from the CPS," in the *Monthly Labor Review,* March 1997).

the experiment in low-wage money management. At eight, Ellen and I grab a snack together standing at the mephitic end of the kitchen counter, but I can only manage two or three mozzarella sticks and lunch had been a mere handful of McNuggets. I am not tired at all, I assure myself, though it may be that there is simply no more "I" left to do the tiredness monitoring. What I would see, if I were more alert to the situation, is that the forces of destruction are already massing against me. There is only one cook on duty, a young man named Jesus ("Hay-Sue," that is) and he is new to the job. And there is Joy, who shows up to take over in the middle of the shift, wearing high heels and a long, clingy white dress and fuming as if she'd just been stood up in some cocktail bar.

Then it comes, the perfect storm. Four of my tables fill up at once. Four tables is nothing for me now, but only so long as they are obligingly staggered. As I bev table 27, tables 25, 28, and 24 are watching enviously. As I bev 25, 24 glowers because their bevs haven't even been ordered. Twenty-eight is four yuppyish types, meaning everything on the side and agonizing instructions as to the chicken Caesars. Twenty-five is a middle-aged black couple, who complain, with some justice, that the iced tea isn't fresh and the tabletop is sticky. But table 24 is the meteorological event of the century: ten British tourists who seem to have made the decision to absorb the American experience entirely by mouth. Here everyone has at least two drinks—iced tea and milk shake, Michelob and water (with lemon slice, please)—and a huge, promiscuous orgy of breakfast specials, mozz sticks, chicken strips, quesadillas, burgers with cheese and without, sides of hash browns with cheddar, with onions, with gravy, seasoned fries, plain fries, banana splits. Poor Jesus! Poor me! Because when I arrive with their first tray of food—after three prior trips just to refill bevs—Princess Di refuses to eat her chicken strips with her pancake-and-sausage special, since, as she now reveals, the strips were meant to be an appetizer. Maybe the others would have accepted their meals, but Di, who is deep into her third Michelob, insists that everything else go back while they work on their starters. Meanwhile, the yuppies are waving me down for more decaf and the black couple looks ready to summon the NAACP.

Much of what happened next is lost in the fog of war. Jesus starts going under. The little printer on the counter in front of him is spewing out orders faster than he can rip them off, much less produce the meals. Even the invincible Ellen is ashen from stress. I bring table 24 their reheated main courses, which they immediately reject as either too cold or fossilized by the microwave. When I return to the kitchen with their trays (three trays in three trips), Joy confronts me with arms akimbo: "What is this?" She means the food—the plates of rejected pancakes, hash browns in assorted flavors, toasts, burgers, sausages, eggs. "Uh, scrambled with cheddar," I try, "and that's…" "NO," she screams in my face. "Is it a traditional, a super-scramble, an eye-opener?" I pretend to study my check for a clue, but entropy has been up to its tricks, not only on the plates but in my head, and I have to admit that the original order is beyond reconstruction. "You don't know an eye-opener from a traditional?" she demands in outrage. All I know, in fact, is that my legs have lost interest in the current venture and have announced their intention to fold. I am saved by a yuppie (mercifully not one of mine) who chooses this moment to charge into the kitchen to bellow that his food is twenty-five minutes late. Joy screams at him to get the hell out of her kitchen, please, and then turns on Jesus in a fury, hurling an empty tray across the room for emphasis.

I leave. I don't walk out, I just leave. I don't finish my side work or pick up my credit-card tips, if any, at the cash register or, of course, ask Joy's permission to go. And the surprising thing is that you *can* walk out without permission, that the door opens, that the thick tropical night air parts to let me pass, that my car is still parked where I left it. There is no vindication in this exit, no fuck-you surge of relief, just an overwhelming dank sense of failure pressing down on me and the entire parking lot. I had gone into this venture in the spirit of science, to test a mathematical proposition, but somewhere along the line, in the tunnel vision imposed by long shifts and relentless concentration, it became a test of myself, and clearly I have failed. Not only had I flamed out as a housekeeper/server, I had even forgotten to give George my tips, and, for reasons perhaps best known to hardworking, generous people like Gail and Ellen, this hurts. I don't cry, but I am in a position to realize, for the first time in many years, that the tear ducts are still there, and still capable of doing their job.

*   *   *

When I moved out of the trailer park, I gave the key to number 46 to Gail and arranged for my deposit to be transferred to her. She told me that Joan is still living in her van and that Stu had been fired from the Hearthside. I never found out what happened to George.

In one month, I had earned approximately $1,040 and spent $517 on food, gas, toiletries, laundry, phone, and utilities. If I had remained in my $500 efficiency, I would have been able to pay the rent and have $22 left over (which is $78 less than the cash I had in my pocket at the start of the month). During this time I bought no clothing except for the required slacks and no prescription drugs or medical care (I did finally buy some vitamin B to compensate for the lack of vegetables in my diet). Perhaps I could have saved a little on food if I had gotten to a supermarket more often, instead of convenience stores, but it should be noted that I lost almost four pounds in four weeks, on a diet weighted heavily toward burgers and fries.

How former welfare recipients and single mothers will (and do) survive in the low-wage workforce, I cannot imagine. Maybe they will figure out how to condense their lives—including child-raising, laundry, romance, and meals—into the couple of hours between full-time jobs. Maybe they will take up residence in their vehicles, if they have one. All I know is that I couldn't hold two jobs and I couldn't make enough money to live on with one. And I had advantages unthinkable to many of the long-term poor—health, stamina, a working car, and no children to care for and support. Certainly nothing in my experience contradicts the conclusion of Kathryn Edin and Laura

Lein, in their recent book *Making Ends Meet: How Single Mothers Survive Welfare and Low-Wage Work*, that low-wage work actually involves more hardship and deprivation than life at the mercy of the welfare state. In the coming months and years, economic conditions for the working poor are bound to worsen, even without the almost inevitable recession. As mentioned earlier, the influx of former welfare recipients into the low-skilled workforce will have a depressing effect on both wages and the number of jobs available. A general economic downturn will only enhance these effects, and the working poor will of course be facing it without the slight, but nonetheless often saving, protection of welfare as a backup.

The thinking behind welfare reform was that even the humblest jobs are morally uplifting and psychologically buoying. In reality they are likely to be fraught with insult and stress. But I did discover one redeeming feature of the most abject low-wage work—the camaraderie of people who are, in almost all cases, far too smart and funny and caring for the work they do and the wages they're paid. The hope, of course, is that someday these people will come to know what they're worth, and take appropriate action.

HOW YOU CAN SAVE WALL STREET

Mother Jones, 1988

W ay back when the Dow Jones first melted down, dozens of important men in pinstriped suits gathered outside the White House to chant: "Wake up, sir! Give us leadership! Quickly, please, before we go back to our fortieth-story offices and hurl our well-nourished bodies onto the Street!" This was foolish, and not just because President Reagan was tied up in his office, memorizing the names of his close friends and cabinet members.

It was foolish because in a free-enterprise system, the economy is none of the president's business. In fact, that is the very definition of the free-enterprise system, which should perhaps be called the "free-president system," since it leaves the president free of all responsibility for the economically anguished, whether they appear at the White House gates in pinstripes or overalls or secondhand blankets.

A free-enterprise economy depends only on *markets*, and, according to the most advanced mathematical macroeconomic theory, markets depend only on *moods*: specifically, the mood of the men in the pinstripes, also known as the Boys on the Street. When the Boys are in a good mood, the market thrives; when they get scared or sullen, it is time for each one of us to look into the retail apple business. For as Franklin Delano Roosevelt once said, "We have nothing to be moody about except a bad mood itself, especially when it strikes someone richer than us."

And what is responsible for the mood of the Boys on the Street? Their wives, their valets, their blood-sugar levels? No; *you* are responsible, because in free enterprise, individual is paramount. What you do in the next few hours will determine whether a few thousand key men on Wall Street have, as we like to say, a nice day. And if *they* don't have a nice day, it'll be 1933 all over again, and you might as well head to the freight yards and check into a nice clean boxcar before the crowd gets there.

Abbie Hoffman had the right idea in 1967, when he and some fellow Yippies gathered in the gallery of the New York Stock Exchange and tossed dollar bills into the pit. At the time, this gesture was widely interpreted as guerrilla theater—some crazed radical attempt at social satire. Actually, it was a desperate and earnest effort to save the economy by propitiating the gods of the market—that is, the Boys in the pit—with their favorite substance. And it worked! They were pleased! They picked up the bills and used them to wipe the perspiration from their furrowed brows. Then they smiled; and they bought low, and they sold high, and the economy surged ahead.

I would say, do it again—change your savings into small bills and toss them like confetti at the men in the pit. Only today it wouldn't work, because although dollars fall very fast, these days they are practically weightless, and the Boys on the Street might be depressed to be in a blizzard of paper worth only pennies in yen or Deutsche Marks. No, you have to be more clever these days, more subtle—which is why I have prepared the following guidelines on What You Can Do to Stabilize World Markets and Guarantee Global Prosperity:

Rule 1: Spend. Now is the time to buy everything you have ever needed or wanted, from a two-dollar porn magazine to a dwarf-shaped hitching post for the front lawn. The reason is that every dollar you spend is a vote of confidence for our free-enterprise economy. Every dollar you spend helps employ someone—in the pornography or lawn-statuary industry or wherever—so that they, too, are enabled to spend. Then the men on Wall Street, sensing the groundswell of confidence around them, will feel happy and confident themselves. Except that...

Reckless consumer spending created our scandalous $2.5 trillion level of personal debt, which alarms certain key men in Tokyo and Bonn, who in turn are likely to call the men on Wall Street and say, "Whaddya got going there, fellas, a Third-World country?" which will bring gloom to Wall Street and penury to the rest of us. Which brings us to:

Rule 2: Save. Sell all your belongings and put the money into a bank, where it will quickly become available to the Boys on the Street for the purposes of leveraged buyouts, corporate takeovers, and other activities that keep them distracted. If you feel queasy about giving up your furniture to provide a larger kitty for those jumpy fellows on the Street, stuff all your assets into a cookie jar. This will help drive up interest rates and make America a more attractive investment to Bonn. However...

The merest upward flutter of interest rates could savage the bond market and reduce the Boys on the Street to craven terror, so it would probably be better to:

Rule 3: Invest all assets in an export-oriented industry— such as nuclear missiles or infant-formula mix. This will shift the balance of trade in our favor and bring cheer to the Boys on the Street. If you have trouble thinking of something that American corporations still know how to produce that someone in the world still might want to buy, remember the pioneering example of pet rocks and the great untapped market of southern Sudan. But be careful not to:

Shift the balance of trade so far in our favor that you upset Toshiba and Mercedes, which means Tokyo and Bonn, so...

"But wait!" you say. "Why should 200 million people pander to the mood swings of a few thousand addicted gamblers?" But that's free enterprise, friends: freedom to gamble and freedom to lose. And the great thing—the truly democratic thing about it—is that you don't even have to be a player to lose.

S&M AS PUBLIC POLICY

The Guardian, 1993

Welfare may turn out to be the domestic equivalent of Saddam Hussein. Already, leading pundits have declared it to be a crucial test of Bill Clinton's manhood: Will he be tough enough to crack down on those lazy sluts who insist on living off government funds, as legions of tweed-jacketed policy wonks demand? Or will he cave in to the welfare wimps—such as, presumably, Donna Shalala—with their squeamish aversion to mass starvation? Meanwhile, no one seems to have noticed that there is an ingenious, low-cost solution that has the potential to please both sides: Allow welfare recipients to continue to collect their miserly checks, but require that they submit, periodically, to public floggings.

Distasteful? Perhaps, but punishment has become a major cultural theme of our time. Consider Madonna's oeuvre, with its emphasis on bondage and whips. Or listen to the nation's leading pundits, as they jump up and down, much like masochists at a sex orgy, demanding that Clinton give us "pain and sacrifice!" On account of the deficit, the reasoning goes, what America needs now is a good sound "spankie." And who better to take the punishment than a social group that has no money, no friends in high places, and not a speck of political clout?

Everyone from neoliberal to neoconservative agrees that something must be done. It's not so much the money (welfare consumes only 1 percent of the federal budget) as the principle of the thing. In dozens of universities and think tanks, scholarly males grow apoplectic at the thought of fifteen-year-olds using pregnancy to get their first rent-free studio apartments. Hence the widespread excitement over Clinton's campaign proposal to limit welfare to two years, during which the recipients will be treated to job training and child care, and after which they will have to scavenge for food as they may.

But a program of welfare plus floggings makes far more sense in every way. First, it will be no less effective at curing poverty than any amount of job training and forced work experience. For decades now, welfare recipients have been subjected to dozens of workfare and work-incentive programs. They have been taught how to dress for job interviews, how to find their way through the want ads, how to process words and tote up numbers. The effects, as now even the most ardent welfare hawks acknowledge, have been negligible: only minuscule gains in income and an inevitable drift back to the welfare rolls. This is not because welfare recipients are incorrigibly lazy. In a labor market where 18 percent of workers already toil full time, year-round, to earn less than poverty-level wages, there are few vacant jobs that offer a living wage, especially women with child-care problems.

Second, the welfare-plus-floggings program will be far cheaper than any work program so far devised. The conservative estimate is that it would cost $50 billion a year to ready the welfare population for the labor market— roughly twice what is spent on welfare in its present form— and that about half of this sum will be spent on child care. So what will really be accomplished by getting welfare recipients trained and out of their houses? The ten million children on welfare, who are now cared for by their mothers at home, will instead be cared for by other poor women called child-care workers—while the mothers take up data entry and burger flipping. The net result, needless to say, will be a surge of commuting among the preschool set.

But the real beauty of the welfare-plus-floggings approach is that it will provide an outlet for the punitive rage now directed at the down-and-out. In a curious inversion of the Sermon on the Mount, no social group attracts more ire than the vaguely termed "underclass." The need to punish the poor is, of course, already built into the present welfare system, which insists that recipients travel from one government office to another, usually with children in tow, and submit to intimate investigations of their finances, sleeping arrangements, and housekeeping habits. Often this bureaucratic harassment reaches fiendish proportions, driving many poor women from the dole. But imagine the much more vivid effect that could be achieved by the actual drawing of blood!

Madonna aside, sadomasochism is entirely consistent with recent political trends. For twelve years now, we've had presidents who have understood the primary function of government to be punishment in one form or another. All available funds have been channeled into the military, which rushes about the world like a schoolmistress armed with a birch rod. Bad countries—like Grenada, Panama, Libya, Iraq—are soundly whipped and sent to stand in their corners. Why, even as he was dragged from the Oval Office, George Bush managed to lash out once again at Saddam—with a "spanking," as *Time* magazine so insightfully put it.

Domestically, too, the punishment theme has been strictly adhered to. While all other domestic functions of government have withered away, the prison system has expanded to the point where the United States is second only to Russia in the percentage of its citizens incarcerated. For poor males, we have prison; for poor females, welfare—and there's no reason why one sex's punishment should be any less onerous than the other's.

It's not that the welfare recipients have done anything wrong. On the contrary, they've been neglected by underfunded schools; abused, in many cases, by husbands and boyfriends; and left to fend for their children in trailer camps or cities that resemble Mogadishu.

But we all know that "welfare reform" means, in plain English, that someone has got to be punished. Programs that throw women off welfare into unemployment or poverty-level jobs will punish, ultimately, their children. Hence the brilliance of the flogging approach: It will make the hawks and the wonks feel much better—without starving a single child.

GOING TO EXTREMES: CEOS VS. SLAVES

The Nation, 2007

Recent findings shed new light on the increasingly unequal terrain of American society. Starting at the top executive level, you may have thought, as I did, that the guys in the C suites operated as a team—or, depending on your point of view, a pack or gang—each getting his fair share of the take. But no, the rising tide in executive pay does not lift all yachts equally. The latest pay gap to worry about is the one between the CEO and his—or very rarely her—third in command.

According to a study by Carola Frydman of the Massachusetts Institute of Technology and Raven E. Saks at the Federal Reserve, thirty to forty years ago the CEOs of major companies earned 80 percent more, on average, than the third-highest-paid executives. By the early part of the twenty-first century, however, the gap between the CEO and the third in command had ballooned up to 260 percent.

Now take a look at what's happening at the very bottom of the economic spectrum, where you might have pictured low-wage workers trudging between food banks or mendicants dwelling in cardboard boxes. It turns out, though, that the bottom is a lot lower than that. In May 2007, a millionaire couple in a woodsy Long Island suburb was charged with keeping two Indonesian domestics as slaves for five years, during which the women were paid $100 a month, fed very little, forced to sleep on mats on the floor, and subjected to beatings, cigarette burns, and other torments.

This is hardly an isolated case. If the new "top" involves pay in the tens or hundreds of millions, a private jet, and a few acres of Marin County, the new bottom is slavery. Some of America's slaves are captive domestics like the Indonesian women on Long Island. Others are sweatshop or restaurant workers, and at least ten thousand are sex slaves lured from their home countries to American brothels by the promise of respectable jobs.

CEOs and slaves: These are the extreme ends of American class polarization. But a parallel splitting is going on in many of the professions. Top-ranked college professors, for example, enjoy salaries of several hundred thousand a year, often augmented by consulting fees and earnings from their patents or biotech companies. At the other end of the professoriate, you have adjunct teachers toiling away for about $5,000 a semester or less, with no benefits or chance of tenure. There was a story a few years ago about an adjunct who commuted to his classes from a homeless shelter in Manhattan, and adjuncts who moonlight as waitresses or cleaning ladies are legion.

Similarly, the legal profession, which is topped by law firm partners billing hundreds of dollars an hour, now has a new proletariat of temp lawyers working for $19–25 an hour in sweatshop conditions. On sites like http:// temporaryattorney.blogspot.com/, temp lawyers report working twelve hours a day, six days a week, in crowded basements with inadequate sanitary facilities. According to an article in *American Lawyer*, a legal temp at a major New York firm reported being "corralled in a windowless basement room littered with dead cockroaches" where six out of seven exits were blocked.

Contemplating the violent and increasing polarization of American society, one cannot help but think of "dark energy," the mysterious force that is propelling the galaxies apart from one another at a speed far greater than can be accounted for by the energy of the original big bang. Cosmic bodies seem to be repelling one another, much as a CEO must look down at his CFO and COO, etc., and think, "They're getting too close. I've got to make more, more, more!"

The difference is that the galaxies don't need one another and are free to go their separate ways nonchalantly. But the CEO presumably depends on his fellow executives, just as the star professor relies on adjuncts to do his or her teaching and the law firm partner is enriched by the sweated labor of legal temps. For all we know, some of those CEOs go home to sip their single malts in mahogany-walled dens that have been cleaned by domestic slaves.

Why is it so hard for the people at the top to graciously acknowledge their dependency on the labor of others? We need some sort of gravitational force to counter the explosive distancing brought about by greed—before our economy imitates the universe and blows itself to smithereens.

ARE ILLEGAL IMMIGRANTS
THE PROBLEM?

Barbara's Blog, 2006

I've been reading with mixed feelings an exchange on my website's forum on the subject of illegal immigration. One contributor writes that "The first step is to deport the illegal aliens and those overstaying their visas. This should open up millions of jobs." He—well, he says he's a male in his mid-thirties—must have been watching Lou Dobbs's strident series on "Our Broken Borders," which blames about 51 percent of our economic woes on illegal immigrants. Though, to give Dobbs his due, he does pin the other 49 percent on "big corporations."

I've traveled across the US-Mexican border, and it didn't seem too broken to me. Peer through the giant fence that runs right to the Pacific Ocean in Tijuana and you see what looks like an armed encampment: That's America, the "land of opportunity," as viewed from the poorer parts of the world. On the way back north, it took fifty minutes to make our way through the US border checkpoint, waiting in bumper-to-bumper traffic as gaunt peddlers, many carrying babies on their backs, went from car to car selling trinkets and snacks.

The amazing thing is that so many Mexicans (and other Latin Americans) risk the border crossing and the hostile culture of the United States—a fact you're reminded of as soon as you enter California and see the first "human crossing" warning signs. These show a silhouetted family running together, reminding you that it's parents and children, not deer, you're likely to collide with just north of the fence.

Now we've been given a glimpse into the lives of one of the biggest categories of illegal Latino immigrants, the day laborers who do jobs like construction, moving, and landscaping. According to a 2006 study, carried out by researchers at three major US universities, about three-fourths of the day laborers in this country lack legal documents. Not surprisingly, they live miserably. Their median earnings are $700 a month, most have no access to health care, and half of them said they'd been stiffed by bosses at one time or another and gone unpaid for their work.

That's what makes undocumented workers so attractive to unscrupulous US employers: When you rip them off, they have no recourse at all. So my first, knee-jerk response to Lou Dobbs et al. would be: If you don't want undocumented immigrants competing with Americans for jobs, stop the *exploitation* of the immigrants and make sure they work under the same laws and regulations as anyone else.

The real surprise in the study is that 49 percent of the day laborers interviewed said they were usually hired not by contractors or companies of any kind, and certainly not "big corporations," but by American homeowners. I'd heard Bay Buchanan (sister of Pat) on Lou Dobbs's show fulminating about the "big corporations" that are hiring all the illegal immigrants, but in fact it's the guy next door who needs his house painted or his lawn mowed.

So there's a sickening level of hypocrisy here. In the last few years, we've seen anti-immigrant protests at day-laborer hiring sites—street corners or, very often, Home Depot parking lots—from Burbank, California, to Suffolk County, Long Island. But how many of those righteous protestors have employed undocumented immigrants themselves, if not as construction and lawn workers, then as nannies or maids?

But I do agree with one forum contributor when he writes: "I get very tired of ivory tower 'professional' types who dismiss the impact of these workers because they're just doing 'jobs nobody else wants to do.'" There's Jimmy, for example, a friend from Buffalo who hasn't had steady employment since he was laid off from an auto plant in the nineties. Now he's getting ready to move to South Florida, where there's still a shortage of workers to repair hurricane damage. His plan? Get a job, or at least hang out at Home Depot, where the pay is low and the possibilities of advancement are negligible—so he might be spotted by potential employers.

With the catastrophic ongoing layoffs in the auto industry, we can expect more American citizens to join the immigrants congregating in Home Depot parking lots. They'll have a choice: to treat the immigrants as competitors and enemies or to band together with them, as coworkers, to fight for better wages and working conditions for all.

Of course, I hope they'll choose the latter. One image haunts me from my border crossing: a thin brown man in tattered clothes trying to sell handmade wooden crosses to the Americans crawling along in their cars. He was carrying one of the larger ones on his back.

WHAT'S SO GREAT ABOUT GATED COMMUNITIES?

Huffington Post, 2007

Another Utopia seems to be biting the dust. The socialist kibbutzim of Israel have vanished or gone increasingly capitalist, and now the paranoid residential ideal represented by gated communities may be in serious trouble. Never exactly cool—remember Jim Carrey in *The Truman Show*?—these pricey enclaves of the white upper-middle class are becoming hotbeds of disillusionment.

At the annual meeting of the American Anthropological Association in Washington in 2007, incoming association president Setha Low painted a picture so dispiriting that the audience guffawed in schadenfreude. The gated community residents Low interviewed had fled from ethnically challenging cities, but they have not managed to escape from their fear. One resident reported that her small daughter has developed a severe case of xenophobia, no doubt communicated by her parents: "We were driving next to a truck with some day laborers and equipment in the back, and we stopped beside them at the light. She [her daughter] wanted to move because she was afraid those people were going to come and get her. They looked scary to her."

Leaving aside the sorry spectacle of homeowners living in fear of their landscapers, there is actually something to worry about. According to Low, gated communities are no less crime-prone than open ones, and Gopal Ahluwalia, senior vice president of research at the National Association of Home Builders, confirms this: "There are studies indicating that there are no differences in the crime in gated communities and nongated communities." The security guards often wave people on in, especially if they look like they're on a legitimate mission—such as the faux moving truck that entered a Fort Myers gated community last spring and left with a houseful of furniture. Or the crime comes from within, as at the Hilton Head Plantation community in South Carolina, where a rash of crime committed by resident teenagers has led to the imposition of a curfew.

Most recently, America's gated communities have been blighted by foreclosures. Yes, even people who were able to put together the down payment on a half-million-dollar house can be ambushed by adjustable-rate mortgages and forced down from the upper- to the lower-middle class. *Newsweek* reports that foreclosures are devastating the gated community of Black Mountain Vistas in Henderson, Nevada, where "yellow patches [now] blot the spartan lawns and phone books lie on front porches, their covers bleached from weeks under the desert sun." Similarly, according to the *Orlando Sentinel*, "Countless homeowners overwhelmed by their mortgages are taking off and leaving behind algae-filled swimming pools and knee-high weeds" in one local gated community.

So for people who sought not just prosperity but perfection, here's another sad end to the American dream, or at least their ethnically cleansed version thereof: boarded-up McMansions, plastic baggies scudding over overgrown lawns, and, in the Orlando case, a foreclosure-induced infestation of snakes. You can turn away the immigrants, the African Americans, the teenagers, and other suspect groups, but there's no fence high enough to keep out the repo man.

All right, some gated communities are doing better than others, and not all of their residents are racists. The communities that allow owners to rent out their houses or that offer homes at middle-class prices of $250,000 or so are more likely to contain a mix of classes and races. The only gated community I have ever visited consisted of dull row houses protected by a slacker guard and a fence, and my host was a writer of modest means and liberal inclinations. But all these places suffer from the delusion that security lies behind physical barriers.

Before we turn all of America into a gated community, with a seven-hundred-mile steel fence running along the southern border, we should consider the mixed history of exclusionary walls. Ancient and medieval European towns huddled behind massive walls, only to face ever more effective catapults, battering rams, and other siege engines. More recently, the Berlin Wall, which the East German government described fondly as a protective "antifascism wall," fell to a rebellious citizenry. Israel, increasingly sealed behind its anti-Palestinian checkpoints and wall, faced an outbreak of neo-Nazi crime in September— coming, strangely enough, from within.

But the market may have the last word on America's internal gated communities. "Hell is a gated community," announced the *Sarasota Herald-Tribune* last June, report-ing that market research by the big home builder Pulte Homes found that no one under fifty wants to live in them, so its latest local development would be ungated. Security, or at least the promise of security, may be one consideration. But there's another old-fashioned Ameri-can imperative at work here, which ought to bear on our national policies as well. As my Montana forebears would have put it: *Don't fence me in!*

IS IT NOW A CRIME TO BE POOR?

New York Times, 2009

I t's too bad so many people are falling into poverty at a
time when it's almost illegal to be poor. You won't be
arrested for shopping in a Dollar Store, but if you are truly,
deeply, in-the-streets poor, you're well advised not to engage in any of the biological necessities of life—like sitting,
sleeping, lying down, or loitering. City officials boast that
there is nothing discriminatory about the ordinances that
afflict the destitute, most of which go back to the dawn of
gentrification in the '80s and '90s. "If you're lying on a sidewalk, whether you're homeless or a millionaire, you're in
violation of the ordinance," a city attorney in St. Petersburg,
Florida, said in June, echoing Anatole France's immortal
observation that "The law, in its majestic equality, forbids
the rich as well as the poor to sleep under bridges."

In defiance of all reason and compassion, the criminalization of poverty has actually been intensifying as the
recession generates ever more poverty. So concludes a new
study from the National Law Center on Homelessness
and Poverty, which found that the number of ordinances

against the publicly poor has been rising since 2006, along with ticketing and arrests for more "neutral" infractions like jaywalking, littering, or carrying an open container of alcohol.

The report lists America's ten "meanest" cities—the largest of which are Honolulu, Los Angeles, and San Francisco—but new contestants are springing up every day. The City Council in Grand Junction, Colorado, has been considering a ban on begging, and at the end of June, Tempe, Arizona, carried out a four-day crackdown on the indigent. How do you know when someone is indigent? As a Las Vegas statute puts it, "An indigent person is a person whom a reasonable ordinary person would believe to be entitled to apply for or receive" public assistance.

That could be me before the blow-drying and eyeliner, and it's definitely Al Szekely at any time of day. A grizzled sixty-two-year-old, he inhabits a wheelchair and is often found on G Street in Washington—the city that is ultimately responsible for the bullet he took in the spine in Fu Bai, Vietnam, in 1972. He had been enjoying the luxury of an indoor bed until last December, when the police swept through the shelter in the middle of the night looking for men with outstanding warrants.

It turned out that Mr. Szekely, who is an ordained minister and does not drink, do drugs, or curse in front of ladies, did indeed have a warrant—for not appearing in court to face a charge of "criminal trespassing" (for sleeping on a sidewalk in a Washington suburb). So he was dragged out of the shelter and put in jail. "Can you imagine?" asked Eric Sheptock, the homeless advocate (himself a shelter resident) who introduced me to Mr. Szekely. "They arrested a homeless man in a shelter for being homeless."

The viciousness of the official animus toward the indigent can be breathtaking. A few years ago, a group called Food Not Bombs started handing out free vegan food to hungry people in public parks around the nation. A number of cities, led by Las Vegas, passed ordinances forbidding the sharing of food with the indigent in public places, and several members of the group were arrested. A federal judge just overturned the antisharing law in Orlando, Florida, but the city is appealing. And now Middletown, Connecticut, is cracking down on food sharing.

If poverty tends to criminalize people, it is also true that criminalization inexorably impoverishes them. Scott Lovell, another homeless man I interviewed in Washington, earned his record by committing a significant crime—by participating in the armed robbery of a steakhouse when he was fifteen. Although Mr. Lovell dresses and speaks more like a summer tourist from Ohio than a felon, his criminal record has made it extremely difficult for him to find a job.

For Al Szekely, the arrest for trespassing meant a further descent down the circles of hell. While in jail, he lost his slot in the shelter and now sleeps outside the Verizon Center sports arena, where the big problem, in addition to the security guards, is mosquitoes. His stick-thin arms are covered with pink crusty sores, which he treats with a regimen of frantic scratching.

For the not-yet-homeless, there are two main paths to criminalization—one involving debt and the other skin color. Anyone of any color or prerecession financial status can fall into debt, and although we pride ourselves on the abolition of debtors' prison, in at least one state, Texas, people who can't afford to pay their traffic fines may be made to "sit out their tickets" in jail.

Often the path to legal trouble begins when one of your creditors has a court issue a summons for you, which you fail to honor for one reason or another. (Maybe your address has changed or you never received it.) Now you're in contempt of court. Or suppose you miss a payment and, before you realize it, your car insurance lapses; then you're stopped for something like a broken headlight. Depending on the state, you may have your car impounded or face a steep fine—again, exposing you to a possible summons. "There's just no end to it once the cycle starts," said Robert Solomon of Yale Law School. "It just keeps accelerating."

By far the most reliable way to be criminalized by poverty is to have the wrong-color skin. Indignation runs high when a celebrity professor encounters racial profiling, but for decades whole communities have been effectively "profiled" for the suspicious combination of being both dark-skinned and poor, thanks to the "broken windows" or "zero tolerance" theory of policing popularized by Rudy Giuliani, when he was mayor of New York City, and his police chief William Bratton.

Flick a cigarette in a heavily patrolled community of color and you're littering; wear the wrong-color T-shirt and you're displaying gang allegiance. Just strolling around in a dodgy neighborhood can mark you as a potential suspect, according to *Let's Get Free: A Hip-Hop Theory of Justice*, an eye-opening new book by Paul Butler, a former federal prosecutor in Washington. If you seem at all evasive, which I suppose is like looking "overly anxious" in an airport, Butler writes, the police "can force you to stop just to investigate why you don't want to talk to them." And don't get grumpy about it or you could be "resisting arrest."

There's no minimum age for being sucked into what the Children's Defense Fund calls "the cradle-to-prison pipeline." In New York City, a teenager caught in public housing without an ID—say, while visiting a friend or relative—can be charged with criminal trespassing and wind up in juvenile detention, Mishi Faruqee, the director of youth justice programs for the Children's Defense Fund of New York, told me. In just the past few months, a growing number of cities have taken to ticketing and sometimes handcuffing teenagers found on the streets during school hours.

In Los Angeles, the fine for truancy is $250; in Dallas, it can be as much as $500—crushing amounts for people living near the poverty level. According to the Los Angeles Bus Riders Union, an advocacy group, twelve thousand students were ticketed for truancy in 2008.

Why does the Bus Riders Union care? Because it estimates that 80 percent of the "truants," especially those who are black or Latino, are merely late for school, thanks to the way that overfilled buses whiz by them without stopping. I met people in Los Angeles who told me they keep their children home if there's the slightest chance of their being late. It's an ingenious antitruancy policy that discourages parents from sending their youngsters to school.

The pattern is to curtail financing for services that might help the poor while ramping up law enforcement: Starve school and public transportation budgets, then make truancy illegal. Shut down public housing, then make it a crime to be homeless. Be sure to harass street vendors when there are few other opportunities for employment. The experience of the poor, and especially poor minorities, comes to resemble that of a rat in a cage scrambling to avoid erratically administered electric shocks.

And if you should make the mistake of trying to escape via a brief marijuana-induced high, it's "gotcha" all over again, because that, of course, is illegal, too. One result is our staggering level of incarceration, the highest in the world. Today the same number of Americans—2.3 million—reside in prison as in public housing.

Meanwhile, the public housing that remains has become ever more prisonlike, with residents subjected to drug testing and random police sweeps. The safety net, or what's left of it, has been transformed into a dragnet.

Some of the community organizers I've talked to around the country think they know why "zero tolerance" policing has ratcheted up since the recession began. Leonardo Vilchis of the Union de Vecinos, a community organization in Los Angeles, suspects that "Poor people have become a source of revenue" for recession-starved cities, and that the police can always find a violation leading to a fine. If so, this is a singularly demented fund-raising strategy. At a congressional hearing in June, the president of the National Association of Criminal Defense Lawyers testified about the pervasive "overcriminalization of crimes that are not a risk to public safety," like sleeping in a cardboard box or jumping turnstiles, which lead to expensively clogged courts and prisons.

A Pew Center study found states spending a record $51.7 billion on corrections, an amount that the center judged, with an excess of moderation, to be "too much."

But will it be enough—the collision of rising prison populations that we can't afford and the criminalization of poverty—to force us to break the mad cycle of poverty and punishment? With the number of people in poverty increasing (some estimates suggest it's up to 45 million to 50 million, from 37 million in 2007), several states are beginning to ease up on the criminalization of poverty—for example, by sending drug offenders to treatment rather than jail, shortening probation and reducing the number of people locked up for technical violations like missed court appointments. But others are tightening the screws: not only increasing the number of "crimes" but also charging prisoners for their room and board—ensuring that they'll be released with potentially criminalizing levels of debt.

Maybe we can't afford the measures that would begin to alleviate America's growing poverty—affordable housing, good schools, reliable public transportation, and so forth. I would argue otherwise, but for now I'd be content with a consensus that, if we can't afford to truly help the poor, neither can we afford to go on tormenting them.

A HOMESPUN SAFETY NET

New York Times, 2009

I f nothing else, the recession is serving as a stress test for the American safety net. How prepared have we been for sudden and violent economic dislocations of the kind that leave millions homeless and jobless? So far, despite some temporary expansions of food stamps and unemployment benefits by the Obama administration, the recession has done for the government safety net pretty much what Hurricane Katrina did for the Federal Emergency Management Agency: It's demonstrated that you can be clinging to your roof with the water rising, and chances are that no one will come to helicopter you out.

Take the case of Kristen and Joe Parente, Delaware residents who had always imagined that people turned to government for help only if "they didn't want to work." Their troubles began well before the recession, when Joe, a fourth-generation pipe fitter, sustained a back injury that left him unfit for even light lifting. He fell into depression for several months, then rallied to ace a state-sponsored retraining course in computer repairs—only to find those skills no longer in demand. The obvious fallback was disability benefits, but—catch-22—when Joe applied he was told he could not qualify without presenting a recent MRI scan. This would cost $800 to $900, which the Parentes do not have, nor has Joe, unlike the rest of the family, been able to qualify for Medicaid.

When Joe and Kristen married as teenagers, the plan had been for Kristen to stay home with the children. But with Joe out of action and three children to support by the middle of this decade, Kristen went to work as a waitress, ending up, in 2008, in a "pretty fancy place on the water." Then the recession struck and in January she was laid off.

Kristen is bright, pretty, and, to judge from her command of her own small kitchen, capable of holding down a dozen tables with precision and grace. In the past she'd always been able to land a new job within days; now there was nothing. Like most laid-off people, she failed to meet the fiendishly complex and sometimes arbitrary eligibility requirements for unemployment benefits. Their car started falling apart.

So in early February, the Parentes turned to the desperate citizen's last resort—Temporary Assistance for Needy Families. Still often called "welfare," the program does not offer cash support to stay-at-home parents as did its predecessor, Aid to Families with Dependent Children. Rather, it provides supplemental income for working parents, based on the sunny assumption that there would always be plenty of jobs for those enterprising enough to get them.

After Kristen applied, nothing happened for six weeks— no money, no phone calls returned. At school, the Parentes' seven-year-old's class was asked to write out what wish they would ask of a genie, should one appear. Brianna's wish was for her mother to find a job because there was nothing to eat in the house, an aspiration that her teacher deemed too disturbing to be posted on the wall with the other children's.

Not until March did the Parentes begin to receive food stamps and some cash assistance. Meanwhile, they were finding out why some recipients have taken to calling the assistance program "Torture and Abuse of Needy Families." From the start, the experience has been "humiliating," Kristen said. The caseworkers "treat you like a bum—they act like every dollar you get is coming out of their own paychecks."

Nationally, according to Kaaryn Gustafson, an associate professor at the University of Connecticut Law School, "applying for welfare is a lot like being booked by the police." There may be a mug shot, fingerprinting, and long interrogations as to one's children's paternity. The ostensible goal is to prevent welfare fraud, but the psychological impact is to turn poverty itself into a kind of crime.

Delaware does not require fingerprints, but the Parentes discovered that they were each expected to apply for forty jobs a week, even though no money was offered for gas, tolls, or babysitting. In addition, Kristen had to drive thirty-five miles a day to attend "job readiness" classes, which she said were "a joke."

With no jobs to be found, Kristen was required to work as a volunteer at a community agency. (God forbid anyone should use government money to let her stay home with her children!) In exchange for $475 a month plus food stamps, the family submits to various forms of "monitoring" to keep them on the straight and narrow. One result is that Kristen lives in constant terror of doing something that would cause the program to report her to Child Protective Services. She worries that the state will remove her children "automatically" if program workers discover that her five-year-old son shares a bedroom with his sisters. No one, of course, is offering to subsidize a larger apartment in the name of child "protection."

It's no secret that the temporary assistance program was designed to repel potential applicants, and at this it has been stunningly successful. The theory is that government assistance encourages a debilitating "culture of poverty," marked by laziness, promiscuity, and addiction, and curable only by a swift cessation of benefits. In the years immediately after welfare "reform," about one and a half million people disappeared from the welfare rolls—often because they'd been "sanctioned" for, say, failing to show up for an appointment with a caseworker. Stories of an erratic and punitive bureaucracy get around, so the recession of 2001 produced no uptick in enrollment, nor, until very recently, did the current recession. As Mark Greenberg, a welfare expert at the Georgetown School of Law, put it, the program has been "strikingly unresponsive" to rising need.

People far more readily turn to food stamps, which have seen a 19 percent surge in enrollment since the recession began. But even these can carry a presumption of guilt or criminal intent. Four states—Arizona, California, New York, and Texas—require that applicants undergo fingerprinting. Furthermore, under a national program called Operation Talon, food stamp offices share applicants' personal data with law enforcement agencies, making it hazardous for anyone who might have an outstanding warrant—for failing to show up for a court hearing on an unpaid debt, for example—to apply.

As in the aftermath of Hurricane Katrina, the most reliable first responders are not government agencies, but family and friends. Kristen and Joe first moved in with her mother and four siblings, and in the weeks before the government came through with a check, she borrowed money from the elderly man whose house she cleans every week, who himself depends on Social Security.

I've never encountered the kind of "culture of poverty" imagined by the framers of welfare reform, but there is a tradition among the American working class of mutual aid, no questions asked. My father, a former miner, advised me as a child that if I ever needed money to "go to a poor man." He liked to tell the story of my great-grandfather, John Howes, who worked in the mines long enough to accumulate a small sum with which to purchase a plot of farmland. But as he was driving out of Butte, Montana, in a horse-drawn wagon, he picked up an Indian woman and her child, and their hard-luck story moved him to give her all his money, turn his horse around and go back to the darkness and danger of the mines.

In her classic study of an African-American community in the late '60s, the anthropologist Carol Stack found rich networks of reciprocal giving and support, and when I worked at low-wage jobs in the 1990s, I was amazed by the generosity of my coworkers, who offered me food, help with my work, and even once a place to stay. Such informal networks—and random acts of kindness—put the official welfare state, with its relentless suspicions and grudging outlays, to shame.

But there are limits to the generosity of relatives and friends. Tensions can arise, as they did between Kristen and her mother, which is what led the Parentes to move to their current apartment in Wilmington. Sandra Smith, a sociologist at the University of California, Berkeley, finds that poverty itself can deplete entire social networks, leaving no one to turn to. While the affluent suffer from "compassion fatigue," the poor simply run out of resources.

At least one influential theory of poverty contends that the poor are *too* mutually dependent, and that this is one of their problems. This perspective is outlined in the book *Bridges Out of Poverty*, cowritten by Ruby K. Payne, a motivational speaker who regularly addresses schoolteachers, social service workers, and members of low-income communities. She argues that the poor need to abandon their dysfunctional culture and emulate the more goal-oriented middle class. Getting out of poverty, according to Payne, is much like overcoming drug addiction, and often requires cutting off contact with those who choose to remain behind: "In order to move from poverty to middle class…an individual must give up relationships for achievement, at least for some period of time." The message from the affluent to the down-and-out: Neither we nor the government is going to do much to help you—and you better not help one another, either. It's every man (or woman or child) for himself.

In the meantime, Kristen has discovered a radically different approach to dealing with poverty. The community agency she volunteered at is Acorn (the Association of Community Organizations for Reform Now), the grassroots organization of low-income people that achieved national notoriety during the 2008 presidential campaign when Republicans attacked it for voter registration fraud (committed by temporary Acorn canvassers and quickly corrected by staff members). Kristen made such a good impression that she was offered a paid job in May, and now, with only a small supplement from the government, she works full time for Acorn, organizing protests against Walgreens for deciding to stop filling Medicaid prescriptions in Delaware, and, in late June, helping turn out thousands of people for a march on Washington to demand universal health insurance.

So the recession tossed Kristen from routine poverty into destitution, and from there, willy-nilly, into a new life as a community organizer and a grassroots leader. I wish I could end the story there, but the Parentes' landlord has just informed them that they'll have to go, because he's decided to sell the building, and they don't have money for a security deposit on a new apartment. "I thought we were good for six months here," Kristen told me, "but every time I let down my guard I just get slammed again."

DEAD, WHITE, AND BLUE: THE GREAT DIE-OFF OF AMERICA'S BLUE-COLLAR WHITE PEOPLE

Guernica, 2015

The white working class, which usually inspires liberal concern only for its paradoxical, Republican-leaning voting habits, has recently become newsworthy for something else: According to economist Anne Case and Angus Deaton, the winner of the latest Nobel Prize in economics, its members in the forty-five- to fifty-four-year-old age group are dying at an immoderate rate. While the life span of affluent white people continues to lengthen, the life span of poor white people has been shrinking. As a result, in just the last four years, the gap between poor white men and wealthier ones has widened by up to four years. The *New York Times* summed up the Deaton and Case study with this headline: "Income Gap, Meet the Longevity Gap."

This was not supposed to happen. For almost a century, the comforting American narrative was that better nutrition and medical care would guarantee longer lives for all. So the great blue-collar die-off has come out of the blue and is, as the *Wall Street Journal* says, "startling."

It was especially not supposed to happen to white people

who, in relation to people of color, have long had the advantage of higher earnings, better access to health care, safer neighborhoods, and, of course, freedom from the daily insults and harms inflicted on the darker-skinned. There has also been a major racial gap in longevity—5.3 years between white and black men and 3.8 years between white and black women—though, hardly noticed, it has been narrowing for the last two decades. Only white people are now dying off in unexpectedly large numbers in middle age, their excess deaths accounted for by suicide, alcoholism, and drug (usually opiate) addiction.

There are some practical reasons why white people are likely to be more efficient than black people at killing themselves. For one thing, they are more likely to be gun owners, and white men favor gunshots as a means of suicide. For another, doctors, undoubtedly acting in part on stereotypes of nonwhite people as drug addicts, are more likely to prescribe powerful opiate painkillers to white people than to people of color. (I've been offered enough oxycodone prescriptions over the years to stock a small illegal business.)

Manual labor—from waitressing to construction work—tends to wear the body down quickly, from knees to back and rotator cuffs, and when Tylenol fails, the doctor may opt for an opiate just to get you through the day.

The Wages of Despair

But something more profound is going on here, too. As *New York Times* columnist Paul Krugman puts it, the "diseases" leading to excess white working-class deaths are those of "despair," and some of the obvious causes are economic. In the last few decades, things have not been going well for working-class people of any color.

I grew up in an America where a man with a strong back—and, better yet, a strong union—could reasonably expect to support a family on his own without a college degree. In 2015, those jobs are long gone, leaving only the kind of work once relegated to women and people of color available in areas like retail, landscaping, and delivery-truck driving. This means that those in the bottom 20 percent of the white income distribution face material circumstances like those long familiar to poor black people, including erratic employment and crowded, hazardous living spaces.

White privilege was never, however, simply a matter of economic advantage. As the great African-American scholar W. E. B. Du Bois wrote in 1935, "It must be remembered that the white group of laborers, while they received a low wage, were compensated in part by a sort of public and psychological wage."

Some of the elements of this invisible wage sound almost quaint today, like Du Bois's assertion that white working-class people were "admitted freely with all classes of white people to public functions, public parks, and the best schools." Today, there are few public spaces that are not open, at least legally speaking, to black people, while the "best" schools are reserved for the affluent—mostly white and Asian American, along with a sprinkling of other people of color to provide the fairy dust of "diversity." While white Americans have lost ground economically, black people have made gains, at least in the de jure sense. As a result, the "psychological wage" awarded to white people has been shrinking.

For most of American history, government could be counted on to maintain white power and privilege by enforcing slavery and later segregation. When the federal government finally weighed in on the side of desegregation, working-class white people were left to defend their own diminishing privilege by moving rightward toward the likes of Alabama Governor (and later presidential candidate) George Wallace and his many white pseudo-populist successors down to Donald Trump.

At the same time, the day-to-day task of upholding white power devolved from the federal government to the state and then local level, specifically to local police forces, which, as we know, have taken it up with such enthusiasm as to become both a national and international scandal. The *Guardian*, for instance, now keeps a running tally of the number of Americans (mostly black) killed by cops (as of this moment, 1,209 for 2015), while black protest, in the form of the Black Lives Matter movement and a wave of on-campus demonstrations, has largely recaptured the moral high ground formerly occupied by the civil rights movement.

The culture, too, has been inching bit by bit toward racial equality, if not, in some limited areas, black ascendency. If the stock image of the early twentieth century "Negro" was the minstrel, the role of rural simpleton in popular culture has been taken over in this century by the characters in *Duck Dynasty* and *Here Comes Honey Boo Boo*. At least in the entertainment world, working-class white people are now regularly portrayed as moronic, while black people are often hyperarticulate, street-smart, and sometimes as wealthy as Kanye West. It's not easy to maintain the usual sense of white superiority when parts of the media are squeezing laughs from the contrast between savvy black people and rural white bumpkins, as in the Tina Fey comedy *Unbreakable Kimmy Schmidt*. White, presumably upper-middle-class people generally conceive of these characters and plot lines, which, to a child of white working-class parents like myself, sting with condescension.

Of course, there was also the election of the first black president. White, native-born Americans began to talk of "taking our country back." The more affluent ones formed the Tea Party; less affluent ones often contented themselves with affixing Confederate flag decals to their trucks.

On the American Downward Slope

All of this means that the maintenance of white privilege, especially among the least privileged white people, has become more difficult and so, for some, more urgent than ever. Poor white people always had the comfort of knowing that someone was worse off and more despised than they were; racial subjugation was the ground under their feet, the rock they stood upon, even when their own situation was deteriorating.

If the government, especially at the federal level, is no longer as reliable an enforcer of white privilege, then it's grassroots initiatives by individuals and small groups that are helping to fill the gap—perpetrating the microaggressions that roil college campuses, the racial slurs yelled from pickup trucks, or, at a deadly extreme, the shooting up of a black church renowned for its efforts in the civil rights era. Dylann Roof, the Charleston killer who did just that, was a jobless high school dropout and reportedly a heavy user of alcohol and opiates. Even without a death sentence hanging over him, Roof was surely headed toward an early demise.

Acts of racial aggression may provide their white perpetrators with a fleeting sense of triumph, but they also take a special kind of effort. It takes effort, for instance, to target a black runner and swerve over to insult her from your truck; it takes such effort—and a strong stomach—to paint a racial slur in excrement on a dormitory bathroom wall. College students may do such things in part out of a sense of economic vulnerability, the knowledge that as soon as school is over their college-debt payments will come due. No matter the effort expended, however, it is especially hard to maintain a feeling of racial superiority while struggling to hold onto one's own place near the bottom of an undependable economy.

While there is no medical evidence that racism is toxic to those who express it—after all, generations of wealthy slave owners survived quite nicely—the combination of downward mobility and racial resentment may be a potent invitation to the kind of despair that leads to suicide in one form or another, whether by gunshots or drugs. You can't break a glass ceiling if you're standing on ice.

It's easy for the liberal intelligentsia to feel righteous in their disgust for lower-class white racism, but the college-educated elite that produces the intelligentsia is in trouble, too, with diminishing prospects and an ever-slipperier slope for the young. Whole professions have fallen on hard times, from college teaching to journalism and the law. One of the worst mistakes this relative elite could make is to try to pump up its own pride by hating on those—of any color or ethnicity—who are falling even faster.

HEALTH

WELCOME TO CANCERLAND

Harper's Magazine, 2001

I was thinking of it as one of those drive-by mammograms, one stop in a series of mundane missions including post office, supermarket, and gym, but I began to lose my nerve in the changing room, and not only because of the kinky necessity of baring my breasts and affixing tiny x-ray opaque stars to the tip of each nipple. I had been in this place only four months earlier, but that visit was just part of the routine cancer surveillance all good citizens of HMOs or health plans are expected to submit to once they reach the age of fifty, and I hadn't really been paying attention then. The results of that earlier session had aroused some "concern" on the part of the radiologist and her confederate, the gynecologist, so I am back now in the role of a suspect, eager to clear my name, alert to medical missteps and unfair allegations. But the changing room, really just a closet off the stark windowless space that houses the mammogram machine, contains something far worse. I notice for the first time now an assumption about who I am, where I am going, and what I will need when I get there. Almost

all of the eye-level space has been filled with photocopied
bits of cuteness and sentimentality: pink ribbons, a cartoon
about a woman with iatrogenically flattened breasts, an
"Ode to a Mammogram," a list of the "Top Ten Things
Only Women Understand" ("Fat Clothes" and "Eyelash
Curlers" among them), and, inescapably, right next to the
door, the poem "I Said a Prayer for You Today," illustrated
with pink roses.

It goes on and on, this mother of all mammograms, cutting into gym time, dinnertime, and lifetime generally.
Sometimes the machine doesn't work, and I get squished
into position to no purpose at all. More often, the x-ray is
successful but apparently alarming to the invisible radiologist, off in some remote office, who calls the shots and never
has the courtesy to show her face with an apology or an
explanation. I try pleading with the technician: I have no
known risk factors, no breast cancer in the family, I had my
babies relatively young and nursed them both. I eat right,
drink sparingly, work out, and doesn't that count for something? But she just gets this tight little professional smile
on her face, either out of guilt for the torture she's inflict-
ing or because she already knows something that I am going
to be sorry to find out for myself. For an hour and a half
the procedure is repeated: the squishing, the snapshot, the
technician bustling off to consult the radiologist and returning with a demand for new angles and more definitive
images. In the intervals while she's off with the doctor I read
the *New York Times* right down to the personally irrelevant
sections like theater and real estate, eschewing the stack of
women's magazines provided for me, much as I ordinarily

enjoy a quick read about sweatproof eyeliners and "fabulous sex tonight," because I have picked up this warning vibe in the changing room, which, in my increasingly anxious state, translates into: Femininity is death. Finally there is nothing left to read but one of the free local weekly newspapers, where I find, buried deep in the classifieds, something even more unsettling than the growing prospect of major disease—a classified ad for a "breast cancer teddy bear" with a pink ribbon stitched to its chest.

Yes, atheists pray in their foxholes—in this case, with a yearning new to me and sharp as lust, for a clean and honorable death by shark bite, lightning strike, sniper fire, car crash. Let me be hacked to death by a madman, is my silent supplication—anything but suffocation by the pink sticky sentiment embodied in that bear and oozing from the walls of the changing room.

My official induction into breast cancer comes about ten days later with the biopsy, which, for reasons I cannot ferret out of the surgeon, has to be a surgical one, performed on an outpatient basis but under general anesthesia, from which I awake to find him standing perpendicular to me, at the far end of the gurney, down near my feet, stating gravely, "Unfortunately, there is a cancer." It takes me all the rest of that drug-addled day to decide that the most heinous thing about that sentence is not the presence of cancer but the absence of me—for I, Barbara, do not enter into it, even as a location, a geographical reference point. Where I once was—not a commanding presence perhaps but nonetheless a standard assemblage of flesh and words and gesture—"there is a cancer." I have been replaced by *it*, is the surgeon's implication. This is what I am now, medically speaking.

In my last act of dignified self-assertion, I request to see the pathology slides myself. This is not difficult to arrange in our small-town hospital, where the pathologist turns out to be a friend of a friend, and my rusty PhD in cell biology (Rockefeller University, 1968) probably helps. He's a jolly fellow, the pathologist, who calls me "hon" and sits me down at one end of the dual-head microscope while he mans the other and moves a pointer through the field. These are the cancer cells, he says, showing up blue because of their overactive DNA. Most of them are arranged in staid semicircular arrays, like suburban houses squeezed into a cul-de-sac, but I also see what I know enough to know I do not want to see: the characteristic "Indian files" of cells on the march. The "enemy," I am supposed to think—an image to save up for future exercises in "visualization" of their violent deaths at the hands of the body's killer cells, the lymphocytes and macrophages. But I am impressed, against all rational self-interest, by the energy of these cellular conga lines, their determination to move on out from the backwater of the breast to colonize lymph nodes, bone marrow, lungs, and brain. These are, after all, the fanatics of Barbaraness, the rebel cells that have realized that the genome they carry, the genetic essence of me, has no further chance of normal reproduction in the postmenopausal body we share, so why not just start multiplying like bunnies and hope for a chance to break out?

It has happened, after all; some genomes have achieved immortality through cancer. When I was a graduate student, I once asked about the strain of tissue-culture cells labeled "HeLa" in the heavy-doored room maintained at body temperature. "HeLa," it turns out, refers to Henrietta Lacks, an African-American woman whose tumor was the progenitor of all HeLa cells, and whose unwitting contribution to science has only recently been recognized. She died; they live, and will go on living until someone gets tired of them or forgets to change their tissue-culture medium and leaves them to starve. Maybe this is what my rebel cells have in mind, and I try beaming them a solemn warning: The chances of your surviving me in tissue culture are nil. Keep up this selfish rampage and you go down, every last one of you, along with the entire Barbara enterprise. But what kind of a role model am I, or are multicellular human organisms generally, for putting the common good above mad anarchistic individual ambition? There is a reason, it occurs to me, why cancer is our metaphor for so many runaway social processes, like corruption and "moral decay": We are no less out of control ourselves.

After the visit to the pathologist, my biological curiosity drops to a lifetime nadir. I know women who followed up their diagnoses with weeks or months of self-study, mastering their options, interviewing doctor after doctor, assessing the damage to be expected from the available treatments. But I can tell from a few hours of investigation that the career of a breast-cancer patient has been pretty well mapped out in advance for me: You may get to negotiate the choice between lumpectomy and mastectomy, but lumpectomy is commonly followed by weeks of radiation, and in either case if the lymph nodes turn out, upon dissection, to be

invaded—or "involved," as it's less threateningly put—
you're doomed to chemotherapy, meaning baldness, nausea,
mouth sores, immunosuppression, and possible anemia.
These interventions do not constitute a "cure" or anything
close, which is why the death rate from breast cancer has
changed very little since the 1930s, when mastectomy was
the only treatment available. Chemotherapy, which became
a routine part of breast-cancer treatment in the eighties,
does not confer anywhere near as decisive an advantage
as patients are often led to believe, especially in postmenopausal women like myself—a two or three percentage
point difference in ten-year survival rates,[1] according to
America's best-known breast-cancer surgeon at the time,
Dr. Susan Love. I know these bleak facts, or sort of know
them, but in the fog of anesthesia that hangs over those
first few weeks, I seem to lose my capacity for self-defense.
The pressure is on, from doctors and loved ones, to do
something right away—kill it, get it out now. The endless
exams, the bone scan to check for metastases, the high-
tech heart test to see if I'm strong enough to withstand
chemotherapy—all these blur the line between selfhood
and thing-hood anyway, organic and inorganic, me and it.
As my cancer career unfolds, I will, the helpful pamphlets
explain, become a composite of the living and the dead—an
implant to replace the breast, a wig to replace the hair. And
then what will I mean when I use the word "I"? I fall into

---

1   In the United States, one in eight women will be diagnosed with breast cancer
at some point. The chances of her surviving for five years are 86.8 percent. For a
black woman this falls to 72 percent; and for a woman of any race whose cancer
has spread to the lymph nodes, to 77.7 percent.

a state of unreasoning passive aggressivity: They diagnosed this, so it's their baby. They found it, let them fix it.

I could take my chances with "alternative" treatments, of course, like punk novelist Kathy Acker, who succumbed to breast cancer in 1997 after a course of alternative therapies in Mexico, or actress and ThighMaster promoter Suzanne Somers, who made tabloid headlines by injecting herself with mistletoe brew. Or I could choose to do nothing at all beyond mentally exhorting my immune system to exterminate the traitorous cellular faction. But I have never admired the "natural" or believed in the "wisdom of the body." Death is as "natural" as anything gets, and the body has always seemed to me like a Siamese twin dragging along behind me, a hysteric really, dangerously overreacting, in my case, to everyday allergens and minute ingestions of sugar. I will put my faith in science, even if this means that the dumb old body is about to be transmogrified into an evil clown—puking, trembling, swelling, surrendering significant parts, and oozing postsurgical fluids. The surgeon—a more genial and forthcoming one this time—can fit me in; the oncologist will see me. Welcome to Cancerland.

Fortunately, no one has to go through this alone. Thirty years ago, before Betty Ford, Rose Kushner, Betty Rollin, and other pioneer patients spoke out, breast cancer was a dread secret, endured in silence and euphemized in obituaries as a "long illness." Something about the conjuncture of "breast," signifying sexuality and nurturance, and that other word, suggesting the claws of a devouring crustacean, spooked almost everyone. Today, however, it's the biggest disease on the cultural map, bigger than AIDS, cystic

fibrosis, or spinal injury, bigger even than those more prolific killers of women—heart disease, lung cancer, and
stroke. There are roughly hundreds of websites devoted to
it, not to mention newsletters, support groups, a whole
genre of first-person breast-cancer books; even, for a while,
a glossy, upper-middle-brow, monthly magazine, *Mamm*.
There are four major national breast-cancer organizations,
of which the mightiest, in financial terms, is the Susan G.
Komen Foundation, headed by breast-cancer veteran and
Bush's nominee for ambassador to Hungary Nancy Brinker.
Komen organizes the annual Race for the Cure, which attracts about a million people—mostly survivors, friends,
and family members. Its website provides a microcosm of
the new breast-cancer culture, offering news of the races,
message boards for accounts of individuals' struggles with
the disease, and a "marketplace" of breast-cancer-related
products to buy.

More so than in the case of any other disease, breast-
cancer organizations and events feed on a generous flow
of corporate support. Nancy Brinker relates how her early
attempts to attract corporate interest in promoting breast
cancer "awareness" were met with rebuff. A bra manufacturer, importuned to affix a mammogram-reminder tag to
his product, more or less wrinkled his nose. Now breast
cancer has blossomed from wallflower to the most popular
girl at the corporate charity prom. While AIDS goes begging and low-rent diseases like tuberculosis have no friends
at all, breast cancer has been able to count on Revlon, Avon,
Ford, Tiffany, Pier 1, Estée Lauder, Ralph Lauren, Lee
Jeans, Saks Fifth Avenue, JCPenney, Boston Market,

Wilson athletic gear—and I apologize to those I've omitted. You can "shop for the cure" during the week when Saks donates 2 percent of sales to a breast-cancer fund; "wear denim for the cure" during Lee National Denim Day, when for a $5 donation you get to wear blue jeans to work. You can even "invest for the cure," in the Kinetics Asset Management's new no-load Medical Fund, which specializes entirely in businesses involved in cancer research.

If you can't run, bike, or climb a mountain for the cure— all of which endeavors are routine beneficiaries of corporate sponsorship—you can always purchase one of the many products with a breast-cancer theme. There are 2.2 million American women in various stages of their breast-cancer careers, who, along with anxious relatives, make up a significant market for all things breast-cancer-related. Bears, for example: I have identified four distinct lines, or species, of these creatures, including "Carol," the Remembrance Bear; "Hope," the Breast Cancer Research Bear, which wears a pink turban as if to conceal chemotherapy-induced baldness; the "Susan Bear," named for Nancy Brinker's deceased sister, Susan; and the new Nick & Nora Wish Upon a Star Bear, available, along with the Susan Bear, at the Komen Foundation website's "marketplace."

And bears are only the tip, so to speak, of the cornucopia of pink-ribbon-themed breast-cancer products. You can dress in pink-beribboned sweatshirts, denim shirts, pajamas, lingerie, aprons, loungewear, shoelaces, and socks; accessorize with pink rhinestone brooches, angel pins, scarves, caps, earrings, and bracelets; brighten up your home with breast-cancer candles, stained-glass pink-ribbon candleholders, coffee mugs, pendants, wind chimes, and night-lights; pay your bills with special BreastChecks or a separate line of Checks for the Cure. "Awareness" beats secrecy and stigma, of course, but I can't help noticing that the existential space in which a friend has earnestly advised me to "confront [my] mortality" bears a striking resemblance to the mall.

This is not, I should point out, a case of cynical merchants exploiting the sick. Some of the breast-cancer tchotchkes and accessories are made by breast-cancer survivors themselves, such as "Janice," creator of the "Daisy Awareness Necklace," among other things, and in most cases a portion of the sales goes to breast-cancer research. Virginia Davis of Aurora, Colorado, was inspired to create the "Remembrance Bear" by a friend's double mastectomy and sees her work as more of a "crusade" than a business. This year she expects to ship 10,000 of these teddies, which are manufactured in China, and send part of the money to the Race for the Cure. If the bears are infantilizing—as I try ever so tactfully to suggest that this is how they may, in rare cases, be perceived—so far no one has complained. "I just get love letters," she tells me, "from people who say, 'God bless you for thinking of us.'"

The ultrafeminine theme of the breast-cancer "marketplace"—the prominence, for example, of cosmetics and jewelry—could be understood as a response to the treatments' disastrous effects on one's looks. But the infantilizing trope is a little harder to account for, and teddy bears are not its only manifestation. A tote bag distributed to breast-cancer patients by the Libby Ross Foundation (through places such as the Columbia Presbyterian Medical Center) contains, among other items, a tube of Estée Lauder Perfumed Body Crème, a hot-pink satin pillowcase, an audiotape "Meditation to Help You with Chemotherapy," a small tin of peppermint pastilles, a set of three small inexpensive rhinestone bracelets, a pink-striped "journal and sketchbook," and—somewhat jarringly—a small box of crayons. Marla Willner, one of the founders of the Libby Ross Foundation, told me that the crayons "go with the journal—for people to express different moods, different thoughts..." though she admitted she has never tried to write with crayons herself. Possibly the idea is that regression to a state of childlike dependency puts one in the best frame of mind with which to endure the prolonged and toxic treatments. Or it may be that, in some versions of the prevailing gender ideology, femininity is by its nature incompatible with full adulthood—a state of arrested development. Certainly men diagnosed with prostate cancer do not receive gifts of Matchbox cars.

But I, no less than the bear huggers, need whatever help I can get, and start wading out into the web in search of practical tips on hair loss, lumpectomy versus mastectomy, how to select a chemotherapy regimen, what to wear after surgery and what to eat when the scent of food sucks. There is, I soon find, far more than I can usefully absorb, for thousands of the afflicted have posted their stories, beginning with the lump or bad mammogram, proceeding through the agony of the treatments; pausing to mention the sustaining forces of family, humor, and religion; and ending, in almost all cases, with warm words of encouragement for the neophyte. Some of these are no more than a paragraph long—brief waves from sister sufferers; others offer almost hour-by-hour logs of breast-deprived, chemotherapized lives:

> **Tuesday, August 15, 2000**: Well, I survived my 4th chemo. Very, very dizzy today. Very nauseated, but no barfing! It's a first.…I break out in a cold sweat and my heart pounds if I stay up longer than 5 minutes.

> **Friday, August 18, 2000**:…By dinnertime, I was full-out nauseated. I took some meds and ate a rice and vegetable bowl from Trader Joe's. It smelled and tasted awful to me, but I ate it anyway.…Rick brought home some Kern's nectars and I'm drinking that. Seems to have settled my stomach a little bit.

I can't seem to get enough of these tales, reading on with panicky fascination about everything that can go wrong—septicemia, ruptured implants, startling recurrences a few years after the completion of treatments, "mets" (metastases) to vital organs, and—what scares me most in the short term—"chemo brain," or the cognitive deterioration that sometimes accompanies chemotherapy. I compare myself with everyone, selfishly impatient with those whose conditions are less menacing, shivering over those who have reached Stage IV ("There is no Stage V," as the main character in the play *Wit*, who has ovarian cancer, explains), constantly assessing my chances.

Feminism helped make the spreading breast-cancer sisterhood possible, and this realization gives me a faint feeling of belonging. Thirty years ago, when the disease went hidden behind euphemism and prostheses, medicine was a solid patriarchy, women's bodies its passive objects of labor. The women's health movement, in which I was an activist in the seventies and eighties, legitimized self-help and mutual support, and encouraged women to network directly, sharing their stories, questioning the doctors, banding together. It is hard now to recall how revolutionary these activities once seemed, and probably few participants in breast-cancer chat rooms and on breast-cancer message boards realize that when postmastectomy patients first proposed meeting in support groups in the mid-1970s, the American Cancer Society responded with a firm and fatherly "no." Now no one leaves the hospital without a brochure directing her to local support groups and, at least in my case, a follow-up call from a social worker to see whether I am safely ensconced in one. This cheers me briefly, until I realize that if support groups have won the stamp of medical approval this may be because they are no longer perceived as seditious.

In fact, aside from the dilute sisterhood of the cyber (and actual) support groups, there is nothing very feminist—in an ideological or activist sense—about the mainstream of breast-cancer culture today. Let me pause to qualify: You can, if you look hard enough, find plenty of genuine, self-identified feminists within the vast pink sea of the breast-cancer crusade, women who are militantly determined to "beat the epidemic" and insistent on more user-friendly approaches to treatment. It was feminist health activists who led the campaign, in the seventies and eighties, against the most savage form of breast-cancer surgery—the Halsted radical mastectomy, which removed chest muscle and lymph nodes as well as breast tissue and left women permanently disabled. It was the women's health movement that put a halt to the surgical practice, common in the seventies, of proceeding directly from biopsy to mastectomy without ever rousing the patient from anesthesia. More recently, feminist advocacy groups such as the San Francisco–based Breast Cancer Action and the Cambridge-based Women's Community Cancer Project helped blow the whistle on "high-dose chemotherapy," in which the bone marrow was removed prior to otherwise lethal doses of chemotherapy and later replaced—to no good effect, as it turned out.

Like everyone else in the breast-cancer world, the feminists want a cure, but they even more ardently demand to know the cause or causes of the disease without which we will never have any means of prevention. "Bad" genes of the inherited variety are thought to account for fewer than 10 percent of breast cancers, and only 30 percent of women diagnosed with breast cancer have any known risk factor (such as delaying childbearing or the late onset of menopause) at all. Bad lifestyle choices like a fatty diet have, after brief popularity with the medical profession, been largely ruled out. Hence suspicion should focus on environmental carcinogens, the feminists argue, such as plastics, pesticides (DDT and PCBs, for example, though banned in this country, are still used in many countries that grow the produce we eat), and the industrial runoff in our groundwater. No carcinogen has been linked definitely to human breast cancer yet, but many have been found to cause the disease in mice, and the inexorable increase of the disease in industrialized nations—about 1 percent a year between the 1950s and the 1990s—further hints at environmental factors, as does the fact that women migrants to industrialized countries quickly develop the same breast-cancer rates as those who are native born. Their emphasis on possible ecological factors, which is not shared by groups such as Komen and the American Cancer Society, puts the feminist breast-cancer activists in league with other, frequently rambunctious, social movements—environmental and anticorporate.

But today theirs are discordant voices in a general chorus of sentimentality and good cheer; after all, breast cancer would hardly be the darling of corporate America if its complexion changed from pink to green. It is the very blandness of breast cancer, at least in mainstream perceptions, that makes it an attractive object of corporate charity and a way for companies to brand themselves friends of the middle-aged female market. With breast cancer, "There was no concern that you might actually turn off your audience because of the lifestyle or sexual connotations that AIDS has," Amy Langer, director of the National Alliance of Breast Cancer Organizations, told the *New York Times* in 1996. "That gives corporations a certain freedom and a certain relief in supporting the cause." Or as Cindy Pearson, director of the National Women's Health Network, the organizational progeny of the women's health movement, puts it more caustically: "Breast cancer provides a way of doing something for women, without being feminist."

In the mainstream of breast-cancer culture, one finds very little anger, no mention of possible environmental causes, few complaints about the fact that, in all but the more advanced, metastasized cases, it is the "treatments," not the disease, that cause illness and pain. The stance toward existing treatments is occasionally critical—in *Mamm*, for example—but more commonly grateful; the overall tone, almost universally upbeat. The Breast Friends website, for example, features a series of inspirational quotes: "Don't cry over anything that can't cry over you," "I can't stop the birds of sorrow from circling my head, but I can stop them from building a nest in my hair," "When life hands out lemons, squeeze out a smile," "Don't wait for your ship to come in...Swim out to meet it," and much more of that ilk. Even in the relatively sophisticated *Mamm*, a columnist bemoans not cancer or chemotherapy but the end of chemotherapy, and humorously proposes to deal with her separation anxiety by pitching a tent outside her oncologist's office. So pervasive is the perkiness of the breast-cancer world that unhappiness requires a kind of apology, as when "Lucy," whose "long-term prognosis is not good," starts her personal narrative on breastcancertalk.org by telling us that her story "is not the usual one, full of sweetness and hope, but true nevertheless."

There is, I discover, no single noun to describe a woman with breast cancer. As in the AIDS movement, upon which breast-cancer activism is partly modeled, the words "patient" and "victim," with their aura of self-pity and passivity, have been ruled un-PC. Instead, we get verbs: Those who are in the midst of their treatments are described as "battling" or "fighting," sometimes intensified with "bravely" or "fiercely"—language suggestive of Katharine Hepburn with her face to the wind. Once the treatments are over, one achieves the status of "survivor," which is how the women in my local support group identify themselves, AA-style, as we convene to share war stories and rejoice in our "survivorhood": "Hi, I'm Kathy and I'm a three-year survivor." For those who cease to be survivors and join the more than 40,000 American women who succumb to breast cancer each year—again, no noun applies. They are said to have "lost their battle" and may be memorialized by photographs carried at races for the cure—our lost, brave sisters, our fallen soldiers. But in the overwhelmingly Darwinian culture that has grown up around breast cancer, martyrs count for little; it is the "survivors" who merit constant honor and acclaim. They, after all, offer living proof that expensive and painful treatments may in some cases actually work.

Scared and medically weakened women can hardly be expected to transform their support groups into bands of activists and rush out into the streets, but the equanimity of breast-cancer culture goes beyond mere absence of anger to what looks, all too often, like a positive embrace of the disease. As "Mary" reports, on the Bosom Buds message board:

> I really believe I am a much more sensitive and thoughtful person now. It might sound funny but I was a real worrier before. Now I don't want to waste my energy on worrying. I enjoy life so much more now and in a lot of aspects I am much happier now.

Or this from "Andee":

This was the hardest year of my life but also in many ways the most rewarding. I got rid of the baggage, made peace with my family, met many amazing people, learned to take very good care of my body so it will take care of me, and reprioritized my life.

Cindy Cherry, quoted in the *Washington Post*, goes further:

If I had to do it over, would I want breast cancer? Absolutely. I'm not the same person I was, and I'm glad I'm not. Money doesn't matter anymore. I've met the most phenomenal people in my life through this. Your friends and family are what matter now.

The First Year of the Rest of Your Life, a collection of brief narratives with a foreword by Nancy Brinker and a share of the royalties going to the Komen Foundation, is filled with such testimonies to the redemptive powers of the disease: "I can honestly say I am happier now than I have ever been in my life—even before the breast cancer." "For me, breast cancer has provided a good kick in the rear to get me started rethinking my life." "I have come out stronger, with a new sense of priorities. Never a complaint about lost time, shattered sexual confidence, or the long-term weakening of the arms caused by lymph-node dissection and radiation. What does not destroy you, to paraphrase Nietzsche, makes you a spunkier, more evolved, sort of person.

The effect of this relentless brightsiding is to transform breast cancer into a rite of passage—not an injustice or a tragedy to rail against, but a normal marker in the life cycle, like menopause or graying hair. Everything in mainstream breast-cancer culture serves, no doubt inadvertently, to tame and normalize the disease: The diagnosis may be disastrous, but there are those cunning pink rhinestone angel pins to buy and races to train for. Even the heavy traffic in personal narratives and practical tips, which I found so useful, bears an implicit acceptance of the disease and the current barbarous approaches to its treatment: You can get so busy comparing attractive head scarves that you forget to question a form of treatment that temporarily renders you both bald and immuno-incompetent. Understood as a rite of passage, breast cancer resembles the initiation rites so exhaustively studied by Mircea Eliade: First there is the selection of the initiates—by age in the tribal situation, by mammogram or palpation here. Then come the requisite ordeals—scarification or circumcision within traditional cultures, surgery and chemotherapy for the cancer patient. Finally, the initiate emerges into a new and higher status— an adult and a warrior—or, in the case of breast cancer, a "survivor."

And in our implacably optimistic breast-cancer culture, the disease offers more than the intangible benefits of spiritual upward mobility. You can defy the inevitable disfigurements and come out, on the survivor side, actually prettier, sexier, more femme. In the lore of the disease— shared with me by oncology nurses as well as by survivors— chemotherapy smooths and tightens the skin; helps you lose weight; and, when your hair comes back, it will be fuller, softer, easier to control, and perhaps a surprising new color. These may be myths, but for those willing to get with the prevailing program, opportunities for self-improvement abound. The American Cancer Society offers the "Look Good…Feel Better" program, "dedicated to teaching women cancer patients beauty techniques to help restore their appearance and self-image during cancer treatment." Thirty thousand women participate a year, each copping a free makeover and bag of makeup donated by the Cosmetic, Toiletry, and Fragrance Association, the trade association of the cosmetics industry. As for that lost breast: After reconstruction, why not bring the other one up to speed? Of the more than 50,000 mastectomy patients who opt for reconstruction each year, 17 percent go on, often at the urging of their plastic surgeons, to get additional surgery so that the remaining breast will "match" the more erect and perhaps larger new structure on the other side.

Not everyone goes for cosmetic deceptions, and the question of wigs versus baldness, reconstruction versus undisguised scar, defines one of the few real disagreements in breast-cancer culture. On the more avant-garde, upper-middle-class side, *Mamm* magazine—which features literary critic Eve Kosofsky Sedgwick as a columnist—tends to favor the "natural" look. Here, mastectomy scars can be "sexy" and baldness something to celebrate. The January 2001 cover story features women who "looked upon their baldness not just as a loss, but also as an opportunity: to indulge their playful sides…to come in contact, in new ways, with their truest selves." One decorates her scalp with temporary tattoos of peace signs, panthers, and frogs; another expresses herself with a shocking purple wig; a third reports that unadorned baldness makes her feel "sensual, powerful, able to re-create myself with every new day." But no hard feelings toward those who choose to hide their condition under wigs or scarves; it's just a matter, *Mamm* tells us, of "different aesthetics." Some go for pink ribbons; others will prefer the Ralph Lauren Pink Pony breast-cancer motif. But everyone agrees that breast cancer is a chance for creative self-transformation—a makeover opportunity, in fact.

Now, cheerfulness, up to and including delusion and false hope, has a recognized place in medicine. There is plenty of evidence that depressed and socially isolated people are more prone to succumb to diseases, cancer included, and a diagnosis of cancer is probably capable of precipitating serious depression all by itself. To be told by authority figures that you have a deadly disease, for which no real cure exists, is to enter a liminal state fraught with perils that go well beyond the disease itself. Consider the phenomenon of "voodoo death"—described by ethnographers among, for example, Australian aborigines—in which a person who has been condemned by a suitably potent curse obligingly shuts down and dies within a day or two. Cancer diagnoses could, and in some cases probably do, have the same kind of fatally dispiriting effect. So, it could be argued, the collectively pumped-up optimism of breast-cancer culture may be just what the doctor ordered. Shop for the Cure, dress in pink-ribbon regalia, organize a run or hike—whatever gets you through the night.

But in the seamless world of breast-cancer culture, where one website links to another—from personal narratives and grassroots endeavors to the glitzy level of corporate sponsors and celebrity spokespeople—cheerfulness is more or less mandatory, dissent a kind of treason. Within this tightly knit world, attitudes are subtly adjusted, doubters gently brought back to the fold. In *The First Year of the Rest of Your Life*, for example, each personal narrative is followed by a study question or tip designed to counter the slightest hint of negativity—and they are very slight hints indeed, since the collection includes no harridans, whiners, or feminist militants:

> Have you given yourself permission to acknowledge you have some anxiety or "blocks" and to ask for help for your emotional well-being?
>
> Is there an area in your life of unresolved internal conflict? Is there an area where you think you might want to do some "healthy mourning"?
>
> Try keeping a list of the things you find "good about today."

As an experiment, I post a statement on the Komen.org message board, under the subject line "angry," briefly listing my own heartfelt complaints about debilitating treatments, recalcitrant insurance companies, environmental carcinogens, and, most daringly, "sappy pink ribbons." I receive a few words of encouragement in my fight with the insurance company, which has taken the position that my biopsy was a kind of optional indulgence, but mostly a chorus of rebukes. "Suzy" writes to say, "I really dislike saying you have a bad attitude toward all of this, but you do, and it's not going to help you in the least." "Mary" is a bit more tolerant, writing, "Barb, at this time in your life, it's so important to put all your energies toward a peaceful, if not happy, existence. Cancer is a rotten thing to have happen and there are no answers for any of us as to why. But to live your life, whether you have one more year or 51, in anger and bitterness is such a waste...I hope you can find some peace. You deserve it. We all do. God bless you and keep you in His loving care. Your sister, Mary."

"Kitty," however, thinks I've gone around the bend: "You need to run, not walk, to some counseling...Please, get yourself some help and I ask everyone on this site to pray for you so you can enjoy life to the fullest."

I do get some reinforcement from "Gerri," who has been through all the treatments and now finds herself in terminal condition: "I am also angry. All the money that is raised, all the smiling faces of survivors who make it sound like it is OK to have breast cancer. IT IS NOT OK!" But Gerri's message, like the others on the message board, is posted under the mocking heading "What does it mean to be a breast-cancer survivor?"

"Culture" is too weak a word to describe all this. What has grown up around breast cancer in just the last fifteen years more nearly resembles a cult—or, given that it numbers more than two million women, their families, and friends—perhaps we should say a full-fledged religion. The products—teddy bears, pink-ribbon brooches, and so forth—serve as amulets and talismans, comforting the sufferer and providing visible evidence of faith. The personal narratives serve as testimonials and follow the same general arc as the confessional autobiographies required of seventeenth-century Puritans: First there is a crisis, often involving a sudden apprehension of mortality (the diagnosis or, in the old Puritan case, a stern word from on high); then comes a prolonged ordeal (the treatment or, in the religious case, internal struggle with the Devil); and finally, the blessed certainty of salvation, or its breast-cancer equivalent, survivorhood. And like most recognized religions, breast cancer has its great epideictic events, its pilgrimages and mass gatherings where the faithful convene and draw strength from their numbers. These are the annual races for a cure, attracting a total of about a million people at more than eighty sites—70,000 of them at the largest event, in Washington, DC, which in recent years has been attended by Dan and Marilyn Quayle and Al and Tipper Gore. Everything comes together at the races: Celebrities and corporate sponsors are showcased; products are hawked; talents, like those of the "Swinging, Singing Survivors" from Syracuse, New York, are displayed. It is at the races, too, that the elect confirm their special status. As one participant wrote in the *Washington Post*:

> I have taken my "battle scarred" breasts to the Mall, donned the pink shirt, visor, pink shoelaces, etc. and walked proudly among my fellow veterans of the breast cancer war. In 1995, at the age of 44, I was diagnosed and treated for Stage II breast cancer. The experience continues to redefine my life.

Feminist breast-cancer activists, who in the early nineties were organizing their own mass outdoor events—demonstrations, not races—to demand increased federal funding for research, tend to keep their distance from these huge, corporate-sponsored, pink gatherings. Ellen Leopold, for example—a member of the Women's Community Cancer Project in Cambridge and author of *A Darker Ribbon: Breast Cancer, Women, and Their Doctors in the Twentieth Century*—has criticized the races as an inefficient way of raising money. She points out that the Avon Breast Cancer Crusade, which sponsors three-day, sixty-mile walks, spends more than a third of the money raised on overhead and advertising, and Komen may similarly fritter away up to 25 percent of its gross. At least one corporate-charity insider agrees. "It would be much easier and more productive," says Rob Wilson, an organizer of charitable races for corporate clients, "if people, instead of running or riding, would write out a check to the charity."

To true believers, such criticisms miss the point, which is always, ultimately, "awareness." Whatever you do to publicize the disease—wear a pink ribbon, buy a teddy bear, attend a race—reminds other women to come forward for their mammograms. Hence, too, they would argue, the cult of the "survivor": If women neglect their annual screenings, it must be because they are afraid that a diagnosis amounts to a death sentence. Beaming survivors, proudly displaying their athletic prowess, are the best possible advertisement for routine screening mammograms, early detection, and the ensuing round of treatments. Yes, miscellaneous businesses—from tiny distributors of breast-cancer wind chimes and note cards to major corporations seeking a woman-friendly image—benefit in the process, not to mention the breast-cancer industry itself, the estimated $12–16 billion-a-year business in surgery, "breast health centers," chemotherapy "infusion suites," radiation treatment centers, mammograms, and drugs ranging from anti-emetics (to help you survive the nausea of chemotherapy) to tamoxifen (the hormonal treatment for women with estrogen-sensitive tumors). But what's to complain about? Seen through pink-tinted lenses, the entire breast-cancer enterprise—from grassroots support groups and websites to the corporate providers of therapies and sponsors of races—looks like a beautiful example of synergy at work: Cult activities, paraphernalia, and testimonies encourage women to undergo the diagnostic procedures, and since a fraction of these diagnoses will be positive, this means more members for the cult as well as more customers for the corporations, both those that provide medical products and services and those that offer charitable sponsorships.

But this view of a life-giving synergy is only as sound as the science of current detection and treatment modalities, and, tragically, that science is fraught with doubt, dissension, and what sometimes looks very much like denial. Routine screening mammograms, for example, are the major goal of "awareness," as when Rosie O'Donnell exhorts us to go out and "get squished." But not all breast-cancer experts are as enthusiastic. At best the evidence for the salutary effects of routine mammograms—as opposed to breast self-examination—is equivocal, with many respectable large-scale studies showing a vanishingly small impact on overall breast-cancer mortality. For one thing, there are an estimated two to four false positives for every cancer detected, leading thousands of healthy women to go through unnecessary biopsies and anxiety. And even if mammograms were 100 percent accurate, the admirable goal of "early" detection is more elusive than the current breast-cancer dogma admits. A small tumor, detectable only by mammogram, is not necessarily young and innocuous; if it has not spread to the lymph nodes, which is the only form of spreading detected in the common surgical procedure of lymph-node dissection, it may have already moved on to colonize other organs via the bloodstream. David Plotkin, director of the Memorial Cancer Research Foundation of Southern California, concludes that the benefits of routine mammography "are not well established; if they do exist, they are not as great as many women hope." Alan Spievack, a surgeon recently retired from the Harvard Medical School, goes further, concluding from his analysis of dozens of studies that routine screening mammography is, in the words of famous British surgeon Dr. Michael Baum, "one of the greatest deceptions perpetrated on the women of the Western world."

Even if foolproof methods for early detection existed,[2] they would, at the present time, serve only as portals to treatments offering dubious protection and considerable collateral damage. Some women diagnosed with breast

---

2 Some improved prognostic tools, involving measuring a tumor's growth rate and the extent to which it is supplied with blood vessels, are being developed but are not yet in use.

cancer will live long enough to die of something else, and some of these lucky ones will indeed owe their longevity to a combination of surgery, chemotherapy, radiation, and/or anti-estrogen drugs such as tamoxifen. Others, though, would have lived untreated or with surgical excision alone, either because their cancers were slow-growing or because their bodies' own defenses were successful. Still others will die of the disease no matter what heroic, cell-destroying therapies are applied. The trouble is, we do not have the means to distinguish between these three groups. So for many of the thousands of women who are diagnosed each year, Plotkin notes, "The sole effect of early detection has been to stretch out the time in which the woman bears the knowledge of her condition." These women do not live longer than they might have without any medical intervention, but more of the time they do live is overshadowed with the threat of death and wasted in debilitating treatments.

To the extent that current methods of detection and treatment fail or fall short, America's breast-cancer cult can be judged as an outbreak of mass delusion, celebrating survivorhood by downplaying mortality and promoting obedience to medical protocols known to have limited efficacy. And although we may imagine ourselves to be well past the era of patriarchal medicine, obedience is the message behind the infantilizing theme in breast-cancer culture, as represented by the teddy bears, the crayons, and the prevailing pinkness. You are encouraged to regress to a little-girl state, to suspend critical judgment, and to accept whatever measures the doctors, as parent surrogates, choose to impose.

Worse, by ignoring or underemphasizing the vexing issue

of environmental causes, the breast-cancer cult turns women into dupes of what could be called the Cancer Industrial Complex: the multinational corporate enterprise that with one hand doles out carcinogens and disease and, with the other, offers expensive, semitoxic pharmaceutical treatments. Breast Cancer Awareness Month, for example, is sponsored by AstraZeneca (the manufacturer of tamoxifen), which, until a corporate reorganization in 2000, was a leading producer of pesticides, including acetochlor, classified by the EPA as a "probable human carcinogen." This particularly nasty conjuncture of interests led the environmentally oriented Cancer Prevention Coalition (CPC) to condemn Breast Cancer Awareness Month as "a public relations invention by a major polluter which puts women in the position of being unwitting allies of the very people who make them sick." Although AstraZeneca no longer manufactures pesticides, CPC has continued to criticize the breast-cancer crusade—and the American Cancer Society—for its unquestioning faith in screening mammograms and careful avoidance of environmental issues. In a June 12, 2001, press release, CPC chairman Samuel S. Epstein, MD, and the well-known physician activist Quentin Young castigated the American Cancer Society for its "longstanding track record of indifference and even hostility to cancer prevention... Recent examples include issuing a joint statement with the Chlorine Institute justifying the continued global use of persistent organochlorine pesticides, and also supporting the industry in trivializing dietary pesticide residues as avoidable risks of childhood cancer. ACS policies are further exemplified by allocating under 0.1 percent of its $700 million annual budget to environmental and occupational causes of cancer."

In the harshest judgment, the breast-cancer cult serves as an accomplice in global poisoning—normalizing cancer, prettying it up, even presenting it, perversely, as a positive and enviable experience.

When, my three months of chemotherapy completed, the oncology nurse calls to congratulate me on my "excellent bloodwork results," I modestly demur. I didn't do anything, I tell her, anything but endure—marking the days off on the calendar, living on Protein Revolution canned vanilla health shakes, escaping into novels and work. Courtesy restrains me from mentioning the fact that the tumor markers she's tested for have little prognostic value, that there's no way to know how many rebel cells survived chemotherapy and may be carving out new colonies right now. She insists I should be proud; I'm a survivor now and entitled to recognition at the Relay for Life being held that very evening in town.

So I show up at the middle-school track where the relay's going on just in time for the Survivors' March: About 100 people, including a few men, since the funds raised will go to cancer research in general, are marching around the track eight to twelve abreast while a loudspeaker announces their names and survival times and a thin line of observers, mostly people staffing the raffle and food booths, applauds. It could be almost any kind of festivity, except for the distinctive stacks of cellophane-wrapped pink Hope Bears for sale in some of the booths. I cannot help but like the kinky small-town gemütlichkeit of the event, especially when the audio system strikes up that universal anthem of solidarity, "We Are Family," and a few people of various ages start twisting to the music on the jerry-rigged stage. But the money raised is going far away, to the American Cancer Society, which will not be asking us for our advice on how to spend it.

I approach a woman I know from other settings, one of our local intellectuals, as it happens, decked out here in a pink-and-yellow survivor T-shirt and with an American Cancer Society "survivor medal" suspended on a purple ribbon around her neck. "When do you date your survivorship from?" I ask her, since the announced time, five and a half years, seems longer than I recall. "From diagnosis or the completion of your treatments?" The question seems to annoy or confuse her, so I do not press on to what I really want to ask: At what point, in a downwardly sloping breast-cancer career, does one put aside one's survivor regalia and admit to being, in fact, a die-er? For the dead are with us even here, though in much diminished form. A series of paper bags, each about the right size for a junior burger and fries, line the track. On them are the names of the dead, and inside each is a candle that will be lit later, after dark, when the actual relay race begins.

My friend introduces me to a knot of other women in survivor gear, breast-cancer victims all, I learn, though of course I would not use the V-word here. "Does anyone else have trouble with the term 'survivor'?" I ask, and, surprisingly, two or three speak up. It could be "unlucky," one tells me; it "tempts fate," says another, shuddering slightly. After all, the cancer can recur at any time, either in the breast or in some more strategic site. No one brings up my own objection to the term, though: that the mindless triumphalism of "survivorhood" denigrates the dead and the dying. Did we who live "fight" harder than those who've died? Can we claim to be "braver," better, people than the dead? And why is there no room in this cult for some gracious acceptance of death, when the time comes, which it surely will, through cancer or some other misfortune?

No, this is not my sisterhood. For me at least, breast cancer will never be a source of identity or pride. As my dying correspondent Gerri wrote: "IT IS NOT OK!" What it is, along with cancer generally or any slow and painful way of dying, is an abomination, and, to the extent that it's human-made, also a crime. This is the one great truth that I bring out of the breast-cancer experience, which did not, I can now report, make me prettier or stronger, more feminine or spiritual—only more deeply angry. What sustained me through the "treatments" is a purifying rage, a resolve, framed in the sleepless nights of chemotherapy, to see the last polluter, along with, say, the last smug health insurance operative, strangled with the last pink ribbon. Cancer or no cancer, I will not live that long, of course. But I know this much right now for sure: I will not go into that last good night with a teddy bear tucked under my arm.

THE NAKED TRUTH
ABOUT FITNESS

Lear's, 1990

The conversation has all the earmarks of a serious moral debate. The man is holding out for the pleasures of this life, few as they are and short as it is. The woman (we assume his wife, since they are having breakfast together and this is a prime-time television commercial) defends the high road of virtue and self-denial. We know there will be a solution, that it will taste like fresh-baked cookies and will simultaneously lower cholesterol, fight osteoporosis, and melt off unwholesome flab. We *know* this. What we have almost forgotten to wonder about is this: Since when is breakfast cereal a *moral* issue?

Morality is no longer a prominent feature of civil society. In the 1980s, politicians abandoned it, Wall Street discarded it, televangelists defiled it. Figuratively speaking, we went for the sucrose rush and forgot the challenge of fiber. But only figuratively. For as virtue drained out of our public lives, it reappeared in our cereal bowls, our exercise regimens, and our militant responses to cigarette smoke, strong drink, and greasy food.

We redefined virtue as health. And considering the probable state of our souls, this was not a bad move. By relocating the seat of virtue from the soul to the pecs, the abs, and the coronary arteries, we may not have become the most virtuous people on earth, but we surely became the most desperate for grace. We spend $5 billion a year on our health-club memberships, $2 billion on vitamins, nearly $1 billion on home-exercise equipment, and $6 billion on sneakers to wear out on our treadmills and StairMasters. We rejoice in activities that leave a hangover of muscle pain and in foods that might, in more temperate times, have been classified as fodder. To say we want to be healthy is to gravely understate the case. We want to be *good*.

Consider my own breakfast cereal, a tasteless, colorless substance that clings to the stomach lining with the avidity of Krazy Glue. Quite wisely, the box makes no promise of good taste or visual charm. Even the supposed health benefits are modestly outlined in tiny print. No, the incentive here is of a higher nature. "It is the right thing to do," the manufacturer intones on the back of the box, knowing that, however alluring our temptations to evil, we all want to do the right thing.

The same confusion of the moral and the physical pervades my health club. "Commit to get fit!" is the current slogan, the verb reminding us of the moral tenacity that has become so elusive in our human relationships. In the locker room we sound like the inmates of a miraculously rehabilitative women's prison, always repenting, forever resolving: "I shouldn't have had that doughnut this morning." "I wasn't here for two weeks and now I'm going to pay the price." Ours is a hierarchy of hardness. The soft, the slow, the easily tired rate no compassion, only the coldest of snubs.

Health is almost universally recognized as a *kind* of virtue. At least, most cultures strong enough to leave an ethnographic trace have discouraged forms of behavior that are believed to be unhealthy. Nevertheless, most of us recognize that health is not an accomplishment so much as it is a *potential*. My upper-body musculature, developed largely on Nautilus machines, means that I probably *can* chop wood or unload trucks, not that I ever *will*. Human cultures have valued many things—courage, fertility, craftsmanship, and deadly aim among them—but ours is almost alone in valuing not the deed itself but the mere capacity to perform it.

So what is it that drives us to run, lift, strain, and monitor our metabolisms as if we were really accomplishing something—something pure, that is, and noble? Sociologist Robert Crawford argues that outbreaks of American "healthism" coincide with bouts of middle-class anxiety. It was near the turn of the century, a time of economic turmoil and violent labor struggles, that white-collar Americans embarked on their first 1980s-style health craze. They hiked, rode bikes, lifted weights, and otherwise heeded Teddy Roosevelt's call for "the strenuous life." They filtered their water and fussed about bran (though sweets were heavily favored as a source of energy). On the loonier fringe, they tried "electric belts," vibrating chairs, testicle supporters, "water cures," prolonged mastication, and copious enemas—moralizing all the while about "right living" and "the divine laws of health."

Our own health-and-fitness craze began in another period of economic anxiety—the 1970s, when the economy slid into "stagflation" and a college degree suddenly ceased to guarantee a career above the cab-driving level. In another decade—say, the 1930s or the 1960s—we might have mobilized for economic change. But the 1970s was the era of *How to Be Your Own Best Friend* and *Looking Out for Number One*, a time in which it seemed more important, or more feasible, to reform our bodies than to change the world. Bit by bit and with the best of intentions, we began to set aside the public morality of participation and protest for the personal morality of health.

Our fascination with fitness has paid off. Fewer Americans smoke; they drink less hard liquor, eat more fiber and less fat. Our rate of heart disease keeps declining, our life expectancy is on the rise. We are less dependent on doctors, more aware of our own responsibility for our health. No doubt we feel better, too, at least those of us who have the means and the motivation to give up bourbon for Evian and poker for racquetball. I personally am more confident and probably more durable as a fitness devotee than I ever was in my former life as a chairwarmer.

But there's a difference between health and healthism, between health as a reasonable goal and health as a transcendent value. By confusing health and virtue, we've gotten testier, less tolerant, and ultimately less capable of confronting the sources of disease that do *not* lie within our individual control. Victim blaming, for example, is an almost inevitable side effect of healthism. If health is our personal responsibility, the reasoning goes, then disease must be our *fault*.

I think of the friend—a thoroughly intelligent, compassionate, and (need I say?) ultrafit person—who called to tell me that her sister was facing surgery for a uterine tumor. "I can't understand it," my friend confided. "I'm sure she's been working out." *Not quite enough* was the implication, despite the absence of even the frailest connection between fibroids and muscle tone. But like sixteenth-century Christians, we've come to see every illness as a punishment for past transgressions. When Chicago mayor Harold Washington died of a heart attack, some eulogizers offered baleful mutterings about his penchant for unreformed, high-cholesterol, soul food. When we hear of someone getting cancer, we mentally scan their lifestyle for the fatal flaw—fatty foods, smoking, even "repressed anger."

There are whole categories of disease that cannot, in good conscience, be blamed on the lifestyles or moral shortcomings of their victims. An estimated 25,000 cancer deaths a year, for example, result from exposure to the pesticides applied so lavishly in agribusiness. Ten thousand Americans are killed every year in industrial accidents; an estimated 20,000 more die from exposure to carcinogens in the workplace—asbestos, toxic solvents, radiation. These deaths are preventable, but not with any amount of oat bran or low-impact aerobics. Environmental and occupational diseases will require a far more rigorous social and political regimen of citizen action, legislation, and enforcement.

Even unhealthy lifestyles can have "environmental" as well as personal origins. Take the matter of diet and smoking. It's easy for the middle-class fiber enthusiast to look down on the ghetto dweller who smokes cigarettes and spends her food stamps on Doritos and soda pop. But in low-income neighborhoods convenience stores and fast-food joints are often the only sources of food, while billboards and TV commercials are the primary sources of nutritional "information." Motivation is another problem. It's one thing to give up smoking and sucrose when life seems long and promising, quite another when it might well be short and brutal.

Statistically speaking, the joggers and bran eaters are concentrated in the white-collar upper-middle class. Blue-and pink-collar people still tend to prefer Bud to Evian and meat loaf to poached salmon. And they still smoke—at a rate of 51 percent, compared with 35 percent for people in professional and managerial occupations. These facts should excite our concern: Why not special cardiovascular-fitness programs for the assembly-line worker as well as the executive? Reduced-rate health-club memberships for truck drivers and typists? Nutritional supplements for the down-and-out? Instead, healthism tends to reinforce long-standing prejudices. If healthy habits are an expression of moral excellence, then the working class is not only "tacky," ill-mannered, or whatever else we've been encouraged to believe—it's morally deficient.

Thus, perversely, does healthism ease the anxieties of the affluent. No amount of straining against muscle machines can save laid-off workers; no aerobic exercises can reduce the price of a private-school education. But fitness *can* give its practitioners a sense of superiority over the potbellied masses. On the other side of victim blaming is an odious mood of self-congratulation: "We" may not be any smarter or more secure about our futures. But surely we are more disciplined and pure.

In the end, though—and the end does come—no one is well served by victim blaming. The victim isn't always "someone else," someone fatter, lazier, or more addicted to smoke and grease. The fact is that we do die, all of us, and that almost all of us will encounter disease, disability, and considerable discomfort either in the process or along the way. The final tragedy of healthism is that it leaves us so ill prepared for the inevitable. If we believe that health is a sign of moral purity and anything less is a species of sin, then death condemns us all as failures. Longevity is not a resoundingly interesting lifetime achievement, just as working out is not exactly a life's work.

Somehow, we need to find our way back to being healthy without being health*ist*. Health is great. It makes us bouncier and probably happier. Better yet, it can make us fit *for* something: strong enough to fight the big-time polluters, for example, the corporate waste dumpers; tough enough to take on economic arrangements that condemn so many to poverty and to dangerous occupations; lean and powerful enough to demand a more nurturing, less anxiety-ridden social order.

Health is good. But it is not, as even the ancient and athletic Greeks would have said, *the* good.

GOT GREASE?

Los Angeles Times, 2002

I t's not only the stock market that has the upper classes biting their fingernails. In the last few years, the low-fat, high-carb way of life that was central to the self-esteem of the affluent has been all but discredited. If avarice was the principal vice of the bourgeoisie, a commitment to low fat was its counterbalancing virtue. You can bet, for example, that those CEOs who cooked the books and ransacked their companies' assets did not start the day with two eggs over easy, a rasher of bacon, and a side of hash browns. No, unbuttered low-fat muffins and delicate slices of melon fueled the crimes of Wall Street: Grease was for proles.

But that dogma no longer holds up. A large number of nutritionists now deny that the low-fat approach will make you slim and resistant to heart disease. As we know, the onset of the American epidemic of obesity coincided precisely with the arrival of the antifat campaign in the 1980s, accompanied by a cornucopia of low-fat cookies, cakes, potato chips, and frozen pot-roast dinners. Millions of Americans began to pig out on "guilt-free" feasts of ungarnished carbs—with perverse and often debilitating results, especially among those unable to afford health club memberships and long hours on the elliptical trainer.

I have confirmed these findings with my own scientific study, which draws on a sample of exactly two: Jane Brody, the *New York Times* health columnist and tireless opponent of all foodstuffs other than veggies and starch, and me. It was Brody, more than anyone else, who promoted the low-fat way of life to the masses, from the eighties on, with headlines like "Our Excessive Protein Intake Can Hurt Liver, Kidneys, Bone," "Fill Up on Bread to Lose Weight," and "Chemicals in Food Less Harmful Than Fat."

As she revealed in a 1999 column, Brody was herself raised on a high-carb, low-fat diet of "shredded wheat, oatmeal, challah, Jewish rye and bagels," the last, presumably, unblemished by the customary "shmear" of cream cheese. I, meanwhile, was raised on a diet that might strain even an Inuit's gallbladder. We ate eggs every morning, meat for lunch, and meat again for dinner, invariably accompanied by gravy or at least pan drippings. We buttered everything from broccoli to brownies and would have buttered butter itself if it were not for the problems of traction presented by the butter-butter interface.

And how did Brody and I exit from our dietarily opposite childhoods? She, by her own admission, was a veritable butterball by her mid-twenties—a size 14 at just under five feet tall. I, at five-foot-seven, weighed in at a gaunt and geeky 110 pounds.

Fast-forwarding to the present, we assume Brody is now admirably trim, if only because of her exercise regimen, since otherwise she wouldn't have dared to promote the low-fat dogma in person. For my part, I no longer butter my brownies, perhaps in part because of Brody's tireless preaching. But the amount of fat she recommends for an entire day—one tablespoon—wouldn't dress a small salad for me or lubricate a single Triscuit. I still regard bread as a vehicle for butter and chicken as an excuse for gravy or, when served cold, mayonnaise. The result? I'm a size 6 and have a cholesterol level that an envious doctor once denounced as "too low." Case closed.

But if that doesn't convince you, there's now a solid medical explanation for why the low-fat, high-carb approach is actually fattening. A meal of carbs—especially those derived from sugar and refined flour—is followed by a surge of blood sugar, then, as insulin is released in response, a sudden collapse, leaving you often light-headed, cranky, headachy, and certainly hungrier than before you ate. Fats and protein can make you fat, too, of course, if ingested in sufficient quantity, but at least they fulfill the conventional role of anything designated as a foodstuff, which is to say that they leave you feeling like you've actually eaten something.

As long as people want to lose weight, we'll probably have dueling diet doctors. But now that it's apparent that the prevailing low-fat wisdom is bunk, why would anyone opt for a diet with a mouthfeel that mimics sawdust?

Perhaps because facts don't matter when a dogma so flattering to the affluent is at stake. In the last couple of decades, the low-fat way of life has become an important indicator of social rank, along with whole-grain—as opposed to white—bread and natural fibers versus polyester. If you doubt this, consider the multiple meanings of grease, as in *greaser* and *greasy spoon*. Among the nutritionally correct upper-middle-class people of my acquaintance, a dinner of French bread and pasta has long been considered a suitable offering for guests—followed by a plate of bone-dry biscotti. And don't bother asking for the butter.

What has made the low-fat dogma especially impervious to critique, though, is the overclass identification of low-fat with virtue and fat with the long-suspected underclass tendency to self-indulgence. Low-fat is the flip side of avarice for a reason: Thanks to America's deep streak of Puritanism—perhaps mixed with a dollop of democratic idealism—ours has been a culture in which everyone wants to be rich but no one wants to be known as a "fat cat." We might be hogging the earth's resources, the affluent seem to be saying, but at least we're not indulging the ancient human craving for fat. So the low-fat diet has been the hair shirt under the fur coat—the daily deprivation that offsets the endless greed.

I wouldn't go so far as to blame the financial shenanigans of the last few years on Brody, but clearly there is a connection. The long-term effects of a low-fat, low-protein diet are easy to guess—a perpetual feeling of insatiety, a relentless, gnawing hunger for more. No doubt, for many thousands of low-fat, high-earning people, money became a substitute, however unfulfilling, for dietary fat. The effect was naturally strongest in Silicon Valley, where dot-commania collided with the northern California, Berkeley-based carbo cult, to disastrous effect. That "irrational exuberance" of the late nineties was in fact the giddiness of hypoglycemia, induced by a diet of boutique muffins and $5-a-loaf "artisan bread."

My advice to the fat-deprived execs: Take a break from the markets and go out and get yourself a bacon cheeseburger and fries or, if you still have a few bucks to toss around, a nice pancetta-rich plate of spaghetti carbonara. Eat every last drop. Then lean back, with the grease dripping down your chin, smile at the people around you, and appreciate, perhaps for the very first time, what it feels like to have enough.

OUR BROKEN MENTAL HEALTH SYSTEM

The Nation, 2007

On April 16, 2007, a withdrawn, silent kid named Cho Seung-Hui opened fire on the Virginia Tech campus, killing thirty-two people. Leaving aside the issue of WMM (Weapons of Mass Murder, aka guns), the massacre has something to teach us about the American mental health system. It's farcically easy for an American to be diagnosed as mentally ill: All you have to do is squirm in your fourth-grade seat and you're likely to be hit with the label of ADHD and a prescription for an antipsychotic. But when a genuine whack job comes along—the kind of guy who calls himself "Question Mark" and turns in essays on bloodbaths—there's apparently nothing to be done.

While Cho Seung-Hui quietly—very quietly—pursued his studies, millions of ordinary, nonviolent folks were being subjected to heavy-duty labels ripped from the DSM-IV. An estimated 20 percent of American children and teenagers are diagnosed as mentally ill in the course of a year, and adults need not feel left out of the labeling spree: Watch enough commercials and you'll learn that you suffer from social

phobia, depression, stress, or some form of sexual indifference (at least I find it hard to believe that all this "erectile
dysfunction" is purely physical in origin).

Consider the essay "Manufacturing Depression" that appeared in *Harper's*. Hoping to qualify for a study on "Minor Depression" at the Massachusetts General Hospital,
the author, Gary Greenberg, presented a list of his problems, including "the stalled writing projects and the weedy
garden, the dwindling bank accounts and the difficulties of
parenthood," in other words, "the typical plaint and worry
and disappointment of a middle-aged, middle-class American life." Alas, it turned out he did not qualify for the
Minor Depression study. "What you have," the doctor told
him, "is Major Depression."

A number of psychiatrists have pointed out that the real
business of the mental health system is social control. Normal, physically active nine-year-olds have to be taught to
sit still. Adults facing "dwindling bank accounts" have to
be drugged or disciplined into accepting their fate. What
therapy aims to achieve is not "health" but compliance with
social norms. The idea still rings true every time I've been
confronted with a "pre-employment personality test" that
reads like a police interrogation: How much have you
stolen from previous employers? Do you have any objections to selling cocaine? Is it "easier to work when you're a
little bit high"?

Then there is the ubiquitous Myers-Briggs test, which
seems obsessed with weeding out loners. Presumably, someone in the HR department can use your test results to
determine whether you're a good "fit." (Incidentally, Myers-

Briggs possesses no category for and no means of detecting the person who might show up at work one day with an automatic weapon.)

But for all the attention to "personality" and garden-variety neurosis, we are left with the problem of the aforementioned psychotics, and the painful question remains: If Cho Seung-Hui's oddities had been noted earlier—say, when he was still under eighteen—could he have been successfully diagnosed and treated? Journalist Paul Raeburn's 2004 book, *Acquainted with the Night: A Parent's Quest to Understand Depression and Bipolar Disorder in His Children*, suggests that the answer is a resounding no.

When his own children started acting up, Raeburn found that there are scores of therapists listed in the Yellow Pages, as well as quite a few inpatient facilities for the flamboyantly symptomatic. But nothing linked these various elements of potential care into anything that could be called a "system." The therapists, who all march to their own theoretical and pharmaceutical drummers, have no reliable connections to the hospitals, nor do the hospitals have any means of providing follow-up care for patients after they are discharged.

Then there is the matter of payment. As managed-care plans gained ground in the health care system in the 1990s, Raeburn reports, they cut their spending on psychiatric treatment by 55 percent, putting mental health services almost out of the reach of the middle class, never mind the poor. Hence, no doubt, the fact that three-quarters of children and teenagers who receive a diagnosis of mental illness get no care for it at all.

If we have no working mental health system, and no means of detecting or treating the murderously disturbed, then here's yet another argument for doing what we should do anyway: Limit access to the tools of murder, end the casual sale of handguns.

LIPOSUCTION: THE KEY TO ENERGY INDEPENDENCE

The Nation, 2008

Everyone talks about our terrible dependency on oil—foreign and otherwise—but hardly anyone mentions what it *is*. Fossil fuel, all right, but whose fossils? Mostly tiny plants called diatoms, but quite possibly a few Barney-like creatures went into the mix, like stegosaurus, brontosaurus, or other giant reptiles that shared the Jurassic period with all those diatoms. What we are burning in our cars and using to heat or cool our homes is, in other words, a highly processed version of corpse juice.

Think of this for a moment, if only out of respect for the dead: There you were, about a hundred million years ago, maybe a contented little diatom or a great big brontosaurus stumbling around the edge of a tar pit—a lord of the earth. And what are you now? A sludge of long-chain carbon molecules that will be burned so that some mammalian biped can make a CVS run for Mountain Dew and chips.

It's an old human habit, living off the roadkill of the planet. There's evidence, for example, that early humans were engaged in scavenging before they figured out how to hunt for themselves. They'd scan the sky for circling vultures, dash off to the kill site—hoping that the leopard that did the actual hunting had sauntered off for a nap—and gobble up what remained of the prey. It was risky, but it beat doing your own antelope tracking.

We continue our career as scavengers today, attracted not by vultures but by signs saying Safeway or Giant. Inside these sites, we find bits of dead animals wrapped neatly in plastic. The killing has already been done for us—usually by underpaid immigrant workers rather than leopards.

I say to my fellow humans: It's time to stop feeding off the dead and grow up! I don't know about food, but I have a plan for achieving fuel self-sufficiency in less time than it takes to say "Arctic National Wildlife Refuge." The idea came to me from reports of the growing crime of french-fry-oil theft: Certain desperate individuals are stealing restaurants' discarded cooking oil, which can then be used to fuel cars. So the idea is this: Why not skip the french-fry phase and harvest high-energy hydrocarbons right from ourselves?

I'm talking about liposuction, of course, and it's a mystery to me why it hasn't occurred to any of those geniuses who are constantly opining about fuel prices on MSNBC. The average liposuction procedure removes about half a gallon of liquid fat, which may not seem like much. But think of the vast reserves our nation is literally sitting on! Thirty percent of Americans are obese, or about 90 million individuals or 45 million gallons of easily available fat—not from dead diatoms but from our very own bellies and butts.

This is the humane alternative to biofuels derived directly from erstwhile foodstuffs like corn. Biofuels, as you might have noticed, are exacerbating the global food crisis by turning edible plants into gasoline. But we could put humans back in the loop by first turning the corn into Fritos and hence into liposuctionable body fat. There would be a reason to live again, even a patriotic rationale for packing on the pounds.

True, liposuction is not risk-free, as the numerous doctors' websites on the subject inform us. And those of us who insist on driving gas guzzlers may quickly deplete their personal fat reserves, much as heroin addicts run out of usable veins. But the gaunt, punctured look could become a fashion statement. Already, the combination of a tiny waist and a huge carbon footprint—generated by one's Hummer and private jet—is considered a sign of great wealth.

And think what it would do for our nation's self-esteem. We may not lead the world in scientific innovation, educational achievement, or low infant mortality, but we are the global champions of obesity. Go to http://www.nation master.com/graph/hea_obe-health-obesity and you'll find America well ahead of the pack when it comes to personal body fat, while those renowned oil producers—Saudi Arabia, Venezuela, and Iran—aren't even among the top twenty-nine. All we need is a healthy dose of fat pride and for CVS to start marketing home liposuction kits. That run for Mountain Dew and chips could soon be an energy-neutral proposition.

THE SELFISH SIDE OF GRATITUDE

New York Times, 2015

This holiday season, there was something in the air that was even more inescapable than the scent of pumpkin spice: gratitude.

In November, NPR issued a number of brief exhortations to cultivate gratitude, culminating in an hourlong special on the "science of gratitude," narrated by Susan Sarandon. Writers in *Time* magazine, the *New York Times*, and *Scientific American* recommended it as a surefire ticket to happiness and even better health. Robert Emmons, a psychology professor at the University of California, Davis, who studies the "science of gratitude," argues that it leads to a stronger immune system and lower blood pressure, as well as "more joy and pleasure."

It's good to express our thanks, of course, to those who deserve recognition. But this holiday gratitude is all about you, and how you can feel better about yourself.

Gratitude is hardly a fresh face on the self-improvement scene. By the turn of the twenty-first century, Oprah Winfrey and other motivational figures were promoting an "attitude of gratitude." Martin Seligman, the father of "positive psychology," which is often enlisted to provide some sort of scientific basis for "positive thinking," has been offering instruction in gratitude for more than a decade. In the logic of positive self-improvement, anything that feels good—from scenic walks to family gatherings to expressing gratitude—is worth repeating.

Positive thinking was in part undone by its own silliness, glaringly displayed in the 2006 best seller *The Secret*, which announced that you could have anything, like the expensive necklace you'd been coveting, simply by "visualizing" it in your possession.

The financial crash of 2008 further dimmed the luster of positive thinking, which had done so much to lure would-be homeowners and predatory mortgage lenders into a speculative frenzy. This left the self-improvement field open to more cautious stances, like mindfulness and resilience, and—for those who could still muster it—gratitude.

Gratitude is at least potentially more prosocial than the alternative self-improvement techniques. You have to be grateful to *someone*, who could be an invisible God, but might as well be a friend, mentor, or family member. The gratitude literature often advises loving, human interactions: writing a "gratitude letter" to a helpful colleague, for example, or taking time to tell a family member how wonderful they are. These are good things to do, in a moral sense, and the new gratitude gurus are here to tell us that they also *feel* good.

But is gratitude always appropriate? The answer depends on who's giving it and who's getting it or, very commonly in our divided society, how much of the wealth gap it's expected to bridge. Suppose you were an $8-an-hour Walmart employee who saw her base pay elevated this year, by company fiat, to $9 an hour. Should you be grateful to the Waltons, who are the richest family in America? Or to Walmart's chief executive, whose annual base pay is close to $1 million and whose home sits on nearly 100 acres of land in Bentonville, Arkansas? Reflexively grateful people are easily dismissed as "chumps," and in this hypothetical case, the term would seem to apply.

Perhaps it's no surprise that gratitude's rise to self-help celebrity status owes a lot to the conservative-leaning John Templeton Foundation. At the start of this decade, the foundation, which promotes free-market capitalism, gave $5.6 million to Dr. Emmons, the gratitude researcher. It also funded a $3 million initiative called Expanding the Science and Practice of Gratitude through the Greater Good Science Center at the University of California, Berkeley, which coproduced the special that aired on NPR. The foundation does not fund projects to directly improve the lives of poor individuals, but it has spent a great deal, through efforts like these, to improve their attitudes.

It's a safe guess, though, that most of the people targeted by gratitude exhortations actually have something to be grateful for, such as Janice Kaplan, the author of the memoir *The Gratitude Diaries*, who spent a year appreciating her high-earning husband and successful grown children. And it is here that the prosocial promise of gratitude begins to dim. True, saying "thank-you" is widely encouraged, but much of the gratitude advice involves no communication or interaction of any kind.

Consider this, from a yoga instructor on CNN.com: "Cultivate your sense of gratitude by incorporating giving thanks into a personal morning ritual, such as writing in a gratitude journal, repeating an affirmation, or practicing a meditation. It could even be as simple as writing what you give thanks for on a sticky note and posting it on your mirror or computer. To help you establish a daily routine, create a 'thankfulness' reminder on your phone or computer to pop up every morning and prompt you."

Who is interacting here? "You" and "you."

The *Harvard Mental Health Letter* begins its list of gratitude interventions with the advice that you should send a thank-you letter as often as once a month, but all the other suggested exercises can be undertaken without human contact: "Thank someone mentally," "Keep a gratitude journal," "Count your blessings," "Meditate" and, for those who are so inclined, "Pray."

So it's possible to achieve the recommended levels of gratitude without spending a penny or uttering a word. All you have to do is to generate, within yourself, the good feelings associated with gratitude, and then bask in its warm, comforting glow. If there is any loving involved in this, it is self-love, and the current hoopla around gratitude is a celebration of onanism.

Yet there is a need for more gratitude, especially from those who have a roof over their heads and food on their table. Only it should be a more vigorous and inclusive sort of gratitude than what is being urged on us now. Who picked the lettuce in the fields, processed the standing rib roast, drove these products to the stores, stacked them on the supermarket shelves, and, of course, prepared them and brought them to the table? Saying grace to an abstract God is an evasion; there are crowds, whole communities of actual people, many of them with aching backs and tenuous finances, who made the meal possible.

The real challenge of gratitude lies in figuring out how to express our debt to them, whether through generous tips or, say, by supporting their demands for decent pay and better working conditions. But now we're not talking about gratitude, we're talking about a far more muscular impulse—and this is, to use the old-fashioned term, "solidarity"—which may involve getting up off the yoga mat.

MEN

HOW "NATURAL" IS RAPE?

Time, 2000

It was cute the first time around: when the president lost his head over Monica's thong undies, that is, and the evolutionary psychologists declared that he was just following the innate biological urge to, tee-hee, spread his seed. Natural selection favors the reproductively gifted, right? But the latest daffy Darwinist attempt to explain male bad behavior is not quite so amusing. Rape, according to evolutionary theorists Randy Thornhill and Craig T. Palmer, represents just another seed-spreading technique favored by natural selection. Sure it's nasty, brutish, and short on foreplay. But it gets the job done.

Thornhill and Palmer aren't endorsing rape, of course. In their article in the latest issue of the *Sciences*—which is already generating a high volume of buzz although their book, *A Natural History of Rape*, won't be out until April— they say they just want to correct the feminist fallacy that "rape is not about sex," it's about violence and domination. The authors argue, among other things, that since the majority of victims are women of childbearing age, the motive must be lust and the intent, however unconscious, must be to impregnate. Hence rape is not an act of pathology, but a venerable old strategy for procreation. What's "natural" isn't always nice.

Now, there are people who reject any attempt to apply evolutionary theory to human behavior, and, as far as I'm concerned, they can go back to composing their annual letters to Santa Claus. Obviously, humans have been shaped by natural selection (though it's not always so obvious how). We are not the descendants of the kindest or wisest of hominids—only of those who managed, by cunning or luck, to produce a few living offspring. But is rape really an effective strategy for guys who, deep down in their genes, just want to be fruitful and multiply?

There are plenty of evolutionary psychologists who would answer with a resounding no. They emphasize the evolutionary value of the human male's "parental investment"—his tendency to stick around after the act of impregnation and help out with the kids. Prehistoric dads may not have read many bedtime stories, but, in this account, they very likely brought home the occasional antelope haunch, and they almost certainly played a major role in defending the family from four-legged predators. In contrast, the rapist generally operates on a hit-and-run basis—which may be all right for stocking sperm banks, but is not quite so effective if the goal is to produce offspring who will survive in a challenging environment. The children of guys who raped-and-ran must have been a scrawny lot and doomed to end up on some leopard's lunch menu.

There's another problem with rape—again, from a

strictly Darwinian perspective. Even if it isn't "about violence," as feminists have claimed, it almost always involves violence or at least the threat thereof; otherwise, it isn't rape. Thornhill and Palmer downplay the amount of physical violence accompanying rape, claiming that no more than 22 percent of victims suffer any "gratuitous" violence beyond that necessary to subdue them. But we are still talking about appalling levels of damage to the mother of the rapist's prospective offspring. Most rape victims suffer long-term emotional consequences—like depression and memory loss—that are hardly conducive to successful motherhood. It's a pretty dumb Darwinian specimen who can't plant his seed without breaking the "vessel" in the process.

Thornhill and Palmer's insistence that the rapist isn't a psychopath, just an ordinary fellow who's in touch with his inner caveman, leads to some dubious prescriptions. They want to institute formal training for boys in how to resist their "natural" sexual impulses to rape. Well, sure, kids should learn that rape is wrong, along with all other forms of assault. But the emphasis on rape as a natural male sexual impulse is bound to baffle those boys—and I would like to think there are more than a few of them out there—whose sexual fantasies have never drifted in a rape-ward direction.

As for the girls, Thornhill and Palmer want them to realize that since rape is really "about sex," it very much matters how they dress. But where is the evidence that women in miniskirts are more likely to be raped than women in dirndls? Women were raped by the thousands in Bosnia, for example, and few if any of them were wearing bikinis or bustiers.

Yes, rape is "about sex," in that it involves a certain sexlike act. But it's a pretty dismal kind of "sex" in which one person's pain, and possible permanent injury, is the occasion for the other one's pleasure. What most of us mean by sex is something mutual and participatory, loving and uplifting, or at least flirty and fun. In fact, making the world safe for plunging necklines and thong undies is a goal that enlightened members of both sexes ought to be able to get behind. As for those guys who can't distinguish between sex and rape, I don't care whether they're as "natural" as granola, they don't deserve to live in the company of women.

THE WARRIOR CULTURE

Time, 1990

I n what we like to think of as "primitive" warrior cultures, the passage to manhood requires the blooding of
a spear, the taking of a scalp or head. Among the Masai of
eastern Africa and dozens of other human cultures, a man
could not marry until he had demonstrated his capacity to
kill in battle. Leadership, too, in a warrior society is typically contingent on military prowess and wrapped in the
mystique of death. In the Solomon Islands, a chief's importance could be reckoned by the number of skulls posted
around his door, and it was the duty of the Aztec kings to
nourish the gods with the hearts of human captives.

All warrior peoples have fought for the same high-
sounding reasons: honor, glory, or revenge. The nature of
their real and perhaps not conscious motivations is a subject of much debate. Some anthropologists postulate a
murderous instinct, almost unique among living species,
in human males. Others discern a materialistic motive behind every fray: a need for slaves, grazing land, or even
human flesh to eat. Still others point to the similarities

between war and other male pastimes—the hunt and out-door sports—and suggest that it is boredom, ultimately, that stirs men to fight.

But in a warrior culture it hardly matters which motive is most basic. Aggressive behavior is rewarded whether or not it is innate to the human psyche. Shortages of resources are habitually taken as occasions for armed offensives, rather than for hard thought and innovation. And war, to a war-rior people, is of course the highest adventure, the surest antidote to malaise, the endlessly repeated theme of legend, song, religious myth, and personal quest for meaning. It is how men die and what they find to live for.

"You must understand that Americans are a warrior na-tion," Senator Daniel Patrick Moynihan told a group of Arab leaders in 1990. He said this proudly, and he may, without thinking through the ugly implications, have told the truth. In many ways, in outlook and behavior, the United States has begun to act like a "primitive" warrior culture.

We seem to believe that leadership is expressed, in no small part, by a willingness to cause the deaths of others. After the US invasion of Panama, President Bush exulted that no one could call him "timid"; he was at last a "macho man." The press, in even more primal language, hailed him for succeeding in an "initiation rite" by demonstrating his "willingness to shed blood."

For lesser offices, too, we apply the standards of a warrior culture. Female candidates are routinely advised to over-come the handicap of their gender by talking "tough." Thus, for example, Dianne Feinstein embraced capital punishment, while Colorado senatorial candidate Josie Heath found it necessary to announce that although she is the mother of an eighteen-year-old son, she is prepared to vote for war. Male candidates are finding their military records under scrutiny. No one expects them, as elected officials in a civilian government, to pick up a spear or a sling and fight. But they must state, at least, their willingness to have another human being killed.

More tellingly, we are unnerved by peace and seem to find it boring. When the cold war ended, we found no reason to celebrate. Instead we heated up the "war on drugs." What should have been a public-health campaign, focused on the persistent shame of poverty, became a new occasion for martial rhetoric and muscle flexing. Months later, when the Berlin Wall fell and communism collapsed throughout Europe, we Americans did not dance in the streets. What we did, according to the networks, was change the channel to avoid the news. Nonviolent revolutions do not uplift us, and the loss of mortal enemies only seems to leave us empty and bereft.

Our collective fantasies center on mayhem, cruelty, and violent death. Loving images of the human body—especially of bodies seeking pleasure or expressing love—inspire us with the urge to censor. Our preference is for warrior themes: the lone fighting man, bandoliers across his naked chest, mowing down lesser men in gusts of automatic-weapon fire. Only a real war seems to revive our interest in real events. With the Iraqi crisis, the networks report, ratings for news shows rose again—even higher than they were for Panama.

And as in any warrior culture, our warrior elite takes pride of place. Social crises multiply numbingly—homelessness, illiteracy, epidemic disease—and our leaders tell us solemnly that nothing can be done. There is no money. We are poor, not rich, a debtor nation. Meanwhile, nearly a third of the federal budget flows, even in moments of peace, to the warriors and their weapon-makers. When those priorities are questioned, some new "crisis" dutifully arises to serve as another occasion for armed and often unilateral intervention.

With Operation Desert Shield, our leaders were reduced to begging foreign powers for the means to support our warrior class. It does not seem to occur to us that the other great northern powers—Japan, Germany, the Soviet Union—might not have found the stakes so high or the crisis quite so threatening. It has not penetrated our imagination that in a world where the powerful, industrialized nation-states are at last at peace, there might be other ways to face down a pint-size third-world warrior state than with massive force of arms. Nor have we begun to see what an anachronism we are in danger of becoming: a warrior nation in a world that pines for peace, a high-tech state with the values of a roving warrior band.

A leftist might blame "imperialism"; a right-winger would call our problem "internationalism." But an anthropologist, taking the long view, might say this is just what warriors do. Intoxicated by their own drumbeats and war songs, fascinated by the glint of steel and the prospect of blood, they will go forth, time and again, to war.

AT LAST, A NEW MAN

New York Times, 1984

There have been waves of "new women" arriving on cue almost every decade for the last thirty years or so—from the civic-minded housewife, to the liberated single, to the dressed-for-success executive. But men, like masculinity itself, were thought to be made of more durable stuff. Change, if it came at all, would come only in response to some feminine—or feminist—initiative.

In the 1970s, for example, it had become an article of liberal faith that a new man would eventually rise up to match the new feminist woman, that he would be more androgynous than any "old" variety of man, and that the change, which was routinely expressed as an evolutionary leap from John Wayne to Alan Alda, would be an unambiguous improvement.

Today a new man is at last emerging, and I say this as someone who is not much given to such announcements. A new man, like a new sexuality or a new conservatism, is more likely to turn out to be a journalistic artifact than a cultural sea change.

But this time something has happened, both to our common expectations of what constitutes manhood and to the way many men are choosing to live.

I see the change in the popular images that define masculinity, and I see it in the men I know, mostly in their thirties, who are conscious of possessing a sensibility and even a way of life that is radically different from that of their fathers. These men have been, in a word, feminized, but without necessarily becoming more feminist. In fact, I do not think that those of us who are feminists either can or, for the most part, would want to take credit for the change.

If we had not all been so transfixed by the changes in women in the last fifteen or twenty years, far more attention would have been paid to the new man by this time. We can recall—with nostalgia or relief—the feminine ideal of less than a generation ago: the full-time homemaker who derived her status as well as her livelihood from her husband and considered paid employment a misfortune visited only on the opposite sex or the unwed. So sudden was her demise, at least as an ideal for most girls to aspire to, that we sometimes forget the notion of manhood that went along with that "feminine mystique."

I think of the men of my father's generation, men who came of age in the 1950s and who, like my own father, defined their masculinity, if not their identity, in terms of their ability to make a living and support a family. This was a matter of convention as much as of choice, for the man who failed to marry and become a reliable provider was considered a failure, and those who failed to marry at all

(that is, by the age of thirty or so) were candidates for the label of "latent homosexual." Men of this generation were encouraged to equate effeminacy with un-Americanism and
to use their leisure to escape—into sports, hunting, or simply the basement—from women and all things feminine.

We recognize that for the most part men aren't like that
anymore and those who are seem grievously out of style.
Usually, we think of the change simply as a movement away
from the old norm—an opening up of possibilities. But the
new man emerging today is not simply the old one minus
the old prohibitions and anxieties. There is a new complex
of traits and attitudes that has come to define manhood and
a kind of new masculine gentility.

Taking his mid-1950s progenitor as a benchmark, the
most striking characteristic of the new man is that he no
longer anchors his identity in his role as family breadwinner. He may *be* the family breadwinner, or imagine becoming one someday, but his ability to do so has ceased to be
the urgent and necessary proof of his maturity or of his
heterosexuality. In fact, he may postpone or avoid marriage
indefinitely—which is why the women's magazines complain so much about the male "lack of commitment" and
"refusal to grow up."

But if the old responsibilities have declined, the pressure
is not off: The old man expressed his status through his
house and the wife who presided over it; the new man expects to express his status through his own efforts and is
deeply anxious about the self he presents to the world. Typically, he is concerned—some might say obsessed—with
his physical health and fitness. He is an avid and style-

conscious consumer, not only of clothes but of food, home furnishings, and visible displays of culture. Finally, and in a marked reversal of the old masculinity, he is concerned that people find him, not forbearing or strong, but genuine, open, and sensitive.

These traits do not always occur together; in individual men, in fact, we are probably more used to encountering them separately, scattered among men of the middle and upper-middle classes. For example, on a spring lunch hour in the nation's capital, you will find scores of ruddy, middle-aged men, jogging resolutely on the banks of the Potomac, and I doubt that many of them are practitioners of the new sensitivity. On the other hand, sensitivity is now fairly well dispersed throughout the male population, so that it is not uncommon to encounter it in married breadwinners with children, where it may take the form of a somewhat fatuous volubility on the subject of fathering. Then, too, rejection of the breadwinner role—at least as reflected in the high rate of default on child-support payments by men who could well afford to pay them—is so endemic that it cannot be confined to a special new type of man. There are men who are otherwise old-fashioned but have taken up a formerly feminine activity like cooking; just as there must be (though I have not met one) upscale bachelors who eschew physical exercise and designer shirts.

But it is possible, increasingly, to find men who qualify as prototypical new males. They are likely to be from twenty-five to forty years old, single, affluent, and living in a city, for it is among such men that the most decisive break in the old masculine values is occurring. In these men, the traits that define the new masculinity are beginning to form a pattern and even to frame a new kind of conformity—one that is vastly different, however, from the gray-flannel blues that bedeviled an earlier generation of middle-class American men.

Jeffrey A. Greenberg was one of a number of young men interviewed by me and my assistant, Harriet Bernstein, a market researcher, who helped me locate single affluent men who were willing to discuss their interests and values. Greenberg is a thirty-two-year-old resident in neurosurgery who lives and works in Washington. He puts in eighty to a hundred hours a week as a doctor, works out in a gym three times a week, and otherwise devotes himself to "the study and acquisition of art." Cooking is his latest enthusiasm: "I thought I wasn't creative in that aspect, but I found that I'm definitely OK. I know what tastes good and I'm able to do that." He entertains at least once a week, which gives him a chance to show off his paintings and eclectic music collection. He indicated that, while there were women in his life, he did not yet "have the ability to make a firm commitment."

Thirty or even twenty years ago, a man like Jeffrey Greenberg would have been a self-conscious minority of "older" bachelors—probably envied by his married friends, and, at the same time, faintly suspected for his "effeminate" tastes.

Today [1984] he is part of a demographic trend that fascinates market researchers and delights the purveyors of upscale consumer goods. There are 7.5 million men living alone (twice as many as there were in 1970). And as the home-furnishings expert Joan Kron observes in her recent book *Home-Psych*, single men are less likely to view their condition as one of temporary deprivation, marked by canned-hash dinners and orange-crate furniture. They cook; they furnish; they may even decorate. *Home Furnishings Daily* has declared them the "New Target," and the magazines that guide their consumption decisions are proliferating and expanding. Significantly, the genre of men's magazine that has done the best in the last few years is the one (represented by *Esquire*, *GQ*, and *M*) that does not depend on the lure of sexy female images, only page after page of slender, confident-looking male models.

What accounts for this change in men? Or, perhaps I should ask more broadly, for this change in our notion of masculinity—a change that affects not only single, affluent young men but potentially the married, middle-aged, and financially immobile male? Sheldon Kotel, a Long Island accountant in his early forties who was my host on a local radio talk show, attributes any change in men to a prior revolution among women. From the early 1970s, he says, "You could see what was happening with women, and we had to get our act together, too. They didn't want to be in their traditional role anymore, and I didn't want to go on being a meal ticket for some woman."

Certainly the new man's unwillingness to "commit himself," in the old-fashioned sense, could be interpreted as a peevish reaction to feminist women—just as his androgynous bent could be interpreted as a positive adjustment, an attempt, as the advocates of men's liberation would say, to "get in touch with one's feminine side." Spokesmen for men's liberation, from Warren Farrell in the early 1970s to

AT LAST, A NEW MAN   161

Donald H. Bell, whose book *Being a Man: The Paradox of Masculinity*, was published in 1982, depict themselves and their fellows as wrestling with the challenge of feminism— giving up a little privilege here, gaining a little sensitivity there, to emerge more "whole" and "self-nurturing."

But for the most part, the new men one is likely to encounter today in our urban singles' enclaves (or on the pages of a men's fashion magazine) bear no marks of arduous self-transformation. No ideological struggle—pro- or antifeminist—seems to have shaped their decision to step out of the traditional male role; in a day-to-day sense, they simply seem to have other things on their minds. Stephen G. Dent, for example, is a twenty-nine-year-old member of a private New York investment firm who was also interviewed by Harriet Bernstein. Dent defines his goals in terms of his career and making money, "because that's how the score is kept." To this end, he rations his time carefully: more than ten hours a day for work and approximately half an hour a day for calisthenics and running. Women definitely figure in his life, and he is pleased to have reduced the time spent arranging dates to an efficient five minutes a day.

Dent feels that "Sensitivity is very important to being a man. It's easy for people to become so caught up in their career challenges that they don't stop to be sensitive to certain things." By that he said he meant "being able to appreciate things that girls appreciate. Like being able to window- shop, for example. An insensitive guy probably won't stop and look at a dress in a window."

For Brian Clarke, like Stephen Dent, the pressures of

upward mobility have pushed marriage into the distant future. He is thirty-three and works fourteen hours a day as a production assistant for a major network television show.

Feminism has not figured much in his life; he discussed it respectfully, but as if it were an idiosyncracy he had not encountered before. Yet he agreed enthusiastically to being identified as a new man. "I'm going uphill, and I don't see the top of the hill yet. So for now there is no one woman in my life....I say it on the first date, 'No commitments!'" He is, furthermore, an ardent and tasteful consumer who remains au courant by reading *GQ, M, Interior Design*, and *Playboy*, this last, he reassured me, "for the fashions."

So I do not think there is a one-word explanation—like feminism—for the new manhood. Rather, I would argue, at least a part of what looks new has been a long time in the making and predates the recent revival of feminism by many decades. Male resistance to marriage, for example, is a venerable theme in American culture, whether in the form of low humor (Li'l Abner's annual Sadie Hawkins Day escape from Daisy Mae) or high art (the perpetual bachelorhood of heroes like Ishmael or the Deerslayer). As Leslie Fiedler argued in 1955 in *An End to Innocence*, the classics of American literature are, by and large, propaganda for boyish adventure rather than the "mature heterosexuality" so admired by mid-twentieth-century psychoanalysts.

The sources of male resentment are not hard to find: In a frontier society, women were cast as the tamers and civilizers of men; in an increasingly urban, industrial society, they became, in addition, the financial dependents of men. From a cynical male point of view, marriage was an arrangement through which men gave up their freedom for the dubious privilege of supporting a woman. Or, as H. L. Mencken put it, marriage was an occasion for a man "to yield up his liberty, his property, and his soul to the first woman who, in despair of finding better game, turns her appraising eye upon him." After all, the traditional female contributions to marriage have been menial, like housework, or intangible, like emotional support. The husband's traditional contribution, his wage or at least a good share of it, was indispensable, measurable, and, of course, portable—whether to the local tavern or the next liaison.

But before male resentment of marriage could become anything more than a cultural undercurrent of grumbling and misogynist humor, three things had to happen. First, it had to become not only physically possible but reasonably comfortable for men to live on their own. In nineteenth-century homes, even simple tasks like making breakfast or laundering a shirt could absorb long hours of labor. Bachelorhood was a privileged state, sustained by servants or a supply of maiden sisters; the average man either married or settled for boardinghouse life. As a second condition for freedom from marriage, men had to discover better ways of spending their money than on the support of a family. The historic male alternatives were drinking and gambling, but these have long been associated, for good reason, with precipitate downward mobility. Third, the penalties levied against the nonconforming male—charges of immaturity, irresponsibility, and latent sexual deviancy—had to be neutralized or inverted.

Within the last few decades, all of these conditions for male freedom have been met. Domestic appliances, plus a rapid rise in the number of apartment dwellings and low-price restaurants, made it possible for a man of average means to contemplate bachelorhood as something other than extended vagrancy. As Philip Roth observed of the 1950s in *My Life as a Man*, it had become entirely feasible—though not yet acceptable—for a young man to "eat out of cans or in cafeterias, sweep his own floor, make his own bed, and come and go with no binding legal attachments." In addition, that decade saw two innovations that boosted the potential autonomy of even the most domestically incompetent males—frozen foods and drip-dry clothes.

Perhaps more important, the consumer-goods market, which had focused on a bland assemblage of family-oriented products, began to show the first signs of serious segmentation. *Playboy*'s success in the 1950s instigated a revival of sophisticated men's magazines (sophisticated, that is, compared with *True*, *Police Gazette*, or *Popular Mechanics*) that delivered an audience of millions of independent-minded men to the advertisers of liquor, sports cars, stereo equipment, and vacations.

In *Playboy*'s case, the ads were complemented by editorial exhortations to male revolt and feature articles portraying wives as "parasites" and husbands as "slaves." There were better ways to spend money than on power mowers and patio furniture, as Hugh Hefner insinuated in his magazine's very first issue: "We like our apartment....We enjoy mixing up cocktails and an hors d'oeuvre or two, putting a little mood music on the phonograph, and inviting in a female acquaintance for a quiet discussion of Picasso, Nietzsche, jazz, sex." And in case that sounded suspiciously effete for 1953, the centerfolds testified to an exuberant, even defiant, heterosexuality.

No sooner had the new, more individualistic male lifestyle become physically possible and reasonably attractive than it began also to gain respectability. Starting in the 1960s, expert opinion began to retreat from what had been a unanimous endorsement of marriage and traditional sex roles. Psychology, transformed by the human-potential movement, switched from "maturity" as a standard for mental health to the more expansive notion of "growth." "Maturity" had been a code word, even in the professional literature, for marriage and settling down; "growth" implied a plurality of legitimate options, if not a positive imperative to keep moving from one insight or experience to the next. Meanwhile, medicine—alarmed by what appeared to be an epidemic of male heart disease—had begun to speak of men as the "weaker sex" and to hint that men's greater vulnerability was due, in part, to the burden of breadwinning.

The connection was scientifically unwarranted, but it cast a lasting shadow over conventional sex roles: The full-time homemaker, who had been merely a parasite on resentful males, became a potential accomplice to murder, with the hardworking, role-abiding breadwinner as her victim. By the 1970s, no salvo of male resentment—or men's liberation—failed to mention that the cost of the traditional male role was not only psychic stagnation and sexual monotony, but ulcers, heart disease, and an early death.

Today, the old aspersions directed at the unmarried male have largely lost their sting. Images of healthy, hardworking men with no apparent attachments abound in the media, such as, for example, the genial-looking bicyclist in the advertisement for *TV Guide*, whose caption announces invitingly, "Zero Dependents."

Perhaps most important, a man can now quite adequately express his status without entering into a lifelong partnership with a female consumer. The ranch house on a quarter acre of grass is still a key indicator of social rank, but it is not the only one. A well-decorated apartment, a knowledge of wines, or a flair for cooking can be an equally valid proof of middle-class (or upper-middle-class) membership, and these can now be achieved without the entanglement of marriage or the risk of being thought a little "queer."

Certainly feminism contributed to the case against the old style of male conformity. On the ideological front, the women's movement popularized the sociological vocabulary of "roles"—a linguistic breakthrough that highlighted the social artifice involved in masculinity, as we had known it, as well as femininity. More practically, feminists envisioned a world in which neither sex would be automatically dependent and both might be breadwinners. Betty Friedan speculated that "Perhaps men may live longer in America when women carry more of the burden of the battle with the world, instead of being a burden themselves," and Gloria Steinem urged men to support the cause because they "have nothing to lose but their coronaries." Yet feminism only delivered the coup de grâce to the old man, who married young, worked hard, withheld his emotions, and "died in the harness." By the time of the feminist revival in the late 1960s and '70s, American culture was already prepared to welcome a new man, and to find him—not caddish or queer—but healthy and psychologically enlightened.

But if the new man's resistance to commitment grows out of longstanding male resentment, there are other features of the new manhood that cannot be explained as a product of the battle of the sexes, no matter which side is presumed to have taken the initiative. Married or single, the preoccupations of these men suggest anxiety rather than liberation, and I think the anxiety stems from very real and relatively recent insecurities about class.

The professional-managerial middle class, which is the breeding ground for social ideals like the new man or new woman, has become an embattled group. In the 1950s and '60s, young men of this class could look forward to secure, high-status careers, provided only that they acquired some credentials and showed up for work. Professional-level job slots were increasing, along with the expansion of corporate and governmental administrative apparatuses, and jobs in higher education increased to keep pace with the growing demand for managerial and "mental" workers.

Then came the long economic downturn of the 1970s and whole occupations—from public administration to college history teaching—closed their ranks and lost ground. One whole segment of formerly middle-class, educated youth drifted downward to become taxi drivers, waiters, or carpenters. As other people crowded into the most vocationally promising areas—medicine, law, management—those too became hazardously overpopulated. According to recent studies of the "disappearing middle class," the erst-while middle-class majority is tumbling down and out (both because of a lack of jobs and because those that remain have not held their own against inflation), while a minority is scrambling up to become the new high-finance, high-tech gentry. Our new men are mainly in the latter category, or are at least holding on by their fingernails.

Times of rapid class realignment magnify the attention paid to class insignia—the little cues that tell us who is a social equal and who is not. In the prosperous 1960s and early '70s, the counterculture had temporarily blurred class lines among American men, mixing Ivy League dropouts with young veterans, hip professionals with un-schooled street kids. Avant-garde male fashion was demo-cratic: blue jeans, gold chains, and shoulder-length hair could equally well be affected by middle-aged psychia-trists, young truck drivers, or off-duty tax lawyers. Thanks to Army-surplus chic and its rock-star embellishments, there was no sure way to distinguish the upward bound from the permanently down-and-out.

By the insecure 1980s, class lines were being hastily re-drawn, and many features of the new manhood can best be understood as efforts to stay on the right side of the line separating "in" from "out," and upscale from merely middle-class. The new male consumerism, for example, is self-consciously elitist: Italian-knit sweaters and double-breasted blazers have replaced the voluntary simplicity of flannel shirts and denim jackets. *Esquire* announced a "return to el-egant dressing" that excludes not only the polyester set but the rumpled professor and any leftover bohemians.

Food fashions, too, have been steadily gentrified, and the traditional masculine culinary repertory of chili and grilled meats would be merely boorish today. A recent issue of *GQ* magazine gave its readers the following advice, which I would have thought almost too precious for the pages of *Gourmet*: "To turn dinner for two into an affair, break open the caviar again—this time over oysters or spooned into baked potatoes with melted butter, a dollop of crème fraîche and a sprinkling of minced green onion. Or offer truffles—black or white…tossed with pasta, cream and butter." Real men may not eat quiche—which has been adopted by the proletariat anyway—but new men are enthusiasts of sushi and cold pasta salads, and are prepared to move on as soon as these, too, find their way to more plebeian palates. As *M* magazine half-facetiously warned its readers, sushi may already be "out," along with pesto dishes and white-wine spritzers.

Consumer tastes are only the most obvious class cues that define the new man and set him off, not only from the old white-collar man but from the less fortunate members of his own generation. Another is his devotion to physical exercise, especially in its most solitary and public form— running. Running is a new activity, dating from the 1970s, and it is solidly upscale. Fred Lebow, the president of the New York Road Runners Club, describes the average marathon runner as a male, "34 years old, college-educated, physically fit and well-off," and a *New York Times* poll found that 46 percent of the participants in the 1983 New York City Marathon earned more than $40,000 a year (85 percent of the participants were male). The old man smoked, drank martinis to excess, and puttered at golf. The new man is a nonsmoker (among men, smoking is becoming a blue-collar trait), a cautious drinker, and, if not a runner, a patron of gyms and spas.

I would not argue that men run in order to establish their social status—certainly not at a conscious level. Running is one manifestation of the general obsession with fitness that gripped the middle class in the 1970s and for which there is still no satisfactory sociological explanation. On one level, running is a straightforward response to the cardiac anxiety that has haunted American men since the 1950s; it may also be a response to the occupational insecurity of the 1970s and '80s. Then, too, some men run to get away from their wives—transforming Rabbit Angstrom's cross-country dash in the final scene of John Updike's *Rabbit, Run* into an acceptable daily ritual. Donald Bell says he took up running (and vegetarianism) "to escape somewhat from the pain and frustration which I felt in this less than perfect marriage."

But whatever the individual motivations, running has become sufficiently identified as an upper-middle-class habit to serve as a reliable insignia of class membership: Running is public testimony to a sedentary occupation, and it has all but replaced the more democratic sports, such as softball and basketball, that once promoted inter-class male mingling.

Finally, there is that most promising of new male traits—sensitivity. I have no hesitation about categorizing this as an upscale-class cue if only because new men so firmly believe that it is. For more than a decade, sensitivity has been supposed to be the inner quality that distinguishes an educated, middle-class male from his unregenerate blue-collar brothers: "They" are Archie Bunkers; "we" are represented by his more liberal, articulate son-in-law. As thoughtful a scholar as Joseph H. Pleck, program director of the Wellesley College Center for Research on Women, who has written extensively on the male sex role, simply restates (in a 1976 issue of the *Journal of Social Issues*) the prejudice that blue-collar men are trapped in the "traditional" male role, "where interpersonal and emotional skills are relatively undeveloped."

No one, of course, has measured sensitivity and plotted it as a function of social class, but Judith Langer, a market researcher, reports that, in her studies, it is blue-collar men who express less "traditional" or "macho" values, both in response to products and in speaking of their relationships with women. "Certainly I'm not suggesting that *only* blue-collar men show such openness," she concludes, "but rather that the stereotype of blue-collar workers can be limited."

To the extent that some special form of sensitivity is located in educated and upwardly mobile males, I suspect it may be largely a verbal accomplishment. The vocabulary of sensitivity, at least, has become part of the new masculine politesse; certainly no new man would admit to being insensitive or willfully "out of touch with his feelings." Quite possibly, as sensitivity has spread, it has lost its moorings in the therapeutic experience and come to signify the heightened receptivity associated with consumerism: a vague appreciation that lends itself to aimless shopping.

None of these tastes and proclivities of the new man

serve to differentiate him from the occasional affluent woman of his class. Women in the skirted-suit set tend to postpone marriage and childbearing; to work long hours and budget their time scrupulously; to follow fashions in food and clothing; and to pursue fitness where once slimness would have sufficed. As Paul Fussell observes in *Class: A Guide through the American Status System*, the upper-middle class—and I would include all those struggling to remain in the upper part of the crumbling middle class—is "the most 'role reversed' of all." And herein lies one of the key differences between the old and the new versions of the American ideal of masculinity: The old masculinity defined itself against femininity and expressed anxiety—over conformity or the rat race—in metaphors of castration. The new masculinity seems more concerned to preserve the tenuous boundary between the classes than to delineate distinctions between the sexes. Today's upper-middle-class or upwardly mobile male is less terrified about moving down the slope toward genderlessness than he is about sliding downscale.

The fact that the new man is likely to remain single well into his prime career years—or, if married, is unlikely to be judged by his wife's appearance and tastes—only intensifies his status consciousness. The old man of the middle class might worry about money, but he could safely leave the details of keeping up with the Joneses to his wife. He did not have to comprehend casseroles or canapés, because she would, nor did he have to feel his way through complex social situations, since sensitivity also lay in her domain. But our new man of the 1980s, married or not, knows that he may be judged solely on the basis of his own savoir faire, his ability to "relate," his figure, and possibly his muscle tone. Without a wife, or at least without a visible helpmate, he has had to appropriate the status-setting activities that once were seen as feminine. The androgynous affect is part of making it.

The question for feminists is: Is this new man what we wanted? Just a few years ago, feminists were, on the whole, disposed to welcome any change in a direction away from traditional manhood. Betty Friedan, in *The Second Stage*, saw "the quiet movement of American men" as "a momentous change in their very identity as men, going beyond the change catalyzed by the women's movement," and she suggested that it might amount to a "massive, evolutionary development."

That was written in a more innocent time, when feminists were debating the "Cinderella complex," as Colette Dowling termed women's atavistic dependencies on men, rather than the "Peter Pan syndrome," which is how another best seller describes the male aversion to commitment. In recent months, there has been a small flurry of feminist attacks on the new male or on assorted new-male characteristics.

The *Washington City Paper* carried a much-discussed and thoroughly acid article on "Wormboys," described by writer Deborah Laake as men who are "passive" in relation to women, who "shrink from marriage" and children, and "cannot be depended on during tough times." According to one woman she quotes, these new men are so fearful of commitment that they even hesitate to ask a woman out to dinner: "They're more interested in saying, 'Why don't you meet me for a drink?' because it implies so much less commitment on their part." I wouldn't exaggerate the extent of the backlash, but it has been sufficient to send several male colleagues my way to ask, with nervous laughter, whether I was writing a new contribution to the "war on wimps."

I don't blame them for being nervous. My generation of feminists insisted that men change, but we were not always directive—or patient—enough to say how. We applauded every sign of male sensitivity or growth as if it were an evolutionary advance. We even welcomed the feminization of male tastes, expecting that the man who was a good cook and a tasteful decorator at twenty-five would be a devoted father and partner in midlife. We did not understand that men were changing along a trajectory of their own and that they might end up being less like what we *are* than like what we were once expected to be—vain and shallow and status-conscious.

But since these are times when any hint of revisionism easily becomes grist for conservatism, it is important to emphasize that if we don't like the new male, neither are we inclined to return to the old one. If the new man tends to be a fop, the old man was (and is), at worst, a tyrant and a bully. At best, he was merely dull, which is why, during the peak years of male conformity, when the test of manhood lay in being a loyal breadwinner, so many of us lusted secretly for those few males—from James Dean and Elvis Presley to Jack Kerouac—who represented unattainable adventure. In our fantasies, as least, we did not want to enslave men, as *Playboy's* writers liked to think, but to share the adventure.

Today, thanks to the women's movement, we have half a chance: Individualism, adventure—that "battle with the world" that Friedan held out to women—is no longer a male prerogative. But if it is to be a shared adventure, then men will have to change, and change in ways that are not, so far, in evidence. Up until now, we have been content to ask them to become more like women—less aggressive, more emotionally connected with themselves and others. That message, which we once thought revolutionary, has gotten lost in the androgynous drift of the consumer culture. It is the marketplace that calls most clearly for men to be softer, more narcissistic and receptive, and the new man is the result.

So it is not enough, anymore, to ask that men become more like women; we should ask instead that they become more like what both men and women *might* be. My new man, if I could design one, would be capable of appreciation, sensitivity, intimacy—values that have been, for too long, feminine. But he would also be capable of commitment, to use that much-abused word, and I mean by that commitment not only to friends and family but to a broad and generous vision of how we might all live together. As a feminist, I would say that vision includes equality between men and women and also—to mention a social goal that seems almost to have been forgotten—equality among men.

PATRIARCHY DEFLATED

The Baffler, 2018

Sometimes it takes a slovenly alt-right "strategist" to put things in proper historical perspective. In a recent chat with a journalist, Steve Bannon called the #MeToo movement an "anti-patriarchy movement" that is "going to undo ten thousand years of recorded history." That much is true. But the implication that patriarchy is somehow the same as civilization gets more implausible with every me-too revelation.

We have been encouraged to think of patriarchy as a solemn undertaking, a millennia-old system designed to keep women down and young men from getting out of line. Its favorite notions, over the centuries, have been Honor, Tradition, Power, and Glory. Its material manifestations range from pyramids to skyscrapers, from the simple lines of ancient Greek temples to the neoclassical architectural majesty of nineteenth-century European capitals. It accessorizes its most hallowed rituals with columns of uniformed soldiers and stirring martial music.

The Naked and the Daft

But how silly patriarchy is looking at this moment, as one rich and powerful man after another falls victim to the #MeToo movement. We've learned that the fatuous centrist Charlie Rose, whose wardrobe includes Versace slacks, liked to swan around among his female office staff in the nude, as did the deep-closeted casino billionaire Steve Wynn. Matt Lauer, whose job was to lend gravitas to the *Today* show, kept a bag full of sex toys in his office, so he'd have something to play with should he manage to lure a young woman in. The president of the most powerful nation in the world, it has been alleged, employed prostitutes to pee on a Moscow hotel bed and enjoyed being spanked with a copy of *Forbes* magazine featuring his likeness on the cover.

Feminists have, of course, seen through the clouds of glory trailing patriarchy to expose its intrinsic cruelty and violence. But one thing we have seldom questioned is its seriousness. Consider the feminist dictum that rape is not about sex, but power. The rapist isn't having fun; he's simply enforcing the age-old power of men. That is, he's doing a kind of work—a service to the other elite men who are his peers. Sex, and hence the possibility of pleasure, at least for men, seldom enters into the feminist discourse on male violence, which has treated rape and sexual assault as an enactment of male domination, and perhaps a necessary warning to women—a kind of public service announcement.

But the mounting accusations of sexual harassment by

powerful men suggest that feminism has been taking patriarchy a bit too seriously. Maybe it's not about the endless
reproduction of power relationships; maybe it's about guys
just having fun. Out of sight of nannies and governesses
and wives, they are stealing treats. One of the accusers of
Hillary Clinton's lecherous former "faith consultant" says
he looked at her "like she was a snack"—not a person or
even a pretty girl but a handy between-meals treat. Certainly Harvey Weinstein treated women this way, hiring a
pimp disguised as a colleague to line up women in the foreign cities he visited so that the great mogul would never
have to go without sustenance. The sheer entitlement on
display here puts one in mind of Newt Gingrich's statement
that he feels like "a happy four-year-old who gets up every
morning hoping to find a cookie."

The Treats of Power

In theory, we might be able to extend a grudging smidgen
of sympathy to the downtrodden working-class man who
comes home to beat or rape his wife. How else is he going to
experience power? But many of the men starring in today's
sexual-harassment scandals already wield plenty of power,
through their positions or their money and can hardly
claim to be deprived of pleasure and flattery in their daily
lives. This is the class that stays in five-star hotels, flies in private jets, and expects their every whim to be gratified by a
staff of eager underlings.

Still, they need their sexual treats. The Presidents Club

in London drew hundreds of bankers and millionaires to pester the short-skirted young women who were paid to serve their drinks. Think, too, of Dominique Strauss-Kahn's sex parties, featuring pliant prostitutes for all-male groups of businessmen and IMF officials. The list goes on: Berlusconi's orgies. Trump's pussy-grabbing. Bill Clinton. Or, going back to the 1950s, Hugh Hefner's empire based on the idea that the "playboy" needs an endless supply of "playmates."

Fun has never been considered a major force in history, but perhaps it—and "the pursuit of pleasure" in general—should be. Gaze up again at the great architectural relics of empire you can find in London or Madrid. Where did the wealth come from to build these marvels? From war, of course—wars of conquest. And what is war? Well, it's hell, or so it is said. But it's also the supreme male adventure, especially for those males who get to ride, not tramp, to the battlefields.

For the last ten thousand years, from the Roman conquests through the Viking raids to the Crusades that followed them and on to the global wars of the twentieth century, war has been an opportunity for taking both treasure and pleasure—rape and pillage. It offers plenty of glory and honor, too, if only posthumously, but it hardly amounts to "civilization."

So, what is a twenty-first-century woman to think as she picks her way through the rubble of patriarchy? First, she should laugh out loud at every instance of male and class-based pomposity she encounters, remember that the president—or the esteemed artist or academic—likes to wag his penis at women in private. She should recall that the Wizard of Oz is an evil clown but still a clown. Then she might consider a suitable punishment for our dethroned patriarchs. Maybe they should be confined to one big locked room stocked with high-tech sex toys and left to fuck themselves sick.

With that accomplished, women—and male dissidents from patriarchy should be included here—might want to turn their attention to what a world shaped by the *female* pursuit of pleasure might look like. Would it be gentle and rainbow-colored? Or would it pulse with its own kinds of ecstasy and transgression?

WOMEN

ARE WOMEN GETTING SADDER? OR ARE WE ALL JUST GETTING A LOT MORE GULLIBLE?

Los Angeles Times, 2009

Feminism made women miserable. This, anyway, seems to be the most popular takeaway from "The Paradox of Declining Female Happiness," a recent study by Betsey Stevenson and Justin Wolfers, which purports to show that women have become steadily unhappier since 1972. Maureen Dowd and Arianna Huffington greeted the news with somber perplexity, but the more common response has been a triumphant: *I told you so.*

On Slate's DoubleX website, a columnist concluded from the study that "The feminist movement of the 1960s and 1970s gave us a steady stream of women's complaints disguised as manifestos...and a brand of female sexual power so promiscuous that it celebrates everything from prostitution to nipple piercing as a feminist act—in other words, whine, womyn, and thongs." Or as Phyllis Schlafly put it, more soberly: "The feminist movement taught women to see themselves as victims of an oppressive patriarchy in which their true worth will never be recognized and any success is beyond their reach…Self-imposed victimhood is not a recipe for happiness."

But it's a little too soon to blame Gloria Steinem for our dependence on SSRIs. For all the high-level head-scratching induced by the Stevenson and Wolfers study, hardly anyone has pointed out (1) that there are some issues with happiness studies in general, (2) that there are some reasons to doubt this study in particular, or (3) that, even if you take this study at face value, it has nothing at all to say about the impact of feminism on anyone's happiness.

For starters, happiness is an inherently slippery thing to measure or define. Philosophers have debated what it is for centuries, and even if we were to define it simply as a greater frequency of positive feelings than negative ones, when we ask people if they are happy, we are asking them to arrive at some sort of average over many moods and moments. Maybe I was upset earlier in the day after I opened the bills, but then was cheered up by a call from a friend, so what am I really?

In one well-known psychological experiment, subjects were asked to answer a questionnaire on life satisfaction, but only after they had performed the apparently irrelevant task of photocopying a sheet of paper for the experimenter. For a randomly chosen half of the subjects, a dime had been left for them to find on the copy machine. As two econ-omists summarize the results: "Reported satisfaction with life was raised substantially by the discovery of the coin on the copy machine—clearly not an income effect."

As for the particular happiness study under discussion, the red flags start popping up as soon as you look at the data. Not to be anti-intellectual about it, but the raw data on how men and women respond to the survey reveal no discernible trend to the naked eyeball. Only by performing an occult statistical manipulation called "ordered probit estimates," do the authors manage to tease out any trend at all, and it is a tiny one: "Women were one percentage point less likely than men to say they were not too happy at the beginning of the sample [1972]; by 2006 women were one percentage point more likely to report being in this category." Differences of that magnitude would be stunning if you were measuring, for example, the speed of light under different physical circumstances, but when the subject is as elusive as happiness—well, we are not talking about paradigm-shifting results.

Furthermore, the idea that women have been sliding toward despair is contradicted by the one *objective* measure of unhappiness the authors offer: suicide rates. Happiness is, of course, a subjective state, but suicide is a cold, hard fact, and the suicide rate has been the gold standard of misery since sociologist Emile Durkheim wrote the book on it in 1897. As Stevenson and Wolfers report—somewhat sheepishly, we must imagine—"Contrary to the subjective well-being trends we document, female suicide rates have been falling, even as male suicide rates have remained roughly constant through most of our sample [1972–2006]." Women may get the blues; men are more likely to get a bullet through the temple.

Another distracting little data point that no one, including the authors, seems to have much to say about is that, while "women" have been getting marginally sadder, black women have been getting happier and happier. To quote the authors: "...happiness has trended quite strongly upward for both female and male African Americans... Indeed, the point estimates suggest that well-being may have risen more strongly for black women than for black men." The study should more accurately be titled "The Paradox of Declining White Female Happiness," only that might have suggested that the problem could be cured with melanin and Restylane.

But let's assume the study is sound and that (white) women have become less happy relative to men since 1972. Does that mean that feminism ruined their lives?

Not according to Stevenson and Wolfers, who find that "The relative decline in women's well-being...holds for both working and stay-at-home mothers, for those married and divorced, for the old and the young, and across the education distribution"—as well as for both mothers and the childless. If feminism were the problem, you might expect divorced women to be less happy than married ones and employed women to be less happy than stay-at-homes. As for having children, the presumed premier source of female fulfillment: They actually make women *less* happy.

And if the women's movement was such a big downer, you'd expect the saddest women to be those who had some direct exposure to the noxious effects of second wave feminism. As the authors report, however, "There is no evidence that women who experienced the protests and enthusiasm in the 1970s have seen their happiness gap widen by more than for those women who were just being born during that period."

What this study shows, if anything, is that neither marriage nor children make women happy. (The results are not in yet on nipple piercing.) Nor, for that matter, does there seem to be any problem with "too many choices," "work-life balance," or the "second shift." If you believe Stevenson and Wolfers, women's happiness is supremely indifferent to the actual conditions of their lives, including poverty and racial discrimination. Whatever "happiness" is…

So why all the sudden fuss about the Wharton study, which first leaked out two years ago anyway? Mostly because it's become a launching pad for a new book by the prolific management consultant Marcus Buckingham, best known for *First, Break All the Rules* and *Now, Discover Your Strengths*. His new book, *Find Your Strongest Life: What the Happiest and Most Successful Women Do Differently*, is a cookie-cutter classic of the positive-thinking self-help genre: First, the heart-wrenching quotes from unhappy women identified only by their email names (Countess1, Luveyduvy, etc.), then the stories of "successful" women, followed by the obligatory self-administered test to discover "the role you were bound to play" (Creator, Caretaker, Influencer, etc.), all bookended with an ad for the many related products you can buy, including a "video introduction" from Buckingham, a "participant's guide" containing "exercises" to get you to happiness, and a handsome set of "Eight Strong Life Plans" to pick from. The *Huffington Post* has given Buckingham a column in which to continue his marketing campaign.

It's an old story: If you want to sell something, first find the terrible affliction that it cures. In the 1980s, as silicone implants were taking off, the doctors discovered "micromastia"—the "disease" of small-breastedness. More recently, as big pharma searches furiously for a female Viagra, an amazingly high 43 percent of women have been found to suffer from "Female Sexual Dysfunction," or FSD. Now, it's unhappiness, and the range of potential "cures" is dazzling: Seagrams, Godiva, and Harlequin, take note.

OUR NEIGHBORHOOD PORN COMMITTEE

Mother Jones, 1986

E ver since the attorney general declared open season on smut, I've had my work cut out for me. I'm referring, of course, to the Meese commission's report on pornography, which urges groups of private citizens to go out and fight the vile stuff with every means at hand—spray paint, acetylene torches, garlic, and crucifixes. In the finest spirit of grassroots democracy, the commission is leaving it up to us to decide what to slash and burn and what to leave on the library shelves. Not that we are completely without guidance in this matter, for Commissioner Frederick Schauer ("golden Schauer" to those wild and crazy boys at *Penthouse*) quotes approvingly a deceased judge's definition of hard-core porn: "I know it when I see it."

Well, so do I, thanks to the report's thoughtful assertions that pornography is something that "hurts women" and, in particular, "bears a causal relationship to the incidence of various nonviolent forms of discrimination against or subordination of women in our society." My little group of citizens—recruited from the PTA, Parents without Partners, and the YWCA aerobics class—decided to go straight to the heart of the matter: all written, scrawled, and otherwise-depicted manifestations of sexism, whether found on daytime TV, in the great classics of Western civilization, or in the published opinions of Donald ("Women can't understand arms control") Regan.

I can understand why the commission decided to restrict its own inquiry to the sexier varieties of sexism, commonly known as pornography. How often, after all, does a group composed largely of white male Republicans (you will pardon the redundancy) get to spend months poring over material that would normally only be available in dark little shops on the seamy, low-rent side of town, and to do so entirely at public expense?

But with all due respect, I believe they erred by so limiting themselves. Violence against women, to take the most unpleasant form of "subordination," predates the commercial porn industry by several millennia. Those Romans who perpetrated the rape of the Sabines, for example, did not work themselves up for the deed by screening *Debbie Does Dallas*, and the monkish types who burned thousands of witches in the Middle Ages had almost certainly not come across *Boobs and Buns* or related periodicals.

I thought my citizens' group should start its search for materials damaging to women with the Bible, on the simple theory that anything read by so many people must have something to do with all the wickedness in the world. "Gather around," I said to my fellow citizens. "If those brave souls on the Meese commission could wade through the likes of *Fellatio Frolics* and *Fun with Whips and Chains*, we can certainly get through Genesis."

It was rough going, let me tell you, what with the incest (Lot and his daughters), mass circumcisions, adultery, and various spillings of seed. But duty triumphed over modesty, and we were soon rewarded with examples of sexism so crude and so nasty that they would make *The Story of O* look like suffragist propaganda. There was the part about Eve and her daughters being condemned to bring forth their offspring in sorrow, and numerous hints that the bringing forth of offspring is in fact the only thing women have any business doing. There were injunctions against public speaking by women, and approving descriptions of a patriarchal dynasty extending, without the least concern for affirmative action, for countless generations from Isaac on. And then there were the truly kinky passages on the necessity of "submitting" to one's husband—an obvious invitation to domestic mayhem.

We wasted no time in calling the newly installed Meese commission hotline to report we had discovered material— widely advertised as "family" reading—that would bring a blush to the cheek of dear Dr. Ruth and worry lines to the smooth brow of Gloria Steinem. "Well, yes," said the commissioner who picked up the phone, "but could this material be used as a masturbatory aid? Is it designed to induce sexual arousal in all but the most priggish Presbyterian? Because it's the arousal, you know, that *reinforces* the sexism, transforming normal, everyday male chauvinism into raging misogyny."

We argued that we had seen a number of TV preachers

in states of arousal induced by this book, and that, furthermore, religious ecstasy might be far more effective at reinforcing sexism than any mere tickle of genital response. But we reluctantly agreed to stop our backyard Bible burnings and to try to focus on material that is more violent, up-to-date, and, preferably, with better visuals.

A week later we called the hotline to report we'd seen *Cobra*, *Raw Deal*, three episodes of *Miami Vice*, and a presidential address on the importance of Star Wars, and felt we now had material that was not only damaging to women but disrespectful of human life in all forms, male and female, born and unborn. "But is it dirty?" asked a weary commissioner. "You know, *sexy*?" And we had to admit that neither the sight of Arnold Schwarzenegger without a shirt nor the president in pancake makeup had ever aroused in us any feeling other than mild intestinal upset.

Now I think we're finally getting the hang of it. The problem, as identified by the Meese commission, isn't violence, sexism, or even sexual violence. The problem is sex, particularly those varieties of sex that might in any way involve women. So in the last few weeks, our citizens' anti-smut group has short-circuited six vibrators, burned three hundred of those lurid little inserts found in Tampax boxes, and shredded half the local supply of *Our Bodies, Ourselves*. It's a tough job, believe me, but as Ed Meese keeps telling us, someone's got to do it.

STRATEGIES OF
CORPORATE WOMEN

New Republic, 1986

S ome of us are old enough to recall when the stereotype of a "liberated woman" was a disheveled radical,
notoriously braless, and usually hoarse from denouncing
the twin evils of capitalism and patriarchy. Today the
stereotype is more likely to be a tidy executive who carries
an attaché case and is skilled in discussing market shares
and leveraged buyouts. In fact, thanks in no small part to
the anger of the earlier, radical feminists, women have
gained a real toehold in the corporate world: About 30 percent of managerial employees are women, as are 40 percent
of the current [1986] MBA graduates. We have come a long
way, as the expression goes, though clearly not in the same
direction we set out on.

The influx of women into the corporate world has generated its own small industry of advice and inspiration.
Magazines like *Savvy* and *Working Woman* offer tips on
everything from sex to software, plus the occasional in-
structive tale about a woman who rises effortlessly from
managing a boutique to being the CEO of a multinational

corporation. Scores of books published since the mid-1970s have told the aspiring managerial woman what to wear, how to flatter superiors, and, when necessary, fire subordinates. Even old-fashioned radicals like myself, for whom "CD" still means civil disobedience rather than an 8 percent interest rate, can expect to receive a volume of second-class mail inviting them to join their corporate sisters at a "networking brunch" or to share the privileges available to the female frequent flier.

But for all the attention lavished on them, all the six-figure promotion possibilities and tiny perks once known only to the men in gray flannel, there is a malaise in the world of the corporate woman. The continuing boom in the advice industry is in itself an indication of some kind of trouble. To take an example from a related field, there would not be a book published almost weekly on how to run a corporation along newly discovered Asian principles if American business knew how to hold its own against the international competition. Similarly, if women were confident about their role in the corporate world, I do not think they would pay to be told how to comport themselves in such minute detail. ("Enter the bar with a briefcase or some files...Hold your head high, with a pleasant expression on your face...After you have ordered your drink, shuffle through a paper or two, to further establish yourself [as a businesswoman]," advises *Letitia Baldrige's Complete Guide to Executive Manners*.)

Nor, if women were not still nervous newcomers, would there be a market for so much overtly conflicting advice:

how to be more impersonal and masculine (Charlene Mitchell and Thomas Burdick's *The Right Moves*) or more nurturing and intuitive (Marilyn Loden's *Feminine Leadership*); how to assemble the standard skirted, suited uniform (de rigueur until approximately 1982) or move beyond it for the softness and individuality of a dress; how to conquer stress or how to transform it into drive; how to repress the least hint of sexuality, or, alternatively, how to "focus the increase in energy that derives from sexual excitement so that you are more productive on the job" (Leslie Aldridge Westoff's *Corporate Romance*). When we find so much contradictory advice, we must assume that much of it is not working.

There is a more direct sign of trouble. A small but significant number of women are deciding not to have it all after all, and are dropping out of the corporate world to apply their management skills to kitchen decor and baby care. Not surprisingly, these retro women have been providing a feast for a certain "I told you so" style of journalism; hardly a month goes by without a story about another couple that decided to make do on his $75,000 a year while she joins the other mommies in the playground. But the trend is real. The editors of the big business–oriented women's magazines are worried about it. So is Liz Roman Gallese, the former *Wall Street Journal* reporter who interviewed the alumnae of Harvard Business School, class of '75, to write *Women Like Us*.

The women Gallese interviewed are not, for the most part, actual dropouts, but they are not doing as well as might have been expected for the first cohort of women to wield the talismanic Harvard MBA. Certainly they are not doing as well as their male contemporaries, and the gap widens with every year since graduation. Nor do they seem to be a very happy or likable group. Suzanne, the most successful of them, is contemptuous of women who have family obligations. Phoebe, who is perhaps the brightest, has an almost pathological impulse to dominate others. Maureen does not seem to like her infant daughter. Of the eighty-two women surveyed, thirty-five had been in therapy since graduation; four had been married to violently abusive men; three had suffered from anorexia or bulimia; and two had become Christian fundamentalists. Perhaps not surprisingly, given the high incidence of personal misery, two-fifths of the group were "ambivalent or frankly not ambitious for their careers."

What is happening to our corporate women? The obvious antifeminist answer, that biology is incompatible with business success, is not borne out by Gallese's study. Women with children were no less likely to be ambitious and do well than more mobile, single women (although in 1982, when the interviews were carried out, very few of the women had husbands or children). But the obvious feminist answer—that women are being discouraged or driven out by sexism—does gain considerable support from *Women Like Us*. Many of the women from the class of '75 report having been snubbed, insulted, or passed over for promotions by their male coworkers. Under these circumstances, even the most determined feminist would begin to suffer from what Dr. Herbert J. Freudenberger and Gail North (in their book *Women's Burnout*) call "business burnout." For nonfeminists, or, more precisely, postfeminists—like Gallese and her respondents, sexism must be all the more wounding for being so invisible and nameless. What you cannot name, except as apparently random incidents of "discrimination," you cannot hope to do much about.

Gallese suggests another problem, potentially far harder to eradicate than any form of discrimination. There may be a poor fit between the impersonal bureaucratic culture of the corporation and what is, whether as a result of hormones or history, the female personality. The exception that seems to prove the rule is Suzanne, who is the most successful of the alumnae and who is also a monster of detachment from her fellow human beings. In contrast, Gallese observes that men who rise to the top are often thoroughly dull and "ordinary"—as men go—but perhaps ideally suited to a work world in which interpersonal attachments are shallow and all attention must focus on the famed bottom line.

To judge from the advice books, however, the corporate culture is not as impersonal, in a stern Weberian sense, as we have been led to believe. For example, *The Right Moves*, which is a good representative of the "how to be more like the boys" genre of books for corporate women, tells us to "eliminate the notion that the people with whom you work are your friends"—sound advice for anyone who aspires to the bureaucratic personality. But it also insists that it is necessary to cultivate the "illusion of friendship," lest coworkers find you "aloof and arrogant." You must, in other words, dissemble in order to effect the kind of personality—

artificially warm but never actually friendly—that suits the corporate culture.

Now, in a task-oriented meritocratic organization—or, let us just say, a thoroughly capitalist organization dedicated to the maximization of profit—it should not be necessary to cultivate "illusions" of any kind. It should be enough just to get the job done. But as *The Right Moves* explains, and the stories in *Women Like Us* illustrate, it is never enough just to get the job done; if it were, far more women would no doubt be at the top. You have to impress people, win them over, and in general project an aura of success far more potent than any actual accomplishment. The problem may not be that women lack the capacity for businesslike detachment, but that, as women, they can never entirely fit into the boyish, glad-handed corporate culture so well described three decades ago in *The Lonely Crowd*.

There may also be a deeper, more existential, reason for the corporate woman's malaise. It is impossible to sample the advice literature without beginning to wonder what, after all, is the point of all this striving. Why not be content to stop at $40,000 or $50,000 a year, some stock options, and an IRA? Perhaps the most striking thing about the literature for and about the corporate woman is how little it has to say about the purposes, other than personal advancement, of the corporate "game." Not one among the Harvard graduates or the anonymous women quoted in the advice books ever voices a transcendent commitment to, say, producing a better widget. And if that is too much to expect from postindustrial corporate America, we might at least hope for some lofty organizational goals—to make X Corp. the biggest damn conglomerate in the Western world, or some such. But no one seems to have a vast and guiding vision of the corporate life, much less a fashionably conservative belief in the moral purposefulness of capitalism. Instead, we find successful corporate women asking, "Why am I doing what I'm doing? What's the point here?" or confiding bleakly that "Something's missing."

In fact, from the occasional glimpses we get, the actual content of an executive's daily labors can be shockingly trivial. Consider Phoebe's moment of glory at Harvard Business School. The class had been confronted with a real-life corporate problem to solve. Recognizing the difficulty of getting catsup out of a bottle, should Smucker and Co. start selling catsup out of a wide-mouthed container suitable for inserting a spoon into? No, was Phoebe's answer, because people like the challenge of pounding catsup out of the bottle; a more accessible catsup would never sell. Now, I am not surprised that this was the right answer, but I am surprised that it was greeted with such apparent awe and amazement by a professor and a roomful of smart young students. Maybe for a corporate man, the catsup problem is a daunting intellectual challenge. But a woman must ask herself: Is *this* what we left the kitchen for?

Many years ago, when America was more innocent but everything else was pretty much the same, Paul Goodman wrote, "There is nearly 'full employment'...but there get to be fewer jobs that are necessary or unquestionably useful; that require energy and draw on some of one's best capacities; and that can be done keeping one's honor and dignity."

Goodman, a utopian socialist, had unusually strict criteria for what counted as useful enough to be "man's work," but he spoke for a generation of men who were beginning to question, in less radical ways, the corporate work world described by William H. Whyte, David Riesman, Alan Harrington, and others. Most of the alienated white-collar men of the 1950s withdrew into drink or early coronaries, but a few turned to Zen or jazz, and thousands of their sons and daughters eventually joined with Goodman to help create the anticorporate and, indeed, anticareerist counterculture of the 1960s. It was the counterculture, as much as anything else, that nourished the feminist movement of the late 1960s and early 1970s, which is where our story began.

In the early years, feminism was torn between radical and assimilationist tendencies. In fact, our first sense of division was between the "bourgeois" feminists who wanted to scale the occupational hierarchy created by men, and the radical feminists who wanted to level it. Assimilation won out, as it probably must among any economically disadvantaged group. Networks replaced consciousness-raising groups; Michael Korda became a more valuable guide to action than Shulamith Firestone. The old radical, anarchistic vision was replaced by the vague hope (well articulated in *Feminine Leadership*) that, in the process of assimilating, women would somehow "humanize" the cold and ruthless world of men. Today, of course, there are still radical feminists, but the only capitalist institution they seem bent on destroying is the local adult bookstore.

*   *   *

As feminism loses its critical edge, it becomes, ironically, less capable of interpreting the experience of its pioneer assimilationists, the new corporate women. Contemporary mainstream feminism can understand their malaise insofar as it is caused by sexist obstacles, but has no way of addressing the sad emptiness of "success" itself. Even the well-worn term "alienation," as applied to human labor, rings no bells among the corporate feminists I have talked to recently, although most thought it an arresting notion. So we are in more or less the same epistemological situation Betty Friedan found herself in describing the misery—and, yes, alienation—of middle-class housewives in the early 1960s; better words would be forthcoming, but she had to refer to "the problem without a name."

Men are just as likely as women to grasp the ultimate pointlessness of the corporate game and the foolishness of many of the players, but only women have a socially acceptable way out. They can go back to the split-level homes and well-appointed nurseries where Friedan first found them. (That is assuming, of course, they can find a well-heeled husband, and they haven't used up all their childbearing years in the pursuit of a more masculine model of success.) In fact, this may well be a more personally satisfying option than a work life spent contemplating, say, the fluid dynamics of catsup. As Paul Goodman explained, with as much insight as insensitivity, girls didn't have to worry about "growing up absurd" because they had intrinsically meaningful work cut out for them—motherhood and home-making.

There is no doubt, from the interviews in *Women Like*

Us as well as my own anecdotal sources, that some successful women are indeed using babies as a polite excuse for abandoning the rat race. This is too bad from many perspectives, and certainly for the children who will become the sole focus of their mothers' displaced ambitions. The dropouts themselves would do well to take a look at Peggy J. Berry's *Corporate Couple*, which advises executive wives on the classic problems such as: how to adjust to the annual relocation, how to overcome one's jealousy of a husband's svelte and single female coworkers, and how to help a husband survive his own inevitable existential crisis.

Someday, I believe, a brilliantly successful corporate woman will suddenly look down at her desk littered with spreadsheets and interoffice memos and exclaim, "Is this really worth my time?" At the very same moment, a housewife, casting her eyes around a kitchen befouled by toddlers, will ask herself the identical question. As the corporate woman flees out through the corporate atrium, she will run headlong into the housewife, fleeing into it. The two will talk. And in no time at all they will reunite those two distinctly American strands of radicalism—the utopianism of Goodman and the feminism of Friedan. They may also, if they talk long enough, invent some sweet new notion like equal pay for...meaningful work.

WHAT ABU GHRAIB TAUGHT ME

Los Angeles Times, 2004

Even those people we might have thought were impervious to shame, like the secretary of defense, admit that the photos of abuse in Iraq's Abu Ghraib prison turned their stomachs.

The photos did something else to me, as a feminist: They broke my heart. I had no illusions about the US mission in Iraq—whatever exactly it is—but it turns out that I did have some illusions about women.

Of the seven US soldiers now charged with sickening forms of abuse in Abu Ghraib, three are women: Specialist Megan Ambuhl, Private First Class Lynndie England, and Specialist Sabrina Harman.

It was Harman we saw smiling an impish little smile and giving the thumbs-up sign from behind a pile of hooded, naked Iraqi men—as if to say, "Hi Mom, here I am in Abu Ghraib!" It was England we saw with a naked Iraqi man on a leash. If you were doing PR for Al Qaeda, you couldn't have staged a better picture to galvanize misogynist Islamic fundamentalists around the world.

Here, in these photos from Abu Ghraib, you have everything that the Islamic fundamentalists believe characterizes
Western culture, all nicely arranged in one hideous image—
imperial arrogance, sexual depravity...and gender equality.

Maybe I shouldn't have been so shocked. We know that
good people can do terrible things under the right circumstances. This is what psychologist Stanley Milgram found
in his famous experiments in the 1960s. In all likelihood,
Ambuhl, England, and Harman are not congenitally evil
people. They are working-class women who wanted an
education and knew that the military could be a stepping-
stone in that direction. Once they had joined, they wanted
to fit in.

And I also shouldn't be surprised because I never believed that women were innately gentler and less aggressive
than men. Like most feminists, I have supported full opportunity for women within the military—(1) because I knew
women could fight, and (2) because the military is one of
the few options around for low-income young people.

Although I opposed the 1991 Persian Gulf War, I was
proud of our servicewomen and delighted that their presence irked their Saudi hosts. Secretly, I hoped that the
presence of women would over time change the military,
making it more respectful of other people and cultures,
more capable of genuine peacekeeping. That's what I
thought, but I don't think that anymore.

A certain kind of feminism, or perhaps I should say a
certain kind of feminist naiveté, died in Abu Ghraib. It
was a feminism that saw men as the perpetual perpetrators,
women as the perpetual victims and male sexual violence

against women as the root of all injustice. Rape has repeatedly been an instrument of war and, to some feminists, it was beginning to look as if war was an extension of rape. There seemed to be at least some evidence that male sexual sadism was connected to our species' tragic propensity for violence. That was before we had seen female sexual sadism in action.

But it's not just the theory of this naive feminism that was wrong. So was its strategy and vision for change. That strategy and vision rested on the assumption, implicit or stated outright, that women were morally superior to men. We had a lot of debates over whether it was biology or conditioning that gave women the moral edge—or simply the experience of being a woman in a sexist culture. But the assumption of superiority, or at least a lesser inclination toward cruelty and violence, was more or less beyond debate. After all, women do most of the caring work in our culture, and in polls are consistently less inclined toward war than men.

I'm not the only one wrestling with that assumption today. Mary Jo Melone, a columnist for the *St. Petersburg* (Florida) *Times*, wrote on May 7, 2004: "I can't get that picture of England [pointing at a hooded Iraqi man's genitals] out of my head because this is not how women are expected to behave. Feminism taught me 30 years ago that not only had women gotten a raw deal from men, we were morally superior to them."

If that assumption had been accurate, then all we would have had to do to make the world a better place—kinder, less violent, more just—would have been to assimilate into what had been, for so many centuries, the world of men. We would fight so that women could become the generals, CEOs, senators, professors, and opinion-makers—and that was really the only fight we had to undertake. Because once they gained power and authority, once they had achieved a critical mass within the institutions of society, women would naturally work for change. That's what we thought, even if we thought it unconsciously—and it's just not true. Women can do the unthinkable.

You can't even argue, in the case of Abu Ghraib, that the problem was that there just weren't enough women in the military hierarchy to stop the abuses. The prison was directed by a woman, General Janis Karpinski. The top US intelligence officer in Iraq, who also was responsible for reviewing the status of detainees before their release, was Major General Barbara Fast. And the US official ultimately responsible for managing the occupation of Iraq since October 2003 was Condoleezza Rice. Like Donald H. Rumsfeld, she ignored repeated reports of abuse and torture until the undeniable photographic evidence emerged.

What we have learned from Abu Ghraib, once and for all, is that a uterus is not a substitute for a conscience. This doesn't mean gender equality isn't worth fighting for for its own sake. It is. If we believe in democracy, then we believe in a woman's right to do and achieve whatever men can do and achieve, even the bad things. It's just that gender equality cannot, all alone, bring about a just and peaceful world.

In fact, we have to realize, in all humility, that the kind of feminism based on an assumption of female moral superiority is not only naive; it also is a lazy and self-indulgent form of feminism. Self-indulgent because it assumes that a victory for a woman—a promotion, a college degree, the right to serve alongside men in the military—is by its very nature a victory for all of humanity. And lazy because it assumes that we have only one struggle—the struggle for gender equality—when in fact we have many more.

The struggles for peace and social justice and against imperialist and racist arrogance, cannot, I am truly sorry to say, be folded into the struggle for gender equality.

What we need is a tough new kind of feminism with no illusions. Women do not change institutions simply by assimilating into them, only by consciously deciding to fight for change. We need a feminism that teaches a woman to say no—not just to the date rapist or the overly insistent boyfriend but, when necessary, to the military or the corporate hierarchy within which she finds herself.

In short, we need a kind of feminism that aims not just to assimilate into the institutions that men have created over the centuries, but to infiltrate and subvert them.

To cite an old, and far from naive, feminist saying: "If you think equality is the goal, your standards are too low." It is not enough to be equal to men, when the men are acting like beasts. It is not enough to assimilate. We need to create a world worth assimilating into.

MAKING SENSE OF
LA DIFFÉRENCE

Time, 1992

Few areas of science are as littered with intellectual rubbish as the study of innate mental differences between the sexes. In the nineteenth century, biologists held that woman's brain was too small for intellect, but just large enough for household chores. When the tiny-brain theory bit the dust (elephants, after all, have bigger brains than humans), scientists began a long, fruitless attempt to locate the biological basis of male superiority in various brain lobes and chromosomes. By the 1960s, sociobiologists were asserting that natural selection, operating throughout the long human prehistory of hunting and gathering, had predisposed males to leadership and exploration and females to crouching around the campfire with the kids.

Recent studies suggest that there may be some real differences after all. And why not? We have different hormones and body parts; it would be odd if our brains were a hundred percent unisex. The question, as ever, is, What do these differences augur for our social roles?—meaning, in particular, the division of power and opportunity between the sexes.

Don't look to the Flintstones for an answer. However human beings whiled away their first 100,000 or so years of existence, few of us today make a living by tracking down mammoths or digging up tasty roots. In fact, much of our genetic legacy of sex differences has already been rendered moot by that uniquely human invention: technology. Military prowess no longer depends on superior musculature or those bursts of aggressive fury that prime the body for combat at ax range. As for exploration, women—with their lower body weight and oxygen consumption—may be the more "natural" astronauts.

But suppose that the feminists' worst-case scenario turns out to be true, and that males really are better, on average, at certain mathematical tasks. If this tempts you to shunt the girls all back to Home Ec—the only acceptable realm for would-be female scientists eighty years ago—you probably need remedial work in the statistics of "averages" yourself. Just as some women are taller and stronger than some men, some are swifter at solid geometry and abstract algebra. Many of the pioneers in the field of x-ray crystallography— which involves three-dimensional visualization and heavy doses of math—were female, including biophysicist Rosalind Franklin, whose work was indispensable to the discovery of the double-helical structure of DNA.

Then there is the problem that haunts all studies of "innate" sex differences: the possibility that the observed differences are really the result of lingering cultural factors— pushing females, for example, to "succeed" by dummying up.

Girls' academic achievement, for example, usually takes a nosedive at puberty. Unless nature has selected for smart girls and dumb women, something is going very wrong at about the middle-school level. Part of the problem may be that males, having been the dominant sex for a few millennia, still tend to prefer females who make them feel stronger and smarter. Any girl who is bright enough to solve a quadratic equation is also smart enough to bat her eyelashes and pretend that she can't.

Teachers too may play a larger role than nature in differentiating the sexes. Studies show that they tend to favor boys by calling on them more often, making eye contact with them more frequently, and pushing them harder to perform. Myra and David Sadker, professors of education at American University, have found that girls do better when teachers are sensitized to gender bias and refrain from sexist language, such as the use of "man" to mean all of us. Single-sex classes in math and science also boost female performance, presumably by eliminating favoritism and male disapproval of female achievement.

The success, so far, of such simple educational reforms only underscores the basic social issue: Given that there may be real innate mental differences between the sexes, what are we going to do about them? A female advantage in reading emotions could be interpreted to mean that males should be barred from psychiatry—or that they need more coaching. A male advantage in math could be used to confine girls to essays and sonnets—or the decision could be made to compensate by putting more effort into girls' math education. In effect, we already compensate for boys' apparent handicap in verbal skills by making reading the centerpiece of grade-school education.

We are cultural animals, and these are cultural decisions of the kind that our genes can't make for us. In fact, the whole discussion of innate sex differences is itself heavily shaped by cultural factors. Why, for example, is the study of innate differences such a sexy, well-funded topic right now, which happens to be a time of organized feminist challenge to the ancient sexual division of power? Why do the media tend to get excited when scientists find an area of difference, and ignore the many reputable studies that come up with no differences at all?

Whatever science eventually defines it as, *la différence* can be amplified or minimized by human cultural arrangements: The choice is up to us, not our genes.

OUTCLASSED:
SEXUAL HARASSMENT

The Guardian, 2017

With Alissa Quart

The number of women in the entertainment industry coming forward with charges of sexual harassment is starting to feel endless. They include stars like Gwyneth Paltrow and Angelina Jolie but also heads of tech start-ups and journalists, gallerists, and producers.

But it is women working in far less glamorous occupations who really bear the brunt of male lechery and assault: the housekeepers, waitresses, and farmworkers. A paper in the journal *Gender, Work & Organization*, based on interviews with female workers at five-star hotels, found almost all experiencing some kind of inappropriate sexual advance from a guest. In another study, 80 percent of waitresses reported sexual harassment. A mind-boggling 88 percent of female construction workers did, too.

If you look at these numbers, you recognize that most victims are not so glamorous.

And yet, the current conversation about harassment is deeply skewed by social class. There are far too many think pieces about high-level actresses and far too few about the waitress at your local diner.

Why? For starters, most working-class women don't hire publicists or lawyers, and they aren't able to cultivate friends in high places. (They are very rarely applauded for that word of the year, "bravery," in public forums.) Most of these women never go public at all. After all, if you're earning $8 to $10 an hour, you cannot afford to go without a paycheck for the weeks it would take to find a new job. Any expression of dissatisfaction with a hostile workplace can lead to a legal firing on the grounds of, for example, having a bad attitude.

Blue-collar and retail workers may well be happy to see the issue of sexual harassment getting attention, yet they might also be irritated at celebs receiving all the attention and respond accordingly. Talk to a hairdresser, a waitress, or a domestic worker, and you're likely to encounter a deep vein of resentment.

We put the studies aside and actually heard from women on social media. "I've been sexually harassed in minimum and low-wage jobs: Choices were to put up with it or quit. Every single time, I quit. But I was young & single. Many women don't have that option," Pittsburgh artist Amie Gillingham wrote on Barbara's Twitter feed.

Or as writer Julie Rea put it to us, "When I was a waitress, there was sexual harassment/innuendo/verbal abuse from the chefs, the barmen, the kitchen porters, the drunk customers, AND the male managers!"

Another former waitress in Michigan wrote on Twitter, "As a waitress I experienced harassment daily. No HR dept to report it to. Manager & owner were biggest offenders. It was keep quiet or lose my job. Needed that job."

As Cecilia, who worked as a minibar attendant at a Chicago hotel, told the *Huffington Post*, she was asked to come into a room by a male guest who was masturbating to his computer when she entered. He wanted her to see him—this was by design.

Indeed, the "business trip" has gotten so hazardous that two cities—Seattle and New York—have passed initiatives that mandate that hotels supply their housekeepers with panic buttons. Harassment is so common that a hospitality careers website offers a checklist, albeit a toothless one, of what maids and cleaning women can do to protect themselves at work.

Threats involve creepy guests whacking off, grabbing them by their aprons, or throwing them down on the bed, as former IMF managing director Dominique Strauss-Kahn allegedly did to a hotel maid in 2011.

And if you think stronger unions always offer better protection for workers on this score, think again. According to a recent report, even staff at the Service Employees International Union (SEIU) have faced charges of sexual harassment—and that's the largest service workers' union.

There certainly is room for outrage about both the mistreatment of thespians and models, and the manhandling of waitresses or women picking berries in the fields. (We should try for a both/and campaign. It could be called #MostofThem!)

Then again, that inclusive strategy rests on a tacit assumption that the airing of the pain of, say, actor Mira

Sorvino will inevitably help less well-born women. And we think the associative property here is probably a fallacy. It's basically a trickle-down theory of female empowerment. We know how well trickle-down theories of all kinds tend to pan out.

So how can we excavate the vast iceberg of sexual harassment that lies beneath the glittering tip of celebrity abuse?

This is a powerful moment for sharing our stories, but it can sometimes feel like we are only reproducing class divisions that have long existed in the feminist movement— where we are aware of the elegant suffering of celebrity comics, businesswomen, and starlets but not those of the working mothers who are handing us our fries or fluffing our pillows. We are not seeing the way the latter are harassed in so many other ways. Working-class women regularly have their purses searched (ostensibly for stolen goods) or are expected to work overtime without pay. This kind of casual hassling is part of the general humiliation that most low-wage workplaces inflict.

Obviously, working women need safe spaces in which to share their experiences, which unions and affluent feminists could help provide—speak-outs and other public forums to spread the word that sexual harassment is not only pervasive but also, fortunately, illegal.

There is a statewide California bill requiring employers to train cleaning and security employees and managers in the basics of preventing sexual harassment. Not-for-profit organizations like Modern Alliance are working to bring many professions together against worker sexual harassment. The Local 1 union in Chicago has pushed for legislation with the brilliantly seamy hashtag #HandsOff PantsOn.

We should certainly put more pressure on local and federal government for similar bills and language in contracts around the country. But these are still small slaps at the many male hands groping at America's female workforce.

GOD, SCIENCE, AND JOY

MIND YOUR OWN BUSINESS

The Baffler, 2015

At about the beginning of this decade, mass-market mindfulness rolled out of the Bay Area like a brand-new app. Very much like an app, in fact, or a whole swarm of apps. Previous self-improvement trends had been transmitted via books, inspirational speakers, and CDs; now, mindfulness could be carried around on a smartphone. There are hundreds of them, these mindfulness apps, bearing names like Smiling Mind and Buddhify. A typical example features timed stretches of meditation, as brief as one minute, accompanied by soothing voices, soporific music, and images of forests and waterfalls.

This is Buddhism sliced up and commodified, and, in case the connection to the tech industry is unclear, a Silicon Valley venture capitalist blurbed a seminal mindfulness manual by calling it "the instruction manual that should come with our iPhones and BlackBerries." It's enough to make you think that the actual Buddha devoted all his time under the Bodhi Tree to product testing. In the mindfulness lexicon, the word "enlightenment" doesn't have a place.

In California, at least, mindfulness and other conveniently accessible derivatives of Buddhism flourished well before BlackBerries. I first heard the word in 1998 from a wealthy landlady in Berkeley, advising me to be "mindful" of the suffocating Martha Stewart-ish decor of the apartment I was renting from her, which of course I was doing everything possible to un-see. A possible connection between her "mindfulness" and Buddhism emerged only when I had to turn to a tenants' rights group to collect my security deposit. She countered with a letter accusing people like me—leftists, I suppose, or renters—of oppressing Tibetans and disrespecting the Dalai Lama.

During the same stint in the Bay Area, I learned that rich locals liked to unwind at Buddhist monasteries in the hills, where, for a few thousand dollars, they could spend a weekend doing manual labor for the monks. Buddhism, or some adaptation thereof, was becoming a class signifier, among a subset of Caucasians anyway, and nowhere was it more ostentatious than in Silicon Valley, where star player Steve Jobs had been a Buddhist or perhaps a Hindu—he seems not to have made much of a distinction—even before it was fashionable for CEOs to claim a spiritual life. Mindfulness guru and promoter Soren Gordhamer noticed in 2013 that tech leaders from Google, LinkedIn, Twitter, and other major tech companies seemed to be "tapped into an inner dimension that guides their work." He called it "wisdom" and named his annual conferences Wisdom 2.0—helpful shorthand, as it happens, for describing the inner smugness of the Bay Area elite.

Today, mindfulness has far outgrown Silicon Valley and its signature industry, becoming another numbingly ubiquitous feature of the verbal landscape, as "positive thinking" once was. While an earlier, more arduous, version of Buddhism attracted few celebrities other than Richard Gere, mindfulness boasts a host of prominent practitioners—Arianna Huffington, Gwyneth Paltrow, and Anderson Cooper among them. "Mindful leadership" debuted at Davos in 2013 to an overflow crowd, and Wisdom 2.0 conferences have taken place in New York and Dublin as well as San Francisco, with attendees fanning out to become missionaries for the new mind-set. This year's event in San Francisco advertises not only familiar faces from Google and Facebook, but also speeches by corporate representatives of Starbucks and Eileen Fisher. Aetna, a Fortune 100 health insurance company, offers its 34,000 employees a twelve-week meditation class, and its CEO dreams of expanding the program to include all its customers, who will presumably be made healthier by clearing their minds. Even General Mills, which dates back to the nineteenth century, has added meditation rooms to its buildings, finding that a seven-week course produces striking results. According to the *Financial Times*,

> 83 percent of participants said they were "taking time each day to optimize my personal productivity"—up from 23 percent before the course. Eighty-two percent said they now make time to eliminate tasks with limited productivity value—up from 32 percent before the course.

Productivity is only one objective of the new miniaturized meditation; there are also the more profound-sounding goals of "wisdom" and "compassion," which are not normally associated with Silicon Valley or American business in general. Just a few years ago, say in 2005, the tech industry exemplified a very different kind of corporate ideology, featuring multitasking and perpetually divided attention—think an incoming call conducted while scanning a new product design, checking email, and deflecting the interruptions of subalterns. It was madness, but the business self-help literature encouraged people to "surf the chaos," nourishing themselves on caffeine and adrenaline. If we needed to unclutter our minds, we were directed to the gym and an hour or so of intense physical activity. A trim muscular body, combined with an ever-flickering gaze, signified executive status.

The backlash against chaos surfing came on quickly, as if The Wolf of Wall Street had been forced to drink a soothing bowl of milk. Studies were piling up to suggest that a lifestyle dependent on multiple devices and double-shot espressos might be toxic to the human mind, impeding concentration and undermining human connectedness. There was wild talk of "unplugging" and fleeing offline. In northern California in 2013, a group called Digital Detox began offering Camp Grounded, a well-publicized summer camp for adults, at which all devices (and alcohol and children and real names) were prohibited, the better to encourage "play" and conversation. We had once imagined that human attention was infinitely divisible, with each particle of it potentially available to advertisers, entertainers, and employers. But it was turning out to be fragile, even endangered, and in need of constant repair.

Where brilliance and creativity had formerly reigned, there were, by the turn of the millennium, suspicions of pathology. Child psychiatrists began to drop "bipolarity" as a default diagnosis and turn their attention to attention itself. Too many children were deficient in it, just as their plugged-in parents were often guilty of "distracted parenting." The switch from bipolarity to attention deficit disorder is hard to date exactly, in part because these conditions are now said to be frequently "comorbid," or overlapping. But as we began to spend more and more of our time interacting with mood-less programs and devices, psychiatry seems to have turned from emotional concerns like bipolarity, which is a "mood disorder," to cognitive problems like ADD and ADHD.

At the same time, diagnoses of autism and Asperger's syndrome were skyrocketing—especially, as a 2001 article in *Wired* pointed out, in Santa Clara County, home of Silicon Valley. Among the adult population, surely something was wrong with Steve Jobs, who alternated between obsessive attention to details and complete withdrawal into himself, between a spiritual aloofness and uncontrolled temper tantrums. Some observers thought they detected a hint of autism in the unblinking, almost affect-free Bill Gates, and the characters in HBO's *Silicon Valley* are portrayed as well "within the spectrum."

So Silicon Valley embraced mindfulness with a twinge of contrition. Not only did its corporate culture encourage something called "geek syndrome," but its products seemed to spread that same derangement to everyone else. The devices that were supposed to make us smarter and more connected to other humans were actually messing with our minds, causing "net brain" and "monkey mind," as well as physical disorders associated with long hours of sitting. As we click between Twitter and Facebook, text and hypertext, one link and another, synapses are being formed and then broken with febrile inconstancy—or so a growing number of experts, such as MIT's Sherry Turkle, warn us—leaving the neuronal scaffolding too fragile to house large thoughts.

A less arrogant industry might have settled for warning labels on its phones and pads, but Silicon Valley wanted an instant cure, preferably one that was high-tech and marketable. The great advantage of mindfulness was that it seemed to be based firmly on science; no "hippie bullshit" or other "woo woo" was involved. A neuroscientist reported that Buddhist monks with about ten thousand hours of meditation under their belts had altered brain functions; shorter bouts of meditation seemed to work at least temporary changes in novices. The field of "contemplative neuroscience" was born, and Silicon Valley seized on it for a much-needed "neural hack." Through meditation, monastic or app-guided, anyone could reach directly into their own moist brain tissue and "resculpt" it in a calmer, more attentive direction. Mindfulness, as its promoters put it, fosters "neuroplasticity."

No one questions that the brain changes with the experiences the mind undergoes. If thought has a physical basis, as scientists assume, then it produces physical alterations in the brain. Trauma and addiction can lead to lasting problems; even fleeting events may leave the chemical changes in the brain that we experience as memory. In fact, "plasticity" is a pallid descriptor for the constant, ongoing transformation of brain tissue. Neurons reach out to each other through tiny membranous protrusions, often forming new synapses. Synapses that fire frequently grow stronger, while the inactive ones wither. Well-connected neurons thrive, while neglected ones die. There is even some evidence that neurons in mature animals can reproduce.

What there is no evidence for, however, is any particularly salubrious effect of meditation, especially in byte-sized doses. This was established through a mammoth, federally sponsored "meta-analysis" of existing studies, published in 2014, which found that meditation programs can help treat stress-related symptoms but are no more effective in doing so than other interventions, such as muscle relaxation, medication, or psychotherapy. There is no excuse for ignoring this study, which achieved worldwide attention. So maybe meditation does have a calming, "centering" effect, but so does an hour of concentration on a math problem or a glass of wine with friends. As for Silicon Valley's unique contribution, mindfulness apps, a recent study concluded that there is an almost complete lack of evidence supporting the usefulness of those applications. We found no randomized clinical trials evaluating the impact of these applications on mindfulness training or health indicators, and the potential for mobile mindfulness applications remains largely unexplored.

For an industry based on empirical science and employing large numbers of engineers, Silicon Valley has been remarkably incurious about the scientific basis of mindfulness, probably because the "neuroplasticity" concept is just too alluring. If the brain can be resculpted through conscious effort, then mindfulness is as imperative as physical exercise; the brain is a "muscle" and, like any muscle, in need of training. Google's chief motivator Chade-Meng Tan was an early adopter, setting up the company's mindfulness training program, Search Inside Yourself, in 2007, and later telling the *Guardian*:

> If you are a company leader who says employees should be encouraged to exercise, nobody looks at you funny.... The same thing is happening to meditation and mindfulness, because now that it's become scientific, it has been demystified. It's going to be seen as fitness for the mind.

One popular and highly rated mindfulness app, Get Some Headspace, advertises itself as a "gym membership for the mind." Only it's easier than working out, of course, or even yoga. As one enthusiastic software entrepreneur said of the Headspace app, "You don't have to sit in a lotus position. You just press 'play' and chill out."

Outside of meditation, which can take just a few minutes a day, the daily practice of mindfulness can be summarized as pay attention, or better yet, pay attention to one thing at a time. Take out the earphones when the children are trying to talk to you. Listen carefully to colleagues, look them in the eyes, and attempt to comprehend things from their point of view. Do not multitask; just sink yourself into "the moment," one task at a time. What could be simpler?

Left unanswered in all of this is the question of what to be mindful of. Yes, the children. But what do you do when one of them is trying to confide in you and the other one is screaming from the bedroom? Or say you're at a business lunch. You have to be mindful of your companion while simultaneously attempting to eat without spilling or choking—and I say you would be remiss if you failed to notice the sad-eyed busboy who is refilling the water glasses. Divided attention far predates the advent of smartphones and is intrinsic to many human activities, such as child-raising, cooking a large meal, and waiting on tables. Or take one of the most ancient human occupations—war—which is relevant because the mindfulness promoters are beginning to market their product to the US military. Incoming fire can come from any direction, at unexpected times and speeds. Morale must be considered, as well as changing instructions from the strategists in command. There is no danger of soldiers distractedly checking their Facebook pages; the issue is whether they have the mental bandwidth demanded by the exigencies of battle.

Silicon Valley got its own tiny taste of combat at the 2014 Wisdom 2.0 conference in San Francisco. The panel on "3 Steps to Build Corporate Mindfulness the Google Way" had just begun when a small group of protesters walked onstage and unfurled a banner saying "Eviction-Free San Francisco," a reference to the savage gentrification that Google, among others, has inflicted on the city. After security pushed the protesters offstage and started a tug-of-war for the banner, a Google mindfulness representative intoned, "We can use this as a moment of practice. Check in with your body and see what's happening, what it's like to be around conflict and people with heartfelt ideas that may be different than what we're thinking." Zen-like, the panel rolled on, undistracted by the brief glimpse of mass evictions and homelessness.

THE ANIMAL CURE

The Baffler, 2012

Encounters with lions, mountain goats, grizzly bears, dolphins, and whales are not least among the exotic experiences offered by the tourism industry. The attractions are obvious: a chance to be outdoors in stunning scenery, to see creatures you may have known only as two-dimensional images, and to feel ecologically high-minded in the process.

But current marketing for the wildlife encounter industry offers something grander, something that people have more commonly sought through meditation, fasting, or prayer. Surf the numerous websites for the booming worldwide whale-watching business, for example, and you will find companies from Baja to Sydney to Reykjavik promising whale-mediated "spiritual experiences."

Satisfied customers report having undergone life-altering changes, or at least fighting back tears: the vacation as vision quest. Or, within Britain, you can experience the "spiritual event" of a Big Cat Encounter—with the big cats conveniently caged. After treating wild animals as nuisances or meat for many centuries, humans are elevating them to the status of the numinous.

Fortunately, it is not necessary to spend a lot of money or endure seasickness to have a spiritual encounter with an animal. In a pinch, pets will do, and the internet offers a rich literature on the uplifting effects of ordinary dogs and cats. In her 2002 book *Mystical Dogs: Animals as Guides to Our Inner Life*, New Age writer Jean Houston promoted dogs not only for their ability to engender serenity in stressed humans, but to lead us to the experience of cosmic unity. As she instructs:

> Proceed with your dog guide down and down until you reach the deepest level of all, the spiritual realm....Often at this level one feels oneself in the presence of God or, if you prefer, the Mind of the Universe. In this realm, images, thoughts, body sensations, and emotions are fused in what is felt as a meaningful process culminating in a sense of self-understanding, self-transformation, spiritual enlightenment and possibly mystical union. Again, record your unique experience.

Cats, she said in an interview with Beliefnet, are "equally evocative of our spiritual depths," pointing out that the Dalai Lama's house is fairly crawling with them. For the spiritually attuned, almost any animal—insect, bird, butterfly—can serve as a doorman to the realm of enlightenment.

Dogs have been particularly nimble at seizing the new opportunities for animals as spirit guides, shamans, and healers. Long confined to blue-collar work as draft animals or security guards, they can now supplement their domestic roles with professional careers—for example, as "therapy dogs." One of the new canine professionals, Bella the Boxer, has written a business advice book titled *Secrets of a Working Dog: Unleash Your Potential and Create Success*, which recommends the power of "pawsitive" thinking. Her credentials? After bemoaning the limited opportunities formerly available to dogs, she urges the reader to shake off his stereotypes and wake up to the existence of a "new breed of working dog that relies on business savvy and brains. Rather than herd sheep, we're joining the human white-collar workforce."

One out of five corporations, Bella reports, now allows dogs at work, where they are tasked with raising human morale, increasing creativity, and reducing stress. Her own ambition is to become one of America's tens of thousands of registered therapy dogs and minister to patients in hospices and nursing homes.

Premonotheistic societies would have found nothing odd about animal healers or animal-induced epiphanies. They worshipped animals, animal-human hybrids (such as Sekhmet, the lion-bodied goddess of predynastic Egypt), and human-shaped deities with animal familiars (such as the Hindu goddess Durga, who rides a tiger). Even the anthropomorphized Greek deities could take animal form, as when Zeus became a swan to rape Leda, and seem to have originated as animal gods. Almost every large and potent animal species—bears, bulls, lions, sharks, snakes—have been an object of human cultic veneration. Before the

Christian missionaries arrived, my Celtic ancestors wor-shipped the goddess Epona, who took the form of a horse. The Makah people of Alaska worship "Whale," who pro-vides them with both physical and spiritual sustenance.

In fact, the connection between animals and religiosity may predate fully evolved *Homo sapiens*. Why do humans tend to imagine that there are gods at all? Because, accord-ing to the latest from the field of cognitive science, there was a survival advantage in imagining that every stirring in the tall grass meant that a leopard—or some such po-tentially hazardous life-form—might be closing in for an attack. Our brains are what the cognitive scientists call "hy-peractive agency detection devices": We see faces in clouds, hear denunciations in thunder, and sense transcendent be-ings all around us because we evolved on a planet densely occupied by other "agents"—animals that could destroy us with the slash of a claw or the splash of a fin, arbitrarily and in seconds.

The rise of the monotheistic religions, featuring either anthropomorphic gods like the Christian "father" or deities so abstract that they are impervious to representation, drove the animals, so to speak, from the temple of the hu-man imagination. This change, occurring between roughly 2000 BCE and 700 CE, has long been celebrated as a huge step forward for humankind—the "axial transformation"—propelling us from the unseemly worship of savage beasts to the refined and dignified adoration of a god who is both perfect and perfectly good. But it was a tragic demotion for animals. The axial religions determined that some of them were ritually "unclean" and reclassified all of them as the inferiors of humans. In *The Others: How Animals Made Us Human*, Paul Shepard traced the "humanization" of the so-called world religions—the expunging of animal imagery from religious sites and the association, especially within Christianity, of animals with demons. There were exceptions like St. Francis of Assisi, but Shepard cites a thirteenth-century priest who defeathered a living sparrow in front of his congregation in order to punish the poor bird for being a bird, with all the innate wretchedness and iniquity that such status entails.

Are animals, at least those not designated as meat, finally making a comeback? We may not worship golden calves or offer human sacrifices to jaguar gods, but Americans spend approximately $50 billion a year on our pets. We have an animal rights movement dedicated loosely to the proposition that "animals are people too" and a burgeoning academic field of Animal Studies, which prepares students for careers in veterinary science or, less auspiciously, for fields like "swine management." There is serious talk of "rewilding" large sections of North American real estate by restoring the original Pleistocene flora and fauna—mastodons, or something resembling them, included.

Implicit in much of the new attention to animals is the commendably liberal idea that they are not—intellectually, emotionally, or morally—all that different from humans. Hollywood animal heroes like Remy the rat chef, Rango the cowboy chameleon, and the Kung Fu Panda aspire, scheme, set long-term goals, and, of course, communicate in the voices of human movie stars. In real life, as observed by scientists, animals have been found to be trespassing egregiously on capabilities once thought to be uniquely human: They can use simple tools; they can be altruistic; they can create what they seem to regard as works of art; they can reason and remember; they can fall into what looks like depression. Language is widespread in the nonhuman world, and not only among birds, dolphins, and whales. Very recent research reveals that American prairie dogs, who are closely related to squirrels, can issue calls informing each other about what kind of human, or other creature, might be approaching. "Here comes the tall human in the blue [shirt]," they can say, or "Here comes the short human in the yellow [shirt]." The human-animal distinction disappears almost completely within the new field of Critical Animal Studies, which seeks to advance "a holistic understanding of the commonality of oppressions, such that speciesism, sexism, racism, ableism, statism, classism, militarism, and other hierarchical ideologies and institutions are viewed as parts of a larger, interlocking, global system of domination." Animals are not only like humans, but they are also specifically like oppressed and marginalized categories of humans. One of the founders of Critical Animal Studies expects that, "within a decade [of 2009]," his field will take its "rightful place alongside women's studies, African-American studies, Chicano/a studies, disability studies, and queer studies."

But the current emphasis on animal-human similarities does not necessarily signal the approach of a new Eden, in which vegetarian lions will lie down with lambs. There is an unseemly coziness to much of this enlightened discourse, an assumption that animals are not only like humans, but that they *like* us, or at least bear no active grudges. Everyone has heard, as the Arlington (Virginia) Animal Welfare League puts it, that "there's no need to fear wildlife. If you don't bother them, they generally won't bother you." Hikers in the national parks are reassured that bears are unlikely to attack unless they are startled or have reason to fear a threat to their young. Even whales, who have suffered mightily at human hands, can be anthropomorphized and, at least in imagination, rendered completely tame. As the website for a Baja whale-watching service opines:

> Whales are amazing creatures. Not only are they among the largest creatures on Earth (Blue whales ARE the largest living creatures on the planet!) but they are also among the most gentle and friendly, and very family oriented. Whales were given a bad rap by whale hunters (who called them "devilfish") starting in the 1600s, because some mother whales were violent in the water when protecting their young from harpoons, but what good mother WOULDN'T do anything to protect her baby?

Fortunately, "The whales have been very forgiving of their earlier slaughter by humans."

But when humans rest too much on the goodwill of animals, or simply let down their guard, things can go very wrong. The poster child for presumptuousness would have to be Timothy Treadwell, who was immortalized by Werner Herzog in the documentary *Grizzly Man*. Having spent thirteen summers living among grizzly bears in the Alaska wilderness—talking to them, reading to them, and occasionally petting them—he came to believe he was "a fully accepted wild animal—brother to these bears." A few weeks after arriving at that triumphant conclusion, he and his girlfriend were killed and partially eaten by one of his ursine siblings. Or we might cite the numerous humans in the life of chimpanzee Nim Chimpsky who taught him to sign more than one hundred words, while at the same time encouraging him to enjoy alcohol, marijuana, and light cross-species sexual intimacies. Perhaps frustrated by his inconsistent and ever-changing human companions, Nim attacked one and bit off nearly half her face.

Another well-documented case of human-animal intimacy gone wrong involves the novelist and short story writer Joy Williams and her German shepherd Hawk, whom she described in an essay as "my sweetie pie, my honey, my handsome boy, my love." As she was leading Hawk into a kennel for one of her rare trips without him, he suddenly leaped on her, biting her breast and hands until "there was blood everywhere." Hawk was subsequently "put down," but Joy survived to become a vegetarian and an animal rights advocate.

The problem is not that animals *are* different from humans in some generalizable way—less gracious, perhaps, or more impulsive and unpredictable—but that it makes very little sense to say what animals are like or not like. There are so many species of animals that any analysis based on the human-animal division is as eccentric, in its own way, as a hypothetical biology based on the jellyfish-nonjellyfish distinction would be. Within species, too, animals differ as individuals, just as humans differ—hence the difficulty in prescribing the best way to avoid a bear attack. Hikers are advised to deflect charging grizzlies by lying down and playing dead, but, sadly, some grizzlies are encouraged by this behavior. Nor can all cases of animal hostility be attributed to human error. Treadwell and Williams may have crossed a line into undue intimacy, but there is no such explanation for the fatal goring of a hiker by a mountain goat in 2011. The man was an experienced hiker, and the goat— who, it has been suggested, may have been harassed by a park ranger in the past—had no apparent proximate *casus belli*. And what are we to make of the occasional whale who attacks a boat—in some cases, even a whale-watching boat, brimming with interspecies goodwill?

So, before engaging a therapy dog, maybe especially a Jungian one, you might want to consider that, in addition to much friendly cooperation, there are serious issues between our species. Humans abuse dogs in many gratuitous ways and, despite much well-intentioned propaganda to the contrary, wolves—who are the ancestors of all dogs, including the "toy" ones—have long been a deadly threat to humans. From Russia to Italy, thousands of people—often children—were lost to wolves between the seventeenth and nineteenth centuries. In late eighteenth-century France, the frequency of wolf attacks on humans necessitated state-sponsored wolf hunts, and when these were suspended during the Revolution, the attacks resumed in full force.

More recently, in 1996, there was a rash of fatal wolf attacks on villagers in Uttar Pradesh. In early 2011 an unprecedented four-hundred-strong wolf pack—or, perhaps we should say army, since the horde represented an alliance of many packs—laid siege to a village in Siberia, although they restricted themselves to eating livestock. One wolf expert speculated that they were not wolves at all, but "a cross between domestic dogs and the wild animal." If so, he wrote, we are faced with "the nightmare possibility that an entirely new creature has been created which, while less wary of humans, also possesses the natural vulpine instinct for hunting and eating as a pack." And plenty of pet dogs other than Hawk have launched individual attacks on their apparently indulgent owners. To cite a couple of random examples, in the last five years a British woman lost her nose to her greyhound while she slept, and a Manhattan woman's scalp was torn open when she bent to give her Rottweiler a good-morning pat.

None of which is to say that animals may not make fine "spirit guides" or, to the extent that we need them, even deities. I once found myself well away from land and escorted by a couple of dolphins, each of them about the size of my kayak. They appeared to be playing with me, diving under the kayak and popping up on the other side, grinning their fixed, unreadable grins. It would have been easy enough for them to flip the kayak over and, if they were so minded, to push me under water until I drowned, but that was not the game they were playing that day. On another occasion, I had a chance to see a tiger, illuminated only by flashlight, at a distance of about three feet. Despite the sturdy fence between us, I found myself experiencing what zoologist Konrad Lorenz called the *heiliger Schauer*, or "holy shiver" of awe that predators inspire in their prey. There is something deeply uncanny about looking into the eyes of a powerful, intelligent, alien being. Maybe you could even call it spiritual.

Besides, it's long past time to admit that the "all-good" and "all-perfect" deities of monotheism have not worked out very well, discredited as they are by earthquakes, floods, tsunamis, and epidemics, not to mention all the murders committed in their names. And what about the built-in biological evil of predation, which has been a driving force of evolution at least since the Cambrian era, about 500 million years ago? If nature is "red in tooth and claw," it must be because the supreme deity, should there be one, prefers this color scheme.

You don't have to be an atheist to see that theodicy, or the effort to excuse God for evil, is a species of idiocy. There is no way to be both all good and all powerful, not in this region of the multiverse anyway. If there is a God or gods—a possibility I am not ruling out—clearly he, she, or they are not, in any human way, "good." At least with animals or zoomorphic deities we know where we are—which is with creatures in whom, as Michael Pollan puts it, we can glimpse "something unmistakably familiar (pain, fear, tenderness) and something irretrievably alien."

But these glimpses are rare. As the entrepreneurs of wildlife tourism understand, most of us are unlikely to encounter a free, self-determining animal larger than a raccoon unless we are willing to pay for the experience. The massive extinctions of megafauna—both through killing for food and killing for sport—that began twelve thousand years ago as humans spread out over the earth have accelerated drastically in the past century or two, leaving us a very lonely species. We try to compensate by seeking out the rare wild animals who have survived our depredations, or by imagining an invisible super being or God who will befriend and comfort us. Or we scan the galaxy for habitable planets, searching for the kind of company—quirky, diverse, and sometimes awe-inspiring—that we once found thick upon this earth.

THE MISSIONARY POSITION

The Baffler, 2012

M ost critics have regarded Ridley Scott's *Prometheus* in much the same way that Arthur Miller probably thought of Marilyn Monroe—gorgeous, but intellectually way out of her depth. No one denies the film's visual glory, which begins the moment a giant chalk-white alien strides out into the Icelandic wasteland, guzzles some gunk from a can, and splits open to release thousands of wriggling worm-like DNA strands into a waterfall. But when it comes to metaphysical coherence, the critical consensus is that *Prometheus* has nothing to offer. "There are no revelations," the *New York Times* opines, "only what are called, in the cynical jargon of commercial storytelling, 'reveals,' bits of momentarily surprising information bereft of meaning or resonance." In its refusal to offer an adequate accounting of the universe and our place in it, the film can even be accused of anti-intellectualism. "We were never really in the realm of working out logical solutions to difficult problems," Geoffrey O'Brien complains in the *New York Review of Books*, just a "cauldron" of "juicily irrational ingredients."

But *Prometheus* does have a clear-cut metaphysical proposition to offer, one so terrible as to be almost inadmissible. Consider the basic plot, minus the many alien invasions of human flesh, the references to corporate greed and alien WMDs, and the enigma of the devious HAL-like android: Guided by archeological clues found in prehistoric rock art, a group of humans set out on a trillion-dollar expedition to visit the planet (actually a moon) that the giant white alien came from. There, among innumerable horrors, since under its bleak surface this moon seems to be a breeding ground for lethal predators of the dark and squirmy variety, they find a cryogenically preserved clone or sibling of that original alien "creator" who seeded earth with DNA. The humans foolishly awaken him, perhaps expecting some sort of seminar on the purpose of life. Instead, the alien starts knocking heads off and strides away to resume his pre-nap project of traveling to and destroying the planet earth. This, and not the DIY abortion of a squid-like alien fetus, is the emotional climax of the film, the point when Noomi Rapace screams at the homicidal alien, "I need to know why! What did we do wrong? Why do you hate us?"

True, we don't know whether the big white aliens are gods, manifestations of a single God, or operatives working for some higher power. But just how much theological clarity can you expect from a Hollywood action film? It doesn't take any great imaginative leap to see that Scott and his writers are confronting us with the possibility that there may be a God, and that He (or She or It or They) *is not good*.

This is not atheism. It is a strand of religious dissidence

that usually flies well under the radar of both philosophers and cultural critics. For example, it took about five years before the critics noticed that Philip Pullman's popular trilogy *His Dark Materials* was not just about a dodgy or unreliable God, but about one who is actively malevolent. Atheism has become a respectable intellectual position, in some settings almost de rigueur, but as Bernard Schweizer explains in his enlightening 2010 book *Hating God: The Untold Story of Misotheism*, morally inspired opposition to God remains almost too radical to acknowledge. How many of Elie Wiesel's admirers know that he said, "Although I know I will never defeat God, I still fight him"? Or that Rebecca West declaimed that "the human will should [not] be degraded by bowing to this master criminal," and that she was echoing a sentiment already expressed by Zora Neale Hurston?

Barred from more respectable realms of speculation, the idea of an un-good God has been pretty much left to propagate in the fertile wetlands of science fiction. One of the early sci-fi classics of the twentieth century, H. P. Lovecraft's 1931 *At the Mountains of Madness*, offers a plotline that eerily prefigures Prometheus. An Antarctic expedition uncovers the ruins of a millions-of-years-old civilization created by extraterrestrial aliens, who awaken and kill most of the explorers. A couple of humans survive to determine, through a careful study of the ruins, that the aliens had "filtered down from the stars and concocted earth life as a joke or mistake." Not all sci-fi deities are so nasty. C. S. Lewis offered a Christ-like lion god in the Narnia series; *Battlestar Galactica's* climax featured a vision of a benevolent, and oddly Luddite, god. But many of the great sci-fi epics derive their philosophical frisson from a callous or outright wicked deity: the impertinent Vulcan god of *Star Trek V: The Final Frontier*, the tyrannical worm-god of *God Emperor of Dune*, the trickster sea god of *Solaris*.

There are less satanic sci-fi gods too—more ethereal, universal, and even intermittently nonviolent. Olaf Stapledon's 1937 *Star Maker* ends with its far-traveling human protagonist encountering the eponymous "eternal spirit": "Here was no pity, no proffer of salvation, no kindly aid. Or here were all pity and all love, but mastered by a frosty ecstasy." In Arthur C. Clarke's 1953 short story "The Nine Billion Names of God," Tibetan monks who have set themselves the task of generating all the possible names of God finally get some assistance from a computer brought to them by Western technicians. As the technicians make their way back down the mountainside from the monastery, they look up at the night sky to see that "without any fuss, the stars were going out." The monks had been right: The universe existed for the sole purpose of listing the names of God and, once this task was accomplished, there was no reason for the universe to go on. The theme of an über-Being who uses humans for its own inscrutable purposes is developed more fully in Clarke's novel *Childhood's End*, in which an "Overmind" of remote extraterrestrial provenance sets humans on a course toward ecstatic communion with each other—and, somehow, at the same time, with it. When that goal is achieved, the earth blows itself up, along with the last human on it, after which the Overmind presumably moves on to find a fresh planet—and species—to fulfill its peculiar cravings.

The idea of an un-good God, whether indifferent or actively sadistic, flies in the face of at least two thousand years of pro-God PR, much of it irrational and coming from professed "people of faith." God is perfectly good and loving, they assert with an almost infantile sense of entitlement; he "has a plan" for us, no matter how murky or misguided that plan often seems. Otherwise, they ask, as if evaluating a health care provider, what comfort does he have to offer us? Or they petulantly demand a "perfect" God—all-good, omnipotent, and omniscient—in the name of what amounts to human vanity. If we, the top dogs on our planet, are to worship some invisible Other, he had better be unimaginably perfect.

But you don't have to be a theist to insist on the goodness of God. Generations of secular social scientists and others writing in the social-science tradition have insisted that a good God, whether He exists or not, is good for us. The argument takes the form of a historical narrative: In the ancient past—and its seeming equivalent in small-scale or "primitive" societies—deities were plural, female as well as male, and often of no detectable moral valence. The ancient deities of Mediterranean peoples, for example, a pantheon that ranges from Zeus to Yahweh and Baal, were psycho-gods—insatiable consumers of blood sacrifice, abettors of genocide, even, in the case of Zeus, a serial rapist. They offered no rationales for their behavior, and when Job insisted on an explanation for the travails visited upon him, he was told, in effect, "Because I can." Further back, in prehistory, lurk deities too wild and bloody-minded to take fully human form. They were predatory animals like Sekhmet, the lion-headed goddess of ancient Egypt, and the man-eating goddess Kali, who wears a tiger skin.

Then, the official narrative continues, somewhere between 900 and 200 BCE, the so-called "Axial Age," God underwent a major makeover. Blood sacrifice was gradually abandoned; diverse and multiple gods fused into a single male entity; a divine concern for peace and order supposedly came to permeate the universe. In the often-told story of divine redemption, Yahweh matures into the kindly shepherd of the Psalms and finally into the all-loving person of Jesus, who is himself offered up as a sacrifice. Comparable changes occur outside the Mediterranean world, including in persistently polytheistic Hinduism, which gives up animal sacrifice and reaches for a sublime über-Deity. What brought about this transformation?

Religious historian Karen Armstrong, probably the best-known living celebrant of axial progress, proposes in her 2006 book *The Great Transformation* that people simply got tired of the bad old gods' violence and immorality. Speaking of the late Vedic period in India, she writes that the traditional gods "were beginning to seem crude and unsatisfactory," leading to the search for a god "who was more worthy of worship." As people became nicer and more sensitive, they lost interest in the grand spectacles of animal sacrifice that constituted preaxial religious ritual and sought a more "spiritual" experience. (She also mentions, but only in passing, that in some parts of the world people had a less exalted reason for abandoning blood sacrifice: they were running out of animals to sacrifice.) To

Armstrong, the axial transformation had only one flaw—
its "indifference to women," which is a pretty wan way to
describe a theological shift that eliminated most of the
planet's goddesses. But she humbly accepts the limits set by
patriarchal monotheism: "Precisely because the question of
women was so peripheral to the Axial Age, I found that any
sustained discussion of this topic was distracting."

In his 2009 book *The Evolution of God*, the polymathic
scholar Robert Wright offered what promised to be an even
more objective and secular explanation for God's "transformation." He argues that, for various reasons, people, or at
least key peoples, were becoming more cosmopolitan and
tolerant, hence in need of a single, universal, morally admirable deity. This seems like a useful approach, until you
recall that the ultracosmopolitan and theologically tolerant
Romans readily absorbed the gods of conquered peoples
into their own polytheistic pantheon. But Wright hardly
needs any concrete historical forces, because "moral
progress…turns out to be embedded in the very logic of
religion as mediated by the basic direction of social
evolution"—which I suppose is a way of saying that things
could only get better, because such is their "logic" and "basic direction." As Wright informs us, "cultural evolution
was all along pushing divinity, and hence humanity, toward
moral enlightenment."

The "New Atheists"—Christopher Hitchens, Richard
Dawkins, Sam Harris, and Daniel Dennett—easily flicked
away the argument that God's axial upgrade was accompanied by a general increase in human goodness and mercy.
They note that the new-model deities, with prophets like

Jesus and Muhammad, have proved just as effective at abetting cruelty and war as the old ones. If the gods have any of their reputed powers, and if they got nicer while humans did not, then we have to question the depth and sincerity of the gods' transformation—or whether it occurred at all. Interestingly, though, neither Armstrong nor Wright cedes any power or agency to the God whose growing goodness they applaud: To do so would be to give up their own claims to scholarly detachment. Their God is presented as nothing more than a projection of human needs and desires, an assessment no atheist could disagree with.

There is another theory of how humans became attached to "good" and increasingly monotheistic gods—and one that is refreshingly free of sweetness and optimism. As Jürgen Habermas and, more recently, in rich historical detail, Robert Bellah have pointed out, the "Axial Period" was a time of endemic warfare, intensified by the introduction of iron weapons across Eurasia. The maintenance of armies and the practice of war require strong central authorities—kings and eventually emperors—who discover that it is both risky and inefficient to try to rule their domestic populations entirely by force. Far easier to persuade the public that the king or the emperor is *deserving* of obedience because the deity he represents, or even embodies, is himself so transcendentally good. The autocrat who rules by divine right—from Constantine to Hirohito, the God-emperor of Japanese State Shintoism—demands not only obedience, but gratitude and love.

The good, post-axial God has not, of course, always been a reliable ally of tyrants. Christianity has again and again helped inspire movements against the powerful, such as the abolitionists and the twentieth-century civil rights movement. But this does not mean that the good God is necessarily good for us, or at least for the downtrodden majority of us. The unforgiveable crime of the post-axial religions is to encourage the conflation of authority and benevolence, of hierarchy and justice. When the pious bow down before the powerful or, in our own time, the megachurches celebrate wealth and its owners, the "good" God is just doing his job of what Habermas called "legitimation."

In 1974, Philip K. Dick experienced a theophany—a "self-disclosure by the divine"—which deftly summarizes science fiction's contribution to theology. It was a shattering revelation, leaving him feeling more like "a hit-and-run accident victim than a Buddha." He disintegrated into mental illness, at least to the point of earning a bed in a locked psychiatric ward for several weeks. As related in his novel *Valis*, in which the author figures as the protagonist, he fought back by working obsessively to understand and communicate his encounter with a deity of extraterrestrial origin that is *"in no way like mortal creatures"* (his italics). This deity or deities—for there may be at least a half dozen of them in Dick's idiosyncratic cosmogony—bear some resemblance to biological creatures: They have their own agendas, and what they seek, through their self-disclosures to humans, is "interspecies symbiosis."

If God is an alternative life-form or member of an alien species, then we have no reason to believe that It is (or They are), in any humanly recognizable sense of the word, "good." Human conceptions of morality almost all derive from the intensely social nature of the human species: Our young require years of caretaking, and we have, over the course of evolution, depended on each other's cooperation for mutual defense. Thus we have lived, for most of our existence as a species, in highly interdependent bands that have had good reasons to emphasize the values of loyalty and heroism, even altruism and compassion. But these virtues, if not unique to us, are far from universal in the animal world (or, of course, the human one). Why should a Being whose purview supposedly includes the entire universe share the tribal values of a particular group of terrestrial primates?

Besides, Dick may have been optimistic in suggesting that what the deity hungers for is "interspecies symbiosis." Symbiosis is not the only possible long-term relationship between different species. Parasitism, as hideously displayed in Ridley Scott's *Alien* series, must also be considered, along with its quicker-acting version, predation. In fact, if anything undermines the notion of a benevolent deity, it has to be the ubiquity of predation in the human and nonhuman animal worlds. Who would a "good" God favor—the antelope or the lion with hungry cubs waiting in its den, the hunter or the fawn? For Charles Darwin, the deal breaker was the Ichneumon wasp, which stings its prey in order to paralyze them so that they may be eaten alive by the wasp's larvae. "I cannot persuade myself," wrote Darwin, "that a beneficent and omnipotent God would have designedly created the Ichneumonidae with the express intention of their feeding within the living bodies of Caterpillars, or that a cat should play with mice." Or, as we may ask more generally: What is kindness or love in a biological world shaped by interspecies predation? "Morality is of the highest importance," Albert Einstein once said, "but for us, not for God."

In *Prometheus*, the first alien releases DNA on earth about 500 million years ago, on the eve, in many viewers' interpretation, of what has been called the Precambrian evolutionary explosion. If so, it was not life that the alien initiated on earth, because life predated the Precambrian. What he did may have been far worse; he may have infected the earth with the code or script for interspecies predation. Before the "explosion," terrestrial life was mostly unicellular and, judging from the low frequency of claws, shells, and other forms of weaponry found in the fossil record, relatively peaceful. Afterwards, living creatures became bigger, more diverse, better armed, and probably either meaner or a lot more frightened: The "arms race" between predator and prey had begun. The causality remains in question here, with scientists still puzzling over the origins of predation and its role in triggering the runaway evolutionary process that led, from the Cambrian on, to humans, to science fiction, and to the idea of God.

If the doughy aliens are not the ultimate deities whose morality we need to assess, then who or what is? Who do these aliens work for—or against? At the end of the movie, with all of their human comrades dead, the android and the Noomi Rapace character rebuild an alien spaceship and set off to find the planet that, according to the android's research, the aliens themselves originally came from. The possibility of a good God or gods, signaled by the cross

Noomi wears around her neck, remains open—as it must, of course, for the sequel.

But, contra so many of the critics, we have learned an important lesson from the magnificent muddle of *Prometheus*: If you see something that looks like a god—say, something descending from the sky in a flaming chariot, accompanied by celestial choir sounds and trailing great clouds of stardust—do not assume that it is either a friend or a savior. Keep a wary eye on the intruder. By all means, do not fall down on your knees.

THE NEW CREATIONISM:
BIOLOGY UNDER ATTACK

The Nation, 1997

With Janet McIntosh

When social psychologist Phoebe Ellsworth took the podium at a recent interdisciplinary seminar on emotions, she was already feeling rattled. Colleagues who'd presented earlier had warned her that the crowd was tough and had little patience for the reduction of human experience to numbers or bold generalizations about emotions across cultures. Ellsworth had a plan: She would preempt criticism by playing the critic, offering a social history of psychological approaches to the topic. But no sooner had the word "experiment" passed her lips than the hands shot up. Audience members pointed out that the experimental method is the brainchild of white Victorian males. Ellsworth agreed that white Victorian males had done their share of damage in the world but noted that, nonetheless, their efforts had led to the discovery of DNA. This short-lived dialogue between paradigms ground to a halt with the retort: "You believe in DNA?"

More grist for the academic right? No doubt, but this exchange reflects a tension in academia that goes far deeper than spats over "political correctness." Ellsworth's experience illustrates the trend—in anthropology, sociology, cultural studies, and other departments across the nation—to dismiss the possibility that there are any biologically based commonalities that cut across cultural differences. This aversion to biological or, as they are often branded, "reductionist" explanations, commonly operates as an informal ethos limiting what can be said in seminars, asked at lectures or incorporated into social theory. Extreme antiinnatism has had formal institutional consequences as well: At some universities, like the University of California, Berkeley, the biological subdivision of the anthropology department has been relocated to a separate building—a spatial metaphor for an epistemological gap.

Although some of the strongest rejections of the biological have come from scholars with a left or feminist perspective, antipathy toward innatist theories does not always score neatly along political lines. Consider a recent review essay by centrist sociologist Alan Wolfe in the *New Republic*. Wolfe makes quick work of Frank Sulloway's dodgy Darwinist claims (in *Born to Rebel: Birth Order, Family Dynamics, and Creative Lives*) about the influence of birth order on personality, but can't resist going on to impugn the motives of anyone who would apply biology to the human condition: In general, he asserts, "The biologizing of human beings is not only bad humanism, but also bad science."

For many social theorists, innate biology can be let in only as a constraint—"a set of natural limits on human functioning," as anthropologist Marshall Sahlins has written. It has, from this point of view, no positive insights to offer into how humans think, act, or arrange their cultures. For others, the study of innate human properties is not merely uninteresting but deeply misguided. Stanford philosopher of science John Dupré, for example, argues that it is "essentialist" even to think that we are a biological species in the usual sense—that is, a group possessing any common tendencies or "universal properties" that might shed some light on our behavior. As feminist theorist Judith Butler puts it, "The very category of the universal has begun to be exposed for its own highly ethnocentric biases."

But the notion that humans have no shared, biologically based "nature" constitutes a theory of human nature itself. No one, after all, is challenging the idea that chimpanzees have a chimpanzee nature—that is, a set of genetically scripted tendencies and potential responses that evolved along with the physical characteristics we recognize as chimpanzee-like. To set humans apart from even our closest animal relatives as the one species that is exempt from the influences of biology is to suggest that we do indeed possess a defining "essence," and that it is defined by our unique and miraculous freedom from biology. The result is an ideological outlook eerily similar to that of religious creationism. Like their fundamentalist Christian counterparts, the most extreme antibiologists suggest that humans occupy a status utterly different from and clearly "above" that of all other living beings. And, like the religious fundamentalists, the new academic creationists defend their stance as if all of human dignity—and all hope for the future—were at stake.

The new secular creationism emerged as an understandable reaction to excess. Since the nineteenth century, conservatives have routinely deployed supposed biological differences as immutable barriers to the achievement of a more egalitarian social order. Darwinism was quickly appropriated as social Darwinism—a handy defense of economic inequality and colonialism. In the twentieth century, from the early eugenicists to *The Bell Curve*, pseudo-biology has served the cause of white supremacy. Most recently, evolutionary psychology has become, in some hands, a font of patriarchal social prescriptions. Alas, in the past few years such simplistic biological reductionism has tapped a media nerve, with the result that, among many Americans, schlock genetics has become the default explanation for every aspect of human behavior from homosexuality to male promiscuity, from depression to "criminality."

Clearly science needs close and ongoing scrutiny, and in the past decade or two there has been a healthy boom in science studies and criticism. Scholars such as Evelyn Fox Keller, Sandra Harding, Emily Martin, and Donna Haraway have offered useful critiques of the biases and ethnocentric metaphors that can skew everything from hypothesis formation to data-collection techniques. Feminists (one of the authors included) have deconstructed medicine and psychology for patriarchal biases; left-leaning biologists such as Stephen Jay Gould, Richard Lewontin, and Ruth Hubbard have exposed misapplications of biology to questions of social policy. However, contemporary antibiologists decry a vast range of academic pursuits coming from very different theoretical corners—from hypotheses about the effects of genes and hormones, to arguments about innate cognitive modules and grammar, to explorations of universal ritual form and patterns of linguistic interaction. All these can be branded as "essentialist," hence wrongheaded and politically mischievous. Paradoxically, assertions about universal human traits and tendencies are usually targeted just as vehemently as assertions about differences: There are no differences between groups, seems to be the message, but there is no sameness among them, either.

Within anthropology, the social science traditionally friendliest to biology and now the one most bitterly divided over it, nineteenth-century claims about universal human nature were supplanted in the early twentieth century by Franz Boas and colleagues, who conducted detailed studies of particular cultures. By the mid-1960s, any role for biological commonalities in cultural anthropology was effectively foreclosed when Clifford Geertz remarked that "Our ideas, our values, our acts, even our emotions are, like our nervous system itself, cultural products."

As neo-Marxist and behaviorist theories of the tabula rasa human gained ground over the next decade, other disciplines followed anthropology's lead. So completely was sociology purged of biology that when Nicholas Petryszak analyzed twenty-four introductory sociology textbooks in 1979, he found that all assumed that "any consideration of biological factors believed to be innate to the human species is completely irrelevant in understanding the nature of human behavior and society." In general, by the seventies, antibiologism had become the rallying cry of academic liberals and feminists—and the apparent defense of human freedom against the iron chains of nature.

It was only with the arrival of the intellectual movements lumped under the term "postmodernism" that academic antibiologism began to sound perilously like religious creationism. Postmodernist perspectives go beyond a critique of the misuses of biology to offer a critique of biology itself, extending to all of science and often to the very notion of rational thought. In the simplified form it often takes in casual academic talk, postmodernism can be summed up as a series of tenets that include a wariness of metanarratives (meaning grand explanatory theories), a horror of essentialism (extending to the idea of any innate human traits), and a fixation on "power" as the only force limiting human freedom—which at maximum strength precludes claims about any universal human traits while casting doubt on the use of science to study our species or anything at all. Glibly applied, postmodernism portrays evolutionary theory as nothing more than a sexist and racist story line created by Western white men.

The deepest motives behind this new secular version of creationism are understandable. We *are* different from other animals. Language makes us more plastic and semiotically sophisticated, and renders us deeply susceptible to meanings and ideas. As for power, Foucault was right: It's everywhere, and it shapes our preferences and categories of thought, as well as our life chances. Many dimensions of human life that feel utterly "natural" are in fact locally constructed, a hard-earned lesson too easy to forget and too important not to publicize. The problem is that the combined vigor of antibiologism and simplified postmodernism has tended to obliterate the possibility that human beings have anything in common, and to silence efforts to explore this domain. Hence we have gone, in the space of a decade or two, from what began as a healthy skepticism about the misuses of biology to a new form of dogma.

As a biologically oriented researcher who has made controversial innatist claims, Rutgers social theorist Robin Fox notes with irony that secular creationist academics seem to have replaced the church as the leading opponents of Darwinism: "It's like they're responding to heresy." Stephen Jay Gould, who has devoted much of his career to critiquing misuses of biology, also detects parallels between religious and academic creationist zeal. While holding that many aspects of human life are local and contingent, he adds, "Some facts and theories are truly universal (and true)— and no variety of cultural traditions can change that...we can't let a supposedly friendly left-wing source be exempt from criticism from anti-intellectual positions."

The new creationism is not simply a case of well-intended politics gone awry; it represents a grave misunderstanding of biology and science generally. Ironically, the creationists invest the natural sciences with a determinative potency no thoughtful scientist would want to claim. Biology is rhetorically yoked to "determinism," a concept that threatens to clip our wings and lay waste to our utopian visions, while culture is viewed as a domain where power relations with other humans are the only obstacle to freedom.

But these stereotypes of biological determinism and cultural malleability don't hold up under scrutiny. For one thing, biology is not a dictatorship—genes work probabilistically, and their expression depends on interaction with their environment. As even Richard Dawkins, author of *The Selfish Gene* and a veritable Antichrist to contemporary creationists of both the secular and Christian varieties, makes clear: "It is perfectly possible to hold that genes exert a statistical influence on human behaviour while at the same time believing that this influence can be modified, overridden or reversed by other influences." And if biology is not a dictatorship, neither is culture a realm of perfect plasticity. The accumulated lessons of ethnography—and, paradoxically, postmodern theories of power themselves—suggest that even in the absence of biological constraints, it is not easy to remold human cultures to suit our utopian visions. In fact, in the extreme constructivist scenario borrowed by secular creationists, it's hard to imagine who would have the will or the ability to orchestrate real change: the people in power, who have no motivation to alter the status quo, or the oppressed, whose choices, preferences, and sentiments have been so thoroughly shaped by the cultural hegemony of the elite? Judged solely as a political stance, secular creationism is no less pessimistic than the biologism it seeks to uproot.

Milder versions of the "nature/nurture" debate begat a synthesis: "There is no biology that is not culturally mediated." But giving biology its due while taking cultural mediation into account requires inclusive and complex thinking—as Phoebe Ellsworth puts it: "You need a high tolerance of ambiguity to believe both that culture shapes things and that we have a lot in common." Despite the ham-fisted efforts of early sociobiologists, many (probably most) biologically based human universals are not obvious to the naked eye or accessible to common sense.

Finally, many secular creationists are a few decades out of date on the kind of "human nature" that evolutionary biology threatens to impose on us. Feminists and liberal academics were perhaps understandably alarmed by the aggressive "man the hunter" image that prevailed in the sixties and seventies; and a major reason for denying the relevance of evolution was a horror of the nasty, brutish cavemen we had supposedly evolved from. But today, evolutionary theory has moved to a more modest assessment of the economic contribution of big-game hunting (as opposed to gathering and scavenging) and a new emphasis on the cooperative—even altruistic—traits that underlie human sociality and intelligence. We don't have to like what biology has to tell us about our ancestors, but the fact is that they have become a lot more likable than they used to be.

In portraying human beings as pure products of cultural context, the secular creationist standpoint not only commits biological errors but defies common sense. In the exaggerated postmodernist perspective appropriated by secular creationists, no real understanding or communication is possible between cultures. Since the meaning of any human practice is inextricable from its locally spun semiotic web, to pluck a phenomenon such as "ritual" or "fear" out of its cultural context is, in effect, to destroy it. Certainly such categories have different properties from place to place, and careful contextualization is necessary to grasp their local implications. But as Ellsworth asks: "At the level of detail of 'sameness' that postmodernists are demanding, what makes them think that two people in the same culture will understand each other?" The ultimate postmodern retort would be, of course, that we do not, but this nihilism does not stand up to either common sense or deeper scrutiny. We manage to grasp things about each other—emotions, motives, nuanced (if imperfect) linguistic meanings—that couldn't survive communicative transmission if we didn't have some basic emotional and cognitive tendencies in common.

The creationist rejection of innate human universals threatens not only an intellectual dead end but a practical one. In writing off any biologically based human commonality, secular creationists undermine the very bedrock of the politics they claim to uphold. As Barbara Epstein of the History of Consciousness Program at the University of California, Santa Cruz, remarks: "If there is no human nature outside social construction, no needs or capacities other than those constructed by a particular discourse, then there is no basis for social criticism and no reason for protest or rebellion." In fact, tacit assumptions of human similarity are embedded in the theories of even such ostensible social constructionists as Marx, whose theory of alienation assumes (in some interpretations, anyway) that there are authentic human needs that capitalism fails to meet.

Would it really be so destructive to our self-esteem as a species to acknowledge that we, like our primate relatives, are possessed of an inherited repertory of potential responses and mental structures? Would we forfeit all sense of agency and revolutionary possibility if we admitted that we, like our primate relatives, are subject to the rules of DNA replication (not to mention the law of gravity)? In their horror of "determinism," academic creationists seem to forget postmodernism's finest insight: that, whatever else we may be, we are indeed creatures of symbol and "text." We may be, in many ways, constrained by our DNA, but we are also the discoverers of DNA—and, beyond that, the only living creature capable of representing its biological legacy in such brilliant and vastly condensed symbols as "DNA."

The good news is that a break may be coming. In spite of the nose-thumbing inspired by the Alan Sokal/Social Text hoax, constructive debates and conversations between scientists and social theorists have been initiated in newsletters, journals, and conferences across the country. A few anthropology departments, including those at Northwestern, Penn State, and Emory, are encouraging communication between their cultural and biological subfields. And although interactionist work has not had adequate space to flourish, achievements so far suggest that, regardless of creationist disclaimers, biological and cognitive universals may be acutely relevant to social theory. Ann Stoler, an anthropologist, historian, and scholar of Foucault at the University of Michigan, agrees. By failing to take our innate cognitive tendencies seriously, she writes, social constructionists may be dodging the "uncomfortable question" as to whether oppressive ideologies like racism and sexism "acquire the weight...they do...because of the ways in which they feed off and build upon [universal] categories of the mind." As Ellsworth says, the meeting of human universals and culture is "where the interesting questions begin."

But for the time being it takes more than a nuanced mind to deal with the interface of culture and biology. It takes courage. This climate of intolerance, often imposed by scholars associated with the left, ill suits an academic tradition rhetorically committed to human freedom. What's worse, it provides intellectual backup for a political outlook that sees no real basis for common ground among humans of different sexes, races, and cultures.

UP CLOSE AT
TRINIDAD'S CARNIVAL

Smithsonian Magazine, 2009

W hen Northerners think of the Caribbean, Trinidad isn't usually the first place that comes to mind. Until recently, Trinidad had few tourist-oriented hotels or restaurants, and its crime rate is so high that visitors are advised not to venture outdoors wearing watches or jewelry, and definitely not at night. What Trinidad does have is carnival—a centuries-old blowout reputedly so wild and intense that it makes Mardi Gras look like a Veterans Day parade.

I had a reason beyond hedonism for making the trip. I'd spent nine years researching a book on the carnival tradition, *Dancing in the Streets: A History of Collective Joy*. Prehistoric rock drawings suggest that costuming and group dancing date back to the Paleolithic. In the nineteenth century, Western explorers found it going strong among indigenous peoples worldwide, including Polynesians, Inuits, West Africans, Aboriginal Australians, and villagers in India. In Europe, however, it had been suppressed when Protestantism and the Counter-Reformation wiped out most public festivities, which, over the years, had become flash points for popular unrest.

The European experience in Trinidad is a case in point: Eighteenth-century French settlers brought the tradition of a pre-Lenten festival, in which they found it amusing to dress up and dance like their African slaves. The enslaved peoples found it even more amusing to use the confusion of carnival as an occasion for uprisings. Long after slavery was abolished by the British in 1838, the colonial administration continued to fight the now-Africanized carnival piece by piece—banning, at one time or another, drums, masks, and dancing in the streets.

But carnival survived, and my question was: What compromises had it made to do so? I had watched Key West's version of carnival—October's Fantasy Fest—go downhill over the years, blanched by commercialization and robbed of artistry as the point of it became to bare one's (painted) breasts and drink oneself sick. Had Trinidad managed to keep carnival's traditional creativity and political charge alive? Most of my years of research had been sedentary, in hushed libraries and poorly lit archives. In February 2008 I decided to go dancing in the streets myself.

I arrived in Port of Spain two days before the official start of carnival, giving me plenty of time to see that "mas," as the Trinidadians call it (from "masquerade"), isn't just a diversion. It's practically a national mobilization. Tens of thousands of people poured into the squat, mountain-ringed city, most of them native-born "Trinis," home from other parts of the world, with a few European tourists thrown in. Banners flying over downtown streets advised, for safety's sake, to "stay with your lime," your lime being the friends you came with. Newspapers offered front-page reports of bitter rivalries in the pre-carnival soca music competitions, screaming headlines like "'No One Will Spoil Dis Mas,' Warns Police Commissioner Paul" and earnest editorials on exactly the kind of questions that concerned me, such as whether the predominance of foreign-made bikini costumes has reduced carnival to a girlie show.

The festivities begin at 4 a.m. on the Monday before Ash Wednesday with a ritual called Jouvay, from either the French *jour ouvert* ("opening day") or the Creole *jou ouvé?* ("Is it daybreak yet?"). I had no idea of what I was getting into when I "registered" at the 3canal storefront center the day before. 3canal is both a musical band and one of the many small production companies that stage carnival; the name, according to one of the musicians, Roger Roberts, derives from a type of machete used by cane cutters and, he says, is "a metaphor for cutting and clearing a path and space for vibes to flow and grow." Despite assurances that no one really has to pay, I'd plunked down 60 Trinidadian dollars (about $10 US) for a bag containing a 3canal badge, a white tank top, a square of silver lamé cloth and—ominously—a plastic water bottle filled with white paint.

A little after 4 a.m, I returned to the 3canal storefront with my little lime of four—two Trinis and two other Americans—to find hundreds of people milling around a flatbed truck from which the 3canal musicians were blasting the band's heavy beat into the darkness. Around Port of Spain, people were assembling into fourteen other Jouvay bands, each several hundred to a thousand strong, and each with its own music and colors.

When the flatbed truck started rolling, the crowd danced along behind it or, more precisely, "chipped," which is Trinidadian for moving individually to music. At first I chipped in my resolute white-lady way, conscious of my status as the only visible blue-eyed person in the crowd. But then the paint came into play, hurled from bottles and dabbed on any body at hand. A plastic bottle of rough whiskey was passed around. There was a moment of near-panic when a police car forced its way through the crowd, and I learned later that in the pushing and shoving a knife fight had broken out just behind us. But still, the vibe here was overwhelmingly sweet. A teenager planted himself in front of me and announced that I looked "too nice," a condition he corrected by gently anointing my face with fresh paint. I don't know the origins of this orgy of body-painting, and I am glad I hadn't joined one of the Jouvay bands that use chocolate or mud instead, but I know its effect: Race was dissolved; even age and gender became theoretical concepts.

In the tradition of Western sociology, crowds are dangerous because they can turn into mobs. So when a contingent from our procession broke away to chase a group of Chinese men watching from the sidelines, I ran along anxiously behind them. Was there resentment of these workers, imported to build downtown skyscrapers? No. Would there be violence? No, the Jouvay celebrants just wanted to cover the foreigners in paint, and the Chinese were doubling over with laughter as they escaped. This was the true and ancient

spirit of carnival: There can be no spectators, only participants, and everyone must be anointed.

Sunrise found us in a small public square, and in a condition far from the one we'd started in. We'd been moving
through the streets for over three hours, powered by beers
passed from hand to hand, and even my ultra-buff American friend was beginning to sag. People were still chipping
away, raising their heads toward the already-hot blue sky in
a kind of triumph. Hardly anyone was noticeably drunk,
but we were annihilated, as individuals anyway—footsore,
bone-tired, dripping with paint and sweat. We were, in
some transcendent way, perfected.

But carnival has many faces and many moods, with different towns observing it in their own special ways. At dusk
we were in the tiny mountain town of Paramin, sitting at an
outdoor fried-chicken place. The townspeople were slowly
assembling on the edge of the road, drinking beer and chipping to a sound system that had been erected just behind
our table. At nightfall, the sound system fell silent, and ten
men beating drums made out of biscuit tins emerged from
the darkness—a reminder of the Trinidadian ingenuity at
drawing music out of industrial detritus, like the island's
steel drums, traditionally crafted from oil barrels. Behind
the drummers came twenty people of indeterminate age
and gender, covered in blue paint, some wearing grotesque
devil masks, others leering hideously, leaping and writhing.
Then another band of drummers, followed by another contingent from hell.

Some of the devils were pulling others on ropes or mock-
beating them with sticks in what is thought to be an

evocation of the work-'em-till-they-die slavery of early Trinidad. Certainly, there was an edge of menace here. When a Blue Devil approached and stabbed his finger at you, you had to give him a Trinidadian dollar (worth 16 US cents), or he would pull you up against his freshly painted body. The onlookers laughed and shrieked and ran, and in the end I didn't run fast enough. Having used up my dollars, partly in defense of two genuinely frightened little girls, I was slimed blue. As the devils eased up on their attacks, the crowd swelled and surged toward the town's central square, where vendors were selling beer and rum amid the ongoing chipping. But I was too sticky with paint to continue—and too shaken, I have to admit, by the mimed hostility of the devils, with its echoes of historical rage.

Shrove Tuesday, the second day, is when the mas bands parade through Port of Spain to be judged on their costumes and music. If there was a time to witness the corrupting effects of commercialism, this "pretty mas"—so called to distinguish it from the first day's "old mas"—would be it. There are about two hundred mas bands on the island, and each was offering, for the equivalent of several hundred US dollars, a costume and such essentials as a day's worth of food and drink and private security. A pre-carnival article in the *Sunday Express* estimated that the big bands, with 3,500 or more members, would each gross ten million Trinidadian dollars, not counting donations from corporate sponsors, such as the ubiquitous cell-phone company bmobile. This isn't just partying; this is business.

According to historian (and soca star) Hollis Liverpool, pretty mas grew out of the upper classes' efforts to tamp down the African-derived aspects of traditional mas, which they saw as vulgar and unruly. To an extent, they have succeeded: The price of admission limits participation to the more affluent, such as Nadia John, a thirty-year-old lawyer I met in her apartment on the Sunday before carnival. For John, it was all about the costume. She modeled the one she would wear with the Island People mas band: a bikini made of wire, feathers, and jewels, so minimal that she dared not let her mother see it.

Not that the poor don't try to crash the party—hence the need for all the private security that surrounds each band as it moves through the streets. According to Wyatt Gallery, one of the owners of the Island People band, this is because "We're very serious about the competition and don't want to look bad," as they might if a lot of uncostumed people slipped in.

So I wasn't expecting much, beyond a chance to see Nadia John in her glory, when we walked from our hotel to the part of town where the mas bands would march and found a place on the curb to sit. But it turned out that even pretty mas is impossible to tame. Despite all the "owners" and "producers," people were still creating carnival themselves, in the streets and on the sidelines—chipping, drinking, eating, and smoking ganja. Then the bands began to drift by, each with its own trucks for music, food, and drink. The marchers were chatting, chipping, and, most notably, "wining." This is like grinding in American dance culture, only the pelvic motions are quicker, more fluttery— an artistic rendition of sex rather than a simulation—and it can involve up to three people at a time. Probably not quite what the British meant by "pretty." One costumed woman sticks in my mind, lost in her own chip, throwing her head back, her face gleaming with exultation and sweat. As Goethe wrote of the eighteenth-century Roman carnival, it "is a festival that is not actually given to the people, but which the people give to themselves."

Yes, Trinidadian carnival has been commercialized—or "Brazilianized," as they say locally—with too much money and booty involved. But as Che Lovelace, a young artist told me, carnival "can't go back, it must go forward." The money helps support hundreds of Trinidadian artists, musicians, and entrepreneurs, and, he says, "helps drive the economy and create jobs." In Trinidad, commercialization is not the death of carnival, but part of how it perpetuates itself.

Scorecard for carnival 2008: In a win for Trinidad's persistent devils, a preliminary body count came to 5 dead and 20 others stabbed or shot. But in a triumph for artistry and social relevance, the title of best mas band went to the Mac-Farlane band with the apocalyptic theme "Earth: Cries of Despair, Wings of Hope." Its call for planetwide renewal and its towering, avant-garde costumes—giant structures pulled by the wearer and wreathed in colored smoke—stole the show.

THE HUMANOID STAIN

The Baffler, 2019

In 1940, four teenage boys stumbled, almost literally, from German-occupied France into the Paleolithic Age. As the story goes, and there are many versions of it, they had been taking a walk in the woods near the town of Montignac when the dog accompanying them suddenly disappeared. A quick search revealed that their animal companion had fallen into a hole in the ground, so—in the spirit of Tintin, with whom they were probably familiar—the boys made the perilous fifty-foot descent down to find it. They found the dog and much more, especially on return visits illuminated with paraffin lamps. The hole led to a cave, the walls and ceilings of which were covered with brightly colored paintings of animals unknown to the twentieth-century Dordogne—bison, aurochs, and lions. One of the boys, an apprentice mechanic, later reported that, stunned and elated, they began to dart around the cave like "a band of savages doing a war dance." Another recalled that the painted animals in the flickering light of the boys' lamps also seemed to be moving. "We were completely crazy," yet another said, although the buildup of carbon dioxide in a poorly ventilated cave may have had something to do with that.

This was the famous and touristically magnetic Lascaux cave, which eventually had to be closed to visitors, lest their exhalations spoil the artwork. Today, almost a century later, we know that Lascaux is part of a global phenomenon, originally referred to as "decorated caves." They have been found on every continent except Antarctica—at least 350 of them in Europe alone, thanks to the cave-rich Pyrenees—with the most recent discoveries in Borneo (2018) and the Balkans (April 2019). Uncannily, given the distances that separate them, all these caves are adorned with similar "decorations": handprints or stencils of human hands, abstract designs containing dots and crosshatched lines, and large animals, both carnivores and herbivores, most of them now extinct. Not all of these images appear in each of the decorated caves—some feature only handprints or megafauna. Scholars of paleoarcheology infer that the paintings were made by our distant ancestors, although the caves contain no depictions of humans doing any kind of painting.

There are humanlike creatures, though, or what some archeologists cautiously call "humanoids," referring to the bipedal stick figures that can sometimes be found on the margins of the panels containing animal shapes. The non-human animals are painted with almost supernatural attention to facial and muscular detail, but, no doubt to the disappointment of tourists, the humanoids painted on cave walls have no faces.

This struck me with unexpected force, no doubt because of my own particular historical situation almost twenty thousand years after the creation of the cave art in question. In about 2002 we had entered the age of "selfies," in which everyone seemed fascinated by their electronic self-portraits—clothed or unclothed, made-up or natural, partying or pensive—and determined to propagate them as widely as possible. Then in 2016 America acquired a president of whom the kindest thing that can be said is that he is a narcissist. This is a sloppily defined psychological condition, I admit, but fitting for a man so infatuated with his own image that he decorated his golf clubs with fake *Time* magazine covers featuring himself. On top of all this, we have been served an eviction notice from our own planet: the polar regions are turning into meltwater. The residents of the southern hemisphere are pouring northward toward climates more hospitable to crops. In July, the temperature in Paris reached a record-breaking 108.7 degrees Fahrenheit.

You could say that my sudden obsession with cave art was a pallid version of the boys' descent from Nazi-dominated France into the Lascaux cave. Articles in the *New York Times* urged [after the 2016 election] distressed readers to take refuge in "self-care" measures like meditation, nature walks, and massages, but none of that appealed to me. Instead, I took intermittent breaks from what we presumed to call "the Resistance" by throwing myself down the rabbit hole of paleoarcheological scholarship. In my case, it was not only a matter of escape. I found myself exhilarated by our comparatively ego-free ancestors who went to great lengths, and depths, to create some of the world's most breathtaking art—and didn't even bother to sign their names.

Auroch Bites Man

Cave art had a profound effect on its twentieth-century viewers, including the young discoverers of Lascaux, at least one of whom camped at the hole leading to the cave over the winter of 1940–41 to protect it from vandals and perhaps Germans. More illustrious visitors had similar reactions. In 1928, the artist and critic Amédée Ozenfant wrote of the art in the Les Eyzies caves, "Ah, those hands! Those silhouettes of hands, spread out and stenciled on an ochre ground! Go and see them. I promise you the most intense emotion you have ever experienced." He credited the Paleolithic artists with inspiring modern art, and to a certain degree they did. Jackson Pollock honored them by leaving handprints along the top edge of at least two of his paintings. Pablo Picasso reportedly visited the famous Altamira cave before fleeing Spain in 1934, and emerged saying, "Beyond Altamira, all is decadence."

Of course, cave art also inspired the question raised by all truly arresting artistic productions: "But what does it *mean*?" Who was its intended audience and what were they supposed to derive from it? The boy discoverers of Lascaux took their questions to one of their schoolmasters, who roped in Henri Breuil, a priest familiar enough with all things prehistoric to be known as "the pope of prehistory." Unsurprisingly, he offered a "magico-religious" interpretation, with the prefix "magico" serving as a slur to distinguish Paleolithic beliefs, whatever they may have been, from the reigning monotheism of the modern world. More practically, he proposed that the painted animals were meant to magically attract the actual animals they represented, the better for humans to hunt and eat them.

Unfortunately for this theory, it turns out that the animals on cave walls were not the kinds that the artists usually dined on. The creators of the Lascaux art, for example, ate reindeer, not the much more formidable herbivores pictured in the cave, which would have been difficult for humans armed with flint-tipped spears to bring down without being trampled. Today, many scholars answer the question of meaning with what amounts to a shrug: "We may never know."

If sheer curiosity, of the kind that drove the Lascaux discoverers, isn't enough to motivate a search for better answers, there is a moral parable reaching out to us from the cave at Lascaux. Shortly after its discovery, the one Jewish boy in the group was apprehended and sent, along with his parents, to a detention center that served as a stop on the way to Buchenwald. Miraculously, he was rescued by the French Red Cross, emerging from captivity as perhaps the only person on earth who had witnessed both the hellscape of twentieth-century Fascism and the artistic remnants of the Paleolithic Age. The latter offered no glimpse of an earthly paradise such as modern keto-drunk paleophiles like to imagine, in which our distant ancestors lounged around making up dance tunes and gnawing on ungulate bones. As we know from the archeological record, it was a time of relative peace among humans. No doubt there were homicides and tensions between and within human bands, but it would be at least another ten thousand years before the invention of war as an organized collective activity. The cave art suggests that humans once had better ways to spend their time.

If they were humans; and the worldwide gallery of known cave art offers so few stick figures or bipeds of any kind that we cannot be entirely sure. If the Paleolithic cave painters could create such perfectly naturalistic animals, why not give us a glimpse of the painters themselves? Almost as strange as the absence of human images in caves is the low level of scientific interest in their absence. In his book *What Is Paleolithic Art?*, the world-class paleoarcheologist Jean Clottes devotes only a couple of pages to the issue, concluding that: "The essential role played by animals evidently explains the small number of representations of human beings. In the Paleolithic world, humans were not at the center of the stage." A paper published, oddly enough, by the Centers for Disease Control and Prevention, expresses puzzlement over the omission of naturalistic depictions of humans, attributing it to Paleolithic people's "inexplicable fascination with wildlife" (not that there were any non-wild animals around at the time).

The marginality of human figures in cave paintings suggests that, at least from a human point of view, the central drama of the Paleolithic went on between the various megafauna—carnivores and large herbivores. So depleted is our own world of megafauna that it is hard to imagine how thick on the ground large mammals once were. Even the herbivores could be dangerous for humans, if mythology offers any clues: Think of the buffalo demon killed by the Hindu goddess Durga, or of the Cretan half-man, half-bull Minotaur who could only be subdued by confining him to a labyrinth, which

was, incidentally, a kind of cave. Just as potentially edible herbivores like aurochs (giant, now-extinct cattle) could be dangerous, death-dealing carnivores could be inadvertently helpful to humans and their humanlike kin, for example, by leaving their half-devoured prey behind for humans to finish off.
The Paleolithic landscape offered a lot of large animals to
watch and plenty of reasons to keep a close eye on them. Some
could be eaten—after, for example, being corralled into a trap
by a band of humans; many others would readily eat humans.

Yet despite the tricky and life-threatening relationship
between Paleolithic humans and the megafauna that comprised so much of their environment, twentieth-century
scholars tended to claim cave art as evidence of an un-
alloyed triumph for our species. It was a "great spiritual
symbol," one famed art historian, himself an escapee from
Nazism, proclaimed, of a time when "man had just emerged
from a purely zoological existence, when instead of being
dominated by animals, he began to dominate them." But
the stick figures found in caves like Lascaux and Chauvet do
not radiate triumph. By the standards of our own time, they
are excessively self-effacing and, compared to the animals
portrayed around them, pathetically weak. If these faceless
creatures were actually grinning in triumph, we would of
course have no way of knowing it.

Meatheads

We are left with one tenuous clue as to the cave artists' sense
of their status in the Paleolithic universe. While twentieth-

century archeologists tended to solemnize prehistoric art as "magico-religious" or "shamanic," today's more secular viewers sometimes detect a vein of sheer silliness. For example, shifting to another time and painting surface, India's Mesolithic rock art portrays few human stick figures; those that are portrayed have been described by modern viewers as "comical," "animalized," and "grotesque." Or consider the famed "birdman" image at Lascaux, in which a stick figure with a long skinny erection falls backwards at the approach of a bison. As Joseph Campbell described it, operating from within the magico-religious paradigm:

> A large bison bull, eviscerated by a spear that has transfixed its anus and emerged through its sexual organ, stands before a prostrate man. The latter (the only crudely drawn figure, and the only human figure in the cave) is rapt in a shamanistic trance. He wears a bird mask; his phallus, erect, is pointing at the pierced bull; a throwing stick lies on the ground at his feet; and beside him stands a wand or staff, bearing on its tip the image of a bird. And then, behind this prostrate shaman, is a large rhinoceros, apparently defecating as it walks away.

Take out the words "shaman" and "shamanistic" and you have a description of a crude—very crude—interaction of a humanoid with two much larger and more powerful animals. Is he, the humanoid, in a trance or just momentarily overcome by the strength and beauty of the other animals? And what qualifies him as a shaman anyway—the bird motif, which paleoanthropologists, drawing on studies of extant Siberian cultures, automatically associated with shamanism? Similarly, a bipedal figure with a stag's head, found in the Trois Frères cave in France, is awarded shamanic status, making him or her a kind of priest, although objectively speaking they might as well be wearing a party hat. As Judith Thurman wrote in the essay that inspired Werner Herzog's film *The Cave of Forgotten Dreams*, "Paleolithic artists, despite their penchant for naturalism, rarely chose to depict human beings, and then did so with a crudeness that smacks of mockery."

But who are they mocking, other than themselves and, by extension, their distant descendants, ourselves? Of course, our reactions to Paleolithic art may bear no connection to the intentions or feelings of the artists. Yet there are reasons to believe that Paleolithic people had a sense of humor not all that dissimilar from our own. After all, we do seem to share an aesthetic sensibility with them, as evidenced by modern reactions to the gorgeous Paleolithic depictions of animals. As for possible jokes, we have a geologist's 2018 report of a series of fossilized footprints found in New Mexico. They are the prints of a giant sloth, with much smaller human footprints *inside* them, suggesting that the humans were deliberately matching the sloth's stride and following it from a close distance. Practice for hunting? Or, as one science writer for *The Atlantic* suggested, is there "something almost playful" about the superimposed footprints, suggesting "a bunch of teenage kids harassing the sloths for kicks"?

Then there is the mystery of the exploding Venuses, where we once again encounter the thin line between the religious ("magico," of course) and the ridiculous. In the 1920s, in what is now the Czech Republic, archeologists discovered the site of a Paleolithic ceramics workshop that seemed to specialize in carefully crafted little figures of animals and, intriguingly, of fat women with huge breasts and buttocks (although, consistent with the fashion of the times, no faces). These were the "Venuses," originally judged to be either "fertility symbols" or examples of Paleolithic pornography. To the consternation of generations of researchers, the carefully crafted female and animal figures consisted almost entirely of fragments. Shoddy craftsmanship, perhaps? An overheated kiln? Then, in 1989, an ingenious team of archeologists figured out that the clay used to make the figurines had been deliberately treated so that it would explode when tossed into a fire, creating what an art historian called a loud—and, one would think, dangerous—display of "Paleolithic pyrotechnics." This, the *Washington Post*'s account concluded ominously, is "the earliest evidence that man created imagery only to destroy it."

Or we could look at the behavior of extant Stone Age people, which is by no means a reliable guide to the behavior of our distant ancestors but may contain clues as to their comical abilities. Evolutionary psychiatrists point out that anthropologists, contacting previously isolated peoples like nineteenth-century Australian aborigines, found them joking in ways comprehensible even to anthropologists. Furthermore, anthropologists report that many of the remaining hunter-gatherers are "fiercely egalitarian," deploying humor to subdue the ego of anyone who gets out of line:

Yes, when a young man kills much meat he comes to think of himself as a chief or a big man, and he thinks of the rest of us as his servants or inferiors. We can't accept this. We refuse one who boasts, for someday his pride will make him kill somebody. So we always speak of his meat as worthless. This way we cool his heart and make him gentle.

Some lucky hunters don't wait to be ridiculed, choosing instead to disparage the meat they have acquired as soon as they arrive back at base camp. In the context of a close-knit human group, self-mockery can be self-protective.

In the Paleolithic, humans were probably less concerned about the opinions of their conspecifics than with actions and intentions of the far more numerous megafauna around them. Would the herd of bison stop at a certain watering hole? Would lions show up to attack them? Would it be safe for humans to grab at whatever scraps of bison were left over from the lions' meal? The vein of silliness that seems to run through Paleolithic art may grow out of an accurate perception of humans' place in the world. Our ancestors occupied a lowly spot in the food chain, at least compared to the megafauna, but at the same time they were capable of understanding and depicting how lowly it was. They knew they were meat, and they also seemed to *know* that they knew they were meat—meat that could think. And that, if you think about it long enough, is almost funny.

Eyes without a Face

Paleolithic people were definitely capable of depicting more realistic humans than stick figures—human figures with faces, muscles, and curves formed by pregnancy or fat. Tiles found on the floor of the La Marche cave in France are etched with distinctive faces, some topped with caps, and have been dated to fourteen to fifteen thousand years ago. A solemn, oddly triangular, female face carved in ivory was found in late nineteenth-century France and recently dated to about twenty-four thousand years ago. Then there are the above-mentioned "Venus" figurines found scattered about Eurasia from about the same time. But all these bits of artwork are small and were apparently meant to be carried around, like amulets perhaps, as cave paintings obviously could not be. Cave paintings stay in their caves.

What is it about caves? The attraction of caves as art studios and galleries does not stem from the fact that they were convenient for the artists. In fact, there is no evidence of continuous human habitation in the decorated caves, and certainly none in the deepest, hardest-to-access crannies reserved for the most spectacular animal paintings. Cave artists are not to be confused with "cavemen."

Nor do we need to posit any special human affinity for caves, since the art they contain came down to us through a simple process of natural selection: outdoor art, such as figurines and painted rocks, is exposed to the elements and unlikely to last for tens of thousands of years. Paleolithic people seem to have painted all kinds of surfaces, including leather derived from animals as well as their own bodies and faces, with the same kinds of ochre they used on cave walls. The difference is that the paintings on cave walls were well enough protected from rain and wind and climate change to survive for tens of millennia. If there was something special about caves, it was that they are ideal storage lockers. "Caves," as paleoarcheologist April Nowell puts it, "are funny little microcosms that protect paint."

If the painters of Lascaux were aware of the preservative properties of caves, did they anticipate future visits to the same site, either by themselves or others? Before the intrusion of civilization into their territories, hunter-gatherers were "nonsedentary" people, meaning perpetual wanderers. They moved to follow seasonal animal migrations and the ripening of fruits, probably even to escape from the human feces that inevitably piled up around their campsites. These smaller migrations, reinforced by intense and oscillating climate change in the Horn of Africa, added up to the prolonged exodus from that continent to the Arabian Peninsula and hence to the rest of the globe. With so much churning and relocating going on, it's possible that Paleolithic people could conceive of returning to a decorated cave or, in an even greater leap of the imagination, foresee visits by others like themselves. If so, the cave art should be thought of as a sort of hard drive and the paintings as information: not just "here are some of the animals you will encounter around here," but *Here we are, creatures like yourselves, and this is what we know.*

Multiple visits by different groups of humans, perhaps over long periods of time, could explain the strange fact that, as the intrepid French boys observed, the animals painted on cave walls seem to be moving. There is nothing supernatural at work here. Look closely, and you see that the animal figures are usually composed of superimposed lines, suggesting that new arrivals in the cave painted over the lines that were already there, more or less like children learning to write the letters of the alphabet. So the cave was not merely a museum. It was an art school where people learned to paint from those who had come before them and went on to apply their skills to the next suitable cave they came across. In the process, and with some help from flickering lights, they created animation. The movement of bands of people across the landscape led to the apparent movement of animals on the cave walls. As humans painted over older artwork, moved on, and painted again, over tens of thousands of years, cave art—or, in the absence of caves, rock art—became a global meme.

There is something else about caves. Not only were they storage spaces for precious artwork, they were also gathering places for humans, possibly up to a hundred at a time in some of the larger chambers. To paleoanthropologists, especially those leaning toward magico-religious explanations, such spaces inevitably suggest *rituals*, making the decorated cave a kind of cathedral within which humans communed with a higher power. Visual art may have been only one part of the uplifting spectacle; recently, much attention has been paid to the acoustical properties of decorated caves and how they may have generated awe-inspiring reverberant sounds. People sang, chanted, or drummed, stared at the lifelike animals around them, and perhaps got high: the cave as an ideal venue for a rave. Or maybe they took, say, "magic mushrooms" they found growing wild, and *then* painted the animals, a possibility suggested by a few modern reports from African San rock artists who dance themselves into a trance state before getting down to work.

Each decoration of a new cave, or redecoration of an old one, required the collective effort of tens or possibly scores of people. Twentieth-century archeologists liked to imagine they were seeing the work of especially talented individuals—artists or shamans. But as Gregory Curtis points out in his book *The Cave Painters*, it took a crowd to decorate a cave—people to inspect the cave walls for cracks and protuberances suggestive of megafauna shapes, people to haul logs into the cave to construct the scaffolding from which the artists worked, people to mix the ochre paint, and still others to provide the workers with food and water. Careful analysis of the handprints found in so many caves reveals that the participants included both women and men, adults and children. If cave art had a function other than preserving information and enhancing ecstatic rituals, it was to teach the value of cooperation, and cooperation—to the point of self-sacrifice—was essential for both communal hunting and collective defense.

In his book *Sapiens*, Yuval Noah Harari emphasizes the importance of collective effort in the evolution of modern humans. Individual skill and courage helped, but so did the willingness to stand with one's band: not to scatter when a dangerous animal approached, not to climb a tree and leave the baby behind. Maybe, in the ever-challenging context of an animal-dominated planet, the demand for human solidarity so far exceeded the need for individual recognition that, at least in artistic representation, humans didn't need faces.

As the Paint Peels

All this cave painting, migrating, and repainting of newly found caves came to an end roughly twelve thousand years ago, with what has been applauded as the "Neolithic Revolution." Lacking pack animals and perhaps tired of walking, humans began to settle down in villages and eventually walled cities; they invented agriculture and domesticated many of the wild animals whose ancestors had figured so prominently in cave art. They learned to weave, brew beer, smelt ore, and craft ever-sharper blades.

But whatever comforts sedentism brought came at a terrible price: property, in the form of stored grain and edible herds, segmented societies into classes—a process anthropologists prudently term "social stratification"—and seduced humans into warfare. War led to the institution of slavery, especially for the women of the defeated side (defeated males were usually slaughtered) and stamped the entire female gender with the stigma attached to concubines and domestic servants. Men did better, at least a few of them, with the most outstanding commanders rising to the status of kings and eventually emperors. Wherever sedentism and agriculture took hold, from China to South and Central America, coercion by the powerful replaced cooperation among equals. In Jared Diamond's blunt assessment, the Neolithic Revolution was "the worst mistake in the history of the human race."

At least it gave us faces. Starting with the implacable "mother goddesses" of the Neolithic Middle East and moving on to the sudden proliferation of kings and heroes in the Bronze Age, the emergence of human faces seems to mark a characterological change—from the solidaristic ethos of small, migrating bands to what we now know as narcissism. Kings and occasionally their consorts were the first to enjoy the new marks of personal superiority— crowns, jewelry, masses of slaves, and the arrogance that went along with these appurtenances. Over the centuries, narcissism spread downward to the bourgeoisie, who, in seventeenth-century Europe, were beginning to write mem- oirs and commission their own portraits. In our own time, anyone who can afford a smartphone can propagate their own image, "publish" their most fleeting thoughts on social media, and burnish their unique "brand." Narcissism has been democratized and is available, at least in crumb-sized morsels, to us all.

So what do we need decorated caves for anymore? One disturbing possible use for them has arisen in just the last decade or so—as shelters to hide out in until the apocalypse blows over. With the seas rising, the weather turning into a series of psycho-storms, and the world's poor becoming ever more restive, the super-rich are buying up abandoned nuclear silos and converting them into "doomsday bunkers" that can house up to a dozen families, plus guards and ser- vants, at a time. These are fake caves, of course, but they are wondrously outfitted—with swimming pools, gyms, shoot- ing ranges, "outdoor" cafes—and decorated with precious artworks and huge LED screens displaying what remains of the outside world.

But it's the Paleolithic caves we need to return to, and not just because they are still capable of inspiring transcendent experiences and connecting us with the long-lost "natural world." We should be drawn back to them for the message they have reliably preserved for over ten thousand generations. All right, it was not intended for us, this message, nor could its authors have imagined such perverse and self-destructive descendants as we have become. But it's in our hands now, still illegible unless we push back hard against the artificial dividing line between history and prehistory, hieroglyphs and petroglyphs, between the "primitive" and the "advanced." This will take all of our skills and knowledge—from art history to uranium-thorium dating techniques to best practices for international cooperation. But it will be worth the effort because our Paleolithic ancestors, with their faceless humanoids and capacity for silliness seem to have known something we strain to imagine.

They knew where they stood in the scheme of things, which was not very high, and this seems to have made them laugh. I strongly suspect that we will not survive the mass extinction we have prepared for ourselves unless we too finally get the joke.

BOURGEOIS
BLUNDERS

FAMILY VALUES

The Worst Years of Our Lives, 1990

Sometime in the eighties, Americans had a new set of "traditional values" installed. It was part of what may someday be known as the "Reagan renovation," that finely balanced mix of cosmetic refinement and moral coarseness that brought $200,000 china to the White House dinner table and mayhem to the beleaguered peasantry of Central America. All of the new traditions had venerable sources. In economics, we borrowed from the Bourbons; in foreign policy, we drew on themes fashioned by the nomad warriors of the Eurasian steppes. In spiritual matters, we emulated the braying intolerance of our archenemies and esteemed customers, the Shi'ite fundamentalists.

A case could be made, of course, for the genuine American provenance of all these new "traditions." We've had our own robber barons, military adventurers, and certainly more than our share of enterprising evangelists promoting ignorance and parochialism as a state of grace. From the vantage point of the continent's original residents, or, for example, the captive African laborers who made America a great agricultural power, our "traditional values" have always been bigotry, greed, and belligerence, buttressed by wanton appeals to a God of love.

The kindest—though from some angles most perverse—of the era's new values was "family." I could have lived with "flag" and "faith" as neotraditional values—not happily, but I could have managed—until "family" was press-ganged into joining them. Throughout the eighties, the winning political faction has been aggressively "profamily." They have invoked "the family" when they trample on the rights of those who hold actual families together, that is, women. They have used it to justify racial segregation and the formation of white-only, "Christian" schools. And they have brought it out, along with flag and faith, to silence any voices they found obscene, offensive, disturbing, or merely different.

Now, I come from a family—was raised in one, in fact—and one salubrious effect of right-wing righteousness has been to make me hew ever more firmly to the traditional values of my own progenitors. These were not people who could be accused of questionable politics or ethnicity. Nor were they members of the "liberal elite" so hated by our current conservative elite. They were blue-eyed, Scotch-Irish Democrats. They were small farmers, railroad workers, miners, shopkeepers, and migrant farmworkers. In short, they fit the stereotype of "real" Americans; and their values, no matter how unpopular among today's opinion-shapers, are part of America's tradition, too. To my mind, of course, the finest part.

But let me introduce some of my family, beginning with

my father, who was, along with my mother, the ultimate source of much of my radicalism, feminism, and, by the standards of the eighties, all-around bad attitude.

One of the first questions in a test of mental competency is "Who is the president of the United States?" Even deep into the indignities of Alzheimer's disease, my father always did well on that one. His blue eyes would widen incredulously, surprised at the neurologist's ignorance, then he would snort in majestic indignation, "Reagan, that dumb son of a bitch." It seemed to me a good deal—two people tested for the price of one.

Like so many of the Alzheimer's patients he came to know, my father enjoyed watching the president on television. Most programming left him impassive, but when the old codger came on, his little eyes twinkling piggishly above the disciplined sincerity of his lower face, my father would lean forward and commence a wickedly delighted cackle. I think he was prepared, more than the rest of us, to get the joke.

But the funniest thing was Ollie North. For an ailing man, my father did a fine parody. He would slap his hand over his heart, stare rigidly at attention, and pronounce, in his deepest bass rumble, "God Bless Am-ar-ica!" I'm sure he couldn't follow North's testimony—who can honestly say that they did?—but the main themes were clear enough in pantomime: the watery-eyed patriotism, the extravagant self-pity, the touching servility toward higher-ranking males. When I told my father that many people considered North a hero, a representative of the finest American traditions, he scowled and swatted at the air. Ollie North was the kind of man my father had warned me about, many years ago, when my father was the smartest man on earth.

My father had started out as a copper miner in Butte, Montana, a tiny mountain city famed for its bars, its brawls, and its distinctly unservile workforce. In his view, which remained eagle-sharp even after a stint of higher education, there were only a few major categories of human beings. There were "phonies" and "decent" people, the latter group having hardly any well-known representatives outside of Franklin Delano Roosevelt and John L. Lewis, the militant and brilliantly eloquent leader of the miners' union. "Phonies," however, were rampant, and, for reasons I would not understand until later in life, could be found clustered especially thick in the vicinity of money or power.

Well before he taught me other useful things, like how to distinguish fool's gold, or iron pyrite, from the real thing, he gave me some tips on the detection of phonies. For one thing, they broadened the *e* in "America" to a reverent *ahh*. They were the first to leap from their seats at the playing of "The Star Spangled Banner," the most visibly moved participants in any prayer. They espoused clean living and admired war. They preached hard work and paid for it with nickels and dimes. They loved their country above all, but despised the low-paid and usually invisible men and women who built it, fed it, and kept it running.

Two other important categories figured in my father's scheme of things. There were dumb people and smart ones: a distinction that had nothing to do with class or formal education, the dumb being simply all those who were taken in by the phonies. In his view, dumbness was rampant, and seemed to increase in proportion to the distance from Butte, where at least a certain hard-boiled irreverence leavened the atmosphere. The best prophylactic was to study and learn all you could, however you could, and, as he adjured me over and over: Always ask *why*.

Finally, there were the rich and the poor. While poverty was not seen as an automatic virtue—my parents struggled mightily to escape it—wealth always carried a presumption of malfeasance. I was instructed that, in the presence of the rich, it was wise to keep one's hand on one's wallet. "Well," my father fairly growled, "how do you think they got their money in the first place?"

It was my mother who translated these lessons into practical politics. A miner's daughter herself, she offered two overarching rules for comportment: Never vote Republican and never cross a union picket line. The pinnacle of her activist career came in 1964, when she attended the Democratic Convention as an alternate delegate and joined the sit-in staged by civil rights leaders and the Mississippi Freedom Democratic Party. This was not the action of a "guilt-ridden" white liberal. She classified racial prejudice along with superstition and other manifestations of backward thinking, like organized religion and overcooked vegetables. The worst thing she could find to say about a certain in-law was that he was a Republican and a churchgoer, though when I investigated these charges later in life, I was relieved to find them baseless.

My mother and father, it should be explained, were hardly rebels. The values they imparted to me had been "traditional" for at least a generation before my parents came along. According to my father, the first great steps out of mental passivity had been taken by his maternal grand-parents, John Howes and Mamie McLaughlin Howes, sometime late in the last century. You might think their rebellions small stuff, but they provided our family with its "myth of origins" and a certain standard to uphold.

I knew little about Mamie McLaughlin except that she was raised as a Catholic and ended up in western Montana sometime in the 1880s. Her father, very likely, was one of those itinerant breadwinners who went west to prospect and settled for mining. At any rate, the story begins when her father lay dying, and Mamie dutifully sent to the next town for a priest. The message came back that the priest would come only if $25 was sent in advance. This being the West at its wildest, he may have been justified in avoiding house calls. But not in the price, which was probably more cash than my great-grandmother had ever had at one time. It was on account of its greed that the church lost the souls of Mamie McLaughlin and all of her descendents, right down to the present time. Furthermore, whether out of filial deference or natural intelligence, most of us have continued to avoid organized religion, secret societies, astrology, and New Age adventures in spirituality.

As the story continues, Mamie McLaughlin herself lay dying a few years later. She was only thirty-one, the mother of three small children, one of them an infant whose birth, apparently, led to a mortal attack of pneumonia. This time, a priest appeared unsummoned. Because she was too weak to hold the crucifix, he placed it on her chest and proceeded to administer the last rites. But Mamie was not dead yet. She pulled herself together at the last moment, flung the crucifix across the room, fell back, and died.

This was my great-grandmother. Her husband, John Howes, is a figure of folkloric proportions in my memory, well known in Butte many decades ago as a powerful miner and a lethal fighter. There are many stories about John Howes, all of which point to a profound inability to accept authority in any of its manifestations, earthly or divine. As a young miner, for example, he caught the eye of the mine owner for his skill at handling horses. The boss promoted him to an aboveground driving job, which was a great career leap for the time. Then the boss committed a foolish and arrogant error. He asked John to break in a team of horses for his wife's carriage. Most people would probably be flattered by such a request, but not in Butte, and certainly not John Howes. He declared that he was no man's servant, and quit on the spot.

Like his own wife, John Howes was an atheist or, as they more likely put it at the time, a freethinker. He, too, had been raised as a Catholic—on a farm in Ontario—and he, too, had had a dramatic, though somehow less glorious, falling out with the local clergy. According to legend, he once abused his position as an altar boy by urinating, covertly of course, in the holy water. This so enhanced his enjoyment of the Easter communion service that he could not resist letting a few friends in on the secret. Soon the priest found out and young John was defrocked as an altar boy and condemned to eternal damnation.

The full weight of this transgression hit a few years later, when he became engaged to a local woman. The priest refused to marry them and forbade the young woman to marry John anywhere, on pain of excommunication. There was nothing to do but head west for the Rockies, but not before settling his score with the church. According to legend, John's last act in Ontario was to drag the priest down from his pulpit and slug him, with his brother, presumably, holding the scandalized congregation at bay.

I have often wondered whether my great-grandfather was caught up in the radicalism of Butte in its heyday: whether he was an admirer of Joe Hill, Big Bill Haywood, or Mary "Mother" Jones, all of whom passed through Butte to agitate, and generally left with the Pinkertons on their tails. But the record is silent on this point. All I know is one last story about him, which was told often enough to have the ring of another "traditional value."

According to my father, John Howes worked on and off in the mines after his children were grown, eventually saving enough to buy a small plot of land and retire to farming. This was his dream, anyway, and a powerful one it must have been for a man who had spent so much of his life underground in the dark.

Far be it from me to interpret this gesture for my great-grandfather, whom I knew only as a whiskery, sweat-smelling, but straight-backed old man in his eighties. Perhaps he was enacting his own uncompromising version of Christian virtue, even atoning a little for his youthful offenses to the faithful. But at another level I like to think that this was one more gesture of defiance of the mine owners who doled out their own dollars so grudgingly—a way of saying, perhaps, that whatever they had to offer, he didn't really need all that much.

So these were the values, sanctified by tradition and family loyalty, that I brought with me to adulthood. Through much of my growing-up, I thought of them as some mutant strain of Americanism, an idiosyncrasy that seemed to grow rarer as we clambered into the middle class. Only in the sixties did I begin to learn that my family's militant skepticism and oddball rebelliousness were part of a much larger stream of American dissent. I discovered feminism, the antiwar movement, the civil rights movement. I learned that millions of Americans, before me and around me, were "smart" enough, in my father's terms, to have asked "Why?"—and, beyond that, the far more radical question, "Why not?"

These are also the values I brought into the Reagan-Bush era, when all the dangers I had been alerted to as a child were suddenly realized. The "phonies" came to power on the strength, aptly enough, of a professional actor's finest performance. The "dumb" were being led and abetted by low-life preachers and intellectuals with expensively squandered educations. And the rich, as my father predicted, used the occasion to dip deep into the wallets of the desperate and the distracted.

It's been hard times for a traditionalist of my persuasion. Long-standing moral values—usually claimed as "Judeo-Christian" but actually of much broader lineage—were summarily tossed, along with most familiar forms of logic. We were told, at one time or another, by the president or his henchpersons, that trees cause pollution, that welfare causes poverty, and that a bomber designed for mass destruction may be aptly named the *Peacemaker*. "Terrorism" replaced missing children to become our national bugaboo and—simultaneously—one of our most potent instruments of foreign policy. At home, the poor and the middle class were shaken down, and their loose change funneled blithely upward to the already overfed.

Greed, the ancient lubricant of commerce, was declared a wholesome stimulant. Nancy Reagan observed the deep recession of '82 and '83 by redecorating the White House, and continued with this Marie Antoinette theme while advising the underprivileged, the alienated, and the addicted to "say no." Young people, mindful of their elders' Wall Street capers, abandoned the study of useful things for investment banking and other occupations derived, ultimately, from three-card monte. While the poor donned plastic outerwear and cardboard coverings, the affluent ran nearly naked through the streets, working off power meals of goat cheese, walnut oil, and crème fraîche.

Religion, which even I had hoped would provide a calming influence and reminder of mortal folly, decided to join the fun. In an upsurge of piety, millions of Americans threw their souls and their savings into evangelical empires designed on the principle of pyramid scams. Even the sleazy downfall of our telemessiahs—caught masturbating in the company of $10 prostitutes or fornicating in their Christian theme parks—did not discourage the faithful. The unhappily pregnant were mobbed as "baby-killers"; sexual nonconformists—gay and lesbian—were denounced as "child molesters"; atheists found themselves lumped with "satanists," communists, and consumers of human flesh.

Yet somehow, despite it all, a trickle of dissent continued. There were homeless people who refused to be shelved in mental hospitals for the crime of poverty, strikers who refused to join the celebration of unions in faraway countries and scabs at home, women who insisted that their lives be valued above those of accidental embryos, parents who packed up their babies and marched for peace, students who protested the ongoing inversion of normal, nursery-school-level values in the name of a more habitable world.

I am proud to add my voice to all these. For dissent is also a "traditional value," and in a republic founded by revolution, a more deeply native one than smug-faced conservatism can ever be. Feminism was practically invented here, and ought to be regarded as one of our proudest exports to the world. Likewise, it tickles my sense of patriotism that insurgents in developing nations have often borrowed the ideas of our own civil rights movement. And in what ought to be a source of shame to some and pride to others, our history of labor struggle is one of the hardest-fought and bloodiest in the world.

No matter that patriotism is too often the refuge of scoundrels. Dissent, rebellion, and all-around hell-raising remain the true duty of patriots.

THE CULT OF BUSYNESS

New York Times, 1985

Not too long ago a former friend and soon-to-be acquaintance called me up to tell me how busy she was. A major report, upon which her professional future depended, was due in three days; her secretary was on strike; her housekeeper had fallen into the hands of the Immigration Department; she had two hours to prepare a dinner party for eight; and she was late for her time-management class. Stress was taking its toll, she told me: Her children resented the fact that she sometimes got their names mixed up, and she had taken to abusing white wine.

All this put me at a distinct disadvantage, since the only thing I was doing at the time was holding the phone with one hand and attempting to touch the opposite toe with the other hand, a pastime that I had perfected during previous telephone monologues. Not that I'm not busy, too: as I listened to her, I was on the alert for the moment the dryer would shut itself off and I would have to rush to fold the clothes before they settled into a mass of incorrigible wrinkles. But if I mentioned this little deadline of mine, she might think I wasn't busy enough to need a housekeeper, so I just kept on patiently saying "Hmm" until she got to her parting line: "Look, this isn't a good time for me to talk, I've got to go now."

I don't know when the cult of conspicuous busyness began, but it has swept up almost all the upwardly mobile, professional women I know. Already, it is getting hard to recall the days when, for example, "Let's have lunch" meant something other than "I've got more important things to do than talk to you right now." There was even a time when people used to get together without the excuse of needing something to eat—when, in fact, it was considered rude to talk with your mouth full. In the old days, hardly anybody had an appointment book, and when people wanted to know what the day held in store for them, they consulted a horoscope.

It's not only women, of course; for both sexes, busyness has become an important insignia of upper-middle-class status. Nobody, these days, admits to having a hobby, although two or more careers—say, neurosurgery and an art dealership—is not uncommon, and I am sure we will soon be hearing more about the tribulations of the four-paycheck couple. Even those who can manage only one occupation at a time would be embarrassed to be caught doing only one *thing* at a time. Those young men who jog with their headsets on are not, as you might innocently guess, rocking out, but are absorbing the principles of international finance law or a lecture on one-minute management. Even eating, I read recently, is giving way to "grazing"—the conscious ingestion of unidentified foods while drafting a legal brief, cajoling a client on the phone, and, in ambitious cases, doing calf-toning exercises under the desk.

But for women, there's more at stake than conforming to another upscale standard. If you want to attract men, for example, it no longer helps to be a bimbo with time on your hands. Upscale young men seem to go for the kind of woman who plays with a full deck of credit cards, who won't cry when she's knocked to the ground while trying to board the six o'clock Delta shuttle, and whose schedule doesn't allow for a sexual encounter lasting more than twelve minutes. Then there is the economic reality: Any woman who doesn't want to wind up a case study in the feminization of poverty has to be successful at something more demanding than fingernail maintenance or come-hither looks. Hence all the bustle, my busy friends would explain—they want to succeed.

But if success is the goal, it seems clear to me that the fast track is headed the wrong way. Think of the people who are genuinely successful—pathbreaking scientists, best-selling novelists, and designers of major new software. They are not, on the whole, the kind of people who keep glancing shiftily at their watches or making small lists titled "To Do." On the contrary, many of these people appear to be in a daze, like the distinguished professor I once had who, in the middle of a lecture on electron spin, became so fascinated by the dispersion properties of chalk dust that he could not go on. These truly successful people are childlike, easily dis-tractable, fey sorts, whose usual demeanor resembles that of a recently fed hobo on a warm summer evening.

The secret of the truly successful, I believe, is that they learned very early in life how *not* to be busy. They saw through that adage, repeated to me so often in childhood, that anything worth doing is worth doing well. The truth is, many things are worth doing only in the most slovenly, half-hearted fashion possible, and many other things are not worth doing at all. Balancing a checkbook, for example. For some reason, in our culture, this dreary exercise is regarded as the supreme test of personal maturity, business acumen, and the ability to cope with math anxiety. Yet it is a form of busyness which is exceeded in futility only by going to the additional trouble of computerizing one's checking account—and that, in turn, is only slightly less silly than taking the time to discuss, with anyone, what brand of personal computer one owns, or is thinking of buying, or has heard of others using.

If the truly successful manage never to be busy, it is also true that many of the busiest people will never be successful. I know this firsthand from my experience, many years ago, as a waitress. Any executive who thinks the ultimate in busyness consists of having two important phone calls on hold and a major deadline in twenty minutes, should try facing six tablefuls of clients simultaneously demanding that you give them their checks, fresh coffee, a baby seat, and a warm, spontaneous smile. Even when she's not busy, a waitress has to look busy—refilling the salt shakers and polishing all the chrome in sight—but the only reward is the minimum wage and any change that gets left on the tables. Much the same is true of other high-stress jobs, like working as a telephone operator, or doing data entry on one of the new machines that monitors your speed as you work: "Success" means surviving the shift.

Although busyness does not lead to success, I am willing to believe that success—especially when visited on the unprepared—can cause busyness. Anyone who has invented a better mousetrap, or the contemporary equivalent, can expect to be harassed by strangers demanding that you read their unpublished manuscripts or undergo the humiliation of public speaking, usually on remote Midwestern campuses. But if it is true that success leads to more busyness and less time for worthwhile activities—like talking (and listening) to friends, reading novels, or putting in some volunteer time for a good cause—then who needs it? It would be sad to have come so far—or at least to have run so hard—only to lose each other.

DEATH OF A YUPPIE DREAM

Journal der Rosa Luxemburg Stiftung, 2013

With John Ehrenreich

Every would-be populist in American politics purports to defend the "middle class," although there is no agreement on what it is. Just in the last couple of years, the "middle class" has variously been defined as everybody, everybody minus the 15 percent living below the federal poverty level; or everybody minus the very richest Americans. Mitt Romney famously excluded "those in the low end" but included himself (2010 income $21.6 million) along with "80 to 90 percent" of Americans. The Department of Commerce has given up on income-based definitions, announcing in a 2010 report that "middle class families" are defined "by their aspirations more than their income....Middle class families aspire to home ownership, a car, college education for their children, health and retirement security and occasional family vacations"—which excludes almost no one.

Class itself is a muddled concept, perhaps especially in America, where any allusion to the different interests of different occupational and income groups is likely to attract the charge of "class warfare." If class requires some sort of "consciousness," or capacity for concerted action, then a "middle class" conceived of as a sort of default class—what you are left with after you subtract the rich and the poor— is not very interesting.

But there is another, potentially more productive, interpretation of what has been going on in the mid-income range. In 1977, we first proposed the existence of a "professional-managerial class," distinct from both the "working class," from the "old" middle class of small business owners, as well as from the wealthy class of owners.

The Origins of the Professional-Managerial Class

The notion of the "PMC" was an effort to explain the largely "middle-class" roots of the New Left in the sixties and the tensions that were emerging between that group and the old working class in the seventies, culminating in the political backlash that led to the election of Reagan. The right embraced a caricature of this notion of a "new class," proposing that college-educated professionals— especially lawyers, professors, journalists, and artists—make up a power-hungry "liberal elite" bent on imposing its version of socialism on everyone else.

The PMC grew rapidly. From 1870 to 1910 alone, while the whole population of the United States increased two-and-one-third times and the old middle class of business entrepreneurs and independent professionals doubled, the number of people in what could be seen as PMC jobs grew almost eightfold. And in the years that followed, that growth only accelerated. Although a variety of practical and theoretical obstacles keep us from making any precise analysis, we estimate that as late as 1930, people in PMC occupations still made up less than 1 percent of total employment. By 1972, about 24 percent of American jobs were in PMC occupations. By 1983 the number had risen to 28 percent and by 2006, just before the Great Recession, to 35 percent.

The relationship between the emerging PMC and the traditional working class was, from the start, riven with tensions. It was the occupational role of managers and engineers, along with many other professionals, to manage, regulate, and control the life of the working class. They designed the division of labor and the machines that controlled workers' minute-by-minute existence on the factory floor, manipulated their desire for commodities and their opinions, socialized their children, and even mediated their relationship with their own bodies.

At the same time, though, the role of the PMC as "rationalizers" of society often placed them in direct conflict with the capitalist class. Like the workers, the PMC were themselves employees and subordinate to the owners, but since what was truly "rational" in the productive process was not always identical to what was most immediately profitable, the PMC often sought autonomy and freedom from their own bosses.

By the mid-twentieth century, jobs for the PMC were

proliferating. Public education was expanding, the modern university came into being, local governments expanded in size and role, charitable agencies merged, newspaper circulation soared, traditional forms of recreation gave way to the popular culture, entertainment, and sports industries, etc.—and all of these developments created jobs for highly educated professionals, including journalists, social workers, professors, doctors, lawyers, and "entertainers" (artists and writers, among others).

Some of these occupations managed to retain a measure of autonomy and, with it, the possibility of opposition to business domination. The so-called "liberal professions," particularly medicine and law, remained largely outside the corporate framework until well past the middle of the twentieth century. Most doctors, many nurses, and the majority of lawyers worked in independent (private) practices.

In the 1960s, for the first time since the Progressive Era, a large segment of the PMC had the self-confidence to take on a critical, even oppositional, political role. Jobs were plentiful, a college education did not yet lead to a lifetime of debt, and materialism was briefly out of style. College students quickly moved on from supporting the civil rights movement in the South and opposing the war in Vietnam to confronting the raw fact of corporate power throughout American society—from the prowar inclinations of the weapons industry to the governance of the university. The revolt soon spread beyond students. By the end of the sixties, almost all of the liberal professions had "radical caucuses," demanding that access to the professions be opened up to those traditionally excluded (such as women and minorities), and that the service ethics the professions claimed to uphold actually be applied in practice.

The Capitalist Offensive

Beginning in the seventies, the capitalist class decisively reasserted itself. The ensuing capitalist offensive was so geographically widespread and thoroughgoing that it introduced what many left-wing theorists today describe as a new form of capitalism, "neoliberalism."

The new management strategy was to raise profits by single-mindedly reducing labor costs, most directly by simply moving manufacturing offshore to find cheaper labor. Those workers who remained employed in the United States faced a series of initiatives designed to discipline and control them ever more tightly: intensified supervision in the workplace, drug tests to eliminate slackers, and increasingly professionalized efforts to prevent unionization. Cuts in the welfare state also had a disciplining function, making it harder for workers to imagine surviving job loss.

Most of these antilabor measures also had an effect, directly or indirectly, on elements of the PMC. Government spending cuts hurt the job prospects of social workers, teachers, and others in the "helping professions," while the decimation of the US-based industrial working class reduced the need for mid-level professional managers, who found themselves increasingly targeted for downsizing. But there was a special animus against the liberal professions, surpassed only by neoliberal hostility to what conservatives

described as the "underclass." Crushing this liberal elite—
by "defunding the left" or attacking liberal-leaning nonprofit organizations—became a major neoliberal project.

Of course, not all the forces undermining the liberal professions since the 1980s can be traced to conscious neoliberal policies. Technological innovation, rising demand for
services, and ruthless profit-taking all contributed to an increasingly challenging environment for the liberal professions, including the "creative ones."

The internet is often blamed for the plight of journalists,
writers, and editors, but economic change preceded technological transformation. Journalism jobs began to disappear as corporations, responding in part to Wall Street
investors, tried to squeeze higher profit margins out of
newspapers and TV news programs. The effects of these
changes on the traditionally creative professions have been
dire. Staff writers, editors, photographers, announcers, and
the like faced massive layoffs (more than 25 percent of
newsroom staff alone since 2001), increased workloads,
salary cuts, and buyouts.

Then, in just the last dozen years, the PMC began to suffer
the fate of the industrial class in the 1980s: replacement by
cheap foreign labor. It came as a shock to many when, in the
2000s, businesses began to avail themselves of new high-
speed transmission technologies to outsource professional
functions.

By the time of the financial meltdown and deep recession
of the post-2008 period, the pain inflicted by neoliberal
policies, both public and corporate, extended well beyond

the old industrial working class and into core segments of the PMC. Unemployed and underemployed professional workers—from IT to journalism, academia, and eventually law—became a regular feature of the social landscape. Young people did not lose faith in the value of an education, but they learned quickly that it makes more sense to study finance rather than physics or "communications" rather than literature. The old PMC dream of a society ruled by impartial "experts" gave way to the reality of inescapable corporate domination.

But the PMC was not only a victim of more powerful groups. It had also fallen into a trap of its own making. The prolonged, expensive, and specialized education required for professional employment had always been a challenge to PMC families—as well, of course, as an often-insuperable barrier to the working class. Higher degrees and licenses are no longer a guarantee of PMC status. Hence the iconic figure of the Occupy Wall Street movement: the college graduate with tens of thousands of dollars in student loan debts and a job paying about $10 a hour, or no job at all.

Whither Class Consciousness?

So in the hundred years since its emergence, the PMC has not managed to hold its own as a class. At its wealthier end, skilled professionals continue to jump ship for more lucrative posts in direct service to capital: Scientists give up their research to become "quants" on Wall Street; physicians can double their incomes by finding work as investment analysts for the finance industry or by setting up "concierge" practices serving the wealthy. At the less fortunate end of the spectrum, journalists and PhDs in sociology or literature spiral down into the retail workforce. In between, health workers and lawyers and professors find their work lives more and more hemmed in and regulated by corporation-like enterprises. The center has not held. Conceived as "the middle class" and as the supposed repository of civic virtue and occupational dedication, the PMC lies in ruins.

More profoundly, the PMC's original dream—of a society ruled by reason and led by public-spirited professionals—has been discredited. Globally, the socialist societies that seemed to come closest to this goal either degenerated into heavily militarized dictatorships or, more recently, into authoritarian capitalist states. Within the United States, the grotesque failure of socialism in China and the Soviet Union became a propaganda weapon in the neoliberal war against the public sector in its most innocuous forms and a core argument for the privatization of just about everything.

But the PMC has also managed to discredit itself as an advocate for the common good. Consider our gleaming towers of medical research and high-technology care—all too often abutting urban neighborhoods characterized by extreme poverty and foreshortened life spans.

Should we mourn the fate of the PMC or rejoice that there is one less smug, self-styled, elite to stand in the way of a more egalitarian future? On the one hand, the PMC has played a major role in the oppression and disempowering of the old working class. It has offered little resistance to (and, in fact, supplied the manpower for) the right's campaign against any measure that might ease the lives of the poor and the working class.

On the other hand, the PMC has at times been a "liberal" force, defending the values of scholarship and human service in the face of the relentless pursuit of profit. In this respect, its role in the last century bears some analogy to the role of monasteries in medieval Europe, which kept literacy and at least some form of inquiry alive while the barbarians raged outside.

As we face the deepening ruin brought on by neoliberal aggression, the question may be: Who, among the survivors, will uphold those values today? And, more profoundly, is there any way to salvage the dream of reason—or at least the idea of a society in which reasonableness can occasionally prevail—from the accretion of elitism it acquired from the PMC?

Any renewal of oppositional spirit among the professional-managerial class, or what remains of it, needs to start from an awareness that what has happened to the professional middle class has long since happened to the blue-collar working class. The debt-ridden unemployed and underemployed college graduates, the revenue-starved teachers, the overworked and underpaid service professionals, even the occasional whistle-blowing scientist or engineer—all face the same kind of situation that confronted skilled craft-workers in the early twentieth century and all American industrial workers in the late twentieth century.

In the coming years, we expect to see the remnants of the PMC increasingly making common cause with the remnants of the traditional working class for, at a minimum, representation in the political process. This is the project that the Occupy movement initiated and spread, for a time anyway, worldwide.

THE UNBEARABLE BEING
OF WHITENESS

Mother Jones, 1988

This column is addressed to my fellow white people
and contains material that we would prefer to keep
among ourselves. God knows we have suffered enough already from the unique problems that have confronted
white people over the centuries: the burden of bringing
Christianity to heathens so benighted that they usually preferred death. The agony of sunburn. But now we face what
may be the biggest problem of all. You know what I mean,
brothers and sisters, *low self-esteem*.

It started with the Asian menace. Many years ago, "Made
in Japan" applied chiefly to windup toys and samurai
movies. No one thought twice about sending their children
off to school with the sons and daughters of laundrymen
and chop suey chefs. But now, alas, the average white person cannot comprehend the inner workings of the simplest
product from Asia, much less read the owner's manual.

In the realm of business, our most brilliant blue-eyed
MBAs admit they are like children compared to the
shoguns of Mitsubishi and Toshiba. As for education,

well, the local high school is offering a full scholarship to the first Caucasian to make valedictorian. And what white parents have not—when pressed to the limit by their brutish, ignorant, dope-fiend children—screamed, "Goddamn it, Stacey [or Sean], why can't you act more like an Asian-American?"

Yes, I know the conventional explanation: White people lack convincing role models. Consider President Reagan, whose own son grew up believing—hoping?—that his true parents were the black help. Or consider the vice president, George Bush, a man so bedeviled by bladder problems that he managed, for the last eight years, to be in the men's room whenever an important illegal decision was made. Or consider how long it took, following the defeat of Robert Bork [as a Supreme Court nominee], for the conservatives to find a white man who was clean-shaven, drug-free, and had also passed his bar exam.

Then there were the nonblack Democratic candidates, who might be considered the very flower of white manhood. For months, none of them could think of anything to say. Political discourse fell to the level of white street talk, as in "Have a nice day."

Then, stealthily, one by one, they began to model themselves after Jesse Jackson. Even the patrician Al Gore, surely one of the whitest men ever to seek public office, donned a windbreaker and declared himself the champion of the working people. Richard Gephardt borrowed Jackson's rhyme about how corporations "merge" with each other and "purge" the workers. Soon he was telling moving stories about his youth as a poor black boy in the South, and how he had inexplicably turned white, clear up to and including his eyebrows.

Confronted with the obvious superiority of the black candidate, many white voters became perplexed and withdrawn. We had liked to think of black people as simple folk with large thighs and small brains—a race of Head Start dropouts, suitable for sweeping floors and assisting blond cops on TV. In fact, there is clear evidence of black intellectual superiority: In 1984, 92 percent of black people voted to retire Ronald Reagan, compared to only 36 percent of white people.

Or compare the two most prominent men of television, Bill Cosby and Morton Downey Jr. Millions of white Americans have grown up with no other father figure than "Cos." Market researchers have determined that we would buy any product he endorses, even if it were a skin-lightener. No one, on the other hand, would buy anything from Downey, unless it was something advertised anonymously in the classified section of *Soldier of Fortune*.

Perhaps it is true, as many white people have secretly and shamefully concluded, that these facts can only be explained by resorting to genetic theories of IQ. But I still like to think there are environmental explanations. A generation ago, for example, hordes of white people fled the challenging, interracial atmosphere of the cities and settled in the whites-only suburbs. Little did we know that a lifestyle devoted to lawn maintenance and shrub pruning would, in no time at all, engender the thick-witted peasant mentality now so common among our people.

At the same time, the white elite walled themselves up in

places like Harvard to preserve white culture in its purest form. Still others, the brightest of our race, retired to Los Alamos to figure out how to bring the whole thing to a prompt conclusion. Unfortunately, our extreme isolation from people of alternative races meant there was never anyone around to point out the self-destructive tendencies inherent in white behavior, which is still known collectively as "Western civilization."

Let's face it, we became ingrown, clannish, and stupid. Cut off from the mainstream of humanity, we came to believe that pink is "flesh-color," that mayonnaise is a nutrient, and that Barry Manilow is a musician. Little did we know that all over the world, people were amusing each other with tales beginning, "Did you hear the one about the Caucasian who…"

I know. It hurts. Low self-esteem is a terrible thing. Some white men, driven mad by the feeling that people are laughing at them, have taken to running around the streets and beating on random people of color or threatening to vote Republican.

Believe me, that kind of acting out won't help. If white people are ever to stand tall, we're going to have to leave our cramped little ghetto and stride out into the world again. Of course, there'll be the inevitable embarrassments at first: the fear of saying the wrong thing, of making mathematical errors, of forgetting the geography of the southern hemisphere. But gather up little Sean and Stacey and tell them, "We can do it! If we study and try very hard, even we can *be somebody*!"

IS THE MIDDLE CLASS DOOMED?

New York Times, 1986

Most of us are "middle-class," or so we like to believe. But there are signs that America is becoming a more divided society: Over the last decade, the rich have been getting richer; the poor have been getting more numerous; and those in the middle do not appear to be doing as well as they used to. If America is "coming back," as President Reagan reassured us in the wake of the economic malaise of the early 1980s, it may be coming back in a harsh and alien form.

It was in the late sixties that American society began to lurch off the track leading to the American dream. No one could have known it at the time, but, according to the economists Bennett Harrison, Chris Tilly, and Barry Bluestone, those were the last years in which economic inequality among Americans declined. Since then, in a sharp reversal of the equalizing trend that had been under way since shortly after World War II, the extremes of wealth have grown further apart and the middle has lost ground. In 1984, according to a report by Congress's Joint Economic

Committee, the share of the national income received by the wealthiest 40 percent of families in the United States rose to 67.3 percent, while the poorest 40 percent received 15.7 percent (the smallest share since 1947); the share of the middle 20 percent declined to 17 percent.

Some economists have even predicted that the middle class, which has traditionally represented the majority of Americans and defined the nation's identity and goals, will disappear altogether, leaving the country torn, like many developing societies, between an affluent minority and a horde of the desperately poor.

At least in the area of consumer options, we seem already in the process of becoming a "two-tier society." The middle is disappearing from the retail industry, for example. Korvettes and Gimbels are gone. Sears, Roebuck and JCPenney are anxiously trying to reposition themselves to survive in an ever more deeply segmented market. The stores that are prospering are the ones that have learned to specialize in one extreme of wealth or the other: Nordstrom's and Neiman-Marcus for the affluent; Kmart for those constrained by poverty or thrift. Whether one looks at food, clothing, or furnishings, two cultures are emerging: natural fibers versus synthetics; handcrafted wood cabinets versus mass-produced maple; David's Cookies versus Mister Donuts.

The political implications of the shift toward a two-tier society—if this is what is really happening—are ominous. Felix Rohatyn, the investment banker and civic leader, has observed: "A democracy, to survive, must at the very least appear to be fair. This is no longer the case in America." We may have outgrown the conceit that America is a uniformly "middle-class" society, but we have expected the extremes of wealth and poverty to be buffered by a vast and stable middle class. If the extremes swell, and if the economic center cannot hold, then our identity and future as a nation may be endangered.

Because the stakes are so high, the subject of class polarization has itself become bitterly polarized. On what could be called the "pessimistic" side is a group of mostly young, though highly acclaimed, economists who tend to be based in the relatively prosperous state of Massachusetts. The other side, which is represented at two research organizations, the Brookings Institution, in Washington, and the Conference Board, in New York City, argues that there are no fundamental flaws in the economy, and that the shift toward greater inequality will be short-lived.

Though much of the debate has been numbingly technical, the differences sometimes seem to have more to do with ideology than statistics. Fabian Linden of the Conference Board, for example, says of "the pessimists": "There are always people who think that this is an imperfect world and has to be changed....It's awfully arrogant, if you think about it."

But no one, however humble, denies that there has been a profound change in the class contours of American society. No matter how you slice up the population—whether you compare the top fifth to the bottom fifth, or the top 40 percent to the poorest 40 percent—and no matter whether you look at individual earnings or household earnings, the have-nots are getting by on less and the haves are doing better than ever.

The change is particularly striking when families with children are compared over time. In 1968, the poorest one-fifth of such families received 7.4 percent of the total income for all families; in 1983, their share was only 4.8 percent, down by one-third. During the same period, the richest fifth increased its share from 33.8 percent to 38.1 percent. The result, according to the Census Bureau, is that the income gap between the richest families and the poorest is now wider than it has been at any time since the bureau began keeping such statistics in 1947.

So far, the middle class is still a statistical reality. At least a graph of income distribution still comes out as a bell-shaped curve, with most people hovering near the mean income rather than at either extreme. (If the middle class disappeared, the curve would have two humps rather than one in the middle.) But in the last decade, the income distribution curve has slumped toward the lower end and flattened a little on top, so that it begins to look less like a weathered hill and more like a beached whale. To the untrained eye, the shift is not alarming, but as economist Jeff Faux, president of the Economic Policy Institute in Washington, says: "These numbers are very slow to move, really glacial. So when you do get a change you better pay attention."

The optimists in the debate attribute the downward shift in earnings chiefly to the baby boomers—the 78-million-member generation that began to crowd into the labor market in the 1960s and '70s, presumably driving down wages by their sheer numbers. As the boomers age, the argument goes, their incomes will rise and America will once again be a solidly middle-class society. But a recent analysis by the economists Bennett Harrison and Chris Tilly at the Massachusetts Institute of Technology and Barry Bluestone at Boston College suggests that the bulge in the labor force created by the baby boom and business-cycle effects can account for less than one-third of the increase in income inequality that has occurred since 1978.

In fact, baby boomers may find it much more difficult to make their incomes grow over time than did their parents' generation. A study by the economists Frank S. Levy and Richard C. Michel shows that, in earlier decades, men could expect their earnings to increase by about 30 percent as they aged from forty to fifty. But men who became forty in 1973 saw their earnings actually decline by 14 percent by the time they reached fifty. If this trend continues, the baby boomers will find little solace in seniority.

The fate of the baby boomers is central to the debate about America's economic future in another way, too. Contrary to the popular stereotype, the baby boomers are not all upwardly mobile, fresh-faced consumers of mesquite cuisine and exercise equipment. The baby boom is defined as those born between 1946 and 1964, and only 5 percent of them qualify as "yuppies" (young urban professional or managerial workers earning over $30,000 a year each, or $40,000 or more for a couple). Most of them, like most Americans, are "middle-class," in the limited sense that they fall somewhere near the middle of the income distribution, rather than at either extreme. Whether they can hold on to, or achieve, middle-class status—however defined—will be a test of whether the

American middle class is still capable of reproducing itself from one generation to the next.

"Middle-class" can be defined in several ways. Statistically, the middle class is simply the part of the population that earns near the median income—say, the 20 percent that earns just above the median income plus the 20 percent whose earnings fall just below it. But in colloquial understanding, "middle-class" is a matter of status as well as income, and is signaled by subtler cues—how we live, what we spend our money on, what expectations we have for the future. Since the postwar period, middle-class status has been defined by home ownership, college education (at least for the children), and the ability to afford amenities such as a second car and family vacations.

In the matter of home ownership, the baby boomers are clearly not doing as well as their parents. Levy and Michel calculate that the typical father of today's boomers faced housing costs that were equivalent to about 14 percent of his gross monthly pay. In 1984, a thirty-year-old man who purchased a median-priced home had to set aside a staggering 44 percent of his income for carrying charges. The recent decline in interest rates has helped some, but it has been largely offset by continuing inflation in the price of homes. The problem is not only that housing costs have escalated, but that the median income has actually been declining. According to the National Association of Homebuilders, a family today [1986] needs an income of approximately $37,000 to afford a median-priced home. In 1985, according to census figures, the median family income was $27,735—almost $10,000 short.

* * *

If the baby-boom bulge in the workforce is not the cause—or the sole cause—of America's slide toward greater economic inequality, what is? Public policy is one obvious contributing factor. In the 1960s and early '70s, public policy—and political rhetoric—favored a downward redistribution of wealth. Ronald Reagan reversed the trend and instituted policies that resulted in the government's first major upward redistribution of wealth since World War II. As a result of the combination of reduced taxes for the better-off and reduced social spending for the poor, the richest one-fifth of American families gained $25 billion in disposable income between 1980 and 1984, while the poorest one-fifth lost $7 billion. The current [1986] tax-revision bill would correct some of these inequities. But at the same time, according to a number of the bill's critics, including Richard A. Musgrave, professor emeritus of political economy at Harvard, it also represents a retreat from the very principle of progressivity in taxation in that it reduces the maximum rate of taxation for the very rich.

The drift toward a two-tier society actually began before the Republicans took office in 1981, and must have been set in motion by changes that go deeper than political trends. Some of these changes may be more social than economic; divorce, for example, can have the effect of splitting the members of individual families into different social classes since, in most cases, the woman ends up with the children and most of the responsibility for supporting them. Single mothers now account for almost half the household heads in poverty.

But if divorce is a factor in the emerging pattern of inequality, so is marriage. Mimi Lieber, a New York–based marketing consultant who has been following the impact of class polarization on consumer choices, says that we are seeing "a changing pattern of marriage; today, the doctor marries another doctor, not a nurse." The result is that marriage is less likely to offer women a chance at upward mobility.

On the whole, however, marriage is probably a stabilizing factor, at least if it is a "nontraditional" form of marriage. Seventy percent of baby-boom women are in the workforce—compared with about 30 percent in their mothers' generation—and the earnings of working wives are all that hold a growing number of families in the middle class. A study prepared by Sheldon Danziger and Peter Gottschalk for the Joint Economic Committee of Congress shows that most of the income gains made by white two-parent families with children since 1967 can be accounted for by increased earnings by wives. On a husband's earnings alone, the average family (of any race) would fall below the median income; on the wife's earnings alone, it would fall to the poverty level of $10,990 for a family of four.

Whatever else is changing in our patterns of marriage and divorce, something has happened to the average American's ability to support a family. According to Bluestone and Harrison, the economy is simply not generating enough well-paying jobs anymore: Between 1963 and 1978, only 23 percent of all new jobs paid poverty-level or "near-poverty-level" wages; but of the jobs generated between 1978 and 1984, almost half—48 percent—paid near-poverty-level wages. Here again, public policy is partly to blame. The minimum wage has not gone up since 1981, and now amounts to $6,700 for full-time, year-round work—almost $4,000 short of the poverty level for a family of four.

There are no doubt deeper—or, as the economists say, "structural"—reasons for the average American's sagging earning power. For one thing, the economy has been "globalized." In some industries, such as garments, toys, and electronics, American workers are competing—directly or indirectly—with workers in the southern hemisphere whose wages are a few dollars per day, rather than per hour. In a related development, the American economy has been "deindustrializing," or shifting from manufacturing to services, fast enough to displace 11.5 million Americans from blue-collar jobs (many in highly paid, unionized industries, such as auto and steel) since 1979. For the most part, service jobs tend to be lower-paying and nonunionized. Finally, there has been the technological revolution. Computers are eating away at many skilled, mid-level occupations—middle managers, department store buyers, machinists—as well as traditionally low-paid occupations, such as bank teller and telephone operator.

It is on the role of the "structural" changes that the economists are most fiercely divided, and, it seems to me, confused. The optimists insist that the causes of class polarization are more ephemeral than structural—if not the baby-boom bulge, then the strong dollar, or some other factor equally likely to go away by itself. Not long ago, the pessimists were convinced that polarization was the straightforward result of globalization, deindustrialization, and high technology, the combination of which, at least theoretically, could be expected to produce a nation of low-skilled helots dominated by a tiny technical-managerial elite.

Now some of them are not so sure. "It's incontestable," says David Smith, an economist on Senator Edward M. Kennedy's staff, "that as a service economy, we won't be able to sustain the level of growth required to maintain our standard of living." But, he says, recent data suggest that high technology does not necessarily bring about occupational polarization. As for international competition, he asks sarcastically, "Who the hell are we competing with in the insurance industry?"

There is no question, though, that American workers are less able than they were in the recent past to hold their own at the bargaining table—and most of them (the more than 80 percent who are not union members) never even get to the bargaining table. In the last decade, citing the need to compete in the newly global marketplace, employers have launched an aggressive campaign to cut labor costs, demanding—and frequently getting—wage givebacks, two-tier contracts, and other concessions. While wage-earning workers tighten their belts, top executives are reaping salaries that might once have been considered obscenely high. According to the social critic Michael Harrington: "We're seeing a savage attack on workers' wages and living standards. In the long run, no one's going to win because a low-wage society cannot be an affluent society."

*   *   *

Whatever the reasons for the growing polarization of American society, polarization creates its own dynamics, and perversely, they tend to make things worse, not better. For one thing, the affluent (say, the upper fifth) do what they can to avoid contact with the desperate and the downwardly mobile. They abandon public services and public spaces—schools, parks, mass transit—which then deteriorate. One result is that the living conditions and opportunities available to the poor (and many in the middle range of income) worsen. And, of course, as the poor sink lower, the affluent have all the more reason to withdraw further into their own "good" neighborhoods and private services.

As the better-off cease to utilize public services, they also tend to withdraw political support for public spending designed to benefit the community as a whole. If you send your children to private school, commute to work by taxi, and find your clean air at Aspen, you are likely to prefer a tax cut to an expansion of government services. This may be one reason for the decline of liberalism among America's upper-middle class. The liberal "effete snobs" that Spiro T. Agnew railed against are as rare today as Republicans on the welfare rolls.

There is another way in which class polarization tends to become self-reinforcing. As the Columbia University economist Saskia Sassen says: "The growth of the new urban upper middle class stimulates the proliferation of low-wage jobs. We're seeing the growth in the cities of a kind of 'servant class' that prepares the gourmet take-out food for the wealthy, stitches their designer clothes, and helps manufacture their customized furniture."

Traditional middle-class patterns of consumption, she notes, had a more egalitarian impact. When everyone bought their furniture at Sears and their food at the A&P, they were generating employment for workers in mass-production industries that were likely to be unionized and to pay well. In contrast, today's upscale consumer shops are boutique-scale outlets for items that are produced, or prepared, by relatively small, nonunionized companies.

The polarization of the extremes—the urban upper-middle class versus the "underclass"—inevitably makes it harder for those in the middle range of income to survive. As the rich get richer, they are able to bid up the costs of goods that middle-income people also consume, particularly housing. Wildly inflated housing costs hurt the affluent upper fifth, too, but they are far more likely than middle-income people to be able to command salary increases to match their escalating cost of living.

For those in the "new collar class," as Ralph Whitehead Jr., a University of Massachusetts professor, terms the non-yuppie plurality of baby boomers, a mortgage may be out of reach, much less a designer style of consumption. But we are all subjected to the blandishments of the booming market for upscale goods.

To be demonstrably "middle-class" in today's culture, a family needs not only the traditional house and car, but at least some of the regalia of the well-advertised upscale lifestyle—beers that cost $5 a six-pack for guests, and $60 sweatshirts for the teenage and preteen children. In order to be "middle-class" as our culture is coming to understand the term, one almost has to be rich.

So far, the hard-pressed families in the middle range of income have found a variety of ways to cope. They delay childbearing; and, even after the children come, both spouses are likely to hold jobs. They are ingenious about finding Kmart look-alikes for Bloomingdale's status goods; and, for the really big expenditures, they are likely to turn to parents for help. But these stratagems have their own costs, one of them being leisure for the kind of family life many of us were raised to expect. "We are seeing the standard two-income family," says Ethel Klein, a Columbia University political-science professor, "and the next step will probably be the three-income family, with the husband having to take a second job in order to keep up."

Karl Marx predicted that capitalist society would eventually be torn apart by the conflict between a greedy bourgeoisie and a vast, rebellious proletariat. He did not foresee the emergence, within capitalism, of a mass middle class that would mediate between the extremes and create a stable social order. But with that middle class in apparent decline and with the extremes diverging further from each other, it would be easy to conclude that the Marxist vision at last fits America's future.

But America is unique in ways that still make any prediction foolhardy. For one thing, Americans are notorious for their lack of class consciousness or even class awareness. In the face of the most brutal personal dislocations, we lack a vocabulary to express our dismay. Furthermore, at least at this point, we seem to lack political leadership capable of articulating both the distress of the have-nots and the malaise in the middle.

Thus there is no sure way to predict which way America's embattled middle class will turn. Some groups that are being displaced from the middle class seem to be moving leftward. Downwardly mobile single mothers, for example, may have helped create the gender gap that emerged, for the first time, in 1980 and was still prominent in the 1984 election, in which a greater proportion of women than men voted for the losing Democratic ticket. But the nation's debt-ridden farmers, another formerly middle-class group, have gone in all directions: some responding to Jesse Jackson's liberal populist message; others moving toward extreme right-wing fringe groups. The financially squeezed middle-income baby boomers are perhaps the most enigmatic of all. After much lush speculation as to their political inclinations, we know only that they tend to be liberal on social issues and more conservative on economic issues, and that they admire both Ronald Reagan and Bruce Springsteen.

Only at the extremes of wealth is political behavior becoming true to Marxist form. Thomas Byrne Edsall, author of *The New Politics of Inequality*, has documented an "extraordinary intensification of class-voting" in the eighties as compared with the previous two decades. For example, in 1956 Dwight D. Eisenhower won by nearly the same margin in all income groups, but in 1980 Reagan won among the rich but was soundly rejected by those in the bottom 40 percent of the income distribution. Party affiliation is

becoming equally polarized, with the haves more monolith-
ically Republican than at any time since the 1930s, and the
have-nots more solidly Democratic.

It is not clear that either party, though, is willing to advance the kinds of programs that might halt America's slide
toward a two-tier society. Admittedly, it will be hard to
get at the fundamental causes of class polarization until
we know what they are. But there is no question that the
dominant policy direction of the last few years has only ex-
acerbated the trend. If we want to avert the polarization of
American society, there is no choice, it seems to me, but to
use public policy to redistribute wealth, and opportunity,
downward again: not from the middle class to the poor, as
Lyndon B. Johnson's Great Society programs tended to do,
but from the very rich to everyone else.

We could start, for example, by raising the minimum
wage, which would not only help the working poor but
would also have a buoyant effect on middle-level wages. We
could enact long-overdue measures, such as national health
insurance and a system of subsidized child care, to help
struggling young families. We could institute tax reforms
that would both generate income for federal spending *and*
relieve those in the middle brackets. A truly progressive income tax, combined with more generous public spending
for education and social-welfare programs, would go a long
way toward smoothing out the widening inequalities of opportunity.

Everyone has a stake in creating a less anxious, more
egalitarian society. In fact, from the point of view of the
currently affluent, the greatest danger is not that a class-

conscious, left-leaning political alternative will arise, but that it will not. For without a potent political alternative, we are likely to continue our slide toward a society divided between the hungry and the overfed, the hopeless and the have-it-alls. What is worse, there will be no mainstream, peaceable political outlets for the frustration of the declining middle class or the desperation of those at the bottom. Instead, it is safe to predict that there will be more crime, more exotic forms of political and religious sectarianism, and ultimately, that we will no longer be one nation, but two.

WELCOME TO FLEECE U.

Mother Jones, 1987

This fall, my lovely and brilliant daughter will matriculate at a famous Ivy League college. Naturally, I am brokenhearted. You see, this fabulously prestigious institution, which for purposes of anonymity, I will call "Fleece U.," charges $20,000 a year—or more than two-thirds the median annual family income—to provide one's child with a bunk bed, cafeteria meals, and a chance to socialize with the future arbitrageurs and racehorse breeders of America.

Like any thrifty parent, I had done everything I could to discourage her from turning into "college material." I hid her schoolbooks. I tried to interest her in cosmetology, teen pregnancy, televison viewing. I even took her to visit a few campuses in the hope that she would be repelled by the bands of frat boys chasing minority students and beating on them with their marketing textbooks. I warned her that collegiate sexism has gotten so bad that the more enlightened colleges are now offering free rape crisis counseling as part of the freshman orientation package. "Oh, Mom," is all I got, "why don't you lighten *up?*"

When the college acceptance letters started pouring in last April, I sent them back stamped "Addressee Unknown," little realizing how determined these places can be when they're closing in on a sale. Brooke Shields called from Princeton to invite my daughter to a taffy pull. Henry Kissinger dropped by in a Learjet to discuss the undergraduate curriculum at Harvard. Benno Schmidt offered her a 15 percent discount at Yale and a date with a leading literary deconstructionist. I was flattered, but I could see I was trapped, like the time I accepted a coupon for a free margarita and found out I had obligated myself to attend a six-hour presentation on time-sharing options in the Poconos.

And don't tell me about financial aid. I had high hopes for that until I started filling out the application form. Question 12 inquired whether I had, in addition to my present income and home furnishings, any viable organs for donation. Question 34 solicited an inventory of the silverware. Question 92 demanded a list of rock stars who could plausibly be hit with a paternity suit.

Why does college cost so much? Or, more precisely, just where is the money going? The mystery deepens when you consider that $20,000 a year is approximately what it would cost to live full time in a downtown hotel with color TV and complimentary continental breakfast. Yet Fleece U., I happen to know, does not even offer room service. Alternatively, $20,000 is what it would cost to institutionalize some poor soul in a facility providing twenty-four-hour nursing service. Yet Fleece U., as everyone knows, has extraordinarily high standards and accepts only those students who have already learned to wash and dress themselves with a minimum of help.

Certainly, the money is not going to enrich the faculty. Except for a few celebrity profs, who have their own gene-splicing firms on the side or who moonlight as Pentagon consultants, most college faculty are a scruffy, ill-nourished lot, who are not above supplementing their income by panhandling on the steps of the student union. Nor can the money be going to the support staff. Even at venerable Fleece U., which has an endowment the size of the federal deficit, secretaries' wages are calculated on the basis of the minimum daily caloric requirement of the human female—any larger sum being considered an incitement to immorality.

Finally, we can rule out the possibility that the money is being used to support poor students who might otherwise go straight into burger flipping. With tuition rising twice as fast as inflation, poor students are no longer welcome at places like Fleece U., even in token numbers. Nationwide, the enrollment of black students peaked in 1980 but is now in decline due to cutbacks in federal aid programs. Meanwhile, the upper-middle class is fleeing the private colleges and beginning to crowd the working class out of state universities, which—at the astonishingly low price of $10,000 or so a year—are the best bargain since double coupons.

This leaves two possibilities: One is that the money is finding its way into the Iran-contra-Brunei triangle, from which no money has ever been known to reemerge. Of course, I have no logical reason for suspecting this. It is just that so much money these days starts out in the checkbooks of wealthy Connecticut widows or the royal family of Saudi Arabia and ends up hovering inaccessibly between Panama, Georgetown, and Zurich—perhaps to turn up someday as an Italian silk suit for Adolfo Calero or a spray of gardenias for Fawn Hall.

The second possibility, and the one that I personally consider more likely, is that the money is going to Don Regan. Not just Don Regan, of course, but G. Gordon Liddy, H. R. Haldeman, and possibly, in a year or two, Oliver North. For what do these fellows do after a period of public service followed, in some cases, by a relaxing spell in a minimum security prison? They repair to the college lecture circuit where, as I read recently, Don Regan pulls down $20,000 a night—the exact amount of my daughter's tuition at Fleece U.!

You can imagine how I feel about paying a sum of this magnitude to the man who almost drove Nancy Reagan to join a feminist support group. Yet I am gradually beginning to believe that the college experience will be important for my daughter. I realize that, even if she never opens a book, college will give her an opportunity I was never able to provide in our home: the chance to be around rich people—almost all of them young and attractive—continuously, twenty-four hours a day. Nor do I have to fear that she will lose the common touch. By the time she graduates, there will be at least one desperately poor person in her circle of acquaintances—myself.

PREWATCHED TV

The Guardian, 1994

Everything else has been automated, so why not that most commonplace of human activities— watching TV? This is the true secret of *Beavis and Butt-Head*'s megasuccess: not that they satisfy a young person's normal interest in arson and the torture of small animals and elderly people—which they do, of course, as has often been noted—but that they take the last bit of effort out of watching TV. For anyone so culturally impaired as not yet to have seen it, their show consists largely of two cartoon figures watching TV on a screen that fills up one's own. *They* make the ironic comments; *they* change the channel whenever a video threatens to drag. Hence the little pimple-butts' great gift to humankind— prewatched TV.

They're beginning to make prewatched commercials, too. Just as one's index finger moves to ward off the oncoming "message"—"Zap!"—the channel appears to change to something more entertaining. Then another virtual zap, and the product, whatever it is, returns. This is automated channel surfing—TV-viewing minus the last little vestige of muscular exertion.

At first we loved channel surfing on our own, accessing the collective mind, as it were, by tapping the buttons on the remote. People took pride in their craftsmanship— splicing scenes of hyena predation from the Discovery Channel in with the president's State of the Union address, for example, or alleviating the gloom of Bosnia with nacho recipes from the nearby Food Channel. Creative viewers mixed Hillary on health care with Tonya on skates, or cut into their favorite televangelist with the human sacrifice scene from *The Temple of Doom*. It was all there at one's fingertips: sprightly political chatter, singing transvestites, warnings about Satan, instructions for making béchamel sauce or rehabilitating a codependent relationship.

But then we went into overload. In my neighborhood, the breaking point came when the cable TV company upgraded us from forty to sixty channels, which meant there would now be not only twenty-four-hour news channels but channels offering continuous weather, shopping-by-phone, and trials of celebrity felons. The first casualty was a neighbor who developed a repetitive stress injury by overusing his remote. Now both of his index fingers are in finger-sized casts, and he has been reduced to changing channels with his nose.

Plus, it must be acknowledged that channel surfing was one of the factors undermining the American family. Once, it had been a simple matter to settle on the evening's entertainment—sex or violence, X-rated or R. After a brief, usually bloodless tussle, the victors settled down to enjoy and the losers resigned themselves to making irritating comments and exotic eructations, much as Beavis and Butthead now do for us. But when viewing became surfing, the fights got nastier. Children demanded their own TVs, often at gunpoint; spouses dueled with matching his-and-hers remotes. One theory has it that Lorena Bobbitt only went for the penis because the index finger, grossly thickened through overuse, resisted the knife.

Channel surfing has been destroying the nation as well. What, after all, are the fissures that really divide us? White versus black, right versus left, or some such archaic dispute? No, of course not. The real divisions are between those who watch MTV and those who favor Christian broadcasting, between CNN viewers and fans of Fox Network. But why let these transitory preferences come between us? American culture is not one or the other—Christian programming or writhing pelvises, "hard" news or Michael Jackson. American culture is everything running in together—béchamel sauce mixed with the Red Hot Chili Peppers, Pat Robertson a microsecond away from RuPaul.

Some say we should throw our remotes into the recycling bin and go back to the old days, when changing a channel involved walking from couch to set, twisting a knob, and returning, on foot, to couch. But the national attention span has gotten much too short for such arduous interruptions. It's far better to have the channel switching done for us, by some godlike invisible hand. Families, communities, nations will draw closer together as we all watch, i.e., rewatch, the same even-handed, prewatched blur.

THE RECESSION'S RACIAL DIVIDE

New York Times, 2009

With Dedrick Muhammad

What do you get when you combine the worst economic downturn since the Depression with the first black president? A surge of white racial resentment, loosely disguised as a populist revolt. An article on the Fox News website has put forth the theory that health reform is a stealth version of reparations for slavery: White people will foot the bill and, by some undisclosed mechanism, black people will get all the care. President Obama, in such fantasies, is a dictator and, in one image circulated among the antitax, anti–health reform "tea parties," he is depicted as a befeathered African witch doctor with little tusks coming out of his nostrils. When you're going down, as the white middle class has been doing for several years now, it's all too easy to imagine that it's because someone else is climbing up over your back.

Despite the sense of white grievance, though, black people are the ones who are taking the brunt of the recession, with disproportionately high levels of foreclosures and unemployment. And they weren't doing so well to begin with. At the start of the recession, 33 percent of the black middle class was already in danger of falling to a lower economic level, according to a study by the Institute on Assets and Social Policy at Brandeis University and Demos, a nonpartisan public policy research organization.

In fact, you could say that for African Americans the recession is over. It occurred from 2000 to 2007, as black employment decreased by 2.4 percent and incomes declined by 2.9 percent. During those seven years, one-third of black children lived in poverty, and black unemployment—even among college graduates—consistently ran at about twice the level of white unemployment.

That was the black recession. What's happening now is more like a depression. Nauvata and James, a middle-aged African-American couple living in Prince George's County, Maryland, who asked that their last name not be published, had never recovered from the first recession of the '00s when the second one came along. In 2003 Nauvata was laid off from a $25-an-hour administrative job at Aetna, and in 2007 she wound up in a $10.50-an-hour job at a car-rental company. James has had a steady union job as a building equipment operator, but the two couldn't earn enough to save themselves from predatory lending schemes.

They were paying off a $524 dining set bought on credit from the furniture store Levitz when it went out of business, and their debt swelled inexplicably as it was sold from one creditor to another. The couple ultimately spent a total of $3,800 to both pay it off and hire a lawyer to clear their credit rating. But to do this they had to refinance their home—not once, but with a series of mortgage lenders. Now they face foreclosure.

Nauvata, who is forty-seven, has since seen her blood pressure soar, and James, fifty-six, has developed heart palpitations. "There is no middle class anymore," he told us, "just a top and a bottom."

Plenty of formerly middle- or working-class white people have followed similar paths to ruin: the layoff or reduced hours, the credit traps and ever-rising debts, the lost home. But one thing distinguishes hard-pressed African Americans as a group: Thanks to a legacy of a discrimination in both hiring and lending, they're less likely than white people to be cushioned against the blows by wealthy relatives or well-stocked savings accounts. In 2008, on the cusp of the recession, the typical African-American family had only a dime for every dollar of wealth possessed by the typical white family. Only 18 percent of black people and Latinos had retirement accounts, compared with 43.4 percent of white people.

Racial asymmetry was stamped on this recession from the beginning. Wall Street's reckless infatuation with subprime mortgages led to the global financial crash of 2007, which depleted home values and 401(k)s across the racial spectrum. People of all races got sucked into subprime and adjustable-rate mortgages, but even high-income black people were almost twice as likely to end up with subprime home-purchase loans as low-income white people—even when they qualified for prime mortgages, even when they offered down payments.

According to a 2008 report by United for a Fair Economy, a research and advocacy group, from 1998 to 2006 (before the subprime crisis), black people lost $71 billion to $93 billion in home-value wealth from subprime loans. The researchers called this family net-worth catastrophe the "greatest loss of wealth in recent history for people of color." And the worst was yet to come.

In a new documentary film about the subprime crisis, *American Casino*, solid black citizens—a high school social studies teacher, a psychotherapist, a minister—relate how they lost their homes when their monthly mortgage payments exploded. Watching the parts of the film set in Baltimore is a little like watching the TV series *The Wire*, except that the bad guys don't live in the projects; they hover over computer screens on Wall Street.

It's not easy to get people to talk about their subprime experiences. There's the humiliation of having been "played" by distant, mysterious forces. "I don't feel very good about myself," says the teacher in *American Casino*. "I kind of feel like a failure."

Even people who know better tend to blame themselves—like Melonie Griffith, a forty-year-old African American who works with the Boston group City Life/La Vida Urbana helping other people avoid foreclosure and eviction. She criticizes herself for having been "naive" enough to trust the mortgage lender who, in 2004, told her not to worry about the high monthly payments she was signing on for because the mortgage would be refinanced in "a couple of months." The lender then disappeared, leaving Griffith in foreclosure, with "nowhere for my kids and me to go." Only when she went public with her story did she find that she wasn't the only one. "There is a consistent pattern here," she told us.

Mortgage lenders like Countrywide and Wells Fargo sought out minority home buyers for the heartbreakingly simple reason that, for decades, black people had been denied mortgages on racial grounds, and were thus a ready-made market for the gonzo mortgage products of the mid-'00s. Banks replaced the old racist practice of redlining with "reverse redlining"—intensive marketing aimed at black neighborhoods in the name of extending home ownership to the historically excluded. Countrywide, which prided itself on being a dream factory for previously disadvantaged home buyers, rolled out commercials showing canny black women talking their husbands into signing mortgages.

At Wells Fargo, Elizabeth Jacobson, a former loan officer at the company, recently revealed—in an affidavit in a lawsuit by the City of Baltimore—that salesmen were encouraged to try to persuade black preachers to hold "wealth-building seminars" in their churches. For every loan that resulted from these seminars, whether to buy a new home or refinance one, Wells Fargo promised to donate $350 to the customer's favorite charity, usually the church. (Wells Fargo denied any effort to market subprime loans specifically to black people.) Another former loan officer, Tony Paschal, reported that at the same time cynicism was rampant within Wells Fargo, with some employees referring to subprimes as "ghetto loans" and to minority customers as "mud people."

If any cultural factor predisposed black people to fall for risky loans, it was one widely shared with white people—

a penchant for "positive thinking" and unwarranted optimism, which takes the theological form of the "prosperity gospel." Since "God wants to prosper you," all you have to do to get something is "name it and claim it." A 2000 DVD from the black evangelist Creflo Dollar featured African-American parishioners shouting, "I want my stuff—right now!"

Joel Osteen, the white megachurch pastor who draws 40,000 worshippers each Sunday, about two-thirds of them black and Latino, likes to relate how he himself succumbed to God's urgings—conveyed by his wife—to upgrade to a larger house. According to Jonathan Walton, a religion professor at the University of California, Riverside, pastors like Osteen reassured people about subprime mortgages by getting them to believe that "God caused the bank to ignore my credit score and bless me with my first house." If African Americans made any collective mistake in the mid-'00s, it was to embrace white culture too enthusiastically, and substitute the individual wish fulfillment promoted by Norman Vincent Peale for the collective-action message of Martin Luther King.

But you didn't need a dodgy mortgage to be wiped out by the subprime crisis and ensuing recession. Black unemployment is now at 15.1 percent, compared with 8.9 percent for white people. In New York City, black unemployment has been rising four times as fast as that of white people. By 2010, according to Lawrence Mishel of the Economic Policy Institute, 40 percent of African Americans nationwide will have endured patches of unemployment or underemployment.

One result is that black people are being hit by a second wave of foreclosures caused by unemployment. Willett Thomas, a neat, wiry forty-seven-year-old in Washington who describes herself as a "fiscal conservative," told us that until a year ago she thought she'd "figured out a way to live my dream." Not only did she have a job and a house, but she had a rental property in Gainesville, Florida, leaving her with the flexibility to pursue a part-time writing career.

Then she became ill, lost her job, and fell behind on the fixed-rate mortgage on her home. The tenants in Florida had financial problems of their own and stopped paying rent. Now, although she manages to have an interview a week and regularly upgrades her résumé, Thomas cannot find a new job. The house she lives in is in foreclosure.

Mulugeta Yimer of Alexandria, Virginia, still has his taxi-driving job, but it no longer pays enough to live on. A thin, tall man with worry written all over his face, Yimer came to this country in 1981 as a refugee from Ethiopia, firmly believing in the American dream. In 2003, when Wells Fargo offered him an adjustable-rate mortgage, he calculated that he'd be able to deal with the higher interest rate when it kicked in. But the recession delivered a near-mortal blow to the taxi industry, even in the still relatively affluent Washington suburbs. He's now putting in nineteen-hour days, with occasional naps in his taxi, while his wife works thirty-two hours a week at a convenience store, but they still don't earn enough to cover expenses: $400 a month for health insurance, $800 for child care, and $1,700 for the mortgage. What will Yimer do if he ends up losing his house? "We'll go to a shelter, I guess," he said, throwing open his hands, "if we can find one."

So despite the right-wing perception of black power grabs, this recession is on track to leave black people even more economically disadvantaged than they were. Does a black president who is inclined toward bipartisanship dare address this destruction of the black middle class? Probably not. But if Americans of all races don't get some economic relief soon, the pain will only increase and, with it, perversely, the unfounded sense of white racial grievance.

DIVISIONS OF LABOR

New York Times, 2017

The working class, or at least the white part, has emerged as our great national mystery. Traditionally Democratic, they helped elect a flamboyantly ostentatious billionaire to the presidency. "What's wrong with them?" the liberal pundits keep asking. Why do they believe Trump's promises? Are they stupid or just deplorably racist? Why did the working class align itself against its own interests?

I was born into this elusive class and remain firmly connected to it through friendships and family. In the 1980s, for example, I personally anchored a working-class cultural hub in my own home on Long Island. The attraction was not me but my husband (then) and longtime friend Gary Stevenson, a former warehouse worker who had become an organizer for the Teamsters Union. You may think of the Long Island suburbs as a bedroom community for Manhattan commuters or a portal to the Hamptons, but they were then also an industrial center, with more than 20,000 workers employed at Grumman alone. When my sister moved into our basement from Colorado, she quickly found a job in a factory within a mile of our house, as did thousands of other people, some of them bused in from the Bronx. Mostly we hosted local residents who passed through our house for evening meetings or weekend gatherings—truck drivers, factory workers, janitors, and eventually nurses. My job was to make chili and keep room in the fridge for the baked ziti others would invariably bring. I once tried to explain the concept of "democratic socialism" to some machine-shop workers and went off on a brief peroration against the Soviet Union. They stared at me glumly across the kitchen counter until one growled, "At least they have health care over there."

By the time my little crew was gathering in the ranch house, working-class aspirations were everywhere being trampled underfoot. In 1981, President Reagan busted the air traffic controllers' union by firing more than 11,000 striking workers—a clear signal of what was to come. A few years later, we hosted a picnic for Jim Guyette, the leader of a militant meatpacking local in Minnesota that had undertaken a wildcat strike against Hormel (and, of course, no Hormel products were served at our picnic). But labor had entered into an age of givebacks and concessions. Grovel was the message, or go without a job. Even the "mighty mighty" unions of the old labor chant, the ones that our little group had struggled both to build and to democratize, were threatened with extinction. Within a year, the wildcat local was crushed by its own parent union, the United Food and Commercial Workers.

Steel mills went quiet, the mines where my father and

grandfather had worked shut down, factories fled south of the border. Much more was lost in the process than just the jobs; an entire way of life, central to the American mythos, was coming to an end. The available jobs, in fields like retail sales and health care, were ill paid, making it harder for a man without a college education to support a family on his own. I could see this in my own extended family, where the grandsons of miners and railroad workers were taking jobs as delivery-truck drivers and fast-food restaurant managers or even competing with their wives to become retail workers or practical nurses. As Susan Faludi observed in her 1999 book *Stiffed*, the deindustrialization of America led to a profound masculinity crisis: What did it mean to be a man when a man could no longer support a family?

It wasn't just a way of life that was dying but also many of those who had lived it. Research in 2015 by Angus Deaton, a Nobel laureate in economics, with his wife, economist Anne Case, showed that the mortality gap between college-educated and non-college-educated had been widening rapidly since 1999. A couple of months later, economists at the Brookings Institution found that for men born in 1920, there was a six-year difference in life expectancy between the top 10 percent of earners and the bottom 10 percent. For men born in 1950, that difference more than doubled, to 14 years. Smoking, which is now mostly a working-class habit, could account for only a third of the excess deaths. The rest were apparently attributable to alcoholism, drug overdoses, and suicide, usually by gunshot—what are often called "diseases of despair."

In the new economic landscape of low-paid service jobs,

some of the old nostrums of the left have stopped making sense. "Full employment," for example, was the mantra of the unions for decades, but what did it mean when so many jobs no longer paid enough to live on? The idea had been that if everyone who wanted a job could get one, employers would have to raise wages to attract new workers. But when I went out as an undercover journalist in the late 1990s to test the viability of entry-level jobs, I found my coworkers—waitstaff, nursing-home workers, maids with a cleaning service, Walmart "associates"—living for the most part in poverty. As I reported in the resulting book, *Nickel and Dimed*, some were homeless and slept in their cars, while others skipped lunch because they couldn't afford anything more than a snack-size bag of Doritos. They were full-time workers, and this was a time, like the present, of nearly full employment.

The other popular solution to the crisis of the working class was job retraining. If ours is a "knowledge economy"— which sounds so much better than a "low-wage economy"— unemployed workers would just have to get their game on and upgrade to more useful skills. President Obama promoted job retraining, as did Hillary Clinton as a presidential candidate, along with many Republicans. The problem was that no one was sure what to train people in; computer skills were in vogue in the '90s, welding has gone in and out of style, and careers in the still-growing health sector are supposed to be the best bets now. Nor is there any clear measure of the effectiveness of existing retraining programs. In 2011, the Government Accountability Office found the federal government supporting forty-seven job-training projects as of 2009, of which only five had been evaluated in the previous five years. Paul Ryan has repeatedly praised a program in his hometown, Janesville, Wisconsin, but a 2012 ProPublica study found that laid-off people who went through it were less likely to find jobs than those who did not.

No matter how good the retraining program, the idea that people should be endlessly malleable and ready to re-create themselves to accommodate every change in the job market is probably not realistic and certainly not respectful of existing skills. In the early '90s, I had dinner at a Pizza Hut with a laid-off miner in Butte, Montana (actually, there are no other kinds of miners in Butte). He was in his fifties, and he chuckled when he told me that he was being advised to get a degree in nursing. I couldn't help laughing, too—not at the gender incongruity but at the notion that a man whose tools had been a pickax and dynamite should now so radically change his relation to the world. No wonder that when blue-collar workers were given the choice between job retraining, as proffered by Clinton, and somehow, miraculously, bringing their old jobs back, as proposed by Trump, they went for the latter.

Now when politicians invoke "the working class," they are likely to gesture, anachronistically, to an abandoned factory. They might more accurately use a hospital or a fast-food restaurant as a prop. The new working class contains many of the traditional blue-collar occupations—truck driver, electrician, plumber—but by and large its members are more likely to wield mops than hammers, and bedpans rather than trowels. Demographically, too, the working class has evolved from the heavily white male grouping that used to assemble at my house in the 1980s; black and Hispanic people have long been a big, if unacknowledged, part of the working class, and now it's more female and contains many more immigrants as well. If the stereotype of the old working class was a man in a hard hat, the new one is better represented as a woman chanting, "*El pueblo unido jamás será vencido!*" (The people united will never be defeated!)

The old jobs aren't coming back, but there is another way to address the crisis brought about by deindustrialization: Pay all workers better. The big labor innovation of the twenty-first century has been campaigns seeking to raise local or state minimum wages. Activists have succeeded in passing living-wage laws in more than a hundred counties and municipalities since 1994 by appealing to a simple sense of justice: Why should someone work full time, year-round, and not make enough to pay for rent and other basics? Surveys found large majorities favoring an increase in the minimum wage; college students, church members, and unions rallied to local campaigns. Unions started taking on formerly neglected constituencies like janitors, home health aides, and day laborers. And where the unions have faltered, entirely new kinds of organizations sprang up: associations sometimes backed by unions and sometimes by philanthropic foundations—Our Walmart, the National Domestic Workers Alliance, and the Restaurant Opportunities Centers United.

Our old scene on Long Island is long gone: the house sold, the old friendships frayed by age and distance. I miss it. As a group, we had no particular ideology, but our vision, which was articulated through our parties rather than any manifesto, was utopian, especially in the context of Long Island, where if you wanted any help from the county, you had to be a registered Republican. If we had a single theme, it could be summed up in the old-fashioned word "solidarity": If you join my picket line, I'll join yours, and maybe we'll all go protest together, along with the kids, at the chemical plant that was oozing toxins into our soil—followed by a barbecue in my backyard. We were not interested in small-P politics. We wanted a world in which everyone's work was honored and every voice heard.

I never expected to be part of anything like that again until, in 2004, I discovered a similar, far-better-organized group in Fort Wayne, Indiana. The Northeast Indiana Central Labor Council, as it was then called, brought together Mexican immigrant construction workers and the native-born building-trade union members they had been brought in to replace, laid-off foundry workers and Burmese factory workers, adjunct professors and janitors. Their goal, according to the president at the time, Tom Lewandowski, a former General Electric factory worker who served in the 1990s as the AFL-CIO's liaison to the Polish insurgent movement Solidarnosc, was to create a "culture of solidarity." They were inspired by the realization that it's not enough to organize people with jobs; you have to organize the unemployed as well as the "anxiously employed"—meaning potentially the entire community. Their not-so-secret tactic was parties and picnics, some of which I was lucky enough to attend.

The scene in Fort Wayne featured people of all colors and collar colors, legal and undocumented workers, liberals and political conservatives, some of whom supported Trump in the last election. It showed that a new kind of solidarity was within reach, even if the old unions may not be ready. In 2016, the ailing AFL-CIO, which for more than six decades has struggled to hold the labor movement together, suddenly dissolved the Northeast Indiana Central Labor Council, citing obscure bureaucratic imperatives. But the labor council was undaunted. It promptly reinvented itself as the Workers' Project and drew more than 6,000 people to the local Labor Day picnic, despite having lost its internet access and office equipment to the AFL-CIO.

When I last talked to Tom Lewandowski, in early February 2017, the Workers' Project had just succeeded in organizing twenty Costco contract workers into a collective unit of their own and were planning to celebrate with, of course, a party. The human urge to make common cause—and have a good time doing it—is hard to suppress.

THROW THEM OUT WITH THE TRASH: WHY HOMELESSNESS IS BECOMING AN OCCUPY WALL STREET ISSUE

Huffington Post, 2011

As anyone knows who has ever had to set up a military encampment or build a village from the ground up, occupations pose staggering logistical problems. Large numbers of people must be fed and kept reasonably warm and dry. Trash has to be removed; medical care and rudimentary security provided—to which ends a dozen or more committees may toil night and day. But for the individual occupier, one problem often overshadows everything else, including job loss, the destruction of the middle class, and the reign of the 1 percent. And that is the single question: *Where am I going to pee?*

Some of the Occupy Wall Street encampments now spreading across the United States have access to Port-o-Potties (Freedom Plaza in Washington, DC) or, better yet, restrooms with sinks and running water (Fort Wayne, Indiana). Others require their residents to forage on their own. At Zuccotti Park, just blocks from Wall Street, this means long waits for the restroom at a nearby Burger King or somewhat shorter ones at a Starbucks a block away.

At McPherson Square in DC, a twenty-something occupier showed me the pizza parlor where she can cop a pee during the hours it's open, as well as the alley where she crouches late at night. Anyone with restroom-related issues—arising from age, pregnancy, prostate problems, or irritable bowel syndrome—should prepare to join the revolution in diapers.

Of course, political protesters do not face the challenges of urban camping alone. Homeless people confront the same issues every day: how to scrape together meals, keep warm at night by covering themselves with cardboard or tarp, and relieve themselves without committing a crime. Public restrooms are sparse in American cities—"as if the need to go to the bathroom does not exist," travel expert Arthur Frommer once observed. And yet to yield to bladder pressure is to risk arrest. A report titled "Criminalizing Crisis," released by the National Law Center on Homelessness and Poverty, recounts the following story from Wenatchee, Washington:

> Toward the end of 2010, a family of two parents and three children who had been experiencing homelessness for a year and a half applied for a two-bedroom apartment. The day before a scheduled meeting with the apartment manager during the final stages of acquiring the lease, the father of the family was arrested for public urination. The arrest occurred at an hour when no public restrooms were available for use. Due to the arrest, the father was unable to make the appointment with the apartment manager and the property was rented out to another person. As of

March 2011, the family was still homeless and searching for housing.

What the Occupy Wall Streeters are beginning to discover, and homeless people have known all along, is that most ordinary, biologically necessary activities are illegal when performed in American streets—not just peeing, but sitting, lying down, and sleeping. While the laws vary from city to city, one of the harshest is in Sarasota, Florida, which passed an ordinance in 2005 that makes it illegal to "engage in digging or earth-breaking activities"—that is, to build a latrine—cook, make a fire, or be asleep and "when awakened state that he or she has no other place to live."

It is illegal, in other words, to be homeless or live outdoors for any other reason. It should be noted, though, that there are no laws requiring cities to provide food, shelter, or restrooms for their indigent citizens.

The current prohibition on homelessness began to take shape in the 1980s, along with the ferocious growth of the financial industry (Wall Street and all its tributaries throughout the nation). That was also the era in which we stopped being a nation that manufactured much beyond weightless, invisible "financial products," leaving the old industrial working class to carve out a livelihood at places like Walmart.

As it turned out, the captains of the new "casino economy"—the stock brokers and investment bankers—were highly sensitive, one might say finicky, individuals, easily offended by having to step over the homeless in the streets or bypass them in commuter train stations. In an economy where a centimillionaire could turn into a billionaire overnight, the poor and unwashed were a major buzzkill. Starting with Mayor Rudy Giuliani in New York, city after city passed "broken windows" or "quality of life" ordinances, making it dangerous for the homeless to loiter or, in some cases, even look "indigent," in public spaces.

No one has yet tallied all the suffering occasioned by this crackdown—the deaths from cold and exposure—but "Criminalizing Crisis" offers this story about a homeless pregnant woman in Columbia, South Carolina:

> During daytime hours, when she could not be inside of a shelter, she attempted to spend time in a museum and was told to leave. She then attempted to sit on a bench outside the museum and was again told to relocate. In several other instances, still during her pregnancy, the woman was told that she could not sit in a local park during the day because she would be "squatting." In early 2011, about six months into her pregnancy, the homeless woman began to feel unwell, went to a hospital, and delivered a stillborn child.

Well before Tahrir Square was a twinkle in anyone's eye, and even before the recent recession, homeless Americans had begun to act in their own defense, creating organized encampments, usually tent cities, in vacant lots or wooded areas. These communities often feature various elementary forms of self-governance: food from local charities has to be distributed, latrines dug, rules—such as no drugs, weapons, or violence—enforced. With all due credit to the Egyptian democracy movement, the Spanish *indignados*, and rebels all over the world, tent cities are the domestic progenitors of the American occupation movement.

There is nothing "political" about these settlements of the homeless—no signs denouncing greed or visits from left-wing luminaries—but they have been treated with far less official forbearance than the occupation encampments of the "American autumn." LA's Skid Row endures constant police harassment, for example, but when it rained, Mayor Antonio Villaraigosa had ponchos distributed to nearby Occupy LA.

All over the country, in the last few years, police have moved in on the tent cities of the homeless, one by one, from Seattle to Wooster, Sacramento to Providence, in raids that often leave the former occupants without even their minimal possessions. In Chattanooga, Tennessee, last summer, a charity outreach worker explained the forcible dispersion of a local tent city by saying, "The city will not tolerate a tent city. That's been made very clear to us. The camps have to be out of sight."

What occupiers from all walks of life are discovering, at least every time they contemplate taking a leak, is that to be homeless in America is to live like a fugitive. The destitute are our own native-born "illegals," facing prohibitions on the most basic activities of survival. They are not supposed to soil public space with their urine, their feces, or their exhausted bodies. Nor are they supposed to spoil the landscape with their unusual wardrobe choices or body odors. They are, in fact, supposed to die, and preferably to do so without leaving a corpse for the dwindling public sector to transport, process, and burn.

But the occupiers are not from *all* walks of life, just from those walks that slope downwards—from debt, joblessness, and foreclosure—leading eventually to pauperism and the streets. Some of the present occupiers were homeless to start with, attracted to the occupation encampments by the prospect of free food and at least temporary shelter from police harassment. Many others are drawn from the borderline-homeless "nouveau poor," and normally encamp on friends' couches or parents' folding beds.

In Portland, Austin, and Philadelphia, the Occupy Wall Street movement is taking up the cause of the homeless as its own, which of course it is. Homelessness is not a side issue unconnected to plutocracy and greed. It's where we're all eventually headed—the 99 percent, or at least the 70 percent, of us, every debt-loaded college grad, out-of-work schoolteacher, and impoverished senior—unless this revolution succeeds.

ACKNOWLEDGMENTS

Grateful acknowledgment is made to the following for permission to reprint previously published material.

HAVES AND HAVE-NOTS

"Nickel-and-Dimed: On (Not) Getting By in America" (*Harper's Magazine*, 1999)
"How You Can Save Wall Street" (*Mother Jones*, 1988)
"S&M As Public Policy" (*The Guardian*, 1993)
"Going to Extremes: CEOs vs. Slaves" originally published as "CEOs vs. Slaves" (*The Nation*, 2007)
"Are Illegal Immigrants the Problem?" (*Barbara's Blog*, 2006)
"What's So Great about Gated Communities?" (*Huffington Post*, 2007)
"Is It Now a Crime to be Poor?" (*New York Times*, 2009)
"A Homespun Safety Net" (*New York Times*, 2009)
"Dead, White, and Blue" (*Guernica*, 2015)

HEALTH

"Welcome to Cancerland" (*Harper's Magazine*, 2001)
"The Naked Truth about Fitness" (*Lear's*, 1990)
"Got Grease?" (*Los Angeles Times*, 2002)
"Our Broken Mental Health System" (*The Nation*, 2007)
"Liposuction: The Key to Energy Independence" (*The Nation*, 2008)
"The Selfish Side of Gratitude" (*New York Times*, 2015)

MEN

"How 'Natural' is Rape?" (*Time*, 2000)
"The Warrior Culture" (*Time*, 1990)
"At Last, a New Man" originally published as "A Feminist's View of the New Man" (*New York Times*, 1984)
"Patriarchy Deflated" (*The Baffler*, 2018)

WOMEN

"Are Women Getting Sadder?" originally published as "The Sad Truth" (*Los Angeles Times*, 2009)
"Our Neighborhood Porn Committee" originally published as "The Story of Ed" (*Mother Jones*, 1986)
"Strategies of Corporate Women" (*New Republic*, 1986)
"Feminism's Assumptions Upended" originally published as "What Abu Ghraib Taught Me" (*Los Angeles Times*, 2004)

"Making Sense of la Différence" (*Time*, 1992)
"Outclassed: Sexual Harassment" originally published
as "Sexual Harassment Doesn't Just Happen to Actors or
Journalists. Talk to a Waitress, or a Cleaner" (*The
Guardian*, 2017)

GOD, SCIENCE, AND JOY

"Mind Your Own Business" (*The Baffler*, 2015)
"The Animal Cure" (*The Baffler*, 2012)
"The Missionary Position" (*The Baffler*, 2012)
"The New Creationism: Biology under Attack" (*The
Nation*, 1997)
"Up Close at Trinidad's Carnival" (*Smithsonian Magazine*,
2009)
"The Humanoid Stain" (*The Baffler*, 2019)

BOURGEOIS BLUNDERS

"Family Values" (Introduction to *The Worst Years of Our
Lives* [Pantheon, 1990])
"The Cult of Busyness" originally published as "Hers"
(*New York Times*, 1985)
"Death of a Yuppie Dream" (*Journal der Rosa Luxemburg
Stiftung*, 2013)
"The Unbearable Being of Whiteness" (*Mother Jones*,
1988)
"Is the Middle Class Doomed?" (*New York Times*, 1986)

"Welcome to Fleece U." (*Mother Jones*, 1987)

"Prewatched TV" (*The Guardian*, 1994)

"The Recession's Racial Divide" (*New York Times*, 2009)

"Divisions of Labor" (*New York Times*, 2017)

"Throw Them Out with the Trash: Why Homelessness Is Becoming an Occupy Wall Street Issue" (*Huffington Post*, 2011)

INDEX

ABOUT THE AUTHOR

BARBARA EHRENREICH is the author of more than a dozen books, including the *New York Times* bestsellers *Nickel and Dimed* and *Natural Causes*. She has a PhD in cellular immunology from Rockefeller University and writes frequently about health care and medical science, among many other subjects. She lives in Virginia.

B
105
.C74
A84
2015

Ashton, Kevin,
author.
How to fly a horse

MAR 1 2 2018

DISCARD

Praise for

"An inspiring vision of creativity that's littered with practical advice, and is a cracking read to boot."   —*BBC Focus*

"[An] entertaining and inspiring meditation on the nature of creative innovation. . . . Fans of Malcolm Gladwell and Steven Levitt will enjoy Ashton's hybrid nonfiction style, which builds a compelling cultural treatise from a coalescence of engaging anecdotes."   —*Booklist*

"If you have ever wondered what it takes to create something, read this inspiring and insightful book. Using examples ranging from Mozart to the Muppets, Kevin Ashton shows how to tap the creative abilities that lurk in us all. There are no secrets, no shortcuts; just ordinary steps we can all take to bring something new into the world. Ashton's message is direct and hopeful: creativity isn't just for geniuses—it's for   ."
                            —Joseph T. Hallinan, author of *Wh*

"A detailed and persuasive argument for how creativity a
not through magical bursts of inspiration but with ca
dogged problem-solving, and hard-won insight. Ashton
wealth of illuminating and entertaining stories from the ann
ness, science, and the arts to show how any of us can apply thi
to our own work."

                      —Mason Currey, author of *Daily Rituals: How Artists*

If you consider yourself a curious person then you will love this book. Ashton shares so many delightful stories of where things come from and how things came to be, I seriously believe that it will make anyone who reads it smarter."
　　　　　　　　　　　　　—Simon Sinek, *New York Times* bestselling author of *Start with Why* and *Leaders Eat Last*

"*How to Fly a Horse* solves the mysteries of invention. Kevin Ashton, the innovator who coined the [term] 'Internet of Things,' shows that creativity is more often the result of ordinary steps than extraordinary leaps. With engrossing stories, provocative studies, and lucid writing, this book is not to be missed."
　　—Adam Grant, professor of management at the Wharton School and *New York Times* bestselling author of *Give and Take*

"Ashton's beautifully written exploration of creativity explodes so many myths and opens so many doors that readers, like me, will be left reeling with possibilities. We can all create, we can all innovate. Move over, Malcolm Gladwell; Ashton has done you one better."
　　　　　　　　—Larry Downes, author of the *New York Times* bestseller *Unleashing the Killer App* and coauthor of *Big Bang Disruption*

"Kevin Ashton's new book *How to Fly a Horse* is all about the creative sorcery and motivational magic necessary to make impossible things happen in teams or as individuals. Through numerous examples of creative genius ranging from Einstein to the creators of *South Park* to the invention of jet planes and concertos, Ashton reveals the secrets of the great scientists, artists, and industrialists of the last few centuries."
　　　　　　　—John Maeda, author of *The Laws of Simplicity* and founder of the SIMPLICITY Consortium at the MIT Media Lab

KEVIN ASHTON

HOW TO FLY A HORSE

Kevin Ashton led pioneering work on RFID (radio frequency identification) networks, for which he coined the term "the Internet of Things," and cofounded the Auto-ID Center at MIT. His writing about innovation and technology has appeared in *Quartz*, *Medium*, *The Atlantic*, and *The New York Times*.

www.howtoflyahorse.com

HOW TO
FLY A HORSE

THE SECRET HISTORY OF CREATION,

INVENTION, AND DISCOVERY

KEVIN ASHTON

ANCHOR BOOKS

A DIVISION OF PENGUIN RANDOM HOUSE LLC

NEW YORK

FIRST ANCHOR BOOKS EDITION, SEPTEMBER 2015

Copyright © 2015 by Kevin Ashton

All rights reserved. Published in the United States by Anchor Books,
a division of Penguin Random House LLC, New York, and distributed
in Canada by Random House of Canada, a division of Penguin Random
House Ltd., Toronto. Originally published in hardcover in the United
States by Doubleday, a division of Penguin Random House LLC,
New York, in 2015.

Anchor Books and colophon are registered trademarks of Penguin
Random House LLC.

The Library of Congress has cataloged the Doubleday edition as
follows:
Ashton, Kevin.
How to fly a horse : the secret history of creation, invention, and
discovery / Kevin Ashton
pages cm
1. Creative ability—History.   2. Inventions—History.
3. Success—History.   1. Title.
B105.C74A84 2015   609—dc23   2014030841

Anchor Books Trade Paperback ISBN: 978-0-8041-7006-2
eBook ISBN: 978-0-385-53860-2

Author photograph © hayeshayes.com
Book design by Pei Loi Koay

www.anchorbooks.com

Printed in the United States of America
10   9   8   7   6

FOR SASHA, ARLO, AND THEO

A genius is the one most like himself.

— THELONIOUS MONK

Work your best at being you. That's where home is.

— BILL MURRAY

CONTENTS

PREFACE: THE MYTH

In 1815, Germany's *General Music Journal* published a letter in which Mozart described his creative process:

> When I am, as it were, completely myself, entirely alone, and of good cheer; say traveling in a carriage, or walking after a good meal, or during the night when I cannot sleep; it is on such occasions that my ideas flow best and most abundantly. All this fires my soul, and provided I am not disturbed, my subject enlarges itself, becomes methodized and defined, and the whole, though it be long, stands almost finished and complete in my mind, so that I can survey it, like a fine picture or a beautiful statue, at a glance. Nor do I hear in my imagination the parts successively, but I hear them, as it were, all at once. When I proceed to write down my ideas the committing to paper is done quickly enough, for everything is, as I said before, already finished; and it rarely differs on paper from what it was in my imagination.

In other words, Mozart's greatest symphonies, concertos, and operas came to him complete when he was alone and in a good mood. He needed no tools to compose them. Once he had finished imagining his masterpieces, all he had to do was write them down.

This letter has been used to explain creation many times. Parts of it appear in *The Mathematician's Mind,* written by Jacques Hadamard in 1945, in *Creativity: Selected Readings,* edited by Philip Vernon in 1976, in Roger Penrose's award-winning 1989 book, *The Emperor's New Mind,* and it is alluded to in Jonah Lehrer's 2012 bestseller *Imagine.* It influenced the poets Pushkin and Goethe and the playwright Peter Shaffer. Directly and indirectly, it helped shape common beliefs about creating.

But there is a problem. Mozart did not write this letter. It is a forgery. This was first shown in 1856 by Mozart's biographer Otto Jahn and has been confirmed by other scholars since.

Mozart's real letters—to his father, to his sister, and to others—reveal his true creative process. He was exceptionally talented, but he did not write by magic. He sketched his compositions, revised them, and sometimes got stuck. He could not work without a piano or harpsichord. He would set work aside and return to it later. He considered theory and craft while writing, and he thought a lot about rhythm, melody, and harmony. Even though his talent and a lifetime of practice made him fast and fluent, his work was exactly that: work. Masterpieces did not come to him complete in uninterrupted streams of imagination, nor without an instrument, nor did he write them down whole and unchanged. The letter is not only forged, it is false.

It lives on because it appeals to romantic prejudices about invention. There is a myth about how something new comes to be. Geniuses have dramatic moments of insight where great things and thoughts are born whole. Poems are written in dreams. Symphonies are composed complete. Science is accomplished with eureka shrieks. Businesses are built by magic touch. Something is not, then is. We do not see the road from nothing to new, and maybe we do not want to. Artistry must be misty magic, not sweat and grind. It dulls the luster to think that every elegant equation, beautiful painting, and brilliant machine is born of effort and error, the progeny of false starts and failures, and that each maker is as flawed, small, and mortal as the rest of us. It is seductive to conclude that great innovation is delivered to us by miracle via genius. And so the myth.

The myth has shaped how we think about creating for as long as creating has been thought about. In ancient civilizations, people believed that things could be discovered but not created. For them, everything had *already* been created; they shared the perspective of Carl Sagan's joke on this topic: "If you want to make an apple pie from scratch, you must first invent the universe." In the Middle Ages, creation was possible but was reserved for divinity and those with divine inspiration. In the Renaissance, humans were finally thought capable of creation, but they had to be *great men*—Leonardo, Michelangelo, Botticelli, and the like. As the nineteenth century turned into the twentieth, creating became a subject for philosophical, then psychological investigation. The question being investigated was "How do the great men do it?" and the answer had the residue of medieval divine intervention. A lot of the meat of the myth was added at this time, with the same few anecdotes about epiphanies and genius—including hoaxes like Mozart's letter— being circulated and recirculated. In 1926, Alfred North Whitehead made a noun from a verb and gave the myth its name: *creativity*.

The creativity myth implies that few people can be creative, that any successful creator will experience dramatic flashes of insight, and that creating is more like magic than work. A rare few have what it takes, and for them it comes easy. Anybody else's creative efforts are doomed.

How to Fly a Horse is about why the myth is wrong.

I believed the myth until 1999. My early career—at London University's student newspaper, at a Bloomsbury noodle start-up called Wagamama, and at a soap and paper company called Procter &

Gamble—suggested that I was not good at creating. I struggled to execute my ideas. When I tried, people got angry. When I succeeded, they forgot that the idea was mine. I read every book I could find about creation, and each one said the same thing: ideas come magically, people greet them warmly, and creators are winners. My ideas came gradually, people greeted them with heat instead of warmth, and I felt like a loser. My performance reviews were bad. I was always in danger of being fired. I could not understand why my creative experiences were not like the ones in the books.

It first occurred to me that the books might be wrong in 1997, when I was trying to solve an apparently boring problem that turned out to be interesting. I could not keep a popular shade of Procter & Gamble lipstick on store shelves. Half of all stores were out of stock at any given time. After much research, I discovered that the cause of the problem was insufficient information. The only way to see what was on a shelf at any moment was to go look. This was a fundamental limit of twentieth-century information technology. Almost all the data entered into computers in the 1900s came from people typing on keyboards or, sometimes, scanning bar codes. Store workers did not have time to stare at shelves all day, then enter data about what they saw, so every store's computer system was blind. Shopkeepers did not discover that my lipstick was out of stock; shoppers did. The shoppers shrugged and picked a different one, in which case I probably lost the sale, or they did not buy lipstick at all, in which case the store lost the sale, too. The missing lipstick was one of the world's smallest problems, but it was a symptom of one of the world's *biggest* problems: computers were brains without senses.

This was so obvious that few people noticed it. Computers were fifty years old in 1997. Most people had grown up with them and had grown used to how they worked. Computers processed data that people entered. As their name confirmed, computers were regarded as thinking machines, not sensing machines.

But this is not how intelligent machines were originally conceived. In 1950, Alan Turing, computing's inventor, wrote, "Machines will eventually compete with men in all purely intellectual fields. But which are the best ones to start with? Many people think that a very abstract activity, like the playing of chess, would be best. It can also be maintained that it is best to provide the machine with the best sense organs that money can buy. Both approaches should be tried."

Yet few people tried that second approach. In the twentieth century, computers got faster and smaller and were connected together, but they did not get "the best sense organs that money can buy." They did not get any "sense organs" at all. And so in May 1997, a computer called Deep Blue could beat the reigning human chess world champion, Garry Kasparov, for the first time ever, but there was no way a computer could see if a lipstick was on a shelf. This was the problem I wanted to solve.

I put a tiny radio microchip into a lipstick and an antenna into a shelf; this, under the catchall name "Storage System," became my first patented invention. The microchip saved money and memory by connecting to the Internet, newly public in the 1990s, and saving its data there. To help Procter & Gamble executives understand this system for connecting things like lipstick—and diapers, laundry detergent, potato chips, or any other object—to the Internet, I gave it a short and ungrammatical name: "the Internet of Things." To help make it real, I started working with Sanjay Sarma, David Brock, and Sunny Siu at the Massachusetts Institute of Technology. In 1999, we cofounded a research center, and I emigrated from England to the United States to become its executive director.

In 2003, our research had 103 corporate sponsors, plus additional labs in universities in Australia, China, England, Japan, and Switzerland, and the Massachusetts Institute of Technology signed a lucrative license deal to make our technology commercially available.

In 2013, my phrase "Internet of Things" was added to the Oxford

Dictionaries, which defined it as "a proposed development of the Internet in which everyday objects have network connectivity, allowing them to send and receive data."

Nothing about this experience resembled the stories in the "creativity" books I had read. There was no magic, and there had been few flashes of inspiration—just tens of thousands of hours of work. Building the Internet of Things was slow and hard, fraught with politics, infested with mistakes, unconnected to grand plans or strategies. I learned to succeed by learning to fail. I learned to expect conflict. I learned not to be surprised by adversity but to prepare for it.

I used what I discovered to help build technology businesses. One was named one of the ten "Most Innovative Companies in the Internet of Things" in 2014, and two were sold to bigger companies—one less than a year after I started it.

I also gave talks about my experiences of creating. My most popular talk attracted so many people with so many questions that, each time I gave it, I had to plan to stay for at least an hour afterward to answer questions from audience members. That talk is the foundation of this book. Each chapter tells the true story of a creative person; each story comes from a different place, time, and creative field and highlights an important insight about creating. There are tales within the tales, and departures into science, history, and philosophy.

Taken together, the stories reveal a pattern for how humans make new things, one that is both encouraging and challenging. The encouraging part is that everyone can create, and we can show that fairly conclusively. The challenging part is that there is no magic moment of creation. Creators spend almost all their time creating, persevering despite doubt, failure, ridicule, and rejection until they succeed in making something new and useful. There are no tricks, shortcuts, or get-creative-quick schemes. The process is ordinary, even if the outcome is not.

Creating is not magic but work.

HOW TO
FLY A HORSE

CHAPTER I

CREATING IS ORDINARY

1 | EDMOND

In the Indian Ocean, fifteen hundred miles east of Africa and four thousand miles west of Australia, lies an island that the Portuguese knew as Santa Apolónia, the British as Bourbon, and the French, for a time, as Île Bonaparte. Today it is called Réunion. A bronze statue stands in Sainte-Suzanne, one of Réunion's oldest towns. It shows an African boy in 1841, dressed as if for church, in a single-breasted jacket, bow tie, and flat-front pants that gather on the ground. He wears no shoes. He holds out his right hand, not in greeting but with his thumb and fingers coiled against his palm, perhaps about to flip a coin. He is twelve years old, an orphan and a slave, and his name is Edmond.

The world has few statues of Africa's enslaved children. To understand why Edmond stands here, on this lonely ocean speck, his hand held just so, we must travel west and back, thousands of miles and hundreds of years.

On Mexico's Gulf Coast, the people of Papantla have dried the fruit of a vinelike orchid and used it as a spice for more millennia than they remember. In 1400, the Aztecs took it as tax and called it "black flower." In 1519, the Spanish introduced it to Europe and called it "little pod," or *vainilla*. In 1703, French botanist Charles Plumier renamed it "vanilla."

Vanilla is hard to farm. Vanilla orchids are great creeping plants, not at all like the *Phalaenopsis* flowers we put in our homes. They can live for centuries and grow large, sometimes covering thousands of square feet or climbing five stories high. It has been said that lady's slippers are the tallest orchids and tigers the most massive, but vanilla dwarfs them both. For thousands of years, its flower was a secret known only to the people who grew it. It is not black, as the Aztecs were led to believe, but a pale tube that blooms once a year and dies in a morning. If a flower is pollinated, it produces a long, green, beanlike capsule that takes nine months to ripen. It must be picked at precisely the right time. Too soon and it will be too small; too late and it will split and spoil. Picked beans are left in the sun for days, until they stop ripening. They do not smell of vanilla yet. That aroma develops during curing: two weeks on wool blankets outdoors each day before being wrapped to sweat each night. Then the beans are dried for four months and finished by hand with straightening and massage. The result is oily black lashes worth their weight in silver or gold.

Vanilla captivated the Europeans. Anne of Austria, daughter of Spain's King Philip III, drank it in hot chocolate. Queen Elizabeth I of England ate it in puddings. King Henry IV of France made adulterating it a criminal offense punishable by a beating. Thomas Jefferson discovered it in Paris and wrote America's first recipe for vanilla ice cream.

But no one outside Mexico could make it grow. For three hundred years, vines transported to Europe would not flower. It was only in 1806 that vanilla first bloomed in a London greenhouse and three more decades before a plant in Belgium bore Europe's first fruit.

The missing ingredient was whatever pollinated the orchid in the wild. The flower in London was a chance occurrence. The fruit in Belgium came from complicated artificial pollination. It was not until late in the nineteenth century that Charles Darwin inferred that a Mexican insect must be vanilla's pollinator, and not until late in the twentieth century that the insect was identified as a glossy green bee called *Euglossa viridissima.* Without the pollinator, Europe had a problem. Demand for vanilla was increasing, but Mexico was producing only one or two tons a year. The Europeans needed another source of supply. The Spanish hoped vanilla would thrive in the Philippines. The Dutch planted it in Java. The British sent it to India. All attempts failed.

This is where Edmond enters. He was born in Sainte-Suzanne in 1829. At that time Réunion was called Bourbon. His mother, Mélise, died in childbirth. He did not know his father. Slaves did not have last names—he was simply "Edmond." When Edmond was a few years old, his owner, Elvire Bellier-Beaumont, gave him to her brother Ferréol in nearby Belle-Vue. Ferréol owned a plantation. Edmond grew up following Ferréol Bellier-Beaumont around the estate, learning about its fruits, vegetables, and flowers, including one of its oddities—a vanilla vine Ferréol had kept alive since 1822.

Like all the vanilla on Réunion, Ferréol's vine was sterile. French colonists had been trying to grow the plant on the island since 1819. After a few false starts—some orchids were the wrong species, some soon died—they eventually had a hundred live vines. But Réunion saw no more success with vanilla than Europe's other colonies had. The orchids seldom flowered and never bore fruit.

Then, one morning late in 1841, as the spring of the Southern Hemisphere came to the island, Ferréol took his customary walk with Edmond and was surprised to find two green capsules hanging from the vine. His orchid, barren for twenty years, had fruit. What came next surprised him even more. Twelve-year-old Edmond said he had pollinated the plant himself.

To this day there are people in Réunion who do not believe it. It seems impossible to them that a child, a slave, and, above all, an *African,* could have solved the problem that beat Europe for hundreds of years. They say it was an accident—that he was trying to damage the flowers after an argument with Ferréol or he was busy seducing a girl in the gardens when it happened.

Ferréol did not believe the boy at first. But when more fruit appeared, days later, he asked for a demonstration. Edmond pulled back the lip of a vanilla flower and, using a toothpick-sized piece of bamboo to lift the part that prevents self-fertilization, he gently pinched its pollen-bearing anther and pollen-receiving stigma together. Today the French call this *le geste d'Edmond*—Edmond's gesture. Ferréol called the other plantation owners together, and soon Edmond was traveling the island teaching other slaves how to pollinate vanilla orchids. After seven years, Réunion's annual production was a hundred pounds of dried vanilla pods. After ten years, it was two tons. By the end of the century, it was two *hundred* tons and had surpassed the output of Mexico.

Ferréol freed Edmond in June 1848, six months before most of Réunion's other slaves. Edmond was given the last name Albius, the Latin word for "whiter." Some suspect this was a compliment in racially charged Réunion. Others think it was an insult from the naming registry. Whatever the intention, things went badly. Edmond left the plantation for the city and was imprisoned for theft. Ferréol was unable to prevent the incarceration but succeeded in getting Edmond released after three years instead of five. Edmond died in 1880, at the age of fifty-one. A small story in a Réunion newspaper, *Le Moniteur,* described it as a "destitute and miserable end."

Edmond's innovation spread to Mauritius, the Seychelles, and the huge island to Réunion's west, Madagascar. Madagascar has a perfect environment for vanilla. By the twentieth century, it was producing most of the world's vanilla, with a crop that in some years was worth more than $100 million.

The demand for vanilla increased with the supply. Today it is the world's most popular spice and, after saffron, the second most expensive. It has become an ingredient in thousands of things, some obvious, some not. Over a third of the world's ice cream is Jefferson's original flavor, vanilla. Vanilla is the principal flavoring in Coke, and the Coca-Cola Company is said to be the world's largest vanilla buyer. The fine fragrances Chanel No. 5, Opium, and Angel use the world's most expensive vanilla, worth $10,000 a pound. Most chocolate contains vanilla. So do many cleaning products, beauty products, and candles. In 1841, on the day of Edmond's demonstration to Ferréol, the world produced fewer than two thousand vanilla beans, all in Mexico, all the result of pollination by bees. On the same day in 2010, the world produced more than five million vanilla beans, in countries including Indonesia, China, and Kenya, almost all of them—including the ones grown in Mexico—the result of *le geste d'Edmond*.

2 | COUNTING CREATORS

What is unusual about Edmond's story is not that a young slave created something important but that he got the credit for it. Ferréol worked hard to ensure that Edmond was remembered. He told Réunion's plantation owners that it was Edmond who first pollinated vanilla. He lobbied on Edmond's behalf, saying, "This young negro deserves recognition from this country. It owes him a debt, for starting up a new industry with a fabulous product." When Jean Michel Claude Richard, director of Réunion's botanical gardens, said he had developed the technique and shown it to Edmond, Ferréol intervened. "Through old age, faulty memory or some other cause," he wrote, "Mr. Richard now imagines that he himself discovered the secret of how to pollinate vanilla, and imagines that he taught the technique to the person who discovered it! Let us leave him to his fantasies." Without Ferréol's great effort, the truth would have been lost.

In most cases, the truth *has* been lost. We do not know, for example, who first realized that the fruit of an orchid could be cured until it tastes good. Vanilla is an innovation inherited from people long forgotten. This is not exceptional; it is normal. Most of our world is made of innovations inherited from people long forgotten—not people who were rare but people who were common.

Before the Renaissance, concepts like authorship, inventorship, or claiming credit barely existed. Until the early fifteenth century, "author" meant "father," from the Latin word for "master," *auctor*. *Auctor*-ship implied authority, something that, in most of the world, had been the divine right of kings and religious leaders since Gilgamesh ruled Uruk four thousand years earlier. It was not to be shared with mere mortals. An "inventor," from *invenire*, "find," was a discoverer, not a creator, until the 1550s. "Credit," from *credo*, "trust," did not mean "acknowledgment" until the late sixteenth century.

This is one reason we know so little about who made what before the late 1300s. It is not that no records were made—writing has been around for millennia. Nor is it that there was no creation—everything we use today has roots stretching back to the beginning of humanity. The problem is that, until the Renaissance, people who created things didn't matter much. The idea that at least *some* people who create things should be recognized was a big step forward. It is why we know that Johannes Gutenberg invented printing in Germany in 1440 but not who invented windmills in England in 1185, and that Giunta Pisano painted the crucifix in Bologna's Basilica of San Domenico in 1250 but not who made the mosaic of Saint Demetrios in Kiev's Golden-Domed Monastery in 1110.

There are exceptions. We know the names of hundreds of ancient Greek philosophers, from Acrion to Zeno, as well as a few Greek engineers of the same period, such as Eupalinos, Philo, and Ctesibius. We also know of a number of Chinese artists from around 400 C.E. onward, including the calligrapher Wei Shuo and her student Wang Xizhi. But the general principle holds. Broadly speaking, our knowledge of who created what started around the middle of the thirteenth century, increased during the European Renaissance of the fourteenth to seventeenth centuries, and has kept increasing ever since. The reasons for the change are complicated and the subject of debate among historians—they include power struggles within the churches of Europe, the rise of science, and the rediscovery of ancient philosophy—but there is little doubt that most creators started getting credit for their creations only after the year 1200.

One way this happened was through patents, which give credit within rigorous constraints. The first patents were issued in Italy in the fifteenth century, in Britain and the United States in the seventeenth century, and in France in the eighteenth century. The modern U.S. Patent and Trademark Office granted its first patent on July 31, 1790. It granted its *eight millionth* patent on August 16, 2011. The patent office does not keep records of how many different people have been granted patents, but economist Manuel Trajtenberg developed a way of working it out. He analyzed names phonetically and compared matches with zip codes, coinventors, and other information to identify each unique inventor. Trajtenberg's data suggests that more than six million distinct individuals had received U.S. patents by the end of 2011.

The inventors are not distributed evenly across the years. Their numbers are increasing. The first million inventors took 130 years to get their patents, the second million 35 years, the third million 22 years, the fourth million 17 years, the fifth million 10 years, and the sixth million inventors took 8 years. Even with foreign inventors removed and adjustments for population increase, the trend is unmistakable. In 1800, about one in every 175,000 Americans was granted a first patent. In 2000, one in every 4,000 Americans received one.

Not all creations get a patent. Books, songs, plays, movies, and other works of art are protected by copyright instead, which in the United States is managed by the Copyright Office, part of the Library of Congress. Copyrights show the same growth as patents. In 1870, 5,600 works were registered for copyright. In 1886, the number grew to more than 31,000, and Ainsworth Spofford, the librarian of Congress, had to plead for more space. "Again it becomes necessary to refer to the difficulty and embarrassment of prosecuting the annual enumeration of the books and pamphlets recently completed," he wrote in a report to Congress. "Each year and each month adds to the painfully overcrowded condition of the collections, and although many rooms have been filled with the overflow from the main Library, the difficulty of handling so large an accumulation of unshelved books is constantly growing." This became a refrain. In 1946, register of copyrights Sam Bass Warner reported that "the number of registrations of copyright claims rose to 202,144 the greatest number in the history of the Copyright Office, and a number so far beyond the capacities of the existing staff that Congress, responding to the need, generously provided for additional personnel." In 1991, copyright registrations reached a peak of more than 600,000. As with patents, the increase exceeded population growth. In 1870, there was one copyright registration for every 7,000 U.S. citizens. In 1991, there was one copyright registration for every 400 U.S. citizens.

More credit is given for creation in science, too. The *Science Citation Index* tracks the world's leading peer-reviewed journals in science and technology. For 1955, the index lists 125,000 new scientific papers—about one for every 1,350 U.S. citizens. For 2005, it lists more than 1,250,000 scientific papers—one for every 250 U.S. citizens.

Patents, copyrights, and peer-reviewed papers are imperfect proxies. Their growth is driven by money as well as knowledge. Not all work that gets this recognition is necessarily good. And, as we shall see later, giving credit to individuals is misleading. Creation is a chain reaction: thousands of people contribute, most of them anonymous, all of them creative. But, with numbers so big, and even though we miscount and undercount, the point is hard to miss: over the last few centuries, more people from more fields have been getting more credit as creators.

We have not become more creative. The people of the Renaissance were born into a world enriched by tens of thousands of years of human invention: clothes, cathedrals, mathematics, writing, art, agriculture, ships, roads, pets, houses, bread, and beer, to name a fraction. The second half of the twentieth century and the first decades of the twenty-first century may appear to be a time of unprecedented innovation, but there are other reasons for this, and we will discuss them later. What the numbers show is something else: when we start counting creators, we find that a lot of people create. In 2011, almost as many Americans received their first patent as attended a typical NASCAR race. Creating is not for an elite few. It is not even *close* to being for an elite few.

The question is not whether invention is the sole province of a tiny minority but the opposite: how many of us are creative? The answer, hidden in plain sight, is all of us. Resistance to the possibility that Edmond, a boy with no formal education, could create something important is grounded in the myth that creating is extraordinary. Creating is not extraordinary, even if its results sometimes are. Creation is human. It is all of us. It is everybody.

3 | THE SPECIES OF NEW

Even without numbers, it is easy to see that creation is not the exclusive domain of rare geniuses with occasional inspiration. Creation surrounds us. Everything we see and feel is a result of it or has been touched by it. There is too much creation for creating to be infrequent.

This book is creation. You probably heard about it via creation, or the person who told you about it did. It was written using creation, and creation is one reason you can understand it. You are either lit by creation now or you will be, come sundown. You are heated or cooled or at least insulated by creation—by clothes and walls and windows. The sky above you is softened by fumes and smog in the day and polluted by electric light at night—all results of creation. Watch, and it will be crossed by an airplane or a satellite or the slow dissolve of a vapor trail. Apples, cows, and all other things agricultural, apparently natural, are also creation: the result of tens of thousands of years of innovation in trading, breeding, feeding, farming, and—unless you live on the farm—preservation and transportation.

You are a result of creation. It helped your parents meet. It likely assisted your birth, gestation, and maybe conception. Before you were born, it eradicated diseases and dangers that could have killed you. After, it inoculated and protected you against others. It treated the illnesses you caught. It helps heal your wounds and relieve your pain. It did the same for your parents and their parents. It recently cleaned you, fed you, and quenched your thirst. It is why you are where you are. Cars, shoes, saddles, or ships transported you, your parents, or your grandparents to the place you now call home, which was less habitable before creation—too hot in the summer or too cold in the winter or too wet or too swampy or too far from potable water or freely growing food or prowled by predators or all of the above.

Listen, and you hear creation. It is in the sound of passing sirens; distant music; church bells; cell phones; lawn mowers and snow blowers; basketballs and bicycles; waves on breakers; hammers and saws; the creak and crackle of melting ice cubes; even the bark of a dog, a wolf changed by millennia of selective breeding by humans; or the purr of a cat, the descendant of one of just five African wildcats that humans have been selectively breeding for ten thousand years. Anything that is as it is due to conscious human intervention is invention, creation, new.

Creation is so around and inside us that we cannot look without seeing it or listen without hearing it. As a result, we do not notice it at all. We live in symbiosis with new. It is not something we do; it is something we are. It affects our life expectancy, our height and weight and gait, our way of life, where we live, and the things we think and do. We change our technology, and our technology changes us. This is true for every human being on the planet. It has been true for two thousand generations; ever since the moment our species started thinking about improving its tools.

Anything we create is a tool—a fabrication with purpose. There is nothing special about species with tools. Beavers make dams. Birds build nests. Dolphins use sponges to hunt for fish. Chimpanzees use sticks to dig for roots and stone hammers to open hard-shelled food. Otters use rocks to break open crabs. Elephants repel flies by making branches into switches they wave with their trunks. Clearly our tools are better. The Hoover Dam beats the beaver dam. But why?

Our tools have not been better for long. Six million years ago, evolution forked. One path led to chimpanzees—distant relatives, but the closest living ones we have. The other path led to us. Unknown numbers of human species emerged. There was *Homo habilis, Homo heidelbergensis, Homo ergaster, Homo rudolfensis,* and many others, some whose status is still controversial, some still to be discovered. All human. None us.

Like other species, these humans used tools. The earliest were pointed stones used to cut nuts, fruit, and maybe meat. Later, some human species made two-sided hand axes requiring careful masonry and nearly perfect symmetry. But apart from minor adjustments, human tools were monotonous for a million years, unchanged no matter when or where they were used, passed through twenty-five thousand generations without modification. Despite the mental focus needed to make it, the design of that early human hand ax, like the design of a beaver dam or bird's nest, came from instinct, not thought.

Humans that looked like us first appeared 200,000 years ago. This was the species called *Homo sapiens*. Members of *Homo sapiens* did not act like us in one important way: their tools were simple and did not change. We do not know why. Their brains were the same size as ours. They had our opposable thumbs, our senses, and our strength. Yet for 150,000 years, like the other human species of their time, they made nothing new.

Then, 50,000 years ago, something happened. The crude, barely recognizable stone tools *Homo sapiens* had been using began to change—and change quickly. Until this moment, this species, like all other animals, did not innovate. Their tools were the same as their parents' tools and their grandparents' tools and their great-grandparents' tools. They made them, but they didn't make them better. The tools were inherited, instinctive, and immutable—products of evolution, not conscious creation.

Then came by far the most important moment in human history—the day one member of the species looked at a tool and thought, "I can make this better." The descendants of this individual are called *Homo sapiens sapiens*. They are our ancestors. They are us. What the human race created was creation itself.

The ability to change anything was the change that changed everything. The urge to make better tools gave us a massive advantage over all other species, including rival species of humans. Within a few tens of thousands of years, all other humans were extinct, displaced by an anatomically similar species with only one important difference: ever-improving technology.

What makes our species different and dominant is innovation. What is special about us is not the size of our brains, speech, or the mere fact that we use tools. It is that each of us is in our own way driven to make things better. We occupy the evolutionary niche of new. The niche of new is not the property of a privileged few. It is what makes humans human.

We do not know exactly what evolutionary spark caused the ignition of innovation 50,000 years ago. It left no trace in the fossil record. We do know that our bodies, including our brain size, did not change—our immediate pre-innovation ancestor, *Homo sapiens,* looked exactly like us. That makes the prime suspect our mind: the precise arrangement of, and connections between, our brain cells. Something structural seems to have changed there—perhaps as a result of 150,000 years of fine-tuning. Whatever it was, it had profound implications, and today it lives on in everyone. Behavioral neurologist Richard Caselli says, "Despite great qualitative and quantitative differences between individuals, the neurobiologic principles of creative behavior are the same from the least to the most creative among us." Put simply, we all have creative minds.

This is one reason the creativity myth is so terribly wrong. Creating is not rare. We are all born to do it. If it seems magical, it is because it is innate. If it seems like some of us are better at it than others, that is because it is part of being human, like talking or walking. We are not all equally creative, just as we are not all equally gifted orators or athletes. But we can all create.

The human race's creative power is distributed in all of us, not concentrated in some of us. Our creations are too great and too numerous to come from a few steps by a few people. They must come from many steps by many people. Invention is incremental—a series of slight and constant changes. Some changes open doors to new worlds of opportunity and we call them breakthroughs. Others are marginal. But when we look carefully, we will always find one small change leading to another, sometimes within one mind, often among several, sometimes across continents or between generations, sometimes taking hours or days and occasionally centuries, the baton of innovation passing in an endless relay of renewal. Creating accretes and compounds, and as a consequence, every day, each human life is made possible by the sum of all previous human creations. Every object in our life, however old or new, however apparently humble or simple, holds the stories, thoughts, and courage of thousands of people, some living, most dead—the accumulated new of fifty thousand years. Our tools and art are our humanity, our inheritance, and the everlasting legacy of our ancestors. The things we make are the speech of our species: stories of triumph, courage, and creation, of optimism, adaptation, and hope; tales not of one person here and there but of one people everywhere; written in a common language, not African, American, Asian, or European but human.

There are many beautiful things about creating being human and innate. One is that we all create in more or less the same way. Our individual strengths and tendencies of course cause differences, but they are small and few relative to the similarities, which are great and many. We are more like Leonardo, Mozart, and Einstein than not.

4 | AN END TO GENIUS

The Renaissance belief that creating is reserved for genius survived through the Enlightenment of the seventeenth century, the Romanticism of the eighteenth century, and the Industrial Revolution of the nineteenth century. It was not until the middle of the twentieth century that the alternative position—that everyone is capable of creation—first emerged from early studies of the brain.

In the 1940s, the brain was an enigma. The body's secrets had been revealed by several centuries of medicine, but the brain, producing consciousness without moving parts, remained a puzzle. Here is one reason theories of creation resorted to magic: the brain, throne of creation, was three pounds of gray and impenetrable mystery.

As the West recovered from World War II, new technologies appeared. One was the computer. This mechanical mind made understanding the brain seem possible for the first time. In 1952, Ross Ashby synthesized the excitement in a book called *Design for a Brain*. He summarized the new thinking elegantly:

> The most fundamental facts are that the earth is over 2,000,000,000 years old and that natural selection has been winnowing the living organisms incessantly. As a result they are today highly specialized in the arts of survival, and among these arts has been the development of a brain, an organ that has been developed in evolution as a specialized means to survival. The nervous system, and living matter in general, will be assumed to be essentially similar to all other matter. No *deus ex machina* will be invoked.

Put simply: brains don't need magic.

A San Franciscan named Allen Newell came of academic age during this period. Drawn by the energy of the era, he abandoned his plan to become a forest ranger (in part because his first job was feeding gangrenous calves' livers to fingerling trout), became a scientist instead, and then, one Friday afternoon in November 1954, experienced what he would later call a "conversion experience" during a seminar on mechanical pattern recognition. He decided to devote his life to a single scientific question: "How can the human mind occur in the physical universe?"

"We now know that the world is governed by physics," he explained, "and we now understand the way biology nestles comfortably within that. The issue is how does the mind do that as well? The answer must have the details. I've got to know how the gears clank, how the pistons go and all of that."

As he embarked on this work, Newell became one of the first people to realize that creating did not require genius. In a 1959 paper called "The Processes of Creative Thinking," he reviewed what little psychological data there was about creative work, then set out his radical idea: "Creative thinking is simply a special kind of problem-solving behavior." He made the point in the understated language academics use when they know they are onto something:

> The data currently available about the processes involved in creative and non-creative thinking show no particular differences between the two. It is impossible to distinguish, by looking at the statistics describing the processes, the highly skilled practitioner from the rank amateur. Creative activity appears simply to be a special class of problem-solving activity characterized by novelty, unconventionality, persistence, and difficulty in problem formulation.

It was the beginning of the end for genius and creation. Making intelligent machines forced new rigor on the study of thought. The capacity to create was starting to look more and more like an innate function of the human brain—possible with standard equipment, no genius necessary.

Newell did not claim that everyone was equally creative. Creating, like any human ability, comes in a spectrum of competence. But everybody can do it. There is no electric fence between those who can create and those who cannot, with genius on one side and the general population on the other.

Newell's work, along with the work of others in the artificial intelligence community, undermined the myth of creativity. As a result, some of the next generation of scientists started to think about creation differently. One of the most important of these was Robert Weisberg, a cognitive psychologist at Philadelphia's Temple University.

Weisberg was an undergraduate during the first years of the artificial intelligence revolution, spending the early 1960s in New York before getting his PhD from Princeton and joining the faculty at Temple in 1967. He spent his career proving that creating is innate, ordinary, and for everybody.

Weisberg's view is simple. He builds on Newell's contention that creative thinking is the same as problem solving, then extends it to say that creative thinking is the same as thinking in general but with a creative result. In Weisberg's words, "when one says of someone that he or she is 'thinking creatively,' one is commenting on the outcome of the process, not on the process itself. Although the impact of creative ideas and products can sometimes be profound, the mechanisms through which an innovation comes about can be very ordinary."

Said another way, normal thinking is rich and complex—so rich and complex that it can sometimes yield extraordinary—or "creative"—results. We do not need other processes. Weisberg shows this in two ways: with carefully designed experiments and detailed case studies of creative acts—from the painting of Picasso's *Guernica* to the discovery of DNA and the music of Billie Holiday. In each example, by using a combination of experiment and history, Weisberg demonstrates how creating can be explained without resorting to genius and great leaps of the imagination.

Weisberg has not written about Edmond, but his theory works for Edmond's story. At first, Edmond's discovery of how to pollinate vanilla came from nowhere and seemed miraculous. But toward the end of his life, Ferréol Bellier-Beaumont revealed how the young slave solved the mystery of the black flower.

Ferréol began his story in 1793, when German naturalist Konrad Sprengel discovered that plants reproduced sexually. Sprengel called it "the secret of nature." The secret was not well received. Sprengel's peers did not want to hear that flowers had a sex life. His findings spread anyway, especially among botanists and farmers who were more interested in growing good plants than in judging floral morality. And so Ferréol knew how to manually fertilize watermelon, by "marrying the male and female parts together." He showed this to Edmond, who, as Ferréol described it, later "realized that the vanilla flower also had male and female elements, and worked out for himself how to join them together." Edmond's discovery, despite its huge economic impact, was an incremental step. It is no less creative as a result. All great discoveries, even ones that look like transforming leaps, are short hops.

Weisberg's work, with subtitles like *Genius and Other Myths* and *Beyond the Myth of Genius,* did not eliminate the magical view of creation nor the idea that people who create are a breed apart. It is easier to sell secrets. Titles available in today's bookstores include *10 Things Nobody Told You About Being Creative, 39 Keys to Creativity, 52 Ways to Get and Keep Your Creativity Flowing, 62 Exercises to Unlock Your Most Creative Ideas, 100 What-Ifs of Creativity,* and *250 Exercises to Wake Up Your Brain.* Weisberg's books are out of print. The myth of creativity does not die easily.

But it is becoming less fashionable, and Weisberg is not the only expert advocating for an epiphany-free, everybody-can theory of creation. Ken Robinson was awarded a knighthood for his work on creation and education and is known for the moving, funny talks he gives at an annual conference in California called TED (for technology, entertainment, and design). One of his themes is how education suppresses creation. He describes "the really extraordinary capacity that children have, their capacity for innovation," and says that "all kids have tremendous talents and we squander them, pretty ruthlessly." Robinson's conclusion is that "creativity now is as important in education as literacy, and we should treat it with the same status." Cartoonist Hugh MacLeod makes the same point more colorfully: "Everyone is born creative; everyone is given a box of crayons in kindergarten. Being suddenly hit years later with the 'creative bug' is just a wee voice telling you, 'I'd like my crayons back, please.'"

If genius is a prerequisite for creating, it should be possible to identify creative ability in advance. The experiment has been tried many times. The best-known version was started in 1921 by Lewis Terman and still continues. Terman, a cognitive psychologist born in the nineteenth century, was a eugenicist who believed the human race could be improved with selective breeding, a classifier of individuals according to their abilities as he perceived them. His most famous classification system was the Stanford-Binet IQ test, which placed children on a scale "ranging from idiocy on the one hand to genius on the other," with classifications in between including "retarded," "feebleminded," "delinquent," "dull normal," "average," "superior," and "very superior." Terman was so sure of his test's accuracy that he thought its results revealed immutable destiny. He also believed, like all eugenicists, that African Americans, Mexicans, and others were genetically inferior to English-speaking white people. He described them as "the world's hewers of wood and drawers of water" who lacked the ability to be "intelligent voters or capable citizens." The children, he said, "should be segregated in special classes." The adults should "not be allowed to reproduce." *Unlike* almost all eugenicists, Terman set out to prove his prejudices.

His experiment was called Genetic Studies of Genius. It was a longitudinal study—meaning it would follow its subjects for a long period of time. It tracked more than 1,500 children who lived in California, all of whom were identified as "gifted" by Terman's IQ test or some similar scheme. Nearly all the participants were white and from upper- or middle-class families. The majority of them were male. This is unsurprising: of the 168,000 children considered for that pool of 1,500, only one was black, one was Indian, one was Mexican, and four were Japanese. The selectees, who had an average IQ of 151, called themselves "Termites." Data about the progress of their lives were collected every five years. After Terman died, in 1956, others took up his research, aiming to continue the work until the last participant either withdrew or died.

Thirty-five years into the experiment, Terman proudly enumerated the success of "his children":

> Nearly 2,000 scientific and technical papers and articles and some 60 books and monographs in the sciences, literature, arts, and humanities. Patents granted amount to at least 230. Other writings include 33 novels, about 375 short stories, novelettes, and plays; 60 or more essays, critiques, and sketches; and 265 miscellaneous articles. Hundreds of publications by journalists that classify as news stories, editorials, or newspaper columns. Hundreds, if not thousands, of radio, television, or motion picture scripts.

The identity of most of the Termites is confidential. Around thirty have disclosed their participation. Some were notable creators. Jess Oppenheimer worked in television and was a principal developer of a top-ranked, Emmy Award–winning comedy called *I Love Lucy*. Edward Dmytryk was a film director, making more than fifty Hollywood movies, including *The Caine Mutiny,* which was nominated for several Oscars, starred Humphrey Bogart, and was the second most watched film of 1954.

Other participants fared less well. They found more ordinary work as policemen, technicians, truck drivers, and secretaries. One was a potter who was eventually committed to a mental hospital; another cleaned swimming pools; several collected welfare. By 1947, Terman was forced to conclude, "We have seen that intellect and achievement are far from perfectly correlated." This was despite Terman actively helping his participants by writing letters of recommendation and providing mentorship and references. Movie director Dmytryk benefited from a letter at age fourteen, after he ran away from his violent father. Terman explained to the Los Angeles juvenile authorities that Dmytryk was "gifted" and his case deserved special consideration. He was saved from his abusive childhood and placed into a good foster home. TV producer Oppenheimer was a coat salesman until Terman helped him get into Stanford University. Some Termites landed careers in Terman's field of educational psychology, and many were admitted to Stanford, where he was an eminent professor. One Termite took over the study after Terman died.

The study's flaws and biases are beside the point. What matters is what happened to the children Terman excluded. The genius theory of creating predicts that the only creators among the children will be the ones Terman deemed geniuses. None of those excluded should have done anything creative: after all, they were not geniuses.

This is where Terman's study falls flat. Terman did not create a control group of non-geniuses for comparison. We know a lot about the hundreds of children who were selected and only a little about the tens of thousands who were not. But what we do know is sufficient to undermine the genius theory. One child Terman considered and rejected was a boy named William Shockley. Another was a boy named Luis Alvarez. Both grew up to win Nobel Prizes for physics— Shockley for coinventing the transistor, Alvarez for his work in nuclear magnetic resonance. Shockley started Shockley Semiconductor, one of the first electronics companies in Silicon Valley. Employees of Shockley's went on to found Fairchild Semiconductor, Intel, and Advanced Micro Devices. Working with his son Walter, Alvarez was the first to propose that an asteroid caused the extinction of the dinosaurs—the "Alvarez hypothesis"—which, after decades of controversy, scientists now accept as fact.

Terman's failure to identify these innovators does not close the coffin on the genius hypothesis. Perhaps his definition of genius was insufficient or Shockley and Alvarez's tests were wrongly administered. But the magnitude of their achievements begs us to consider another conclusion: genius does not predict creative ability because it is not a prerequisite.

Subsequent studies tried to correct this by measuring creative ability specifically. Starting in 1958, psychologist Ellis Paul Torrance administered a set of tests later known as the Torrance Tests of Creative Thinking to schoolchildren in Minnesota. Tasks included coming up with unusual ways to use a brick, having ideas for improving a toy, and improvising a drawing based on a given shape, such as a triangle. The researchers assessed the creative ability of each child by looking at how many ideas he or she generated, how different the ideas were from the others, how unusual they were, and how much detail they included. The difference in thinking about thinking that characterized psychology after World War II is evident in Torrance's work. Torrance suspected that creation was "within the reach of everyday people in everyday life" and eventually tried to modify his tests to eliminate racial and socioeconomic bias. Unlike Terman, Torrance did not expect his method to be a reliable predictor of future outcomes. "A high degree of these abilities does not guarantee that the possessor will behave in a highly creative manner," he wrote. "A high level of these abilities, however, increases a person's chances of behaving creatively."

How did these more modest expectations play out for Torrance's Minnesotan children? The first follow-up research came in 1966, using children who were tested in 1959. They were asked to select the three classmates who had the best ideas and then complete a questionnaire about their own creative work. The answers were compared with the data from seven years earlier. The correlation was not bad. It was certainly better than Terman's. The results were much the same after a second follow-up test, in 1971. The Torrance Tests seemed to be a reasonable way to predict creative ability.

The moment of truth came after fifty years, when the participants were ending their careers and had demonstrated whatever creative ability they possessed. The results were simple. Sixty participants responded. None of the high-scoring individuals had created anything that had achieved public recognition. Many had done things Torrance and his followers called "personal achievements" of creation, such as forming an action group, building a house, or pursuing a creative hobby. The Torrance Tests had achieved the modest goal of predicting who might have a somewhat creative life. They had done nothing to foresee who might have a creative career.

Without meaning to, Torrance had done something else. He had reinforced what Terman's results showed but Terman stubbornly ignored: that genius has nothing to do with creative ability, even when creative ability is broadly defined and generously measured. Torrance had recorded the IQ of all his participants. His results showed no connection between creative ability and general intelligence. Whatever Terman was measuring had nothing to do with creating, which is why he missed the Nobel laureates Shockley and Alvarez. We may call them creative geniuses now, but if creative genius is apparent only after creation, it is just another way of saying "creative."

6 | ORDINARY ACTS

The case against genius is clear: too many creators, too many creations, and too little predetermination. So how does creation happen?

The answer lies in the stories of people who have created things. Stories of creation follow a path. Creation is destination, the consequence of acts that appear inconsequential by themselves but that, when accumulated, change the world. Creating is an ordinary act, creation its extraordinary outcome.

Was Edmond's story ordinary or extraordinary? If we could travel back to Ferréol's estate in the Réunion of 1841, we would see ordinary acts: a boy following an old man around a garden, a conversation about watermelons, the boy poking around inside a flower. If we returned in

1899, we would see an extraordinary outcome: the island transformed, the world transforming. Knowing the outcome tempts us to retrofit the acts with extraordinariness—to picture Edmond awake all night wrestling with the problem of pollination, having a moment of epiphany in the moonlight, and an enslaved twelve-year-old orphan revolutionizing Réunion and the world.

But creation comes from *ordinary* acts. Edmond learned about botany through boyish curiosity and daily walks with Ferréol. Ferréol kept up with developments in the science of plants, including the work of Charles Darwin and Konrad Sprengel. Edmond applied this knowledge to vanilla, with the help of a bamboo tool and a child's small fingers. When we look behind creation's curtain, we find people like us doing things we can do.

This does not make creating easy. Magic is instant, genius an accident of birth. Take them away and what is left is work.

Work is the soul of creation. Work is getting up early and going home late, turning down dates and giving up weekends, writing and rewriting, reviewing and revising, rote and routine, staring down the doubt of the blank page, beginning when we do not know where to start, and not stopping when we cannot go on. It is not fun, romantic, or, most of the time, even interesting. If we want to create, we must, in the words of Paul Gallico, open our veins and bleed.

There are no secrets. When we ask writers about their process or scientists about their methods or inventors where they get their ideas from, we are hoping for something that doesn't exist: a trick, recipe, or ritual to summon the magic—an alternative to work. There isn't one. To create is to work. It is that easy and that hard.

With the myth gone, we have a choice. If we can create without genius or epiphany, then the only thing stopping us from creating is us. There is an arsenal of ways to say no to creating. One, *it is not easy,* has already been addressed. It is not easy. It is work.

Another is *I have no time.* But time is the great equalizer, the same for all: twenty-four hours every day, seven days every week, every life a length unknown, for richest and poorest and all between. We mean *we have no spare time,* a blunt blade in a world whose bestselling literary series was begun by a single mother writing in Edinburgh's cafés when her infant daughter slept, where a career more than fifty novels long was started by a laundry worker in the furnace room of a trailer in Maine, where world-changing philosophy was composed in a Parisian jail by a prisoner awaiting the guillotine, and where three centuries of physics were overturned in a year by a man with a permanent position as a patent examiner. There is time.

The third no is the big one, the gun to the head of our dreams. Its endless variations all say the same thing: *I can't.* Here is the sour fruit of the myth that only the special can create. None of us think we are special, not in the middle of the night, when our faces fluoresce in the bathroom mirror. *I can't,* we say. *I can't because I am not special.*

We *are* special, but that does not matter right now. What matters is that we do not have to be. The creativity myth is a mistake born of a need to explain extraordinary outcomes with extraordinary acts and extraordinary characters, a misunderstanding of the truth that creation comes from ordinary people and ordinary work. Special is not necessary.

All that is necessary is to begin. *I can't* is not true once we begin. Our first creative step is unlikely to be good. Imagination needs iteration. New things do not flow finished into the world. Ideas that seem powerful in the privacy of our head teeter weakly when we set them on our desk. But every beginning is beautiful. The virtue of a first sketch is that it breaks the blank page. It is the spark of life in the swamp. Its quality is not important. The only bad draft is the one we do not write.

How to create? Why create? The rest of the book is about how and why. What to create? Only you can decide that. You may know. You may have an idea like an itch. But if you do not, don't worry. How and what are connected: one leads to the other.

CHAPTER 2

THINKING IS LIKE WALKING

1 | KARL

Berlin once stood at the center of the creative world. The city's theaters reverberated with debuts by Max Reinhardt and Bertolt Brecht. Its nightclubs hosted bawdy burlesque *Kabarett*. Albert Einstein ascended its Academy of Sciences. Thomas Mann prophesied the perils of National Socialism. The movies *Metropolis* and *Nosferatu* premiered to packed houses. Berliners called it the Golden Age: the years of Marlene Dietrich, Greta Garbo, Joseph Pilates, Rudolf Steiner, and Fritz Lang.

It was a time and place for thinking about thinking. In Berlin, German psychologists were having radical thoughts about how the human mind works. Otto Selz, a professor in Mannheim, far to the southwest, sowed the seed: he was among the first to propose that thinking was a process that could be scrutinized and described. For most of his contemporaries, the mind was magic and mystery. For Selz, it was mechanism.

But as the 1930s began, Otto Selz heard the boots of doom

approaching. He was Jewish. Hitler was rising. Berlin's celebration of creation was turning apocalyptic. Destruction was coming.

Selz had been asking psychological questions: How did a mind work? Could he measure it? What could he prove? Now he was also asking practical ones: What was going to happen to him? Could he escape it? How much time remained?

And—equally important to him—would his thoughts survive if he did not? His chance to pass them on was brief. In 1933, the Nazis prevented him from working and prohibited others from citing him. His name disappeared from the literature.

But at least one Berliner knew Selz's work. Karl Duncker was thirty years old when the Nazis banned Otto Selz. Duncker was not Jewish. His appearance was Aryan: fair skin, flaxen hair, and faceted jaw. He was no safer for it. His ex-wife was Jewish, and his parents were Communists. He made two applications to become a professor at the University of Berlin. Both were rejected despite his excellent academic record. In 1935, the school fired him from his job as a researcher. He published his masterwork, *On Problem Solving*—in which he defied the Nazis by citing Selz ten times—and fled to the United States.

The Golden Age was over. Novelist Christopher Isherwood, teaching English in Berlin, captured its passing:

Today the sun is brilliantly shining; it is quite mild and warm. I go out for my last morning walk, without an overcoat or hat. The sun shines, and Hitler is master of this city. The sun shines, and dozens of my friends—my pupils at the Workers' School, the men and women I met are in prison, possibly dead or being tortured to death. I catch sight of my face in the mirror of a shop, and am horrified to see that I am smiling. You can't help smiling, in such beautiful weather. The trams are going up and down the Kleist-strasse, just as usual. They, and the people on the pavement, and the tea-cosy dome of the Nollendorfplatz station have an air of curious familiarity, of striking resemblance to something one remembers as normal and pleasant in the past.

Duncker took a position in the psychology department of Swarthmore College, in Pennsylvania. In 1939, he produced his first paper since arriving in America, coauthored with Isadore Krechevsky, an immigrant who'd left the tiny Lithuanian village of Sventijánskas as a young boy to escape Russian anti-Semitism. Krechevsky, whose encounters with prejudice in the United States had brought him to the edge of abandoning his academic career, was the first American Duncker inspired.

The joint paper, "On Solution-Achievement," published in *Psychological Review,* marks the moment in the history of the mind when America met Berlin. Krechevsky, in the American style of the time, studied learning in rats. Duncker studied thinking in humans. This was so unusual that Duncker had to clarify what thinking meant: "The functional sense of problem-solving, not a special, e.g., imageless, kind of representation."

In the paper, the two men agreed that solving problems required "a number of intermediate steps," but Krechevsky noted a crucial difference between Duncker's ideas and the ones that were prevalent in America: "There is in Duncker's analysis one major concept which does not find a close parallel in American psychology: in his experiments, the solution to the problem is a meaningful one. The organism can bring to bear experiences from other occasions and comparatively few general experiences can be utilized for problem-solving."

Duncker had made his first mark. American psychologists experimented on animals and spoke of *organisms:* train-your-rat psychology. Duncker cared about human minds and meaningful problems. He put his foot to a shovel and broke ground for a cognitive revolution that would take twenty years to build.

In Germany, the Nazis arrested Otto Selz and took him to Dachau, their first concentration camp. They held him there for five weeks.

Duncker published his second paper, on the relationship between familiarity and perception, in the *American Journal of Psychology*.

In Russia, his brother Wolfgang was captured in Stalin's Great Purge and murdered in the gulag.

Duncker's third paper of the year was published in the pioneering journal of philosophy and psychology *Mind*. His subject was the psychology of ethics. Duncker wanted to understand why people's moral values varied so much. The paper was nuanced, comprehensive, and poignant. A man devoted to discovering how humans think was trying to make sense of the end of Berlin:

> The motive "for the benefit of the State" depends upon whether the State is felt to be the embodiment of the highest values of life or merely a sort of police-station. On the whole moral judgments are based upon the standard meanings of the society in question. Its chief aim is not to be "just," but to instigate and to enforce its standard meanings and conducts. It is this function which interferes with a purely ethical conduct.

Here was his answer. States can replace ethics with edicts.

At the end of February 1940, Karl Duncker wrote something else.

Dear Mother,

You have been good to me.
*   Don't condemn me.*

He drove to nearby Fullerton and, while sitting in his car, shot himself in the head with a pistol. He was thirty-seven.

In Amsterdam, the Nazis captured Otto Selz, took him to Auschwitz, and murdered him.

In Berkeley, the University of California awarded a professorship in psychology to a man named David Krech. He had changed his name from Isadore Krechevsky. He was Duncker's first American coauthor. He went on to have a storied thirty-year career specializing in the mechanics of memory and stimulation.

Krech was one of many people Duncker influenced. Duncker carried Germany's best and most radical ideas about thinking to the United States and started a revolution he did not live to see. He was a message in a bottle cast from the shores of a dying Berlin. The bottle broke, but not before it had delivered its message.

2 | THE QUESTION OF FINDING

Duncker's monograph *On Problem Solving*, which he published in 1935 as he was fleeing Germany, led to a transformation in the science of brain and mind known as the "cognitive revolution" that laid the foundation for our understanding of how people create. For many reasons, including its references to Otto Selz, *On Problem Solving* was verboten in Hitler's nation. War arrived. Berlin burned. Copies became rare.

Then, five years after Duncker's suicide, one of his former students, Lynne Lees, revived the monograph by translating it into English and presenting his bold agenda—"to study productive thinking"—to the world.

Duncker rejected studies of great thinkers. He likened them to lightning—a dramatic display of something "better investigated in little sparks within the laboratory." He used "practical and mathematical problems because such material is more suitable for experimentation," but he made it clear that he was studying *thought,* not puzzles or math.

It did not matter what someone was thinking *about*—the "essential features of problem-solving are independent of the thought-material."

For millennia, people had been herded into categories: civilized and savage, Caucasian and Negro, man and woman, Gentile and Jew, rich and poor, capitalist and Communist, genius and dullard, gifted and non-gifted. Category determined capacity. By the 1940s, these divisions had been reinforced by "scientists" who evoked the innate potential to organize the human race like a zoo and lock "different" people into cages, sometimes literal ones. Then a Gentile who married a Jew, a son of Communists who emigrated to live among capitalists, a man who collaborated with Jews and women and who had witnessed the horrors caused by the fraud of measuring humanity, showed that human thought has an essence unaffected by scale, subject, or thinker—that our minds all work the same way.

It was radical and controversial, and it shifted the shape of psychology. Duncker's approach was simple. He gave people problems and asked them to think aloud as they tried to solve them. In this way, he saw the structure of thought.

Thinking is finding a way to achieve a goal that cannot be attained by an obvious action. We want to accomplish something but do not know how, so before we can act we must think. But *how* do we think? Or, as Duncker phrased it, what is the answer to "the specific question of finding: In what way can a meaningful solution be found?"

We all use the same process for thinking, just as we all use the same process for walking. It is the same whether the problem is big or small, whether the solution is something new or something logical, whether the thinker is a Nobel laureate or a child. There is no "creative thinking," just as there is no "creative walking." Creation is a *result*—a place thinking may lead us. Before we can know how to create, we must know how to think.

Duncker deployed an array of experiments. They included the

Abcabc Problem, which asked high school students to work out why numbers in the form 123,123 and 234,234 are always divisible by 13; the Stick Problem, in which babies as young as eight months old were given a stick that enabled them to reach a remote toy; the Cork Problem, where a piece of wood had to be inserted into a door frame even though it was not as long as the door was wide; and the Box Problem, where candles had to be attached to a wall by selecting from objects including thumb tacks and various boxes. Duncker varied his experiments many times until he understood how people think, what helps, and what gets in the way.

One of his conclusions: "If a situation is introduced in a certain perceptual structure, thinking achieves a contrary structure only against the resistance of the former structure."

Or: old ideas obstruct new ones.

And this was the case with Duncker's work. Few psychologists read or understood *On Problem Solving* in its entirety—not because it was complicated but because old ideas made them resist it. Today the monograph is known mostly for the Box Problem, which has been given the misnomer the Candle Problem and also redesigned. It attracted more attention than all the others. Psychologists and people who write about creation have been discussing it for more than fifty years. Here is its modern incarnation:

Picture yourself in a room with a wooden door. The room contains a candle, a book of matches, and a box of tacks. Using only these things, how would you attach the candle to the door so that you can light it, have it burn normally, and create light to read by?

People usually think of three solutions. One is to melt part of the candle and use the melted wax to fix the candle to the door. Another is to tack the candle to the door. Both work, but not very well. The third solution, which occurs to only a minority of people, is to empty out the tack box, tack *that* to the wall, and use it to hold the candle.

This last solution has a feature the others do not: one of the items, the box, is used for something other than its original purpose. At some point the person solving the problem stops seeing it as a thing for holding the tacks and starts seeing it as a thing for holding the candle.

This shift, sometimes called an *insight,* is considered important by some people who think about creating. They suspect that there is something remarkable about seeing the box differently, that the shift is a leap like the one we experience when we look at that picture of a vase that might be two faces or the old lady that could be a young lady or the duck that may be a rabbit. Once we make this "leap," the problem is solved.

Following Duncker's lead, psychologists have created many similar puzzles. Examples include the Charlie Problem:

Dan comes home one night after work, as usual. He opens the door and steps into the living room. On the floor he sees Charlie lying dead. There is water on the floor, as well as some pieces of glass. Tom is also in the room. Dan takes one quick glance at the scene and immediately knows what happened. How did Charlie die?

And the Prisoner and Rope Problem:

A prisoner was attempting to escape from a tower. He found in his cell a rope that was half long enough to permit him to reach the ground safely. He divided the rope in half, tied the two parts together, and escaped. How could he have done this?

And the Nine-Dot Problem:

Picture three rows of three dots, evenly spaced to resemble a square. Join the dots using only four straight lines without taking your pencil or pen off the paper.

All are solved the same way: by the equivalent of realizing that the faces are also a vase. Charlie is not a person but a fish. Tom is not a person but a cat. Tom knocked over Charlie's fish bowl, and Charlie died. The prisoner did not "divide" the rope in half widthwise, as we naturally imagine, but lengthwise. The nine dots are joined by drawing lines that extend beyond the "square" created by the dots. This is the source of the cliché "thinking outside the box."

Does this mean minds leap? We can answer that question with one more problem, the Speckled Band:

Julia sleeps in a locked room. Beside her bed is a bell pull for summoning the housekeeper. Above the bell pull is a ventilator that connects to the room next door. That room contains a safe, a dog leash, and a saucer of milk. One night Julia screams. There is a whistle and a clang. She is found dying with a burnt match in her hand. There are no signs of violence. There are no pets in the house. Her room had remained locked. Her last words are "the speckled band." How did Julia die?

This is not a psychology problem. It is a summary of a Sherlock Holmes story written by Arthur Conan Doyle in 1892. Julia died from the bite of a poisonous snake trained to crawl through the ventilator and down the bell pull, then return when her murderer whistled. He kept the snake on the leash and fed it the milk. The clang is the sound of him hiding the snake in the safe after the murder. Upon being bitten, Julia lit a match for illumination and glimpsed the snake, which looked to her like a "speckled band."

Holmes works this out by observing that the only way into the locked room is through the ventilator. He deduces that because Julia died quickly and without obvious signs of violence, she was probably poisoned. Something small and poisonous therefore passed through the ventilator. The dog leash suggests an animal, rather than a gas, and the saucer of milk rules out an insect such as a spider. Julia's dying words about a speckled band, which initially seem cryptic, now sound like a description of the most likely remaining solution: a snake, trained to respond to its master's whistle. The clang shows that the snake is in the safe.

Holmes is a fictional character famous for detection, not creation.

He describes his process as "observation and deduction: eliminate all other factors, and the one which remains must be the truth." He does not solve Julia's murder with a creative leap. The "insight" that begins his process of deduction—that the only way into the locked room is via the ventilator—is an observation. The surprising solution that a snake killed her follows.

Minds do not leap. Observation, evaluation, and iteration, not sudden shifts of perception, solve problems and lead us to creation. We can see this using Duncker's technique: observing people solving his most famous problem.

3 | STEPS, NOT LEAPS

Many people do not think using words, but we can all verbalize our thoughts without affecting our problem-solving skills. Listening to the mind shows how thinking works. Robert Weisberg asked people to think aloud as they worked on Duncker's Box Problem. He changed the problem by including nails as well as tacks and substituting a piece of cardboard for the wooden door. The people he worked with had the objects in front of them. They were asked to imagine solutions but not build them.

Here are the thoughts of three people who did *not* think of using the tack box as a candleholder:

PERSON 1: "Melt the candle and try to stick it up. Candle coming out vertically on a nail, but it will break. Put the candle sideways and nail it up. The candle looks heavy. Put a nail or two nails in the side of the candle, but it might not stay up. I could . . . no, I couldn't do that."

PERSON 2: "I'm looking at the nails, but they won't penetrate but otherwise how will the candle stick? Put a nail through the vertical candle. Put a nail through the candle held horizontal. Can't use the matches. Put nails in the wick and under the candle . . ."

PERSON 3: "I was thinking you could take a nail and bang it through, but that would split the candle, so use the matches to melt enough wax, then use the nails—no good. Bang the nails in close together and put the candle on them. . . ."

And here are the thoughts of three people who *did* think of using the tack box to hold the candle:

PERSON 4: "Candle has to burn straight, so if I took a nail and put it through the candle and cardboard . . . [10 second pause] . . . if I took several nails and made a row and set the candle on that. If I took the nails out of the box, nailed the box to the wall."

PERSON 5: "Melt wax and use it to stick the candle up. Take a nail—the nail won't go through the candle. Put nails around the candle or under the candle to hold it. Put the candle in the nail box—it wouldn't work, the box would rip."

PERSON 6: "Light a match and see if I could get wax up on the cardboard. Push a nail through the candle into the cardboard. I'm looking at the matches to see if the idea would work. I'm trying to get more combinations with the nails. Build a base for the candle with the nails like a rectangle. Better yet, use the box. Put two nails into the cardboard, put the box on them, melt some wax and put the candle into the box with the wax and it'll stand."

This is how we think. *Everyone* who thinks of using the tack box gets there the same way. After eliminating other ideas, they think of building a platform out of nails, then think of using the tack box as the platform. There is no sudden shift of perception. We move from known to new in small steps. In every case, the pattern is the same: begin with something familiar, evaluate it, solve any problems, and repeat until a satisfactory solution is found. Duncker discovered this in the 1930s:

"Successful people arrived at the solution in this way: they started from tacks and looked for a 'platform to be fastened to the door with tacks.'"

Evaluation directs iteration. Person 3 decides to "bang the nails in close together and put the candle on them" and evaluates this as satisfactory. Person 4 evaluates this as *un*satisfactory so takes one more step: use the tack box. Person 5 also takes this step, the solution Duncker sought for his problem, but makes the opposite evaluation: it won't work. Person 6 takes the most steps of all and, as a result, improves Duncker's solution by using melted wax to stabilize the candle.

Creating is taking steps, not making leaps: find a problem, solve it, and repeat. Most steps wins. The best artists, scientists, engineers, inventors, entrepreneurs, and other creators are the ones who keep taking steps by finding new problems, new solutions, and then new problems again. The root of innovation is exactly the same as it was when our species was born: looking at something and thinking, "I can make this better."

Six undergraduates talking their way through a puzzle is not enough for generalization, nor is twenty-five, which is how many Weisberg asked to talk out loud, nor even 376, which is how many tried the Box Problem in his experiment. But these results do undermine a vital premise of the creativity myth: that creating requires leaps of extraordinary thinking. It does not. Ordinary thinking works.

4 | AHA!

There is an alternative to the theory that creation comes from ordinary thinking: the idea, proposed by psychologists Pamela Auble,

Jeffrey Franks, and Salvatore Soraci, writer Jonah Lehrer, and many others, that many of the best creations come from an extraordinary moment of sudden inspiration, sometimes called the "eureka effect" or "aha! moment." Ideas start as caterpillars of the conscious mind, become cocoons in the unconscious, then fly out like butterflies. This moment results in excitement and possibly exclamation. The key to creating is to cultivate more of these moments.

People who believe this will have many reasonable objections to the proposal that creation comes from ordinary thinking. There are documented cases of great creators having aha! moments. Many people have experienced frustration with a problem and set it aside only to have the solution come to them. Neurologists seeking the source of such moments are discovering interesting things. The aha! moment is woven into our world. Oprah Winfrey has trademarked it. How can ordinary thinking explain this?

The most frequently cited story of an aha! moment was first made famous by a Roman architect named Vitruvius.

Vitruvius says that when the Greek general Hiero was crowned king of Syracuse, in Sicily, twenty-three hundred years ago, he celebrated by giving a craftsman some gold and asking him to create a golden wreath. The craftsman duly delivered a wreath with the same weight as the gold that Hiero had provided, but Hiero suspected that he had been tricked and that most of the wreath was made of silver. Hiero asked Syracuse's greatest thinker, a twenty-two-year-old named Archimedes, to find the truth: was the wreath pure gold or a mixture of gold and silver? According to Vitruvius, Archimedes then took a bath. The lower he sank, the more the water overflowed. This gave him an idea. Archimedes ran home naked, shouting, *"Eureka, eureka!"*—"I have found it, I have found it!" He made two objects that were both the same weight as the wreath, one in gold and one in silver, and submerged each of them in water and measured how much water overflowed. The silver object displaced more water than the gold object. Then Archimedes submerged Hiero's "golden" wreath into the water. It displaced more water than the same weight of pure gold, proving that it had been adulterated with silver or some other substance.

This story about Archimedes, which Vitruvius told two centuries after the fact, is almost certainly not true. The method Vitruvius describes does not work, as Archimedes would have known. Galileo pointed this out in a paper called "La Bilancetta" ("The Little Balance"), which calls the method of comparing gold and silver Vitruvius describes "altogether false." The tiny differences in the amount of water displaced by the gold, the silver, and the wreath would have been too hard to measure. Surface tension and drops of water that remained on the wreath would have caused other problems. Galileo's paper shows the method Archimedes probably used, based on Archimedes's own work: weighing the wreath underwater. Buoyancy, not displacement, is the key to solving the problem. Overflowing a bath is unlikely to have inspired this.

But let's take Vitruvius's story at face value. He says that Archimedes, "while the case was still on his mind, happened to go to the bath, and on getting into a tub observed that the more his body sank into it, the more water ran out over the tub. As this pointed out the way to explain the case in question, without a moment's delay, and transported with joy, he jumped out of the tub and rushed home naked, crying with a loud voice that he had found what he was seeking; for as he ran he shouted repeatedly in Greek, 'Eureka, eureka.'"

Or: Archimedes's eureka moment came from an observation he made *while thinking about the problem*. At best, the bath is like the platform of nails in the Weisberg experiments: it is the one thing that leads to another. If it happened at all, Archimedes's legendary shout of *"Eureka"* did not come from an aha! moment but from the simple joy of solving a problem with ordinary thinking.

Another famous example of an aha! moment comes from Samuel

Taylor Coleridge, who claimed his poem "Kubla Khan" was written in a dream. According to Coleridge's preface:

> In the summer of the year 1797, the Author, then in ill health, had retired to a lonely farmhouse. An anodyne had been prescribed, from the effects of which he fell asleep in his chair at the moment that he was reading, "Here the Khan Kubla commanded a palace to be built, and a stately garden thereunto. And thus ten miles of fertile ground were inclosed with a wall." The author continued for about three hours in a profound sleep during which time he could not have composed less than from two to three hundred lines without any sensation or consciousness of effort. On awaking he eagerly wrote down the lines; at this moment he was unfortunately called out by a person on business from Porlock and on his return to his room, found all the rest had passed away.

This gave the poem—subtitled "A Vision in a Dream"—an aura of mystery and romance that continues to this day. But Coleridge is misleading us. The anodyne, or painkiller, which he says he had been prescribed was opium dissolved in alcohol—a substance to which Coleridge was addicted. A trance of three to four hours is a classic opium-induced state, which can be euphoric and hallucinogenic. Coleridge's movements in the summer of 1797 are well known. He had no time to retire to a lonely farmhouse. The person from Porlock may have been fictitious and an excuse for not finishing the poem. Coleridge used a similar device—a fake letter from a friend—to excuse the incompleteness of another work, his *Biographia Literaria*. The preface claims the poem was composed during sleep, then written automatically. But in 1934, an earlier manuscript of "Kubla Khan" was found that differs from the published poem. Among many changes, "From forth this Chasm with hideous turmoil seething" became "*And from* this chasm, with *ceaseless* turmoil seething"; "So twice six miles of fertile ground /

With Walls and Towers were compass'd round" was changed to "So twice *five* miles of fertile ground / With walls and towers were *girdled* round"; "mount Amora" was rewritten as "mount *Amara*"—a reference to Milton's *Paradise Lost*—then, finally, "mount *Abora*." The origin story changed, too. Coleridge says the poem was "composed in a sort of reverie brought on by two grains of opium" in the fall, rather than appearing complete during a sleep in the summer.

These are minor changes, but they show conscious thought, not unconscious automation. "Kubla Khan" may or may not have started in a dream, but ordinary thinking finished it.

A third frequently told story about an aha! moment comes from 1865, when chemist August Kekulé discovered the ringlike structure of benzene. Twenty-five years after making this discovery, Kekulé said, in a speech to the German Chemical Society:

> I was sitting writing at my textbook but the work did not progress; my thoughts were elsewhere. I turned my chair to the fire and dozed. Again the atoms were gamboling before my eyes. This time the smaller groups kept modestly in the background. My mental eye, rendered more acute by repeated visions of the kind, could now distinguish larger structures of manifold conformation: long rows, sometimes more closely fitted together all twining and twisting in snake-like motion. But look! What was that? One of the snakes had seized hold of its own tail, and the form whirled mockingly before my eyes. As if by a flash of lightning I awoke; and this time also I spent the rest of the night in working out the consequences of the hypothesis.

Robert Weisberg points out that the word Kekulé used was *halbschlaf,* or "half-sleep," which is often translated as "reverie." Kekulé was not sleeping. He was daydreaming. His dream is often described as a vision of a snake biting its tail. But Kekulé says he saw *atoms* twisting in a *snake-like motion*. When he later describes one of the snakes seizing its tail, he is referring back to his analogy. He is not seeing a snake. This is a case of visual imagination helping solve a problem, not an aha! moment happening in a dream.

A sudden revelation has also been attributed to Einstein, who was stuck for a year while developing the special theory of relativity and went to a friend for help. "It was a beautiful day when I visited him with this problem," he said. "I started the conversation with him in the following way: 'Recently I have been working on a difficult problem. Today I come here to battle against that problem with you.' We discussed every aspect of this problem. Then suddenly I understood where the key to this problem lay. Next day, I came back to him again and said to him, without even saying hello, 'Thank you. I've completely solved the problem.'"

Was this a flash of inspiration? No. In Einstein's own words: "I was led to it by steps." All stories of aha! moments—and there are surprisingly few—are like these: anecdotal, often apocryphal, and unable to survive scrutiny.

And there has been a lot of scrutiny: in the last few decades of the twentieth century, many psychologists believed that creation comes from a period of unconscious thinking they called "incubation," followed by an emotion they called "the feeling of knowing," followed by an aha! moment, or "insight." These psychologists conducted hundreds of experiments designed to validate their hypothesis.

For example, in 1982, two researchers at the University of Colorado tested the feeling of knowing with thirty people in an experiment lasting nineteen days. They showed the subjects pictures of entertainers and asked them to recall the entertainers' names. Only 4 percent of memories were recovered spontaneously, most of them by the same four people. All the other memories were recovered by ordinary thinking: gradually working through the problem by remembering, for example, that the entertainer was a movie star in the 1950s, that he had appeared in an Alfred Hitchcock movie where he was chased by a crop duster, that the movie was called *North by Northwest,* and, finally, that his name was Cary Grant. The study's conclusion? Even the "spontaneous" memories had probably also come from ordinary thinking, and there was no support for unconscious mental processing as a way of recovering memories. Other studies into the feeling of knowing have had similar results.

And what of incubation? An academic named Robert Olton spent many years at the University of California, Berkeley, trying to prove that incubation exists. In one experiment he sorted 160 people into ten groups and asked them to solve an insight problem called the Farm Problem, which involves dividing an L-shaped "farm" into four parts of the same size and shape. The solution is novel—you have to make four smaller L shapes in various orientations. Every subject was tested individually and given thirty minutes to solve the problem. To see if taking a break from thinking—that is, incubating—made a difference, some subjects were given a fifteen-minute break. During this break, some people could do whatever they wanted; others were given mental work like counting backward in threes, or were asked to talk about the problem out loud, or were told to relax in a room with a comfortable chair, dim lights, and soft music. Each activity tested a different idea about how incubation works.

But the results were the same for every group. People who worked continuously performed as well as people given a period for incubation. People given a period for incubation performed as well as one another, regardless of what they did during incubation. Olton sliced the data many ways, looking for evidence that incubation worked, but was forced to conclude, "The major finding of this study is that no evidence of incubation was apparent under any condition, even under those where its appearance would seem most likely." He called this "an inexorably negative finding." He was also unable to replicate any of the positive results others had reported. "To our knowledge," he wrote, "no study reporting evidence of incubation in problem solving has survived replication by an independent investigator."

Olton suggested that one explanation for the lack of evidence supporting incubation was flawed experiments. But he added, "A second, more radical, explanation of our results is to accept them at face value and to question the existence of incubation as an objectively demonstrable phenomenon. That is, incubation may be something of an illusion, perhaps rendered impressive by selective recall of the few but vivid occasions on which great progress followed separation from a problem and forgetting of the many occasions when it did not."

To his credit, Robert Olton did not give up. He designed a different study, this time using experts trying to solve a problem in their area of expertise—chess players and a chess problem—in the hope that this would give better results than undergraduates with an insight problem. Half his subjects worked continuously and half were given a break, during which they were asked not to think about the problem. Again, the break made no difference. Both groups performed equally well. Olton, initially a believer in incubation, was forced to doubt its existence. His despair was evident in the subtitle of the paper he wrote about the study: "Searching for the Elusive." The paper concluded, "We simply didn't find incubation."

Most researchers now regard incubation as folk psychology—a popular belief but wrong. Almost all of the evidence suggests the same thing: Caterpillars do not cocoon in the unconscious mind. The butterflies of creation come from conscious thinking.

5 | THE SECRET OF STEVE

Karl Duncker wrote that the act of creation starts with one of two questions: " 'Why doesn't it work?' or, 'What should I change to make it work?' "

These sound simple, but answering them can lead to extraordinary results. One of the best examples comes from Steve Jobs, cofounder and CEO of Apple Inc. When Jobs announced Apple's first cell phone, the iPhone, in 2007, he said:

> The most advanced phones are called smartphones. They are definitely a little smarter, but they actually are harder to use. They all have these keyboards that are there whether you need them or not. How do you solve this? We solved it in computers 20 years ago. We solved it with a screen that could display anything. What we're going to do is get rid of all these buttons and just make a giant screen. We don't want to carry around a mouse. We're going to use a stylus. No. You have to get them and put them away, and you lose them. We're going to use our fingers.

It is no coincidence that Jobs sounds like one of Duncker's subjects thinking aloud while trying to attach a candle to a door. The step-by-step process is the same. Problem: Smarter phones are harder to use because they have permanent keyboards. Solution: A big screen and a pointer. Problem: What kind of pointer? Solution: A mouse. Problem: We don't want to carry a mouse around. Solution: A stylus. Problem: A stylus might get lost. Solution: Use our fingers.

Apple sold 4 million phones in 2007, 14 million in 2008, 29 million in 2009, 40 million in 2010, and 82 million in 2011, for a total of 169 million sold in its first five years in the phone business, despite charging a higher price than its competitors did. How?

For several years, starting around 2002, I was a member of the research advisory board of a company that made cell phones. Every year it gave me its latest phone. I found each one harder to use than the last, as did other board members. It was no secret that Apple might enter the cell phone market, but the risk was always dismissed, since Apple had never made a phone. A few months after Apple's phone became available, the board met and I asked what the company thought of it. The chief engineer said, "It has a really bad microphone."

This was true, irrelevant, and revealing. This company thought smartphones were phones, only smarter. They had made some of the first cell phones, which, of course, had buttons on them. These had been successful. So, as they added smarts, they added buttons. They thought a good phone provided a good phone call and the smart stuff was a bonus.

Apple made computers. For Apple, as Jobs's announcement made clear, a smartphone was not a phone. It was a computer for your pocket that, among other things, made calls. Making computers was a problem that Apple, as Jobs described it, had "solved" twenty years ago. It did not matter that Apple had never made a phone. It did matter that phone makers had never made a computer. The company I was advising, once a leading phone manufacturer, lost a large amount of money in 2007, saw its market share collapse, and was eventually sold.

"Why doesn't it work?" deceives us with its simplicity. The first challenge is to ask it. The chief engineer did not ask this question about his phones. He saw rising sales and happy customers and so assumed that nothing was broken and there was nothing to fix.

But Sales + Customers = Nothing Broken is a formula for corporate cyanide. Most big companies that die kill themselves drinking it. Complacency is an enemy. "If it ain't broke, don't fix it" is an impossible idiom. No matter the sales and customer satisfaction, there is always something to fix. Asking, "Why doesn't it work?" is creation inhaling. Answering is creation breathing out. Innovation suffocates without it.

"Why doesn't it work?" has the pull of a polestar. It sets creation's direction. For Jobs and the iPhone, the critical point of departure was not finding a solution but seeing a problem: the problem of keyboards making smarter phones harder to use. Everything else followed.

Apple was not unique. Korean electronics giant LG launched a product much like the iPhone before the iPhone was announced.

The LG Prada had a full-sized touch screen, won design awards, and sold a million units. When Apple's very similar direction—a big touch screen—was revealed, competitors built near replicas within months. These other companies could make an iPhone, but they could not conceive one. They could not look at their existing products and ask, "Why doesn't it work?"

The secret of Steve was evident in 1983, during the sunrise of the personal computer, when he spoke at a design conference in Aspen, Colorado. There was no stage, and there were no visual aids. Jobs stood behind a lectern with yearbook hair, a thin white shirt, its sleeves folded as far as his forearms, and—"they paid me sixty dollars, so I wore a tie"—a pink-and-green bow tie. The audience was small. He gestured widely as he envisioned "portable computers with radio links," "electronic mailboxes," and "electronic maps." Apple Computer, of which Jobs was then cofounder and a director, was a six-year-old startup playing David to IBM's Goliath. Apple's sling was sales; it had sold more personal computers than any other company in 1981 and 1982. But despite his optimism, Jobs was dissatisfied:

> If you look at computers, they look like garbage. All the great product designers are off designing automobiles or buildings but hardly any of them are designing computers. We're going to sell ten million computers in 1986. Whether they look like a piece a shit or they look great. There are going to be these new objects in everyone's working environment, in everyone's educational environment, in everyone's home environment. And we have a shot at putting a great object there. Or if we don't, we're going to put one more piece of junk there. By 1986 or 1987 people are going to be spending more time interacting with these machines than they spend in a car. And so industrial design, software design, and how people interact with these things must be given the consideration that we give automobiles today, if not a lot more.

Twenty-eight years later, Walt Mossberg, technology columnist for the *Wall Street Journal,* described a similar discussion that happened near the end of Jobs's life: "One minute he'd be talking about sweeping ideas for the digital revolution. The next about why Apple's current products were awful, and how a color, or angle, or curve, or icon was embarrassing."

A good salesman sells everybody. A great salesman sells everybody but himself. What made Steve Jobs think differently was not genius, passion, or vision. It was his refusal to believe that sales and customers meant nothing was broken. He enshrined this in the name of the street encircling Apple's campus: Infinite Loop. The secret of Steve was that he was never satisfied. He devoted his life to asking, "Why doesn't it work?" and "What should I change to make it work?"

But hang on. Surely there is an alternative to starting by asking, "Why doesn't it work?" What if you simply start with a good idea?

Ideas are a staple of myths about creating; they even have their own symbol, the lightbulb. That comes from 1919, the age of silent movies, a decade before Mickey Mouse, when the world's favorite animated animal was Felix the Cat. Felix was black, white, and mischievous. Symbols and numbers would appear above his head, and sometimes he would grab them to use as props. Question marks became ladders, musical notes became vehicles, exclamation points became baseball bats, and the number 3 became horns he used to turn the tables on a bull. One symbol lived long after the cat: when Felix had an idea, a lightbulb appeared above his head. Lightbulbs have represented ideas ever since. Psychologists adopted the image: after 1926, they often called having an idea *illumination.*

The creativity myth confuses having ideas with the actual work of creating. Books with titles like *Making Ideas Happen, How to Get Ideas, The Idea Hunter,* and *IdeaSpotting* emphasize idea generation, and idea-generation techniques abound. The most famous is brainstorming, invented by advertising executive Alex Osborn in 1939 and first published in 1942 in his book *How to Think Up.* This is a typical description, from James Manktelow, founder and CEO of MindTools, a company that promotes brainstorming as a way to "develop creative solutions to business problems":

> Brainstorming is often used in a business setting to encourage teams to come up with original ideas. It's a freewheeling meeting format, in which the leader sets out the problem that needs to be solved. Participants then suggest ideas for solving the problem, and build on ideas suggested by others. A firm rule is that ideas must not be criticized—they can be completely wacky and way out. This frees people up to explore ideas creatively and break out of established thinking patterns. As well as generating some great solutions to specific problems, brainstorming can be a lot of fun.

Osborn claimed significant success for his technique. As one example of brainstorming's effectiveness, he cited a group of United States Treasury employees who came up with 103 ideas for selling savings bonds in forty minutes. Corporations and institutions including DuPont, IBM, and the United States government soon adopted brainstorming. By the end of the twentieth century, its origins forgotten, brainstorming had become a reflex approach to creating in many organizations and had entered the jargon of business as both a noun and a verb. It is now so common that few people question it. Everybody brainstorms; therefore, brainstorming is good.

But does it work?

Claims about the success of brainstorming rest on easily tested assumptions. One assumption is that groups produce more ideas than individuals. Researchers in Minnesota tested this with scientists and advertising executives from the 3M Company. Half the subjects worked in groups of four. The other half worked alone, and then their results were randomly combined as if they had worked in a group, with duplicate ideas counted only once. In every case, four people working individually generated between 30 to 40 percent more ideas than four people working in a group. Their results were of a higher quality, too: independent judges assessed the work and found that the individuals produced better ideas than the groups.

Follow-up research tested whether larger groups performed any better. In one study, 168 people were either divided into teams of five, seven, or nine or asked to work individually. The research confirmed that working individually is more productive than working in groups. It also showed that productivity decreases as group size increases. The conclusion: "Group brainstorming, over a wide range of group sizes, inhibits rather than facilitates creative thinking." The groups produced fewer and worse results because they were more likely to get fixated on one idea and because, despite all exhortations to the contrary, some members felt inhibited and refrained from full participation.

Another assumption of brainstorming is that suspending judgment is better than assessing ideas as they appear. Researchers in Indiana tested this by asking groups of students to think of brand names for three different products. Half of the groups were told to refrain from criticism and half were told to criticize as they went along. Once again, independent judges assessed the quality of each idea. The groups that did not stop to criticize produced more ideas, but both groups produced the same number of good ideas. Deferring criticism added only bad ideas. Subsequent studies have reinforced this.

Research into brainstorming has a clear conclusion. The best way to create is to work alone and evaluate solutions as they occur. The worst way to create is to work in large groups and defer criticism. Steve Wozniak, Steve Jobs's cofounder at Apple and the inventor of its first computer, offers the same advice: "Work alone. You're going to be best able to design revolutionary products and features if you're working on your own. Not on a committee. Not on a team."

Brainstorming fails because it is an explicit rejection of ordinary thinking—all leaps and no steps—and because of its unstated assumption that having ideas is the same as creating. Partly as a result, almost everybody has the idea that ideas are important. According to novelist Stephen King, the question authors signing books get asked most often—and are least able to answer—is "Where do you get your ideas from?"

Ideas are like seeds: they are abundant, and most of them never grow into anything. Also, ideas are seldom original. Ask several independent groups to brainstorm on the same topic at the same time, and you will likely get many of the same ideas. This is not a limitation of brainstorming; it is true of all creation. Because everything arises from steps, not leaps, most things are invented in several places simultaneously when different people walk the same path, each unaware of the others. For example, four different people discovered sunspots independently in 1611; five people invented the steamboat between 1802 and 1807; six people conceived of the electric railroad between 1835 and 1850; and two people invented the silicon chip in 1957. When political scientists William Ogburn and Dorothy Thomas studied this phenomenon, they found 148 cases of big ideas coming to many people at the same time and concluded that their list would grow longer with more research.

Having ideas is not the same thing as being creative. Creation is execution, not inspiration. Many people have ideas; few take the steps to make the thing they imagine. One of the best examples is the airplane. The brothers Orville and Wilbur Wright were not the first people to have the idea of building a flying machine, nor were they the first people to begin building one, but they were the first people to fly.

The Wright brothers' story begins in Germany's Rhinow Hills on Sunday, August 9, 1896. The sky stretched clean as a sheet, the moon chewed the sun in a partial solar eclipse, and a white shape soared between the peaks. It had the spoked wings of a bat and a crescent tail. A bearded man hung beneath: Otto Lilienthal, piloting a new glider, maneuvering by shifting his weight, aiming to create a powered flying machine. A gust of wind caught the glider and tilted it up. He swung his body but was unable to right it. His great white bat fell fifty feet, and Lilienthal thrashed in its jaws. His back was broken, and he died the next day. His last words were "Sacrifices must be made."

Orville and Wilbur Wright read the news at their Wright Cycle Company store in Dayton, Ohio. Lilienthal's sacrifice seemed senseless to them. No one should drive a vehicle he cannot steer, especially not in the sky.

Cycling was a new fashion in the 1890s. Bicycles are miracles of equilibrium. They are not easy to build or ride. When we cycle, we make constant adjustments to stay balanced. When we turn, we abandon this balance by steering and leaning, then recover it once our turn is complete. The problem of the bicycle is not motion; it is balance. Lilienthal's death showed the Wrights that the same was true of aircraft. In their book *The Early History of the Airplane,* the brothers wrote:

> The balancing of a flyer may seem, at first thought, to be a very simple matter, yet almost every experimenter had found in this one point which he could not satisfactorily master. Some experimenters placed the center of gravity far below the wings. Like the pendulum, it tended to seek the lowest point; but also, like the pendulum, it tended to oscillate in a manner destructive of all stability. A more satisfactory system was that of arranging the

wings in the shape of a broad V, but in practice it had two serious defects: first, it tended to keep the machine oscillating; and second, its usefulness was restricted to calm air. Notwithstanding the known limitations of this principle, it had been embodied in almost every prominent flying machine that had been built. We reached the conclusion that a flyer founded upon it might be of interest from a scientific point of view, but could be of no value in a practical way.

In the same book, Wilbur added: "When this one feature has been worked out the age of flying machines will have arrived, for all other difficulties are of minor importance."

This observation set the Wright brothers on the path to the world's first flight. They saw an airplane as "a bicycle with wings." The problem of the aircraft is not flying: like the bicycle, it is balance. Otto Lilienthal died because he succeeded at the first and failed at the second.

The Wrights solved the problem by studying birds. A bird is buffeted by wind when it glides. It balances by raising one wingtip and lowering the other. The wind turns the wings like sails on a windmill until the bird regains equilibrium. Wilbur again:

To mention all the things the bird must constantly keep in mind in order to fly securely through the air would take a very considerable treatise. If I take a piece of paper, and after placing it parallel with the ground, quickly let it fall, it will not settle steadily down as a staid, sensible piece of paper ought to do, but it insists on contravening every recognized rule of decorum, turning over and darting hither and thither in the most erratic manner, much after the style of an untrained horse. Yet this is the style of steed that men must learn to manage before flying can become an everyday sport. The bird has learned this art of equilibrium, and learned it so thoroughly that its skill is not apparent to our sight. We only learn to appreciate it when we try to imitate it.

That is, when we try to fly a horse.

These were the Wrights' first mental steps. *Problem:* Balance a bucking aircraft. *Solution:* Imitate gliding birds.

The next problem was how to reproduce a bird's balance mechanically. Their first solution required metal rods and gears. This caused the next problem: it was too heavy to fly. Wilbur discovered the solution in the Wrights' bicycle shop while playing with a long, thin cardboard box that had once contained an inner tube—something roughly the same size and shape as a box of tin foil or Saran Wrap. When Wilbur twisted the box, one corner dipped slightly and the other rose by the same amount. It was a motion similar to a gliding bird's wingtips, but it used so little force that it could be achieved with cables. The distinctive double wings on the brothers' airplanes were based on this box; they called the twisting that made the tips go up and down "wing warping."

As young boys, the Wrights had loved to make and fly kites—"a sport to which we had devoted so much attention that we were regarded as experts." Despite their fascination, they stopped during their teenage years because it was "unbecoming to boys of our ages." And yet, twenty years later, Wilbur found himself cycling through Dayton as fast as he could with a five-foot kite across his handlebars. He had built it with wings that warped to prove the idea worked. He was hurrying to show it to Orville. The brothers had completed their second step.

And so it continued. The Wright brothers' great inventive leap was not a great mental leap. Despite its extraordinary outcome, their story is a litany of little steps.

For example, they spent two years trying to make Wilbur's kite big enough to carry a pilot before discovering that the aerodynamic data they were using was worthless.

"Having set out with absolute faith in the existing scientific data," they wrote, "we were driven to doubt one thing after another, till finally, after two years of experiment, we cast it all aside, and decided to rely entirely upon our own investigations."

The Wrights had started flying as a hobby and with little interest in "the scientific side of it." But they were ingenious and easily intrigued. By the time they realized that all the published data was wrong—"little better than guesswork"—they had also discovered what knowledge was needed to design wings that would fly. In 1901, they built a bicycle-mounted test platform to simulate airplanes in flight, then a belt-driven wind tunnel they used to create their own data. Many of the results surprised them—their findings, they wrote, were "so anomalous that we were almost ready to doubt our own measurements."

But they eventually concluded that *everybody else's* measurements were wrong. One of the biggest sources of error was the Smeaton coefficient, a number developed by eighteenth-century engineer John Smeaton to determine the relationship between wing size and lift. Smeaton's number was 0.005. The Wrights calculated that the correct figure was actually 0.0033. Wings needed to be much bigger than anybody had realized if an airplane was ever going to fly.

The Wrights used the same data to design propellers. Propellers had been built for boats but never for aircraft. Just as the brothers thought of an airplane as a bicycle that flew, they thought of a propeller as a wing that rotated. The lessons from their wind tunnel enabled them to design a near-perfect propeller on their first attempt. Modern propellers are only marginally better.

The Wrights' aircraft are the best evidence that they took steps, not leaps. Their glider of 1900 looked like their kite of 1899. Their glider of 1901 looked like their glider of 1900 but with a few new elements. Their glider of 1902 was their glider of 1901, bigger and with a rudder. Their 1903 *Flyer*—the aircraft that flew from Kitty Hawk's sands—was their 1902 glider made bigger again with propellers and an engine added. Orville and Wilbur Wright did not leap into the sky. They walked there one step at a time.

Thinking might make planes and phones, but surely art flows from soul to eye? Karl Duncker's mental steps may apply to the calculation of engineering, but do they also describe the majesty of art? To answer this question, we return to a Berlin on the brink of war.

On November 1, 1913, Franz Kluxen entered Berlin's Galerie Der Sturm to buy a painting. Kluxen was one of Germany's foremost collectors of modern art. He owned works by Marc Chagall, August Macke, Franz Marc, and a dozen Picassos. On this day another artist caught his eye—a controversial figure pushing painting to become ever more unreal: Wassily Kandinsky. The picture Kluxen bought was an abstract of contorting shapes and penetrating lines dominated by blues, browns, reds, and greens called *Bild mit weißem Rand,* or *Painting with White Border.*

A few months before Kluxen walked up to the finished painting in Berlin, Kandinsky had walked up to its blank canvas in Munich with a single piece of charcoal in his hand. The canvas was covered in a white paint made from five layers of zinc, chalk, and lead. Kandinsky had specified the paint precisely. He forbade artificial chalk made from gypsum and demanded more expensive natural chalk made from fossilized cells a hundred million years old.

Kandinsky drew a picture with the charcoal. Then he mixed paints using as many as ten pigments per color—his purple was made of white, vermilion, black, green, two yellows, and three blues, for example—and brushed them on in layers from lightest to darkest without pausing or missing a stroke. The picture covered thirty square feet, but Kandinsky finished it quickly. This speed and certainty created an impression of spontaneity. It was as if he awoke that morning and rushed to record a vanishing fragment of dream.

Art is the mastery of making appearance deceive. Kandinsky spent five months planning every stroke of his apparently spontaneous painting and years developing the method and theory that took him to it. Kandinsky was a Russian immigrant living in Germany. He visited his native Moscow in the fall of 1912 just as the First Balkan War began. To Russia's south, the Balkan League of Serbia, Greece, Bulgaria, and Montenegro was attacking Turkey, then called the Ottoman Empire. It was a brief, brutal war that started at the time of Kandinsky's trip and finished as he completed *Painting with White Border,* in May 1913. He returned to Germany packing a problem: how to paint the emotion of the moment—the "extremely powerful impressions I had experienced in Moscow—or more correctly, of Moscow itself."

He started by painting a sketch in oils he called *Mascau,* later renamed *Sketch 1 for Painting with White Border.* It was a constricted thicket of velveteen green with cadmium red accents and dark hemming lines. A trio of black curves oozed toward the top left corner, evoking the three-horse sled called a troika, a common Kandinsky motif and a symbol used by other Russians, including Nikolai Gogol, to represent their nation's divinity.

His second sketch, barely different, diffused the lines until they were more stain than stroke—in his words, "dissolving the colors and forms." More sketches followed. Kandinsky burnished his picture on paper, card, and canvas. He scrawled in pencil, mapping which colors would go where using letters and words. He brushed some studies with watercolor, others with gouache—a blend of gum and pigment halfway between watercolor and oil—and India ink. He crayoned. He made twenty sketches, each no more than one or two steps different from the last. The process took five months. The twenty-first picture— Kandinsky's finished work—is very similar to the first. *Painting with White Border* is the old friend you run into after a few years. *Sketch 1* is how the friend used to look. But vast differences hide beneath the surface of each piece. They tell the true story of artistic creation.

The green ground of *Sketch 1* is a mix of seven colors: green, umber, ocher, black, yellow, blue, and white. At the painting's center, Kandinsky first applied a yellow made from five colors: cadmium yellow, yellow ocher, red ocher, yellow lake, and chalk. Then, when the yellow was dry, he painted it over with green. These steps were not artistic: the canvas of *Sketch 1* had already been used, and Kandinsky had to cover an existing painting. He did such a good job that it was not until almost a hundred years later, after the advent of infrared imaging, that a team of conservators working for New York's Guggenheim Museum, which owns *Painting with White Border*, and Washington, D.C.'s Phillips Collection, which owns *Sketch 1*, discovered that there was a picture beneath the picture.

Once he had prepared the canvas, Kandinsky continued *Sketch 1* by layering colors from dark to light, rearranging and repainting the picture many times as he worked. This is partly visible from a close inspection of his brushstrokes and has been fully exposed by X-ray, which undresses a painting layer by layer. An X-ray of *Sketch 1* shows a blur: Kandinsky reworked the image so many times that only a few elements of the finished piece can be seen. He painted over almost everything on the canvas in fits of iteration that lasted until he solved his first problem: how to capture "the extremely powerful impressions I had experienced in Moscow."

When *Sketch 1* was complete, Kandinsky identified remaining problems one at a time. He rotated the image from portrait to landscape, softened the colors, and changed the ground from dark green to luminous white. One sketch shows twenty variations of the troika as Kandinsky tuned its curves like strings on a cello. And then there was the eponymous white border:

> I made slow progress with the white edge. My sketches did little
> to help, that is, the individual forms became clear within me—and

yet, I could still not bring myself to paint the picture. It tormented me. After several weeks, I would bring out the sketches again, and still I felt unprepared. It is only over the years that I have learned to exercise patience in such moments and not smash the picture over my knee.

Thus, it was not until after nearly five months that I was sitting in the twilight looking at the second large-scale study, when it suddenly dawned on me what was missing—the white edge. Since this white edge proved the solution to the picture, I named the whole picture after it.

With this final problem solved, Kandinsky ordered the canvas. When he first touched it with his charcoal, he knew exactly what he was about to make. Where an X-ray of *Sketch 1* shows a blur of painted work and rework, an X-ray of *Painting with White Border* is exactly like the painting itself. This is how we know he did not hesitate. After five months and twenty steps, Kandinsky was ready to paint.

The twenty steps are only part of the story. Kandinsky's journey did not begin with *Sketch 1,* and it did not end with *Painting with White Border.* His first works, painted in 1904, were colorful, realistic landscapes. His last, painted in 1944, were atonal, geometric abstracts. His first and last pictures look wholly unalike, but everything Kandinsky painted in the intervening years was a small step along the road that unites them. *Painting with White Border* marks a slight move toward more abstract images and is part of Kandinsky's transition from dark to light. Even in a lifetime of art, creation is a continuum.

As Karl Duncker showed, all creation, whether painting, plane, or phone, has the same foundation: gradual steps where a problem leads to a solution that leads to a problem. Creating is the result of thinking like walking. Left foot, problem. Right foot, solution. Repeat until you arrive. It is not the size of your strides that determines your success but how many you take.

CHAPTER 3

EXPECT ADVERSITY

1 | JUDAH

One summer night in 1994, a five-year-old named Jennifer crept downstairs to tell her mother her ear hurt. Jennifer's pediatrician prescribed eardrops. The pain got worse. One side of her face bulged. The pediatrician doubled her dose. The swelling grew. X-rays revealed nothing. The lump got bigger than a baseball. Jennifer glowed with fever, her head inflated, she lost weight. Surgeons removed the lump. It came back. They took half of Jennifer's jaw. Still the lump returned. It was removed again. It came a fourth time, reaching toward her skull to kill her. Medicine did not work. Jennifer's one chance was radiation. Nobody knew if it would affect the tumor. Everybody knew it would stop half her face from growing. Children with that condition often kill themselves.

As Jennifer's parents contemplated their choice, her doctor heard rumors of a researcher with a controversial theory that tumors create their own blood supply. This man said growths like Jennifer's could be destroyed by cutting off their access to blood. Very few people believed him, and his approach was so experimental that it was practically quackery. The man's name was Judah Folkman.

Jennifer's doctor told her parents about this unproven theory. He warned them that Folkman was a controversial man with a mixed reputation, possibly more fantasist than scientist. Jennifer's parents felt they had little to lose. "Fantasy" is just another word for hope with long odds. It is better than no hope. Jennifer's father signed a consent form and put his daughter's life in Judah Folkman's hands.

Folkman prescribed injections of a new, unproven drug. Jennifer's father, a machinist, gave her the shots. Her mother, who worked at a grocery store, held her. For weeks they stuck needles into Jennifer's arm, over her tear-soaked cries of protest. Folkman's shots made her worse. They boiled the disfigured, dying little girl in fever and terrified her with visions. Neighbors heard her screaming during the night and remembered her in their prayers.

Folkman called his theory *angiogenesis*—Latin for "growth of new blood vessels." He had conceived it more than thirty years earlier when one of his experiments went wrong. He was an enlisted man, a surgeon required to spend time in the navy researching new ways to store blood on long voyages. To see what methods might work, he built a maze of tubes that circulated blood substitutes through a rabbit gland and injected the gland with the fastest-growing things he knew of: cancer cells from a mouse. He expected the cells to either grow or die. But something else happened. The cells grew as big as dots on dice, then stopped. They were still alive; when Folkman put them back in the mice, they swelled into deadly tumors. Here was mystery. Why would cancer stop on a gland but kill in a mouse?

Folkman noticed that the tumors in the mice were full of blood and the tumors on the glands were not. In the mice, new blood vessels reached out, greeting the tumors, feeding and growing them.

Other navy lab scientists found this mildly interesting. Judah Folkman thought it was life-changing. He felt sure he had discovered something important. What if the tumors were creating these new vessels, weaving themselves a bloody web in which to grow? What if you could stop that from happening? Would it kill the tumors?

Folkman was a surgeon. Wrist-deep in living flesh, surgeons see things lab scientists do not. To a surgeon, a tumor is a wet red mess, like fat on a steak. To a scientist, it is dry and white, like a cauliflower. "I had seen and handled cancers, and they were hot and red and bloody," Folkman said. "And so when critics would say, 'Well, we don't see any blood vessels in these tumors,' I knew they were looking at tumors that had been taken out. All the blood was drained. They were specimens."

After leaving the navy, Folkman joined City Hospital in Boston. His lab was tiny, and the only natural light that dribbled in was from windows near the high ceiling.

He worked alone for years. When he finally recruited a team, it consisted of one medical student and one undergraduate. They worked nights and weekends on a debut paper about how blood vessels depend on cell fragments called platelets. It was published in *Nature* in 1969.

After that, Folkman's work was rejected. *Cell Biology, Experimental Cell Research,* and the *British Journal of Cancer* refused to print his papers on the connections between tumors and blood. His requests for grants were denied. Reviewers said his conclusions went beyond the data, that what he saw in his lab would not be seen in patients, and that his experiments were poorly designed. Some called him crazy.

In the 1960s and '70s, no one in cancer cared about blood. All the glory went to tumor killers wielding radiation and poison. Doctors targeted malignant cells as if they were marauding armies and attacked them with treatments inspired by war. Chemotherapy was developed from the chemical weapons of World War I; radiation resembled the nuclear weapons of World War II. Folkman imagined cancer as a disease of regeneration, not degeneration—a condition caused by the body growing, unlike most other illnesses, which are caused by the body decaying or failing. He did not picture tumors as invaders. He thought they were naturally communicating cells, having what his first research assistant, Michael Gimbrone, called a "dynamic dialogue" with the body. Folkman was convinced that he could stop this communication and make tumors die of natural causes.

One reason Folkman faced skepticism was that he was a surgeon. Scientists had little respect for surgeons. A surgeon's place was in the butcher's shop of the operating room, not the library of the laboratory. But Folkman said that seeing cancer in living people helped his work. He once rushed to the lab inspired by a patient whose ovarian cancer had spread beyond her ovaries. During the surgical procedure to save her, he had found a large tumor full of blood orbited by small white tumors that had not yet signaled for a supply. He thought life was confirming his ideas even though all the experts were rejecting them.

And their rejection was fierce. At best, Folkman's talks were met with apathy. At worst, audiences walked out when it was his turn to speak, leaving him facing an empty room. A member of one grant committee wrote that he was "working on dirt." Another said he was on "a hopeless search." A professor at Yale called him "a charlatan." Researchers were advised not to join his lab. Members of the board of Boston Children's Hospital, where he had been surgeon in chief, worried that Folkman was damaging their hospital's reputation. They cut his salary in half and forced him to quit performing surgery. One day in 1981, he repaired the deformed throat of a newborn baby girl, scrubbed out, and was never allowed to operate again.

The attacks from outside Folkman's lab were matched by disappointments within it. Trying to prove his hypothesis meant monotonous experiments, most of which were unsuccessful. He put a sign on his wall excusing his lack of progress. It said: "Innovation is a series of repetitive failures."

One Saturday in November 1985, Folkman's researcher Donald Ingber found fungus contaminating one of his experiments. This is not uncommon in laboratories. Scientists follow a strict protocol: they throw contaminated experiments away. Ingber did not do this. He examined the blood vessels growing in the petri dish. The fungus was forcing them to retreat.

Ingber and Folkman experimented with the fungus, watching as it blocked the growth of blood vessels in culture dishes, then chicken embryos, then mice.

Enter Jennifer. Folkman tried to exorcise her tumor to prove his crackpot theory of angiogenesis. As Jennifer twisted and screamed under the torture of Folkman's "treatment," her family came to realize why Folkman could not get published, funded, or perform surgery. It was the same reason other scientists called him a crazy charlatan on a hopeless search, walked out of his talks, said he was working on dirt, and told researchers to avoid him.

The reason was that his idea was new.

After the first few weeks of agonizing treatment, Jennifer's fevers cooled. Her hallucinations passed. The lump in her head shrank away until it left her forever. Her jaw grew back. She was a pretty little girl again. Judah Folkman had saved her life.

2 | FAIL

There are no shortcuts to creation. The path is one of many steps, neither straight nor winding but in the shape of a maze.

Judah Folkman walked the maze. It is easy to enter and difficult to stay.

Creation is not a moment of inspiration but a lifetime of endurance. The drawers of the world are full of things begun. Unfinished sketches, pieces of invention, incomplete product ideas, notebooks with half-formulated hypotheses, abandoned patents, partial manuscripts. Creating is more monotony than adventure. It is early mornings and late nights: long hours doing work that will likely fail or be deleted or erased—a process without progress that must be repeated daily for years. Beginning is hard, but continuing is harder. Those who seek a glamorous life should not pursue art, science, innovation, invention, or anything else that needs new. Creation is a long journey where most turns are wrong and most ends are dead. The most important thing creators do is work. The most important thing they don't do is quit.

The only way to be productive is to produce when the product is bad. Bad is the path to good. Until he saved Jennifer's life, Folkman described his work as "a series of repetitive failures." Those failures did not come easily. There were gory experiments with rabbit eyes, chicken embryos, and puppy intestines. Some ideas needed vast quantities of cow cartilage, others gallons of mouse urine. Many experiments had to be repeated many times. Some went wrong and were thrown away. Some went right but yielded unhelpful results. Much of the work took nights and weekends. Long periods of effort produced nothing. Folkman once wondered about the difference between futility and tenacity and came to a conclusion that became his mantra: "If your idea succeeds, everybody says you're persistent. If it doesn't succeed, you're stubborn."

Folkman saved more lives after Jennifer's. Angiogenesis became an important theory in the treatment of cancer. Doctors and scientists regarded Folkman as more than persistent—he was lauded as a genius. But he received that distinction only after he proved his hypothesis. Surely either he had been a genius all along or he was no genius at all?

Donald Ingber's fungus was not the miraculous coincidence it might seem to be. Endurance often finds fortune. Folkman and his team worked for years to discover ways to culture blood vessels, to test for blocking agents, and to understand the nature of tumor growth. Ingber was a brilliant scientist, working on a Saturday, prepared for chance. In any other lab, the fungus would have been thrown out. In other labs, doing different research, it almost certainly already had been. That event was a culmination, not a revelation. Luck favors work.

We enter creation's maze with problems at every turn. Folkman's beginning, working alone in a badly lit lab barely bigger than a toll-booth, was not auspicious. Neither were his first experiments. He started with more questions than answers. We will, too. Some we ask ourselves. Some are asked by others. We will not know the answers or even how to find them. Creation demands belief beyond reason. Our foothold is faith—in ourselves, in our dream, in our odds of success, and in the cumulative, compound, creative power of work. Folkman had no reason to know he was right and countless reasons to believe he was wrong—many of them provided by his peers. He continued because of faith.

Faith is how we face failure. Not faith in a higher power—although we may choose that, too—but faith that there is a way forward. Creators redefine failure. Failure is not final. It carries no judgment and yields no conclusions. The word comes from the Latin *fallere,* to deceive. Failure is deceit. It aims to defeat us. We must not be fooled. Failure is lesson, not loss; it is gain, not shame. A journey of a thousand miles ends with a single step. Is every other step a failure?

Stephen Wolfram, scientist, author, and entrepreneur, is best known for his geeky software program Mathematica. In addition to writing books and code, he obsessively gathers information about his life. He has amassed what he says is "one of the world's largest collections of personal data." He knows how many e-mails he has sent since 1989, how many meetings he has had since 2000, how many phone calls he has made since 2003, and how many steps he has taken since 2010. He knows these things precisely. Since 2002 he has logged every key he has ever pressed on his computer's keyboard. He made over one hundred million keystrokes in the ten years between 2002 and 2012 and was surprised to find that the key he pressed most often was Delete. He had used it more than seven million times: he erased seven out of every hundred characters he typed, a year and a half of writing, then deleting.

Wolfram's measurement includes around two hundred thousand e-mails. He found he deleted most often when he was writing for publication. This is true for professional writers, too. Stephen King, for example, has published more than eighty books, most of them fiction. He says he writes two thousand words a day. Between the beginning of 1980 and the end of 1999, he published thirty-nine new books, totaling more than five million words. But writing two thousand words a day for twenty years yields *fourteen* million words: King must erase almost two words for every one he keeps. He says, "That DELETE key is on your machine for a good reason."

Where do Stephen King's deleted words go? They are not all lost to rephrasing. One of King's most popular books is a novel called *The Stand,* published in 1978. The finished manuscript, submitted after he had made all his deletions, was, he says, "twelve hundred pages long and weighed twelve pounds, the same weight as the sort of bowling ball I favor."

His publishers were worried that such a long book would not sell, so King made more deletions: three hundred pages' worth. But his most telling revelation is that he might never have traveled that far: around the halfway point in the writing, after more than five hundred single-spaced pages, King got stuck: "If I'd had two or even three hundred pages I would have abandoned *The Stand* and gone on to something else—God knows I had done it before. But five hundred pages was too great an investment, both in time and in creative energy."

King will throw away three hundred single-spaced typewritten pages, about sixty thousand words, which will have taken him more than a month to write, if he feels they are not good enough.

Success is the culmination of many failures. When James Dyson, an inventor, finds a problem, he immediately builds something that does not solve it, an approach he calls "make, break, make, break." What the world calls a failure the engineer calls a prototype. From Dyson's website:

There's a misconception that invention is about having a great idea, tinkering with it in the tool shed for a few days, then appearing with the finished design. In fact, it's usually a far longer and iterative process—trying something over and over, changing one small variable at a time. Trial and error.

Dyson describes himself as "just an ordinary person. I get angry about things that don't work." The thing that made him so angry it changed his life was a vacuum cleaner that lost suction as its bag filled. He was thinking about it as he drove past a factory with a dust extractor that works based on a principal called "cyclonic separation." Cyclonic separators, or cyclones, spin air in a spiral and move anything else—like dust and dirt—around until it eventually drops down. This is is how Dorothy got to Oz:

> The north and south winds met where the house stood, and made it the exact center of the cyclone. In the middle of a cyclone the air is generally still, but the great pressure of the wind on every side of the house raised it up higher and higher, until it was at the very top of the cyclone. The little girl gave a cry of amazement and looked about her. The cyclone had set the house down very gently—for a cyclone—in the midst of a country of marvelous beauty.

The beauty of dust extraction by cyclone is simple: there is no filter to clog, which means nothing reduces the suction. Filters were the reason most vacuum cleaners sucked—or, rather, did not. Dyson's idea was equally simple: make a vacuum cleaner that used a cyclone instead of sucking dust and air through a filter.

Cyclone math is *not* simple—it combines fluid mechanics to describe the movement of air with particle transport equations to predict the behavior of dust. Dyson did not waste much time on this math. Like the Wright brothers, he made an observation, then went straight to making. And the first thing he made—out of cardboard and a disassembled vacuum cleaner—did not work. Neither did the second, third, or fourth.

Dyson faced many problems. He had to make the world's smallest cyclone. It had to be capable of extracting house dust particles about a millionth of a meter wide. And he had to make it suitable for home use and mass production.

It took more than five *thousand* prototypes, constructed over five years, to create a working cyclone-based vacuum cleaner. He says, "I'm a huge failure because I made 5,126 mistakes." And, on another occasion:

> I wanted to give up almost every day. A lot of people give up when the world seems to be against them, but that's the point when you should push a little harder. I use the analogy of running a race. It seems as though you can't carry on, but if you just get through the pain barrier, you'll see the end and be okay. Often, just around the corner is where the solution will happen.

Dyson's solution was—eventually—a working cyclone-based vacuum cleaner that created a multibillion-dollar business and a personal fortune of more than $5 billion.

Judah Folkman's observation that "innovation is a series of repetitive failures" applies to every field of creation and every creator. Nothing good is created the first time. The step-by-step approach to problem solving Karl Duncker observed does not apply only to *forward* movements like Kandinsky's sketches. Some steps go *backward*. But persistence turns everything into progress. Writer Linda Rubright's definition of "Iterative Process" is "Total fail. Repeat." Creators must be willing to fail and repeat until they find the step that arrives. Samuel Beckett said it best: "Try again. Fail again. Fail better."

Failure is not wasteful but useful. Time spent failing is time spent well. Wandering creation's maze is never a waste of time. Only leaving it is.

A Hungarian psychology professor once wrote to famous creators, asking them to be interviewed for a book he was writing. One of the most interesting things about his project was how many people said no.

Management writer Peter Drucker: "One of the secrets of productivity (in which I believe whereas I do not believe in creativity) is to have a VERY BIG waste paper basket to take care of ALL invitations such as yours—productivity in my experience consists of NOT doing anything that helps the work of other people but to spend all one's time on the work the Good Lord has fitted one to do, and to do well."

Secretary to novelist Saul Bellow: "Mr. Bellow informed me that he remains creative in the second half of life, at least in part, because he does not allow himself to be a part of other people's 'studies.'"

Photographer Richard Avedon: "Sorry—too little time left."

Secretary to composer György Ligeti: "He is creative and, because of this, totally overworked. Therefore, the very reason you wish to study his creative process is also the reason why he (unfortunately) does not have time to help you in this study. He would also like to add that he cannot answer your letter personally because he is trying desperately to finish a Violin Concerto which will be premiered in the Fall."

The professor contacted 275 creative people. A third of them said no. Their reason was lack of time. A third said nothing. We can assume their reason for not even saying no was also lack of time and possibly lack of a secretary.

Time is the raw material of creation. Wipe away the magic and myth of creating and all that remains is work: the work of becoming expert through study and practice, the work of finding solutions to problems and then problems with those solutions, the work of trial and error, the work of thinking and perfecting, the work of *creating*. Creating consumes. It is all day, every day. It knows neither weekends nor vacations. It is not when we feel like it. It is habit, compulsion, obsession, and vocation. The common thread that links creators is how they spend their time. No matter what you read, no matter what they claim, nearly all creators spend nearly all their time on the work of creation. There are few overnight successes and many up-all-night successes.

Saying no has more creative power than ideas, insights, and talent combined. Saying no guards time, the thread from which we weave our creations. The math of time is simple: you have less than you think and need more than you know.

We are not taught to say no. We are taught *not* to say no. No is rude. No is a rebuff, a rebuttal, a minor act of verbal violence. No is for drugs and strangers with candy.

But consider the Hungarian professor: famous, distinguished, politely and personally requesting a small amount of time from people who had already found creative success. And two-thirds of them declined, in most cases saying nothing or having someone else say no for them, wasting not even a minute to reply.

Creators do not ask how much time something takes but how much creation it costs. This interview, this letter, this trip to the movies, this dinner with friends, this party, this last day of summer. How much less will I create unless I say no? A sketch? A stanza? A paragraph? An experiment? Twenty lines of code? The answer is always the same: yes makes less. We do not have enough time as it is. There are groceries to buy, gas tanks to fill, families to love, and day jobs to do.

People who create know this. They know the world is all strangers with candy. They know how to say no, and they know how to suffer the consequences. Charles Dickens, rejecting an invitation from a friend:

"It is only half an hour"—"It is only an afternoon"—"It is only an evening," people say to me over and over again; but they don't know that it is impossible to command one's self sometimes to any stipulated and set disposal of five minutes—or that the mere consciousness of an engagement will sometime worry a whole day. Who ever is devoted to an art must be content to deliver himself wholly up to it, and to find his recompense in it. I am grieved if you suspect me of not wanting to see you, but I can't help it; I must go in my way whether or no.

No makes us aloof, boring, impolite, unfriendly, selfish, antisocial, uncaring, lonely, and an arsenal of other insults. But no is the button that keeps us on.

4 | NOW WASH YOUR HANDS

Failure is often followed by rejection.

In 1846, large numbers of women and babies were dying during childbirth in Vienna. The cause of death was puerperal fever, a disease that swells then kills its victims. Vienna's General Hospital had two maternity clinics. Mothers and newborns were dying in only one of them. Pregnant women waited outside the hospital, begging not to be taken to the deadly clinic, often giving birth in the street if they were refused. More women and babies survived labor in the street than in the clinic. All the deaths came at the hands of doctors. In the other clinic, midwives delivered the babies.

Vienna General was a teaching hospital where doctors learned their trade by cutting up cadavers. They often delivered babies after dissecting corpses. One of the doctors, a Hungarian named Ignaz Semmelweis, started to wonder if the puerperal fever was somehow being carried from the corpses to the women in labor. Most of his peers thought the question preposterous. Carl Edvard Marius Levy, a Danish obstetrician, for instance, wrote that Semmelweis's "beliefs are too unclear, his observations too volatile, his experiences too uncertain, for the deduction of scientific results." Levy was offended by the lack of theory behind Semmelweis's work. Semmelweis speculated that some kind of organic matter was being transferred from the morgue to the mothers, but he did not know what it was. Levy said this made the whole idea unsatisfactory from a "scientific point of view."

But, from a *clinical* point of view, Semmelweis had convincing data to support his hypothesis. At a time when doctors did not scrub in or out of the operating room, and were so proud of the blood on their gowns that they let it build up throughout their careers, Semmelweis persuaded the doctors of Vienna to *wash their hands* before delivering babies, and the results were immediate. In April 1847, 57 women died giving birth in Vienna General's deadly First Clinic—18 percent of all patients. In the middle of May, Semmelweis introduced hand-washing. In June, 6 women died, a death rate of 2 percent, the same as the untroubled Second Clinic. The death rate stayed low, and in some months fell to zero. In the following two years, Semmelweis saved the lives of around 500 women, and an unknown number of children.

This was not enough to overcome the skepticism. Charles Delucena Meigs, an American obstetrician, typified the outrage. He told his students that a doctor's hands could not possibly carry disease because doctors are gentlemen and "a gentleman's hands are clean."

Semmelweis did not know why hand-washing before delivery saved lives—he only knew that it did. And if you do not know *why* something saves lives, why do it? For Levy, Meigs, and Semmelweis's other "gentlemen" contemporaries, preventing the deaths of thousands of women and their babies was not reason enough.

As the medical community rejected Semmelweis's ideas, his morale and behavior declined. He had been a rising star at the hospital until he proposed hand-washing. After a few years, he lost his job and started showing signs of mental illness. He was lured to a lunatic asylum, put in a straitjacket, and beaten. He died two weeks later. Few attended his funeral. Without Semmelweis's supervision, the doctors at Vienna General Hospital stopped washing their hands. The death rate for women and babies at the maternity clinic rose by 600 percent.

Even in a field as apparently empirical and scientific as medicine, even when the results are as fundamental as life not death, and even when the creation is as simple as asking people to wash their hands, creators may not be welcome.

Why? Because powerful antibodies of the status quo mass against change. When you bring something truly new to the world, brace. Having an impact is not usually a pleasant experience. Sometimes the hardest part of creating is not having an idea but saving an idea, ideally while also saving yourself.

Semmelweis's idea challenged two millennia of medical dogma. Since the time of Hippocrates, doctors had been trained in humorism: the belief that the body is made up of four fluids, or humors: black bile, yellow bile, phlegm, and blood. Humorism lives in our language today. In Latin, black bile is *melan chole*. People with too much of it were said to suffer from *melancholy*. Too much yellow bile, *chole,* made a person irritable, or *choleric*. An excess of blood, *sanguis,* made them optimistic, or *sanguine*. Phlegm made them stoic, or *phlegmatic*. Good health meant these humors were in balance. Disease and disability came from imbalances caused by inhaling vapors or "bad air," an idea known as "miasma theory." Diseases were treated by removing blood. In the nineteenth century, doctors removed blood by placing leeches on their patients' bodies, a treatment called "hirudotherapy." The leeches attached themselves to the patient's skin using a sucker, behind which lay a three-bladed, propeller-shaped jaw. Once the sucker was in place, the leech latched on by biting, injected anesthetic and blood thinners into the patient; then it sucked the patient's blood. Once full, it dropped off to begin digestion. The process took up to two hours. It was important to wait. If the leech was removed prematurely, it would vomit into the patient's open wound.

Semmelweis's idea that puerperal fever might be carried by doctors from corpses to patients and could therefore be prevented by hand-washing contradicted the ancient trinity of humorism, miasma, and hirudotherapy. How could hygiene impact health when disease was generated spontaneously inside the body?

As Semmelweis lay dying, another creator, Louis Pasteur, answered this question. Where Semmelweis pointed to the number of women who did not die and expected common sense to prevail, Pasteur used carefully designed experiments to advance what became known as "germ theory." He produced incontrovertible evidence to show that living microorganisms caused many diseases. Pasteur was well aware of the controversial nature of his theory and possibly also of the hostile rejection that proponents like Semmelweis had suffered. Humorism's true believers had been fighting rumors about germs for centuries. Pasteur was meticulous with his evidence, persistent with his claims, and eventually convinced most of Europe. Semmelweis's clinical results hinted at the truth, but they were not enough to overcome two thousand years of belief in something else. A new idea needs much better evidence than an old one, as some of our best thinkers have pointed out.

David Hume: "A wise man proportions his belief to the evidence."

Pierre-Simon Laplace: "The weight of evidence for an extraordinary claim must be proportioned to its strangeness."

Marcello Truzzi: "An extraordinary claim requires extraordinary proof."

Carl Sagan: "Extraordinary claims require extraordinary evidence."

Prevailing ideas are fortified by incumbency and familiarity, no matter how ridiculous they may seem later. They can only be changed by people ready to meet rejection with evidence, patience, and stamina. Semmelweis believed that saving hundreds of women was enough.

One reason for Semmelweis's collapse was that he did not expect such a good idea to be so soundly rejected and was shocked at the vicious and sometimes personal attacks. But creation is the infiltration of the old by the new, a stone in the shoe of the status quo, and this makes creators threats, at least to some. As a consequence, creation is seldom welcome.

Still, Semmelweis's surprise is typical. The most common misconception about creation is that good ideas are celebrated—partly because of something that happened in Concord, Massachusetts, in 1855.

5 | BETTER MOUSETRAPS

In a long, flowing hand that joined words as well as letters, Ralph Waldo Emerson wrote in his journal, "If a man has good corn, or wood, or boards, or pigs, to sell, or can make better chairs or knives, crucibles, or church organs, than anybody else, you will find a broad, hard beaten road to his house, though it be in the woods." By 1889, several years after Emerson's death, the line was being misquoted as "If a man can write a better book, preach a better sermon, or make a better mousetrap than his neighbor, though he builds his house in the woods, the world will make a beaten path to his door." Later it was changed again, to "Build a better mousetrap and the world will beat a path to your door," and became famous.

These words did more than cause a misunderstanding about the popularity of new things in general. Many people take them literally, and as a result, the mousetrap has become one of the most frequently patented and reinvented devices in America. Around four hundred applications for mousetrap patents are made every year. About forty patents are granted. More than five thousand mousetrap patents have been issued in total—so many that the U.S. Patent and Trademark Office has thirty-nine subclasses for mousetraps, including "Impaling," "Choking or Squeezing," and "Electrocuting and Explosive." Independent inventors hold nearly all mousetrap patents. Almost all of them cite the quotation they believe is Emerson's. But the world does not beat a path to their door. Fewer than twenty of the five thousand mousetrap patents have ever made any money.

The saying was not intended to inspire better mousetraps. Rather, a better mousetrap inspired it. Emerson could not have written it: he died before commercial mousetraps were invented. I know the story well in part because my great-grandfather, who lived at the same time as Emerson, made his living as a rat catcher. His principal tools were dogs: Jack Russell terriers, a relatively new breed in those days and one developed specifically for hunting vermin. Other mouse-trapping techniques included cats—actually less effective than dogs, despite their reputation—as well as cages and drowning. This changed in the late 1880s, when an inventor from Illinois named William C. Hooker created the first mass-production mousetrap. And not long after that, my family's trade changed, too. There was little demand for rat catchers when people could buy cheap traps. Hooker's trap is the one we know today: a spring-loaded bar released by a trigger when a mouse takes the bait. This is the "better mousetrap" referred to in the 1889 revision of Emerson's words. It does not need building: William Hooker has already built it.

Hooker's "snap trap" was perfected within a few years. It was cheap, easy, and effective. It remains the dominant design today. It traps a quarter of a billion mice a year, outsells all its competitors combined by a factor of two to one, and costs less than a dollar. Almost all of the five thousand mousetraps created since Hooker's have been rejected.

The idea that creators are hailed as heroes is as wrong today as it was when Emerson did not write it. Emerson's actual point was about what he called "common fame"—the success a person has in their community if they provide valuable goods or services. If he were writing today, Emerson might have said, "Open the best coffee shop in town and your neighbors will wait in line for a cup." He is not exhorting us to invent an alternative to coffee.

The mistaken belief that the world awaits a better mousetrap has yielded more than mousetraps. It has given rise to an industry of predators. Businesses called "invention promotion companies" advertise on television and radio and in newspapers and magazines, promising to evaluate people's ideas, patent them, and sell them to manufacturers and retailers. They charge an initial fee of hundreds of dollars for "evaluation." The evaluation almost always concludes that a person's idea is patentable and valuable. Then the companies demand thousands of dollars for legal and marketing services. Inventors are made to feel that their idea has been specially selected. They are given the impression that the invention promotion company will be investing its own time and money in their idea so it can earn royalties. In fact, the companies make all their money from the up-front fees. They have little success marketing inventions or helping inventors.

In 1999, the U.S. federal government intervened to protect the "Nation's most precious natural resource: the independent inventor." The American Inventor's Protection Act was signed into law by President Clinton, and the Federal Trade Commission filed lawsuits against invention promotion companies operating under names including National Idea Center, American Invention Associates, National Idea Network, National Invention Network, and Eureka Solutions International. In a moment of knowing poetry, the FTC called its program Project Mousetrap.

One company, Davison & Associates, settled with the FTC by making a payment of $11 million and promising not to misrepresent its services. The company has since changed its name to Davison Design. It has an amusement park–like "factory" called Inventionland, complete with a castle, pirate ship, and tree house hidden behind a false bookcase in its offices in O'Hara, Pennsylvania. Inventionland is staffed by employees called "Inventionmen." Their creations include a pan for making meatballs, a rail for storing flip-flops, and clothes for dogs. Many of their inventions are based on Davison's own ideas, even though they are billed as "client products."

Inventionland is where we find the truth about better mousetraps. The FTC settlement forced Davison to disclose how many of its clients make money. According to the company's November 2012 report, an average of eleven thousand people a year sign its agreements. Of these, three make a profit. In the twenty-three years between Davison's founding, in 1989, and 2012, twenty-seven people have made money using the company's services, barely more than one a year. How much money? Davison has to disclose its prices. Its customers multiplied by its prices equals sales of $45 million a year. Davison says the money it makes on sales of its customers' products is 0.001 percent of its revenue and that this represents a 10 percent royalty on what its customers make. If this is correct, Davison makes $450 a year from royalties and Davison's customers all added together receive a total of $4,050 a year for the $45 million a year they spend on the company's services—less than one dollar returned for every ten thousand invested.

Davison offers to sign up more than sixty thousand ideas a year. This alone should make an inventor suspicious—and it might but for the myth of the better mousetrap. Unfortunately, anyone who loves your idea the first time they hear it either loves you or wants something. What to expect when you're inventing is rejection. Build a better mousetrap and the world will not beat a path to your door. You must beat a path to the world.

6 | THE MOST DECISIVE OF DENIALS

Rejection hurts, but it is not the worst thing that can happen. On February 22, 1911, Gaston Hervieu grasped the railing on the first platform of the Eiffel Tower and looked down. He was almost two hundred feet above Paris. The people watching him from the ground looked smaller than his fingernails.

Hervieu was an inventor of parachutes and airships. In 1906, he was part of a team that tried to reach the North Pole by airship; in 1909, he developed a parachute to slow the descent of aircraft. Hervieu had climbed the Eiffel Tower to test a new emergency parachute for pilots. He checked the wind, took a nervous breath, and began the test. His parachute opened as soon as it cleared the platform. The silk filled with air, making a hemisphere in the sky, then sailed safely to the ground. A photographer from the Dutch newsweekly *Het Leven* captured the moment: a figure descending gracefully, silhouetted beneath the tower's northwestern arch, with the watching crowd and the Palais du Trocadéro in the background.

There was a catch, though. Hervieu did not make the jump himself; he used a 160-pound test dummy instead. To most people this seemed prudent, but for at least one man, it was an outrage. Franz Reichelt was an Austrian tailor who was developing a parachute of his own. He denounced Hervieu's use of a dummy as a "sham" and, one year later, on the morning of Sunday, February 4, 1912, arrived at the Eiffel Tower to conduct an experiment of his own.

Reichelt had made sure his test would be publicized. Photographers, journalists, and a cameraman from the Pathé news service were all waiting to meet him. He posed for pictures, doffed his black beret, and then made an announcement that took most people by surprise. He would not be using a dummy or even a safety harness. He said, "I am so convinced my device will work properly that I will jump myself."

Gaston Hervieu, who had come to the Eiffel Tower to watch Reichelt's test, tried to stop him. Hervieu claimed there were technical reasons why Reichelt's parachute would not work. The two men had a heated discussion until, finally, Reichelt turned away and walked to the tower's staircase. As he began his ascent, he looked back and said, "My parachute will give your arguments the most decisive of denials."

Hervieu had carried a parachute and a dummy up the 360 steps to the tower's first floor, but Reichelt carried nothing: he was *wearing* his parachute, just as a pilot would if he were about to leap from a crashing airplane. Reichelt's description of the concept appeared in news stories the following day: "My invention has nothing in common with similar devices. It is partly waterproof fabric and partly pure silk. The first serves as clothing and adapts to the body like ordinary clothes; the second consists of a parachute which is folded behind the pilot like a backpack."

Two assistants were waiting for him when he reached the top of the staircase. They set a chair on a table so that Reichelt could stand above the railing and jump. For more than a minute, he stayed with one foot on the chair and the other on the railing, looking down, checking the wind, and making last-minute adjustments. It was below freezing in Paris, and his breaths came out as steamy plumes. Then he stepped off the railing, into the void.

A photographer from *Het Leven* waited beneath the tower's northwestern arch, ready to take a picture exactly like the one of Hervieu's test, only showing a living man, not a dummy.

That picture does show a living man, but it is different from the one taken a year earlier in another way. Where the photograph of Hervieu's test shows a perfect parachute, the photograph of Reichelt's test shows a blur like a broken umbrella. The broken umbrella is Reichelt. His "parachute" did not work. It was a suit of clothes intended to turn the person wearing it into something like a flying squirrel. Large silk sheets connected Reichelt's arms to his ankles, and a hood stood above his head. Reichelt fell for four seconds, accelerating constantly, until he hit the ground at sixty miles an hour, making a cloud of frost and dust and a dent six inches deep. He was killed on impact.

Modern parachutes use 700 square feet of fabric and should be deployed only above 250 feet; Reichelt's parachute used less than 350 square feet of fabric, and he deployed it at 187 feet. He had neither the surface area nor the altitude needed to make a successful jump; this was why Hervieu had tried to stop him.

Hervieu was not the only one who had told Reichelt that his parachute suit would not work; it had also been rejected by experts at the Aéro-Club de France, who had written, "The surface of your device is too small. You will break your neck."

Reichelt ignored all these rejections until the only thing left to reject him was reality. And, as physicist Richard Feynman said seventy-four years later, "For a successful technology, reality must take precedence over public relations, for nature cannot be fooled."

Dramatic ending aside, Reichelt's story is the story of most would-be creators. We hear about creation's few wins and never know its many losses. Tales like Ignaz Semmelweis's are carefully chosen cherries. Much of their power comes from dramatic irony: we know the creator will be vindicated in the end. This can make creators seem like heroes and rejecters seem like villains. But rejecters are nearly always sincere. They want to stop wrong and dangerous thinking. They believe they are right, and they usually are. If Reichelt had landed, we would read his story differently. Reichelt would seem like a hero, Hervieu a jealous rival, and the Aéro-Club de France a group of out-of-touch obstructionists. But only the outcome would be different. The motives of Reichelt's rejecters would be unchanged.

Rejection has value.

Judah Folkman was rejected for decades. His grants were denied, his papers returned, his audiences hostile. He endured lawsuits, demotion, innuendo, and insult. But he was a charming man. He inspired his researchers, was always available to patients, and told his wife he loved her every day. Folkman was not rejected because he was bad or because his ideas were bad. He was rejected because rejection is a natural consequence of new.

Why? Because we fear new as much as we need it.

In the 1950s, two psychologists, Jacob Getzels and Phillip Jackson, studied a group of high school students. All the students had higher-than-average IQs, but Getzels and Jackson found that the most creative students tended to have lower IQs than the least creative students. As part of the study, the students wrote brief autobiographies. One higher-IQ student wrote:

> My autobiography is neither interesting or exciting and I see
> very little reason for writing it. However I shall attempt to write
> a certain amount of material which would be constructive. I was
> born May 8, 1943, in Atlanta, Georgia, USA. I am descended from
> a long line of ancestry which is mostly Scotch and English, with a
> few exceptions here and there. Most of my recent ancestors have
> lived in the southern US for a good while, though some are from
> New York. After being born, I remained in Georgia six weeks,
> after which I moved to Fairfax, Virginia. During my four-year stay
> there, I had few adventures of any kind.

One highly creative student wrote:

> In 1943 I was born. I have been living without interruption ever
> since. My parents are my mother and father—an arrangement
> I have found increasingly convenient over the years. My father
> is a physician and surgeon—at least that's what the sign on his
> office door says. Of course, he's not anymore for Dad's past the
> age where men ought to enjoy the rest of his life. He retired from

Mercy Hospital Christmas before last. Got a fountain-pen for 27 years of service.

The difference between these two passages is typical of the differences the study found between the high-IQ children and the highly creative children. The highly creative children were funnier, more playful, less predictable, and less conventional than the high-IQ children. This was no surprise. The surprise was the teachers: they liked the high-IQ children, but they did *not* like the creative children. Getzels and Jackson were amazed. They had expected the opposite, because their experiment had revealed something else: the highly creative children were delivering academic results as good as or better than the high-IQ children—a performance far better than the twenty-three-point deficit in their IQ scores would predict. If you believed in IQ scores—and all the teachers in this school did—the highly creative children were beating the odds. But, even though the highly creative children were star performers who were exceeding expectations, the teachers did not like them. They preferred the less creative children who were performing as expected.

This was not a freak result. It has been repeated many times, and it remains the same today. The vast majority—98 percent—of teachers say creating is so important that it should be taught daily, but when tested, they nearly always favor less creative children over more creative children.

The Getzels-Jackson effect is not restricted to schools, and it persists into adulthood. Decision makers and authority figures in business, science, and government all say they value creation, but when tested, they do not value creators.

Why? Because people who are more creative also tend to be more playful, unconventional, and unpredictable, and all of this makes them harder to control. No matter how much we say we value creation, deep down, most of us value control more. And so we fear change and favor familiarity. Rejecting is a reflex.

We do not only reject other people's creative instincts; often, we reject our own, too.

In one experiment, Dutch psychologist Eric Rietzschel asked people to score ideas based on how "feasible," "original," and "creative" they were, and then asked them which ones were "the best." The ideas people selected as "the best" ideas were almost always the ones they had scored as the least "creative."

When Rietzschel asked people to assess their own work, he got the same result: almost everybody thought their least "creative" ideas were their "best" ideas.

The findings are highly repeatable. Decades of data all show the same thing: even though we say we want creation, we tend to reject it.

8 | THE NATURE OF NO

The tendency to welcome new ideas in principle then reject them in practice is a feature, not a bug. Every species has its niche, and every niche has its risk and reward. The human race's niche is the niche of new. Our reward is rapid adaptation: we can change our tools faster than evolution can change our bodies. Our risk is that the footsteps of new lead into darkness. Creating something new may kill us; creating nothing new certainly will. This makes us creatures of contradiction: we need and fear change. No one is only progressive or only conservative. Each of us is both. And so we say we want new, then choose same.

Our innate drive for new would make us extinct if it were unrestrained. Everyone would die trying everything. The instinct to reject is evolution's solution to our problem of needing to make new while needing to take care.

We are wired to reject new things, or at least be suspicious of them. When we are in familiar situations, cells in our brain's seahorse-shaped core, the hippocampus, fire hundreds of times faster than they do when we are in new situations. The hippocampus is connected to two tiny balls of neurons called amygdalae—from the Greek for "almonds"— that drive our emotions. The connection between the hippocampus and the amygdalae is one reason that same feels good and new may not.

As our brains react, so do we. We swerve from what feels bad to what feels better. When something is new, our hippocampus finds few matching memories. It signals unfamiliarity to our amygdalae, which give us feelings of uncertainty. Uncertainty is an aversive state: we avoid it if we can. Psychologists can show this in experiments. Feelings of uncertainty bias us against new things, make us prefer familiarity, and stop us from recognizing creative ideas. This happens even when we value creation or think we are good at creating.

To make matters worse, we fear rejection, too. As anyone who has lost a lover knows, rejection hurts. We use phrases like "broken-hearted," "bruised egos," and "hurt feelings," because we feel physical pain when spurned—a word that, not coincidentally, comes from the Old English *spurnen,* "to kick." In 1958, psychologist Harry Harlow proved something Aristotle had proposed twenty-five hundred years earlier: we need love like we need air. In experiments no ethics committee would allow today, Harlow separated newborn monkeys from their mothers. The babies preferred a soft, cloth surrogate mother doll to a wire surrogate, even though the wire version delivered food. Monkeys deprived of a soft surrogate often died, despite having enough food and water. Harlow called his paper "The Nature of Love" and concluded that physical contact is more important than calories. His finding extends to humans. We would rather die hungry than lonely.

Our primal need for connection doubles the dilemma of novelty. We are biased against new experiences, but it is hard to admit that we feel this way, even to ourselves, because we also face social pressure to make positive statements about creative ideas. We know we should not suggest that being creative is bad. We may even self-identify as "creative." The bias against new is a prejudice a bit like sexism and racism: we know it is socially unacceptable to "dislike" creation, we sincerely believe we "like" creation, but when presented with a specific creative idea, we are more likely to reject it than we realize. And, when we present a creative idea to others, *they* are much more likely to reject it than *they* realize. It is human nature to say no to new.

Sexism and racism are famous prejudices. The bias against new is not. No one talks about *newism*. "Luddism," our closest word, is a misunderstanding. The Luddites—about whom much more later—were English weavers who destroyed automatic looms to protect their jobs during the late eighteenth and early nineteenth centuries. Although Luddism was, in the words of Thomas Pynchon, an effort to "deny the machine," the attack on new technology was incidental. The Luddites were not fighting against new. They were fighting for their livelihoods. Yet their name fills the void in our vocabulary where there is a fear without a noun.

The bias against new is no less real because it goes unnamed; if anything, its anonymity makes it worse. Labels make things visible. Women and racial minorities are not surprised by prejudice against them. The words "sexism" and "racism" signal that sexism and racism exist. Newism comes with no such warning. When companies, academies, and societies revere creation in public and then reject it in private, creators *are* surprised and wonder what they did wrong.

Boston Children's Hospital's rejection of Judah Folkman is typical. Children's is one of America's highest-ranked hospitals and part of Harvard University, the oldest institute of higher learning in the United States. The hospital houses more than a thousand scientists and has produced Nobel laureates and Lasker Award winners. It is a place where new ideas should be welcomed. Yet Children's punished Folkman for having a theory about cancer that his contemporaries found controversial. The hospital is proud of him now. But in 1981, when it stopped him from being a surgeon and reduced his pay, it was not. I chose Folkman's story because it shows how flowers are sometimes mistaken for weeds. The point is not that Boston Children's Hospital did something wrong. The point is that it did something normal.

What is *not* normal about Folkman's story is his tenacity. It is hard to withstand repeated rejection. But we cannot create unless we know what to do with no.

9 | ESCAPING THE MAZE

How do we escape this maze of rejection, failure, and distraction?

Rejection is a reflex that evolved to protect us. No matter what we may gain, our first reactions to new are suspicion, skepticism, and fear. This is the right response: most ideas are bad. Stephen Jay Gould: "A man does not attain the status of Galileo merely because he is persecuted; he must also be right."

Creators must expect rejection. The only way to avoid rejection is to avoid making anything new. Rejection is not a ticket to quit. It does not mean the work is bad. It does not mean *we* are bad. Rejection is about as personal as gravity.

At its best, rejection is information. It shows us what to do next. When Judah Folkman's early critics argued that he was seeing inflammation, not blood vessels, he designed experiments to exclude inflammation. Rejection is not persecution. Drain it of its poison and what remains may be useful.

Franz Reichelt, the parachutist who leapt to his death, did not listen to the lessons of rejection or failure. He not only ignored experts who pointed out the flaws in his design, he ignored his own data. He tested his parachute using dummies, and they crashed. He tested his parachute by jumping thirty feet into a haystack, and *he* crashed. He tested his parachute by jumping twenty feet *without* a haystack, and he crashed *and* broke his leg. Instead of changing his invention again and again until it worked, he clung to his bad idea in the face of all evidence and stopped thinking at the first solution he'd found.

The creation is not the creator. Great creators do not extend their belief in themselves to their work. A creation can be changed. The problem-solution loop never ends. Reichelt's loop ended soon after it began. His tragedy is a metaphor for the problem with leaps. He saw a problem and tried to solve it not with a series of steps but with a leap both literal and figurative. He was not an artist of new but a martyr to same.

Ignaz Semmelweis, the hand-washing obstetrician so vexed by rejection that he lost his job, then his life, missed a huge opportunity. Semmelweis had found something of world-changing importance: a link between cadavers and disease. His critics complained that he did not know what it was. He believed that saving lives was convincing enough. But it was not. If he had taken his rejection less personally and fought back by devoting himself to understanding more, he, not Louis Pasteur, might have discovered germs, and his contribution might have saved lives everywhere forever, instead of in one place for a few years.

Failure is a kind of rejection best done in private. The greatest creators are their own greatest critics. They look at their work even more deeply than other people will, and they test it against more exacting standards. They reject most of what they make either in part (as Stephen King does when he throws away two-thirds of his words) or in whole (as James Dyson does when he condemns yet another prototype) many times before anybody else gets to. The world is already inclined to reject you. Do not give it more reasons than necessary. Never have a failure in public that you could have in private. Private failures are faster, cheaper, and less painful.

Our nature does not help us. In addition to the discomfort with ambiguity that pushes us to want to find solutions quickly, there is also the problem of pride. Pride and its opposite, shame, can make us fearful of failure and resentful of rejection. Our ego does not want to hear no. We want to be right the first time, make a quick buck, be an overnight success. The creativity myth, with its roots in genius, aha! moments, and other magic, appeals to the part of us that wants to win without work, get without sweat, make no mistakes. None of these things are possible. Do not take pride in your work. Earn it.

We can learn a lot from what people do when they get lost in *real* mazes—along backcountry hiking routes, on terrain crossed with old trails, and in other places where losing your way can be deadly. This is only somewhat metaphorical. Whether we are creating or walking, we are trying to get somewhere by taking steps and making choices.

William Syrotuck analyzed 229 cases of people who became lost, 25 of whom died. He found that when we are lost, most of us act the same way. First, we deny that we are going in the wrong direction. Then, as the realization that we are in trouble seeps in, we press on, hoping chance will lead us. We are least likely to do the thing that is most likely to save us: turn around. We know our path is wrong, yet we rush along it, compelled to save face, to resolve the ambiguity, to achieve the goal. Pride propels us. Shame stops us from saving ourselves.

Great creators know that the best step forward is often a step back—to scrutinize, analyze, and assess, to find faults and flaws, to challenge and to change. You cannot escape a maze if you only move forward. Sometimes the path ahead is behind.

Rejection educates. Failure teaches. Both hurt. Only distraction comforts. And of these, only distraction can lead to destruction. Rejection and failure can nourish us, but wasted time is a tiny death. What determines whether we will succeed as creators is not how intelligent we are, how talented we are, or how hard we work, but how we respond to the adversity of creation.

Why is changing the world so hard? Because the world does not want to change.

CHAPTER 4

HOW WE SEE

1 | ROBIN

June 1979 was a cold, wet month in Western Australia. The worst day was Monday, June 11. An inch of rain fell, blown by a mean wind that turned windows into drums. Behind a loud window in Perth, a man with a silver beard and bolo tie looked through his microscope and saw something that would change the world.

Robin Warren was a pathologist at the Royal Perth Hospital. What he saw were bacteria in a patient's stomach. Scientists had known that bacteria could not grow in the stomach since the beginning of bacteriology. Stomachs are acidic, so they had to be sterile. The bacteria Warren saw were curved like croissants. They flattened the brushy surface of the stomach's lining. Warren could see them at magnifications of one hundred, but his colleagues could not. He showed them images magnified one thousand times, then some taken with a high-power electron microscope. They eventually saw the bacteria but not the point. Only Warren thought the discovery meant something, although he did not know what.

He did not rush to judgment, like Ignaz Semmelweis, nor did he disregard possible objections, like Franz Reichelt, nor did he allow his rejection instinct to delete the gleam of something new. Warren was a quieter, shier man than Judah Folkman, but his response to being the only person in the lab who thought he had seen something significant was Folkmanesque. He believed what he saw, he believed it might be important, and he would not be dissuaded. In his report of that day's biopsy, he wrote: "It contains numerous bacteria. They appear to be actively growing and not a contaminant. I am not sure of the significance of these unusual findings, but further investigation may be worthwhile."

Having seen the bacteria once, he saw them often. They were in one out of every three stomachs. The dogma of the sterile stomach said bacteria could not live in the gut. No one else had ever seen bacteria there. "The apparent absence of any previous report was given to me as one of the main reasons why they could not be there at all," he said.

Warren collected samples of the bacteria that were not there for two years, until he found someone who believed him.

Barry Marshall was a newly hired gastroenterologist who needed a research project. Warren, like all pathologists, did not see patients. He worked with samples clinicians gave him, most of which were from ulcers and lesions. This made seeing the bacteria harder: activity around the wounds added noise. Marshall agreed to send Warren biopsies from ulcer-free sites, and the two men started to collaborate.

Within a year, Warren and Marshall had one hundred clean samples. They found that 90 percent of patients who had the bacteria had ulcers. *Every* patient with a duodenal ulcer—erosion in the lining of the acidic passage at the start of the intestine, immediately after the stomach—had the bacteria.

The two men tried and failed to grow the bacteria in the hospital's lab. For six months they started with live samples and ended with nothing.

Then, during Easter 1982, a drug-resistant superbug contaminated the hospital and overwhelmed its lab. Warren and Marshall's samples were forgotten for five days. The lab staff had been discarding the samples after two. The bacteria grew in the extra three. All they had needed was more time.

The bacterium was new. It was eventually given the name *Helicobacter pylori,* or *H. pylori* for short. Warren and Marshall wrote about their discovery in a 1984 letter to the *Lancet,* one of the world's highest-impact medical journals. They concluded that the bacteria, which "appeared to be a new species, were present in almost all patients with active chronic gastritis, duodenal ulcer, or gastric ulcer and thus may be an important factor in these diseases."

The *Lancet*'s editor, Ian Munro, could not find any reviewers who agreed. Everybody knew bacteria could not grow in the stomach. The results had to be wrong. Fortunately for Warren and Marshall—and all of us—Ian Munro was no ordinary journal editor; he was a radical thinker who, among other things, campaigned for human rights, nuclear disarmament, and medicine for the poor. In an unusual and impactful moment of science as it should be, Munro published the letter over the objections of his reviewers, even adding a note saying, "If the authors' hypothesis should prove valid this work is very important indeed."

Warren and Marshall went on to show that *H. pylori* causes ulcers. Others, building on their work, learned how to cure ulcers by killing *H. pylori* with antibiotics. In 2004, Warren and Marshall won the Nobel Prize "for their discovery of the bacterium *Helicobacter pylori* and its role in gastritis and peptic ulcer disease." We now know that there are hundreds of species of bacteria in the stomach and that, among other things, they play an essential role in keeping the digestive system stable.

There is something strange about this story.

What Robin Warren saw on that cold, wet Monday was not something no one had seen. It was something everyone had seen. The only thing he did that no one else had done was believe it. By 1979, Warren had spent seventeen years mastering the complex science of pathology—the careful preservation and examination of human tissue—especially analyzing stomach biopsies. These became common in the 1970s, after the invention of the flexible endoscope—a tube with a light, camera, and cutting tool that doctors could feed down the throat of a patient and use to extract tissue. Before this, most samples were either from whole stomachs that had been removed or from cadavers. These were difficult to process. Information was lost while the samples were made ready for analysis. It was these bad samples that had led to every doctor and scientist being taught that bacteria do not live in the stomach. Warren said, "This was taken as so obvious as to barely rate a mention." His biopsies told a different story.

"As my knowledge of medicine and then pathology increased, I found that there are often exceptions to 'known facts,'" he said.

Also, "I preferred to believe my eyes, not the medical textbooks or the medical fraternity."

He makes it sound simple. Yet flexible endoscopes were being used all over the world. Thousands of pathologists were looking at stomach biopsies. *H. pylori* was staring them all in the face. But they saw dogma, not bacteria.

In June 1979, the month Warren first noticed *H. pylori,* a group of American scientists published a paper about an epidemic of stomach disease among participants in a research study. The volunteers were healthy at the start of the project; then half of them became ill with stomach pain, followed by a loss of stomach acidity. The illness was almost certainly infectious. The scientists tested the patients' blood and stomach fluid. They looked for a virus—because they knew bacteria could not grow in the stomach—and they did not find one. Their conclusion was: "We have been unable to isolate an infectious agent, nor have we been able to establish a viral or bacterial cause." These were not beginners; they were led by a decorated professor of medicine who was also editor in chief of the journal *Gastroenterology*. After Warren and Marshall's work was published, these scientists revisited their biopsies. *H. pylori* was clearly visible. They had seen it and not seen it. Their patients had been suffering from an acute infection of the bacteria. One of the scientists said, "Failing to discover *H. pylori* was my biggest mistake."

In 1967, Susumu Ito, a professor at Harvard Medical School, had biopsied his own stomach and used an electron microscope to take a perfect photograph of *H. pylori*. It appeared labeled as a "spirillum," but without further comment or attempt at identification, in that year's American Physiological Society *Handbook of Physiology*. Tens of thousands of scientists saw the picture. None of them saw *H. pylori*.

In 1940, Harvard researcher Stone Freedberg had found *H. pylori* in more than a third of ulcer patients. His supervisor told him he was wrong and made him stop his research.

Only Robin Warren believed and would not be dissuaded. He maintained a lonely vigil over *H. pylori* for two years, until Marshall arrived.

H. pylori has now been found in medical literature dating back to 1875. When Robin Warren discovered it, it had been seen and not believed for 104 years.

2 | WHAT YOU SEE IS NOT WHAT YOU GET

H. pylori's tiny boomerangs hid in plain sight for more than a century because of a problem called "inattentional blindness." The name comes from perception psychologists Arien Mack and Irvin Rock, but the best definition comes from novelist Douglas Adams:

> Something that we can't see, or don't see, or our brain doesn't let us see, because we think that it's somebody else's problem. The

brain just edits it out; it's like a blind spot. If you look at it directly you won't see it unless you know precisely what it is. It relies on people's natural predisposition not to see anything they don't want to, weren't expecting or can't explain.

Adams uses this definition in his book *Life, the Universe and Everything* in a scene where nobody notices that an alien spacecraft has landed in the middle of a cricket match. The story is comic, but the concept is real: the brain is the secret censor of the senses. It takes steps between sensing and thinking that we do not notice.

The path from eye to mind is long. Each eye has two optic nerves, one for the right half of the brain and one for the left. They travel as far back as they can possibly go—to an outside layer at the back of the brain called the visual cortex. Touch the back of your head, and your hand is next to the part of your brain that connects to your eyes. The visual cortex compresses what your eyes see by a factor of ten, then passes the information to the center of the brain, the striatum. The information is compressed again, this time by a factor of three hundred, as it travels to its next stop, the basal nuclei at the striatum's core. This is where we discover what the eyes have seen and decide what to do about it. Only one three-thousandth of what is rendered on the retina gets this far. The brain selects what gets through by adding prior knowledge and making assumptions about how things behave. It subtracts what does not matter and what has not changed. It determines what we will and will not know. This preprocessing is powerful. What the brain adds seems real. What it subtracts may as well not exist.

This is why it is a bad idea to have a phone conversation while driving. Using a phone halves the amount of sensory information that enters our mind. Our eyes stare at the same things for the same length of time, but our brain edits out most of the information as unimportant. The information may be important for driving, but our brain preprocesses it based on what is important for our phone call. This does not happen when we are listening to the radio, because the radio does not expect us to talk back. It does not happen when we are talking to a passenger, because the passenger is in the same space we are. But studies show that when we talk on the phone, we get inattentional blindness. The conversation is our problem. That child unexpectedly crossing the street in front of us is somebody else's problem. Our brain does not let us see her. As Douglas Adams described it, our brain blinds our mind to the unusual.

This is also true when we are walking. In one study, researchers put a clown on a unicycle in the path of pedestrians. The researchers asked people who walked past the clown if they had noticed anything unusual. Everybody saw him unless they had been on their cell phone. Three out of every four people who had been using their phone did not see the clown. They looked back in astonishment, unable to believe they had missed him. They had looked straight at him but had not registered his presence. The unicycling clown crossed their paths but not their minds.

Harvard researchers Trafton Drew and Jeremy Wolfe did a similar experiment with radiologists by adding a picture of a gorilla to X-rays of lungs. An X-ray section of a lung looks like a black-and-white picture of a bowl of miso soup. As radiologists flick through images, they see progressive slices of the lungs, as if they are looking deeper into the soup. In Drew and Wolfe's images, a crudely cut out black-and-white picture of a man in a gorilla suit had been added to the top right corner of some of the layers, as if he were floating on his back there. The radiologists saw the tiny nodules that indicated whether each lung was cancerous, but almost all of them missed the gorilla, even though it was shaking its fist at them and would have occupied as much space as a matchbox if it had actually been present in the lungs. Each radiologist who did not see the gorilla looked at it for about half a second.

Inattentional blindness is not an experimental effect. In 2004, a forty-three-year-old woman went to the emergency room suffering from fainting and other symptoms. The doctors suspected heart and lung problems, so they put a catheter into her body using a guidewire that went from her thigh to her chest. The doctors forgot to remove the guidewire. Five days passed before anybody found it. The woman spent all that time in intensive care, where she had three X-rays and a CT scan as attempts were made to stabilize her. A dozen doctors looked at the images. The guidewire in her chest—which, fortunately, did not contribute to her condition—was obvious on all of them, but nobody noticed it.

3 | OBVIOUS FACTS

When Robin Warren accepted his Nobel Prize, he quoted Sherlock Holmes: "There is nothing more deceptive than an obvious fact."

It was an "obvious fact" that bacteria do not live in the stomach, just as it was an "obvious fact" that emergency room doctors remember to remove guidewires and an "obvious fact" that there are no gorillas in pictures of lungs.

Radiologists are experts in seeing. Years of training and practice make what is invisible to us obvious to them. They can diagnose a disease after looking at a chest X-ray for a fifth of a second, the time it takes to make a single voluntary eye movement. If you or I were to look at an X-ray of a lung, we would scan the whole thing, searching for irregularities. This is also what novice radiologists do. But as they become more trained, they move their eyes less, until all they have to do is glance at a few locations for a few moments to find the information they need.

This is called "selective attention." It is a hallmark of expertise. "Expert" has the same Latin root as "experience." Aldous Huxley, writing in his 1932 book *Texts and Pretexts,* says: "Experience is a matter of sensibility and intuition, of seeing and hearing the significant things, of paying attention at the right moments, of understanding and coordinating."

Adriaan de Groot, a chess master and psychologist, studied expertise by showing a chess position to players of different ranks, including grandmasters and world champions, and asking them to think aloud as they considered their move. De Groot had two expectations. First, that better players would make better moves. Second, that better players would make more calculations. What he found surprised him.

The first thing he noticed was the same problem-solution loop undergraduates used to solve the candle problem, Apple used to design the iPhone, and the Wright brothers used to invent the airplane.

A chess expert's first step is to evaluate the problem. One master started like this:

"Difficult: this is my first impression. The second is that by actual numbers I should be badly off, but it is a pleasant position."

The second step is to think of a move:

"I can do a whole lot of things. Get my Rook into it, at the Pawns."

Each move is evaluated after it is generated:

"No, a touch of fantasy. Not worth much. No good. Maybe not so crazy."

De Groot discovered several things. First, unfamiliar problems are solved with slow loops that are easily verbalized. Second, everybody revisits and reevaluates some solutions. This is not indecision: each evaluation goes deeper.

What surprised De Groot was how the problem-solution loop differed between players of different ranks. He'd expected grandmasters to make the best moves, and they did. But he had thought that this would be due to more analysis. What he found was the opposite. Grandmasters evaluated fewer moves and reevaluated them less often than other players did. One grandmaster evaluated one move twice, then evaluated another and played it. It was the best possible move. This was generally true: despite evaluating fewer moves fewer times, four of the five grandmasters in the study made the best possible move. The other grandmaster made the second best possible move. Grandmasters did not consider any moves that were not in the top five best moves. Lower-ranked players considered moves as poor as the twenty-second best. The less expert the player, the more options they considered, the more evaluations they made, and the worse their eventual move was.

Less thinking led to better solutions. More thinking led to worse solutions. Was this evidence of genius and epiphany? Were grandmasters making their moves by inspiration?

No. De Groot noticed something odd as he listened to grandmasters thinking aloud. Here is a typical comment from a grandmaster:

"First impression: an isolated Pawn; White has more freedom of movement."

Compare this to a master, a skilled player just one rank down, talking about the same position:

"The first thing that strikes me is the weakness of the Black King's wing, particularly the weakness at KB6. Only after that a general picture of the position. Finally, the complications in the center are rather striking: possibilities for exchange in connection with the loose Bishop on K7. Still later: my Pawn on QN2 is *en prise*."

En prise means the piece is vulnerable to being taken—this is the "isolated Pawn" the grandmaster mentioned first. We do not need to understand chess to see that the grandmaster came to an instant conclusion where the master took more time. De Groot hypothesized that the grandmasters' "remarks represent but a fraction of what has, in reality, been perceived. By far the largest part of what the subject 'sees' remains unsaid."

Experts do not think less. They think more efficiently. The practiced brain eliminates poor solutions so quickly that they barely reach the attention of the conscious mind.

De Groot showed this with another experiment. Grandmaster Max Euwe (a world champion), a master (De Groot himself, with his wife acting as experimenter), an expert-level player, and a class-level player were shown a position for five seconds, then asked to reconstruct it and think about a move. For Euwe, the grandmaster, this was trivial—he reconstructed the board easily. De Groot, the master, put nearly all the pieces in the right place but argued with his wife because he thought she had made a mistake setting up the board: "Is there really a Black Knight on KB2? That would be rather curious!" The expert-level player remembered three-quarters of the board; the class-level player, less than half.

Was grandmaster Euwe a genius? Did he have a photographic memory? No. As De Groot suspected, forcing Euwe to reconstruct the position showed he was thinking in fast loops:

"First impression: awfully rotten position, strong compressed attack by White. The order in which I saw the pieces was about King on K1, Knight on Q2, White Queen on QB3, Queen on K2, Pawns on K3 and his on K4, White Rook on Q8, White Knight on QN4, Rook on QN5—that funny Rook that doesn't do anything—Knight on KB2, Bishop on KB1, Rook on KR1, Pawns on KR2 and KN3. I didn't look at the other side very much, but I presume there is another Pawn on QR2. The rest for White: King on KN8, Rook on KB8, Pawns on KB7, KN7, KR7, and QR7, QN7."

In the five seconds he was given to look at the board, Euwe had seen the pieces in priority order, understood the logic of the position, and started reasoning about his move. He was doing ordinary thinking extraordinarily fast. His speed came from experience. It enabled him to see similarities to other games and connections between pieces. He did not *remember* the positions of the pieces—he *inferred* them. For example, he reconstructed the position that De Groot had assumed was a mistake by inference and without doubt: "Another piece is on

KB2—the King was completely closed in—that must be a Knight then."

The position reminded him of another game—"there's a vague recollection of a Fine-Flohr game in the back of my mind"—and all the similarities he saw gave him "a certain feeling of being familiar with this sort of situation." Experience enabled him to find a solution almost instantly.

Grandmasters have not been grandmasters forever. When they were masters, they played like masters, evaluating more moves more times. When they were expert-level players, they played like expert-level players—evaluating even more moves even more times. Because they have evaluated so many moves and accumulated so much experience, grandmasters can pay very selective attention to a game. The expert's first impression is not a first impression at all. It is the latest in a series of millions.

Creating is thinking. Attention is what we think *about*. The more we experience, the less we think—whether in chess, radiography, painting, science, or anything else. Expertise is efficiency: experts use fewer problem-solution loops because experts do not consider unlikely solutions.

Which means "selective attention" is another way of saying "obvious facts." As Robin Warren and Sherlock Holmes remind us, obvious facts can deceive. They are all we will see with the blindness of inattention. Developing expertise is essential, but it can block us from seeing the unexpected.

Becoming an expert is only the first step to becoming creative. As we are about to find out, the second step is surprising, confusing, and perhaps even intimidating: it is becoming a beginner.

In 1960, twelve elderly Japanese Americans waited at a gate in San Francisco International Airport. It had been nineteen years since the Japanese navy had attacked America's Pacific Fleet in Pearl Harbor. After the attack, these men and women were imprisoned in stables at a horse track in San Bruno. Three years later, the American government set each of them free with twenty-five dollars and a train ticket, then dropped atom bombs on Japan. They were Zen Buddhists and congregants of Sokoji, or the San Francisco Temple, which they had built in an abandoned synagogue near the Golden Gate Bridge in the calm before the war. They had continued to pay the mortgage while imprisoned. They were at the airport to meet their new priest.

As the sun rose, a silver-and-white Japan Air Lines Pacific Courier arrived from Honolulu, where it had stopped for fuel on its twenty-four-hour journey from Tokyo. Passengers started down stairs behind its port-side wing. Only one traveler, a tiny man in robes, sandals, and socks, looked energetic: Shunryu Suzuki, the priest.

Suzuki arrived in America when it was on the cusp of the 1960s. Children of the war were coming of age, animosity toward Japan was becoming curiosity, and young San Franciscans had started visiting Sokoji to ask about Zen Buddhism. Suzuki gave them all the same answer: "I sit at 5:45 in the morning. Please join me."

It was an invitation to the seated meditation called *zazen* in Japanese and *dhyāna* in Sanskrit. People in India and East Asia had sat in quiet contemplation for thousands of years, but the practice was little known in America. The few Americans who had tried it used chairs. Suzuki made his students sit on the floor with their legs crossed, backs upright, and eyes half-open. If he suspected they were sleeping, he struck them with a stick called a *kyōsaku*.

The class grew throughout the 1960s. In 1970, Suzuki's American students published his teachings in a book. The next year, a little more than a decade after his arrival, he died. The book, *Zen Mind, Beginner's Mind*, was as small, modest, and inspiring as he was. His was American Buddhism's first voice. His book is still in print.

Beginner's mind, *shoshin* in Japanese, was the essence of Suzuki's teaching. He described it simply: "In the beginner's mind there are many possibilities, but in the expert's there are few."

In Zen, simple words can have deep meanings. Beginner's mind is not the mind of the beginner but the mind of the master. It is an attention beyond the selection and blindness of expertise, one that notices everything without assumption. Beginner's mind is not mystical or spiritual but practical. It is Edmond Albius looking at a flower, Wilbur and Orville Wright looking at a bird, Wassily Kandinsky looking at a canvas, Steve Jobs looking at a phone, Judah Folkman looking at a tumor, Robin Warren looking at a bacterium. It is seeing what is there instead of seeing what we think.

Nyogen Senzaki, one of the first Zen monks in America, explained beginner's mind with a story, or *kōan:*

Nan-in, a Japanese master, received a university professor who came to inquire about Zen.

Nan-in served tea. He poured his visitor's cup full, and then kept on pouring.

The professor watched the overflow until he no longer could restrain himself. "It is overfull. No more will go in!"

"Like this cup," Nan-in said, "you are full of your own opinions and speculations. How can I show you Zen unless you first empty your cup?"

David Foster Wallace made the same point with a joke:

There are these two young fish swimming along and they happen to meet an older fish swimming the other way, who nods at them and says, "Morning, boys. How's the water?" And the two young fish swim on for a bit, and then eventually one of them looks over at the other and goes "What the hell is water?"

Creation is attention. It is seeing new problems, noticing the unnoticed, finding inattentional blind spots. If, in retrospect, a discovery or invention seems so obvious we feel as if it was staring us in the face all along, we are probably right. The answer to the question "Why didn't I think of that?" is "beginner's mind."

Or as Suzuki writes in *Zen Mind, Beginner's Mind:* "The real secret of the arts is to always be a beginner."

To see the unexpected, expect nothing.

5 | STRUCTURE

While Shunryu Suzuki was teaching Eastern philosophy at Sokoji, Thomas Kuhn was teaching Western philosophy on the other side of San Francisco Bay, in Berkeley. Kuhn was recovering from a great disappointment. He had spent sixteen years at Harvard University, earned three degrees in physics, and become a member of the university's elite Society of Fellows, but had been denied a position as a tenured professor. He had come to California to rebuild his career.

Kuhn's problem was that he had changed his mind. His degrees were in physics, but while working on his PhD, he had developed an interest in philosophy, a subject for which he had passion but no training. He also taught an undergraduate course on the history of science. He was not a scientist, philosopher, or historian but some odd combination of all three. Harvard was not sure what to do with him, and, he soon discovered, neither was the University of California, which hired him as a professor of philosophy, then changed his role to include history. It was clear he was no longer a scientist. The rest was fog.

This change in Kuhn's path started one summer afternoon when he first read Aristotle's *Physics*. The conventional view was that the book laid a foundation for all the physics that followed, but Kuhn could not see it. For example, Aristotle says:

> Everything that is in locomotion is moved either by itself or by something else. In the case of things that are moved by themselves it is evident that the moved and the movement are together: for they contain within themselves their first movement, so that there is nothing in between. The motion of things that are moved by something else must proceed in one of four ways: pulling, pushing, carrying, and twirling. All forms of locomotion are reducible to these.

This is not imprecise Newtonian physics or incomplete Newtonian physics; it is not Newtonian physics at all. The more Kuhn read old science, the more he realized that it was not connected to the science that followed it. Science is not a continuum, he concluded, but something else.

So, Kuhn wondered, what are we to make of these old theories? Were they not science and the people who practiced them not scientists? Did Newtonian physics also cease to be scientific when Einsteinian physics replaced it? How does science move from one set of theories to another, if not by gradually building on the work of the past?

By 1962, after fifteen years of research, Kuhn had his answer. He published it in a book called *The Structure of Scientific Revolutions*. He proposed that science proceeded in a series of revolutions where ways of thinking changed completely. He called these ways of thinking "paradigms." A paradigm is stable for a time, and scientists work on proving things that the paradigm predicts, but eventually exceptions appear. Scientists treat the exceptions as unanswered questions at first, but if enough of them are discovered and the questions are important enough, their paradigm is thrown into "crisis." The crisis continues until a new paradigm emerges. Then the cycle begins again. In Kuhn's view, a new paradigm is not an improved version of its predecessor. New paradigms vanquish old paradigms altogether. This is why it is impossible to understand scientists like Aristotle through a modern lens: they were working in a paradigm that has since been overthrown by scientific revolutions.

Despite its obscure topic, Kuhn's book has sold more than a million copies and is one of the most cited works in the world. Science writer James Gleick called it "the most influential work of philosophy in the latter half of the 20th century."

Paradigms are a form of selective attention. What changes during one of Kuhn's "scientific revolutions" is what scientists see. In Kuhn's words: "During revolutions scientists see new and different things when looking with familiar instruments in places they have looked before. What were ducks in the scientist's world before the revolution are rabbits afterwards."

Robin Warren's "discovery" of the bacterium *H. pylori,* which occurred after Kuhn's book was published, may be the clearest example of scientists seeing what they expect, not what is there. After Warren, scientists looked at images they had looked at before and were amazed to see things they had not previously seen. Their expertise—the system of beliefs, experiences, and assumptions Kuhn calls a paradigm— had blinded them.

Seeing is not the same as looking. Knowing changes what we see as much as seeing changes what we know—not in a metaphorical or metaphysical way but literally. People on cell phones did not see the unicycling clown. Radiologists did not see the gorilla. Generations of scientists did not see *H. pylori*. This is not because the mind plays tricks but because the mind *is* a trick. Seeing and believing evolved because making sense of the world enabled species to survive and reproduce. Later, we became conscious and creative and wanted more from our senses, but as soon they were good enough for survival and reproduction, they were good enough for everything. We may want to believe that we inhabit a stable, objective universe and that our senses and minds render it fully and accurately—that what we perceive is "real"— and we may need to believe this so we can feel sane enough and safe enough to get on with our lives, but it is not true. If we want to understand the world enough to change it, we must understand that our senses do not give us the whole picture. Neil deGrasse Tyson, speaking at the Salk Institute in 2006, said:

There is so much praise for the human eye, but anyone who has seen the full breadth of the electromagnetic spectrum will recognize how blind we are. We cannot see magnetic fields, ionizing radiation, or radon. We cannot smell or taste carbon monoxide, carbon dioxide, or methane, but if we breathe them in we are dead.

We know that these things exist because we have developed tools that sense them. But whether we use senses or sensors or both, our perception will always be limited by what we can detect and how we understand it. The first limitation is obvious—we know our eyes cannot see without light, for example—but the second, understanding, is not. There is a line between eye and mind. Not everything makes it across.

Creating means opening this border: reshaping our understanding so we notice things we have not noticed before. They do not have to be big or extraordinary. David Foster Wallace told his joke about fish to introduce something apparently mundane:

> After work you have to get in your car and drive to the supermarket. The supermarket is very crowded. And the store is hideously lit and infused with soul-killing Muzak. It's pretty much the last place you want to be. And who are all these people in my way? Look at how repulsive most of them are, and how stupid and cowlike and dead-eyed and nonhuman they seem, or at how annoying and rude it is that people are talking loudly on cell phones. Look at how deeply and personally unfair this is. Thinking this way is my natural default setting. It's the automatic way that I experience the boring, frustrating, crowded parts of life.
>
> But there are totally different ways to think about these kinds of situations. You can choose to look differently at this fat, dead-eyed, over-made-up lady who just screamed at her kid in the checkout line. Maybe she's not usually like this. Maybe she's been up three straight nights holding the hand of a husband who is dying of bone cancer. If you really learn how to pay attention, it will actually be within your power to experience a crowded, consumer-hell type situation as not only meaningful, but sacred. You get to consciously decide what has meaning and what doesn't.

When we change what has meaning, we change what we see. Wallace offers an alternative paradigm for the line at the grocery store. The lady's appearance stays the same, but he sees her differently. His second interpretation—that her husband has bone cancer—is speculative and probably wrong, but it is not more speculative or more likely to be wrong than his first. It is probably closer to the truth: few of us are generally mean, but all of us have difficult days that make us look mean to strangers. Wallace directs his selective attention to select something else. He can do this because he recognizes that his "natural default" way of seeing is not his *only* way of seeing. It is a choice. His ability to choose to see ordinary things differently—"as not only meaningful, but sacred"—made him one of the greatest writers of his generation.

Beginner's mind and expertise sound like opposites, but they are not. Western philosophy has conditioned us to see things in opposing pairs—black and white, left and right, good and evil, yin and yang (as opposed to the original Chinese idea of yin-yang), beginner and expert—a paradigm called "dualism." We do not have to see things this way. We can see them as connected, not opposed. Beginner's mind is *connected to,* not *opposite to,* expertise because the greatest experts understand that they are working within the constraints of a paradigm and they know how those constraints arose. In science, for example, some constraints are the result of available tools and techniques. Robin Warren had developed enough expertise as a pathologist to know that the dogma of the sterile stomach predated the invention of the flexible endoscope and might be a wrong assumption caused by a lack of technology. Judah Folkman knew that assumptions about tumors were based on specimens, not surgery. The Wright brothers knew that the Smeaton coefficient for calculating the relationship between wing size and lift was an assumption developed in the eighteenth century that might be wrong. The greatest test of your expertise is how explicitly you understand your assumptions.

There are no true beginners. We start building paradigms as soon as we are born. We inherit some, we are taught some, and we infer some. When we first create, we are already David Foster Wallace's fish, swimming in a sea of assumptions we have not yet noticed. The final step of expertise is the first step to beginner's mind: knowing what you assume, why, and when to suspend your assumptions.

There is a problem with seeing things no one else sees. How do we know we are right? What's the difference between necessary confidence and dangerous certainty—between discovery and delusion?

In the summer of 1894, Percival Lowell looked through the telescope in his new observatory for the first time. He had already announced he was starting "an investigation into the condition of life on other worlds," with "strong reason to believe that we are on the eve of a pretty definite discovery in the matter."

Lowell watched the ice on the south pole of Mars melt in the summer heat. Other astronomers had seen straight lines crossing the Martian desert. As the ice melted, the lines changed color, becoming lighter in the south and darker in the north. As far as Lowell was concerned, there was only one possible explanation: the lines were artificial canals—an "amazing blue network on Mars that hints that one planet besides our own is actually inhabited now."

Lowell inspired a century of science fiction starring marauding Martians. Many matched Lowell's descriptions. For example, in *Under the Moons of Mars,* Edgar Rice Burroughs wrote, "The people had found it necessary to follow the receding waters until necessity had forced upon them their ultimate salvation, the so-called Martian canals."

Scientists were less convinced. One of Lowell's opponents was Alfred Wallace, known for his work on evolution. Wallace did not challenge Lowell's maps. The Lowell Observatory was one of the best in the world, and Wallace had no reason to doubt what Lowell saw. Instead Wallace attacked Lowell's conclusions with a list of logical flaws, including:

> The totally inadequate water-supply for such worldwide irrigation;
> the extreme irrationality of constructing so vast a canal-system
> the waste from which, by evaporation, would use up ten times the

probable supply; how the Martians could have lived before this great system was planned and executed; why they did not first utilize and render fertile the belt of land adjacent to the limits of the polar snows; the fact that the only intelligent and practical way to convey a limited quantity of water such great distances would be by a system of water-tight and air-tight tubes laid *under the ground;* and only a dense population with ample means of subsistence could possibly have constructed such gigantic works—even if they were likely to be of any use.

The argument was resolved in Wallace's favor in 1965 when NASA's *Mariner 4* spacecraft took pictures of Mars that showed, in the words of the mission's imaging engineer, a surface "like that of our own Moon, deeply cratered, and unchanged over time. No water, no canals, no life."

But there was still one mystery. Whenever other astronomers said they could not see canals on Mars, Lowell pointed out that he had a better observatory. This was largely true. Few people had access to Lowell's private observatory while he was alive, but after he died, astronomers were finally able to look through his telescope. Still, no one could see any canals. What had Lowell been seeing?

The answer turned out to be his own eyes. Lowell was not an experienced astronomer. He had mistakenly made the aperture of his telescope so small that it worked like an ophthalmoscope, the handheld device doctors use to shine light into the eyes of patients. The veins on Lowell's retina were reflecting onto the lens of his telescope's eyepiece. His maps of Martian canals are mirror images of the tree of blood vessels we all have on the backs of our eyes—as are the "spokes" he saw on Venus, the "cracks" he saw in Mercury, the "lines" he saw on Jupiter's moons, and the "tores" he saw on Saturn.

Lowell was looking at a projection from inside his head. No telescope is more powerful than the prejudice of the person looking through it. We can see what we expect when it does not exist just as well as we can ignore the unexpected when it does.

Seeing what we expect shares the same root as inattentional blindness. When we prime our eyes with preconception, we do not have beginner's mind. Lowell could have avoided his errors. A. E. Douglass, his assistant, pointed out the risk of making the telescope's aperture so small not long after Lowell started using it: "Perhaps the most harmful imperfection of the eye is within the lens. Under proper conditions it displays irregular circles and radial lines resembling a spider-web. These become visible when the pencil of light entering the eye is extremely minute."

Douglass tested his hypothesis by hanging white globes a mile from the observatory. When he looked at them through the telescope, he saw the same lines Lowell was mapping onto planets. Lowell's response was to fire Douglass—soon to become a distinguished astronomer—for disloyalty.

We can change direction when we take steps but not when we make leaps. Lowell made a *leap* when he said he would find life on Mars. He committed himself to canals, not truth. Robin Warren took a *step* when he said there were bacteria in the stomach. He made that modest note in his lab report: "I am not sure of the significance of these unusual findings, but further investigation may be worthwhile." Then he took more steps. They led to the Nobel Prize.

Warren did not lack confidence—he was not, for example, deterred by colleagues who said the bacteria were of no significance—but he did lack something Lowell had in abundance: certainty.

Confidence is belief in yourself. Certainty is belief in your beliefs. Confidence is a bridge. Certainty is a barricade.

Certainty is even easier to create than illusion. Our brains are electrochemical. The feeling of certainty, like any other feeling, comes from the electrochemistry in our heads. Chemical and electrical stimulation can make us feel certain. Ketamine, phencyclidine, and methamphetamine create feelings of certainty, as does applying electricity to the entorhinal cortex, a part of the brain a few inches behind the nose.

False certainty is common in everyday life. In a study of memory, cognitive psychologists Ulric Neisser and Nicole Harsch tested false certainty by asking students how they first heard about the explosion of the space shuttle *Challenger.* One student's answer was: "I was in my religion class and some people walked in and started talking about it. I didn't know any details except that it had exploded and the school-teacher's students had all been watching which I thought was so sad."

Another response was: "I was sitting in my freshman dorm room with my roommate and we were watching TV. It came on a news flash and we were both totally shocked."

Both answers are from the same student. Neisser and Harsch first asked her the question the day after the event, then tracked her down two years later and asked the question again. She felt "absolutely certain" about the second answer.

Of the forty people in the *Challenger* study, twelve were wrong about everything they recalled, and most were wrong about most things. Thirty-three were sure they had never been asked the question before. There was no relationship between the subjects' feelings of certainty and their accuracy. Being wrong, even being *shown* we are wrong, does not stop us from feeling certain.

Nor does irrefutable evidence—in fact, there is no such thing. Everybody continued to believe their second, incorrect memory even when shown the answers they had handwritten the day after the explosion. One response: "I still think of it as the other way around."

Once we become certain, we can remain certain, even when the evidence that we are mistaken should be overwhelming. This unshakable certainty was first studied in 1954, when psychic and spiritualist Dorothy Martin said aliens had warned her that the world would be destroyed on December 21. Psychologists Leon Festinger, Stanley Schachter, Henry Riecken, and others posed as believers, joined her group of followers, and watched what happened when her prophecy did not come true.

Martin had made specific predictions. One, delivered via trance by an alien called "the Creator," said a "spaceman" would arrive at midnight on December 20 to rescue Martin and her followers in a "flying saucer." The group made preparations, including learning passwords, cutting the zippers out of their pants, and removing their bras. Festinger, Shachter, and Riecken's book about the experience, *When Prophecy Fails,* describes what happened when the spaceman failed to appear:

> The group began reexamining the original message which had stated that at midnight they would be put into parked cars and taken to the saucer. The first attempt at reinterpretation came quickly. One member pointed out that the message must be symbolic, because it said they were to be put into parked cars but parked cars do not move and hence could not take the group anywhere. The Creator then announced that the message was indeed symbolic, but the "parked cars" referred to their own physical bodies, which had obviously been there at midnight. The flying saucer, he went on, symbolized the inner light each member of the group had. So eager was the group for an explanation of any kind that many actually began to accept this one.

The aliens' big prediction had been the end of the world. But Martin received a new message from the aliens shortly before this was due to occur: "From the mouth of death have ye been delivered. Not since the beginning of time upon this Earth has there been such a force of Good and light as now floods this room."

The group had saved the world! The cataclysm was canceled. Members started calling newspapers to announce the news. They did not even consider the possibility that Martin's prophecies were false.

One of the undercover psychiatrists, Leon Festinger, named this gap between certainty and reality "dissonance." When what we know contradicts what we believe, we can either change our beliefs to fit the facts or change the facts to fit our beliefs. People suffering from certainty are more likely to change the facts than their beliefs.

Next, Festinger studied dissonance in ordinary people. In one experiment, he gave volunteers a mundane task, then asked what they thought of it. Each one said it was boring. Despite this, he persuaded them to tell the next volunteer to arrive that it was fun. After people told someone else the task was fun, their memory of it altered. They "remembered" thinking that the task was fun. They changed what they knew to fit something they had initially only pretended to believe.

Once we become certain, we need the world to become and remain consistent with our certainty. We see things that do not exist and ignore things that do in order to keep life in line with our beliefs. Festinger writes in his 1957 book, *A Theory of Cognitive Dissonance:* "When dissonance is present, in addition to trying to reduce it, the person will actively avoid situations and information which would likely increase the dissonance."

Knowing that dissonance exists does not help prevent it. We can have dissonance about our dissonance. Dorothy Martin had a long career communicating with aliens after her prophecy failed and even after the study about her was published. Some of Martin's followers interpreted the psychologists' research as *proof* of her powers. For example, "Natalina," an "explorer of the supernatural" from Tulsa, Oklahoma, wrote on her website "Extreme Intelligence": "The psychologists determined that when people have a strong enough faith in something, they will often do exactly the opposite of what we would expect when their faith is tested."

How can we know we are seeing something real, and not being deluded by dissonance—that we are like Robin Warren and Judah Folkman, not Percival Lowell and Dorothy Martin?

That's easy: delusion comforts when truth hurts. When you feel sure, feel wary. You may be suffering from certainty.

Delusion's comfort comes from certainty. Certainty is the low road past questions and problems. Certainty is cowardice—the flight from the possibility that we might be wrong. If we already know we are right, why confront queries or qualms? Just climb the Eiffel Tower and fly already.

Confidence is a cycle, not a steady state, a muscle that must be strengthened daily, a feeling we renew and increase by enduring the adversity of creation. Certainty is constant. Confidence comes and goes.

Make an enemy of certainty and befriend doubt. When you can change your mind, you can change anything.

CHAPTER 5

WHERE CREDIT IS DUE

1 | ROSALIND

Sleet like crystal tears fell on cobbles of black umbrellas at the United Jewish Cemetery in London. It was April 17, 1958. Across the sea in Brussels, the World's Fair opened with a scale model of a virus as the main attraction. In the cemetery, a casket containing the body of the scientist who built the model was put in the ground. Her name was Rosalind Franklin. She had died of cancer the day before, aged thirty-seven. Her work was understanding the mechanics of life.

With its gas chambers, guided missiles, and fission bombs, World War II was an apex for the engineering of death. After the war, scientists sought a new summit. Physicist Erwin Schrödinger captured the spirit of the age with a series of talks in Dublin called "What Is Life?" He said the laws of physics are based on entropy: the "tendency of matter to go over into disorder." Yet life resists entropy, "avoiding the rapid decay into the inert," by means then enigmatic. Schrödinger set a bold goal for the science of the rest of the century: to discover how life lives.

Of all the things in the universe, only life escapes inertia and decay, however briefly. An individual organism delays destruction by consuming matter from the environment—by breathing, eating, and drinking, for example—and using it to replenish itself. A species delays destruction by transferring its blueprint from parent to child. Life itself delays destruction by adapting and diversifying these blueprints. At the start of the 1950s, life's mechanism was a mystery; by the end of the decade, much of the mystery had been solved. Rosalind Franklin's model of a virus at the World's Fair was a celebration of that triumph.

The model showed the tobacco mosaic virus, known to scientists as "TMV" and studied throughout the world because it is easy to obtain, highly infectious, and relatively simple. TMV was named for the destruction it wreaks on tobacco leaves, which it stains in a brown patchwork like a mosaic. In 1898, Dutch botanist Martinus Beijerinck showed that the infection was not caused by bacteria, which are relatively large and cellular, but by something smaller and cell-less. He called it a "virus," using the Latin word for "poison."

Bacteria are cells that divide to reproduce, like the cells in other life-forms. A virus has no cells. It occupies, or infects, cells and repurposes their engines of reproduction to make copies of itself—it is a microbiological cuckoo. A virus contains the information it needs to make a copy of itself and little else. But how is the information stored? How does the virus duplicate the information in a new cell without giving away its only copy?

The questions were more important than tobacco or viruses. *All* reproduction is like viral reproduction. Parents do not cut themselves in half to make a child. Like viruses, fathers provide information only: a sperm is a message wrapped in matter. To understand a virus is to understand life.

Life's information is a series of instructions that give cells particular functions. A child is not, as scientists of the nineteenth century believed, a blend of its parents; it inherits discrete instructions from each parent. These discrete instructions are called "genes."

Genes were discovered in 1865 by Gregor Mendel, a friar at St. Thomas's Abbey in Brünn, now part of the Czech Republic. Mendel grew, cross-fertilized, and analyzed tens of thousands of pea plants and found that traits present in one plant could be introduced into its offspring but, in most cases, could not be blended. For example, peas could either be round or wrinkled but could not be both; nor could they be of some intermediate form. When Mendel crossed round and wrinkled peas, their descendants were always round and never wrinkled. The instruction "Be round" dominated the instruction "Be wrinkled." Mendel called these instructions "characters"; today we call them "genes."

Mendel's work was ignored—even Darwin was unaware of it—until 1902, when it was rediscovered and became the basis of "chromosome theory." Chromosomes are packets of protein and acid found in the nuclei of living cells. Their name comes from one of the first things discovered about them—that they become brightly colored when stained during scientific experiments: *chroma* is Greek for "color," and *soma* is Greek for "body." Chromosome theory, developed in parallel by Walter Sutton and Theophilus Painter and formalized by Edmund Beecher Wilson, explained what chromosomes do: they carry the genes that enable life to reproduce.

At first, scientists assumed the chromosome's proteins were the source of life's information. Proteins are long, complicated molecules. Acids, the other component of chromosomes, are relatively simple.

Rosalind Franklin believed life's messengers might be the chromosome's acids, not its proteins. She came to the subject indirectly. During her college years, she developed an interest in crystals and learned how to study them using X-rays. She became an expert on the structure of coal—or, as she called it, "holes in coal"—which gave her a reputation as a talented X-ray crystallographer. This led her to two research positions at the University of London, where she analyzed biological samples instead of geological samples. It was during her second appointment, at Birkbeck College, that she studied the tobacco mosaic virus.

The word "crystal" evokes brittle things like snowflakes, diamonds, and salt, but in science, a crystal is any solid with atoms or molecules arranged in a three-dimensional repeating pattern. Both of the acids found in chromosomes, deoxyribonucleic acid and ribonucleic acid, or DNA and RNA, are crystals.

Crystal molecules are tightly packed: the gap between them is a few ten-billionths of a meter long. Light waves are hundreds of times longer than this, so light cannot be used to analyze a crystal's structure—it cannot pass through the crystal's gaps. But the waves of an X-ray are the same size as the crystal's gaps. They can pass through the crystal's lattice, and as they do so, they are diverted (or "refracted") every time they hit one of the crystal's atoms. X-ray crystallographers deduce the structure of a crystal by sending X-rays through it from every possible angle, then analyzing the results. The work requires precision, attention to detail, and an ability to imagine in three dimensions. Franklin was a master crystallographer.

She needed all her skill to solve the problem of how viruses reproduce. Unlike bacteria, viruses are metabolically inert—meaning that they don't change in any way or "do" anything—if they have not penetrated a cell. The tobacco mosaic virus, for example, is just a tube of motionless protein molecules until it infects a plant—a tube that contains deadly instructions, encoded in RNA. By the time Franklin took on the problem, it had already been determined that there was nothing but empty space in the center of the tobacco mosaic virus. So where were the deadly instructions?

The answer, she discovered, was that the virus is structured like a drill bit: its protein exterior is twisted with grooves, and its core is scored with spirals of acid. This weaponlike form also shows how viruses work. The protein punctures the cell, and then the RNA unspools and takes over the reproductive machinery in the nucleus of the cell, cloning itself and so spreading infection.

Franklin published her results at the start of 1958. She did the work despite being treated for cancer, from which she had been suffering since 1956. The tumors went away, then returned to kill her. She made the model for the World's Fair while she was dying.

Her death was noted in the *New York Times* and the London *Times*. Both newspapers described her as a skilled crystallographer who helped discover the nature of viruses.

Then, in the years after her death, a new truth was told. Rosalind Franklin's contribution to humanity was far greater than her work on the tobacco mosaic virus. For a long time, the only people who knew what she had really accomplished were the three men who had secretly stolen her work: James Watson, Francis Crick, and Maurice Wilkins.

2 | THE WRONG CHROMOSOMES

Watson and Crick were researchers at Cambridge University. Wilkins had been Franklin's colleague and supervisor during her first University of London appointment, at King's College. All three men wanted to be first to answer the question of the age: what is the structure of DNA, the acid that carries the information of life, and how does it work? The men saw themselves in competition. Wilkins called the trio "rats" and wished the other two "happy racing."

Rosalind Franklin was aware of the race but did not compete in it. She believed racing made hasty science, and she had a handicap: she was a woman.

From a genetic perspective, the difference between a man and a woman is one of forty-six chromosomes. Women have two X chromosomes. Men have an X and a Y chromosome. The Y chromosome carries 454 genes, fewer than 1 percent of the total number in a human being. Because of this tiny difference, the creative potential of women has been suppressed for most of human history.

In some ways, Rosalind Franklin was lucky. She was educated at Cambridge University's Newnham College. Had she been born a few generations earlier, she would not have been admitted to Cambridge. Newnham was founded in 1871, the second of the university's women-only colleges. The other, Girton, was founded in 1869. Cambridge University was founded in 1209. For its first 660 years—more than 80 percent of its existence—no women were admitted. Even when they were admitted, women were not equal to men. Despite placing first in the university's entrance exam for chemistry, Franklin could not be a member of the university or an undergraduate. Women were "students of Girton and Newnham Colleges." They could not earn a degree. And even this place in the university's underbelly was a privilege. The number of women allowed to attend Cambridge was capped at five hundred, to ensure that 90 percent of students were men.

Science, while pretending to be dispassionate and rational, has long been an active oppressor of women. Britain's Royal Society of scientists barred women for almost three hundred years, on grounds including the argument that women were not "legal persons." The first women were admitted to the society in 1945. Both were from fields similar to Franklin's: Kathleen Lonsdale was a crystallographer, Marjory Stephenson a microbiologist.

Marie Curie, history's most famous female scientist, did no better. The French Academy of Sciences—the equivalent of Britain's Royal Society—rejected her application for membership. Harvard University refused to award her an honorary degree because, in the words of Charles Eliot, then president emeritus, "Credit does not entirely belong to her." Eliot assumed that her husband, Pierre, did all her work; so did almost all her male peers. They had no such problems assuming that credit "entirely belonged to" any of the men they wanted to honor.

These rejections came despite Curie being the first woman to win a Nobel Prize in science and the only person, male or female, to win Nobel Prizes in two different sciences (for physics in 1903 and chemistry in 1911). The prizes were, in part, a result of her fighting for the credit she deserved. When she accepted her second Nobel Prize, Curie used the word "me" seven times at the start of her speech, stressing, "The chemical work aimed at isolating radium in the state of the pure salt, and at characterizing it as a new element, was carried out specially by me." The second woman to win a Nobel Prize in science was Curie's daughter Irène. Both women shared their prizes with their husbands, except for Marie's chemistry prize, which was awarded after Pierre Curie's death.

The Curies' success did not help Lise Meitner. She discovered nuclear fission only to see her collaborator Otto Hahn receive the 1944 Nobel Prize for her work. The third woman to win a Nobel in science—and the first non-Curie—was biochemist Gerty Cori, in 1947, who, like both the Curies, shared the prize with her husband. The first woman to win without her husband was physicist Maria Goeppert-Mayer, in 1963. In total, only 15 women have won Nobel Prizes in science, compared to 540 men, making women 36 times less likely to win than a man. The odds have changed little since Marie Curie's day: a female scientist wins a Nobel about once every seven years. Only two women other than Curie have won a prize by themselves; there has been only one year, 2009, when women have won prizes in two of the three science categories at the same time; women have never won science prizes in the same category in two consecutive years; and ten of the sixteen prizes given to women have been in the "medicine or physiology category." Only two women not named Curie have won Nobel Prizes in Chemistry. Only one woman not named Curie has won a Nobel Prize in Physics.

This is not because women have less aptitude for science. Rosalind Franklin, for example, took better pictures of DNA than anyone had taken before, then used a complex mathematical equation called the "Patterson function" to analyze them. The equation, developed by Arthur Lindo Patterson in 1935, is a classic technique in X-ray crystallography. The two main properties of electromagnetic waves are their intensity, or "amplitude," and their length, or "phase." The image created by an X-ray shows amplitude but not phase, which can also be a rich source of information. The Patterson function overcomes this limitation by calculating the phase based on the amplitude. In the 1950s, before computers or even calculators, this work took months. Franklin had to use a slide rule, pieces of paper, and hand calculations to work out the phases for every image, each one of which represented a slice of the three-dimensional crystal molecule she was analyzing.

While Franklin was concluding this work, her King's College colleague Maurice Wilkins showed her data and pictures to James Watson and Francis Crick, without her consent or knowledge. Watson and Crick leapt to the conclusion Franklin was diligently proving—that the structure of DNA was a double helix—published it, then shared the Nobel Prize with their secret source, Wilkins. When Rosalind Franklin died, she did not know the three men had stolen her work. Even after she was dead, they did not give her credit. She was not thanked in their Nobel acceptance speech, unlike several men who made lesser contributions. Wilkins referred to Franklin only once in his Nobel lecture and misrepresented her importance by saying that she made "very valuable contributions to the X-ray analysis," rather than confessing that she did *all* the X-ray analysis and far more besides. Watson and Crick did not mention her at all in their Nobel lectures.

3 | THE TRUTH IN CHAINS

Rosalind Franklin was the most important person in the story of DNA's discovery. She was the first-ever member of the human race—or any other species on earth—to see the secret of life. She answered Schrödinger's question "What Is Life?" with a photograph she took on May 1, 1952. She pointed her camera at a single strand of DNA fifteen millimeters, or five-eighths of an inch, from the lens, set the exposure time for one hundred hours, and opened the shutter. It really was *her* camera. She had designed it and overseen its construction in the King's College workshop. It tilted precisely so she could take pictures of DNA specimens at different angles. It was able to take photographs at very close range. It protected DNA specimens from humidity with a brass-and-rubber seal that also allowed Franklin to remove the air around a sample and replace it with hydrogen, a better medium for crystallography. There was nothing else like it anywhere in the world.

Four days later, the picture was ready. It is one of the most important images in history. To any but the most trained eye, it does not look like much: a shadowy circle around something like a ghostly face, its eyes, eyebrows, nostrils, and dimples symmetrically and diagonally aligned, smiling like a Buddha or perhaps God Him- or Herself.

It was clear to Franklin what the picture showed. DNA had the shape of two helixes, like a spiral staircase with no central support. The shape gave a clear indication of how life reproduced. The spiral staircase could copy itself by unwinding and replicating.

Franklin knew what she had, but she did not run through the King's College corridors shouting some equivalent of "Eureka!" She was determined not to leap to conclusions. She wanted to work through the math and have proof before she published, and she was determined to keep an open mind until she had gathered all the data. So she gave the image the serial number 51 and continued her work. She was still completing her Patterson function calculations, and there were many more pictures to take. Then Maurice Wilkins showed picture 51 to James Watson and Francis Crick, and the three men were awarded the Nobel Prize for a woman's work.

It was the same when Marietta Blau, an unpaid woman working at the University of Vienna, developed a technique for photographing atomic particles. Blau could not get a paid position anywhere, even though her work was a major advance in particle physics. C. F. Powell, a man who "adopted and improved" her techniques, was awarded the Nobel Prize in 1950. Agnes Pockels was denied a college education because she was a woman, taught herself science from her brother's textbooks, created a laboratory in her kitchen, and used it to make fundamental discoveries about the chemistry of liquids. Her work was "adopted" by Irving Langmuir, who won a Nobel Prize for it in 1932. There are many similar stories. A lot of men have won Nobel Prizes in science for discoveries made in whole or part by women.

4 | THE HARRIET EFFECT

Even in our new post-genomic age, the game of claims is rigged in favor of white men. One reason is an imbalance first recorded fifty years ago by a sociologist named Harriet Zuckerman. Zuckerman was trying to find out if scientists were more successful alone or in teams. She interviewed forty-one Nobel Prize winners and discovered something that forever changed the direction of her research: that, after winning the prize, many Nobel laureates became wary of joining teams because they find they receive too much individual credit for things the group has done. One said, "The world is peculiar in this matter of how it gives credit. It tends to give the credit to already famous people." Another: "The man who's best known gets more credit, an inordinate amount of credit." Almost every Nobel Prize–winning scientist said the same thing.

Until Zuckerman, most scholars assumed that the strata of science were more or less meritocratic. Zuckerman showed that they are not. More-recognized scientists get more recognition, and less-recognized scientists get less recognition, no matter who does the work.

Zuckerman's discovery is known as the Matthew effect, after Matthew 25:29 — "For whoever has will be given more, and they will have an abundance. Whoever does not have, even what they have will be taken from them." This was the name Robert Merton, a far more eminent sociologist, gave Zuckerman's findings. Zuckerman discovered the effect, then experienced it: the credit for Zuckerman's work went to Merton. Merton gave Zuckerman full acknowledgment, but it made little difference. As she'd predicted, he had recognition and so was given more. There were no hard feelings. Zuckerman collaborated with Merton, then married him.

The Matthew effect—or perhaps more correctly the Harriet effect—is part of the broader problem of seeing what we think, instead of seeing what is. It is unusual that the scientists in Zuckerman's study were honest enough to know they were getting credit they did not deserve. As we are prejudiced about others, so we are prejudiced about ourselves. For centuries, white men have tried to persuade other people that white men are superior. In the process, many white men have become convinced of their own superiority. People often give and take credit based on their prejudices. If there is a person from a "superior" group in the room when something is created, members of the group often assume that the "superior" person did most of the work, even when the opposite is true. Most of the time, the "superior" person makes the same assumption.

I was once forwarded an e-mail that a senior, white, male scientist had sent to a junior, non-white, female scientist. She was applying for a patent. The male scientist demanded to be listed as an inventor on her patent, on the grounds that her research might have been "connected" to him. He claimed he had no interest in getting credit—he was only "making sure she did things correctly." Patent law is complicated, but the patent office's definition of inventorship is not. "Unless a person contributes to the conception of the invention," it reads, "he is not an inventor." If the female scientist named the male scientist as an inventor, she risked invalidating her patent. If she did not, she risked her career. The male scientist's ploy works: he is named as an inventor on nearly fifty patents, an improbable number, especially as most of the patents have many inventors, even though the average number of people who "contribute to the conception" of an invention is two. The man sincerely believed he must have had something to do with the woman's invention, even though the first time he heard of it was when he saw her patent application.

5 | SHOULDERS, NOT GIANTS

Harriet Zuckerman's husband, Robert Merton, was a magnet for credit, and not just because he was a man—he was also one of the most important thinkers of the twentieth century. Merton founded a field called the "sociology of science," which, along with his friend Thomas Kuhn's "philosophy of science," scrutinizes the social aspects of discovery and creation.

Merton dedicated his life to understanding how people create, especially in science. Science claims to be objective and rational, and while its results sometimes are, Merton suspected that its practitioners are not. They are people, capable of being as subjective, emotional, and biased as everybody else. This is why "scientists" have been able to justify so many wrong things, from racial and gender inferiority to canals on Mars and the idea that the body is made of "humors." Scientists, like all creative people, operate in environments—Merton divided them into what he called micro-environments and macroenvironments—which shape what they think and do. The way of seeing that Kuhn called a "paradigm" is part of the macroenvironment; whose contributions are recognized and why is part of the microenvironment.

One of Merton's observations was that the very idea of giving sole credit to any individual is fundamentally flawed. Every creator is surrounded by others in both space and time. There are creators working alongside them, creators working across the hall from them, creators working across the continent from them, and creators long dead or retired who worked before them. Every creator inherits concepts, contexts, tools, methods, data, laws, principles, and models from thousands of other people, dead and alive. Some of that inheritance is readily apparent; some of it is not. But every creative field is a vast community of connection. No creator deserves too much credit because every creator is in so much debt.

In 1676, Isaac Newton described this problem when he wrote, "If I have seen further it is by standing on the shoulders of giants." This may seem like modesty, but Newton used it in a letter where he was arguing with rival scientist Robert Hooke about credit. The comment became famous, and Newton is frequently cited as if he coined the phrase. But Newton was already standing on the shoulders of another when he wrote that sentence. Newton got it from George Herbert, who in 1651 wrote, "A dwarf on a giant's shoulders sees farther of the two." Herbert got it from Robert Burton, who in 1621 wrote, "A dwarf standing on the shoulders of a giant may see farther than a giant himself." Burton got it from a Spanish theologian, Diego de Estella, also known as Didacus Stella, who probably got it from John of Salisbury, 1159: "We are like dwarfs on the shoulders of giants, so that we can see more than they, and things at a greater distance, not by virtue of any sharpness of sight on our part, or any physical distinction, but because we are carried high and raised up by their giant size." John of Salisbury got it from Bernard of Chartres, 1130: "We are like dwarfs standing upon the shoulders of giants, and so able to see more and see farther than the ancients." We do not know from whom Bernard of Chartres got it.

Robert Merton pieced this chain of custody together in a book, *On the Shoulders of Giants,* to exemplify the long, many-handed sequence of gradual improvement that is creation's reality and to show how one person, usually famous, can accumulate credit they do not deserve. Newton's line was, in fact, close to a cliché at the time he wrote it. He was not pretending to be original; it was such a common aphorism that he did not need to cite a source. His reader, Hooke, would have already been familiar with the idea.

But there is a problem with the statement, whether we attribute it to Newton or somebody else: the idea of "giants." If everybody sees further because they are standing on the shoulders of giants, then there are no giants, just a tower of people, each one standing on the shoulders of another. Giants, like geniuses, are a myth.

How many people are holding us up? A human generation is about twenty-five years long. If it was not until fifty thousand years ago that our transition to *Homo sapiens sapiens*—creative people—was complete, then everything we make is built upon two thousand generations of human ingenuity. We do not see further because of giants. We see further because of generations.

6 | INHERITANCE

Rosalind Franklin, master crystallographer, stood on a tower of generations when she became the first person to see the secret of life.

Almost nothing was known about crystals at the start of the twentieth century, but they had been a subject of curiosity at least since the winter of 1610, when Johannes Kepler wondered why snowflakes had six corners. Kepler wrote a book, *The Six-Cornered Snowflake,* in which he speculated that solving the riddle of the snowflake, or "snow crystal," would allow us to "recreate the entire universe."

Many people tried to understand snowflakes, including Robert Hooke, the recipient of Newton's "shoulders of giants" letter. They were drawn, described, and categorized for three centuries, but never explained. No one understood what a snowflake was, because no one understood what a crystal was, because no one understood the physics of solid matter.

The crystals' mysteries are invisible to the eye. To see them, Rosalind Franklin needed a tool that also has its origins in Kepler's time: the X-ray.

While Kepler's curiosity about snowflakes has a clear connection to crystals, the origin of the X-ray starts with something less obvious: improvements in air-pump technology that enabled scientists to wonder about vacuums. One such scientist was Robert Boyle, who used vacuums to try to understand electricity. Others improved on Boyle's work until, almost two hundred years later, German glassblower Heinrich Geissler created the "Geissler tube," a partial vacuum in a bottle that glowed with light whenever an electrical coil connected to it was discharged. Geissler's invention was a novelty, an "interesting scientific toy," during his lifetime, but decades later, it became the basis for neon lighting, incandescent lightbulbs, and the "vacuum tube"—the principal component of early radios, televisions, and computers.

In 1869, English physicist William Crookes built on Geissler's work to create the "Crookes tube," which had a better vacuum than the Geissler tube. The Crookes tube led to the discovery of cathode rays, later renamed "electron beams."

Then, in 1895, German physicist Wilhelm Röntgen noticed a strange shimmering in the dark while he was working with a Crookes tube. He ate and slept in his lab for six weeks while he investigated, then one day positioned his wife's hand on a photographic plate and pointed his Crookes tube at it. When he showed her the result, a picture of her bones, the first ever image of a living skeleton, she said, "I have seen my death." Röntgen named his discovery after the symbol for something unknown: "X-ray."

But what were these unknown rays? Were they particles, like electrons, or waves, like light?

Physicist Max von Laue answered this question in 1912. Laue put crystals between X-rays and photographic plates and found that the X-rays left interference patterns—which are similar to sunlight reflecting off rippling water—on the plates. Particles could not fit through the densely packed molecules of a crystal—and, if they did, they were unlikely to make interference patterns. Therefore, Laue concluded, X-rays were waves.

Within months of hearing about Laue's work, a young physicist named William Bragg showed that the interference patterns also revealed the inner structure of the crystal. In 1915, at the age of twenty-five, he won the Nobel Prize in Physics for his discovery, becoming the youngest ever Nobel laureate. His father, also a physicist called William, received the award too, but this was all "Matthew effect." Bragg the elder played almost no role in his son's discovery.

Bragg's work transformed the study of crystals. Before Bragg, crystallography was a branch of mineralogy, part of the science of mines and mining, and much of the work involved collecting and cataloging; after Bragg, the field became "X-ray crystallography," a wild frontier of physics inhabited by scientists intent on penetrating the mysteries of solid matter.

The sudden shift had an important and unexpected consequence: it advanced the careers of female scientists. In the late 1800s, universities had started admitting women into science classes, albeit reluctantly. Crystallography, a relative backwater, was a field of study where women had been able to find work after graduating. One, a woman named Florence Bascom, was teaching geology at Bryn Mawr College in Pennsylvania, while Bragg was accepting his Nobel Prize. Bascom was the first woman to receive a PhD from Johns Hopkins University, where she was forced to take classes sitting behind a screen so that she would "not distract the men"; she was also the first female geologist appointed by the United States Geological Survey, and had been an expert in crystals long before physicists became interested in them.

When the study of crystals moved from understanding their exterior—mineralogy and chemistry—to understanding their interior—solid-state physics—Bascom followed, taking her female students with her.

One of them was a woman named Polly Porter, who had been forbidden from going to school because her parents did not believe girls should be educated. When Porter was fifteen, her family moved from London to Rome. While her brothers studied, Porter wandered the city, collecting fragments of stone, cataloging the marble the ancient Romans had used to build the capital of their empire. When the family moved to Oxford, Porter found bits of Rome there, too: in Oxford University's Museum of Natural History, which had a collection of ancient Roman marble in need of cleaning and labeling. Henry Miers, Oxford's first professor of mineralogy, noticed Porter's regular visits to the collection and hired her to translate the catalog and reorganize the stones. She discovered crystallography through Miers. He told Porter's parents she should apply for admission to the university, but they would not hear of it.

Porter took a job dusting instead. But not just any dust—the dust in the laboratory of Alfred Tutton, a crystallographer at London's Royal School of Mines. Tutton taught Porter how to make and measure crystals. Then the Porters moved to the United States, so Polly cataloged more stones, first at the Smithsonian Institution, then at Bryn Mawr College, where Florence Bascom discovered her and appealed to Mary Garrett, a suffragist and railroad heiress, for funds so she could study. There she stayed until 1914, the year Bragg's Nobel Prize was announced and crystallography moved from the margins of geology to the foundation of science. At that point, Bascom wrote to Victor Goldschmidt, a mineralogist at Heidelberg University, in Germany:

Dear Professor Goldschmidt:

I have long had the purpose of writing you to interest you in Miss Porter, who is working this year in my laboratory and whom I hope you will welcome in your laboratory next year. Her heart is set upon the study of crystallography and she should go to the fountainhead of inspiration.

Miss Porter's life has been unusual, for she has never been to school or college. There are therefore great gaps in her education, particularly in chemistry and mathematics, but to offset this I believe you will find that she has an unusual aptitude and an intense love of your subject. I want to see her have the opportunities which have so long been denied her. I am both ambitious for her and with faith in her ultimate success.

Yours truly,
Florence Bascom

Goldschmidt welcomed Porter in June 1914.

The next month the First World War started.

Porter succeeded at her work of learning the art of crystallography despite the difficulties of the war and the depression and distraction of Goldschmidt, and three years later, she earned a science degree from Oxford. She stayed at Oxford, conducting research into, and teaching undergraduates about, the crystals that were her passion until she retired, in 1959. One of her most enduring acts was to inspire and encourage a woman who would become one of the world's greatest crystallographers and Rosalind Franklin's mentor: Dorothy Hodgkin.

Hodgkin was a child at the dawn of the crystal revolution. She was two years old when Bragg invented X-ray crystallography, five years old when he and his father won the Nobel Prize, and when she was fifteen, she listened as the elder Bragg gave the Royal Institution's Christmas Lectures for children. In Britain, the lectures, which were started by Michael Faraday in 1825, are as much part of the season as feasting and caroling. Bragg's topic in 1923 was "The Nature of Things"—six lectures describing the recently revealed subatomic world.

"In the last twenty-five years," he noted, "we have been given new eyes. The discoveries of radioactivity and of X-rays have changed the whole situation: which is indeed the reason for the choice of the subject of these lectures. We can now understand so many things that were dim before; and we see a wonderful new world opening out before us, waiting to be explored."

Three of Bragg's lectures were about crystals. He explained their allure: "The crystal has a certain charm due partly to glitter and sparkle, partly to perfect regularity of outline. We feel that some mystery and beauty must underlie the characteristics that please us, and indeed that is the case. Through the crystal we look down into the first structures of nature."

The lectures inspired Dorothy Hodgkin to pursue a career in crystallography, but Oxford disappointed her: crystal structures were a small part of the university's undergraduate science syllabus. It was only in her final year that she met Polly Porter, who was teaching crystallography while also conducting research to classify every crystal in the world. Porter inspired Hodgkin anew and may have even stopped her from straying into another field. Hodgkin wrote, "There was such a mass of material clearly already available on crystal structures that I had not known about—I wondered, for a moment, whether there was anything for me to find out—and gradually realized the limitations of the present which we could pass."

What Hodgkin saw before most other scientists was that X-ray crystallography could be applied not only to rocks but also to living molecules and that it might be able to reveal the secrets of life itself. In 1934, shortly after graduating, she set about proving her idea by analyzing a crystalline human hormone: insulin. The molecule would not yield to the technology of the 1930s. In 1945, she determined the crystal structure of a form of cholesterol, the first ever biomolecular structure to be identified, or "solved," then determined the structure of a second biomolecule, penicillin. In 1954, she worked out the structure of vitamin B_{12}, and for this discovery she was awarded the Nobel Prize.

That same year, Japanese physicist Ukichiro Nakaya solved the mystery of the snowflake. Snowflakes that form at temperatures higher than -40 degrees Celsius are not pure water. They form around another particle, almost always biological, and usually a bacterium. It is a beautiful coincidence that life, in the form of a bacterium, is the nucleus of an abundant crystal, snow, and that a crystal, DNA, is the nucleus of abundant life. Nakaya also showed why snowflakes have six corners: because snowflakes grow from ice crystals, and the crystalline structure of ice is hexagonal.

When Rosalind Franklin started analyzing DNA using X-ray crystallography, she was inheriting a technique pioneered by Dorothy Hodgkin, who was inspired by Polly Porter, who was a protégée of Florence Bascom, who broke ground for all women in science, following work by William Bragg, who was inspired by Max von Laue, who followed Wilhelm Röntgen, who followed William Crookes, who followed Heinrich Geissler, who followed Robert Boyle.

Even the greatest individual contribution is a tiny step on humanity's way. We owe nearly everything to others. Generations are also generators. The point of the fruit is the tree, and the point of the tree is the fruit.

Today, the whole world stands on Rosalind Franklin's shoulders. Everybody benefits from her work; it is a link in the long chain that led to—among many other things—virology, stem-cell research, gene therapy, and DNA-based criminal evidence. Franklin's impact, along with Bragg's, Röntgen's, and all of the others', has even traveled beyond this planet. NASA's robotic rover *Curiosity* analyzes the surface of Mars using onboard X-ray crystallography. Nucleobases, essential components of DNA, have been found in meteorites, and glycolaldehyde, a sugarlike molecule that is a part of RNA, has been discovered orbiting a star four hundred million light-years away from us. Because we have found these buildings blocks so far away, it now seems possible that life is not rare but everywhere. Life was mysterious when Franklin first photographed it; today, we understand it so well we can reasonably suspect that the universe may be full of it.

Rosalind Franklin died because of her DNA. She was an Ashkenazi Jew, descended in part from people who migrated from the Middle East to the shores of Europe's Rhine River during the Middle Ages. Her family name was once Fraenkel; her ancestors were from Wrocław, now in Poland, then the capital of Silesia. Much of her genetic inheritance was European, not Asian: the Ashkenazim began when Jewish men converted European women and survived by prohibiting marriage outside their group. Three of these people had genetic flaws: two of them had mutated breast cancer type 1 tumor suppressor genes, called BRCA1 genes; another had a mutation called 6174delT in his or her breast cancer type 2 tumor suppressor, or BRCA2, gene. Franklin likely inherited one of these mutated genes. The BRCA2 mutation makes a woman fifteen times more likely to get ovarian cancer; the BRCA1 mutation increases her odds by a factor of thirty. Rosalind Franklin died of ovarian cancer.

None of this could have been imagined before she photographed DNA. Today, Ashkenazi Jewish women, all literal cousins of Rosalind Franklin, can get a test to see if they have the BRCA1 or BRCA2 mutations and take preventative measures if they do. These measures are crude: they include surgical removal of both breasts, to reduce the risk of breast cancer, and surgical removal of the ovaries and fallopian tubes, to reduce the risk of ovarian cancer. But in the near future there will likely be a targeted therapy that prevents the mutation from causing cancer, without the need for surgery. This will also be true of other genetic mutations, other cancers, and other diseases. Franklin could not save her own life, but she could and did help save the lives of tens of thousands of other women who were born after her death, many of whom will never know her name.

None of this would have happened, or it would have happened later, if women were still barred from science—not because they are women but because they are human and, thus, as likely to create, invent, or discover as anybody else. The same is true of people who are black, brown, or gay. A species that survives by creating must not limit who can create. More creators means more creations. Equality brings justice to some and wealth to all.

CHAPTER 6

CHAINS OF CONSEQUENCE

1 | WILLIAM

William Cartwright's dog started barking soon after midnight on Sunday, April 12, 1812. There was a single gunshot from the north, one from the south, then one each from the east and the west. Cartwright's watchers awoke at the sounds. Men, unseen and uncounted, came through the night and beat the watchers to the ground in the lee of Cartwright's mill.

Other men broke the mill's windows and pounded on its door with great sledgehammers called "Enochs." Yet more fired pistols through the broken windows, and muskets at the higher floors.

Cartwright, accompanied by five employees and five soldiers, counterattacked, firing muskets from behind raised flagstones and ringing a bell to alert the cavalry stationed one mile away.

The mill door, which Cartwright had reinforced and studded with iron, would not yield to the Enochs. Musket balls smoked up and down. Soon, two men lay dying in the yard. After twenty minutes and

140 shots, the attackers retreated, carrying the wounded, unable to retrieve the dying.

Once the shadows of the mob had disappeared, Cartwright looked out. Hammers and pistols had destroyed his first-floor windows, pane and frame; musket balls had shattered fifty more panes upstairs. His door had been sledged beyond repair. Beyond, two mortally wounded men furled and unfurled among discarded hammers and hatchets, axes, puddles of blood, strips of flesh, and a severed finger.

The object of the attack was Cartwright's automatic loom. The attackers were weavers, trying to destroy the new machine before it destroyed their jobs. They called themselves "Luddites" and had launched similar attacks throughout the north of England. William Cartwright was the first man to ever defeat them.

The Luddites—their name came from the then-famous, possibly fictional machine breaker Ned Ludd—have become icons of both restraint in the face of new technology and entrenched fear of change. They were driven by neither: they were just men desperate to keep their jobs. Their battle was against capital, not technology. The new and improved Enoch sledgehammers they used to wreck looms were named after their inventor, Enoch Taylor, who had also invented the looms that were being wrecked—an irony that was not lost on the Luddites, who chanted, "Enoch did make them, Enoch shall break them."

The Luddites' story is a tale not about right and wrong but about the nuance of new. As our creations advance from generation to generation, they have consequences that, good or bad, are nearly always unforeseen and unintended.

New technology is often called "revolutionary." This is not always hyperbole. The context of that bloody night in England was a collision between two revolutions, one technological and one social.

In the decades before, Europe's monarchs and aristocrats had been besieged. In 1776, thirteen North American colonies had declared independence from King George III of England. The French Revolution started in 1789, and the French king Louis XVI was dead within four years. Thomas Paine summarized the spirit of revolution, and the age, in 1791, when he wrote in *The Rights of Man,* "Governments must have arisen either out of the people or over the people."

At the time of the Luddites, the British government, like the French government that had just been deposed, was one that had arisen *over* the people. The head of state, King George III, was one strand in a cobweb of intermarried, interrelated monarchs covering Europe. George ruled Britain through a tier of intermediaries: hereditary aristocrats who in turn ruled the general population. Recently, a new layer in the social hierarchy had endangered this arrangement: capitalists—men who became wealthy through working and creating work for others, not by accidents of birth. People claiming to be "royal" did not impress the capitalists, who expected political power along with their profits. Their rise was in part a result of inventions like the printing press, which freed information, and labor-saving machines, which freed time. The middle class is a consequence of the creations of the Middle Ages.

The battle at William Cartwright's mill exemplified the new tensions. Cartwright, given but a few of the monarch's soldiers, rang his bell for more, and they never came. The aristocracy was ambivalent about this new industrial class. Many of them recognized the same risk the Luddites saw—that mechanization could concentrate power and wealth in new hands. Technology like Taylor's automatic loom did not threaten one social class. It threatened two.

The Luddites, monarchs, and aristocrats did not fear technology in general so much as the possible consequences of particular technologies for them personally. New tools make new societies.

While the aristocrats were unsure of the threat, the Luddites were certain—so convinced that automatic looms would do them harm that they were willing to risk death, either in their raids or from execution after capture, to stop the rise of the machines. But the longer-term consequences of the looms, a precursor to both computers and robots, were unforeseen, especially by the Luddites. They could never have predicted that their descendants—today's workers—would use information technology and automation to make their living, just as William Cartwright did. In the end, we'll see, it was the working class that gained the most from the new technology. The aristocrats, the only ones who perhaps had the power to keep automation away, did nothing and lost everything.

2 | HUMANITY'S CHOIR

The consequences of technology are mostly unforeseeable, in part because technology is so complex. To understand that complexity, let's step back from Cartwright's mill to consider something apparently all-American and seemingly mundane: a can of Coca-Cola.

The H-E-B grocery store a mile from my home in Austin, Texas, sells twelve cans of Coca-Cola for $4.49.

Each one of those cans originated in a small town of four thousand people on the Murray River in Western Australia called Pinjarra—the site of the world's largest bauxite mine. Bauxite is surface-mined—basically scraped and dug from the top of the ground—and then crushed and washed with hot sodium hydroxide until it separates into aluminum hydroxide and a waste material called "red mud." The aluminum hydroxide is first cooled and then heated to over a thousand degrees Celsius in a kiln, where it becomes aluminum oxide, or alumina. The alumina is dissolved in a molten substance called cryolite, a rare mineral first discovered in Greenland, and turned into pure aluminum using electricity in a process called electrolysis. The pure aluminum sinks to the bottom of the molten cryolite, is drained off, and is placed in a mold. The result is a long, cylindrical bar of aluminum.

Australia's role in the process ends here. The bar is transported west to the port of Bunbury and loaded onto a container ship to begin a month-long journey to—in the case of Coke for sale in Austin—the port of Corpus Christi, on the Texan coast.

After the aluminum bar makes landfall, a truck takes it north on Interstates 37 and 35 to a bottling plant on Burnet Road in Austin, where it is rolled flat in a rolling mill and turned into aluminum sheets. The sheets are punched into circles and shaped into a cup by a mechanical process called drawing and ironing—this not only forms the can but also thins the aluminum. The transition from circle to cylinder takes about a fifth of a second. The outside of the can is decorated using a base layer called "urethane acrylate," then up to seven layers of colored acrylic paint and varnish, which are cured using ultraviolet light. The inside of the can is painted, too—with a chemical called a "comestible polymeric coating," to prevent aluminum from getting into the soda. So far, this vast tool chain has produced only an empty can with no lid. The next step is to fill it up.

Coca-Cola is made from syrup produced by the Coca-Cola Company of Atlanta, Georgia. The syrup is the only thing the Coca-Cola Company provides; the bottling operation belongs to a separate, independent corporation called the Coca-Cola Bottling Company. The main ingredient in the syrup used in the United States is a sweetener called high-fructose corn syrup 55, so named because it is 55 percent fructose, or "fruit sugar," and 42 percent glucose, or "simple sugar"—the same ratio of fructose to glucose as in natural honey. High-fructose corn syrup is made by grinding wet corn until it becomes cornstarch, mixing the cornstarch with an enzyme secreted by a bacillus, a rod-shaped bacterium, and another enzyme, this one secreted by an aspergillus mold, and then using a third enzyme, xylose isomerase, derived from a bacterium called *Streptomyces rubiginosus,* to turn some of the glucose into fructose.

The second ingredient, caramel coloring, gives the drink its distinctive dark brown color. There are four types of caramel coloring; Coca-Cola uses type E150d, which is made by heating sugars with sulfite and ammonia to create bitter brown liquid. The syrup's other principal ingredient is phosphoric acid, which adds acidity and is made by diluting burnt phosphorus (created by heating phosphate rock in an arc furnace) and processing it to remove arsenic.

High-fructose corn syrup and caramel coloring make up most of the syrup, but all they add is sweetness and color. Flavors make up a much smaller proportion of the mixture. These include vanilla, which—as we have already seen—is the fruit of a Mexican orchid that has been dried and cured; cinnamon, which is the inner bark of a Sri Lankan tree; coca leaf, which comes from South America and is processed in a unique U.S. government–authorized factory in New Jersey to remove its addictive stimulant, cocaine; and kola nut, a red nut found on a tree that grows in the African rain forest (this may be the origin of Coca-Cola's distinctive red logo).

The final ingredient, caffeine, is a stimulating alkaloid that can be derived from the kola nut, coffee beans, and other sources.

All these ingredients are combined and boiled down to a concentrate, which is transported from the Coca-Cola Company factory in Atlanta to the Coca-Cola Bottling Company factory in Austin, where it is diluted with local water infused with carbon dioxide. Some of the carbon dioxide turns to gas in the water, and these gas bubbles give the water effervescence, also known as "fizz," after its sound. The final mixture is poured into cans, which still need lids.

The top of the can is carefully engineered: it is aluminum, too, but it has to be thicker and stronger than the rest of the can to withstand the pressure of the carbon dioxide gas, and so it is made from an alloy with more magnesium. The lid is punched and scored, and a tab opening, also made of aluminum, is installed. The finished lid is put on top of the filled can, and the edges of the can are folded over it and welded shut. Twelve of these cans are packaged into a paperboard box called a fridge pack, using a machine capable of producing three hundred such packs a minute.

The finished box is transported by road to my local H-E-B grocery store, where—finally—it can be bought, taken home, chilled, and consumed. This chain, which spans bauxite bulldozers, refrigerators, urethane, bacteria, and cocaine, and touches every continent on the planet except Antarctica, produces seventy million cans of Coca-Cola each day, one of which can be purchased for about a dollar on some close-by street corner, and each of which contains far more than something to drink. Like every other creation, a can of Coke is a product of our world entire and contains inventions that trace all the way back to the origins of our species.

The number of individuals who know how to make a can of Coke is zero. The number of individual nations that could produce a can of Coke is zero. This famously American product is not American at all. Invention and creation, as we have seen, is something we are all in together. Modern tool chains are so long and complex that they bind us into one people and one planet. They are chains of minds: local and foreign, ancient and modern, living and dead—the result of disparate invention and intelligence distributed over time and space. Coca-Cola did not teach the world to sing, no matter what its commercials suggest, yet every can contains humanity's choir.

The story of Coca-Cola is typical. Everything we make depends on tens of thousands of people and two thousand generations of ancestors.

In 1929, Russian Ilya Ehrenburg described how a car was made, much as I have done here for Coca-Cola, in a book called *The Life of the Automobile*. He begins with Frenchman Philippe Lebon developing the first internal combustion engine at the end of the eighteenth century and ends with the emergence of the oil industry. On the way, Ehrenburg shows contributions from, among others, Francis Bacon, Paul

Cézanne, and Benito Mussolini. He writes of Henry Ford's conveyor belts — "It's not even a belt. It's a chain. It's a miracle of technology, a victory of human intelligence, a growth of dividends."

In 1958, Leonard Read traced the history of a yellow "Mongol 482" pencil, made by the Eberhard Faber Pencil Company, from the growth and logging of a cedar tree in Oregon, through its transportation to a milling and painting factory in San Leandro, California, and onward to Wilkes-Barre, Pennsylvania, where it is grooved, laid with lead made from Sri Lankan graphite and Mississippian mud, lacquered with the refined oil of castor beans, and topped with brass and a material called factice, "a rubber-like product made from reacting rape seed oil from the Dutch East Indies with sulphur chloride," to make an eraser.

And, in 1967, Martin Luther King Jr. told a similar story while preaching to the Ebenezer Baptist Church in Atlanta, in a sermon called "Peace on Earth":

> It really boils down to this: that all life is interrelated. We are all caught in an inescapable network of mutuality, tied into a single garment of destiny. Whatever affects one directly, affects all indirectly. We are made to live together because of the interrelated structure of reality. Did you ever stop to think that you can't leave for your job in the morning without being dependent on most of the world? You get up in the morning and go to the bathroom and reach over for the sponge, and that's handed to you by a Pacific islander. You reach for a bar of soap, and that's given to you at the hands of a Frenchman. And then you go into the kitchen to drink your coffee for the morning, and that's poured into your cup by a South American. And maybe you want tea: that's poured into your cup by a Chinese. Or maybe you're desirous of having cocoa for breakfast, and that's poured into your cup by a West African. And then you reach over for your toast, and that's given to you at the

hands of an English-speaking farmer, not to mention the baker. And before you finish eating breakfast in the morning, you've depended on more than half of the world.

Half the world *and* the two thousand generations that came before us. Together, they give us what computer scientists call "tool chains"— the processes, principles, parts, and products that let us create.

King described tool chains to argue for world peace. But the politics and morality of our long and ancient tool chains are complicated. Ilya Ehrenburg described the chain that built the automobile to argue for Marxism: he believed that the industrial processes of mass production endangered and dehumanized workers. Leonard Read saw the pencil's journey as an argument for libertarianism: he claimed that such spontaneous complexity was possible only when people were free of central control from government "masterminds." Clearly we are tempted to ascribe meaning to the complexity of creation. But should we?

3 | AMISH LESSONS

There is a real-life model for exploring the relationship between creation and its consequences: America's Amish people—a group of Mennonite Christians descended from Swiss immigrants. The Amish value small, rural communities, and their way of life includes protecting these communities from external influence. As electrification spread through America during the twentieth century, the Amish resisted it. They did the same with other inventions from the period, notably the car and telephone. As a result, the Amish, particularly traditional or "Old Order" Amish, have a reputation for being old-fashioned, frozen in time, and opposed to technology.

But the Amish do *not* avoid new technology. They are as creative and resourceful as anybody, and more creative and resourceful than most.

They generate electricity with solar panels, have invented sophisticated systems for using batteries and propane gas, use LED lighting, operate machines powered by gas engines or compressed air, make photocopies, refrigerate food, and use computers for word processing and making spreadsheets. The thing they avoid as much as possible is using this technology to connect to the non-Amish, or "English," world. This is why they generate their own power and do not have their own long-distance transportation—they take taxis to travel beyond the range of their horse-drawn buggies—and why their computers do not have Internet access. They are not practicing self-sufficiency. Most of the tools the Amish use are like Coca-Cola: they contain ideas from across the globe; could not be made without large-scale power plants, water-treatment facilities, oil refineries, and information systems; and cannot be sourced locally. The Amish do not have a puritanical preference for manual labor, either: the line between convenience and efficiency is fine, and while the Amish value work, they do not treasure inefficiency. Amish clothes dryers and word processors do things that the Amish could also do—and have previously done—by hand.

Contrary to their reputation, the Amish are among the most conscious, thoughtful tool users in the world. Amish leader Elmo Stoll explains: "We do not consider modern inventions to be evil. A car or television set is a material thing—made of plastic, wood, or metal. Lifestyle changes are made possible by modern technologies. The connection between the two needs to be examined with care."

The Amish approach to technology only seems arbitrary. The Amish are cautious about technology because they are cautious about how it shapes their communities.

The most unusual thing about the Amish may be that they walk their talk. They are not the only people with objections to creation, change, and technology. Some believe that not all technology is good, therefore most technology is bad; that because technology cannot solve all problems, it cannot solve any problems; and that anyone who thinks technology can do good is a naïve optimist, ignorant of technology's harmful consequences. One example is writer and technology critic Evgeny Morozov, who argues against what he calls "the folly of technological solutionism":

> Not everything that could be fixed should be fixed—even if the latest technologies make the fixes easier, cheaper, and harder to resist. Sometimes imperfect is good enough; sometimes, it's much better than perfect. What worries me most is that, nowadays, the very availability of cheap and diverse digital fixes tells us what needs fixing. It's quite simple: the more fixes we have, the more problems we see.

What's more, he says, technology is

> embedded in a world of complex human practices, where even tiny adjustments to seemingly inconsequential acts might lead to profound changes in our behavior. It might very well be that by optimizing our behavior *locally* . . . we'll end up with suboptimal behavior *globally*. . . . One local problem might be solved—but only by triggering several global problems that we can't recognize at the moment.

Morozov is right. "The more fixes we have, the more problems we see" is a good description of Karl Duncker's problem-solution loops, discussed in chapter 2. Problems lead to solutions, which lead to problems, and—Morozov's second point—because solutions are assembled across the world and inherited by future generations, the problems a solution creates may be felt only far away or in the future. Creating can cause problems unintended, unforeseen, and often unknowable, at least in advance. To illustrate, we return to our can of Coca-Cola.

Once we knelt by a stream to scoop water with bare hands. Now we pull a tab on an aluminum can and drink ingredients we cannot name from places we may not know mixed in ways we do not understand.

Coca-Cola is a branch on our fifty-thousand-year-old tree of new. It is there because water is our most important nutrient. If we do not drink water, we die within five days. If we drink the wrong water, we die of waterborne diseases like cyclosporiasis, microsporidiosis, coenurosis, cholera, and dysentery. Thirst should limit us to places within a day or two's walk of potable water and make migration and exploration dangerous. But the two thousand generations developed tools to make water portable and potable and allow us to live far away from rivers and lakes.

Early technologies for carrying and storing water included skins, hollowed gourds called calabashes, and—eighteen thousand years ago—pottery. Ten thousand years ago we developed wells, which allowed constant access to fresh groundwater. Three thousand years ago, people in China started drinking tea, a step that coincided with drinking boiled water, a practice that—coincidentally—killed disease-bearing microorganisms. The existence of these organisms was not discovered for another twenty-five hundred years, but as the technology of tea spread gradually from China through the Middle East and eventually, around 1600 C.E., to Europe, tea drinkers began to suspect that water was healthier when boiled. Boiling also enabled free-ranging travel, as water found along the way could now be made safe.

The best source of pure water is the spring—nature's equivalent of a well, where groundwater flows up from an aquifer. This water, clean and rich in minerals, has been revered for thousands of years; natural springs are often considered sacred sites of healing. Some spring water is naturally effervescent.

As bottles—first developed by the Phoenicians of the Middle East twenty-five hundred years ago—became more common, it was at last possible to transport sacred water, with its healing purity and high mineral content, from springs to other places. Once bottled and transported, these "mineral waters" could also be flavored.

Some of the earliest flavored waters were Persian *sharbats,* or sherbets, made using crushed fruits, herbs, and flower petals, and first described in Ismail Gorgani's twelfth-century medical encyclopedia, *Zakhireye Khwarazmshahi.* About a hundred years later, people in Britain drank water mixed with fermented dandelions and the roots of the burdock plant, which made it effervescent. Hundreds more years later, similar drinks were made in Asia and the Americas, using parts of a prickly Central American vine called sarsaparilla or the roots of sassafras trees. All of these variants on the theme of sparkling water and drinks made with natural ingredients were thought to have health benefits.

In the late 1770s, chemists began to replicate the properties of springwater and herbal drinks. In Sweden, Torbern Bergman made water effervescent using carbon dioxide. In Britain, Joseph Priestley did the same. Johann Jacob Schweppe, a Swiss German, commercialized Priestley's process and started the Schweppes Company in 1783. The mineral content of springwater was replicated with phosphate and citrus to make drinks called orange or lemon "phosphates," or "acids"; these terms were popularly used for flavored effervescent water in the United States into the twentieth century.

As mineralization and carbonation became common, the healing properties associated with springwater receded in favor of remedies and tonics that contained exotic ingredients, such as the fruit of the African baobab tree and roots supposedly extracted from swamps. Many of these "patent medicines" contained cocaine and opium, which made them effective in treating pain (if nothing else) and also addictive.

One of these medicines, invented by chemist John Pemberton in

Georgia in 1865, was made from ingredients including kola nut and coca leaf, as well as alcohol. Twenty years later, when parts of Georgia banned alcohol consumption, Pemberton made a nonalcoholic version, which he called "Coca-Cola." In 1887, he sold the formula to a drugstore clerk named Asa Candler.

A few years earlier, Louis Pasteur, Robert Koch, and other European scientists had discovered that bacteria caused disease, marking the beginning of the end for remedies and tonics. During the next two decades, medicine became scientific, and also regulated. Harvey Washington Wiley, chief chemist at the United States Department of Agriculture, led a crusade that culminated in the signing of the Pure Food and Drug Act in 1906 and the creation of the government agency that became the U.S. Food and Drug Administration.

In retreat as a medicine, Coca-Cola syrup was mixed with carbonated water in drugstores and sold as a beverage, its health claims softened to ambiguous adjectives such as "refreshing" and "invigorating." At first, the carbonated water was added manually, and the drink was available only at soda fountains. Bottling was such a foreign idea that, in 1899, Candler licensed the U.S. bottling rights, in perpetuity, to two young lawyers for one dollar, because he thought that all the money in cola would come from selling the syrup.

This may seem like an amazing mistake, but in 1899 things weren't so obvious. Glass was not easy to mass-produce, and Candler might have assumed that bottling would be a small business forever. But glass and bottling technologies were improving. In 1870, Englishman Hiram Codd developed a soda bottle that used a marble as a stopper—an ingenious approach that took advantage of the pressure from the carbonation to push the marble up the neck of the bottle to form a seal. Today, these Codd bottles sell at auction for thousands of dollars. As bottle technology improved, Coca-Cola bottling increased. Ten years after Candler sold his bottling rights, there were four hundred Coca-Cola bottling plants in the United States. Coca-Cola, once tied to the soda fountain, had become portable, and it would soon migrate again, from the bottle to the can.

The story of the can begins with Napoleon Bonaparte. Napoleon, having lost more soldiers to malnutrition than to combat, had concluded that "an army marches on its stomach." In 1795, the French revolutionary government offered a twelve-thousand-franc prize to anyone who could invent a way to preserve food and make it portable. Nicolas Appert, a Parisian confectioner, spent fifteen years experimenting and ultimately developed a method of preserving food by sealing it in airtight bottles then placing the bottles in boiling water. As with water for tea, the boiling killed bacteria—in this case, the bacteria that caused food to rot, a phenomenon that would not be understood for another hundred years. Appert sent sealed bottles that included eighteen types of food, ranging from partridge to vegetables, to soldiers at sea, who opened them after four months and found unspoiled, apparently fresh food inside. Appert won the prize, and Napoleon awarded it to him personally.

France's enemy, Britain, viewed Appert's preservation technology as a weapon. Preserved food extended Napoleon's reach. The army that marched on its stomach could now march farther. Britain's response was immediate: inventor Peter Durand improved upon Appert's approach by using cans made of tin instead of bottles. King George III awarded him a patent for his invention. Whereas glass bottles were fragile and difficult to transport, Durand's cans were far more likely to survive the march to war. Canned food quickly became popular among travelers. It helped fuel the voyages of German explorer Otto von Kotzebue and British admiral William Edward Parry, as well as the California Gold Rush—which started in 1848 and saw three hundred thousand people move to California, establishing San Francisco as a major city in the process—and it extended the range of both armies in the American Civil War.

In a coincidence that nods to Napoleon and the origins of canning, Coca-Cola developed the first soda cans during the 1950s to supply American soldiers fighting a distant war in Korea. They were manufactured from tin that had been thickened to contain the pressure of carbonation and coated to prevent chemical reactions, steps that made them heavy and expensive. When cheaper, lighter aluminum cans were invented in 1964, Coca-Cola's bottlers adopted them almost immediately.

Coca-Cola exists because we get thirsty. It exists because water can be dangerous and we cannot all live next to a spring. It exists because people got sick and hoped that herbs and roots and tree bark from far-off places might help them. It exists because we sometimes need to travel—to flee, hunt, go to war, or search for better places and ways. Coca-Cola may look like a luxury, but it exists because of a need for life.

Yet, like all creations, Coca-Cola is flawed by unforeseen, unintended, and often distant consequences. Aluminum begins in bauxite surface mines, which are devastating to their local environment. In 2002, a British mining company, Vedanta, requested approval to mine bauxite in the Niyamgiri Hills of East India, home to an indigenous tribal people called the Dongria Kondh. The plan, which was approved by the Indian government, would have destroyed the tribe's way of life, and also their sacred mountain. The tribespeople led international protests that put a stop to the mine, but it was a close call—and one that, of course, had no impact on equally destructive bauxite mines in Australia, Brazil, Guinea, Jamaica, and more than a dozen other countries around the world.

High-fructose corn syrup has been cited as a cause of rising obesity, especially in the United States. Americans ate 113 pounds of sugar per person in 1966. By 2009, this had risen to 130 pounds per person, an increase that may, in part, be due to the introduction of high-fructose corn syrup, which, because of import tariffs, is much cheaper in America than sugar. The average American consumes around forty pounds of high-fructose corn syrup a year.

Caffeine can be intoxicating and addictive if overused and if taken in excess can cause vomiting or diarrhea, which can result in dehydration—the opposite of drinking. Caffeine in soda is a particular problem for children: they now drink an average of 109 milligrams per day—twice as much as children in the 1980s.

Even though aluminum is easily recycled, many aluminum cans are disposed of in landfill sites, where they take hundreds of years to decompose. The production and distribution of each can adds around half a pound of carbon dioxide to the atmosphere, where it contributes to climate change.

The Coca-Cola Company has been an effective proponent of global trade and has succeeded in manufacturing and selling its product all over the world, a strategy that has caused conflict and concern in many countries, including India, China, Mexico, and Colombia. One issue is water rights: the only local ingredient in Coca-Cola is water, and manufacturing twelve ounces of Coke requires far more than twelve ounces of water because of cleaning, cooling, and other industrial processes. When all the processes in Coca-Cola's tool chain are taken into account, a twelve-ounce can uses more than four thousand ounces, or over thirty gallons, of water. It will always be cheaper and more efficient to drink water than Coke, and this is a problem in areas suffering from water shortages.

So, do better tools always lead to a better life? Does making better things always make things better? How can we be sure that making things better won't make things worse?

These are questions we, like the Amish and Evgeny Morozov, must ask. Sometimes technology's flaws are dangerous—even deadly. Coca-Cola's early competitors, root beer and sarsaparilla, were both made with fermented roots of the sassafras tree, an ingredient that is now banned because it is suspected of causing liver disease and cancer. Glass once contained enough lead to cause lead poisoning, one consequence of which can be gout, a painful inflammation that usually affects the joint of the big toe. Gout was long known as the "rich man's disease" because its sufferers were so often from the upper classes of society—people like King Henry VIII, John Milton, Isaac Newton, and Theodore Roosevelt. Benjamin Franklin went so far as to write an essay titled "Dialogue Between Franklin and the Gout." Dated "Midnight, October 22, 1780," the dialogue recounts a conversation in which Franklin asks his gout to explain what he did "to merit these cruel sufferings." He assumed they were the result of too much food and not enough exercise, and "Madam Gout" chides him for his laziness and gluttony. In fact, the cause of the "rich man's disease," for Franklin and all the others, was lead crystal decanters, which were used by the upper classes for storing and serving port, brandy, and whiskey. "Lead crystal" is not crystal at all but glass with a high lead content. The lead can leach from the glass into the alcohol and cause lead poisoning, which causes gout.

Lead poisoning may also have afflicted the majority of Roman emperors, including Claudius, Caligula, and Nero, who drank wine flavored with syrup made in lead pots. This had consequences far beyond gout. Their lead poisoning was so severe that it probably caused organ, tissue, and brain problems—severe symptoms that affected so many emperors that they likely contributed to the end of the Roman Empire.

As Amish leader Elmo Stoll says, new is neutral, neither good nor bad. As Morozov says, new *things* tend to be good for some people and bad for others, or good now and bad later, or both.

Not convinced? Let's return to William Cartwright's mill.

Understanding the impact of the past on the present is as hard as predicting the impact of the present on the future. They probably did not know it, but the weavers who attacked William Cartwright's automatic loom would not have been weavers at all but for automation. Until the thirteenth century, England's textile industry was centered in the southeast. What moved it north to places like Rawfolds, Yorkshire, the site of Cartwright's mill, was mechanization—specifically the mechanization of the cloth-cleaning process known as "fulling." For millennia, fulling cloth was like treading grapes, accomplished by the stomping of naked feet. To pace themselves and stay synchronized, the fullers, usually women, sang special "fulling songs," slow at the beginning when the cloth was tough, then quickening as it became more supple. The women adjusted the length and tempo of their song to fit the size and type of cloth being fulled. For example, from Scotland, originally sung in Gaelic, with nonsense syllables added here and there as needed:

> *Come on, my love,*
> *Keep your promise to me,*
> *Take greetings from me,*
> *Over to Harris,*
> *To John Campbell,*
> *My brown-haired sweetheart,*
> *Hunter of goose,*
> *Seal and swan,*
> *Of leaping trout,*
> *Of bellowing deer,*
> *Wet is the night,*
> *Tonight and cold.*

In England, the tradition of the fulling song was ended by a technology that revolutionized the world between the first and fifteenth centuries: the watermill.

Watermills were invented two thousand years ago, first spinning horizontally, like Frisbees, then vertically, like cart wheels. By the time the millennium turned, they were everywhere, initially used for grinding grain but soon for fulling cloth—as well as tanning, laundering, sawing, crushing, polishing, pulping, and making "milled" coins.

The new importance of rivers changed the value of land. Sites that could deliver energy to mills were now among the most important places in the world. The work went where the energy was.

During the first millennium, England's textile trade was centered in its southeastern counties, but mechanized fulling machines needed a type of waterpower that was available only in the northwest. The textile industry relocated. By the end of the thirteenth century, England's singers of fulling songs were silent.

This revolution in power sowed the seeds of the Enlightenment: the experience of engineering nature's energy led directly to the development of theoretical physics and the scientific revolution. Newton was probably inspired more by a churning watermill than a falling apple.

By the time William Cartwright was born, at the end of the eighteenth century, textile manufacturing was highly automated and had been for centuries. The difference between Cartwright's new loom and his old mill was that the loom replaced mental as well as manual labor. Fulling by treading is a rote task. People supply little more than kinetic energy from their muscles. This is why cranks, cams, and gears attached to waterwheels replaced manual labor so quickly: fulling is mainly applied power. But weaving is mental as well as manual work. It takes mind, not just muscle, to interpret and understand weaving patterns. As waterpower increased the volume of the textile industry, demand for weavers grew, which created a need for workers with better-trained brains. A system of apprenticeship arose to meet this need: master weavers taught teenage children the skill of textile making. Weaving apprenticeships were a common form of schooling in the days before public education: in 1812, the year of the Luddites' attack on William Cartwright's mill, around one in twenty English teenagers living in or near mill towns became weavers' apprentices. It was these same workers with better-trained brains who started to demand political reform during the late eighteenth and early nineteenth centuries.

The automated loom threatened the weavers because it could "think," too, or at least follow directions. Weaving patterns were fed into it using punched cards that could mimic the mind of the weaver, doing his thinking more quickly and precisely, and making him redundant in the process. It was the first programmable machine—in many ways, the first computer. The Luddites were protesting the start of the information revolution.

At the time, the consequences of this revolution seemed bleak. Men descended from manual laborers had been trained to think because mills had reduced the need for manual labor and increased the need for mental work. Now new looms threatened to reduce the need for them, too—perhaps to eliminate the need for workers almost entirely.

What the Luddites could not foresee was that the opposite would happen. The consequence of William Cartwright's victory was entirely unexpected and unintended. The automated loom did not reduce the need for intelligent labor; it increased it. As simple programmable machines took over simple mental tasks, the manufacturing efficiencies that followed created new jobs in a vast new tool chain—jobs like maintaining, designing, and building ever more sophisticated machines; planning production; accounting for income and expenses; and jobs that, less than a century later, would be called "management." These jobs required workers who could do more than think. They required workers who could *read*.

In 1800, one-third of all Europeans could read, in 1850 one-half of all Europeans could read, and in 1900 almost all Europeans could read. After millennia of illiteracy, everything changed in a century. All of your ancestors were probably illiterate until a few generations ago. Why can you read though they could not? The big reason is automation.

The men who attacked Cartwright's mill in 1812 did not learn to read after they lost their campaign against the automated loom, but their children and grandchildren did. Industrialized nations responded to the need for smarter workers by investing in public education. Between 1840 and 1895, school attendance in these countries grew faster than population.

As automation improved and proliferated during the twentieth century, it both drove and was driven by the continued expansion of education. Every year more children were educated to an ever-increasing level. In 1870, America had 7 million elementary school students, 80,000 secondary school students, and awarded 9,000 college degrees. In 1990, America had 30 million elementary school students, 11 million secondary school students, and awarded 1.5 million college degrees. Relative to population, this is almost the same number of children in elementary school but thirty-five times more children in secondary school and twenty-five times more college graduates. The trend toward higher education continues. The number of Americans earning college degrees almost doubled between 1990 and 2010.

The Luddites did not—and could not—foresee this when they tried to wreck Cartwright's loom. Cartwright could not have foreseen it, either. Every man was for himself; none could have imagined the far better future automation would bring to his grandchildren.

Chains of tools have chains of consequences. As creators, we can anticipate some of these consequences, and if they are bad, we should of course take steps to prevent them, up to and including creating something else instead. What we cannot do is stop creating.

This is where self-described technology "heretics" like Evgeny

Morozov go wrong. The answer to invention's problems is not less invention but more. Invention is an act of infinite and imperfect iteration. New solutions beget new problems, which beget new solutions. This is the cycle of our species. We will always make things better. We will never make them best. We should not expect to anticipate all the consequences of our creations, or even most of them, good *or* bad. We have a different responsibility: to actively seek those consequences out, discover them as soon as possible, and, if they are bad, to do what creators do best: welcome them as new problems to solve.

CHAPTER 7

THE GAS IN YOUR TANK

1 | WOODY

In March 2002, Woody Allen did something he had never done. He flew from New York to Los Angeles, put on a bow tie, and attended the Academy of Motion Picture Arts and Sciences annual awards ceremony, the Oscars. Allen had won three Academy Awards and received seventeen other nominations, including more screenwriting nominations than any other writer, yet he had never attended a ceremony. In 2002, his movie *The Curse of the Jade Scorpion* was nominated for nothing. He went anyway. The audience stood and applauded in welcome. He introduced a montage of movie scenes made in New York and encouraged directors to continue working there even though terrorists had attacked the city months earlier. He said, "For New York City, I'll do anything."

Why does Allen avoid the ceremony? He gives several tongue-in-cheek excuses—the two most common being that there is nearly always a good basketball game on that night and that he has to play clarinet every Monday with the Eddy Davis New Orleans Jazz Band.

Neither reason is real. The real reason, which he explains occasionally, is that he believes the Oscars will diminish the quality of his work.

"The whole concept of awards is silly," he says. "I cannot abide by the judgment of other people, because if you accept it when they say you deserve an award, then you have to accept it when they say you don't."

On another occasion: "I think what you get in awards is favoritism. People can say, 'Oh, my favorite movie was *Annie Hall*,' but the implication is that it's the best movie, and I don't think you can make that judgment except for track and field, where one guy runs and you see that he wins; then it's okay. I won those when I was younger, and those were nice because I knew I deserved them."

Whatever motivates Woody Allen, it is not awards. His example is extreme—almost all other Academy Award–nominated writers, directors, and actors attend the Oscars—but it points to something important. Prizes are not always carrots of creation. Sometimes, they can inhibit and impair.

Motives are never simple. We are motivated by a soup of things, some we are aware of and some we are not. Psychologist R. A. Ochse lists eight motivations for creating: the desire for mastery, immortality, money, recognition, self-esteem; the desire to create beauty, to prove oneself, and to discover underlying order. Some of these rewards are internal, some external.

Harvard psychologist Teresa Amabile studies the connection between motivation and creation. Early in her research, she had a suspicion that internal motivation improves creation but external motivation makes it worse.

The external motivator Woody Allen avoids is the evaluation of others. Poet Sylvia Plath admitted to craving what she called "the world's praise," even though she found it made creating harder: "I want to feel my work good and well taken, which ironically freezes me at my work, corrupts my nunnish labor of work-for-itself-as-its-own-reward."

In one of her studies, Amabile asked ninety-five people to make collages. In order to test the role of outside evaluation on the process of creation, some participants were told, "We have five graduate artists from the Stanford Art Department working with us. They will make a detailed evaluation of your design, noting the good points and criticizing the weaknesses. We will send you a copy of each judge's evaluation of your design." Others were given no information about being evaluated.

In fact, all the collages were evaluated on many dimensions by a panel of experts. Work by people expecting evaluation was significantly less creative than work done by people making collages for their own sake. The people expecting evaluation also reported less interest in doing the work—the internal creative drive Plath called "nunnish labor" had been diminished.

Amabile replicated these results in a second experiment with a new variable—an audience. She divided forty people into four groups. She told the first group it was being evaluated by four art students watching from behind a one-way mirror, the second group that it would be evaluated by art students waiting elsewhere, and the third group that behind the mirror people were waiting to begin a different experiment. She did not mention audiences or evaluations to the fourth group. This was the one that did the work that was the most creative. The next most creative group was the other group that had not been told it would be evaluated, while knowing there were people watching. The group that expected to be evaluated but had no audience came in third. The least creative group by a considerable amount was the group that was being both evaluated *and* judged. The evaluated groups reported more anxiety than the nonevaluated groups. The more anxious they were, the less creative they were.

In her next test, Amabile examined written rather than visual creations. She told people they were participating in a handwriting study. As before, there were four groups, some evaluated and some not, some watched and some not. Amabile gave them twenty minutes to write a poem about joy. Once again a panel of experts judged the poems and ranked them from most to least creative. The results were the same. What's more, nonevaluated subjects reported that they were more satisfied with their poems. Evaluated subjects said that writing them felt like work.

Amabile's research validates Woody Allen's reasons for avoiding the Oscars. Allen also skipped high school classes and dropped out of college. Missing award ceremonies is, in his case, part of a pattern of avoiding the potential destruction of external influence.

Allen works at a small desk in the corner of his New York apartment, writing movie scripts on yellow legal paper using a burgundy red Olympia SM2 portable typewriter that he bought when he was sixteen. He says, "It still works like a tank. Cost me forty dollars, I think. I've written every script, every *New Yorker* piece, everything I've ever done on this typewriter."

He keeps a miniature Swingline stapler, two plum-colored staple removers, and scissors alongside the typewriter, and he literally cuts and pastes—or, rather, staples—his writing from one draft to the next: "I have a lot of scissors here, and these little stapling machines. When I come to a nice part, I cut that part off and staple it on."

The result is a mess: a patchwork of paper, each piece either held together with staples or pocked with the acne of staples removed. And covering the mess, in an eleven-point typeface called Continental Elite, colored in a spectrum of grays and blacks that can only come from metal on ribbon, is the screenplay for a movie that will almost certainly be a hit and may, incidentally, win some of the awards Woody Allen avoids.

In 1977, one of these ragged yellow quilts became the movie *Annie Hall*. Allen thought it was terrible: "When I was finished with it, I didn't like the film at all, and I spoke to United Artists at the time and offered to make a film for them for nothing if they would not put it out.

I just thought to myself, 'At this point in my life, if this is the best I can do, they shouldn't give me money to make movies.'"

United Artists released the film anyway. Allen was wrong to doubt it: *Annie Hall* was a great success. Marjorie Baumgarten of the *Austin Chronicle* wrote, "Its comedy, performances, and insights are all dead-on perfect." Vincent Canby of the *New York Times:* "It puts Woody in the league with the best directors we have." Larry David, cocreator of the TV show *Seinfeld:* "It changed the way comedies were going to be made forever."

Allen's views about awards first became clear when *Annie Hall* was nominated for five Academy Awards and he refused to attend the ceremony. He did not even watch it on television. He recalled, "The next morning I got up, and I get the *New York Times* delivered to my apartment, and I noticed on the front page, on the bottom, it said, '*Annie Hall* wins 4 Academy Awards,' so I thought 'Oh, that's great.'"

Two of the awards, for Best Director and Best Screenplay, went to Allen himself. Unimpressed, he insisted that the phrase "Academy Award Winner" could not appear on advertising for the film anywhere within a hundred miles of New York.

Allen's next film was *Stardust Memories.* It underlined his indifference to praise: "It was my least popular film but it was certainly my own personal favorite."

Woody Allen is not alone in wanting to avoid being distracted by the judgment of others. When T. S. Eliot ascended to the highest peak of praise, the Nobel Prize in Literature, he did not want it. Poet John Berryman congratulated him, saying it was "high time." Eliot replied that it was "rather too soon. The Nobel is a ticket to one's own funeral. No one has ever done anything after he got it." His acceptance speech was modest to the point of evasion:

> When I began to think of what I should say, I wished only to
> express very simply my appreciation, but to do this adequately

proved no simple task. Merely to indicate that I was aware of having received the highest international honor that can be bestowed upon a man of letters would be only to say what everyone knows already. To profess my own unworthiness would be to cast doubt upon the wisdom of the Academy; to praise the Academy might suggest that I approved the recognition. May I therefore ask that it be taken for granted, that I experienced, on learning of this award to myself, all the normal emotions of exaltation and vanity that any human being might be expected to feel at such a moment, with enjoyment of the flattery, and exasperation at the inconvenience, of being turned overnight into a public figure? I must therefore try to express myself in an indirect way. I take the award of the Nobel Prize in Literature, when it is given to a poet, to be primarily an assertion of the value of poetry. I stand before you, not on my own merits, but as a symbol, for a time, of the significance of poetry.

Einstein actually *did* evade receiving his Nobel Prize. The award came long after his genius was generally acknowledged and was given not for his work on relativity but a more obscure finding—his proposal that light was sometimes a particle as well as a wave, known as the *photoelectric effect*. He claimed a prior engagement in Japan on the night of the Nobel ceremony, sent apologies to the Awards Committee, and gave an "acceptance speech" the following year in an address to the Nordic Assembly of Naturalists in Gothenburg.

He mentioned neither the photoelectric effect nor the Nobel Prize.

2 | CHOICE OR REWARD

It is February 1976 in the harbor town of Sausalito, California. The days are cold and dry. A strange redwood hut overlooks the still, gray bay. Crudely carved animals decorate its door. A beaver squeezes an accordion. An owl blows a saxophone. A dog picks at the strings of a guitar. There are no windows. Inside the hut, rock band Fleetwood Mac is recording an album called *Yesterday's Gone*. Their mood is as bleak as the weather, the atmosphere as odd as the door. The musicians hate this weird, dark studio with its strange animals. They have fired their producer. Singer Christine McVie and bass player John McVie, the Mac in the band's name, are heading for divorce. Guitarist Lindsey Buckingham and singer Stevie Nicks are riding a bronco of an affair: on again, off again, argumentative. Drummer Mick Fleetwood finds his wife in bed with his best friend. Each day at dusk they haul their emotions past the trippy critters, feast on palliative cocaine, and work past midnight. Christine McVie calls it "a cocktail party."

Fleetwood Mac survives Sausalito for a few months, then decamps to Los Angeles. Singers McVie and Nicks stay away. The Sausalito tapes are a mess. The band cancels its sold-out U.S. tour, and its record label, Warner Bros., postpones the release of *Yesterday's Gone*.

In Hollywood, forensic engineers slowly apply technical salve to the tapes and rescue the project. The band reassembles to listen and is surprised. The album is good—very good. Memories of the bickering in Sausalito inspire John McVie to change its name. He calls it *Rumours*.

Rumours is released to critical ecstasy in February 1977. It spends thirty-one weeks at the top of the *Billboard* chart, sells tens of millions of copies, wins the 1978 Grammy for album of the year, and becomes one of the bestselling records in American history, bigger than anything by the Beatles.

How to follow *Rumours*? Fleetwood Mac rents a studio in West Los Angeles, spends a million dollars, and leaves with a double album called *Tusk,* the most expensive record ever made. It gets tepid reviews; stalls at No. 4 on the charts, sells a few million copies, and sinks. Warner Bros. compares it to the rocket that was *Rumours* and declares it a failure.

A few years later, the pop band Dexys Midnight Runners met a similar fate. Dexys' big success was *Too-Rye-Ay*, an album propelled by a song called "Come On Eileen," which was the biggest-selling single of 1982 in both the United States and the United Kingdom. Like Fleetwood Mac, Dexys recorded *Too-Rye-Ay* during a storm of personal crisis: singer and bandleader Kevin Rowland and violinist Helen O'Hara were falling out of love. The album's success led to an intense world promotional tour. The musicians washed up on England's shores exhausted. Three members quit. The ones that remained went to the studio to record their next album, *Don't Stand Me Down*. It cost more money and took more time than *Too-Rye-Ay*. The photograph on the sleeve showed what was left of the band, known for wearing denim overalls, scrubbed and suited as if for job interviews. Inside were only seven songs, one of which was twelve minutes long and began with two minutes of conversation about nothing. *Don't Stand Me Down* confused reviewers, launched with no single, and did not sell. Dexys Midnight Runners would not record another album for twenty-seven years. Music business veterans call this *second album syndrome*—the one after the breakthrough that costs more, takes longer, tries harder, and fails.

Neither Fleetwood Mac nor Dexys Midnight Runners were made less creative by the emotional pressures they suffered when they recorded *Rumours* and *Too-Rye-Ay*. Like many before them, they made art from angst. But the bloom of success hides thorns of expectation. Big profits have a big price: the implied promise of more, made to a waiting, watching, wanting world.

All creators face this risk. Work we want to do is better than work we must do. Dostoyevsky bewailed the external pressure of a publisher's expectations:

This is my story: *I worked and I was tortured.* You know what it means to compose? No, thank God, you do not! I believe you have never written to order, by the yard, and have never experienced that hellish torture. Having received in advance from the *Russky Viestnik* so much money (Horror! 4,500 rubles). I fully hoped in the beginning of the year that poesy would not desert me, that the poetical idea would flash out and develop artistically towards the end of the year and that I should succeed in satisfying everyone. All through the summer and all through the autumn I selected various ideas (some of them most ingenious), but my experience enabled me always to feel beforehand the falsity, difficulty, or ephemerality of this or that idea. At last I fixed on one and began working, I wrote a great deal; but on the 4th of December I threw it all to the devil. I assure you that the novel might have been tolerable; but I got incredibly sick of it just because it was tolerable, and not *positively good*—I did not want that.

Dostoyevsky's experience was typical. Working "to order, by the yard," is less creative than working by choice.

Harry Harlow was a protégé of Lewis Terman, the father figure of the Termites we met in chapter 1. Terman's influence on Harlow was so great that he persuaded him to change his last name from "Israel" because it sounded "too Jewish." After getting a doctorate in psychology under Terman at Stanford, the newly named Harlow became a professor at the University of Wisconsin–Madison, where he renovated a vacant building and created one of the world's first primate laboratories. Some of his experiments tested the effect of reward on motivation. Harlow left puzzles consisting of a hinge held in place by bolts, pins, and bars in the monkeys' cages. The monkeys could unlock the hinge by releasing the restraints in the right order. When the monkeys opened the puzzles, Harlow reset them. After a week the monkeys had learned to open the puzzles quickly, with few mistakes. During the last five days of the experiment, one monkey opened the puzzle in less than five minutes 157 times. There was no reward: the monkeys opened the puzzles for amusement.

When Harlow introduced a reward—food—into the process, the monkeys' puzzle solving got worse. In his own words: it "tended to disrupt, not facilitate the performances of the experimental subjects." This was a surprising finding. It was one of the first times anybody noticed that external rewards could demotivate rather than invigorate.

But these were monkeys. What about people?

Theresa Amabile asked professional artists to select twenty pieces of their work, ten of which had been commissioned and ten of which had been created without a commission. A panel of independent judges assessed the merits of each piece. They consistently rated the commissioned art less creative than the self-motivated work.

In 1961, Princeton's Sam Glucksberg investigated the question of motivation using the Candle Problem. He told some people that they would win between $5 and $20, depending on how quickly they got the candle on the wall—the equivalent of between $40 and $160 in 2014 dollars. He offered other people no reward. As with Harlow's monkeys and Amabile's artists, reward had a detrimental effect on performance. People offered no reward solved the Candle Problem faster than people with a chance to win $150. Follow-up experiments by Glucksberg and others replicated these results.

The relationship between reward and motivation is not as simple as "rewards reduce performance." There are more than a hundred studies besides Amabile's and Glucksberg's. They reach no consensus. Some find that rewards help, some find that they hurt; some find that they make no difference.

Ken McGraw at the University of Mississippi offered one of the most promising hypotheses to sort out some of the mess: he wondered if tasks involving discovery were disrupted by rewards, but tasks that had one right answer, like math problems, were improved by them. In 1978, he gave students a test with ten questions. The first nine required mathematical thinking, and the tenth needed creative discovery. He offered half of the students $1.50 ($12 in 2014 dollars) if they got the problems right. He offered nothing to the other half. McGraw's results partially confirmed his idea. Reward had *no* effect on the math questions: both groups performed equally well. But it made a big difference on the creative discovery question. The subjects working for rewards took much longer to find the answer. Rewards are only a problem when open-minded thinking is required. They have a positive or neutral effect on other kinds of problem solving, but whether explicit, like Dostoyevsky's advance from the *Russky Viestnik,* or implicit, like the expectations Fleetwood Mac faced after *Rumors,* rewards clog the clockwork of creation.

Amabile explored and extended this finding with two more experiments. In the first, she asked schoolchildren to tell a story based on pictures in a book. Half the children agreed to tell a story in return for a reward—the chance to play with a Polaroid camera—and half did not. She eliminated the possibility that anticipating the reward was interfering with the children's thinking by letting them play with the camera *before* they told their story. Children in the "no reward" group got to play with the camera too, but no connection was made to the task. The children's stories were tape-recorded and judged by an independent group of teachers. The results were clear and as expected: children who'd been expecting no reward told more creative stories.

In the second experiment, Amabile introduced a new variable: *choice.* She told sixty undergraduates that they were participating in a personality test for course credit. In each case, the researcher pretended that her video recorder had broken and the experiment could not be completed. She then told members of one group, called *no choice–no reward,* that they had to make a collage instead. She told subjects in another group, called *no choice–reward,* that they had to make a collage but would be paid $2. She asked people in a third group, *choice–no reward,* if they would mind making a collage but did not offer payment. She asked members of the fourth group, *choice–reward,* if they would mind making a collage for $2. For added emphasis, the reward groups worked with two dollar bills in front of them. An independent panel of experts judged the collages. In this experiment, reward *did* lead to the most creative work—by the *choice–reward* group. But the *least* creative work was also caused by reward—it came from the *no choice–reward* group. Both *no reward* groups scored in the middle, regardless of whether or not they had been given a choice. In creative work, choice transforms the role of reward. The least creative group's problem was easily diagnosed: members of the *no choice–reward* group reported feeling the most pressure.

No choice–reward is the condition most of us are in when we go to work.

3 | THE CROSSROADS

People in America's Deep South tell a story about a musician named Robert Johnson. They say one night when the crickets were quiet and clouds curtained the moon, Johnson stole out of his bed at Will Dockery's plantation cradling his guitar. He followed the Sunflower River by the light of the stars until it brought him to a crossroads in the dust bowl where a tall, dark figure stood waiting. The figure took Johnson's guitar with hands strange and large, tuned it, then played it so the strings wailed and wept with mortal emotion, making a music no man had heard before. When he finished playing, the stranger revealed his identity: he was the Devil. The Devil offered Johnson a trade: the sound of the guitar for Johnson's soul. Johnson took the deal and became the greatest guitarist who ever lived, playing the Devil's music, which was called "the blues," all along the Mississippi Delta until he became legend. After six years, the Devil called in his due and took Robert Johnson's soul. Johnson was twenty-seven.

The story is neither completely true nor completely false. There *was* a man named Robert Johnson. He *did* play the blues along the

Mississippi Delta for six years. He was one of the greatest guitarists who ever lived. His legacy includes blues, rock, and metal. He died at twenty-seven. He did not make a deal with the Devil, but he did come to a crossroads where he had to make a deal with himself. Johnson married at nineteen and, despite his talent as a musician, planned a stable life as a farmer and father. It was only when his wife, Virginia, died in childbirth that he resolved to do what others described as "sell his soul to the Devil" and fully commit to playing the blues.

The story that arose around Robert Johnson's life and talent is partly due to his early death; partly due to his song "Cross Road Blues," which tells a tale about failing to hitch a ride, not a deal with the Devil; and mostly a mixture of ancient German legend and African American myth.

The German legend is the story of Faust, which dates back at least as far as the sixteenth century. It comes in many flavors but has one common theme. Faust is a learned man, typically a doctor, who yearns for knowledge and magical power. He calls upon the Devil and strikes a bargain. Faust gets knowledge and magic, and the Devil gets Faust's soul. Faust enjoys his powers until the Devil returns and takes him to Hell.

According to hoodoo, the folk mythology of African slaves, you can acquire special skills if you meet a dark stranger at a crossroads in the dead of night. The voodoo traditions of Haiti and Louisiana also reserve a special role for the crossroads: they connect the spiritual world to the material world and are guarded by a gatekeeper called Papa Legba. Unlike the legend of Faust, this stranger at the crossroads demands no price.

Robert Johnson's story blends these two mythic archetypes to illuminate a deeper truth: there comes a point in every creative life, no matter what the discipline, when success depends upon committing completely. The commitment has a high price: we must devote ourselves almost entirely to our creative goal. We must say no to distraction when we want to say yes. We must work when we do not know what to do. We must return to our creation every day without excuse. We must continue when we fail.

If any devil is involved, he is not the one demanding commitment. Whatever your higher power, whether God, Allah, Jehovah, Buddha, or the greater good of humanity, this is whom you serve when you commit to a life of creation. What is diabolical is squandering your talents. We sell our soul when we waste our time. We drive neither ourselves nor our world forward if we choose idling over inventing.

When Robert Johnson came to the crossroads at midnight, it was temptation that said, Do not practice, do not play, do not write, do not stretch your hands across the frets until they ache, do not press your fingers into the strings until they bleed, do not play to empty chairs and chattering drunks who boo, do not perfect your music, do not train your voice, do not lie awake with your lyrics until every word sounds right, do not study the skill of every great player you hear, do not invest your every breathing, waking minute pursuing your God-given mission to create. Take it easy, mourn your wife and child, get some rest, have a drink, play some cards, hang with your friends—they do not spend all day and night messing with guitars and music.

And Robert Johnson looked at temptation and said *no*. Then he took his guitar to the Mississippi Delta and for six years played music so great it changed the world, music so great it inspired every guitarist that followed, music so great we are discussing him now not because our topic is guitars or even music but because his story breathes life into the true meaning of creative commitment.

If you are fully immersed in your creative life and the crossroads has long left your rearview mirror, be affirmed. The friends, mothers, fathers, therapists, colleagues, ex-boyfriends, ex-girlfriends, ex-husbands, and ex-wives who said you were crazy and you work too hard and you will never make it and you need more balance were wrong, as are the ones who still do.

If you have not yet reached the crossroads, look around. It is here now. That stranger over there is waiting for the chance to offer you an endless supply of reasons why you should not create a thing.

All he wants in return is your soul.

Some say there is a condition called "writer's block"—a paralysis that prevents people from creating. Writer's block is alleged to cause depression and anxiety. Some researchers have speculated that it has neurological causes. One has even attributed it to "cramping" in the brain. But no one has found any evidence that writer's block is real. It is the inevitable underbelly of that other unproven phenomenon, the aha! moment. If you can create only when you are inspired, then you cannot create when you are not inspired; therefore, creating can be blocked.

Woody Allen makes fun of writer's block. He wrote a play called *Writer's Block,* and he wrote, directed, and starred in a movie, *Deconstructing Harry,* in which the protagonist, Harry Block, tells his therapist: "For the first time in my life I experience writer's block. . . . Now this, to me, is unheard of. . . . I start these short stories and I can't finish them. . . . I can't get into my novel at all . . . because I took an advance."

Allen took the role of Harry, but only as a last resort, two weeks before filming began, because other actors, including Robert De Niro, Dustin Hoffman, Elliott Gould, Albert Brooks, and Dennis Hopper were not available. Allen was afraid people would assume Harry Block was autobiographical, when, in fact, he is antithetical: "He's a New York Jewish writer—that's me—but he's a writer with writer's block—that immediately disqualifies me."

Writer's block immediately disqualifies Harry Block from being Woody Allen because Woody Allen is one of the most productive film makers of his—and possibly any—generation. Between 1965 and 2014, Allen was credited in more than sixty-six films as a director, writer, or actor—often all three. To take writing alone: Allen has written forty-nine full-length theatrical films, eight stage plays, two television films, and two short films in less than sixty years, a rate of over a script a year, despite directing and acting in movies at about the same rate. The only other moviemakers who come close are Ingmar Bergman, who wrote or directed fifty-five films in fifty-nine years but did not act in any of them, and directors from the "factory" studio system of the 1930s, like John Ford, who directed 140 films, sixty-two of them silent, in fifty-one years but did not write or act in any.

Allen's productivity tells two truths about writer's block. The first is about the importance of time:

> I never like to let any time go unused. When I walk somewhere in the morning, I still plan what I'm going to think about, which problem I'm going to tackle. I may say, this morning I'm going to think of titles. When I get in the shower in the morning, I try to use that time. So much of my time is spent thinking because that's the only way to attack these writing problems.

A victim of "writer's block" is *not* unable to write. He or she can still hold the pen, can still press the keys on the typewriter, can still power up the word processor. The only thing a writer suffering from writer's block cannot do is write something they think is good. The condition is not writer's block, it is write-something-I-think-is-good block. The cure is self-evident: write something you think is bad. Writer's block is the mistake of believing in constant peak performance. Peaks cannot be constant; they are, by definition, exceptional. You will have good days and less good days, but the only bad work you can do is the work you do not do. Great creators work whether they feel like it or not, whether they are in the mood or not, whether they are inspired or not. Be chronic, not acute. Success doesn't strike; it accumulates.

Woody Allen learned this early, writing jokes for television, saying: "You couldn't sit in a room and wait for your muse to come and tickle you. Monday morning came, there was a dress rehearsal Thursday, you had to get that thing written. And it was grueling, but you learned to write." And:

> Writing doesn't come easy, it's agonizing work, very hard, and you have to break your neck doing it. I read many years later that Tolstoy said, in effect, "You have to dip your pen in blood." I used to get at it early in the morning and work at it and stay at it and write and rewrite and rethink and tear up my stuff and start over again. I came up with such a hard-line approach—I never waited for inspiration; I always had to go in and do it. You know, you gotta force it.

Writer's block is not the same as getting stuck. Everybody gets stuck. The myth of writer's block may exist partly because not everybody knows how to get unstuck. Allen:

> I've found over the years that any momentary change stimulates a fresh burst of mental energy. So if I'm in this room and then I go into the other room, it helps me. If I go outside to the street, it's a huge help. If I go up and take a shower it's a big help. So I sometimes take extra showers. I'll be in the living room and at an impasse and what will help me is to go upstairs and take a shower. It breaks up everything and relaxes me. I go out on my terrace a lot. One of the best things about my apartment is that it's got a long terrace and I've paced it a million times writing movies. It's such a help to change the atmosphere.

Allen's second truth about writer's block is a confirmation that intrinsic motivation is the only motivation. Inspirational lightning bolts are external—they come from without and are beyond our control. The power to create must come from within. Writer's block is waiting—waiting for something outside of yourself—and just a shinier way to say "procrastination."

Much of the paralysis of writer's block comes from worrying what others will think: write-something-I-think-is-good block is often rooted in write-something-somebody-else-will-think-is-good block. Woody Allen's indifference to other people's opinion about his work is one big reason why he is so productive. He is even indifferent to what other people think of his productivity: "Longevity is an achievement, yes, but the achievement that I'm going for is to try to make a great film. That has eluded me over the decades."

Not only does Allen not go to awards shows, he does not read any of his reviews and has not even been to see all his own movies. The work, specifically the satisfaction he takes from it for himself, is its own statuette: "When you actually sit down to write, it's like eating the meal you've spent all day in the kitchen cooking."

Cook to eat, not to serve.

5 | THE OTHER HALF OF KNOWING

The largest island in the Philippine archipelago is Luzon, which reaches like a wing from Manila toward China and Taiwan. In the east, the Mingan Mountains climb to wild green peaks six thousand feet high. Until the eighteenth century, these mountains kept a secret: an indigenous people called the Abilaos or Italons or, most commonly in English, the Ilongots.

As recently as fifty years ago, the Ilongots had a ferocious reputation. *Popular Science* described them as "savages, treacherous murderers, and wholly untamable." They were known to be headhunters—people who murdered and decapitated their neighbors, keeping their victims' heads, and sometimes heart and lungs, as trophies.

In 1967, Michelle Rosaldo, an anthropologist from New York, went to live with the Ilongots. The Ilongots were doing much less head-hunting in the 1960s, but this was still a brave step. The last anthropologist to live with the Ilongots, William Jones, had been there less than a year when three Ilongots, including the man he shared a hut with, killed him with knives and spears.

What Rosaldo found was a culture with a distinct view of human nature. The Ilongots believe that everything human is the result of two psychological forces: *bēya,* or knowledge, and *liget,* or passion. Success in life comes from tempering passion with knowledge. Passion with knowledge brings creation and love; passion without knowledge brings destruction and hate. Passion, they believe, is innate and dwells in the heart. Knowledge is instilled and found in the head. The purpose of each Ilongot's life was to develop the knowledge they needed to focus their passion into creation for the common good. Headhunting and other forms of violence were the result of too much passion and not enough knowledge. Amazed, Rosaldo captured the Ilongots' insights in a book, *Knowledge and Passion,* now an iconic work of anthropology.

Stories like Woody Allen's and experiments like Teresa Amabile's show us that passion matters but not what passion *is.* The wisdom of the Ilongots fills that gap. Passion is the most extreme state of choice without reward. Or, rather, it is *its own reward,* an energy that is indifferent to outcomes, even when they include missed sleep, becoming poor, losing your friends, bleeding and bruising, even death.

This is not a new definition. The word "passion" comes from the Latin *passio,* for "suffering." In 1677, Dutch philosopher Baruch Spinoza defined passion as a negative state in his masterwork, *Ethica*

Ordine Geometrico Demonstrata, or *The Ethics:* "The force of any passion or emotion can overcome the rest of a man's activities or power, so that the emotion becomes obstinately fixed to him."

Spinoza thought passion was the opposite of reason—a force for madness. French philosopher René Descartes had a different view: "We can't be misled by passions, because they are so close, so internal to our soul, that it can't possibly feel them unless they are truly as it feels them to be. Even when asleep and dreaming we can't feel sad or moved by any other passion unless the soul truly has this passion within it."

Or: passion is the voice of the soul.

The two definitions of passion dueled until the twentieth century, when the positive view became more popular. But is passion always good? The Ilongots show us the answer. Passion is energy; if it does not create, it harms.

6 | ADDICTION, SORT OF

As the Ilongots and their headless victims know, passion that does not create destroys. We are all creative, and whether we have found it yet or not, we all have passion. But so many of us, for one reason or another, do not put our passion into action. Unfulfilled passion creates a cavity between our present and our potential—a void that can drip with destruction and despair. It stagnates. It manifests as might-have-beens. If we do not chase our dreams, they will pursue us as nightmares. Unfulfilled passion creates addicts and criminals.

Daquan Lawrence celebrated his sixteenth birthday incarcerated at the Elliot Hillside Detention Center in Roxbury, part of Boston, Massachusetts. His parents were drug addicts. His Nana Charlesetta rescued him from their home when he was five. He was arrested for the first time at thirteen, for dealing marijuana and crack on the streets of Mattapan, Roxbury's troubled neighbor, known in Boston as "Murderpan." (Roxbury itself has a marginally better reputation. Bostonians only call *that* part of town "Roachbury.") Lawrence careened from one prison to the next for the rest of his childhood, known to all, including himself, as a repeat offender and maker of trouble.

Then, soon after that jailhouse sweet sixteen, a pipe-thin stranger came to Elliot Hillside. His name was Oliver Jacobson. He carried heavy black boxes into the detention center's staff room. Lawrence peered shyly through the door. He saw Jacobson unpacking a piano. Trails of cables connected microphones, keyboards, speakers, and headphones.

Encouraged by Jacobson, Lawrence approached a microphone and tried to rap. It was a moment of revelation for all who saw it: Lawrence, the hopeless young pusher on a treadmill of crime and punishment or worse, had the gift the hip-hop world calls "flow." His rap was fluid, on time, and in tune. He ad-libbed—or "freestyled"—using a range of poetic tricks, from rhyme and repetition to assonance and alliteration:

> *It's the strive from inside that reveals the pride,*
> *But the message from the sky that shows me the guide,*
> *We are leaders, overachievers,*
> *Stuck once in the vision and precision of believers,*
> *Keep looking up to the sky, you keep flowin',*
> *Never stop in the dark, you are glowing.*

Lawrence spent months writing songs with Jacobson. He gave himself the rap name "True." He studied acting, playing Romeo in *Romeo and Juliet* and Othello in *Othello*.

When he got out of jail, at seventeen, he took his first-ever job to pay for acting school—as a door-to-door salesman for an energy company. He passed his General Educational Development test, earning the equivalent of a high school diploma. He started thinking about college and told the *Boston Globe,* "The arts taught me to have a direction, to have a goal, be the best you can be. It feels like I've been productive in every way. I feel like right now, it's real right for me. It's meaningful."

Daquan's story is not unusual. Rappers have a reputation for becoming criminals, but criminals more frequently become rappers, or musicians in other genres, or writers, actors, artists, or creators of some other kind. In 1985, a seventeen-year-old crack cocaine dealer named Shawn Corey Carter borrowed a gun and shot his older brother in an argument about jewelry; in 1999 he was arrested and tried for allegedly stabbing a man in the stomach in a New York nightclub. Carter pleaded guilty to a misdemeanor and was given three years' probation. It was a turning point. He said, "I vowed to never allow myself to be in a situation like that again." Today, Carter is better known as a rapper named Jay-Z. By 2013, after twenty years of success in music and business, he had a personal fortune of around half a billion dollars.

Music has diverted children from crime all over the world. Israel has a program called Music Is the Answer; Australia's Children's Music Foundation has a Disadvantaged Teens program; Oliver Jacobson, Daquan Lawrence's music teacher, was a volunteer for the U.S. nonprofit Genuine Voices; and in Britain, the Irene Taylor Trust, a charity, operates a program called Music in Prisons. In an evaluation of one of its programs, the Irene Taylor Trust claimed that prisoners were 94 percent less likely to commit a crime during the program and 58 percent less likely to commit a crime in the six months after completing it. These numbers are too good to be true—the data is sparse and the research poorly controlled. It would be wrong to say that a few months of music school ends a life of crime: Daquan Lawrence continued to deal drugs, and get caught doing it, for several years after he started to rap. But all the good outcomes make the truth obvious: the more we create, the less we destroy.

We are inclined to regard passion as positive and addiction as negative, but they are indistinguishable apart from their outcomes. Addiction destroys, passion creates, and that is the only difference between them. In the 1950s, George "Shotgun" Shuba hit baseballs for the Brooklyn Dodgers. One night after he retired, Shuba sat in his basement with sportswriter Roger Kahn, drinking cognac and talking about the game. Shuba described how as a boy he had practiced by hanging a length of knotted rope in his backyard and hitting it with a weighted bat. Then, old and slightly drunk, he demonstrated. From a case on the wall he took a bat weighted with lead and prepared to hit an old knotted rope as if it were a ball. Kahn described what happened next:

> The swing was beautiful, and grunting softly he whipped the bat into the clumped string. Level and swift, the bat parted the air and made a whining sound. Again Shuba swung and again, controlled and terribly hard. It was the hardest swing I ever saw that close.
>
> I said, "You're a natural."
>
> "Ah," Shuba said. "You talk like a sportswriter."
>
> He went to the file and pulled out a chart, marked with Xs.
>
> "In the winters," he said, "for fifteen years after loading potatoes or anything else, even when I was in the majors, I'd swing six hundred times. Every night, and after sixty I'd make an X. Ten Xs and I had my six hundred swings. Then I could go to bed.
>
> "You call that natural? I swung a 44-ounce bat 600 times a night, 4,200 times a week, 46,200 swings every winter."

The secret of Shuba's swing was what psychologist William Glasser later called "positive addiction." Shuba was so passionate about baseball that he acted like an addict. He could not sleep unless he had swung his bat six hundred times. His addiction, or passion, became his career.

One way or another, your passion will out. Use it as the courage to create.

Passion must be structured by process. Woody Allen starts with a drawer full of pieces of paper, many torn from matchbooks and magazine corners, all little patches of possibility:

> I'll start with scraps and things that are written on hotel things, and I'll, you know, ponder these things, I'll pull these out and I'll dump them here like this on the bed. I have got to go through this all the time, and every time I start a project I sit here like this, and I look. A note here is "A man inherits all the magic tricks of a great magician." Now that's all I have there, but I could see a story, forming where some little jerk like myself at an auction or at some opportunity buys all those illusions and you know boxes and guillotines and things and it leading me to some kind of interesting adventure going into one of those boxes and maybe suddenly showing up in a different time frame or a different country or in a different place altogether. I'll spend an hour thinking of that and it'll go no place and I'll go on to the next one.

The three most destructive words in the English language may be *before I begin*.

Oscar-winning screenwriter Charlie Kaufman: "To begin, to begin. How to start? I'm hungry. I should get coffee. Coffee would help me think. I should write something first, then I'll reward myself with coffee. Coffee and a muffin. OK, so I need to establish the themes. Maybe banana-nut. That's a good muffin."

The only thing we do before we begin is fail to begin. Whatever form our failure takes, be it a banana-nut muffin, a tidier sock drawer, or a bag of new stationery, it is the same thing: a non-beginning, complete with that dead car sound, all click, no ignition. Having resisted the temptation of others, we must also resist the temptation of us.

The best way to begin is the same as the best way to swim in the sea. No tiptoes. No wading. Go under. Get wet and cold from scalp to sole. Splutter up salt, push the hair from your brow, then stroke and stroke again. Feel the chill change. Do not look back or think ahead. Just go.

In the beginning, all that matters is how much clay you throw on the wheel. Go for as many hours as you can. Repeat every day possible until you die.

The first beginning will feel wrong. We are not used to being with ourselves uninterrupted. We do not know the way first things look. We have imagined our creations finished but never begun. A thing begun is less right than wrong, more flaw than finesse, all problem and no solution. Nothing begins good, but everything good begins. Everything can be revised, erased, or rearranged later. The courage of creation is making bad beginnings.

Russian composer Igor Stravinsky, one of the great innovators of twentieth-century music, played a Bach fugue on the piano every morning. He started every day like this for years. Then he worked for ten hours. Before lunch he composed. After lunch he orchestrated and transcribed. He did not wait for inspiration. He said, "Work brings inspiration if inspiration is not discernible in the beginning."

Ritual is optional, but consistency is not. Creating requires regular hours of solitude. Time is your main ingredient, so use the highest-quality time to create.

At first, creating for an hour is hard. Every five minutes our mind itches for interruption: to stretch, get coffee, check e-mail, pet the dog. We indulge an urge for research, and before we know it we have Googled three links away from where we started and are reminding ourselves of the name of Bill Cosby's wife in *The Cosby Show* (it was Clair) or learning what sound a giraffe makes (giraffes are generally quiet, but they sometimes cough, bellow, snort, bleat, moo, and mew). This is the candy we give ourselves.

What solitude creates interruption destroys. Science describes the destruction unequivocally. Many experiments show the same things: interruption slows us down. No matter how little time is stolen by interruption, we lose even more time reconnecting to our work. Interruption causes twice as many mistakes. Interruption makes us angry. Interruption makes us anxious. These effects are the same among men and women. Creation knows no multitasking.

Interruption, unfortunately, is also addictive. We live in an interruption culture, and it conditions us to crave interruption. Say no to the itch. More "no's" equals fewer itches. The mind is a muscle that starts soft but becomes long and lean with use. The more we focus, the stronger it gets. After that first difficult hour, several seem easy. Then we not only work for hours but also feel wrong if we do not. A change comes. The itch is not for interruption but for concentration.

As we sit with our pen poised above the page we aim to turn into a novel, scientific paper, work of art, patent, poem, or business plan, we can feel paralyzed—and that's only if we can summon up the courage to sit in the first place. While knowing that this is a natural and normal part of the creative process may ease our minds a little, it may not make us more productive. We look around for inspiration. This is the right thing to do, only much of art lies not in what we see but in what we don't. When we envy the perfect creations of others, what we do not see, what we by definition *cannot* see, and what we may also forget when we look back at successful creations of our own, is everything that got thrown away, that failed, that didn't make the cut. When we look at a perfect page, we should put it not on a pedestal but on a pile of imperfect pages, all balled or torn, some of them truly awful, created only to be thrown away. This trash is not failure but foundation, and the perfect page is its progeny.

The most creative force we can conceive of is not us, it is what created us, and we can learn from it. Call it God or evolution; it is undeniably a brutal editor. It destroys almost all of what it makes, through death, extinction, or simple failure to reproduce or be produced, and selects only the best of what is left for survival. Creation is selection.

Everything, whether nature or culture, was created by this process. Every peach, every orchid, every starling, like every successful act of art, or science, or engineering, or business, is made of a thousand failures and extinctions. Creation is selection, iteration, and rejection.

Good writing is bad writing well edited; a good hypothesis is whatever is left after many experiments fail; good cooking is the result of choosing, chopping, skinning, shelling, and reducing; a great movie has as much to do with what ends up on the cutting room floor as what does not. To succeed in the art of new, we must fail freely and frequently. The empty canvas must not stay empty. We have to plunge into it.

What we produce when we do will be bad, or at least not as good as it will become. This is natural. We must learn to be at ease with it. Whenever we begin to invent or create or conceive, whenever we begin to make something new, our heads fill with advocates of same, holding censor's pencils, babbling criticism. We recognize most of them. They are the ghosts of hecklers, judgers, investors, and reviewers past, present, and future, personifications created by our evolved instinct for keeping things the way they are, manifesting to stay our hand and save us from the perils of new.

These characters—all us in disguise, of course—should be welcomed, not rejected. They are important and useful, but they have arrived too early. The time for critical assessment—their time—comes later. For now they must be shown to a room in our mind where they can wait, unheard, until needed for editing, assessing, and redrafting. Otherwise they will not only paralyze us, they will drain our imagination. It takes a lot of energy to script and voice all those naysayers—energy we need for the task at hand.

The same is true of their opposites. Sometimes inner critics are replaced by cheerleaders of new who urge us on with fantasies of fame and glamour. They imagine the first bad stanza we write bringing down the house on Broadway. They script our Nobel acceptance speech while we are drafting the title of our scientific paper. They rehearse the anecdotes we will share on the couches of chat shows while we are writing the first page of our novel. For these voices, anything new we make, or even conceive of, is perfect. Show them to the waiting room, too.

Almost nothing we create will be good the first time. It will seldom be bad. It will probably be a dull shade of average. The main virtue of a first sketch is that it breaks the blank page. It is a spark of life in the swamp, beautiful if only because it is a beginning.

And, somehow, long after the beginning and far into an endless middle, something takes shape. After the tenth prototype, the hundredth experiment, or the thousandth page, there is enough material to enable selection. All that clay thrown on the wheel has the potential to be more than new. It has the potential to be good.

This is the time for those advocates of same, our inner critics and judges, to be let through the door they have been pounding on for so long. They have been eavesdropping all the while and are ready to attack the work with blue pencils as sharp as teeth and claws. Let them be loud. Let them brutally scrutinize the data, or the draft, or the sketch and cut out anything and everything that doesn't need to be there. Selection is a bloody process. Beautiful work, maybe months in the making, is culled in moments.

This is the hardest part of all. We are the sum of our time and dreams and deeds, and our art is all three. Abandoning an idea can seem like losing a limb. But it is not nearly as serious, and it has to be done. The herd must be thinned or it faces extinction, and any new work that does not suffer selection faces an equivalent fate: it is unlikely to pass peer review, or be produced or patented, exhibited, or published. The world will always be more hostile to our work than we are. Ruthless selection gives it less to work with.

When the frenzy is over and only our fittest work, our very best new, has survived, it is time to begin again. The agents of same, sated for now, must retreat so that whatever is left, however slight, can reproduce and grow into a second draft, another prototype, a changed experiment, a rewritten song, stronger and better adapted.

And so it goes on. No eurekas or flashes of inspiration. Innovation is whatever remains when all our failures are removed. The only way to work is to accept our urge to create *and* our desire to keep things the same and make both pull in our favor. The art of new, and perhaps the art of happiness, is not absolute victory for either new or old but balance between them. Birds do not defy gravity or let it bind them to the ground. They use it to fly.

8 | FROM E TO F

Why do more when you can do less? Woody Allen has pondered that, too: "Why opt for a life of grueling work? You delude yourself that there's a reason to lead a productive life of work and struggle and perfection of one's profession or art. My ambitions or my pretensions—to which I freely admit—are not to gain power. I only want to make something that will entertain people, and I'm stretching myself to do it."

New is difference, so difference makes new. When we create, we harvest what is uniquely ours, our speck of special, our very selves, shaped by our genes, by the life that courses over us daily, and, for those of us who have them, our God or gods. We each bring difference to the world. It is inside us from birth to death. Every parent knows that their child is like no other, made from a recipe of talents, tendencies, tics, and loves all his or her own. My first child loved snow before she could walk. My second rejected his first snowfall by crying for a chai latte. He was not yet two. What makes us prefer a chai latte to snow before we are two? Something innate. No matter how many billions breathe

the air of this earth, *you* bear something that has never before been borne and will not be borne again: a gift to be given not kept.

We may not write symphonies or discover laws of science, but new is in all of us. There is a bakery in my old neighborhood in Los Angeles. It is tiny, forty seats or fewer. A woman called Annie Miler created it in 2000. Annie is a pastry chef. She makes blueberry muffins, butterscotch brownies, and grilled cheese sandwiches. The bakery's interior is artful, tasteful, and personal. You can see Annie growing up in pictures hanging along the wall. In the first she is a little redheaded girl shyly displaying an early cake; by the last she stands with her team on her bakery's opening day. Annie's baking binds her community. Her store is where neighbors meet to pet each other's dogs and share small talk over the tang of espresso. The seasons change with the fruit in her tarts and the flavors of her soups. People go to her bakery to kick-start their day, to have first dates, and to salve the pains of life.

Annie's place probably sounds like a place you know. There are many people who, like Annie, have built boutiques, cafés, florists, delis, and thousands of other community businesses that go beyond mere franchises or cookie-cutter stores and have new and unique details because they are reflections of what is new and unique about their creators.

Be like Woody Allen and Annie Miler. Make passion the gas in your tank.

CHAPTER 8

CREATING ORGANIZATIONS

1 | KELLY

In January 1944, Milo Burcham strolled across an airstrip in California's Mojave Desert and climbed into a plane called *Lulu Belle*. *Lulu Belle* looked like an insect: shiny green with stubby wings and no propellers. A crowd of men, swaddled in overcoats, watched in silence. Burcham started the engine, a de Havilland Goblin from England—the only one of its kind in the world—shot a brief glance of mischief at his audience, and then accelerated into the sky. When he reached 502 miles an hour, he dropped *Lulu Belle* low and flew her so close to the men that he could see them startle. They were still watching in silence when he landed and opened the cockpit. He pushed himself out, wearing his best just-another-walk-in-the-park face, fighting a grin and winning, until the men whooped and ran toward him, hollering and clapping as if they had never seen a plane before. Burcham cracked a smile as wide as the sky. It was *Lulu Belle*'s first flight. No American plane had ever flown so fast.

Lulu Belle's official name was the "Lockheed P-80 Shooting Star."

She was the first fighter jet in the United States military. It was forty years since the Wright brothers' first flight at Kitty Hawk and 143 days since the P-80 had been conceived.

If creating is best done alone by people with intrinsic motivation and free choice, how do creative *teams* work? How can anyone build an *organization* that creates?

The team that built the P-80 at the height of World War II faced a hard problem: build a jet-powered airplane that can fight, and build it fast. The urgency was a matter of life and death. In 1943, British code breakers had discovered something horrifying: Hitler's engineers had built a jet-powered fighter plane with a top speed of 600 miles per hour. The plane, called the Messerschmitt Me 262 Schwalbe, or Swallow, was agile and highly maneuverable, despite being armed with four machine guns, rockets, and, if necessary, bombs. It was in mass production. It would be raining death on Europe by early 1944. The Nazis were winning a new kind of war—a war from the sky, using technology that had been inconceivable just a few years earlier.

The man who led the team to counter the threat of the Messerschmitt was Clarence Johnson, an engineer known to all as "Kelly." The urgency and complexity of the challenge were not Johnson's only problems—the United States government was also sure that German spies were listening to its communications. Johnson had to build a secret lab using old boxes and a tent rented from a circus and hide it next to a wind tunnel at the Lockheed plant in Burbank, California. He could not hire secretaries or janitors, and his engineers could not tell anyone, not even their families, what they were doing. One engineer called the place the "Skonk Works," after a factory that ground skunks and shoes into oil in a popular comic strip called *Li'l Abner*. The name stuck until long after the war, and when the secrecy lifted, the comic's publisher made Lockheed change the name. From then on the operation, technically Lockheed's advanced projects division, was called the "Skunk Works."

The circumstances forced on Kelly Johnson seemed adverse but turned out to be fortuitous—he discovered that a small, isolated, highly motivated group is the best kind of team for creation. The United States military gave Johnson and his team six months to design America's first jet fighter. They needed fewer than five. The P-80 was the first plane developed by the engineers at the Skunk Works, and they went on to invent the supersonic F-104 Star Fighter; the U-2 surveillance plane; the Blackbird surveillance plane, which flew at three times the speed of sound; and aircraft that could evade radar detection. In addition to creating planes, Johnson created something else: a model organization for achieving the impossible quickly.

2 | SHOW ME

Kelly Johnson started working at Lockheed in 1933. It was a small airplane manufacturer with only five engineers, restructuring after bankruptcy and struggling to compete with two much larger companies: Boeing and Douglas (later McDonnell Douglas). Johnson's first day at Lockheed could have been his last. He had been hired in part because, as a student at the University of Michigan, he had helped test Lockheed's new Model 10 Electra all-metal airplane in the university's wind tunnel. His professor, Edward Stalker, the head of Michigan's department of aeronautical engineering, had given the Electra a good report. Johnson disagreed. On day one at Lockheed, the twenty-three-year-old, who had only just received his graduate degree in aeronautics and had been hired not as an engineer but to make technical drawings, said so:

> I announced that the new airplane, the first designed by the reorganized company and the one on which its hopes for the future were based, was not a good design, actually was unstable. They were somewhat shaken. It's not the conventional way to begin

employment. It was, in fact, very presumptuous of me to criticize my professors and experienced designers.

There are few companies today where this would be a good career move. In the 1930s, there were probably even fewer. What happened next almost explains Lockheed's success all by itself.

Johnson's boss was Hall Hibbard, Lockheed's chief engineer. Hibbard's aeronautics degree was from the Massachusetts Institute of Technology, then and now one of the world's greatest engineering schools. He wanted what he called "new young blood"—people who were "fresh out of school with newer ideas." Hibbard said, "When Johnson told me that the new airplane we had just sent in to the university wind tunnel was no good, and it was unstable in all directions, I was a little bit taken aback. And I wasn't so sure that we ought to hire the guy. But then I thought better of it. After all, he came from a good school and seemed to be intelligent. So, I thought, let's take a chance."

Instead of firing Johnson for impudence, Hibbard sent him on his first business trip, saying, "Kelly, you've criticized this wind-tunnel report on the Electra signed by two very knowledgeable people. Why don't you go back and see if you can do any better with the airplane?"

Johnson drove twenty-four hundred miles to Michigan with a model of the Electra balanced in the back of his car. He tested it in the wind tunnel seventy-two times, until he solved the problem with an unusual "twin" tail that had a fin on each side of the aircraft and nothing in the center.

Hibbard's response to the new idea was to work late writing Johnson a letter:

Dear Johnson,

You will have to excuse the typing as I am writing here at the factory tonight and this typewriter certainly is not much good.

You may be sure that there was a big celebration around these parts when we got your wires telling about the new find and how simple the solution really was. It is apparently a rather important discovery and I think it is a fine thing that you should be the one to find out the secret. Needless to say, the addition of these parts is a very easy matter; and I think that we shall wait until you get back perhaps before we do much along that line.

Well, I guess I'll quit now. You will be quite surprised at the Electra when you get here, I think. It is coming along quite well.

Sincerely,
Hibbard.

When Johnson returned to Lockheed, he found that he had been promoted. He was now Lockheed's sixth engineer.

The story of the Skunk Works, America's first jet fighter, its supersonic aircraft, stealth technology, and whatever may follow that started with this one act. In almost any other company, or talking to almost any other manager, Johnson would have been laughed out of the room, and possibly out of his job. That was Hibbard's first instinct, too. But Hibbard had a rare trait: he was intellectually secure.

Intellectually secure people do not need to show anyone how smart they are. They are empirical and seek truth. Intellectually *in*secure people need to show *everyone* how smart they are. They are egotistical and seek triumph.

Intellectual security is not related to intellect. People who are more skilled with their hands than their minds are often intellectually secure. They know what they know and enjoy people who know more. Brilliant people are usually intellectually secure, too—and for the same reason.

Intellectual insecurity is most commonly found in the rest of us: people who are neither nonintellectual nor extremely intellectual. Not only are we the vast majority—we are also the people most likely to be made managers. People who are mainly skilled with their hands are no more interested in management than are Nobel laureates. As a result, most managers and executives are intellectually insecure. Hall Hibbard was unusual, and he was in the right place at the right time.

Hibbard's response to his new employee's bold claim that Lockheed's plane was a lemon was the perfect one. One of the most powerful things any manager can say is "Show me."

Frank Filipetti, a producer for musicians including Foreigner, Kiss, Barbra Streisand, George Michael, and James Taylor, uses "show me" to manage creative conflict in the recording studio:

When you're dealing with a creative process, there's always ego involved. I have one philosophy: I never want to get into an argument about, or discuss, how something is going to sound. I've had people sit there and tell me why putting the backgrounds in the first chorus isn't going to work, and they'll expound on that for thirty minutes, when all you've got to do is play the damn thing, and then you'll hear it. And more times than not, everybody agrees, once they hear it. But they'll sit there and they'll argue this thing out without listening to it. You can intellectualize all this stuff until you're blue in the face, but the end result is the way it sounds, and that can really surprise you sometimes. There have been times when I thought I was absolutely right, and then I listen to it, and I have to admit, "That actually sounds pretty good." Once you get to that stage where you say, "Let's just play it," it's really amazing how everybody kind of hears the same thing all of a sudden. And it takes that ego thing out of it, too.

Hibbard's letter was the equivalent of "That actually sounds pretty good." It meant so much to Johnson that he kept it his entire life.

In November 1960, Robert Galambos figured something out. He said out loud, to no one in particular, "I know how the brain works."

A week later, Galambos presented his idea to David Rioch, his manager for the past ten years. The meeting went badly. Rioch did not say, "Show me." Instead, Galambos's idea made Rioch angry. He ordered Galambos not to talk about it in public, or to write about it, and predicted that his career was over. And it nearly was: within months, Galambos was looking for a new job.

Both men were neuroscientists at the Walter Reed Army Institute of Research, in Silver Spring, Maryland. They had worked together closely for a decade, trying to understand how the brain works and how to repair it. They and their colleagues had made Walter Reed one of the world's most respected and prestigious centers of neuroscience. Galambos, then forty-six years old, was more than just an accomplished neuroscientist—he was also a famous one. When he was a researcher at Harvard, he had for the first time conclusively proved, with collaborator Donald Griffin, that bats use echolocation to "see in the dark"—a radical finding that was not immediately accepted by experts but that we now take for granted. Despite this pedigree, and their long history of successfully working together, Rioch quickly forced Galambos out of his job because of his new idea. Six months later, Galambos left Walter Reed forever.

Galambos's idea was apparently simple: he hypothesized that cells called "glia" are crucial to brain function. Forty percent of all brain cells are glia, but in 1960 it was assumed that they didn't do anything but hold the other, more important cells together and perhaps support and protect them. This assumption was built right into their name: the word *glia* is medieval Greek for "glue."

Rioch's problem with Galambos's idea dates back to a nineteenth-century Spaniard, Santiago Ramón y Cajal. Cajal was a Nobel Prize–

winning scientist and a central figure in the development of modern brain science. Around 1899, he concluded that a particular type of electrically excitable cell was the critical unit of brain function. He called this type of cell a "neuron," after the Greek word for "nerve." His idea became known as "Cajal's neuron doctrine." By 1960, everybody in the field believed it. As with glia, the idea was right there in the name—after Cajal, the study of the brain became known as "neuroscience." Robert Galambos's idea that glial cells had an equally important role to play in making the brain work challenged what every neuroscientist, including Dave Rioch, had believed for their whole careers. It questioned the foundations of the field, risked causing a revolution, and threatened the empire of the neuron. Rioch sensed the risk and tried to shut Galambos down.

Since this confrontation, Galambos's idea has become widely accepted. Scientists do not get fired for having ideas about glia anymore. They are more likely to be promoted. There is an increasing body of evidence that Galambos was right and that glial cells play a vital role in signaling and communication within the brain. They secrete fluids with purposes as yet unknown and may have a crucial influence on brain diseases such as Alzheimer's. One type of glia, star-shaped cells called astrocytes, may be more sensitive signalers than neurons. Fifty years after Galambos's confrontation with Rioch, one scientific review concluded, "Quite possibly the most important roles of glia have yet to be imagined."

The fact that Galambos eventually turned out to be right is beside the point. Organizations are not supposed to work this way. Brilliant, innovative thinking is meant to be encouraged. Galambos and his idea should and could have made a beachhead on a whole new continent of fertile research opportunities. Instead, important discoveries about glia and the brain were delayed for decades. We are learning things today that we could have found out in the 1970s. So why would a distinguished scientist like David Rioch be provoked to anger by an idea proposed by an equally distinguished scientist like Robert Galambos?

The problem was not Rioch. Robert Galambos's story is typical—it happens in almost every organization almost all the time. Kelly Johnson's is not. Both men are examples of what management scholars Larry Downes and Paul Nunes call "truth-tellers":

> Truth-tellers are genuinely passionate about solving big problems. They harangue you with their vision, and as a result they rarely stay in one company for very long. They are not model employees—their true loyalty is to the future, not next quarter's profits. They can tell you what's coming, but not necessarily when or how. Truth-tellers are often eccentric and difficult to manage. They speak a strange language, one that isn't focused on incremental change and polite business-speak. Learning to find them is hard. Learning to understand them, and appreciate their value, is even harder.

Truth-tellers are a bit like the glia of organizations: long overlooked, yet essential for regeneration. They may not be popular. The truth is often awkward and unwelcome, and so are the people who tell it.

As we have seen in our discussions of rejection, confrontations about ideas are hardwired into human nature. The hallmark of a creative organization is that it is much more receptive to new thinking than the world in general. A creative organization does not resent conflicts over concepts; it resolves them. But most organizations are not like Lockheed—they are like Walter Reed. So most truth-tellers are not treated like Kelly Johnson—they are treated like Robert Galambos. We do not walk in a welcoming world when we are given the gift of great thoughts. Great thoughts are great threats.

Kelly Johnson's motto was "Be quick, be quiet, be on time." This was never more important than when he was asked to build *Lulu Belle,* America's first jet fighter. *Lulu Belle* not only flew more quickly than other planes; she was designed and developed more quickly than other planes, too. She had to be: the future of the free world depended on her.

During World War II, planes became faster until they hit a mysterious limit: when they reached 500 miles per hour, they either went out of control or broke apart. Lockheed first experienced the problem in its P-38 Lightning fighter plane, which was so effective that the Germans called it the "fork-tailed devil" and the Japanese called it "two planes, one pilot." Several Lockheed test pilots were killed trying to take the P-38 beyond 500 miles an hour. Tony LeVier, one of Lockheed's greatest test pilots, said that when a plane reached that speed, it felt like "a giant hand shook the plane out of the pilot's control." The problem was so severe that it could not be explored experimentally: at high speeds, model planes were thrown about so forcefully that they could damage a wind tunnel.

As Johnson and his team worked to understand the problem, they uncovered something alarming: the Nazis had already solved it.

On August 27, 1939, four days before World War II began, a plane called the Heinkel He 178 took off from Rostock, on Germany's north coast, and flew over the Baltic Ocean. The He 178 was remarkable because it had no propellers. Instead, it had something no plane before it had ever had: a jet engine.

Planes create waves in the air. The waves travel at the speed of sound. The faster the plane goes, the closer the waves become, until they start to merge. In aerodynamics, this merging is called "compressibility." Compressibility creates a brick wall that planes fly into at around 500 miles an hour—but only if they have propellers.

Jet engines pull air through a funnel. When the air is forced out of the back of the engine, an equal and opposite reaction thrusts the plane forward. Jet planes do not fly into the wall of compressibility; they push off from it. Germany's new jet-powered Messerschmitts, the descendants of the He 178, would be able to outmaneuver, and probably destroy, every other plane in the sky, unless the Allies could develop a jet fighter, too.

Kelly Johnson had wanted to build a jet plane for the U.S. Army Air Forces, the predecessor of the United States Air Force, as soon as he found out about the He 178, but the USAAF told him to make the existing planes fly faster instead. It was only much later, when they discovered Germany's imminent introduction of the jet-powered Messerschmitts, that America's air commanders understood that building a jet plane was the *only* way to make planes fly faster.

The British had developed a jet engine, but attaching it to an existing airplane was ineffective. Jet engines needed whole new aircraft. And so, on June 8, 1943, at 1:30 p.m. exactly, the United States Army Air Forces gave Lockheed a contract to build a jet fighter, and only 180 days in which to do it.

Even Kelly Johnson was not sure he could meet this challenge. Lockheed was already building twenty-eight planes a day, working three shifts every day except Sunday, when it did one or two. The company had no extra engineering capacity, no extra space, and its equipment was in constant use. Lockheed's president, Robert Gross, told Johnson, "You brought this on yourself, Kelly. Go ahead and do it. But you've got to rake up your own engineering department and your own production people and figure out where to put this project."

These apparently impossible constraints gave us the model creative organization.

Johnson believed that engineers should be as close to the action as possible, so he used Lockheed's lack of spare capacity as an excuse to build a "lean" organization, where the muscles of his team—the designers, engineers, and mechanics—had direct connections to one another, without the fat of managers and administrative staff keeping them apart.

The lack of extra space, as well as the need for high security, gave him an excuse to build an isolated, insulated organization. No one else was allowed into the Skunk Works' box-and-tent "building." This was not just to keep the project covert. It had another benefit: shared secrets and an exclusive workspace gave the team a unique bond.

Inside the tent, a "scoreboard calendar" counted down the 180 days, keeping everyone focused on creation's most precious resource: time.

The challenges grew toward the end of the project: half the team fell ill because of the workload, the barely heated makeshift building, and colder-than-usual midwinter weather. They had to build the plane without ever seeing its engine—it had been shipped from Britain, but the expert sent with it in secret was arrested on suspicion of spying because he could not explain why he was in America. Then the day before the plane was scheduled to fly, the engine exploded. There was no choice but to wait for another—the only other one in existence.

The proof of the organization was the result. Despite these obstacles, the Skunk Works beat the schedule by thirty-seven days, and *Lulu Belle* flew the first time.

5 | THE SECRET OF BERT AND ERNIE

Mike Oznowicz and his wife, Frances, escaped the Nazis twice during the 1930s. First they fled from Holland to North Africa and then, when the war followed them, they fled from North Africa to England. They had two children while they were in England; the second, Frank, was born in the barracks town of Hereford in May 1944. In 1951, Mike and Frances spent their last dollars moving their family to the United

States, eventually settling in California, where Mike found work dressing windows.

Mike and Frances's passion was puppets. Both were active members of the Puppeteers of America, a nonprofit founded in 1937 to help promote and improve the art of puppetry. In 1960, the Puppeteers' annual Puppetry Festival was held in Detroit, Michigan. Mike and Frances befriended a first-time attendee named Jim Henson. Henson, his wife, and their three-month-old daughter had driven five hundred miles from their home in Bethesda, Maryland, in a Rolls-Royce Silver Shadow to attend the show. One day a friend drove the Rolls-Royce around Detroit while Henson performed puppetry through the sunroof with a hand-and-rod frog he called "Kermit."

Henson became close to the Oznowiczs. In 1961, when the Puppetry Festival was held in Pacific Grove, California, they introduced him to their son Frank, who had just turned seventeen. Frank was a skilled manipulator of the puppets on strings called marionettes, and he won the festival's talent contest, even though he preferred baseball and, he said, practiced puppetry only because he was the child of a family of puppeteers.

Henson was building a successful business making TV commercials with a new style of puppets he called "Muppets." Henson thought Frank had great talent and wanted to hire him. At first, Frank declined—he wanted to be a journalist, not a puppeteer, and he was only seventeen years old. But there was something about Jim Henson, and the meeting, that he could not forget: "Jim was this very quiet, shy guy who did these absolutely fucking amazing puppets that were totally brand new and fresh, that had never been done before."

After Frank finished high school, he agreed to take a part-time position with Henson's company, Muppets, Inc., and also enrolled in City College in New York so he could get an education. But within two semesters, Frank stopped going to college and started working full-time with Henson. Frank said, "What was going on with the Muppets was too exciting."

By 1963, when Frank joined Henson, the Muppets were moving beyond commercials. A popular country music singer named Jimmy Dean was planning a variety show for ABC Television, and he wanted Henson to provide a puppet for the show. Henson created Rowlf, a brown, floppy-eared dog. Rowlf got up to eight minutes of airtime per episode, often upstaged Dean, and received thousands of letters from fans each week.

Rowlf was what is known as a "live-hand Muppet." Some Muppets, like Kermit the Frog, are "hand-and-rod Muppets": a single puppeteer—technically, a "Muppeteer"—puts one hand in the Muppet's head and uses the other to manipulate the Muppet's hands using rods. Live-hand Muppets need *two* Muppeteers: one Muppeteer puts one hand, usually the right one, into the Muppet's head and the other hand into the Muppet's glovelike left hand. A second Muppeteer puts his or her right hand into the Muppet's right hand. The two Muppeteers stand close together and must think and move as one. Henson was Rowlf's voice, head, mouth, and left hand; Frank was Rowlf's right hand. One night, Jimmy Dean, the show's host, stumbled saying "Oznowicz" on air and accidentally gave Frank a more magical name: Oz.

Oz and Henson were at the beginning of what would become a potent creative partnership.

A few years later—partly because of Rowlf—Henson, Oz, and the rest of Muppets, Inc., were recruited to work on a new television series for children to be called *Sesame Street*.

While they were preparing for the first show, Henson and Oz found two new Muppets in the rehearsal room, made and designed by master Muppet maker Don Sahlin, the creator of Rowlf. One was a tall hand-and-rod puppet with a long yellow head like a football about to be kicked, crossed by one thick eyebrow. The other was its opposite, a short live-hand puppet with a squat orange head, no eyebrows, and a meadow of black hair.

Henson took the yellow puppet and Oz took the orange one, trying to discover the characters inhabiting them. The puppets felt wrong. They switched. Henson took the short orange guy with the scared-cat hair; Oz took the tall guy with the unibrow. Everything clicked. The yellow Muppet, played by Oz, became "Bert," careful, serious, and sensible; the orange Muppet, played by Henson, became "Ernie," a playful, funny risk taker. Bert was the kind of guy who wanted to be a journalist, not a puppeteer. Ernie was the kind of guy who would cruise Detroit in a Rolls-Royce waving a frog through the sunroof. And yet, somehow, Bert and Ernie were kindred spirits, worth more together than apart.

The first episode of *Sesame Street* was broadcast on Monday, November 10, 1969. After the words "In Color," two clay animation monsters appear, followed by an archway with the words "Sesame Street." The monsters walk through the arch, the screen fades to black, and the show's theme song, "Can You Tell Me How to Get to Sesame Street?" begins, sung by a choir of children over clips of real urban kids—not the scrubbed and tailored angels normally seen on television at that time—playing in city parks. The title sequence ends, and the show opens on the green street sign that says, "Sesame Street," while an instrumental version of the song, played on harmonica by jazz musician Toots Theilemans, begins. A black schoolteacher named Gordon is showing a little white girl named Sally around the neighborhood. After introducing her to some human characters and an eight-foot-tall full-costume Muppet called "Big Bird," Gordon hears singing coming from the basement of 123 Sesame Street and points to the basement window, saying, "That's Ernie. Ernie lives down in the basement, and he lives there with his friend Bert. Whenever you hear Ernie singing, you can bet he's taking a bath."

The show cuts to Ernie in the bathtub, singing while scrubbing.

ERNIE: Hey, Bert. Can I have a bar of soap?

BERT (*entering*): Yah.

ERNIE: Just toss it into Rosie here.

BERT (*looking around, perplexed*): Who's Rosie?

ERNIE: My bathtub. I call my bathtub Rosie.

BERT: Ernie, why do you call your bathtub Rosie?

ERNIE: What's that?

BERT: I said, why do you call your bathtub Rosie?

ERNIE: Because every time I take a bath, I leave a ring
around Rosie.

Ernie giggles a glottal, staccato giggle. Bert looks at the camera, as if asking the audience whether they can believe this guy. With that sequence, Bert and Ernie became the first puppets to appear on *Sesame Street*. They are still major characters today.

Bert and Ernie's close relationship has often aroused suspicion. What were two male puppets doing together? Why were they so close? Pentecostal pastor Joseph Chambers of Charlotte, North Carolina, thought he knew: "Bert and Ernie are two grown men sharing a house and a bedroom. They share clothes, eat and cook together, and have blatantly effeminate characteristics. In one show Bert teaches Ernie how to sew. In another they tend plants together. If this isn't meant to represent a homosexual union, I can't imagine what it's supposed to represent."

But no, Bert and Ernie are not gay. To discover what the characters represent, we need look no further than the men inside the puppets. Not only were Henson and Oz Bert and Ernie, Bert and Ernie were Henson and Oz. *Sesame Street* writer Jon Stone recalls, "Their relationship reflected the real-life Jim-Frank relationship. Jim was the instigator, the teaser, the cutup. Frank was the conservative, careful victim. But essential to the rapport was the affection and respect which these two men held for each other. Ernie and Bert are best friends; so it was with Jim and Frank."

Some of the greatest creative work comes from people working in twos. The partnership is the most basic unit of creative organization, and it holds many lessons for how to build creative teams. Some creative partners are married, like Pierre and Marie Curie; some are family, like Orville and Wilbur Wright; but most are neither. They may not even be friends. They are people like Simon and Garfunkel, Warren and Marshall, Abbott and Costello, Lennon and McCartney, Page and Brin, Hanna and Barbera, Wozniak and Jobs, Henson and Oz.

As in the story of Bert and Ernie, the intimacy of the creative partnership confuses some people, perhaps because they overestimate the importance of individuals.

The secret of Bert and Ernie is that nothing is created alone. Steve Wozniak's advice to "work alone," mentioned earlier, is not as simple as it seems. As Robert Merton observed, we never act as individuals without interacting with myriad others—by reading their words, remembering their lessons, and using tools they made, at the very least. A partnership puts this interaction into the same room.

6 | WHEN THE ROAD SEEMS LONG

In a creative partnership, the alternating nature of ordinary conversation and the problem-solution loops of ordinary thinking combine: partners use the same creative process as individuals but do their thinking aloud, seeing problems in each other's solutions, and finding solutions to each other's problems.

Trey Parker and Matt Stone have been creative partners since they met at the University of Colorado in 1989. In 2011, they won nine Tony awards for *The Book of Mormon,* a Broadway musical they co-wrote with

Robert Lopez; they have created movies, books, and video games; and they are best known for *South Park,* an animated television series they created in 1997. Parker and Stone have written, produced, and voiced hundreds of episodes of *South Park,* most of them made, from conception to completion, in six days.

The process begins in a conference room in Los Angeles on a Thursday morning, where Parker and Stone discuss ideas with their head writers and start to create the show that will air the following Wednesday. Stone describes the room as "a safe place, because for all the good ideas that we get, there's a hundred not so good ones." No one else is allowed in, but, in 2011, Parker and Stone let filmmaker Arthur Bradford put remote cameras in the room to make a documentary called *6 Days to Air: The Making of South Park.*

On day one of the film, Parker and Stone discuss script ideas, including the Japanese tsunami, bad movie trailers, and college basketball, ad-libbing possible scripts as they go, much like Henson and Oz trying out Bert and Ernie for the first time. By the end of the day, Parker and Stone have nothing—or, at least, nothing they like. Parker is worried. He tells Bradford, "There's a show on this Wednesday. We don't even know what it is. Even though that's the way we've always done it, there's a little voice saying, 'Oh, you're screwed.'"

On the morning of day two, Parker makes a suggestion to Stone: "Let's try this. Let's go to eleven-thirty trying to come up with something completely new; then from eleven-thirty to twelve-thirty we'll pick which of yesterday's ideas we're going to do."

Stone is skeptical: "A whole other show?"

But rather than argue for improving the existing ideas, Stone tries the process. Eventually, Parker throws out an idea about something he finds frustrating: "Last night, I went onto iTunes, and that window came up again that says, 'Your iTunes is out of date,' you know, which happens every time. 'God damn it. Here it goes again. I got to download another version of iTunes.' How many times have I hit 'Agree' to those terms and conditions, and I've never even read one line of them?"

Stone laughs, then suggests how Parker's frustration with iTunes might yield a plot: "The joke is that everyone always reads the terms and conditions except for Kyle." (Kyle is one of the show's main characters.)

Stone, speaking later, explained what happened next: "And then we said, 'Oh wait, this is actually starting to be something.'"

The pattern—Parker directing the process and finding the points of departure, and Stone refining and building on them—is typical of Parker and Stone's working relationship. Partnerships tend not to be hierarchical, in the sense that one person has authority over the other, but they are seldom leaderless. In Parker and Stone's partnership, Parker leads. Stone says, "Even though we're a partnership, and we each bring something different to the table, the way that the stories are expressed is completely through Trey. It's like Trey's the chef. Whatever I've got channels through him."

Parker agrees, but he is under no illusions about Stone's equal importance. Referring to another famous partnership from the rock band Van Halen, Parker says, "You can sit there and say, 'Well, it's all Eddie Van Halen,' but as soon as David Lee Roth leaves, you say, 'Well, forget that band.' Eddie can sit there and say, 'I write everything,' but you're not Van Halen without David Lee Roth."

On Monday, with less than three days until airtime, the script is still not complete. Animation and voice work is under way on the main plot, which features Kyle being forced to do the crazy things he agreed to when he accepted the iTunes terms and conditions. But the show lacks a subplot and an ending. Parker begins the day by describing the remaining problems to Stone: "We are in danger of doing our typical first-show thing where we've just got way too many ingredients; we haven't introduced the idea of apps at all; and I am worried about time—whatever this thing is at the end, it is going to have to be fast."

Parker then starts solving these problems—by, for example, describing a subplot where another main character, Eric, tries to persuade his mother to buy him an iPad. Stone's role here is evaluation: he laughs as Parker acts out the idea.

Parker is worried. That evening, he tells documentary maker Bradford, "I am pretty scared right now because I am up to twenty-eight pages of script and I still have five scenes to write. Each scene's about a minute long usually, so this is going to end up being about a forty-page script, which just becomes brutal, because I have to start taking scenes and figuring out how to do this same thing in half the time."

Even in a partnership, the literal, physical act of writing—choosing the words, rather than having the ideas—is an individual activity. This is what Wozniak means when he says, "Work alone." Two people and a blank page is no formula for creation: a pencil is a one-person device. Stone does not hover on Parker's shoulder trying to be helpful. He is in another room, working on script edits. Parker says, "I hate writing because it is so lonely and sad. I know everyone's waiting for me to get it done, and it is a battle of fighting over lines and trying to figure out what the best way to say things is. I just hate it so much."

As Monday ends, Parker paces while Stone watches from a couch. Both men are rubbing their heads and plucking at the bridges of their noses. Parker summarizes the current problem: "We're a minute short and I have four scenes to write."

In four days, he has gone from worrying about having no material to worrying about having too much. Stone says he hits rock bottom every Sunday and Parker hits rock bottom a day later. Sure enough, on Monday, Parker says, "I feel terrible about the episode. I am embarrassed we are putting this piece of shit on the air."

The laughter of a few days ago is gone. Parker and Stone stalk the studio, hunched and miserable.

Tuesday, the day before the show will air, starts with exhausted animators sleeping under their desks or at their keyboards. At six a.m., while the sun rises, Parker and Stone meet alone in the writers' room. Parker has erased the crude pictures that were on the whiteboard a few days ago; now there is a flat list of scenes with names like "Playground," "Eric's Home," "Jail Scene," and "At the Genius Bar." Parker stands at the whiteboard with a marker while Stone leans back in an armchair, his hands behind his head.

The roles have changed. Parker is no longer leading. He is pitching ideas: "Beginning of act two, we come back, and that's when it's 'Okay, the Geniuses are going to see us now.' And then, act three: we just start with the unveiling of the thing. And then we go to, they're doing the bubble thing, and Gerald flips out, joins Apple. We're back, and that's it."

And Stone is not being led; he is coaching and cajoling. He sounds paternal when he says, "That's great. Yeah, that actually works."

Reinvigorated, Parker returns to the keyboard. An hour later, the animators are being woken up and handed the completed script for *South Park*'s episode 1501: the first of the fifteenth season and the 211th Parker and Stone have written.

The story shows how many creative partnerships work. Parker trusts Stone. Stone complements Parker. Parker may appear to make a greater creative contribution, but Stone enables it, in particular by giving Parker emotional support during the loneliness and stress of creation. Stone creates, too, and Parker enables *that* by providing impetus. Partners create together by helping each other create individually.

7 | THE WRONG TYPE OF ORGANIZATION

The common thread that connects one person creating to two people creating can—or should—extend to larger groups of people, too. Creative partners talking sound a lot like creative individuals thinking aloud, and nothing needs to change when the group gets larger. The purpose of a creative conversation is to identify and solve creative problems, such as "What should this episode be about?" or "What order should these scenes be in?" The only participants in the conversation should be people who can make a contribution to answering these questions, which is why Parker and Stone's writers' room is a "safe place," off-limits to all but a few writers. There is no room for managers, "devil's advocates," or any other species of spectator in a creative conversation. This conversation is the main purpose of creating in a group. The detailed creative work is still done alone, unless help—practical, emotional, or both—is needed to get past the inevitable pressures and failures.

Parker and Stone's company, South Park Digital Studios, is a lot like Lockheed's Skunk Works: it is part of a big corporation, Viacom; it is isolated in its own physical location; and it is capable of working almost impossibly fast. While it takes six days to make an episode of *South Park,* it takes six *months* for most other production companies to make an episode of most animated TV shows.

In the wrong type of organization, Parker and Stone's creative talent can quickly become destructive. In 1998, Viacom asked the two men to make a *South Park* movie with another one of its subsidiaries, Paramount Pictures. Parker and Stone started fighting with the Paramount executives almost as soon as production began. One of their first battles was about the movie's rating. Parker and Stone wanted a movie with themes and language that would make it R-rated—meaning that no one under seventeen would be admitted unless they were accompanied by a parent or adult guardian. Paramount wanted a PG-13 rating—a milder movie that anyone could see, although parents would be warned that some content may be inappropriate for children under thirteen.

Parker rebelled: "After they showed us graphs of how much more money we'd make with a PG-13, we were like, 'R or nothing.'"

Parker declared what he later called "war." Paramount sent them tapes of trailers for the movie; Parker and Stone broke them in half and mailed them back. They sent rude faxes to everyone they knew at Paramount, including one, titled "A Formula for Success," that said, "Cooperation + you doing nothing = success." Parker stole the only copy of a censored promotional videotape to stop it from being broadcast on MTV. After this incident—the tape was the result of several days and nights of hard work by Paramount employees—Paramount threatened to sue Parker and Stone.

Parker and Stone's biggest protest against Paramount was the movie itself. They turned the film into a full-length musical about their frustration with Paramount's attempts to censor them. In *South Park: Bigger, Longer & Uncut,* the United States declares war on Canada because of a Canadian TV show with bad language; a schoolteacher tries to rehabilitate cussing children by singing a song based on *The Sound of Music*'s "Do-Re-Mi"; and characters say things like "This movie has naughty language, and it might make you kids start using bad words," and "I'm sorry! I can't help it!! That movie has warped my fragile little mind."

By the short-term standards of profit and loss, the Paramount–South Park collaboration was a success: the film grossed $83 million against a budget of $21 million, won awards, and Parker and co-writer Marc Shaiman received an Oscar nomination for their song "Blame Canada." But from the longer-term perspective of building a creative organization, the project was a catastrophe, and an expensive one: despite the positive outcome, and despite owning the rights to sequels, Paramount will never be able to make another *South Park* movie.

Parker told *Playboy,* "They couldn't pay us enough to work with them again."

Stone added, "You had marketing battles, legal battles, all these battles. Even with the clout of having this huge franchise that had earned Viacom hundreds of millions of dollars, the studio did everything they could to beat us down and beat the spirit out of the movie."

If Parker and Stone sound childish, it is because they *are* childish—
in the best possible way. The social skills that enable creation through
cooperation—and the antisocial behavior that can result when creation is excessively controlled—are things we all have as children but
that are educated out of most of us as we grow up. We develop our
ability to create in groups when we develop our ability to talk, but
we often lose it during our school years, and we may have lost it completely by the time we start our first job. One of the first people to
discover this was a man in Belarus in the 1920s. One of the best ways to
demonstrate it is with a marshmallow.

In 2006, Peter Skillman, an industrial designer, gave a three-minute
presentation at a conference in Monterey, California. He spoke immediately after former Vice President and future Nobel Prize winner Al
Gore and immediately before spacecraft designer Burt Rutan. Despite
the lack of time and the difficult billing, Skillman's talk made a big
impact. It described what he called "the marshmallow challenge," a
team-building activity he developed with Dennis Boyle, a founding
member of the design consultancy IDEO. The challenge is simple. Each
team is given a brown paper bag containing twenty sticks of uncooked
spaghetti, a yard of string, a yard of masking tape, and a marshmallow.
The goal is to build the tallest possible freestanding structure that can
take the weight of the marshmallow. The team members cannot use the
paper bag, and they cannot mess with the marshmallow—for example,
they cannot make it lighter by eating some of it—but they can break up
the spaghetti, string, and masking tape. They have eighteen minutes,
and they cannot be holding their structure when the time is up.

Skillman's most surprising finding: the best performers are children
aged five and six. Skillman says, "Kindergartners, on every objective

measure, have the highest average score of any group that I've ever tested." Creative professional Tom Wujec confirmed this: he conducted marshmallow challenge workshops more than seventy times between 2006 and 2010 and recorded the results. Kindergartners' towers average twenty-seven inches high. CEOs can only manage twenty-one-inch towers, lawyers build fifteen-inch towers, and the worst scores come from business school students: their towers are typically ten inches high, about one-third the height of the towers built by kindergartners. CEOs, lawyers, and business school students waste minutes on power struggles and planning, leave themselves only enough time to build one tower, and do not uncover the hidden assumption that makes the challenge so challenging: marshmallows are heavier than they look. When they finally figure this out, they have no time left to do anything about it. Wujec recounts those last moments: "Several teams will have the powerful desire to hold on to their structure at the end, usually because the marshmallow, which they just placed onto their structure moments before, is causing the structure to buckle."

Young children win because they collaborate spontaneously. They build towers early and often rather than wasting time fighting for leadership and dominance, they do not sit around talking—or "planning"—before they act, and they discover the problem of the marshmallow's weight quickly, when they have lots of time left to solve it.

Why do children do this? That question is answered by the work of Lev Vygotsky, a psychologist from Belarus. In the 1920s, Vygotsky discovered that the development of language and creative ability are so connected they may even be the same thing.

The first thing we do with speech is organize our surroundings. We name important people, like "Mama" and "Dada," and we name important objects, both natural, like "dog" and "cat," and man-made, like "car" and "cup." The second thing we do with speech is organize our behavior. We can set ourselves goals, like chase the dog or grab the cup, and communicate needs, like ask for Mama. We may have had these goals and needs before we could speak, but words allow us to make them more explicit, both to ourselves and to others. When we know the word for dog, we are more likely to chase a dog, because we are more capable of *deciding* to do so. This is why young children chasing dogs can often be heard saying "dog" to themselves again and again. Words beget wishes. The next thing we do with speech is create: when we can manipulate a word, we can manipulate the world. Or, as Vygotsky said:

> Although children's use of tools during their preverbal period is comparable to that of apes, as soon as speech and the use of signs are incorporated into any action, the action becomes transformed and organized along entirely new lines. The specifically human use of tools is thus realized, going beyond the more limited use of tools possible among the higher animals.

For example, when Vygotsky's research associate Roza Levina asked Milya, a four-year-old girl, to draw a picture of the sentence "The teacher is angry," Milya was unable to complete the task. Levina reports what Milya said:

> "The teacher is angry. I can't draw the teacher. This is how she looks." (She draws, pressing hard with a pencil.) "It is broken. It is broken, the pencil. And Olya has a pencil and a pen." (Child fidgets on her chair.)

Milya's response is typical of a child in the first stage of using language—labeling her world. Her speech is not yet a system of signs that helps her achieve goals; it is a narration of the here and now.

Anya, three years and seven months old, is younger than Milya, but she is in the next stage of development. (Another of Vygotsky's discoveries was something we now take for granted: that children's minds develop at different speeds.) Vygotsky put some candy on top of a cupboard, hung a stick on the wall, and asked Anya to get the candy. At first there was a long silence. Then Anya started talking about, and *working on,* the problem. Vygotsky reports:

> "It's very high." (She climbs up onto the divan and reaches for the candy.) "It's very high." (She reaches.) "You can't get it. It's very high." (She grasps the stick and leans on it, but she does not use it.) "I can't get it. It's very high." (She holds the stick in one hand and reaches for the candy with the other.) "My arm's tired. You can't get it. We have a tall cupboard. Papa puts things up there, and I can't get them." (She reaches.) "No, I can't reach it with my hand. I'm still little." (She stands up on a chair.) "There we go. I can get it better from the chair." (She reaches. She stands on the chair, and swings the stick. She takes aim at the candy.) "Uh-uh." (She laughs and pushes the stick forward. She glances at the candy, smiles, and gets it with the stick.) "There, I got it with the stick. I'll take it home and give it to my cat."

The difference between Anya and Milya is one of development, not ability. Milya will soon be able to do what Anya did: use language not just to label the world but also to manipulate it in pursuit of a goal. Vygotsky did not have to ask Anya to think aloud about reaching the candy—children at her stage do that anyway. Anya's thoughts connect to her actions because we do not manipulate the world, then describe what we did afterward. We manipulate language so we can manipulate the world.

Language and creation are so interconnected that you cannot have one without the other. Language, in this sense, means a system of symbols and rules that allows us to make and manipulate a mental representation of past, present, and possible future states. People who prefer pictures to words, for example, still move symbols around—

some of the symbols just happen to be images. Anya developed this ability relatively early; children normally move from labeling with language to manipulating with language between the ages of four and five.

The connection between language and creating has an important consequence: once children can solve problems by talking about what they are doing, they have the basic skills they need to create with others.

The surprising thing about the marshmallow challenge, then, is not the performance of the children but the performance of the adults. The business students who build a ten-inch tower would have built a twenty-seven-inch tower when they were in kindergarten. Where did those extra seventeen inches go? What happened to the students in the intervening years?

The business students, like most of the rest of us, lost a lot of their capacity to cooperate. The focus on individual accomplishment in their education and environment taught them that it was more valuable to perform individual tasks, especially solving problems with definite answers, than to work on ambiguous things in teams. The natural collaborative ability they developed as children got squashed like their marshmallow towers.

Even worse, by the time children become adults, they have learned that talking is an alternative to doing. At school, most work is done individually and quietly—especially most of the work that gets graded. One of the most common classroom rules is "No talking." The message is clear: you cannot do and talk at the same time.

This division between words and actions persists into the workplace, where groups solve problems by talking—or "planning"—until they agree on what they think is the one best answer, then take action. Children do not hold meetings at school; they discover them as adults, at work. Children see the marshmallow challenge as a chance to collaborate; adults treat it like a meeting. All the children in a team build and experiment, compare results, learn from one another, and create as a community as soon as the clock starts ticking. They do not discuss this in advance. They just get on with it. All the adults in a team do nothing for the first few minutes, because they are talking instead; then most of them do nothing but watch—or "manage"—someone else building a tower for the remainder of the time. According to Tom Wujec's data, kindergartners try putting the marshmallow on the tower an average of five times during the eighteen minutes. Their first attempt usually happens between the fourth and fifth minutes. Business students typically put the marshmallow on the tower once, at the eighteenth—or last—minute.

Vygotsky's research explains why children act when adults plan. The connection between expression and action is stronger when we are younger. This is most obvious in experiments that involve choice. Vygotsky asked four- and five-year-old children to press one of five keys that corresponded to a picture they were shown. The children thought not with words but with actions. Vygotsky notes:

Perhaps the most remarkable result is that the entire process of selection by the child is *external,* and concentrated in the motor sphere. The child does her selecting while carrying out whatever movements the choice requires. Adults make a preliminary decision internally and subsequently carry out the choice in the form of a single movement that executes the plan. The child's movements are replete with diffuse gropings that interrupt and succeed one another. A mere glance at the chart tracing the child's movements is sufficient to convince one of the basic motor nature of the process.

Or: adults think before acting; children think *by* acting.

Talking while acting is useful, but talking *about* acting is *not*—or, at least, not often, and not for long. This is why "Show me" is such a powerful thing to say. "Show me" stops speculation and starts action.

Another thing adults have learned that kindergartners have not is that groups must be hierarchical. Adults start with some team members locking horns for leadership. Children start with everyone working together.

Creative partnerships are barely hierarchical—they would not be "partnerships" if they were—so little or no energy is expended on dominance rituals. Jim Henson was senior to Frank Oz in every way but one: when Henson and Oz created together, they were equals. There is no partnership without equality. Henson and Oz did not waste their time on power struggles; they spent it all on doing, talking aloud like the children in Vygotsky's research, solving problems, and helping each other grow. The birth of Bert and Ernie is a perfect example. Henson and Oz did not hold a meeting or make plans. They picked up the puppets and thought aloud until Bert and Ernie appeared.

9 | WHAT ORGANIZATIONS ARE MADE OF

In 1954, something unprecedented happened at six trials in the U.S. Courthouse in Wichita, Kansas. These were typical trials with typical cases, typical defendants, and typical convictions and acquittals. Only the heating units in the jury room were strange. They contained hidden microphones, put there by University of Chicago researchers, who used them to record the jurors' deliberations. The judge and lawyers knew about the microphones, but the jurors did not.

The recordings were sealed until a final judgment was entered in each case and all appeals were dismissed. Then the researchers analyzed the interactions to learn about group behavior in a jury room. When the findings were published a year later, they caused a nationwide scandal. In one of the first privacy controversies, the Senate Subcommittee on Internal Security subpoenaed the researchers, and more than a hundred newspaper editorials condemned them for threatening the foundation of the American legal system.

The scandal has been forgotten, but the method has not. Harold Garfinkel, one of the researchers who analyzed the jury room tapes, called it "microsociology." Scientists have now conducted thousands of experiments using microphones and video cameras to understand the human behavioral minutiae that compose society.

One reason traditional sociology, or "macrosociology," looks at large groups from afar over long periods of time is technological. When the social sciences were first conceived—in large part by Frenchman Émile Durkheim in the 1890s—there was no practical way to record and observe everyday interactions in detail. Microsociology became possible only in the 1950s, with the invention of the magnetic tape recorder, the transistor, and mass-production electrical microphones.

Like traditional sociologists, business writers—often, by the way, former business school students—typically look at organizations as if they were flying high above them. They see the big picture—the mergers, changes in stock price, and major product launches that are the equivalent of the freeways, neighborhoods, and parks we see through the window of a descending airplane—but, with the exception of a few senior executives, the individuals are invisible.

You cannot learn much by looking at an organization from the sky. Organizations exist only on the ground. They are not, as is commonly claimed, made of people. Organizations are made of people *interacting*. What an organization organizes is everyday human interactions.

Microsociology shows us that these interactions are not trivial. Everything that happens between two or more people is rich in meaning.

Before microsociology, the dominant assumption was that people in groups made decisions using reasoning, in a series of steps something like this:

1. Define the situation.
2. Define the decision to be made.
3. Identify the important criteria.
4. Consider all possible solutions.
5. Calculate the consequences of these solutions versus the criteria.
6. Choose the best option.

Microsociology showed conclusively that we seldom think this way, especially not in groups. In group interactions, our decisions are more likely to be based on unwritten rules and cultural assumptions than on pure reason. Ludwig Wittgenstein, an Austrian British philosopher, said that these interactions, which on the surface look like nothing more than talking, are like a game, because they consist of "moves" and "turns." He called the game *Sprachspiel,* or "the language game."

In a group, words are heard in a context that includes emotion, power, and existing relationships with other group members. We are all social chameleons, adjusting our skin to blend in with, or sometimes stand out from, whatever crowd we happen to be in.

Sociologist Erving Goffman called the moves in the language game "interaction rituals." Later, his colleague Randall Collins called series of these moves "interaction ritual chains." The chain starts with the situation—for example, a business meeting. The way each individual behaves in the meeting will depend on a number of things: their level of authority, their mood, their previous experience in similar meetings, and their current relationships with the other people in the room. All these things change their behavior. They will not act the way they might in a different situation—for example, when they are unwell and visiting the doctor. In the meeting, the greeting "How are you?" signifies nothing more than courtesy. Collins writes, "'How are you?' is not a request for information, and it is a violation of its spirit to reply as if the interlocutor wanted to know details about one's health."

In the other case, when a person is visiting the doctor, the question "How are you?" at the start of the appointment *is* a request for information. It would be a violation *not* to provide details about one's health. The same person being asked the same question gives a different reply because they are participating in a different ritual.

Organizations are made of rituals—millions of small, moments-long transactions between individuals within groups—and it is these rituals that determine how much an organization creates.

10 | RITUALS OF DOING

The biggest lesson from the story of Kelly Johnson and the Skunk Works is that creation is doing, not saying. The most creative organizations prioritize rituals of doing; the least creative organizations prioritize rituals of saying, the most common of which is the meeting. "Meeting" is a euphemism for "talking"; therefore, meetings are an alternative to work. Despite this, the average office worker attends six hour-long meetings a week, almost a full working day. If an organization uses Microsoft's Outlook software to automatically schedule meetings, their employees attend even more meetings—nine hour-long meetings a week. There is no creating in meetings. Creation is action, not conversation. Creative organizations have external meetings—for example, with customers, as Lockheed did to win its wartime contracts to make planes—but the more creative an organization is, the fewer *internal* meetings it tends to have, and the fewer people tend to be at those meetings. The result is more people spending more time at the coal face of creation.

Much of what happens in internal meetings is called "planning," but planning is of limited value, because nothing ever goes according to plan. Kelly Johnson had little use for plans and did not need to know the details of how things were going to happen before doing them.

Engineering plans are important for getting a product built, but engineering plans are doing, not saying. Even then, some engineering plans are made after the product is built. Johnson describes his first day at Lockheed:

> I was assigned to work with Bill Mylan in the tooling department, designing tools for assembly of the Electra. Mylan was an old hand and knew his business. "I'll build them, kid, and you can draw them later," he explained to me.

You cannot control the future. Being too rigid about making things happen the way you planned stops you from reacting to emerging problems and causes you to miss unexpected opportunities. Have high expectations about what and few expectations about how. This is the opposite of the way most organizations operate. Many "executives" spend half of their week in "planning" meetings and the other half preparing for them. You cannot build a plan that predicts your setbacks—like the engine expert being arrested as a spy, or his engine exploding the first time you turn it on—but you can build an organization that executes anyway.

Saying instead of doing is worse than unproductive: it is counterproductive. In 1966, Philip Jackson, one of the psychologists who discovered that teachers do not like creative children, introduced a new term to describe how organizations transmit values and shape behavior: the "hidden curriculum."

Jackson used the term to describe schools:

> The crowds, the praise, and the power that combine to give a distinctive flavor to classroom life collectively form a hidden curriculum, which each student (and teacher) must master if he is to make his way satisfactorily through the school. The demands created by these features of classroom life may be contrasted with

the academic demands—the "official" curriculum, so to speak—to which educators traditionally have paid the most attention.

We learn the hidden curriculum as children, when our minds are eager, we hunger for friends, and we are most afraid of shame. We learn it without knowing: the hidden curriculum is a set of unwritten rules, implied, often at odds with what we are told. We learn the opposite of the official curriculum: that originality ostracizes, imagination isolates, risk is ridiculed. You faced a choice as a child you may not remember: to be yourself and be alone or to be like others and be with others. Education is homogenization. This is why nerds are targets and friends move in herds.

We carry this lesson through life. Education may be forgotten, but experience gets ingrained. What we divide into discrete periods like "high school," "college," and "work" is in fact a continuum. And so the hidden curriculum operates in all organizations, from corporations to nations. Jackson says:

> As institutional settings multiply and become for more and more people the areas in which a significant portion of their life is enacted, we will need to know much more than we do at present about how to achieve a reasonable synthesis between the forces that drive a person to seek individual expression and those that drive him to comply with the wishes of others.

Organizations are a competition between compliance and creation. The leaders of our organizations may ask us to create sometimes, but they demand that we comply always. Compliance is more important than creation in most organizations, no matter how much they pretend otherwise. If you comply but do not create, you may be promoted. If you create but do not comply, you will be fired. When rewards are given for compliance, not contribution, we call it "office politics." We are required to comply not with what the organization *says*, but with what the organization *does*. If a CEO stands up and gives an annual all-company PowerPoint presentation about his love of innovators and risk takers, then allocates most of his company's money to the old product groups and gives all his promotions to the people who manage them, he sends a clear signal to anybody who understands the hidden curriculum: do what the CEO does, not what the CEO says. *Talk about* innovating and taking risks, but do not *do* it. Work in the old product groups and focus your actions on old products. Leave the innovative, risky products to less organizationally adept, more creative people, who will be fired as soon as they fail and who will fail because they are not given any resources. This approach to getting ahead is one many organizations demand, although they do not realize it and will not admit it. Jackson writes:

> No matter what the demand or the personal resources of the person facing it there is at least one strategy open to all. This is the strategy of psychological withdrawal, of gradually reducing personal concern and involvement to a point where neither the demand nor one's success or failure in coping with it is sharply felt.

Can someone both be inventive and follow the hidden curriculum that puts compliance and loyalty over creation and discovery? Perhaps, but the two things are opposites:

> The personal qualities that play a role in intellectual mastery are very different from those that characterize the Company Man. Curiosity, as an instance, is of little value in responding to the demands of conformity. The curious person typically engages in a kind of probing, poking, and exploring that is almost antithetical to the attitude of the passive conformist. Intellectual mastery calls

for sublimated forms of aggression rather than for submission to constraints.

Also, why bother? Why spend the energy and imagination needed to maintain a false identity—to be a conforming Clark Kent so you can keep your creative superself hidden—when you can get equally good results by conforming without creating or by taking your creative abilities somewhere where they will be appreciated? This is the dilemma creative people face everywhere. They seldom choose to resolve it by being secretly creative. Most people resign or become resigned after taking a new idea to their boss for evaluation. Proposing something new is a high-risk transaction. For Kelly Johnson at Lockheed in the 1930s, it worked. For Robert Galambos at the Walter Reed Army Institute of Research in the 1960s, as in most organizations most of the time, it did not.

Building a creative organization is hard, but keeping it creative is many times harder. Why? Because every paradigm changes, and only the best creators can change with the consequences of their creations.

In the summer of 1975, a few months after the fall of Saigon and the end of the Vietnam War, a Skunk Works engineer named Ben Rich presented an idea to Kelly Johnson. It was a design for an airplane shaped like an arrowhead: flat, triangular, and sharply pointed. Rich and his team called it the "Hopeless Diamond." Johnson's initial reaction was not positive. Rich said, "He took one look at the sketch of the Hopeless Diamond and charged into my office. Kelly kicked me in the butt—hard too. Then he crumpled up the proposal and threw it at my feet. 'Ben Rich, you dumb shit,' he stormed, 'have you lost your goddam mind?'"

Kelly Johnson's arrival at Lockheed in 1933 was soon followed by the start of the Second World War. Partly as a result of Johnson's work, World War II was the first major air war: airplanes killed 2.2 million people—more than 90 percent of them, around 2 million people, civilians, mainly women and children. The weapons used to defend against air attacks were crude and ineffective: antiaircraft guns that, on average, fired three thousand shells for each bomber they destroyed. As a result, nearly all bombers reached their targets. In the age of the nuclear bomb, this was a frightening statistic.

Immediately after the war, the new, urgent problem was how to defend against death from the sky, and the solution was surface-to-air missiles, which used the new technologies of computing and radar to locate, pursue, and destroy attacking aircraft. In Vietnam, the next major air war after World War II, surface-to-air missiles destroyed 205 U.S. planes, one for every 28 missiles fired—performance more than ten times better than the antiaircraft guns of World War II. Flying over enemy territory had become so dangerous it was almost suicidal.

This was the context for Ben Rich's "Hopeless Diamond" proposal. The paradigm for understanding aircraft had shifted. The problem now was not how to fly, or how to fly faster, but how to fly in secret.

The Hopeless Diamond was an attempt to solve that problem.

After bursting into Ben Rich's office, kicking him, and throwing his proposal on the floor, Kelly Johnson yelled, "This crap will never get off the ground."

Not every great innovator is a great manager of innovation. Johnson's yelling and screaming might have been the end of Rich's proposal but for one thing: the "Show me" rule.

The Skunk Works engineers had developed a tradition: when there was a dispute about something technical, they bet each other a quarter, then ran an experiment. Johnson and Rich had placed about forty of these bets during their years of working together. Johnson had won them all. There were two things Johnson always seemed to win: arm-wrestling matches—he'd worked as a brick carrier when he was young and had developed arms like thick ropes—and twenty-five-cent technical bets.

Rich said, "Kelly, this diamond is somewhere between ten thousand and one hundred thousand times lower in radar cross section than any U.S. military airplane or any new Russian MiG."

Johnson considered that. Lockheed had some experience building aircraft that evaded radar. In the 1960s, the company had developed an unmanned drone, called the D-21, that took photographs, dropped its camera to be picked up later, then blew itself up. The technology worked, but the program was a commercial failure. Johnson thought about the twelve-year-old drone that had failed, and said, "Ben, I'll bet you a quarter that our old D-21 drone has a lower cross section than that goddam diamond."

Or: "Show me." And so on September 14, 1975, the two men met in creation's equivalent of a duel.

Rich's team put a scale model of the Hopeless Diamond into an electromagnetic chamber and measured how hard it was to detect on radar—a quality the Lockheed engineers had started to call "stealth."

Rich and Johnson received the results and looked at them eagerly. The Hopeless Diamond was a thousand times stealthier than the D-21. Rich had won his first ever bet with Johnson. Johnson flipped Rich a quarter. Then he said, "Don't spend it until you see the damned thing fly."

The plane, code-named "Have Blue," did fly. It was the first-ever stealth aircraft, the parent of every subsequent undetectable aircraft, from the F-117 Nighthawk, to the MH-60 Black Hawk helicopters used in the 2011 raid on Osama bin Laden's compound in Pakistan, to the Lockheed SR-72, an almost invisible plane that flies at over forty-five hundred miles per hour. It was the product of an organization that valued action over talk, spent little time planning and lots of time trying, and resolved disputes about ideas not with arm wrestling or rank pulling but with two simple words: "Show me."

CHAPTER 9

GOOD-BYE, GENIUS

1 | THE INVENTION OF GENIUS

There is a desert more than a thousand miles long on Africa's Atlantic coast. Much of it is a sand sea, or *erg*, where the wind makes dunes twenty miles long and a thousand feet high. The desert is called the Namib, and it is home to a people called the Himba, whose women cover their skin and hair with milk fat, ash, and ocher, both for beauty and to protect themselves from the sun. In 1850, the Himba saw something odd in the dunes: men with white skin, covered in clothing, coming toward them through the sand. One of the men was thin and nervous. In time they found that he had a fetish for counting and measuring, and whenever he removed his Quaker-style "wide-awake" hat, they saw he had combed his hair over a bald spot that rose on his head like the moon. His name was Francis Galton. These people who had learned to live well in one of the world's most desolate places did not impress him. He wrote later that they were "savages" who needed to be "managed," whose food and possessions could be "seized," and who could not "endure the steady labour that we Anglo-Saxons have been bred to support."

Galton was one of the first Europeans to visit the Namib. He took his prejudices about the Himba and other African people he met back with him to England. After his half cousin Charles Darwin published *The Origin of Species,* in 1859, Galton became obsessed with it and started a career measuring and classifying humanity to promote selective breeding, an idea he eventually called "eugenics."

Galton's book *Hereditary Genius,* published in 1869, proposed that human intelligence was inherited directly and diluted by "poor" breeding. He later came to doubt his use of the word "genius" in the title, although it is not entirely clear why:

> There was not the slightest intention on my part to use the word genius in any technical sense, but merely as expressing an ability that was exceptionally high, and at the same time inborn. A person who is a genius is defined as a man endowed with superior faculties. The reader will find a studious abstinence throughout the work from speaking of genius as a special quality. It is freely used as an equivalent for natural ability. There is no confusion of ideas in this respect in the book, but its title seems apt to mislead, and if it could be altered now, it should appear as *Hereditary Ability.*

Geniuses, then, were not a species apart but men (*always* men, of course) with "superior natural ability." Galton is not specific about what geniuses have a superior natural ability *to do,* but he is very clear that *men like him* are far more likely to be endowed with this superior ability, whatever it is, than anyone else: "The natural ability of which this book mainly treats is such as a modern European possesses in a much greater average share than men of the lower races."

Lastly, and most importantly, this ability, while natural and bestowed mainly on "modern Europeans," could be improved with selective breeding: "There is nothing either in the history of domestic animals or in that of evolution to make us doubt that a race of men may be formed who shall be as much superior mentally and morally to the modern European, as the modern European is to the lowest of the Negro races."

Or: we can breed better people in the same way we can breed bigger cows.

The comparison to cows is not trite. Just as cows are graded using a classification system (in Britain, for example, an "E3" carcass is "excellent" and neither too lean nor too fat, while a "–P1" carcass is "poor" and skinny), so Galton proposed a grading system, or "Classification of Men According to Their Natural Gifts," ranging from "a," meaning something like "of below-average quality," to "X," for a one-in-a-million genius. The system, which Galton believed was "no uncertain hypothesis" but "an absolute fact," enabled him to make what he clearly thought were absolute comparisons between "races":

> The negro race has occasionally, but very rarely, produced such men as Toussaint l'Ouverture [the leader of the Haitian revolution of 1791], who are of our class F; that is to say, its X, or its total classes above G, appear to correspond with our F, showing a difference of not less than two grades between the black and white races, and it may be more. In short, classes E and F of the negro may roughly be considered as the equivalent of our C and D—a result which again points to the conclusion, that the average intellectual standard of the negro race is some two grades below our own.

This passage of Galton's makes no sense, and it is representative of his whole book. Without providing any evidence at all, he asserts that the best a black man can be is a "class F" type of cow, whereas the best a white man can be is a "class X" cow; this is two grades higher, and therefore white people are two grades better than black people. The best case against Galton's argument that white men are smarter than everyone else may be Galton's own stupidity.

But Galton was taken seriously. He gave centuries of prejudice a facade of reason and science. His work cast a dreadful shadow across the twentieth century, and into today. Galton's use of the word "genius" gave it the meaning it has now. To us, genius is what Galton said it was: a rare ability gifted by nature to a special few. You were either born with it or, more probably, you were not. But this was at best a secondary definition of genius in Galton's time. It was only because of the rise of eugenics, driven highest by the Nazis' belief in "racial hygiene," that the idea of genius as inherited superiority became common during the end of the nineteenth century and was the only accepted use by the end of the twentieth. There is a straight line from Galton's use of "genius" to Hitler's use of genocide.

A hypothesis is not false because it is offensive or atrocious. Galton's definition of genius as natural exceptional ability, reserved almost exclusively for white men, who then must ensure that only they father children for the good of the species, is not wrong because it is immoral; it is wrong because there is no evidence to support it. Galton's only evidence is self-evidence. His life's work was an elaboration of his prejudices, which were founded, as prejudices always seem to be, upon his conviction that he himself was one of a special breed.

All the evidence supports the opposite case: that natural ability is distributed among people of all types and is not the biggest factor determining our success. From the world-changing work of Edmond Albius, to the world-*saving* work of Kelly Johnson, we see that people everywhere can make differences big and small and that there is no way to guess who they will be in advance. When Rosalind Franklin revealed the human blueprint in DNA, she proved that there was nowhere for Galton's hypothetical racially determined exceptional ability to hide.

Genius as Galton defined it has no place in the twenty-first century—not because genius is not necessary but because we know it does not exist.

Long before Galton and eugenics, everyone had genius. The first definition of "genius" comes from ancient Rome, where the word meant "spirit" or "soul." This is the true definition of creative genius. Creating is to humans as flying is to birds. It is our nature, our spirit. Our purpose as a people and as individuals is to leave a legacy of new and improved art, science, and technology for future generations, just as our two thousand generations of ancestors did before us.

We are each a piece of something connected and complicated, something with such constant presence that it is invisible: the network of love and imagination that is the true fabric of humanity. This is not a fashionable view among people who claim to think. There is a false intellectual tradition of complaint that paints wonder as blunder, mistakes snorts for thoughts, and points at human beings as if they were mainly shameful. "But famine," "but war," "but Hitler," "but climate change": it is easier to look for flies in the soup than to work in the kitchen. But we *are* all connected, and we *are* creative. No one does anything alone. Even the greatest inventors build on the work of thousands. Creation is contribution.

We cannot know the weight of our contribution in advance. We must create for creation's sake, trust that our creations may have impacts we cannot foresee, and know that often the greatest contributions are the ones with the most unimaginable consequences.

The biggest consequence of our creation is us. The human population doubled between 1970 and 2010. In 1970, the average person lived to be fifty-two years old. In 2010, the average person lived to be seventy. Not only are twice as many people each living one-third longer, each individual's consumption of natural resources is increasing. Food intake was eight hundred thousand calories per person per year in 1970 and over a million calories a year in 2010. The amount of water we each consume more than doubled, from 160,000 gallons a year in 1970 to nearly 330,000 gallons a year in 2010. Despite the rise of the Internet and computers and the decline of printed newspapers and books, our use of paper increased from 55 pounds per person per year in 1970 to 120 pounds in 2010. We have more energy-efficient technology than we did in 1970, but we also have *more* technology, and more of the world has access to electricity, so, while we used 1,200 kilowatt-hours per person per year in 1970, we used 2,900 kilowatt-hours in 2010.

These changes are good for individuals right now: they mean more of us are living longer, healthier lives, with enough to eat and drink and a much better chance of avoiding or surviving illness and injury. The same is likely to be true of our children. But increased consumption will be a crisis for our entire species in the near future. It is not only how many of us there are and how much we each consume that is growing; the *rate of growth* of these numbers is growing, too. We are going faster *and* we are still accelerating. Our natural resources cannot grow as fast as our needs. If nothing changes, our species will one day ask for more than our planet can give; the only unknown is when.

These are not new concerns. In 1798, a book called *An Essay on the Principle of Population* was published in Britain. Its pseudonymous author warned of possible disaster:

The power of population is indefinitely greater than the power in the earth to produce subsistence for man. Population, when unchecked, increases in a geometrical ratio. Subsistence increases only in an arithmetical ratio. A slight acquaintance with numbers will show the immensity of the first power in comparison of the second. By that law of our nature which makes food necessary to the life of man, the effects of these two unequal powers must be kept equal. This implies a strong and constantly operating check on population from the difficulty of subsistence. This difficulty must fall some where, and must necessarily be severely felt by a large portion of mankind.

Or: we are producing more people than food, so the majority will soon starve.

The author was Thomas Malthus, a country vicar from the village of Wotton, thirty miles south of London. Malthus's father, inspired by French philosopher Jean-Jacques Rousseau, thought humanity was progressing toward perfection because of science and technology. Malthus the younger disagreed. His essay was a bleak picture painted to prove his father wrong.

Malthus was widely read and remained influential long after his death. Darwin and Keynes mentioned him favorably, Engels and Marx attacked him, and Dickens ridiculed him in *A Christmas Carol*, when Ebenezer Scrooge tells two gentlemen why he does not donate to the poor: "If they would rather die," said Scrooge, "they had better do it, and decrease the surplus population."

Or as Malthus put it:

The power of population is so superior to the power in the earth to produce subsistence for man, that premature death must in some shape or other visit the human race. The vices of mankind are active and able ministers of depopulation. But should they fail in this war of extermination, sickly seasons, epidemics, pestilence, and plague, advance in terrific array, and sweep off their thousands and ten thousands. Should success be still incomplete, gigantic inevitable famine stalks in the rear, and with one mighty blow, levels the population with the food of the world.

And yet we are still here.

Malthus was right about the growth in population—in fact, he greatly underestimated it. But he was wrong about its consequences.

At the close of the eighteenth century, when Malthus wrote his essay, there were almost a billion people in the world, the population having doubled in three centuries. This would have seemed like an alarming rate of growth to him. But in the twentieth century, the world population doubled twice more, reaching *two* billion in 1925 and *four* billion in 1975. According to Malthus's theory, this should have resulted in great famine. In fact, famine declined as population increased. In the twentieth century, 70 million people died due to lack of food, but most of them perished in the first few decades. Between 1950 and 2000, famine was eradicated from everywhere but Africa; since the 1970s, it has been concentrated in two countries: Sudan and Ethiopia. Fewer people are dying of starvation even though there are far more people on the planet.

The only way this famine could have been avoided, according to Malthus, was if "the vices of mankind" killed enough people first. In the first half of the twentieth century, that may have looked right: the First and Second World Wars combined to make the deadliest decades since the Black Death, killing as many as one in every four hundred people per year in the 1940s. But after that, war deaths dropped. From 1400 to 1900, about one in ten thousand people died in war every year, with peaks around 1600 and 1800, during the Wars of Religion and the

Napoleonic Wars. After 1950, that number is close to zero. Contrary to all Malthusian expectations, premature deaths plummet when population soars.

The reason is creation—or, more specifically, creators. When population grows, our ability to create grows even faster. There are more people creating, so there are more people with whom to connect. There are more people creating, so there are more tools in the tool chain. There are more people creating, so we have more time, space, health, education, and information for creating. Population is production. This is why there has been an apparent acceleration of innovation in the last few decades. We have not become innately more creative. There are just more of us.

And this is why we need new. Consumption is a crisis because of math; it is not yet a catastrophe because of creation. We beat change *with* change.

The chain of creation is many links long, and every link—each one a person creating—is essential. All stories of creators tell the same truths: that creating is extraordinary but creators are human; that everything right with us can fix anything wrong with us; and that progress is not an inevitable consequence but an individual choice. Necessity is not the mother of invention. You are.

ACKNOWLEDGMENTS

I owe a great debt to Robert W. Weisberg for his books *Creativity: Understanding Innovation in Problem Solving, Science, Invention, and the Arts* (2006), *Creativity: Beyond the Myth of Genius* (1993), and *Creativity: Genius and Other Myths* (1986); to Google; to Wikipedians everywhere; to the Internet Archive; to Christian Grunenberg, Alan Edwards, and Nathan Douglas for their artificial intelligence–driven database, DevonThink; and to Keith Blount and Ioa Petra'ka of Literature and Latte for Scrivener, their software for authors.

Most of the details in the story of Edmond Albius in chapter 1 come from Tim Ecott's book *Vanilla: Travels in Search of the Ice Cream Orchid*. Ecott did important primary research on Réunion to discover the true story of Edmond Albius.

Chapter 2 draws heavily from Lynne Lees's translation of *On Problem Solving*, by Karl Duncker. The description of a talk by Steve Jobs comes from "The 'Lost' Steve Jobs Speech from 1983," by Marcel Brown, published on Brown's *Life, Liberty and Technology* blog; a cassette tape from John Celuch; a transcript by Andy Fastow; and photographs by Arthur Boden provided by Ivan Boden.

Chapter 3's material about Judah Folkman is mainly from Robert Cooke's 2001 biography *Dr. Folkman's War* and a PBS documentary called *Cancer Warrior.* Stephen King's memoir *On Writing,* and an article titled "A Better Mousetrap," by Jack Hope, published in *American Heritage* magazine in 1996, were also essential sources for this chapter. The book referred to in the section "Strangers with Candy" is *Creativity: Flow and the Psychology of Discovery and Invention,* by Mihaly Csikszentmihalyi.

Robin Warren's 2005 Nobel Lecture, "Helicobacter: The Ease and Difficulty of a New Discovery," inspired chapter 4. Jeremy Wolfe of Brigham and Women's Hospital in Boston gave me an uncorrected prepublication proof of a paper he coauthored, "The Invisible Gorilla Strikes Again: Sustained Inattentional Blindness in Expert Observers," as well as other guidance on the subject of inattentional blindness. Robert Burton's book *On Being Certain* led me to many sources, including "Phantom Flashbulbs: False Recollections of Hearing the News About *Challenger,*" a 1992 paper by Ulric Neisser and Nicole Harsch. The full story of Dorothy Martin is in Festinger, Schachter, and Riecken's book *When Prophecy Fails.* There is more technical detail in Festinger's book *A Theory of Cognitive Dissonance.*

From chapter 5: Brenda Maddox's *Rosalind Franklin: The Dark Lady of DNA* is a wonderful biography of Franklin; Robert Merton's *On the Shoulders of Giants* is insightful and funny.

Chapter 6's description of the battle at William Cartwright's mill is informed by the Luddite Bicentenary blog, at ludditebicentenary .blogspot.co.uk; David Griffiths of the Huddersfield Local History Society in England helped with everything about the Luddites, especially by sending me Alan Brooke's and the late Lesley Kipling's book *Liberty or Death,* as well as many pamphlets. *The Amish,* by Donald Kraybill, Karen Johnson-Weiner, and Steven Nolt, was an invaluable source.

All work on motivation and creation by Teresa Amabile of Harvard

Business School, discussed in chapter 7, is wonderful, especially her 1996 book, *Creativity in Context*. The descriptions of and quotations from Woody Allen come mainly from Robert Weide's *Woody Allen: A Documentary* and Eric Lax's biography *Conversations with Woody Allen*. Annie Miler's café is Clementine, at 1751 Ensley Avenue in Los Angeles, California. I recommend the grilled cheese. Good luck parking.

There are many books about Lockheed's Skunk Works, which is described in chapter 8. Kelly Johnson's autobiography, *Kelly: More Than My Share of It All,* and Ben Rich's *Skunk Works: A Personal Memoir of My Years at Lockheed* both benefit from being by primary sources. Brian Jones's biography of Jim Henson and Michael Davis's *Street Gang* are excellent books about Henson and Oz. Lev Vygotsky's *Mind in Society* is still fascinating today. Tom Wujec maintains a website about the marshmallow challenge at marshmallowchallenge.com; I first heard about the challenge from my wonderful friend Diane Levitt, who learned about it from our mutual colleague Nate Kraft.

The data about famine in chapter 9 comes from *Famine in the Twentieth Century,* by Stephen Devereux, and the data about war comes from *The Better Angels of Our Nature,* by Steven Pinker. "Everything right with us can fix anything wrong with us" is a paraphrase from Bill Clinton's 1993 inaugural address, which was written mostly by Michael Waldman.

Early drafts of the sections "Obvious Facts," "Humanity's Choir," "A Can of Worms," and "Strangers with Candy" appeared in *Medium*.

Other references and sources are listed in the notes and bibliography, below. For additional information, see www.howtoflyahorse.com, which is an interactive companion for this book.

Many of the quotations in this book have been modified, with no change in meaning, to fit the text without the distraction of ellipses and square brackets; wherever possible, complete versions of these quotations are in the notes below. Some descriptive details in the text, such as facial expressions, are imagined or assumed; most, such as weather, are not. Most links in the notes use the URL-shortening service Bitly—indicated by the domain name "bit.ly"—and are simplified so that they can be typed into a web browser easily. The links will expand once entered and take you to the appropriate host site.

Jason Arthur

Arlo Ashton

Sasha Ashton

Theo Ashton

Sydney Ashton

Elle B. Bach

Emma Banton

Julie Barer

Emily Barr

Larry Begley

Lizz Blaise

Aaron Blank

Lyndsey Blessing

Kristin Brief

Dick Cantwell

Katell Carruth

Amanda Carter

Henry Chen

Mark Ciccone

Paolo De Cesare

John Diermanjian

Larry Downes

Benjamin Dreyer

Mike Duke

Esther Dyson

Pete Fij

Stona Fitch

John Fontana

Andrew Garden

Audrey Gato

Tal Goretsky

Sarah Greene

Esther Ha

Alan Haberman

Mich Hansen

Adam Hayes

Nick Hayes

Chloe Healy

Rebecca Ikin

Durk Jager

Anita James

Gemma Jones

Levi Jones

Al Jourgensen

Mitra Kalita

Steve King

Pei Loi Koay

AJ Lafley

Cecilia Lee

Kate Lee

Bill Leigh

Diane Levitt

Maddy Levitt

Roxy Levitt

Gideon Lichfield

Angelina Fae Lukacin

John Maeder

Doireann Maguire

Yael Maguire

Sarah Mannheimer

Sylvia Massy

Sanaz Memarzadeh

Bob Metcalfe

Dan Meyer

Lisa Montebello

Alyssa Mozdzen

Jason Munn

Jun Murai

Eric Myers

Wesley Neff

Nicholas Negroponte

Christoph Niemann

Karen O'Donnell

Maureen Ogle

Ben Oliver

Sasha Orr

Sun Young Park

Shwetak Patel

Arno Penzias

John Pepper

Andrea Perry

Elizabeth Perry

Nancy Pine

Richard Pine

John Pitts

Elizabeth Price

Jamie Price

Kris Puopolo

Sin Quirin

David Rapkin

Nora Reichard

Matt Reynolds

Laura Rigby

Rhonda Rigby

Mark Roberti

Aaron Rossi

Kyle Roth

Eliza Rothstein

Paige Russell

Paul Saffo

Sanjay Sarma

Carsten Schack

Richard Schultz

Toni Scott

Arshia Shirzadi

Elizabeth Shreve

Tim Smucker

Bill Thomas

Bonnie Thompson

Adrian Tuck

Joe Volman

Pete Weiss

Marie Wells

Daniel Wenger

Ev Williams

Yukiko Yumoto

NOTES

PREFACE: THE MYTH

xiii   **In 1815, Germany's *General Music Journal* published a letter:** The letter was
published in *Allgemeine Musikalische Zeitung,* or "General Music Journal," in 1815,
vol. 17, pp. 561–66. For full descriptions of the Mozart letter hoax and its consequences, see Cornell University Library, 2002; Zaslaw, 1994; and Zaslaw, 1997.

xiv   **Mozart's real letters:** Mozart's compositional process is described by Konrad in
Eisen, 2007; by Zaslaw in Morris, 1994; and in Jahn, 2013.

xv   **In 1926, Alfred North Whitehead made a noun:** Many scholars have concluded that Whitehead invented the word "creativity" in Whitehead, 1926, within
the following sentence: "The reason for the temporal character of the actual
world can now be given by reference to the creativity and the creatures." Meyer,
2005, contains an excellent summary of this scholarship.

CHAPTER 1: CREATING IS ORDINARY

1   **A bronze statue stands in Sainte-Suzanne:** There is a picture of the statue of
Edmond Albius at http://bit.ly/albiusstatue.

1   **On Mexico's Gulf Coast, the people of Papantla:** The descriptions of vanilla
and the story of Edmond Albius are based on Ecott, 2005, also Cameron, 2011.

7   **The modern U.S. Patent and Trademark Office:** The first patent issued by
what was then called the U.S. Patent Office was granted to Samuel Hopkins, an

inventor living in Pittsford, Vermont, for an improved way of making potassium carbonate—in those days called "potash"—out of trees, mainly for use in soap, glass, baking, and gunpowder. See Henry M. Paynter "The First Patent" (revised version), http://bit.ly/firstpatent. The eight millionth patent was granted to Robert Greenberg, Kelly McClure, and Arup Roy of Los Angeles for a prosthetic eye that electrically stimulates a blind person's retina. See "Millions of Patents," USPTO, http://bit.ly/patentmillion. Actually, this was probably closer to the 8,000,500th patent issued, as the Patent Office started numbering patents in series only in 1836.

7 **economist Manuel Trajtenberg:** See "The Mobility of Inventors and the Productivity of Research," a presentation by Manuel Trajtenberg, Tel Aviv University, July 2006: http://bit.ly/patentdata. Using a multistage analysis of inventors' names, addresses, coinventors, and citations, Trajtenberg ascertained that the 2,139,313 U.S. patents granted at the time of his analysis had been issued to 1,565,780 distinct inventors. The granted patents had a mean of 2.01 inventors per patent. Trajtenberg's analysis suggests that the average number of patents per inventor is 2.7. By taking the 2011 number of 8,069,662, multiplying it by 2.01 to get the total named inventors, and then dividing by 2.7 to account for the average number of patents per inventor, I calculated that there were around 6,007,415 unique inventors named on granted patents by the end of 2011.

7 **The inventors are not distributed evenly:** This analysis assumes that Trajtenberg's numbers are constants, and so the number of "inventors" scales in exactly the same way as the number of patents, as published by the USPTO and cited above.

7 **Even with foreign inventors removed:** My own analysis, using USPTO data as cited above, U.S. Census data, and Trajtenberg's numbers as constants. The USPTO started tracking patents awarded to foreign residents in 1837. The figure of 1,800 is six in a million, so closer to one in 166,666, but I rounded up to a clean number to keep both statistics as "one in" something.

8 **In 1870, 5,600 works were registered for copyright:** See the Annual Report of the Librarian of Congress, 1886: http://bit.ly/copyrights1866.

8 **In 1946, register of copyrights Sam Bass Warner:** See the 49th Annual Report of the Register of Copyrights, June 30, 1946: http://bit.ly/copyrights1946.

8 **In 1870, there was one copyright registration for every 7,000:** History of registrations taken from Annual Report of the Register of Copyrights, September 30, 2009: http://bit.ly/copyrights2009. The analysis is my own, using U.S. Census data. In 1870, there were three registrations for every in 20,000 people, which I rounded to one registration for every 7,000 people to match the format of following number, one in 400.

8 **one for every 250 U.S. citizens:** Data about the *Science Citation Index* from Eugene Garfield, "Charting the Growth of Science," paper presented at the Chemical Heritage Foundation, May 17, 2007; http://bit.ly/garfieldeugene. The analysis is my own, using U.S. Census data.

9 **a typical NASCAR race:** The average NASCAR race attendance in 2011 was 98,818, based on data from ESPN / Jayksi LLC, at http://bit.ly/nascardata. The number of U.S. residents granted first patents in 2011 was 79,805, based on USPTO data and Trajtenberg's constants.

10 **five African wildcats:** See Driscoll et al., 2007.

11   **Dolphins use sponges to hunt for fish:** Krützen et al., 2005.

11   **human tools were monotonous for a million years:** Mithen, 1996, and Kuhn and Stiner in Mithen, 2014.

13   **"Despite great qualitative and quantitative":** Casseli, 2009.

15   **"The most fundamental facts":** Ashby, 1952.

15   **A San Franciscan named Allen Newell:** See Newell, "Desires and Diversions," a lecture presented at Carnegie Mellon, December 4, 1991; the video is available at http://bit.ly/newelldesires, courtesy of Scott Armstrong.

16   **"The data currently available about the processes":** Newell, 1959. Available at http://bit.ly/newellprocesses.

16   **Weisberg was an undergraduate during the first years:** Robert Weisberg's résumé is available at http://bit.ly/weisbergresume.

17   **"when one says of someone that":** Weisberg, 2006.

17   **Sprengel's peers did not want to hear that flowers had a sex life:** Zepernick and Meretz, 2001.

18   **Titles available in today's bookstores:** Titles found at Amazon.com.

18   **Weisberg's books are out of print:** According to Amazon.com, where only a Kindle edition of Weisberg's last, more academic title, *Creativity: Understanding Innovation in Problem Solving, Science, Invention, and the Arts,* is available "new."

18   **"creativity now is as important in education as literacy":** Ken Robinson, TED talk, June 27, 2006. Transcript at http://bit.ly/robinsonken.

18   **Cartoonist Hugh MacLeod:** MacLeod, 2009.

19   **The best-known version was started in 1921:** See Terman's own work, especially Terman and Oden, 1959. Shurkin, 1992, offers an excellent review of Terman's work.

22   **"within the reach of everyday people in everyday life":** Torrance, 1974, quoted in Cramond, 1994.

24   **open our veins and bleed:** Versions of this comment have been attributed to several writers. According to Garson O'Toole, the original is "It is only when you open your veins and bleed onto the page a little that you establish contact with your reader," from "Confessions of a Story Writer," by Paul Gallico, 1946; http://bit.ly/openavein.

25   **bestselling literary series was begun by a single mother:** J. K. Rowling; see http://bit.ly/rowlingbio.

25   **a career more than fifty novels long:** "Four years before, I had been running sheets in an industrial laundry for $ 1.60 an hour and writing Carrie in the furnace-room of a trailer," King, 2010. See also Lawson, 1979.

25   **world-changing philosophy was composed in a Parisian jail:** Paine, 1794.

25   The **"man with a permanent position as a patent examiner"** was Albert Einstein.

CHAPTER 2: THINKING IS LIKE WALKING

26   **Thomas Mann prophesied the perils of National Socialism:** Mann, 1930.

27   **He made two applications to become a professor:** Now the Humboldt University of Berlin (German: Humboldt-Universität zu Berlin), founded in 1810 as the University of Berlin (Universität zu Berlin). In Duncker's day it was known

as the Frederick William University (Friedrich-Wilhelms-Universität), and later (unofficially) also as the Universität Unter den Linden.

27 **Both were rejected:** This and other Duncker biographical details from Schnall, 1999, published in Valsiner, 2007; see also Simon, 1999, in Valsiner, 2007.

27 **He published his masterwork, *On Problem Solving*:** Duncker, 1935. Translation: Duncker and Lees, 1945.

27 **"Today the sun is brilliantly shining":** Quotation edited for length and clarity from Isherwood, 1939. The unedited passage is: "To-day the sun is brilliantly shining; it is quite mild and warm. I go out for my last morning walk, without an overcoat or hat. The sun shines, and Hitler is master of this city. The sun shines, and dozens of my friends—my pupils at the Workers' School, the men and women I met at the I.A.H.—are in prison, possibly dead. But it isn't of them that I am thinking—the clear-headed ones, the purposeful, the heroic; they recognized and accepted the risks. I am thinking of poor Rudi, in his absurd Russian blouse. Rudi's make-believe, story-book game has become earnest; the Nazis will play it with him. The Nazis won't laugh at him; they'll take him on trust for what he pretended to be. Perhaps at this very moment Rudi is being tortured to death. I catch sight of my face in the mirror of a shop, and am shocked to see that I am smiling. You can't help smiling, in such beautiful weather. The trams are going up and down the *Kleistrsrasse,* just as usual. They, and the people on the pavement, and the teacosy dome of the *Nollendortplatz* station have an air of curious familiarity, of striking resemblance to something one remembers as normal and pleasant in the past—like a very good photograph."

28 **an immigrant who'd left the tiny Lithuanian village of Sventijánskas:** Detail from Kimble, 1998, in which *Sventijánskas* is transliterated as "Swiencianke." Krechevsky was born Yitzhok-Eizik Krechevsky and started using the first name Isadore when he attended school in the United States.

28 **The joint paper, "On Solution-Achievement":** Duncker, 1939.

29 **Duncker published his second paper, on the relationship between familiarity and perception:** Duncker, 1939b.

29 **Duncker's third paper of the year:** Duncker, 1939c.

29 **He drove to nearby Fullerton:** *New York Times,* 1940.

30 **In Berkeley, the University of California awarded:** Rensberger, 1977.

32 **"If a situation is introduced in a certain perceptual structure":** This is my translation—the Lees translation uses "structuration" instead of "structure."

32 **Psychologists and people who write about creation:** Duncker's *On Problem Solving* has around twenty-two hundred citations, according to Google scholar: http://bit.ly/dunckercitations.

33 **How did Charlie die?:** Weisberg, 1986.

33 **the Prisoner and Rope Problem:** Described in Metcalfe, 1987, cited in Chrysikou, 2006, and Weisberg, 2006.

34 **This is the source of the cliché "thinking outside of the box":** See http://bit.ly/outsideofbox. A possible alternative origin story involves a man smuggling bicycles by distracting border guards with a box of sand balanced on the handlebars.

34 **It is a summary of a Sherlock Holmes story:** "The Adventure of the Speckled Band" in Doyle, 2011.

35 **The surprising solution that a snake killed her follows:** Doyle may have

made a mistake in this story. When Doyle wrote "The Adventure of the Speckled Band," in 1892 it was generally believed that snakes were deaf. This led to much speculation among Holmes's enthusiasts about what kind of snake Doyle had in mind, or whether it was in fact, a lizard. Later research, starting in 1923, and culminating as recently as 2008, showed that snakes can hear, via their jaws, despite not having external ears.

35 **Many people do not think using words:** See Weisberg, 1986, and Chrysikou, 2006, for examples of how this has been established.

35 **Robert Weisberg asked people to think aloud:** Weisberg and Suls, 1973.

37 **Six undergraduates talking their way through a puzzle:** Weisberg and Suls, 1973. Weisberg's paper describes six related experiments, one of which was evaluating solutions to the problem rather than solving it; 376 is the number of subjects who participated in the other five experiments.

38 **Oprah Winfrey has trademarked it:** Winfrey's Harpo companies own two "live" trademarks using the phrase "aha! moment," registration number 3805726 and registration number 3728350.

38 **Greek general Hiero was crowned king of Syracuse:** Vitruvius, 1960.

38 **Hiero asked Syracuse's greatest thinker:** Biello, 2006.

39 **Galileo pointed this out in a paper called "La Bilancetta":** Galileo, 2011. Translation from Fermi and Bernardini, 2003.

39 **Buoyancy, not displacement:** This is explained beautifully by Chris Rorres at http://bit.ly/rorres.

39 **But let's take Vitruvius's story at face value:** Vitruvius, 1960.

40 **"In the summer of the year":** Edited from Coleridge, 2011. The complete quotation is:

In the summer of the year 1797, the Author, then in ill health, had retired to a lonely farm-house between Porlock and Linton, on the Exmoor confines of Somerset and Devonshire. In consequence of a slight indisposition, an anodyne had been prescribed, from the effects of which he fell asleep in his chair at the moment that he was reading the following sentence, or words of the same substance, in "Purchas's Pilgrimage": "Here the Khan Kubla commanded a palace to be built, and a stately garden thereunto. And thus ten miles of fertile ground were inclosed with a wall." The Author continued for about three hours in a profound sleep, at least o the external senses, during which time he has the most vivid confidence, that he could not have composed less than from two to three hundred lines; if that indeed can be called composition in which all the images rose up before him as things, with a parallel production of the correspondent expressions, without any sensation or consciousness of effort. On awaking he appeared to himself to have a distinct recollection of the whole, and taking his pen, ink, and paper, instantly and eagerly wrote down the lines that are here preserved. At this moment he was unfortunately called out by a person on business from Porlock, and detained by him above an hour, and on his return to his room, found, to his no small surprise and mortification, that though he still retained some vague and dim recollection of the general purport of the vision, yet, with the exception of some eight or ten scattered lines and images, all the rest had passed away like the images on the surface of a stream into which a stone has been cast, but, alas! without the after restoration of the latter!

40 **Coleridge used a similar device—a fake letter from a friend:** See Coleridge, 1907, where a letter from a "friend" interrupts chapter 13 of his *Biographia Literaria*. Bates, 2012, describes the "friend" as "a humorous gothic counterfeit."

41 **Coleridge says the poem was "composed in a sort of reverie":** Hill, 1984.

41 **"I was sitting writing at my textbook but the work":** Benfey, 1958.

42 **This is a case of visual imagination helping solve a problem:** Based on Weisberg, 1986 and Rothenberg, 1995.

42 **A sudden revelation has also been attributed to Einstein:** Einstein, 1982.

42 **In Einstein's own words: "I was led to it by steps":** Moszkowski, 1973, p. 96. The complete quotation is "But the suddenness with which you assume it to have occurred to me must be denied. Actually I was lead [*sic*] to it by *steps* arising from the *individual* laws."

42 **These psychologists conducted hundreds of experiments:** Hélie, 2012, includes references to many of these experiments. Advocates of the "incubation" hypothesis now use the term "implicit cognition."

42 **They showed the subject pictures of entertainers:** Read, 1982. "The research was initiated while both authors were on study leave at the University of Colorado." Cited and discussed in Weisberg, 1986.

43 **Other studies into the feeling:** e.g., Nisbett, 1977.

43 **In one experiment he sorted 160 people:** Olton and Johnson, 1976.

44 **He designed a different study:** Olton, 1979. Cited in Weisberg, 1993.

44 **Most researchers now regard incubation as folk psychology:** The phrase "folk psychology" is used in Vul, 2007. See also Dorfman et al., 1996; Weisberg, 2006, which contains a thorough review of studies of incubation; Dietrich and Kanso, 2010; and Weisberg, 2013, which critiques attempts to study insight using neural imaging and also analyzes the popularization of incubation by journalist Jonah Lehrer. Incubation is not completely discredited, however; some psychologists are reviving the hypothesis under the name "implicit cognition." Weisberg, 2014, attempts to incorporate theories of incubation into theories of ordinary thinking.

44 **" 'Why doesn't it work?' or, 'What should I change to make it work?' ":** Duncker, 1945. I have adjusted the translation—the Lees translation uses "alter" instead of "change."

45 **When Jobs announced Apple's first cell phone:** Talk by Steve Jobs at MacWorld San Francisco on January 9, 2007. Video: http://bit.ly/keyjobs. Transcript by Todd Bishop and Bernhard Kast: http://bit.ly/kastbernhard.

45 **Apple sold 4 million phones in 2007:** Data from Apple Inc. annual reports summarized at http://bit.ly/salesiphone. Adjusted to convert fiscal years to calendar years and rounded to the nearest million.

46 **This was true, irrelevant, and revealing:** The microphone built into the original iPhone had a narrow frequency response of about 50Hz to about 4kHz, compared, for example, to the subsequent iPhone 3G, which ranged from below 5Hz to 20kHz. Analysis by Benjamin Faber at http://bit.ly/micriphone.

46 **"If it ain't broke, don't fix it":** This phrase was popularized by Bert Lance, director of the Office of Management and Budget in the Carter administration, who used it in 1977. See *Nation's Business,* May 1977, p. 27, at http://bit.ly/dontfix.

46 **Korean electronics giant LG launched:** The LG Prada, or LG KE850, was announced in December 2006 and made available for sale in May 2007. Apple

announced the iPhone in January 2007 and made it available for sale in June 2007. The LG Prada was the first cell phone with a capacitive touch screen. See http://bit.ly/ke850.

47 **The secret of Steve was evident in 1983:** This was the IDCA, or International Design Conference Aspen, 1983. The IDCA is now part of the Aspen Design Summit, organized by the American Institute of Graphic Arts. More at http://bit.ly/aspendesign.

47 **"If you look at computers, they look like garbage":** Brown, 2012, based on a cassette tape from John Celuch of Inland Design and a transcription by Andy Fastow at http://bit.ly/jobs1983. The transcription has been edited slightly for clarity. The description of Jobs's appearance is based on photos by Arthur Boden, posted by Ivan Boden at http://bit.ly/ivanboden.

48 **"One minute he'd be talking about sweeping ideas":** Mossberg, 2012.

48 **One symbol lived long after the cat:** TV Tropes, at http://bit.ly/felixbulb. Many Felix the Cat cartoons showing prop use are available online—see, for example, http://bit.ly/felixcartoon.

48 **Psychologists adopted the image:** Wallas, 1926.

49 **The most famous is brainstorming:** Osborn, 1942. See also http://bit.ly/alexosborn.

49 **"Brainstorming is often used in a business setting":** Extract from "Brainstorming Techniques: How to Get More Out of Brainstorming" at http://bit.ly/mindtoolsvideo. Transcript at http://bit.ly/manktelow.

50 **Researchers in Minnesota tested this:** Dunnette, 1963. Cited in Weisberg, 1986.

50 **Follow-up research tested whether larger groups:** Bouchard, 1970. Cited in Weisberg 1986.

50 **Researchers in Indiana tested this by asking groups of students:** Weisskopf-Joelson and Eliseo, 1961. Cited in Weisberg, 1986.

50 **Subsequent studies have reinforced this:** See, for example, Brilhart, 1964, as discussed by Weisberg, 1986.

50 **Steve Wozniak, Steve Jobs's cofounder at Apple:** Wozniak, 2007. Cited in Cain, 2012.

51 **According to novelist Stephen King:** King, 2001.

51 **political scientists William Ogburn and Dorothy Thomas:** Ogburn and Thomas, 1922.

52 **the moon chewed the sun in a partial solar eclipse:** Eclipse details at http://bit.ly/rhinoweclipse.

52 **"Sacrifices must be made":** Details of Lilienthal's death from Wikipedia, at http://bit.ly/lilienthalotto.

52 **"The balancing of a flyer may seem":** Wright, 2012.

53 **They saw an airplane as "a bicycle with wings":** Heppenheimer, 2003. Cited in Weisberg, 2006.

54 **"a sport to which we had devoted so much attention":** Wright, 2012.

54 **"Having set out" through "our own measurements":** Wright, 2012.

55 **Wings needed to be much bigger:** The Wrights' math was correct. Today, aerodynamicists use a Smeaton coefficient of 0.00327. See Smithsonian National Air and Space Museum at http://bit.ly/smeatoncoeff.

55   **The Wrights' aircraft are the best evidence:** This point is beautifully illustrated in a presentation called "Invention of the Airplane" from NASA's Glenn Research Center, available at http://bit.ly/manywings. See especially slide 56.

56   **On November 1, 1913, Franz Kluxen entered:** Little is known about Franz Kluxen of Münster (also listed in catalogs as Kluxen of Boldixum, a district of Wyk, a town on the German island of Föhr in the North Sea). According to Richardson, 1996, Kluxen may have been "one of the earliest (he started in 1910) and most serious buyers of Picasso in pre-1914 Germany . . . By 1920, all the Kluxen Picassos that can be traced had changed hands. Kluxen may have been a victim of the war or of hard times."

56   **He forbade artificial chalk made from gypsum:** Natural chalk is from the Cretaceous period, circa 145.5 + 4 to 65.5 + 0.3 million years ago; it includes ancient cell fragments visible only by microscope. Steele et al., in Smithgall, 2011.

56   **The picture covered thirty square feet:** *Painting with White Border* is 140 cm x 200 cm = 2.8 square meters = 30.14 square feet.

57   **"extremely powerful impressions I had experienced":** Kandinsky, *"Picture with the White Edge,"* in Lindsay and Vergo, 1994. Cited in Smithgall, 2011.

57   **a common Kandinsky motif and a symbol:** See, for example, Kandinsky's *Painting with Troika,* 1911. The troika symbolizes divinity by recalling the prophet Elijah's fiery chariot ride to heaven.

59   **His first works, painted in 1904:** See, for example, *Russische Schöne in Landschaft,* from around 1904.

59   **His last, painted in 1944:** See, for example, *Gedämpfter Elan,* 1944.

CHAPTER 3: EXPECT ADVERSITY

60   **One summer night in 1994, a five-year-old named Jennifer:** Jennifer is real—I have omitted her last name to help protect her privacy—and so are all the important details of her story. A few narrative details—that she had a pretty face, that her father signed the consent form, that she cried when given her shots—are imagined or assumed. The sources for Judah Folkman's story are Cooke, 2001; Linde, 2001; published academic papers; and Folkman's obituaries.

62   **"I had seen and handled cancers":** Linde, 2001.

63   **Scientists had little respect for surgeons:** Today it is common for the best medical doctors to also do basic research. Judah Folkman is one reason why. For data on the rise of physician-scientists from the 1970s onward, see Zemlo, 2000.

65   **Angiogenesis became an important theory:** One promising line of investigation is whether regular doses of aspirin and other medicines modulate angiogenesis and reduce the risk of, for example, colon cancer, lung cancer, breast cancer, and ovarian cancer. See Albini et al., 2012; Holmes et al., 2013; Tsoref et al., 2014; and Trabert et al., 2014.

66   **A journey of a thousand miles ends with a single step:** The famous line "A journey of a thousand miles starts with single step" is from chapter 64 of the *Tao Te Ching;* Tsu, 1972.

66   **He knows how many e-mails he has sent:** Wolfram, 2012. It is a year and a half or writing and deleting because 7 deletes out of a every 100 keystrokes is 7 per-

cent, but you also have 7 percent of keystrokes then getting deleted; this means 14 percent of keystrokes result in no extra text; 14 percent of ten years rounded up is a year and a half. This assumes that, on average, it takes as long to decide to delete something as it does to decide to write it.

66–67 **Stephen King, for example, has published:** Includes novels, screenplays, collections of short stories, and works of nonfiction. From Wikipedia's Stephen King bibliography at http://bit.ly/kingbibliography.

67 **He says he writes two thousand words a day:** King, 2001. "I like to get ten pages a day, which amounts to 2,000 words."

67 **Between the beginning of 1980 and the end of 1999:** My count of Stephen King's words starts with *Firestarter* (1980) and ends with *The New Lieutenant's Rap* (1999); it excludes the unedited version of *The Stand,* which is essentially a reprint of a prior book, and *Blood & Smoke,* which is King reading stories published elsewhere. I used the page count in the Wikipedia bibliography at http://bit.ly /kingbibliography, which is for the hardback format of each book, and I assumed three hundred words per page. I subtracted six months because King was injured and barely writing after June 1999. King did not begin writing his *Entertainment Weekly* column, "The Pop of King," until 2003, so that does not count toward his word total.

67 **"That DELETE key is on your machine":** King, 2001.

67 **One of King's most popular books:** King, 2001: "This is . . . the one my long-time readers still seem to like the best."

67 **"twelve hundred pages long and weighed twelve pounds":** King, 2010.

67 **"If I'd had two or even three hundred pages":** King, 2001.

67 **"There's a misconception that invention":** From Dyson's website, at http://bit .ly/dysonideas.

68 **"just an ordinary person":** Dyson interviewed at a WIRED Business Conference, 2012. Video at http://bit.ly/videodyson.

68 **"The north and south winds met":** Baum, 2008.

69 **house dust particles about a millionth of a meter wide:** House dust dimensions from "Diameter of a Speck of Dust" in *The Physics Factbook,* edited by Glenn Elert, written by his students at http://bit.ly/dustsize, with sense checking by Matt Reynolds of the University of Washington.

69 **"I'm a huge failure because I made 5,126 mistakes":** Dyson interviewed at a Wired Business Conference, 2012. Video at http://bit.ly/videodyson.

69 **"I wanted to give up almost every day":** Edited from Dyson's website, at http:// bit.ly/dysonstruggle. Full quotation: "I wanted to give up almost every day. But one of the things I did when I was young was long distance running, from a mile up to ten miles. They wouldn't let me run more than ten miles at school—in those days they thought you'd drop down dead or something. And I was quite good at it, not because I was physically good, but because I had more determination. I learned determination from it. A lot of people give up when the world seems to be against them, but that's the point when you should push a little harder. I use the analogy of running a race. It seems as though you can't carry on, but if you just get through the pain barrier, you'll see the end and be okay. Often, just around the corner is where the solution will happen."

69 **a personal fortune of more than $5 billion:** Dyson Ltd.'s 2013 revenues esti-

mated at £6 billion by Wikipedia, at http://bit.ly/dysoncompany. Dyson's net worth was estimated at £3 billion by the *Sunday Times* in 2013. See http://bit.ly /dysonworth.

69 **"Iterative Process"**: Rubright, 2013.

69 **"Try again. Fail again. Fail better"**: Beckett, 1983.

70 **A Hungarian psychology professor once wrote**: Csikszentmihalyi, 1996.

71 **"It is only half an hour"**: Letter from Charles Dickens to Maria Winter, written on April 3, 1855, published in Dickens, 1894. Appears in Amabile, 1996, citing Allen, 1948. The complete quotation is: "I hold my inventive capacity on the stern condition that it must master my whole life, often have complete possession of me, make its own demands upon me, and sometimes, for months together, put everything else away from me. If I had not known long ago that my place could never be held, unless I were at any moment ready to devote myself to it entirely, I should have dropped out of it very soon. All this I can hardly expect you to understand—or the restlessness and waywardness of an author's mind. You have never seen it before you, or lived with it, or had occasion to think or care about it, and you cannot have the necessary consideration for it. 'It is only half an hour,'—'It is only an afternoon,'—'It is only an evening,' people say to me over and over again; but they don't know that it is impossible to command one's self sometimes to any stipulated and set disposal of five minutes,—or that the mere consciousness of an engagement will sometimes worry a whole day. These are the penalties paid for writing books. Whoever is devoted to an art must be content to deliver himself wholly up to it, and to find his recompense in it. I am grieved if you suspect me of not wanting to see you, but I can't help it; I must go my way whether or no."

73 **Semmelweis had convincing data to support his hypothesis**: Ignaz Semmelweis was not the only doctor to suspect that puerperal fever was being transmitted to patients by doctors. He didn't know it, but he was one of several physicians who had reached the same conclusion. Fifty years earlier, in Scotland, a surgeon named Alexander Gordon wrote about it; in 1842, Thomas Watson, a professor at the University of London, started recommending hand-washing; and in 1843, American Oliver Wendell Holmes published a paper about it. All were ignored or condemned.

73 **Semmelweis saved the lives**: Data from Semmelweis, 1859. Semmelweis's numbers are not entirely clear, and there is no way to know exactly how many women would have died without hand-washing. The mean patient death rate in the First Clinic in the fourteen years before hand-washing was introduced was 8 percent, versus 3 percent in the Second Clinic over the same period. The average death rate in the First Clinic dropped to 3 percent in the years 1846 (when hand-washing was introduced in May), 1847 and 1848 (when Semmelweis was terminated in March). If the average death rate in the First Clinic had remained at 8 percent in these three years, then 548 more women would have died. This is the basis for the statement that Semmelweis "saved the lives of around 500 women." This number is undoubtedly low. It does not include the fact that the average death rate only returned to its pre-hand-washing levels several years after Semmelweis's dismissal, nor, as mentioned, does it include babies, as there is not enough data about newborns in Semmelweis's paper to estimate how many

babies were saved. (I have assumed that Semmelweis's use of the term "patients" in his data about deaths means the numbers refer to women only, as this is how he uses the word elsewhere in the paper.)

75 **"A wise man proportions his belief to the evidence":** The Hume quotation is from Hume, 1748; the Sagan quotation is from the opening lines of the PBS television program *Cosmos,* episode 12, first aired on December 14, 1980, available at http://bit.ly/extraordinaryclaims; the Truzzi quotation is from Truzzi, 1978. Laplace's quotation has a more complicated pedigree. The original source is Laplace, 1814, which states, "We are so far from knowing all the agents of nature and their diverse modes of action that it would not be philosophical to deny phenomena solely because they are inexplicable in the actual state of our knowledge. But we ought to examine them with an attention all the more scrupulous as it appears more difficult to admit them." This was rewritten as "The weight of the evidence should be proportioned to the strangeness of the facts" and called "The Principle of Laplace," by Théodore Flournoy in Flournoy, 1900, but is most commonly repeated as "The weight of evidence for an extraordinary claim must be proportioned to its strangeness." All four quotations are cited in the Wikipedia entry for Truzzi, at http://bit.ly/marcellotruzzi; the story of Laplace's quotation is told in the Wikipedia entry for Laplace, at http://bit.ly/laplacepierre.

76 **"If a man has good corn, or wood, or boards":** Emerson, 1909.

76 **"If a man can write a better book":** Yule, 1889. Cited in Hope, 1996.

76 **"Build a better mousetrap":** Much of this section is based on a brilliant article by Jack Hope. Hope, 1996.

76 **More than five thousand mousetrap patents:** Hope, writing in 1996, estimated 4,400 patents, growing at 40 a year. His projection appears to be accurate: by May 2014 there were around 5,190 mousetrap patents, and applications show no sign of slowing down. See: http://bit.ly/mousetraps.

77 **Almost all of them cite the quotation:** Hope, 1996, quoting Joseph H. Bumsted, vice-president of mousetrap manufacturer Woodstream Corporation: "They feel it was written just for them, and they recite it as if that in itself were reason for Woodstream to buy their ideas!"

77 **Emerson could not have written it:** Emerson died in 1882; the first mousetrap patent was issue in 1894.

77 **This changed in the late 1880s:** Hooker's mousetrap has U.S. Patent Number 0528671. See http://bit.ly/hookertrap.

77 **Hooker's "snap trap" was perfected within a few years:** See http://bit.ly /victortrap. In May 2014, you could buy 20 traps for $15, with free shipping.

78 **"Nation's most precious natural resource":** Ergenzinger, 2006.

78 **One company, Davison & Associates:** At first, Davison was ordered to pay $26 million in compensation. The FTC and the company then reached a settlement and Davison made a "non punitive" payment of $10.7 million, which I rounded up to $11 million to keep the prose simple.

79 **Many of their inventions are based on Davison's own ideas:** See, for example, the "Swingers Slotted Spoon" at http://bit.ly/davisonspoon. Despite being listed on the "Samples of Client Products" section of the Davison Web site the product information reveals: "This corporate product was invented and licensed by Davison for its own benefit."

79 **sales of $45 million a year:** This is calculated based on the disclosed number of 11,325 people a year buying a "pre-development agreement" at the published price of $795 and the disclosed number of 3,306 people buying a "new product sample agreement" at $11,500 which is halfway between the published estimated price of $8,000 – $15,000. This adds up to gross annual revenue from these services of $47,022,375. Sources: http://www.davison.com/legal/ads1.html, and http://www.davison.com/legal/aipa.html, viewed and saved on December 31, 2012. "Other public information" refers to Dolan, 2006: "Last year [presumably 2005], he [George Davison] says, his shop netted $2 million on $25 million in revenue." http://bit.ly/dolankerry.

80 **He denounced Hervieu's use of a dummy as a "sham":** The word in French is *chiqué,* which could also be translated as "bluff," or "deception." Reichelt: *"Je veux tenter l'expérience moi-même et sans chiqué [sic], car je tiens à bien prouver la valeur de mon invention."* Le Petit Journal, February 5, 1912, "L'Inventeur Reichelt S'est Tué Hier," at http://bit.ly/petitjournal.

80 **Reichelt had made sure his test:** He met with journalists the evening before the jump; the Pathé news footage of his jump, which was never aired, is at http://bit.ly/reicheltjump. The description of Reichelt's preparations, leap, and subsequent death, are based on this film.

80 **"I am so convinced my device will work properly":** Edited and translated from the French: *"Je suis tellement convaincu que mon appareil, que j'ai déjà experimenté, doit bien fonctionner, que demain matin, après avoir obtenu l'autorisation de la préfecture de police, je tenterai l'expérience du haut de la première platforme de la Tour Eiffel."* From Le Petit Journal, February 5, 1912, "L'Inventeur Reichelt S'est Tué Hier," at http://bit.ly/petitjournal.

81 **Reichelt fell for four seconds:** Calculated from Green Harbor Publications, "Speed, Distance, and Time of Fall for an Average-Sized Adult in Stable Free Fall Position," 2010, at http://bit.ly/fallspeed.

82 **Hervieu was not the only one:** Le Matin, February 5, 1912 (number 10205), *"Expérience tragique,"* at http://bit.ly/lematin: *"La surface de votre appareil est trop faible, lui disait-on; vous vous romprez cou"* — "The surface of your device is too small, he was told; you will break your neck."

82 **"For a successful technology":** From Volume 2, Appendix F, of the United States Presidential Commission on the Space Shuttle Challenger Accident, 1986, at http://bit.ly/feynmanfooled.

83 **In the 1950s, two psychologists:** "High school" is assumed based on the grade level and birth years the children mentioned in their autobiographical essays. Getzels 1962. There were 533 children in total.

83 **Getzels and Jackson found that the most creative students:** These are all bright children to begin with. The mean IQ at the school was around 135. The difference in IQ scores between the "most creative" and "least creative" here is relative to their peers.

84 **It has been repeated many times:** See, for example, Bachtold, 1974; Cropley, 1992; and Dettmer, 1981.

84 **98 percent:** Feldhusen, 1975. Cited in in Westby, 1995. Westby also hypothesizes that teachers favor less creative chilmen over more creative children in part because more creative children tend to be harder to control.

84   **The Getzels-Jackson effect is not restricted:** Staw, 1995.

85   **In one experiment, Dutch psychologist Eric Rietzschel:** Rietzschel, 2010, Study 2.

85   **When Rietzschel asked people to assess their own work:** Rietzschel, 2010, Study 1.

86   **When we are in familiar situations:** Gonzales, 2004: "Normally, hippocampal cells fire perhaps only once every second on average. But at that mapped place, they fire hundreds of times faster."

86   **Uncertainty is an aversive state:** See, for example, Heider, 1958; Whitson, 2008

86   **Psychologists can show this in experiments:** See, for example, Mueller, 2012.

86   **rejection hurts:** For the neural basis of why this is so, see Eisenberger, 2004; Eisenberger, 2005.

86   **comes from the Old English *spurnen,* "to kick":** "Old English" means English spoken from the mid-fifth through mid-twelfth centuries.

86   **In 1958, psychologist Harry Harlow proved:** Aristotle, 2011, VIII.1155a5: "Without friends no one would wish to live, even if he possessed all other goods." Cited in Eisenberger and Lieberman, 2004.

87   **We know we should not suggest:** Flynn and Chatman, 2001; Runco, 2010. Both cited in Mueller et al., 2012.

87   **"Luddism," our closest word:** There is also the word "neophobia," but this is uncommon and normally used only in technical literature. See, for example, Patricia Pliner and Karen Hobden. "Development of a Scale to Measure the Trait of Food Neophobia in Humans." *Appetite* 19, no. 2 (October 1992):105–20.

87   **Luddism was, in the words of Thomas Pynchon:** Pynchon, 1984.

87   **Children's is one of America's highest-ranked hospitals:** As of 2012, *U.S. News & World Report* has ranked Children's near or at the top of its honor roll for more than twenty years. Comarow, 2012.

88   **"A man does not attain the status of Galileo":** From "Velikovsky in Collision," in Gould, 1977.

90   **William Syrotuck analyzed 229 cases:** Syrotuck and Syrotuck, 2000. Cited in Gonzales, 2004.

CHAPTER 4: HOW WE SEE

92   **"It contains numerous bacteria":** Warren, 2005.

92   ***Every* patient with a duodenal ulcer:** A "duodenal ulcer" is sometimes known as a "peptic ulcer." The "acidic passage" is "the duodenum."

93   **It was eventually given the name *Helicobacter pylori*:** *H. pylori* was known as *Campylobacter pylori,* also "pyloric campylobacter," for some years—*H. pylori* is its final and current name.

93   **the *Lancet,* one of the world's highest-impact medical journals:** In the 2011 *Journal Citation Report: Science Edition* (Thompson Reuters, 2012), the *Lancet*'s impact factor was ranked second among general medical journals, at 38.278, after the *New England Journal of Medicine,* at 53.298. From Wikipedia's entry on the *Lancet,* at http://bit.ly/lancetwiki.

93   **"appeared to be a new species":** Marshall and Warren, 1984.

93 Ian Munro was no ordinary journal editor: Freeman, 1997.

93 even adding a note saying: Munro, 1984. Quoted in Van Der Weyden, 2005.

93 We now know that there are hundreds of species of bacteria: See, for example, Sheh, 2013.

94 "As my knowledge of medicine and then pathology increased": Warren, 2005.

94 "I preferred to believe my eyes": Marshall, 2002. Cited in Pincock, 2005.

94 a group of American scientists: Ramsey et al., 1979. Six scientists, variously from the University of Texas, Harvard Medical School, and Stanford University, authored the paper.

95 they were led by a decorated professor of medicine: John S. Fordtran, who is the last-named author on the paper. Biographical details at Boland, 2012.

95 H. pylori was clearly visible: From Munro, 1985: "That outbreak was in a series of volunteers taking part in a study involving multiple gastric intubations and the cause was then assumed to have been viral. However, biopsy specimens have now been examined retrospectively and pyloric campylobacters have been found."

95 "Failing to discover H. pylori was my biggest mistake": W. I. Peterson, in a GastroHep.com profile: "What is the biggest mistake that you have made? Failing to discover H. pylori in 1976." Available at http://bit.ly/walterpeterson.

95 In 1967, Susumo Ito, a professor at Harvard Medical School: Ito, 1967. Cited in Marshall, 2005.

95 In 1940, Harvard researcher Stone Freedberg: Freedberg and Barron, 1940. Cited in Marshall, 2005: "The new spiral organism was not just a strange infection occurring in Western Australia, but was the same as the 'spirochaete' which had been described in the literature several times in the previous 100 years. . . . In 1940, Stone Freedberg from Harvard Medical School had seen spirochaetes in 40% of patients undergoing stomach resection for ulcers or cancer. About 10 years later, the leading US gastroenterologist, Eddie Palmer at Walter Reid [sic] Hospital, had performed blind suction biopsies on more than 1000 patients but had been unable to find the bacteria. His report concluded that bacteria did not exist except as post mortem contaminants." See also Altman, 2005.

95 H. pylori has now been found in medical literature: See Kidd and Modlin, 1998; Unge, 2002; and Marshall, 2002.

95 "inattentional blindness": Mack and Rock, 2000.

95 "Something that we can't see, or don't see": Adams, 2008. The quotation consists of two separate elements edited and combined: "An S.E.P.," he said, "is something that we can't see, or don't see, or our brain doesn't let us see, because we think that it's somebody else's problem. That's what S.E.P. means. Somebody Else's Problem. The brain just edits it out; it's like a blind spot. If you look at it directly you won't see it unless you know precisely what it is. Your only hope is to catch it by surprise out of the corner of your eye," and, later, "The Somebody Else's Problem field is much simpler and more effective, and what is more can be run for over a hundred years on a single flashlight battery. This is because it relies on people's natural predisposition not to see anything they don't want to, weren't expecting or can't explain."

96 The path from eye to mind is long: Description of visual loop based on Seger, 2008.

96 This is why it is a bad idea: The literature on this point is unequivocal: see, for

example: Harbluk et al., 2002; Strayer et al., 2003; Rakauskas et al., 2004; Strayer and Drews, 2004; Strayer et al., 2006; Strayer and Drews, 2007; and Young et al., 2007.

97 **In one study, researchers put a clown on a unicycle:** Hyman et al., 2010.

97 **Harvard researchers Trafton Drew and Jeremy Wolfe:** Drew et al., 2013, "The Invisible Gorilla Strikes Again."

97 **In 2004, a forty-three-year-old woman:** Lum et al., 2005. The incident took place at Strong Memorial Hospital in Rochester, New York. Cited in Drew et al., 2013.

98 **When Robin Warren accepted his Nobel Prize:** Warren, 2005, citing Doyle, 2011, from "The Boscombe Valley Mystery," first published in 1891.

98 **They can diagnose a disease after looking at a chest X-ray:** Drew et al., 2013.

99 **Adriaan de Groot, a chess master and psychologist:** De Groot, 1978. Cited in Weisberg, 1986.

103 **In 1960, twelve elderly Japanese Americans:** Biographical details about Shunryu Suzuki are from Chadwick, 2000.

103 **these men and women were imprisoned:** Americans of Japanese descent living in San Francisco were interred at Tanforan Racetrack, now a shopping mall at 1150 El Camino Real, San Bruno, California, where they were housed in stables and barracks before being moved to other camps farther inland. University of Southern California, 1942; *San Francisco Chronicle,* 1942.

103 **They were Zen Buddhists and congregants of Sokoji:** Chadwick, 2000: "The name he gave the abandoned synagogue had a simple meaning: *Soko* stood for San Francisco and the *ji* meant temple." The original temple was at 1881 Bush Street, four miles southeast of Fort Point and the southern end of the Golden Gate Bridge. The building was originally the Ohabai Shalome synagogue of the Jewish Congregation Ohabai Shalome; it was sold to Japanese American Teruro Kasuga in 1934 after the congregation experienced misfortunes, including a loss of membership due to religious reforms and the murder of its rabbi during what may have been a homosexual encounter. Kasuga turned it into *Sokoji,* also known as the "Soto Zen Center." The congregation moved to larger facilities on Page Street between 1969 and 1972, partly as a result of the increased interest in Zen Buddhism that Shunryu Suzuki had helped create. The building's history is beautifully described in Kenning, 2010.

103 **As the sun rose:** Suzuki arrived on May 23, 1959. Sunrise that day was at around 5:55 a.m. (see http://bit.ly/sfsunrise). Japan Air Lines flight 706 arrived at 6:30 a.m. (http://bit.ly/jaltime). The plane was a DC-6B, with silver-and-white livery, as shown at http://bit.ly/jaldc6; also http://bit.ly/jaldc6b. The "Pacific Courier" designation is from http://bit.ly/jaltime. Suzuki's clothing is described in Chadwick, 2000: "He was wearing his priest's traveling robes with a *rakusu* hanging around his neck, *zori,* and white *tabi* socks."

103 **"I sit at 5:45 in the morning":** Chadwick, 2000.

103 **People in India and East Asia:** From Wikipedia, http://bit.ly/easia: "The UN subregion of Eastern Asia and other common definitions of East Asia contain the entirety of the People's Republic of China, Japan, North Korea, South Korea, Mongolia and Taiwan." According to Everly and Lating, 2002, meditation has been practiced since 1500 B.C.E. Writer Alan W. Watts helped introduce medita-

tion to the United States in the 1959 as the presenter of KQED San Francisco's public television series *Eastern Wisdom and Modern Life*. His episode on meditation, "The Silent Mind," is at http://bit.ly/wattsmind.

103 **Suzuki made his students sit on the floor:** Chadwick, 2000. Picture at http://bit.ly/shunryu.

103 **If he suspected they were sleeping:** The name of the stick is typically transliterated as *keisaku*, but it is called *kyōsaku* in the Soto school, of which Suzuki was a member. Picture at http://bit.ly/kyosaku.

104 **His was American Buddhism's first voice:** Suzuki, 1970. From Fields, 1992: "It was, in fact, an American Buddhist voice, unlike any heard before, and yet utterly familiar. When Suzuki Roshi spoke, it was as if American Buddhists could hear themselves perhaps for the first time." Fields is cited in the 2011 edition of Suzuki, *Zen Mind, Beginner's Mind*.

104 **Nyogen Senzaki, one of the first Zen monks in America:** Senzaki, 1919.

104 **David Foster Wallace made the same point:** Wallace, 2009.

105 **Kuhn was recovering from a great disappointment:** Biographical details about Thomas Kuhn are from Nickles, 2002.

106 **This change in Kuhn's path:** Kuhn, 1977: "One memorable (and very hot) summer day those perplexities suddenly vanished." Nickles, 2002, citing Caneva, 2000, quotes Kuhn describing the event as taking place during an "afternoon," while attending a ceremony at the University of Padua, Italy, in 1992. Weinberg, 1998, also describes talking with Kuhn at this event about his understanding of Aristotle.

106 **The conventional view was that the book:** See, for example, Heidegger, 1956: "Aristotelian 'physics' . . . determines the warp and woof of the whole of Western thinking, even at that place where it, as modern thinking, appears to think at odds with ancient thinking. But opposition is invariably comprised of a decisive, and often even perilous, dependence. Without Aristotle's Physics there would have been no Galileo." Cited in the Wikipedia entry on Aristotle's *Physics*, at http://bit.ly/aristotlephysics.

106 **"Everything that is in locomotion":** Edited from Aristotle, 2012. The complete quotation is: "Everything that is in locomotion is moved either by itself or by something else. In the case of things that are moved by themselves it is evident that the moved and the movement are together: for they contain within themselves their first movement, so that there is nothing in between. The motion of things that are moved by something else must proceed in one of four ways for there are four kinds of locomotion caused by something other than that which is in motion, viz.: pulling, pushing, carrying, and twirling. All forms of locomotion are reducible to these."

106 **Science is not a continuum, he concluded:** Another example, discussed at length by Kuhn, 1962: in 1667, German Johann Joachim Becher published a book called *Physical Education,* in which he first described his theory of how and why things burned. Becher identified a new element called *"terra pinguis,"* which was a part of anything that burned. Burning released *terra pinguis* into the air until the air was so full of *terra pinguis* that it could take no more, at which point the burning stopped. Things that did not burn contained no *terra pinguis.* In the eighteenth century, Georg Ernst Stahl changed the name of *terra pinguis* to "phlogiston," and

the theory dominated physics for almost a hundred years. Phlogiston, or *terra pinguis,* has no modern equivalent—according to current science, it does not exist.

107 **Despite its obscure topic, Kuhn's book:** Garfield, 1987: "The 10 most-cited books, in descending order, are Thomas S. Kuhn's *Structure of Scientific Revolutions . . ."* In May 2014, Google Scholar listed more than seventy thousand citations for the book (http://bit.ly/kuhncitations). In 2012, on the fiftieth anniversary of its release, the University of Chicago Press said, "We had no idea that we had a book on our hands that would sell over 1.4 million copies." Press release at http://bit.ly/1pt4million.

107 **"the most influential work of philosophy":** Gleick, 1996. The book started a debate in philosophy that continues today. Critics have accused Kuhn of using "paradigm" to mean many different things (see, for example Masterman, 1970, in Lakatos et al., 1970; Eckberg and Hill, 1979; Fuller, 2001), but they all add up to one thing: a paradigm is a way of seeing the world. The word "paradigm" also became so well known that it appeared in several cartoons in the *New Yorker,* including one in which a doctor tells a patient, "I'm afraid you've had a paradigm shift" (J. C. Duffy, December 17, 2001, at http://bit.ly/paradigmcartoon1) and one in which one unlucky-looking man says to another, "Good news—I hear the paradigm is shifting" (Charles Barsotti, January 19, 2009, at http://bit.ly /paradigmcartoon2).

107 **"During revolutions scientists see new and different things":** Kuhn, 1962. The sudden appearance of *H. pylori* is not a new phenomenon. One example from Kuhn: in 1690, Britain's astronomer royal John Flamsteed saw a star and called it "34 Tauri." In 1781, William Herschel looked at it through a telescope but saw a comet, not a star. He pointed it out to Nevil Maskelyne, who saw a comet that might be a planet. German Johann Elert Bode saw a planet, too, and this soon led to a consensus: the object was a planet and was eventually called Uranus. Once one new planet had been discovered, the paradigm changed: finding new planets seemed possible. Astronomers, using the same instruments as before to look at the same sky, suddenly found twenty more minor planets and asteroids, including Neptune, which, like Uranus, had looked like a star since the seventeenth century. Something similar happened when Copernicus said the earth revolved around the sun: the previously unchangeable sky suddenly filled with comets that had been made visible not by new instruments but by a new paradigm. Meanwhile, Chinese astronomers, who had never believed that the sky was unchangeable, had been seeing comets for centuries.

108 **Neil deGrasse Tyson, speaking at the Salk Institute:** Tyson, 2006. Video at http://bit.ly/NdGTSalk. Quotation edited from the transcript at http://bit .ly/NdGTsenses. The complete quotation as transcribed is: "And we so much praise about the human eye, but anyone who has seen the full breadth of the electromagnetic spectrum will recognize how blind we are, okay, and part of that blindness means we can't see, we can't detect, magnetic fields, ionizing radiation, radon. We are like sitting ducks for ionizing radiation. We have to eat constantly, because we're warm blooded. Crocodile eat a chicken a month, it's fine. Okay, so we are always looking for food. These gases at the bottom [referring to a slide, with the words CO (carbon monoxide), CH4 (methane), CO2 (carbon dioxide)]: you can't smell them, taste them you breath [*sic*] them in you're dead, okay."

109 **"After work you have to get in your car"**: Heavily edited for length from Wallace, 2009.

110 **the original Chinese idea of yin-yang**: In simplified Chinese: 阴阳; traditional Chinese: 陰陽. The characters mean "sunny-side, shady-side." There is no "and."

111 **"an investigation into the condition"**: Lowell's comments are edited from a quotation in Sheehan, 1996, which cites Strauss, 1994. The original quotation from Sheehan is: "What Percival Lowell hoped to accomplish through this 'speculative, highly sensational and idiosyncratic project' is well documented in an address he gave to the Boston Scientific Society on May 22, 1894, which was printed in the *Boston Commonwealth*. His main object, he stated, was to study the solar system: 'This may be put popularly as an investigation into the condition of life on other worlds, including last but not least their habitability by beings like [or] unlike man. This is not the chimerical search some may suppose. On the contrary, there is strong reason to believe that we are on the eve of pretty definite discovery in the matter.' To Lowell, the implications of the lines that Italian astronomer Giovanni Schiaparelli figuratively called *canali* were self-evident: 'Speculation has been singularly fruitful as to what these markings on our next to nearest neighbor in space may mean. Each astronomer holds a different pet theory on the subject, and pooh-poohs those of all the others. Nevertheless, the most self-evident explanation from the markings themselves is probably the true one; namely, that in them we are looking upon the result of the work of some sort of intelligent beings. . . . The amazing blue network on Mars hints that one planet besides our own is actually inhabited now.'" Sheehan's work is available from the University of Arizona at http://bit.ly/sheehanmars.

111 **Lowell inspired a century of science fiction**: The word "Martian" predated Lowell—it first appeared in 1883, in a story almost certainly inspired by Schiaparelli (Lach-Szyrma, 1883) but did not become famous until 1898, *after* Lowell's announcements, when H. G. Wells published *The War of the Worlds*. Burroughs's *Under the Moons of Mars* was a series of short stories first published in 1912, as a series under the pen name "Norman Bean," and renamed *A Princess of Mars* when released in book form (Burroughs, 1917). The complete quotation is: "The shores of the ancient seas were dotted with just such cities, and lesser ones, in diminishing numbers, were to be found converging toward the center of the oceans, as the people had found it necessary to follow the receding waters until necessity had forced upon them their ultimate salvation, the so-called Martian canals."

111 **One of Lowell's opponents was Alfred Wallace**: Wallace had already concluded that "the Earth is the only habitable planet in the solar system" when Lowell started publishing (Wallace, 1904).

111 **"The totally inadequate water-supply"**: Edited from Wallace, 1907.

112 **The argument was resolved in Wallace's favor**: Momsen, 1996. The complete quotation is: "And then the real wonder came—picture after picture showing that the surface was dotted with craters! It appeared uncannily like that of our own Moon, deeply cratered, and unchanged over time. No water, no canals, no life." Momsen was described as "the imaging engineer for JPL's [Jet Propulsion Laboratory's] Mariner series of missions" by John B. Dobbins on December 12, 2005, in a message to the NASA Spaceflight Forum at http://bit.ly/nasaforum.

112 **His maps of Martian canals are mirror images:** Sheehan and Dobbins, 2003. Lowell describes the "Tores" he saw on Saturn in Lowell, 1907.

113 **"Perhaps the most harmful imperfection of the eye":** See Sheehan and Dobbins, 2003; also Douglass, 1907.

113 **"I am not sure of the significance":** Warren, 2005.

113–114 **Ketamine, phencyclidine, and methamphetamine:** Burton, 2009. Phencyclidine is also known as PCP, or angel dust. Methamphetamine is also known as "meth"; the derivatives MDMA, or ecstasy, and methamphetamine hydrochloride salt, or "crystal meth," can also create feelings of certainty. For more on the effects of entorhinal cortex stimulation, see Bartolomei, 2004.

114 **cognitive psychologists Ulric Neisser and Nicole Harsch:** Neisser and Harsch, 1992. Cited in Burton, 2009.

114 **Thirty-three were sure they had never been asked:** This was actually thirty-three out of forty-four. The study had three parts. In part one, 106 students completed a questionnaire the day after the *Challenger* explosion. In part two, administered two and a half years later, forty-four of those students agreed to complete a follow-up questionnaire. In part three, forty of those students particpated in an interview where the two questionnaires were compared. Part three, the interview, took place six months after part two, the second questionnaire, had been completed. Four students dropped out between the second and third parts of the test, which is why the base size in the test is forty.

114 **This unshakable certainty was first studied in 1954:** Festinger et al., 1956, in which Martin is given the pseudonym "Mrs. Marian Keech" to protect her identity.

115 **"The group began reexamining the original message":** Edited from Festinger et al., 1956. Complete quotation: "At any rate, in the next hour and a half, the group began to come to grips with the fact that no caller had arrived at midnight to take them to the saucer. The problem from here on was to reassure themselves and to find an adequate, satisfying way to reconcile the disconfirmation with their beliefs. They began by re-examining the original message which had stated that at midnight the group would be put into parked cars and taken to the saucer. In response to some of the observers' prodding about that message during the coffee break, the Creator stated that anyone who wished might look up that message. It had been buried away among many others in a large envelope and none of the believers seemed inclined to look for it, but one of the observers volunteered. He found it and read it aloud to the group. The first attempt at reinterpretation came quickly. Daisy Armstrong pointed out that the message must, of course, be symbolic, because it said we were to be put into parked cars; but parked cars do not move and hence could not take the group anywhere. The Creator then announced that the message was indeed symbolic, but the 'parked cars' referred to their own physical bodies, which had obviously been there at midnight. The 'porch' (flying saucer), He went on, symbolized in this message the inner strength, the inner knowing, and inner light which each member of the group had. So eager was the group for an explanation of any kind that many actually began to accept this one."

115 **"From the mouth of death have ye been delivered":** Edited from Festinger et al., 1956. Complete quotation: "And mighty is the word of God—and by his word have ye been saved—for from the mouth of death have ye been delivered

and at no time has there been such a force loosed upon the Earth. Not since the beginning of time upon this Earth has there been such a force of Good and light as now floods this room and that which has been loosed within this room now floods the entire Earth."

116 **Leon Festinger, named this gap:** The term used throughout *When Prophecy Fails* is "dissonance." Later, in Festinger, 1957, the term became "cognitive dissonance."

115 **In one experiment, he gave volunteers:** Festinger, 1962.

116 **"When dissonance is present, in addition to trying to reduce it":** Festinger, 1957.

116 **Dorothy Martin had a long career:** After the events described in the book, Martin moved to the Yucatán Peninsula in Mexico, was involved with "the Brotherhood of the Seven Rays," a group that included another purported "UFO contactee," George Hunt Williamson, and at some point became known as "Sister Thedra." According to another spiritualist, "Dr. Robert Ghost Wolf," while she was in Mexico, Martin "had an experience which changed her in an instant when as it is told by her that [*sic*] Jesus Christ physically appeared to her and spontaneously cured her of cancer. He introduced himself to her by his true, [*sic*] name, 'Sananda Kumara,' thereby revealing his affiliation with the Venusian founders of the Great Solar Brotherhoods. By his command that [*sic*] Sister Thedra went to Peru. Sister Thedra eventually left Peru upon felling [*sic*] her experience there was complete. She then traveled to Mt. Shasta in California and founded the Association of Sananda and Sanat Kumara." Dorothy Martin died in May 1992. She did her last "automatic writing" on May 3, 1992: "Sori Sori: Mine beloved, I am speaking unto thee for the good of all. It is now come the time that ye come out from the place wherein ye are. Ye shall shout for joy! Let it be, for many shall greet thee with glad shouts! So be it, no more pain . . . Amen . . . Sananda." (Ellipses in original.) After Martin's death, the Association of Sananda and Sanat Kumara changed its address to a location next to a pizza restaurant called "Apizza Heaven" in Sedona, Arizona. See http://bit.ly/thedra and http://bit.ly/sananda. Martin's story is also mentioned (rather inaccurately) in Largo, 2010.

116 **"The psychologists determined that when people":** From "Extraordinary Intelligence," a website created by a woman using the pseudonym "Natalina," sometimes "Natalina EI," who lives in Tulsa, Oklahoma; http://bit.ly /whenfaithistested.

CHAPTER 5: WHERE CREDIT IS DUE

118 **Sleet like crystal tears fell on cobbles:** Biographical details about Rosalind Franklin are from Maddox, 2003, and Glynn, 2012.

118 **Physicist Erwin Schrödinger captured the spirit:** Schrödinger gave a series of lectures at the Dublin Institute for Advanced Studies at Trinity College in 1943 (published as a book in 1944) in which he anticipated the discovery of DNA with the statement "the most essential part of a living cell—the chromosome fibre may suitably be called an aperiodic crystal" (Schrödinger, 1944).

120 **Mendel's work was ignored:** Mendel's work did not become widely known until the start of the twentieth century; Darwin died in 1882. Darwin proposed a "pro-

visional hypothesis," quite different from Mendel's, which he called "pangenesis," in Darwin, 1868. "Chromosome theory" is also known as "Boveri-Sutton chromosome theory," "the chromosome theory of inheritance," and "the Sutton-Boveri theory."

120 **Rosalind Franklin believed life's messengers:** It was not until the 1930s that the acids were first considered as candidate information carriers by the Canadian American scientist Oswald Avery Jr. (Maddox, 2003).

121 **a crystal is any solid with atoms or molecules arranged:** A crystal can also consist of a three-dimensional, repeating arrangement of ions; I excluded that point here for clarity and simplicity.

122 **Franklin published her results at the start:** Franklin published regularly on the tobacco mosaic virus between 1955 and 1958 (see works by Franklin and by Franklin with others in the bibliography, below), and her work culminated in two papers published in 1958: "The Radial Density Distribution in Some Strains of Tobacco Mosaic Virus," coauthored with Kenneth Holmes and published before her death (Holmes and Franklin, 1958), and "The Structure of Viruses as Determined by X-ray Diffraction," which was published posthumously (Franklin et al., 1958).

123 **"Credit does not entirely belong to her":** A letter from Charles Eliot to Marie Meloney, December 18, 1920, part of the Marie Mattingly Meloney papers, 1891–1943, Columbia University Library; http://bit.ly/meloney. Quoted in Ham, 2002.

124 **Curie used the word "me" seven times:** See Curie, 1911. The quotation also appears in Emling, 2013.

124 **In total, only 15 women have won:** "Science" means prizes in "chemistry," "physics," or "physiology or medicine." The 15 women (as of 2014) are Maria Goeppert Mayer (physics, 1963), Marie Curie (physics, 1903, and chemistry, 1911), Ada E. Yonath (chemistry, 2009), Dorothy Hodgkin (chemistry, 1964), Irène Joliot-Curie (chemistry, 1935), Elizabeth H. Blackburn (physiology or medicine, 2009), Carol W. Greider (physiology or medicine, 2009), Françoise Barré-Sinoussi (physiology or medicine, 2008), Linda B. Buck (physiology or medicine, 2004), Christiane Nüsslein-Volhard (physiology or medicine, 1995), Gertrude B. Elion (physiology or medicine, 1998), Rita Levi-Montalcini (physiology or medicine, 1986), Barbara McClintock (physiology or medicine, 1983), Rosalyn Yalow (physiology or medicine, 1977), and Gerty Theresa Cori (physiology or medicine, 1947). See http://bit.ly/womenlaureates.

126 **It protected DNA specimens from humidity:** Pictures of Franklin's camera are at http://bit.ly/dnacamera.

127 **There are many similar stories:** These examples are a selection from Byers and Williams, 2010.

127 **One reason is an imbalance first recorded:** Zuckerman, 1965.

127 **"The world is peculiar in this matter":** Quotations are from Merton, 1968.

127 **Until Zuckerman, most scholars assumed:** See, for example, Pareto et al., 1935, discussed in Zuckerman, 1977.

128 **"For whoever has will be given more":** New International Version. Other translations and commentaries at http://bit.ly/matthew2529.

128 **Zuckerman collaborated with Merton, then married him:** Merton and Zuckerman married in 1993. Merton separated from his first wife, Suzanne Carhart,

in 1968, soon after Zuckerman completed her PhD (Hollander, 2003; Calhoun, 2003; and Wikipedia entry on Robert K. Merton at http://bit.ly/mertonrk).

128　**Patent law is complicated:** See U.S. Patent and Trademark Office web page at http://bit.ly/inventorship.

128　**If the female scientist named the male scientist:** See Radack, 1994, for a discussion of the risks of assigning inventorship to non-inventors.

129　**the average number of people who "contribute":** See discussion of Trajtenberg in chapter 1.

129　**part of the macroenvironment:** Merton used the word "paradigm" twenty-five years before Kuhn, but, Merton says, with a less precise, "more limited," meaning. See video of "Robert K. Merton Interviewed by Albert K. Cohen, May 15, 1997," posted by the American Society of Criminology at http://bit.ly/mertoncohen.

130　**In 1676, Isaac Newton described this problem:** Letter from Isaac Newton to Robert Hooke, dated "Cambridge, February 5, 1675–6," published in Brewster, 1860.

130　**Newton got it from George Herbert:** See Merton, 1993. There is an excellent summary of the life of this quotation, written by Joseph Yoon, formerly of NASA, on Aerospace Web at http://bit.ly/josephyoon (although the date given for Didacus Stella's quotation is incorrect). Bernard of Chartres may have found the idea in the work of Talmudic scholars (it appears in the writings of Talmudist Isaiah di Trani, who lived after Bernard, but Isaiah may have inherited it from other, earlier Talmudists, rather than getting it from Bernard); it could also have been inspired by the ancient Greek myth of Cedalion, who rides on the shoulders of the giant Orion.

131　**a subject of curiosity at least since the winter:** There are other, earlier discussions of snowflakes, including Han Ying (韓嬰, 150 B.C.E.), Albertus Magnus (1250), and Olaus Magnus (1555). I start with Kepler because he was one of the first to try to explain snowflakes by connecting them to crystals—"Let the chemists, then, tell us whether there is any salt in snow, and what kind, and what shape it takes"—and crystals, not snowflakes, are the subject of the discussion.

132　**Geissler's invention was a novelty:** Shepardson, 1908.

132　**"I have seen my death":** Markel, 2012.

133　**Were they particles, like electrons:** This question about X-rays was asked before Einstein proposed wave-particle duality.

133　**In 1915, at the age of twenty-five:** Jenkin, 2008, and Authier, 2013.

134　**One of them was a woman named Polly Porter:** Polly was not her real name. She was christened "Mary Winearls Porter" but had always been called "Polly."

134　**While her brothers studied, Porter wandered the city:** The result was a book, *What Rome Was Built With.* See Porter, 1907.

134　**Henry Miers, Oxford's first professor of mineralogy:** Price, 2012.

135　**"Dear Professor Goldschmidt":** Letter dated January 14, 1914, edited from Arnold, 1993. The quotation as it appears in Arnold is: "Dear Professor Goldschmidt: I have long had the purpose of writing you to interest you in Miss Porter, who is working this year in my laboratory and whom I hope you will welcome in your laboratory next year. Her heart is set upon the study of crystallography and I hope she will remain with you for more than one year. Her income is not sufficient for her to live in Bryn Mawr College without earning money. This

Miss Porter is doing now, but her work takes too much time from her studies and besides she should go to the fountainhead of inspiration. . . . Miss Porter thinks she will, in Germany, be able to live upon her income. Miss Porter's life has been unusual, for her parents (her father is corresponding editor of the London Times) have been almost constant travellers and she has never been to school or college save for a very brief period. There are therefore great gaps in her education, particularly in chemistry and mathematics, but to offset this I believe you will find that she has an unusual aptitude for crystal measurement, etc., and certainly an intense love of your subject. I want to see her have the opportunities which have so long been denied her—Miss Porter is perhaps about 26 years of age, very modest and unselfassertive but with a quiet initiative. I hope you will be interested to have her as a student and 1 think she will repay all you may do for her. She must eventually be self-supporting and I hope she will be fitted for the position of curator and crystallographer of some mineral collection. Miss Porter is spending this year only with me and if she does come to you, it will be apparent to you, I fear, that she has but made a beginning. I am, however, both ambitious for her and with faith in her ultimate success. . . ."

135 **She stayed at Oxford, conducting research:** Haines, 2001.

136 **Bragg's topic in 1923:** The title of Bragg's lectures was "Concerning the Nature of Things." Bragg, 1925.

136 **Dorothy Hodgkin:** Biographical details about Dorothy Hodgkin are from Ferry, 2000.

137 **That same year, Japanese physicist Ukichiro Nakaya:** Nakaya, 1954. Summarized in nontechnical terms in Libbrecht, 2001.

137 **They form around another particle:** See Lee, 1995, for more. Christner et al., 2008, "examined IN [ice nucleators—particles that act as a nucleus for ice crystals that form in the atmosphere] in snowfall from mid- and high-latitude locations and found that the most active were biological in origin. Of the IN larger than 0.2 micrometer that were active at temperatures warmer than $-7°C$, 69 to 100% were biological, and a substantial fraction were bacteria."

137 **Nucleobases, essential components of DNA:** Callahan et al., 2011.

137 **glycolaldehyde, a sugarlike molecule:** Jørgensen et al., 2012.

138 **Franklin likely inherited:** Gabai-Kapara, 2014, suggests that only 2 percent of Ashkenazi Jews carry a BRCA mutation, split evenly between the BRCA1 mutation and the BRCA2 mutation. (Only about three in ten thousand Ashkenazim have mutations in both their BRCA1 *and* BRCA2 genes.) Not all women with BRCA mutations develop ovarian cancer, and not all ovarian cancers among Ashkenazi Jewish women are caused by BRCA mutations: only 40 percent of Ashkenazi Jewish women who develop ovarian cancer have BRCA2 mutations. It is Franklin's death from ovarian cancer at such a young age, *combined with* her Ashkenazi Jewish descent, that indicates she was likely to have been a carrier of a mutated BRCA gene.

138 **The BRCA2 mutation makes:** Antinou, 2003. While 1.4 percent of all women develop ovarian cancer, 39 percent of women with a BRCA1 mutation and 11 to 17 percent of women with a BRCA2 mutation develop ovarian cancer. BRCA mutations also increase breast cancer risk: while 12 percent of all women develop breast cancer, 55 to 65 percent of women with a BRCA1 mutation and 45 percent

of women with a BRCA2 mutation develop breast cancer. See the National Cancer Institute at http://bit.ly/ncibrca for more information about the impact of BRCA mutations on both diseases.

138 **all literal cousins of Rosalind Franklin:** According to genetic analysis by Carmi, 2014, all Ashkenazi Jews are descended from a population of about 350 people who lived seven hundred years ago, around 1300 CE. If we assume a generation is, on average, twenty-five years, and the founding people were interrelated, this suggests that all living Ashkenazim are about thirtieth cousins or closer.

CHAPTER 6: CHAINS OF CONSEQUENCE

140 **William Cartwright's dog started barking:** Details of the attack on Cartwright's mill taken from the "Luddite Bicentenary" website at: http://bit.ly/rawfolds.

141 **The new and improved Enoch sledgehammers:** Details about "the Great Enoch" are available on the *Radical History Network* blog at http://bit.ly/greatenoch.

142 **"Governments must have arisen":** Paine, 1791.

146 **He begins with Frenchman Philippe Lebon:** Lebon's patent is dated 1801, but Ehrenburg describes him developing the engine in 1798 (Ehrenburg, 1929).

147 **"It really boils down to this":** Dr. King first delivered this sermon at Ebenezer Baptist Church, where he served as co-pastor. On Christmas Eve 1967, the Canadian Broadcasting Corporation aired the sermon as part of the seventh annual Massey Lectures. Available at http://bit.ly/drkingsermon.

149 **"We do not consider modern inventions to be evil":** This quotation, and other details about the Amish, are from Kraybill et al., 2013.

150 **"Not everything that could be fixed should be fixed":** Morozov, 2013.

156 **When all the processes in Coca-Cola's tool chain:** Analysis based on Ercin et al., 2011.

158 *Come on, my love:* This is the English translation of a traditional Scottish walking, or "waulking," song "Coisich, A Ruin" ("Come On, My Love"), probably from around the fourteenth century. There is a beautiful recording by Catriona MacDonald at http://bit.ly/coisich. Craig Coburn summarizes the tradition of the Scottish walking song at http://bit.ly/craigcoburn. Fulling in England is discussed in Pelham, 1944; Lennard, 1951; Munro, 1999; and Lucas, 2006.

160 **jobs that, less than a century later:** Dating this to Towne, 1886.

161 **Between 1840 and 1895, school attendance:** Cipolla, 1969.

161 **In 1990, America had 30 million:** Statistics from Snyder, 1993, summarized at http://bit.ly/snydersummary; full version at http://bit.ly/snyderthomas.

161 **The number of Americans earning college degrees:** Analysis based on demographic data from InfoPlease, "Population Distribution by Age, Race, and Nativity, 1860–2010" (http://bit.ly/uspopulation); U.S. Census at http://bit.ly/educationfacts; Snyder, 1993 (http://bit.ly/snyderthomas); and Joseph Kish's table "U.S. Population 1776 to Present" (http://bit.ly/kishjoseph).

163 **In March 2002, Woody Allen did something:** Biographical details about
Woody Allen from Wikipedia entry at http://bit.ly/allenwoody. In 2002 he had
won three Academy Awards—two for *Annie Hall* (Best Original Screenplay and
Best Director, 1978) and one for *Hannah and Her Sisters* (Best Original Screenplay,
1987). He had also been nominated for seventeen other awards: *Annie Hall* (Best
Actor in a Leading Role, 1978), *Interiors* (Best Original Screenplay and Best Director, 1979), *Manhattan* (Best Original Screenplay, 1980), *Broadway Danny Rose* (Best
Original Screenplay and Best Director, 1985), *The Purple Rose of Cairo* (Best Original Screenplay, 1986), *Hannah and Her Sisters* (Best Director, 1987), *Radio Days*
(Best Original Screenplay, 1988), *Crimes and Misdemeanors* (Best Original Screenplay and Best Director, 1989), *Alice* (Best Original Screenplay, 1990), *Husbands
and Wives* (Best Original Screenplay, 1993), *Bullets Over Broadway* (Best Original
Screenplay and Best Director, 1994), *Mighty Aphrodite* (Best Original Screenplay,
1996), and *Deconstructing Harry* (Best Original Screenplay, 1998). As of 2014, since
appearing at the 2002 Academy Awards ceremony, he has won a fourth award
for *Midnight in Paris* (Best Original Screenplay, 2011) and received three other
nominations: *Match Point* (Best Original Screenplay, 2006), *Midnight in Paris* (Best
Director, 2011), and *Blue Jasmine* (Best Original Screenplay, 2014). A complete
list of Allen's awards is available at the Internet Movie Database, http://bit.ly
/allenawards. The speech in which he said, "For New York City, I'll do anything"
can be seen on YouTube at http://bit.ly/allenspeech.

163 **He gives several tongue-in-cheek excuses:** From Block and Cornish, 2012:
"Audie Cornish, Host: Woody Allen is a favorite to take home at least one Oscar
for Best Original Screenplay, but don't expect the camera to cut to him when the
nominees' names are announced. Melissa Block, Host: With one exception, Woody
Allen has never attended the Academy Awards. In spite of his previous 21 nominations and three wins, he declines the invites. He's known for it, so notoriously so
that urban myths are told as to why. Cornish: No, it's not because of a standing gig
playing the clarinet at a New York pub. We were assured of that by Eric Lax, who
wrote 'Conversations with Woody Allen.' Eric Lax: It was a polite excuse. I think
that, if he has a gig that night, he can say, well, I had a gig that night. I needed to be
there. You know, that goes all the way back to 'Annie Hall.'" Allen, quoted in Hornaday, 2012: "They always have it on Sunday night. And it's always—you can look
this up—it's always opposite a good basketball game. And I'm a big basketball fan.
So it's a great pleasure for me to come home and get into bed and watch a basketball game. And that's exactly where I was, watching the game."

164 **"The whole concept of awards is silly":** From Lax, 2000: "There are two things
that bother me about [the Academy Awards]," he said in 1974 after Vincent
Canby had written a piece wondering why *Sleeper* had received no nominations.
"They're political and bought and negotiated for—although many worthy people
have deservedly won—and the whole concept of awards is silly. I cannot abide by
the judgment of other people, because if you accept it when they say you deserve
an award, then you have to accept it when they say you don't."

164 **"I think what you get in awards is favoritism":** From Weide, 2011. Video clip
on YouTube at http://bit.ly/whatyougetinawards.

164 **Psychologist R. A. Ochse lists eight motivations:** Ochse, 1990.

164 **"I want to feel my work good and well taken":** Plath, 1982, as quoted in Amabile, 1996.

165 **Amabile asked ninety-five people:** Amabile, 1996.

166 **Olympia SM2 portable typewriter:** Australian blogger Teeritz gives a detailed description of the SM2, with photographs, at http://bit.ly/olympiasm2.

166 **"It still works like a tank":** Woody Allen quotations throughout from Lax, 2000, and Weide, 2011; descriptions (e.g., type of typewriter) based on Weide, 2011.

167 **Poet John Berryman congratulated him:** Simpson, 1982. Cited in Amabile 1983.

167 **"When I began to think of what":** Edited from Eliot, 1948. Full text at http://bit.ly/eliotbanquet.

168 **an address to the Nordic Assembly of Naturalists:** Einstein, 1923.

168 **The days are cold and dry:** Sausalito weather in February 1976 from *Old Farmer's Almanac* at http://bit.ly/pointbonita.

168 **A strange redwood hut:** Record Plant Studios, 2200 Bridgeway, Sausalito, CA 94965. Photographs of the entrance, with carved animals, at http://bit.ly/recordplant.

169 **Christine McVie calls it a "a cocktail party":** Crowe, 1977. Complete quotation: "'Trauma,' Christine groans. 'Trau-*ma*. The sessions were like a cocktail party every night—people everywhere.'"

169 **Warner Bros. compares it to the rocket:** *Tusk* has a mixed reputation now. Some critics, and some members of Fleetwood Mac, regard it as the band's best work.

170 ***Don't Stand Me Down* confused reviewers:** As with *Tusk,* some now consider *Don't Stand Me Down* to be a misunderstood masterpiece. See, for example, comments on the *Guardian* website at http://bit.ly/dontstand, such as, "*Don't Stand Me Down* is the statement of a maverick genius that went over the heads of all but the connoisseurs."

170 **Dexys Midnight Runners would not record:** Details about Dexys Midnight Runners and *Don't Stand Me Down* at Wikipedia: http://bit.ly/dexyswiki and http://bit.ly/dontstandwiki. General discussion of "second album syndrome" in Seale, 2012.

170 **"This is my story":** Dostoyevsky, 1923; partly quoted in Amabile 1983, citing Allen, 1948.

171 **After getting a doctorate in psychology:** Biographical details about Harry Harlow are from Sidowski and Lindsley, 1988, and the Wikipedia entry for Harry Harlow at http://bit.ly/harlowharry.

171 **Harlow left puzzles consisting of a hinge:** See Harlow, 1950.

172 **"tended to disrupt, not facilitate":** Harlow et al., 1950.

172 **They consistently rated the commissioned art:** Amabile, Phillips, and Collins, 1994, cited in Amabile, "Creativity in Context," 1996.

172 **Princeton's Sam Glucksberg investigated the question:** Glucksberg, 1962, cited in Amabile, 1983.

172 **Follow-up experiments by Glucksberg:** For example, McGraw and McCullers, 1979.

172 **There are more than a hundred studies:** See for example, reviews by Cameron and Pierce, 1994; Eisenberger and Cameron, 1996; and Eisenberger et al., 1999.

173 **Rewards are only a problem:** McGraw and McCullers, 1979, cited in Amabile 1983.

173 **Amabile explored and extended this finding:** Amabile,Hennessey, and Gross-man (1986), cited in Amabile, "Creativity in Context," 1996.

174 **People in America's Deep South:** Among many excellent books about Robert Johnson are Wardlow, 1998; Pearson and McCulloch, 2003; and Wald, 2004.

177 **One has even attributed it to "cramping":** Flaherty, 2005.

177 **He wrote a play called *Writer's Block*:** *Writer's Block* is two one-act plays. The description given in many playbills is: "In *Riverside Drive,* a paranoid schizo-phrenic former-screenwriter stalks a newly successful but insecure screenwriter, believing he has stealing not only his ideas but his life. *Old Saybrooke,* a combi-nation of old-fashioned sex farce and an interesting look at a writer's process, involves a group of married couples who have cause to ponder the challenges of commitment." See, for example, Theatre in LA at http://bit.ly/theatreinla and Goldstar at http://bit.ly/goldstarhollywood.

177 **"For the first time in my life":** Transcript of *Deconstructing Harry* corrected from Drew's Script-O-Rama at http://bit.ly/harryblock.

177 **Allen took the role of Harry:** Details about Allen's process, and Allen quota-tions, from Lax, 2000.

179 **"You have to dip your pen in blood":** Allen may be thinking of the following comment, reported by pianist Alexander Goldenveizer in a memoir translated by S. S. Koteliansky and Virginia Woolf as *Talks with Tolstoi,* published by the Hogarth Press in 1923: "One ought only to write when one leaves a piece of one's flesh in the ink-pot each time one dips one's pen." This extract from the memoir is also referenced in Walter Allen's *Writers on Writing,* 1948.

181 ***Popular Science* described them as "savages":** Barrows, 1910.

181 **The last anthropologist to live:** *Boston Evening Transcript,* 1909.

181 **Rosaldo captured the Ilongots' insights in a book:** Rosaldo, 1980.

182 **"The force of any passion or emotion":** Spinoza, 1677.

182 **"We can't be misled by passions":** Descartes, 1649.

182 **Daquan Lawrence celebrated his sixteenth birthday:** Daquan Lawrence's story and lyrics are from Hansen, 2012.

184 **the Irene Taylor Trust claimed:** The claims, which have been repeated in sev-eral of the Trust's publications as well as by other sources, refer to a production of Shakespeare's *Julius Caesar* at Bullingdon Prison in Oxfordshire, England, in May 1999. According to the Trust's original evaluation report, "94% of partici-pants did not offend during the time that they were involved in the Julius Caesar Project" and "There was a 58% decrease in the offence rates of participants in the six months following the project, compared to the offence rates in the six-month period before the project began." The full report, which is called "Julius Caesar—H.M.P Bullingdon," and is undated and attributed only to the "Irene Taylor Trust," can be downloaded from http://bit.ly/taylortrust.

185 **In the 1950s, George "Shotgun" Shuba:** George Shuba story from Kahn, 1972, cited in Glasser, 1977, which mistakenly calls Shuba "Schuba."

185 **what psychologist William Glasser later called:** Glasser, 1976.

186 **"I'll start with scraps and things":** Allen in Weide, 2011.

186 **"To begin, to begin":** From the movie *Adaptation* (2002), directed by Spike Jonze. These lines are written by Charlie Kaufman and said by the character

"Charlie Kaufman," a screen writer struggling with a script, played by Nicholas Cage.

187 **"Work brings inspiration":** Notes about Stravinsky, including this quotation, from Gardner, 2011.

188 **Science describes the destruction unequivocally:** See, for example, Bailey, 2006, which details experimental results and also includes a good literature review.

191 **Woody Allen has pondered that:** Lax, 2010. The complete quotation from Allen is:

"Why not opt for a sensual life instead of a life of grueling work? When you're at heaven's gate, the guy who has spent all his time chasing and catching women and has a sybaritic life gets in, and you get in, too. The only reason I can think of not to is, it's another form of denial of death. You delude yourself that there's a reason to lead a meaningful life, a productive life of work and struggle and perfection of one's profession or art. But the truth is, you could be spending that time indulging yourself—assuming you can afford it—because you both wind up in the same place.

"If I don't like something, it doesn't matter how many awards it's won. It's important to keep your own criteria and not defer to the trends of the marketplace.

"I hope that somewhere along the line it will be perceived that I'm not really a personal malcontent, or that my ambition or my pretensions—which I freely admit to—are not to gain power. I only want to make something that will entertain people, and I'm stretching myself to do it."

CHAPTER 8: CREATING ORGANIZATIONS

193 **In January 1944, Milo Burcham strolled:** Descriptions of the Skunk Works drawn mainly from Johnson, 1990, and Rich, 1994.

193 *Lulu Belle*'s **official name:** To be precise: Lockheed's prototypes, or "experimental" aircraft, had the prefix "X" in their names, so *Lulu Belle*'s full official name was the "XP-80." The P-80 was the name of subsequent production aircraft based on her design.

198 **"When you're dealing with a creative process":** Frank Filipetti quotation from Massey, 2000.

199 **In November 1960, Robert Galambos figured:** Robert Galambos's biographical details from Squire, 1998.

200 **"Quite possibly the most important roles of glia":** Barres, 2008. This quotation also appears in Martin, 2010. For more on the importance of glia, see Barres, 2008; Wang and Bordey, 2008; Allen, 2009; Edwards, 2009; Sofroniew and Vinters, 2010; Steinhäuser and Seifert, 2010; and Eroglu and Barres, 2010.

201 **"Truth-tellers are genuinely passionate":** Edited from a pre-press edition of Downes and Nunes, 2014. Downes and Nunes interviewed me for this part of their book as an example of a "truth-teller."

205 **In 1960, the Puppeteers' annual Puppetry Festival:** There is a photograph of the event program in the Jim Henson Archive at http://bit.ly/puppetry1960.

205 **Mike and Frances befriended a first-time attendee:** Biographical details about Jim Henson and Frank Oz are mainly from Jones, 2013; Davis, 2009; and the Muppet Wiki at http://bit.ly/muppetwiki.

205 **he wanted to be a journalist, not a puppeteer:** Douglas, 2007.

206 **Henson and Oz found two new Muppets:** The story of Bert and Ernie draws from the Wikipedia entry at http://bit.ly/erniebert.

207 **After the words "In Color," two clay animation:** The first episode of *Sesame Street* can be seen on YouTube at http://bit.ly/firstsesamestreet.

208 **"Bert and Ernie are two grown men sharing a house":** Various sources, including the Muppet Wiki, attribute this quotation to a radio broadcast by Chambers in 1994. See http://bit.ly/gayberternie.

210 **an animated television series they created:** *South Park,* the television series, which first aired in 1997, is based on two animated shorts that Parker and Stone created in 1992 and 1995.

210 **Parker and Stone let filmmaker Arthur Bradford:** *Six Days to Air: The Making of South Park* (2011), sometimes known as *Six Days to South Park,* directed by Arthur Bradford.

214 **In 1998, Viacom asked the two men:** Quotations and details about the making of the *South Park* movie from Pond, 2000.

216 **In 2006, Peter Skillman, an industrial designer:** TED (Technology, Entertainment, Design) 2006. Video at http://bit.ly/skillmanTED.

216 **developed with Dennis Boyle:** Skillman gives details on the genesis of the marshmallow challenge on the TED website at http://bit.ly/skillmanbackground.

217 **Creative professional Tom Wujec confirmed this:** Wujec's slides, and a talk he gave at the 2010 TED conference, at http://bit.ly/wujecTED.

217 **"Several teams will have the powerful desire":** From Wujec's marshmallow challenge instructions at http://bit.ly/marshmallowinstructions.

218 **"Although children's use of tools":** Quotations from Vygotsky, 1980.

222 **In 1954, something unprecedented happened:** Cornwell, 2010.

223 **Before microsociology, the dominant assumption:** Model adapted from David McDermott's website Decision Making Confidence at http://bit.ly/mcdermottdavid.

224 **Sociologist Erving Goffman called the moves:** Collins, 2004.

225 **the average office worker attends:** Data from my own online survey of 123 self-described "office workers," working at various levels of their organizations.

225 **the more creative an organization is:** See Mankins et al., 2014.

226 **"I was assigned to work with Bill Mylan":** Johnson, 1990.

226 **In 1966, Philip Jackson:** From Jackson, 1966: "The other curriculum might be described as unofficial or perhaps even hidden, because to date it has received scant attention from educators. This hidden curriculum can also be represented by three R's, but not the familiar one of reading, 'riting, and 'rithmetic. It is, instead, the curriculum of rules, regulations, and routines, of things teachers and students must learn if they are to make their way with minimum pain in the social institution called *the school.*"

226 **"The crowds, the praise, and the power":** Jackson quotations in this section from Jackson, 1968.

228 **"The personal qualities":** The complete quotation from Jackson is:
   "The personal qualities that play a role in intellectual mastery are very different from those that characterize the Company Man. Curiosity, as an instance, is of little value in responding to the demands of conformity. The curious person

typically engages in a kind of probing, poking, and exploring that is almost antithetical to the attitude of the passive conformist. The scholar must develop the habit of challenging authority and questioning the value of tradition. He must insist on explanations for things that are unclear. Scholarship requires discipline, to be sure, but this discipline serves the demands of scholarship rather than the wishes and desires of other people. In short, intellectual mastery calls for sublimated forms of aggression rather than for submission to constraints."

229–230　**airplanes killed 2.2 million people:** Wartime casualty figures are notoriously unreliable and always disputed. To quote statistical historian Matthew White (White, 2013): "The numbers that people want to argue about are casualties." Here, 2.2 million is the sum of casualties and losses listed in the Wikipedia entry "Strategic Bombing During World War II" (http://bit.ly/WW2bombing), which reflects the consenus of historians: 60,595 British civilians; 160,000 airmen in Europe; more than 500,000 Soviet civilians; 67,078 French civilians killed by U.S.-U.K. bombing; 260,000 Chinese civilians; 305,000–600,000 civilians in Germany, including foreign workers; 330,000–500,000 Japanese civilians; 50,000 Italians killed by Allied bombing. Adding these numbers together and taking the high end where there are ranges gives a total of 2,197,673. The sources for these numbers (all of which are listed in the entry itself) include Keegan, 1989; Corvisier and Childs, 1994; and White, 2003.

230　**fired three thousand shells for each bomber:** This number is based on the efficiency of German 88mm guns, or "eighty-eights," at destroying Boeing B-17 Flying Fortresses, which was 2,805 shells per bomber destroyed. Westermann, 2011, cited in Wikipedia at http://bit.ly/surfacetoairmissiles.

231　**the Lockheed SR-72:** Demonstrations of the SR-72 could begin in 2018, with initial flights in 2023, and full service in 2030, according to Brad Leland, Lockheed's portfolio manager for air-breathing hypersonic technologies, in Norris, 2013.

CHAPTER 9: GOOD-BYE, GENIUS

232　**whenever he removed his Quaker-style "wide-awake" hat:** Galton recommends the wide-awake in his book *The Art of Travel* (Galton, 1872)—"I notice that old travellers in both hot and temperate countries have generally adopted a scanty 'wide-awake'"—so I have assumed he may have worn one. The wide-awake is also known as the "Quaker hat." Images at http://bit.ly/wideawakehat.

232　**He wrote later that they were "savages":** Comments from Galton, 1872. For example: "Seizing Food—On arriving at an encampment, the natives commonly run away in fright. If you are hungry, or in serious need of anything that they have, go boldly into their huts, take just what you want, and leave fully adequate payment. It is absurd to be over-scrupulous in these cases."

234　**in Britain, for example, an "E3" carcass is "excellent":** From the EC, or EUROP, classification grid in the U.K. Rural Payments Agency's "Beef Carcase Classification Scheme," available at http://bit.ly/carcase.

234　**"The negro race has occasionally, but very rarely":** Galton, 1869.

237　**In 2010, the average person:** According to the Global Burden of Disease 2010 study (Wang, 2013), the world average life expectency is 67.5 for men and 73.3 for women. The unweighted average of these two values is 70.4, which rounds to 70.

238 **"The power of population is indefinitely greater":** Malthus quotations from Malthus, 1798, and subsequent editions.

239 **famine declined as population increased:** See Devereux and Berge, 2000, for a comprehensive study of famine in the twentieth century.

239 **the First and Second World Wars combined:** Data from Pinker, 2010, which uses Brecke, 1999; Long and Brecke, 2003; and McEvedy and Jones, 1978 as sources.

BIBLIOGRAPHY

Adams, Douglas. *Life, the Universe and Everything (Hitchhiker's Guide to the Galaxy)*. Random House Publishing Group. Kindle Edition, 2008.

Albini, Adriana, Francesca Tosetti, Vincent W. Li, Douglas M. Noonan, and William W. Li. "Cancer Prevention by Targeting Angiogenesis." *Nature Reviews Clinical Oncology* 9, no. 9 (2012): 498–509.

Allen, Nicola J., and Ben A. Barres. "Neuroscience: Glia—More Than Just Brain Glue." *Nature* 457, no. 7230 (2009): 675–77.

Allen, Walter Ernest, ed. *Writers on Writing*. Phoenix House, 1948.

Altman, Lawrence K. "A Scientist, Gazing Toward Stockholm, Ponders 'What If?'" *New York Times,* December 6, 2005.

Amabile, Teresa M. *Creativity and Innovation in Organizations*. Harvard Business School Publishing, 1996.

———. *Creativity in Context: Update to "The Social Psychology of Creativity."* Westview Press, 1996.

———. *How to Kill Creativity*. Harvard Business School Publishing, 1998.

———. "Motivating Creativity in Organizations: On Doing What You Love and Loving What You Do." *California Management Review* 40, no. 1 (1997).

———. "Motivational Synergy: Toward New Conceptualizations of Intrinsic and Extrinsic Motivation in the Workplace." *Human Resource Management Review* 3, no. 3 (1993): 185–201.

———. "The Social Psychology of Creativity: A Componential Conceptualization." *Journal of Personality and Social Psychology* 45, no. 2 (1983): 357.

Amabile, Teresa M., Sigal G. Barsade, Jennifer S. Mueller, and Barry M. Staw. "Affect and Creativity at Work." *Administrative Science Quarterly* 50, no. 3 (2005): 367–403.

Amabile, Teresa M., Regina Conti, Heather Coon, Jeffrey Lazenby, and Michael Herron. "Assessing the Work Environment for Creativity." *Academy of Management Journal* 39, no. 5 (1996): 1154–84.

Amabile, Teresa M., Beth A. Hennessey, and Barbara S. Grossman. "Social Influences on Creativity: The Effects of Contracted-for Reward." *Journal of Personality and Social Psychology* 50, no. 1 (1986): 14.

Amabile, Teresa M., Karl G. Hill, Beth A. Hennessey, and Elizabeth M. Tighe. "The Work Preference Inventory: Assessing Intrinsic and Extrinsic Motivational Orientations." *Journal of Personality and Social Psychology* 66, no. 5 (1994): 950.

Antoniou, Anthony, P. D. P. Pharoah, Steven Narod, Harvey A. Risch, Jorunn E. Eyfjord, J. L. Hopper, Niklas Loman, Håkan Olsson, O. Johannsson, and Åke Borg. "Average Risks of Breast and Ovarian Cancer Associated with BRCA1 or BRCA2 Mutations Detected in Case Series Unselected for Family History: A Combined Analysis of 22 Studies." *The American Journal of Human Genetics* 72, no. 5, (2003): 1117–30.

Aristotle, *Nicomachean Ethics.* Translated by Robert C. Bartlett and Susan D. Collins. University of Chicago Press, 2011.

Arnold, Lois B. "The Bascom-Goldschmidt-Porter Correspondence: 1907 to 1922." *Earth Sciences History* 12, no. 2 (1993): 196–223.

Ashby, Ross. *Design for a Brain.* John Wiley, 1952.

Authier, André. *Early Days of X-Ray Crystallography.* Oxford University Press, 2013.

Bailey, Brian P., and Joseph A. Konstan. "On the Need for Attention-Aware Systems: Measuring Effects of Interruption on Task Performance, Error Rate, and Affective State." *Computers in Human Behavior* 22, no. 4 (2006): 685–708.

Barres, Ben A. "The Mystery and Magic of Glia: A Perspective on Their Roles in Health and Disease." *Neuron* 60, no. 3 (2008): 430–40.

Barrows, David Prescott. *The Ilongot or Ibilao of Luzon.* Science Press, 1910.

Bartolomei, F., E. Barbeau, M. Gavaret, M. Guye, A. McGonigal, J. Regis, and P. Chauvel. "Cortical Stimulation Study of the Role of Rhinal Cortex in Deja Vu and Reminiscence of Memories." *Neurology* 63, no. 5 (2004): 858–64.

Bates, Brian R. "Coleridge's Letter from a 'Friend' in Chapter 13 of the Biographia Literaria." Paper presented at the Rocky Mountain Modern Language Association (RMMLA) Conference. Boulder, CO, October 11–13, 2012.

Baum, L. Frank. *The Wonderful Wizard of Oz.* Oxford University Press, 2008.

Beckett, Samuel. *Worstward Ho.* John Calder, 1983.

Benfey, O. Theodore. "August Kekule and the Birth of the Structural Theory of Organic Chemistry in 1858." *Journal of Chemical Education* 35 (1958): 21.

Biello, David. "Fact or Fiction?: Archimedes Coined the Term 'Eureka!' in the Bath." *Scientific American.* December 8, 2006.

Block, Melissa, and Audie Cornish. "Why Woody Allen Is Always MIA at Oscars." NPR. *All Things Considered.* February 24, 2012.

Boland, C. Richard, Guenter Krejs, Michael Emmett, and Charles Richardson. "A Birthday Celebration for John S. Fordtran, MD." *Proceedings (Baylor University Medical Center)* 25, no. 3 (July 2012): 250–53.

Boston Evening Transcript. "Anthropologist Loses Life." March 31, 1909.

Bragg, William. *Concerning the Nature of Things.* 1925. Reprint, Courier Dover Publications, 2004.

Brecke, P. "The Conflict Dataset: 1400 A.D.–Present." Georgia Institute of Technology, 1999.

Brewster, David. *Memoirs of the Life, Writings, and Discoveries of Sir Isaac Newton.* Vol. 2. Edmonston and Douglas, 1860.

Bronowski, Jacob. *The Ascent of Man.* BBC Books, 2013.

Brooke, Alan, and Lesley Kipling. *Liberty or Death: Radicals, Republicans and Luddites c. 1793–1823.* Workers History Publications, 1993.

Brown, Jonathon D., and Frances M. Gallagher. "Coming to Terms with Failure: Private Self-Enhancement and Public Self-Effacement." *Journal of Experimental Social Psychology* 28, no. 1 (1992): 3–22.

Brown, Marcel. "The 'Lost' Steve Jobs Speech from 1983; Foreshadowing Wireless Networking, the iPad, and the App Store." *Life, Liberty, and Technology.* October 2, 2012. http://lifelibertytech.com/2012/10/02/the-lost-steve-jobs-speech-from-1983-foreshadowing-wireless-networking-the-ipad-and-the-app-store/#.

Burks, Barbara, Dortha Jensen, and Lewis Terman. *The Promise of Youth: Follow-up Studies of a Thousand Gifted Children.* Vol. 3 of *Genetic Studies of Genius Volume.* Stanford University Press, 1930.

Burroughs, Edgar Rice. *A Princess of Mars.* 1917. Reprint, eStar Books, 2012.

Burton, Robert. *On Being Certain: Believing You Are Right Even When You're Not.* St. Martin's Griffin, 2009.

Byers, Nina, and Gary Williams. *Out of the Shadows: Contributions of Twentieth-Century Women to Physics.* Cambridge University Press, 2010.

Cain, Susan. *Quiet: The Power of Introverts in a World That Can't Stop Talking.* Broadway Books, 2013.

———. "The Rise of the New Groupthink." *New York Times,* January 13, 2012.

Calhoun, Craig. "Robert K. Merton Remembered." *Footnotes: Newsletter of the American Sociological Society* 31, no. 33 (2003). http://www.asanet.org/footnotes/mar03/indextwo.html.

Callahan, Michael P., Karen E. Smith, H. James Cleaves, Josef Ruzicka, Jennifer C. Stern, Daniel P. Glavin, Christopher H. House, and Jason P. Dworkin. "Carbonaceous Meteorites Contain a Wide Range of Extraterrestrial Nucleobases." *Proceedings of the National Academy of Sciences* 108, no. 34 (2011): 13995–98.

Cameron, Judy, and W. David Pierce. "Reinforcement, Reward, and Intrinsic Motivation: A Meta-Analysis." *Review of Educational Research* 64, no. 3 (1994): 363–423.

Cameron, Ken. *Vanilla Orchids: Natural History and Cultivation.* Timber Press, 2011.

Caneva, Kenneth L. "Possible Kuhns in the History of Science: Anomalies of Incommensurable Paradigms." *Studies in History and Philosophy of Science* 31, no. 1 (2000): 87–124.

Carmi, Shai, Ken Y. Hui, Ethan Kochav, Xinmin Liu, James Xue, Fillan Grady, Saurav Guha, Kinnari Upadhyay, Dan Ben-Avraham, Semanti Mukherjee, B. Monica Bowen, Tinu Thomas, Joseph Vijai, Marc Cruts, Guy Froyen, Diether Lambrechts, Stéphane Plaisance, Christine Van Broeckhoven, Philip Van Damme, Herwig Van Marck, Nir Barzilai, Ariel Darvasi, Kenneth Offit, Susan Bressman, Laurie J. Ozelius, Inga Peter, Judy H. Cho, Harry Ostrer, Gil Atzmon, Lorraine N. Clark, Todd Lencz, and Itsik Pe'er. "Sequencing an Ashkenazi Reference Panel

Supports Population-Targeted Personal Genomics and Illuminates Jewish and European Origins." *Nature Communications* 5, no 4835 (September 9, 2014).

Carruthers, Peter. "The Cognitive Functions of Language." *Behavioral and Brain Sciences* 25, no. 6 (2002): 657–74.

——. "Creative Action in Mind." *Philosophical Psychology* 24, no. 4 (2011): 437–61.

——. "Human Creativity: Its Cognitive Basis, Its Evolution, and Its Connections with Childhood Pretence." *British Journal for the Philosophy of Science* 53, no. 2 (2002): 225–49.

Carruthers, Peter, and Peter K Smith. *Theories of Theories of Mind.* Cambridge University Press, 1996.

Carus-Wilson, E. M. "The English Cloth Industry in the Late Twelfth and Early Thirteenth Centuries." *Economic History Review* 14, no. 1 (1944): 32–50.

——. "An Industrial Revolution of the Thirteenth Century." *Economic History Review* 11, no. 1 (1941): 39–60.

Caselli, R. J. "Creativity: An Organizational Schema." *Cognitive and Behavioral Neurology* 22, no. 3 (2009): 143–54.

Chadwick, David. *Crooked Cucumber: The Life and Zen Teaching of Shunryu Suzuki.* Harmony, 2000.

Christner, Brent C., Cindy E. Morris, Christine M. Foreman, Rongman Cai, and David C. Sands. "Ubiquity of Biological Ice Nucleators in Snowfall." *Science* 319, no. 5867 (2008): 1214.

Chrysikou, Evangelia G. "When a Shoe Becomes a Hammer: Problem Solving as Goal-Derived, Ad Hoc Categorization." PhD Diss., Temple University, 2006.

Cipolla, Carlo M. *Literacy and Development in the West.* Penguin Books, 1969.

Coleridge, Samuel Taylor. *Biographia Literaria.* 2 vols. Oxford University Press, 1907.

"College Aide Ends Life." *New York Times,* February 24, 1940.

Collins, Randall. *Interaction Ritual Chains.* Princeton University Press, 2004.

——. "Interaction Ritual Chains, Power and Property: The Micro-Macro Connection as an Empirically Based Theoretical Problem." *Micro-Macro Link* (1987): 193–206.

——. "On the Microfoundations of Macrosociology." *American Journal of Sociology* (1981): 984–1014.

Coleridge, Samuel Taylor. 2011. *The Complete Poetical Works of Samuel Taylor Coleridge.* Vols. I and II. Kindle Edition. Public domain.

Cooke, Robert. *Dr. Folkman's War: Angiogenesis and the Struggle to Defeat Cancer.* Random House, 2001.

Comarow, Avery. "Best Children's Hospitals 2013–14: The Honor Roll." *U.S. News & World Report,* June 10, 2014.

Cornell University Library, Division of Rare & Manuscript Collections. "How Did Mozart Compose?" 2002. http://rmc.library.cornell.edu/mozart/compose.htm.

——. "The Mozart Myth: Tales of a Forgery." 2002, http://rmc.library.cornell.edu /mozart/myth.htm.

Cornwell, Erin York. "Opening and Closing the Jury Room Door: A Sociohistorical Consideration of the 1955 Chicago Jury Project Scandal." *Justice System Journal* 31, no. 1 (2010): 49–73.

Corvisier, André, and John Childs. A Dictionary of Military History and the Art of War. Wiley-Blackwell, 1994.

Costa, Marta D., Joana B. Pereira, Maria Pala, Verónica Fernandes, Anna Olivieri, Alessandro Achilli, Ugo A Perego, Sergei Rychkov, Oksana Naumova, and Jiri Hatina. "A Substantial Prehistoric European Ancestry Amongst Ashkenazi Maternal Lineages." *Nature Communications* 4 (2013).

Cox, Catherine Morris. *The Early Mental Traits of Three Hundred Geniuses.* Stanford University Press, 1926.

Cramond, Bonnie. "The Torrance Tests of Creative Thinking: From Design Through Establishment of Predictive Validity." In Rena Faye Subotnik and Karen D. Arnold, eds., *Beyond Terman: Contemporary Longitudinal Studies of Giftedness and Talent.* Greenwood Publishing Group, 1994.

Cropley, Arthur J. *More Ways Than One: Fostering Creativity.* Ablex Publishing, 1992.

Crowe, Cameron. "The True Life Confessions of Fleetwood Mac." *Rolling Stone* 235 (1977).

Csikszentmihalyi, Mihaly. *Creativity: Flow and the Psychology of Discovery and Invention.* Harper Perennial, 1996.

———. *Finding Flow: The Psychology of Engagement with Everyday Life.* Masterminds Series. Basic Books, 1998.

———. *Flow: The Psychology of Optimal Experience.* Harper Perennial Modern Classics, 2008.

Curie, Marie. "Radium and the New Concepts in Chemistry." Nobel lecture, 1911. http://www.nobelprize.org/nobel prizes/chemistry/laureates/1911/marie-curie- lec- ture.html.

Darwin, Charles. *The Variation of Animals and Plants Under Domestication.* John Murray, 1868.

Davis, Michael. *Street Gang: The Complete History of Sesame Street.* Penguin Books, 2009.

De Groot, Adriaan. *Thought and Choice in Chess.* Psychological Studies. Mouton De Gruyter, 1978.

Descartes, René. *The Passions of the Soul.* Hackett, 1989.

Dettmer, Peggy. "Improving Teacher Attitudes Toward Characteristics of the Cre- atively Gifted." *Gifted Child Quarterly* 25, no. 1 (1981): 11–16.

Devereux, Stephen. *Famine in the Twentieth Century.* Brighton: Institute of Develop- ment Studies, 2000.

Dickens, Charles. *A Christmas Carol.* Simon and Schuster, 1843.

Dickens, Charles, and Gilbert Ashville Pierce. *The Writings of Charles Dickens: Life, Let- ters, and Speeches of Charles Dickens; with Biographical Sketches of the Principal Illustra- tors of Dicken's [sic] Works.* Vol. 30. Houghton, Mifflin and Company, 1894.

Dietrich, Arne, and Riam Kanso. "A Review of Eeg, Erp, and Neuroimaging Studies of Creativity and Insight." *Psychological Bulletin* 136, no. 5 (2010): 822.

Dolan, Kerry A. *Inside Inventionland. Forbes* 178, no. 11 (2006): 70ff.

Dorfman, Jennifer, Victor A. Shames, and John F. Kihlstrom. "Intuition, Incubation, and Insight: Implicit Cognition in Problem Solving." *Implicit Cognition* (1996): 257–96.

Dostoyevsky, Fyodor, and Anna Grigoryevna Dostoyevskaya. *Dostoevsky: Letters and Reminiscences.* Books for Libraries Press, 1971.

Douglas, Edward. "A Chat with Frank Oz." ComingSoon.net. August 10, 2007, http:// www.comingsoon.net/news/movienews.php?id=23056.

Douglass, A. E. "The Illusions of Vision and the Canals of Mars." (1907).

Downes, Larry, and Paul Nunes. *Big Bang Disruption: Strategy in the Age of Devastating Innovation.* Portfolio, 2014.

Doyle, Sir Arthur Conan, and the Conan Doyle Estate. "The Complete Sherlock Holmes." 1877. Reprint, Complete Works Collection, 2011.

Drew, Trafton, Karla Evans, Melissa L.-H. Võ, Francine L. Jacobson, and Jeremy M. Wolfe. "Informatics in Radiology: What Can You See in a Single Glance and How Might This Guide Visual Search in Medical Images?" *Radiographics* 33, no. 1 (2013): 263–74.

Drew, Trafton, Melissa L.-H. Võ, and Jeremy M Wolfe. "The Invisible Gorilla Strikes Again: Sustained Inattentional Blindness in Expert Observers." *Psychological Science* 24, no. 9 (2013): 1848–53.

Drews, Frank A. "Profiles in Driver Distraction: Effects of Cell Phone Conversations on Younger and Older Drivers." *Human Factors: The Journal of the Human Factors and Ergonomics Society* 46, no. 4 (2004): 640–49.

Driscoll, Carlos A., Marilyn Menotti-Raymond, Alfred L. Roca, Karsten Hupe, Warren E. Johnson, Eli Geffen, Eric H. Harley, Miguel Delibes, Dominique Pontier, Andrew C. Kitchener, Nobuyuki Yamaguchi, Stephen J. O'Brien, and David W. Macdonald. "The Near Eastern Origin of Cat Domestication." *Science* 317, no. 5837 (2007): 519–23.

Duncker, Karl. *On Problem Solving.* Translated by Lynne S. Lees. *Psychological Monographs* 58 (1945): i–113.

———. "Ethical Relativity? (An Enquiry into the Psychology of Ethics)." *Mind* (1939): 39–57.

———. "The Influence of Past Experience upon Perceptual Properties." *The American Journal of Psychology* (1939): 255–65.

Duncker, Karl, and Isadore Krechevsky. "On Solution-Achievement." *Psychological Review* 46, no. 2 (1939): 176.

Dunnette, Marvin D., John Campbell, and Kay Jaastad. "The Effect of Group Participation on Brainstorming Effectiveness for 2 Industrial Samples." *Journal of Applied Psychology* 47, no. 1 (1963): 30.

Eckberg, Douglas Lee, and Lester Hill Jr. "The Paradigm Concept and Sociology: A Critical Review." *American Sociological Review* (1979): 925–37.

Ecott, Tim. *Vanilla: Travels in Search of the Ice Cream Orchid.* Grove Press, 2005.

Edwards, Robert. "What the Neuron Tells Glia." *Neuron* 61, no. 6 (2009): 811–12.

Ehrenburg, Ilya. *Life of the Automobile.* Serpent's Tail, 1929.

Einstein, Albert. "Fundamental Ideas and Problems of the Theory of Relativity." *Les Prix Nobel 1922* (1923): 482–90.

———. "How I Created the Theory of Relativity." Lecture given in Kyoto, December 14, 1922. Translated by Yoshimasa A. Ono. *Physics Today* 35, no. 8 (1982): 45–47.

Eisen, Cliff, and Simon P. Keefe. *The Cambridge Mozart Encyclopedia.* Cambridge University Press, 2007.

Eisenberger, Naomi I., and M. D. Lieberman. "Why Rejection Hurts: A Common Neural Alarm System for Physical and Social Pain." *Trends in Cognitive Sciences* 8, no. 7 (2004): 294–300.

Eisenberger, Naomi I., and Matthew D. Lieberman. "Why It Hurts to Be Left Out:

The Neurocognitive Overlap Between Physical and Social Pain." In *The Social Outcast: Ostracism, Social Exclusion, Rejection, and Bullying*, edited by Kipling D. Williams, Joseph P. Forgas, and William von Hippel, 109–30. Routledge, 2005.

Eisenberger, Robert, and Judy Cameron. "Detrimental Effects of Reward: Reality or Myth?" *American Psychologist* 51, no. 11 (1996): 1153.

Eisenberger, Robert, W. David Pierce, and Judy Cameron. "Effects of Reward on Intrinsic Motivation—Negative, Neutral, and Positive: Comment on Deci, Koestner, and Ryan (1999)." *Psychological Bulletin* 125, no. 6 (1999): 677–91.

Elias, Scott. *Origins of Human Innovation and Creativity*. Vol. 16, Developments in Quaternary Science. Elsevier, 2012.

Eliot, Thomas Stearns. "Banquet Speech: December 10, 1948." In *Nobel Lectures, Literature 1901–1967*, edited by Horst Frenz. Elsevier Publishing, 1969.

Emerson, Ralph Waldo. *Journals of Ralph Waldo Emerson, with Annotations*. University of Michigan Library, 1909.

Emling, Shelley. *Marie Curie and Her Daughters: The Private Lives of Science's First Family*. Palgrave Macmillan, 2013.

Epstein, Stephan R. "Craft Guilds, Apprenticeship, and Technological Change in Pre-industrial Europe." *Journal of Economic History* 58, no. 3 (1998): 684–713.

Ercin, A. Ertug, Maite Martinez Aldaya, and Arjen Y. Hoekstra. "Corporate Water Footprint Accounting and Impact Assessment: The Case of the Water Footprint of a Sugar-Containing Carbonated Beverage." *Water Resources Management* 25, no. 2 (2011): 721–41.

Ergenzinger, Edward R., Jr. "The American Inventor's Protection Act: A Legislative History." *Wake Forest Intellectual Property Law Journal* 7 (2006): 145.

Eroglu, Cagla, and Ben A. Barres. "Regulation of Synaptic Connectivity by Glia." *Nature* 468, no. 7321 (2010): 223–31.

Everly, George S., Jr., and Jeffrey M. Lating. *A Clinical Guide to the Treatment of the Human Stress Response*. Springer Series on Stress and Coping. Springer, 2002.

Feist, Gregory J. *The Psychology of Science and the Origins of the Scientific Mind*. Yale University Press, 2008.

Feldhusen, John F., and Donald J. Treffinger. "Teachers' Attitudes and Practices in Teaching Creativity and Problem-Solving to Economically Disadvantaged and Minority Children." *Psychological Reports* 37, no. 3f (1975): 1161–62.

Fermi, Laura, and Gilberto Bernardini. *Galileo and the Scientific Revolution*. Dover, 2003.

Ferry, Georgina. *Dorothy Hodgkin: A Life*. Cold Spring Harbor Laboratory Press, 2000.

Festinger, Leon. *Conflict, Decision, and Dissonance*. Stanford University Press, 1964.
———. *A Theory of Cognitive Dissonance*. 1957. Reprint, Stanford University Press, 1962.
———. "Cognitive Dissonance." *Scientific American* 207, no. 4 (1962): 92–102.

Festinger, Leon, Kurt W. Back, and Stanley Schachter. *Social Pressures in Informal Groups: A Study of Human Factors in Housing*. Stanford University Press, 1950.

Festinger, Leon, and James M. Carlsmith. "Cognitive Consequences of Forced Compliance." *Journal of Abnormal and Social Psychology* 58, no. 2 (1959): 203.

Festinger, Leon, Henry W. Riecken, and Stanley Schachter. *When Prophecy Fails: A Social and Psychological Study of a Modern Group That Predicted the Destruction of the World*. Harper Torchbooks, 1956.

Fields, Rick. *How the Swans Came to the Lake*. Shambhala, 1992.

Flaherty, Alice Weaver. *The Midnight Disease: The Drive to Write, Writer's Block, and the Creative Brain*. Mariner Books, 2005.

Flournoy, Théodore. *From India to the Planet Mars: A Study of a Case of Somnambulism*. Harper & Bros., 1900.

Flynn, Francis J., and Jennifer A. Chatman. "Strong Cultures and Innovation: Oxymoron or Opportunity." In *International Handbook of Organizational Culture and Climate* edited by Cary L. Cooper, Sue Cartwright, and P. Christopher Earley. Wiley, 2001, 263–87.

Franklin, Rosalind E. "Location of the Ribonucleic Acid in the Tobacco Mosaic Virus Particle." *Nature* 177, no. 4516 (1956): 929–30.

———. "Structural Resemblance Between Schramm's Repolymerised A-Protein and Tobacco Mosaic Virus." *Biochimica et Biophysica Acta* 18 (1955): 313–14.

———. "Structure of Tobacco Mosaic Virus." *Nature* 175, no. 4452 (1955): 379.

Franklin, Rosalind E., Donald L. D. Caspar, and Aaron Klug. "The Structure of Viruses as Determined by X-Ray Diffraction." *Plant Pathology, Problems and Progress* 1958 (1958): 447–61.

Franklin, Rosalind E., and Barry Commoner. "Abnormal Protein Associated with Tobacco Mosaic Virus; X-Ray Diffraction by an Abnormal Protein (B8) Associated with Tobacco Mosaic Virus." *Nature* 175, no. 4468 (1955): 1076.

Franklin, Rosalind E., and A. Klug. "The Nature of the Helical Groove on the Tobacco Mosaic Virus Particle X-Ray Diffraction Studies." *Biochimica et Biophysica Acta* 19 (1956): 403–16.

———. "The Splitting of Layer Lines in X-Ray Fibre Diagrams of Helical Structures: Application to Tobacco Mosaic Virus." *Acta Crystallographica* 8, no. 12 (1955): 777–80.

Freedberg, A. Stone, and Louis E. Barron. "The Presence of Spirochetes in Human Gastric Mucosa." *American Journal of Digestive Diseases* 7, no. 10 (1940): 443–45.

Freeman, Karen. "Dr. Ian A. H. Munro, 73, Editor of the Lancet Medical Journal." *New York Times*, February 3, 1997.

Fuller, Steve. *Thomas Kuhn: A Philosophical History for Our Times*. University of Chicago Press, 2001.

Gabai-Kapara, Efrat, Amnon Lahad, Bella Kaufman, Eitan Friedman, Shlomo Segev, Paul Renbaum, Rachel Beeri, Moran Gal, Julia Grinshpun-Cohen, Karen Djemal, Jessica B. Mandell, Ming K. Lee, Uziel Beller, Raphael Catane, Mary-Claire King, and Ephrat Levy-Lahad. "Population-Based Screening for Breast and Ovarian Cancer Risk Due to *BRCA1* and *BRCA2*." *Proceedings of the National Academy of Sciences*, September 5, 2014.

Galilei, Galileo. "La Bilancetta." *Galileo and the Scientific Revolution* (1961): 133–43.

Galton, Francis. *The Art of Travel; or, Shifts and Contrivances Available in Wild Countries*. (1872). Digitized June 29, 2006. Google Book.

———. *English Men of Science: Their Nature and Nurture*. D. Appleton, 1875.

———. *Hereditary Genius*. Macmillan, 1869.

———. *Inquiries into Human Faculty and Its Development*. Macmillan, 1883.

———. *Natural Inheritance*. Macmillan, 1889.

Gardner, Howard E. *Creating Minds: An Anatomy of Creativity Seen Through the Lives of Freud, Einstein, Picasso, Stravinsky, Eliot, Graham, and Ghandi*. Basic Books, 2011.

Garfield, Eugene. "A Different Sort of Great-Books List—the 50 20th-Century Works Most Cited in the Arts and Humanities Citation Index, 1976–1983." *Current Contents* 16 (1987): 3–7.

Getzels, Jacob W., and Philip W. Jackson. *Creativity and Intelligence: Explorations with Gifted Students.* Wiley, 1962, pp. xvii, 293.

Glasser, William. *Positive Addiction.* Harper & Row New York, 1976.

———. "Positive Addiction." *Journal of Extension* (May/June 1977): 4–8.

———. "Promoting Client Strength Through Positive Addiction." *Canadian Journal of Counselling and Psychotherapy/Revue Canadienne de Counseling et de Psychothérapie* 11, no. 4 (2012).

Gleick, James. "The Paradigm Shifts." *New York Times Magazine,* December 29, 1996.

Glucksberg, Sam. "The Influence of Strength of Drive on Functional Fixedness and Perceptual Recognition." *Journal of Experimental Psychology* 63, no. 1 (1962): 36.

Glynn, Jenifer. *My Sister Rosalind Franklin: A Family Memoir.* Oxford University Press, 2012.

Gonzales, Laurence. *Deep Survival: Who Lives, Who Dies, and Why.* W. W. Norton, 2004.

Gould, Stephen Jay. *Ever Since Darwin.* W. W. Norton, 1977.

Guralnick, Peter. *Searching for Robert Johnson.* Dutton Adult, 1989.

Hadamard, Jacques. *The Mathematician's Mind.* Princeton University Press, 1996.

Haines, Catharine M. C. *International Women in Science: A Biographical Dictionary to 1950.* ABC-CLIO, 2001.

Ham, Denise. *Marie Sklodowska Curie: The Woman Who Opened the Nuclear Age.* 21st Century Science Associates, 2002.

Hansen, Amy. "Lyrics of Rap and Lines of Stage Help Mattapan Teen Turn to Better Life." *Boston Globe,* December 5, 2012.

Harbluk, Joanne L., Y. Ian Noy, and Moshe Eizenman. *The Impact of Cognitive Distraction on Driver Visual Behaviour and Vehicle Control.* Transport Canada, 2002., http://www.tc.gc.ca/motorvehiclesafety/tp/tp13889/pdf/tp13889es.pdf.

Harlow, Harry F. "Learning and Satiation of Response in Intrinsically Motivated Complex Puzzle Performance by Monkeys." *Journal of Comparative and Physiological Psychology* 43, no. 4 (1950): 289.

———. "The Nature of Love." *American Psychologist* 13, no. 12 (1958): 673.

Harlow, Harry F., Margaret Kuenne Harlow, and Donald R. Meyer. "Learning Motivated by a Manipulation Drive." *Journal of Experimental Psychology* 40, no. 2 (1950): 228.

Hegel, Georg Wilhelm Friedrich. *The Philosophy of History.* Translated by J. Sibree. Courier Dover Publications, 2004.

Heidegger, Martin. *The Principle of Reason.* Studies in Continental Thought. Indiana University Press, 1956.

Heider, F. *The Psychology of Interpersonal Relations.* Psychology Press, 1958.

Heilman, Kenneth M. *Creativity and the Brain.* Psychology Press, 2005.

Hélie, Sebastien, and Ron Sun. "Implicit Cognition in Problem Solving." In *The Psychology of Problem Solving: An Interdisciplinary Approach,* edited by Sebastien Helie. Nova Science Publishing, 2012.

———. "Incubation, Insight, and Creative Problem Solving: A Unified Theory and a Connectionist Model." *Psychological Review* 117, no. 3 (2010): 994.

Hennessey, B. A., and T. M. Amabile. "Creativity." *Annual Review of Psychology* 61 (2010): 569–98.

Hennessey, Beth A., and Teresa M. Amabile. *Creativity and Learning (What Research Says to the Teacher)*. National Education Association, 1987.

Heppenheimer, T. A. *First Flight: The Wright Brothers and the Invention of the Airplane.* Wiley, 2003.

Hill, John Spencer. *A Coleridge Companion: An Introduction to the Major Poems and the "Biographia Literaria."* Prentice Hall College Division, 1984.

Hollander, Jason. "Renowned Columbia Sociologist and National Medal of Science Winner Robert K. Merton Dies at 92." Columbia News: The Public Affairs and Record Home Page, February 5, 2003, http://www.columbia.edu/cu/news/03/02 /robertKMerton.html.

Holmes, Chris E., Jagoda Jasielec, Jamie E. Levis, Joan Skelly, and Hyman B. Muss. "Initiation of Aspirin Therapy Modulates Angiogenic Protein Levels in Women with Breast Cancer Receiving Tamoxifen Therapy." *Clinical and Translational Science* 6, no. 5 (2013): 386–90.

Holmes, K. C., and Rosalind E. Franklin. "The Radial Density Distribution in Some Strains of Tobacco Mosaic Virus." *Virology* 6, no. 2 (1958): 328–36.

Hope, Jack. "A Better Mousetrap." *American Heritage,* October 1996, 90–97.

Hornaday, Anna. "Woody Allen on 'Rome,' Playing Himself and Why He Skips the Oscars." *Washington Post,* June 28, 2012.

Hume, David. *An Enquiry Concerning Human Understanding.* Oxford Philosophical Texts. Oxford University Press, 1748.

Huxley, Aldous. *Texts and Pretexts: An Anthology with Commentaries.* 1932. Reprint, Greenwood, 1976.

Hyman, Ira E., S. Matthew Boss, Breanne M. Wise, Kira E. McKenzie, and Jenna M. Caggiano. "Did You See the Unicycling Clown? Inattentional Blindness While Walking and Talking on a Cell Phone." *Applied Cognitive Psychology* 24, no. 5 (2010): 597–607.

Isherwood, Christopher. *Goodbye to Berlin.* HarperCollins, 1939.

Ito, S. "Anatomic Structure of the Gastric Mucosa." *Handbook of Physiology* 2 (1967): 705–41.

Iyer, Pico. "The Joy of Quiet." *New York Times,* December 29, 2011.

Jackson, Philip W. *Life in Classrooms.* Teachers College Press, 1968.

———. "The Student's World." *Elementary School Journal* (1966): 345–57.

Jahn, Otto. *Life of Mozart.* 3 vols. Cambridge Library Collection: Music. Cambridge University Press, 2013.

Associated Press. "Jap Reception Center Nears Completion." April 4, 1942. University of California Japanese American Relocation Digital Archive Photograph Collection. http://bit.ly/japreception.

Jenkin, John. *William and Lawrence Bragg, Father and Son: The Most Extraordinary Collaboration in Science.* Oxford University Press, 2008.

Johnson, Clarence L. "Kelly," with Maggie Smith. *Kelly: More Than My Share of It All.* Random House, 1990.

Jones, Brian Jay. *Jim Henson: The Biography.* Ballantine Books, 2013.

Jørgensen, Jes K., Cécile Favre, Suzanne E. Bisschop, Tyler L. Bourke, Ewine F. van Dishoeck, and Markus Schmalzl. "Detection of the Simplest Sugar, Glycolaldehyde, in a Solar-Type Protostar with Alma." *Astrophysical Journal Letters* 757, no. 1 (2012): L4.

Kahn, Roger. *The Boys of Summer.* Harper Perennial Modern Classics, 1972.

Kahneman, Daniel. *Thinking, Fast and Slow.* Farrar, Straus and Giroux, 2013.

———. "Attention and Effort." Prentice-Hall, 1973.

———. "Don't Blink! The Hazards of Confidence." *New York Times,* October 23, 2011.

Kahneman, Daniel, and Gary Klein. "Conditions for Intuitive Expertise: A Failure to Disagree." *American Psychologist* 64, no. 6 (2009): 515.

Kahneman, Daniel, and Amos Tversky. "Choices, Values, and Frames." *American Psychologist* 39, no. 4 (1984): 341.

———. "On the Psychology of Prediction." *Psychological Review* 80, no. 4 (1973): 237.

———. "Subjective Probability: A Judgment of Representativeness," *Cognitive Psychology* 3, no. 3 (1972): 430–54.

Kaufman, James C., and Robert J. Sternberg, eds. *The Cambridge Handbook of Creativity* Cambridge Handbooks in Psychology. Cambridge University Press, 2010.

Keegan, John. *The Second World War.* Random House, 1989.

Kenning, Kaleene. "Ohabai Shalome Synagogue." Examiner.com, March 2, 2010.

Kepler, Johannes. *The Six-Cornered Snowflake.* Paul Dry Books, 1966.

Kidd, Mark, and Irvin M. Modlin. "A Century of *Helicobacter pylori.*" *Digestion* 59, no. 1 (1998): 1–15.

Kimble, Gregory A., and Michael Wertheimer. *Portraits of Pioneers in Psychology.* Vol. 3. American Psychological Association, 1998.

King, Stephen. *Danse Macabre.* Gallery Books, 2010.

———. *On Writing: A Memoir of the Craft.* Pocket Books, 2001.

Kleinmuntz, Benjamin. *Formal Representation of Human Judgment.* Carnegie Series on Cognition. John Wiley & Sons, 1968.

Kraybill, Donald B., Karen M. Johnson-Weiner, and Steven M. Nolt. *The Amish.* Johns Hopkins University Press, 2013.

Kroger, S., B. Rutter, R. Stark, S. Windmann, C. Hermann, and A. Abraham. "Using a Shoe as a Plant Pot: Neural Correlates of Passive Conceptual Expansion." *Brain Research* 1430 (2012): 52–61.

Kruger, J., and D. Dunning. "Unskilled and Unaware of It: How Difficulties in Recognizing One's Own Incompetence Lead to Inflated Self-Assessments." *Journal of Personality and Social Psychology* 77, no. 6 (1999): 1121–34.

Krützen, Michael, Janet Mann, Michael R. Heithaus, Richard C. Connor, Lars Bejder, and William B. Sherwin. "Cultural Transmission of Tool Use in Bottlenose Dolphins." *Proceedings of the National Academy of Sciences of the United States of America* 102, no. 25 (2005): 8939–43.

Kuhn, Thomas S. *Black-Body Theory and the Quantum Discontinuity, 1894–1912.* University of Chicago Press, 1987.

———. *The Copernican Revolution: Planetary Astronomy in the Development of Western Thought.* Harvard University Press, 1992.

———. *The Essential Tension: Selected Studies in Scientific Tradition and Change.* University of Chicago Press, 1977.

———. *The Road Since Structure: Philosophical Essays, 1970–1993, with an Autobiographical Interview.* University of Chicago Press, 2002.

———. *The Structure of Scientific Revolutions.* 3rd ed. University of Chicago Press, 1996.

Lach-Szyrma, Wladyslaw Somerville. *Aleriel; or, A Voyage to Other Worlds. A Tale, Etc.* 1883. Reprint, British Library, Historical Print Editions, 2011.

Lakatos, Imre, Thomas S. Kuhn, W. N. Watkins, Stephen Toulmin, L. Pearce Williams, Margaret Masterman, and P. K. Feyerabend. *Criticism and the Growth of Knowledge: Proceedings of the International Colloquium in the Philosophy of Science, London, 1965.* Cambridge University Press, 1970.

Langer, J. S. "Instabilities and Pattern Formation in Crystal Growth." *Reviews of Modern Physics* 52, no. 1 (1980): 1.

Langton, Christopher G., and Katsunori Shimohara. *Artificial Life V: Proceedings of the Fifth International Workshop on the Synthesis and Simulation of Living Systems (Complex Adaptive Systems).* A Bradford Book, 1997.

Laplace, Pierre Simon. *Essai Philosophique sur les Probabilités.* Vve Courcier, 1814.

Largo, Michael. *God's Lunatics: Lost Souls, False Prophets, Martyred Saints, Murderous Cults, Demonic Nuns, and Other Victims of Man's Eternal Search for the Divine.* William Morrow Paperbacks, 2010.

Lawson, Carol. *Behind the Best Sellers: Stephen King.* Westview Press, 1979.

Lax, Eric. *Woody Allen: A Biography.* Da Capo Press, 2000.

———. *Conversations with Woody Allen.* Random House, 2009.

Lee, R. E., Jr., Gareth J. Warren, and Lawrence V. Gusta. *Biological Ice Nucleation and Its Applications.* American Phytopathological Society, 1995.

Lehrer, Jonah. *Imagine: How Creativity Works.* Houghton Mifflin, 2012.

Lennard, Reginald. *Rural England, 1086–1135: A Study of Social and Agrarian Conditions.* Oxford: Clarendon Press, 1959.

———. "Early English Fulling Mills: Additional Examples." *Economic History Review* 3, no. 3 (1951): 342–43.

Libbrecht, Kenneth G. "Morphogenesis on Ice: The Physics of Snow Crystals." *Engineering and Science* 64, no. 1 (2001): 10–19.

Linde, Nancy. *Cancer Warrior.* First aired on February 27, 2001, by PBS. Written, produced and directed by Nancy Linde.

Lindsay, Kenneth C., and Peter Vergo, eds. *Kandinsky: Complete Writings on Art.* Da Capo Press, 1994.

Long, William J., and Peter Brecke. *War and Reconciliation: Reason and Emotion in Conflict Resolution.* MIT Press, 2003.

Lowell, Percival. "Tores of Saturn." *Lowell Observatory Bulletin* 1 (1907): 186–90.

Lucas, Adam. *Wind, Water, Work: Ancient and Medieval Milling Technology.* Leiden, Koninklijke Brill, 2006.

Lum, Timothy E., Rollin J. Fairbanks, Elliot C. Pennington, and Frank L. Zwemer. "Profiles in Patient Safety: Misplaced Femoral Line Guidewire and Multiple Failures to Detect the Foreign Body on Chest Radiography." *Academic Emergency Medicine* 12, no. 7 (2005): 658–62.

Mack, Arien, and Irvin Rock. *Inattentional Blindness.* A Bradford Book, 2000.

MacLeod, Hugh. *Ignore Everybody: And 39 Other Keys to Creativity.* Portfolio Hardcover, 2009.

Maddox, Brenda. *Rosalind Franklin: The Dark Lady of DNA.* Harper Perennial, 2003.

Malthus, Thomas Robert. *An Essay on the Principle of Population, as It Affects the Future Improvement of Society.* Dent, 1973.

Mankins, Michael, Chris Brahm, and Gregory Caimi. "Your Scarcest Resource." *Harvard Business Review* 92, no. 5 (2014): 74–80.

Mann, Thomas. *Deutsche Ansprache: Ein Appell an die Vernunft (An Appeal to Reason)*. S. Fischer, 1930.

Markel, Howard. "'I Have Seen My Death': How the World Discovered the X-Ray." PBS NewsHour: The Rundown, December 20, 2012, http://www.pbs.org /newshour/rundown/i-have-seen-my-death-how-the-world-discovered-the-x-ray.

Marshall, Barry. *Helicobacter Pioneers: Firsthand Accounts from the Scientists Who Discovered Helicobacters, 1892–1982*. Wiley-Blackwell, 2002.

Marshall, Barry J., and J. Robin Warren. "Unidentified Curved Bacilli in the Stomach of Patients with Gastritis and Peptic Ulceration." *Lancet* 323, no. 8390 (1984): 1311–15.

Martin, Douglas. "Robert Galambos, Neuroscientist Who Showed How Bats Navigate, Dies at 96." *New York Times,* July 15, 2010.

Massey, Howard. *Behind the Glass: Top Record Producers Tell How They Craft the Hits*. Backbeat Books, 2000.

Masterman, Margaret. "The Nature of a Paradigm." In Lakatos, Imre, and Alan Musgrave, eds. *Criticism and the Growth of Knowledge*. Cambridge University Press, 1970.

McEvedy, Colin, and Richard Jones. *Atlas of World Population History*. Harmondsworth: Penguin Books, 1978.

McGraw, Kenneth O., and John C. McCullers. "Evidence of a Detrimental Effect of Extrinsic Incentives on Breaking a Mental Set." *Journal of Experimental Social Psychology* 15, no. 3 (1979): 285–94.

Merton, Robert K. *On the Shoulders of Giants: A Shandean Postscript*. University of Chicago Press, 1993.

———. "The Matthew Effect in Science." *Science* 159, no. 3810 (1968): 56–63.

———. "The Matthew Effect in Science, II: Cumulative Advantage and the Symbolism of Intellectual Property." *Isis* (1988): 606–23.

Metcalfe, Janet, and David Wiebe. "Intuition in Insight and Noninsight Problem Solving." *Memory & Cognition* 15, no. 3 (1987): 238–46.

Meyer, Steven J. "Introduction: Whitehead Now." *Configurations* 13 (2005): 1–33.

Mithen, Steven, ed. *Creativity in Human Evolution and Prehistory*. Routledge, 2014.

———. *The Prehistory of the Mind: The Cognitive Origins of Art, Religion and Science*. Thames & Hudson, 1996.

Momsen, Bill. "*Mariner IV:* First Flyby of Mars: Some Personal Experiences." http://bit .ly/billmomsen (2006).

Morozov, Evgeny. *To Save Everything, Click Here: The Folly of Technological Solutionism*. PublicAffairs, 2013.

Morris, James M. *On Mozart*. Woodrow Wilson Center Press and Cambridge University Press, 1994.

Mossberg, Walt. "The Steve Jobs I Knew." *AllThingsD,* October 5, 2012. http:// allthingsd.com/20121005/the-steve-jobs-i-knew/.

Moszkowski, Alexander. *Conversations with Einstein*. Horizon Press, 1973.

Mueller, Jennifer S., Shimul Melwani, and Jack A. Goncalo. "The Bias Against Creativity: Why People Desire but Reject Creative Ideas." *Psychological Science* 23, no. 1 (2012): 13–17.

Munro, Ian. "Pyloric Campylobacter Finds a Volunteer." *Lancet* 1, no. 8436 (1985): 1021–22.

———. "Spirals and Ulcers." *Lancet* 1, no. 8390 (1984): 1336–37.

Munro, John. "The Symbiosis of Towns and Textiles: Urban Institutions and the Changing Fortunes of Cloth Manufacturing in the Low Countries and England, 1270–1570." *Journal of Early Modern History* 3, no. 3 (1999): 1–74.

Munro, John H. "Industrial Energy from Water-Mills in the European Economy, 5th to 18th Centuries: The Limitations of Power." University Library of Munich, 2002.

Nakaya, Ukichiro. *Snow Crystals: Natural and Artificial.* Harvard University Press, 1954.

Neisser, Ulric, and Nicole Harsch. "Phantom Flashbulbs: False Recollections of Hearing the News About *Challenger.*" In *Affect and Accuracy in Recall: Studies of "Flashbulb" Memories,* edited by Eugene Winograd and Ulric Neisser. Cambridge University Press, 1992, pp. 9–31.

Newell, Allen, J. Clifford Shaw, and Herbert Alexander Simon. *The Processes of Creative Thinking.* Rand Corporation, 1959.

Newton, Isaac, I. Bernard Cohen, and Marie Boas Hall. *Isaac Newton's Papers & Letters on Natural Philosophy and Related Documents.* Harvard University Press, 1978.

Nickles, Thomas. *Thomas Kuhn.* Contemporary Philosophy in Focus. Cambridge University Press, 2002.

Nisbett, Richard E., and Timothy D. Wilson. "Telling More Than We Can Know: Verbal Reports on Mental Processes." *Psychological Review* 84, no. 3 (1977): 231.

Norris, Guy. *Skunk Works Reveals SR-71 Successor Plan.* New York: Springer-Verlag, 2013.

Ochse, R. A. *Before the Gates of Excellence: The Determinants of Creative Genius.* Cambridge Greek and Latin Classics. Cambridge University Press, 1990.

Ogburn, William F., and Dorothy Thomas. 1922. "Are Inventions Inevitable? A Note on Social Evolution." *Political Science Quarterly* 37, no. 1 (March 1922): 83–98.

Olton, Robert M. "Experimental Studies of Incubation: Searching for the Elusive." *Journal of Creative Behavior* 13, no. 1 (1979): 9–22.

Olton, Robert M., and David M. Johnson. "Mechanisms of Incubation in Creative Problem Solving." *American Journal of Psychology* (1976): 617–30.

Osborn, Alex F. *Applied Imagination: Principles and Procedures of Creative Problem-Solving.* C. Scribner's Sons, 1957.

———. *How to Think Up.* McGraw-Hill, 1942.

Paine, Thomas. *The Age of Reason.* 1794. Reprint, CreateSpace Independent Publishing Platform, 2008.

———. *Writings of Thomas Paine: (1779–1792), The Rights of Man.* Vol. 2. 1791. Reprint, 2013.

Pareto, Vilfredo, Arthur Livingston, Andrew Bongiorno, and James Harvey Rogers. *A Treatise on General Sociology.* General Publishing Company, 1935.

Pearson, Barry Lee, and Bill McCulloch. *Robert Johnson: Lost and Found.* Music in American Life. University of Illinois Press, 2003.

Pelham, R. A. "The Distribution of Early Fulling Mills in England and Wales." *Geography* (1944): 52–56.

Penn, D. C., K. J. Holyoak, and D. J. Povinelli. "Darwin's Mistake: Explaining the Discontinuity Between Human and Nonhuman Minds." *Behavioral and Brain Sciences* 31, no. 2 (2008): 109–30.

Penrose, Roger, and Martin Gardner. *Emperors New Mind: Concerning Computers, Minds, and the Laws of Physics.* Oxford University Press, 1989.

Pincock, Stephen. "Nobel Prize Winners Robin Warren and Barry Marshall." *Lancet* 366, no. 9495 (2005): 1429.

Pinker, Steven. *The Better Angels of Our Nature: Why Violence Has Declined.* Viking, 2010.

Plath, Slyvia. *Journals of Sylvia Plath.* Dial Press, 1982.

Pollio, Marcus Vitruvius. *The Ten Books on Architecture.* Architecture Classics, 2013.

Pond, Steve. "Trey Parker and Matt Stone: The *Playboy* Interview." *Playboy* 457, no. 7230 (2000): 675–77.

Porter, Mary Winearls. *What Rome Was Built With: A Description of the Stones Employed in Ancient Times for Its Building and Decoration.* University of Michigan Library, 1907.

Price, Monica T. "The Corsi Collection in Oxford." Corsi Collection of Decorative Stones. Oxford University Museum website: http://www.oum.ox.ac.uk/corsi /about/oxford.

Pynchon, Thomas. "Is It O.K. to Be a Luddite?" *New York Times,* October 28, 1984.

Radack, David V. "Getting Inventorship Right the First Time." *JOM* 46, no. 6 (1994): 62.

Rakauskas, Michael E., Leo J. Gugerty, and Nicholas J. Ward. "Effects of Naturalistic Cell Phone Conversations on Driving Performance." *Journal of Safety Research* 35, no. 4 (2004): 453–64.

Ramsey, E. J., K. V. Carey, W. L. Peterson, J. J. Jackson, F. K. Murphy, N. W. Read, K. B. Taylor, J. S. Trier, and J. S. Fordtran. "Epidemic Gastritis with Hypochlorhydria." *Gastroenterology* 76, no. 6 (1979): 1449–57.

Read, J. Don, and Darryl Bruce. "Longitudinal Tracking of Difficult Memory Retrievals." *Cognitive Psychology* 14, no. 2 (1982): 280–300.

Read, Leonard E. "I, Pencil." *Freeman,* December 1958, p. 32.

Renfrew, Colin and Iain Morley. *Becoming Human: Innovation in Prehistoric Material and Spiritual Culture.* Cambridge University Press, 2009.

Rensberger, Boyce. "David Krech, 68, Dies; Psychology Pioneer." *New York Times,* July 16, 1977.

Rich, Ben R., and Leo Janos. *Skunk Works: A Personal Memoir of My Years at Lockheed.* Little Brown, 1994.

Richardson, John. *A Life of Picasso.* Vol. 2, *1907–1917: The Painter of Modern Life.* Random House, 1996.

Rietzschel, Eric F., Bernard A. Nijstad, and Wolfgang Stroebe. "The Selection of Creative Ideas After Individual Idea Generation: Choosing Between Creativity and Impact." *British Journal of Psychology* 101, no. 1 (2010): 47–68.

Rosaldo, Michelle Zimbalist. *Knowledge and Passion.* Cambridge University Press, 1980.

Rothenberg, Albert. "Creative Cognitive Processes in Kekule's Discovery of the Structure of the Benzene Molecule." *American Journal of Psychology* (1995): 419–38.

Rubright, Linda. "D.Inc.tionary." *Medium.* February 16, 2013. https://medium.com /@deliciousday/d-inc-tionary-b8eed806fc6b.

Runco, Mark A. "Creativity Has No Dark Side." In *The Dark Side of Creativity,* edited by David H. Cropley, Arthur J. Cropley, James C. Kaufman, and Mark A. Runco. Cambridge University Press, 2010.

Rutter, B., S. Kroger, H. Hill, S. Windmann, C. Hermann, and A. Abraham. "Can Clouds Dance? Part 2: An Erp Investigation of Passive Conceptual Expansion." *Brain and Cognition* 80, no. 3 (2012): 301–10.

"S.F. Clear of All But 6 Sick Japs." *San Francisco Chronicle.* May 21, 1942, http://www
.sfmuseum.org/hist8/evac19.html.

Sawyer, R. Keith. *Explaining Creativity: The Science of Human Innovation.* Oxford University Press, 2012.

Schnall, Simone. *Life as the Problem: Karl Duncker's Context.* Psychology Today Tapes, 1999.

Schrodinger, Erwin. *What Is Life?: With Mind and Matter and Autobiographical Sketches.* Canto Classics. Cambridge University Press, 1944.

Seale, Jack. "The Joy of Difficult Second (or Third, or Twelfth) Albums." *Radio Times,* May 17, 2012.

Seger, Carol A. "How Do the Basal Ganglia Contribute to Categorization? Their Roles in Generalization, Response Selection, and Learning Via Feedback." *Neuroscience & Biobehavioral Reviews* 32, no. 2 (2008): 265–78.

Semmelweis, Ignaz. *The Etiology, Concept, and Prophylaxis of Childbed Fever.* 1859. Reprint, University of Wisconsin Press, 1983.

Senzaki, Nyogen. *101 Zen Stories.* Kessinger Publishing, 1919.

Sheehan, William. *The Planet Mars: A History of Observation and Discovery.* University of Arizona Press, 1996.

Sheehan, William, and Thomas Dobbins. "The Spokes of Venus: An Illusion Explained." *Journal for the History of Astronomy* 34 (2003): 53–63.

Sheh, Alexander, and James G Fox. "The Role of the Gastrointestinal Microbiome in *Helicobacter pylori* Pathogenesis." *Gut Microbes* 4, no. 6 (2013): 22–47.

Shepardson, George Defrees. *Electrical Catechism: An Introductory Treatise on Electricity and Its Uses.* McGraw-Hill, 1908.

Shurkin, Joel N. *Terman's Kids: The Groundbreaking Study of How the Gifted Grow Up.* Little Brown, 1992.

Sidowski, J. B., and D. B. Lindsley. "Harry Frederick Harlow: October 31, 1905–December 6, 1981." *Biographical Memoirs of the National Academy of Sciences* 58 (1988): 219–57.

Simon, Herbert A. *Karl Duncker and Cognitive Science.* Springer, 1999.

Simon, Herbert A., Allen Newell, and J. C. Shaw. "The Processes of Creative Thinking." Rand Corporation, 1959.

Simonton, Dean Keith. *Greatness: Who Makes History and Why.* Guilford Press, 1994.

——. *Origins of Genius: Darwinian Perspectives on Creativity.* Oxford University Press, 1999.

Simpson, Eileen. *Poets in Their Youth: A Memoir.* Noonday Press, 1982.

Smithgall, Elsa, ed. *Kandinsky and the Harmony of Silence: Painting with White Border (Phillips Collection).* Yale University Press, 2011.

Snyder, Thomas D. *120 Years of American Education: A Statistical Portrait.* National Center for Education Statistics, 1993.

Sofroniew, Michael V. and Harry V. Vinters. "Astrocytes: Biology and Pathology." *Acta Neuropathologica* 119, no. 1 (2010): 7–35.

Spinoza, Benedictus de. *Ethics: Ethica Ordine Geometrico Demonstrata.* 1677. Reprint, Floating Press, 2009.

Squire, Larry R. *The History of Neuroscience in Autobiography.* Vol. 1. Academic Press, 1998.

Staw, Barry M. "Why No One Really Wants Creativity." *Creative Action in Organizations* (1995): 161–66.

Steinhäuser, Christian, and Gerald Seifert. "Astrocyte Dysfunction in Temporal Lobe Epilepsy." *Epilepsia* 51, no. s5 (2010): 54–54.

Strauss, David. "Percival Lowell, W. H. Pickering and the Founding of the Lowell Observatory." *Annals of Science* 51, no. 1 (1994): 37–58.

Strayer, David L., and Frank A. Drews. "Cell-Phone-Induced Driver Distraction." *Current Directions in Psychological Science* 16, no. 3 (2007): 128–31.

Strayer, David L., Frank A. Drews, and Dennis J. Crouch. "A Comparison of the Cell Phone Driver and the Drunk Driver." *Human Factors: The Journal of the Human Factors and Ergonomics Society* 48, no. 2 (2006): 381–91.

Strayer, David L., Frank A. Drews, and William A. Johnston. "Cell Phone–Induced Failures of Visual Attention During Simulated Driving." *Journal of Experimental Psychology: Applied* 9, no. 1 (2003): 23.

Suzuki, Shunryu. *Zen Mind, Beginner's Mind.* 1970. Reprint, Shambhala, 2011.

Syrotuck, William and Syrotuck, Jean Anne. *Analysis of Lost Person Behavior.* Barkleigh Productions, 2000.

Takeuchi, H., Y. Taki, H. Hashizume, Y. Sassa, T. Nagase, R. Nouchi, and R. Kawashima. "The Association Between Resting Functional Connectivity and Creativity." *Cereb Cortex* 22, no. 12 (2012): 2921–29.

———. "Cerebral Blood Flow During Rest Associates with General Intelligence and Creativity." *PLoS One* 6, no. 9 (2011): e25532.

Taylor, Frederick Winslow. *The Principles of Scientific Management.* Harper, 1911.

Terman, Lewis. *Genetic Studies of Genius.* Vol. 1. Stanford Press, 1925.

———. *Genetic Studies of Genius.* Vol. 5. Stanford Press, 1967.

———. *Sex and Personality Studies in Masculinity and Femininity.* Shelley Press, 2007.

———. "Are Scientists Different?" *Scientific American* 192 (1955): 25–29.

———. *Condensed Guide for the Stanford Revision of the Binet-Simon Intelligence Tests.* Nabu Press, 2010.

———. *Genius and Stupidity: A Study of Some of the Intellectual Processes of Seven "Bright" and Seven "Stupid" Boys.* The Pedagogical Seminary 13, no. 3 (1906).

———. *The Intelligence of School Children: How Children Differ in Ability, the Use of Mental Tests in School Grading and the Proper Education of Exceptional Children.* Riverside Textbooks in Education. Houghton Mifflin Company, 1919.

Terman, Lewis M., and M. A. Merrill. *Stanford-Binet Intelligence Scale.* Houghton Mifflin Company, 1960.

Terman, Lewis Madison, and Maud A. Merrill. *Measuring Intelligence: A Guide to the Administration of the New Revised Stanford-Binet Tests of Intelligence.* Riverside Textbooks in Education. Houghton Mifflin, 1937.

Terman, Lewis, and Melita Oden. *The Gifted Child Grows Up: Twenty-Five Years' Follow-up of a Superior Group.* Vol. 4 of *Genetic Studies of Genius.* Stanford University Press, 1947.

Terman, Lewis M., and Melita H. Oden. *The Gifted Group at Mid-Life.* Stanford University Press, 1959.

Torrance, Ellis Paul. *Norms Technical Manual: Torrance Tests of Creative Thinking.* Ginn, 1974.

———. "The Creative Personality and the Ideal Pupil." *Teachers College Record* 65, no. 3 (1963): 220–26.

Towne, Henry R. "Engineer as Economist." *Transactions of the American Society of Mechanical Engineers* 7, no. 1886 (1886): 425ff. Reprinted in *Academy of Management Proceedings* vol. 1986, no. 1: 3–4.

Trabert, Britton, Roberta B. Ness, Wei-Hsuan Lo-Ciganic, Megan A. Murphy, Ellen L. Goode, Elizabeth M. Poole, Louise A. Brinton, Penelope M. Webb, Christina M. Nagle, and Susan J. Jordan. "Aspirin, Nonaspirin Nonsteroidal Anti-Inflammatory Drug, and Acetaminophen Use and Risk of Invasive Epithelial Ovarian Cancer: A Pooled Analysis in the Ovarian Cancer Association Consortium." *Journal of the National Cancer Institute* 106, no. 2 (2014): djt431.

Truzzi, Marcello. "On the Extraordinary: An Attempt at Clarification." *Zetetic Scholar* 1, no. 11 (1978).

Tsoref, Daliah, Tony Panzarella, and Amit Oza. "Aspirin in Prevention of Ovarian Cancer: Are We at the Tipping Point?" *Journal of the National Cancer Institute* 106, no. 2 (2014): djt453.

Tsu, Lao. *Tao Te Ching.* Vintage Books, 1972.

Tversky, Amos, and Daniel Kahneman. "Advances in Prospect Theory: Cumulative Representation of Uncertainty." *Journal of Risk and Uncertainty* 5, no. 4 (1992): 297–323.

———. "Availability: A Heuristic for Judging Frequency and Probability." *Cognitive Psychology* 5, no. 2 (1973): 207–32.

———. "The Framing of Decisions and the Psychology of Choice." *Science* 211, no. 4481 (1981): 453–58.

———. "Judgment Under Uncertainty: Heuristics and Biases." *Science* 185, no. 4157 (1974): 1124–31.

———. "Loss Aversion in Riskless Choice: A Reference-Dependent Model." *Quarterly Journal of Economics* 106, no. 4 (1991): 1039–61.

———. "Rational Choice and the Framing of Decisions." *Journal of Business* (1986): S251–78.

Tyson, Neil deGrasse. "The Perimeter of Ignorance." *Natural History* 114, no. 9 (2005).

———. "The Perimeter of Ignorance." Talk adapated from *Natural History Magazine,* given at the *Beyond Belief: Science, Religion, Reason and Survival* Conference. Salk Institute for Biological Studies, La Jolla, California, November 5, 2006. Video at http://bit.ly/NdGTSalk.

Underwood, Geoffrey D. M. *Implicit Cognition.* Oxford University Press, 1996.

Unge, Peter. "*Helicobacter pylori* Treatment in the Past and in the 21st Century." In *Helicobacter Pioneers: Firsthand Accounts from the Scientists Who Discovered Helicobacter,* edited by Barry Marshall. Wiley, 2002, 203–13.

United States Presidential Commission on the Space Shuttle Challenger Accident. *Report to the President: Actions to Implement the Recommendations of the Presidential Commission on the Space Shuttle Challenger Accident.* National Aeronautics and Space Administration, 1986.

Vallerand, Robert J. "On the Psychology of Passion: In Search of What Makes People's Lives Most Worth Living." *Canadian Psychology/Psychologie Canadienne* 49, no. 1 (2008): 1.

Vallerand, Robert J., Céline Blanchard, Genevieve A. Mageau, Richard Koestner, Catherine Ratelle, Maude Léonard, Marylene Gagné, and Josée Marsolais. "Les Passions de l'Âme: On Obsessive and Harmonious Passion." *Journal of Personality and Social Psychology* 85, no. 4 (2003): 756.

Vallerand, Robert J., and Nathalie Houlfort. "Passion at Work." In *Emerging Perspectives on Values in Organizations,* edited by Stephen W. Gilliland, Dirk D. Steiner, and Daniel P. Skarlicki. Information Age Publishing, 2003, 175–204.

Vallerand, Robert J., Yvan Paquet, Frederick L. Philippe, and Julie Charest. "On the Role of Passion for Work in Burnout: A Process Model." *Journal of Personality* 78, no. 1 (2010): 289–312.

Vallerand, Robert J., Sarah-Jeanne Salvy, Geneviève A. Mageau, Andrew J. Elliot, Pascale L. Denis, Frédéric M. E. Grouzet, and Celine Blanchard. "On the Role of Passion in Performance." *Journal of Personality* 75, no. 3 (2007): 505–34.

Valsiner, Jaan, ed. *Thinking in Psychological Science: Ideas and Their Makers.* Transaction Publishers, 2007.

Van Der Weyden, Martin B., Ruth M. Armstrong, and Ann T. Gregory. "The 2005 Nobel Prize in Physiology or Medicine." *Medical Journal of Australia* 183, nos. 11–12 (2005): 612.

Vernon, P. E., ed. *Creativity: Selected Readings.* Penguin Books, 1970.

Vul, Edward, and Harold Pashler. "Incubation Benefits Only After People Have Been Misdirected." *Memory & Cognition* 35, no. 4 (2007): 701–10.

Vygotsky, Lev S. *Mind in Society: The Development of Higher Psychological Processes.* Harvard University Press, 1980.

Wald, Elijah. *Escaping the Delta: Robert Johnson and the Invention of the Blues.* Amistad, 2004.

Wallace, Alfred Russel. *Is Mars Habitable? A Critical Examination of Professor Percival Lowell's Book "Mars and Its Canals," with an Alternative Explanation.* Macmillan, 1907.

———. *Man's Place in the Universe: A Study of the Results of Scientific Research in Relation to the Unity or Plurality of Worlds.* Chapman and Hall, 1904.

Wallace, David Foster. *This Is Water: Some Thoughts, Delivered on a Significant Occasion, About Living a Compassionate Life.* Little, Brown, 2009.

Wallas, Graham. *The Art of Thought.* Harcourt, Brace, 1926.

Wang, Doris D. and Angélique Bordey. "The Astrocyte Odyssey." *Progress in Neurobiology* 86, no. 4 (2008): 342–67.

Wang, Haidong, Laura Dwyer-Lindgren, Katherine T. Lofgren, Julie Knoll Rajaratnam, Jacob R. Marcus, Alison Levin-Rector, Carly E. Levitz, Alan D. Lopez, and Christopher J. L. Murray. "Age-Specific and Sex-Specific Mortality in 187 Countries, 1970–2010: A Systematic Analysis for the Global Burden of Disease Study 2010." *The Lancet* 380, no. 9859 (2013): 2071–94.

Wardlow, Gayle Dean. *Chasin' That Devil Music: Searching for the Blues.* Backbeat Books, 1998.

Warren, Robin J. "Helicobacter: The Ease and Difficulty of a New Discovery." Nobel lecture, December 8, 2005. http://www.nobelprize.org/nobel_prizes/medicine/laureates/2005/warren-lecture.pdf.

Weide, Robert B. *Woody Allen: A Documentary.* PBS "American Masters" documentary originally aired on television in 2011. Video on Demand release dated 2013.

Weinberg, Steven. "The Revolution That Didn't Happen." *New York Review of Books* 25, no. 3 (1998): 250–53.

Weisberg, Robert, and Jerry M. Suls. "An Information-Processing Model of Duncker's Candle Problem." *Cognitive Psychology* 4, no. 2 (1973): 255–76.

Weisberg, Robert W. *Creativity: Beyond the Myth of Genius.* W. H. Freeman, 1993.

———. *Creativity: Genius and Other Myths.* Series of Books in Psychology. W. H. Freeman, 1986.

———. *Creativity: Understanding Innovation in Problem Solving, Science, Invention, and the Arts.* Wiley, 2006.

———. "On the 'Demystification' of Insight: A Critique of Neuroimaging Studies of Insight." *Creativity Research Journal* 25, no. 1 (2013): 1–14.

———. "Toward an Integrated Theory of Insight in Problem Solving." *Thinking & Reasoning.* February 24, 2014, http://www.tandfonline.com/doi/abs/10.1080/13546783.2014.886625#.U9u-vYBdW6i.

Weisskopf-Joelson, Edith, and Thomas S. Eliseo. "An Experimental Study of the Effectiveness of Brainstorming." *Journal of Applied Psychology* 45, no. 1 (1961): 45.

Werrell, Kenneth P. "The Strategic Bombing of Germany in World War II: Costs and Accomplishments." *Journal of American History* 73, no. 3 (December 1986): 702–13.

Westby, Erik L., and V. L. Dawson. "Creativity: Asset or Burden in the Classroom?" *Creativity Research Journal* 8, no. 1 (1995): 1–10.

Westermann, Edward B. *Flak: German Anti-Aircraft Defenses, 1914–1945.* University Press of Kansas, 2001.

White, Matthew. *Atrocities: The 100 Deadliest Episodes in Human History.* W. W. Norton, 2013.

———. *Historical Atlas of the Twentieth Century.* Matthew White, 2003, http://users.erols.com/mwhite28/20century.htm.

Whitehead, Alfred North. *Religion in the Making: Lowell Lectures 1926.* 1926. Reprint, Fordham University Press, 1996.

Whitson, Jennifer A., and Adam D. Galinsky. "Lacking Control Increases Illusory Pattern Perception." *Science* 322, no. 5898 (2008): 115–17.

Wolfram, Stephen. "The Personal Analytics of My Life." Stephen Wolfram blog, March 8, 2012. http://bit.ly/wolframanalytics.

Wozniak, Steve, with Gina Smith. *iWoz: Computer Geek to Cult Icon; How I Invented the Personal Computer, Co-Founded Apple, and Had Fun Doing It.* W. W. Norton, 2007.

Wright, Orville, and Wilbur Wright. *The Early History of the Airplane.* Dayton-Wright Airplane Company, 1922. https://archive.org/details/earlyhistoryofai00wrigrich.

Young, Kristie, Michael Regan, and M. Hammer. "Driver Distraction: A Review of the Literature." In *Distracted Driving,* 379–405. Australasian College of Road Safety, 2007.

Yule, Sarah S. B. *Borrowings: A Collection of Helpful and Beautiful Thoughts.* New York: Dodge Publishing, 1889.

Zaslaw, Neal. "Recent Mozart Research and *Der neue Köchel.*" In *Musicology and Sister Disciplines: Past, Present, Future. Proceedings of the 16th International Congress of the International Musicological Society, London, 1997.* Oxford University Press, 2000.

———. "Mozart as a Working Stiff." Essay published on the "Apropos Mozart" web site, 1994. http://bit.ly/zaslaw.

Zemlo, Tamara R., Howard H. Garrison, Nicola C. Partridge, and Timothy J. Ley. "The Physician-Scientist: Career Issues and Challenges at the Year 2000." *FASEB Journal* 14, no. 2 (2000): 221–30.

Zepernick, Bernhard, and Wolfgang Meretz. "Christian Konrad Sprengel's Life in Relation to His Family and His Time: On the Occasion of His 250th Birthday." *Willdenowia-Annals of the Botanic Garden and Botanical Museum Berlin-Dahlem* 31, no. 1 (2001): 141–52.

Zuckerman, Harriet. *Scientific Elite: Nobel Laureates in the United States.* Transaction Publishers, 1977.

Zuckerman, Harriet Anne. *Nobel Laureates in the United States: A Sociological Study of Scientific Collaboration.* PhD diss. Columbia University, 1965.

INDEX

Apple Computer, 47
Apple Inc., 45–46, 47, 48, 50, 99
Archimedes, 38–39
Aristotle, 86, 106, 107, 262*n*
Armstrong, Daisy, 265*n*
Army Air Forces (USAAF), U.S., 203
art:
    from angst, 169–70
    creation of, 56–59
    music and, 169–70, 174–75, 183–84
artificial intelligence, 16
Ashby, Ross, 15
Ashkenazi Jews, 138, 269*n*, 270*n*
Aspen, Colo., 47
astrocytes, 200
astronomy, 111–13, 263*n*, 264*n*
Atlanta, Ga., 144, 145, 147
Auble, Pamela, 37
Auschwitz, 30
Austin, Tex., 143, 144, 145
Austin Chronicle, 167
Australia, 91–93, 143–44, 184
authorship, 6
    as misleading, 9, 122, 123–24, 125
    records of, 6–7
    see also credit; inventors; patents
automation, 143, 158, 161
    see also looms, automatic
Avedon, Richard, 70
awards, *see* rewards
Aztecs, 2

Bach, Johann Sebastian, 187
Bacon, Francis, 146
bacteria, 137, 153, 260*n*
    Helicobacter pylori, 93, 94, 95, 107
    in stomachs, 91–95, 98, 113
    ulcers and, 92, 93, 95
    viruses vs., 119, 121
Balkan War, First, 57
Bascom, Florence, 133–35, 137
Basilica of San Domenico, 6
Baumgarten, Marjorie, 167
bauxite, 143, 155
Beatles, 169
Becher, Johann Joachim, 262*n*
Beckett, Samuel, 69
beginner's mind, 104–5, 110, 113
Beijerinck, Martinus, 119
Belarus, 217
Belgium, 2–3

beliefs, 66, 116
Belle-Vue, Réunion, 3
Bellier-Beaumont, Elvire, 3
Bellier-Beaumont, Ferréol, 3–4, 5–6,
    17–18, 23, 24
Bellow, Saul, 70
Bergman, Ingmar, 178
Bergman, Torbern, 152
Berlin, Germany, 26–27, 29, 30, 56
Berlin, University of, 27
Berryman, John, 167
Bert and Ernie (Muppets), 207–9, 210,
    222
bicycles, 52, 53, 55
Big Bird (Muppet), 207
"Bilancetta, La" (Galileo), 39
Billboard, 169
bin Laden, Osama, 231
Biographia Literaria (Coleridge), 40
Birkbeck College, 121
Blackbird surveillance plane, 195
Black Death, 239
Blau, Marietta, 126–27
Block, Harry (char.), 177
blood, 74
    tumors and, 60–63
blood vessels, 61–62, 64, 65
Bloomsbury, England, xv
blues, 174–75
Bode, Johann Elert, 263*n*
Boeing, 195
Bogart, Humphrey, 20
Book of Mormon, The (musical), 209–10
Boston, Mass., 182–83
Boston Children's Hospital, 63, 87–88
Boston City Hospital, 62
Boston Globe, 184
Botticelli, Sandro, xv
bottles, bottling, 151–52, 154
Box Problem (Candle Problem), 32, 35–37,
    172
Boyle, Dennis, 216
Boyle, Robert, 132, 137
Bradford, Arthur, 210, 212
Bragg, William, Jr., 133, 134, 135–36, 137
Bragg, William, Sr., 133, 135
brain, 14–15, 30, 86, 114, 199–200
    inattentional blindness and, 96–97
    see also mind
brainstorming, 49–51
BRCA genes, 138, 269*n*–70*n*
Brecht, Bertolt, 26